World's Largest Countries By Population

Rank	Country	Millions
1	China	1 330
2	India	1 173
3	United States	310
4	Indonesia	243
5	Brazil	201
6	Pakistan	184
7	Bangladesh	156
8	Nigeria	152
9	Russia	139
10	Japan	127

Source: CIA—World Factbook 2011.

World's Most Expensive Cities

Rank	City	Country
1	Tokyo	Japan
2	Osaka Kobe	Japan
3	Paris	France
4	Copenhagen	Denmark
5	Oslo	Norway
6	Zurich	Switzerland
7	Frankfurt	Germany
8	Helsinki	Finland
9	Geneva	Switzerland
10	Singapore	Singapore

Source: The Economist January 2011

World's Highest Unemployment Rates

Rank	Country	Unemployment Rate (%)
1	Zimbabwe	95
2	Nauru	90
3	Liberia	85
4	Burkina Faso	77
5	Turkmenistan	60
6	Cocos (Keeling) Islands	60
7	Djibouti	59
8	Namibia	51
9	Zambia	50
10	Senegal	48

Source: CIA—World Factbook 2011.

INSTRUCTORS...

Would you like your **students** to show up for class **more prepared**?
(Let's face it, class is much more fun if everyone is engaged and prepared...)

Want an **easy way to assign** homework online and track student **progress**?
(Less time grading means more time teaching...)

Want an **instant view** of student or class performance?
(No more wondering if students understand...)

Need to **collect data and generate reports** required for administration or accreditation?
(Say goodbye to manually tracking student learning outcomes...)

Want to **record and post your lectures** for students to view online?
(The more students can see, hear, and experience class resources, the better they learn...)

 ## With **McGraw-Hill's *Connect*,**

INSTRUCTORS GET:

- Simple **assignment management**, allowing you to spend more time teaching.
- **Auto-graded** assignments, quizzes, and tests.
- **Detailed visual reporting** where student and section results can be viewed and analyzed.
- Sophisticated **online testing** capability.
- A **filtering and reporting** function that allows you to easily assign and report on materials that are correlated to learning objectives and Bloom's taxonomy.
- An easy-to-use **lecture capture** tool.
- The option to **upload course documents** for student access.

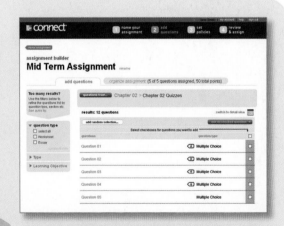

PRINCIPLES OF
MICROECONOMICS

SEVENTH EDITION

PRINCIPLES OF
MICROECONOMICS

JOHN E. SAYRE

ALAN J. MORRIS
Capilano University

McGraw-Hill Ryerson
Connect. Learn. Succeed.

PRINCIPLES OF MICROECONOMICS
Seventh Edition

Copyright © 2012, 2009, 2006, 2004, 2001, 1999, 1996 by McGraw-Hill Ryerson Limited, a Subsidiary of The McGraw-Hill Companies. All rights reserved. No part of this publication may be reproduced or transmitted in any form or by any means, or stored in a data base or retrieval system, without the prior written permission of McGraw-Hill Ryerson Limited, or in the case of photocopying or other reprographic copying, a licence from The Canadian Copyright Licensing Agency (Access Copyright). For an Access Copyright licence, visit www.accesscopyright.ca or call toll free to 1-800-893-5777.

Statistics Canada information is used with the permission of Statistics Canada. Users are forbidden to copy this material and/or redisseminate the data, in an original or modified form, for commercial purposes, without the expressed permission of Statistics Canada. Information on the availability of the wide range of data from Statistics Canada can be obtained from Statistics Canada's Regional Offices, its World Wide Web site at http://www.statcan.ca and its toll-free access number 1-800-263-1136.

ISBN 13: 978-0-07-038546-7
ISBN 10: 0-07-038546-7

2 3 4 5 6 7 8 9   CTPS   1 9 8 7 6 5 4 3

Printed and bound in China.

Care has been taken to trace ownership of copyright material contained in this text; however, the publisher will welcome any information that enables them to rectify any reference or credit for subsequent editions.

SPONSORING EDITOR: James Booty
MARKETING MANAGER: Jeremy Guimond
SENIOR DEVELOPMENTAL EDITOR: Maria Chu
EDITORIAL ASSOCIATE: Erin Catto
FREELANCE PERMISSIONS EDITOR: Lynn McIntyre
SUPERVISING EDITORS: Joanne Limebeer, Katie McHale
COPY EDITOR: Judy Sturrup
PROOFREADER: Rohini Herbert
PRODUCTION COORDINATOR: Sheryl MacAdam
INSIDE DESIGN: Sarah Orr/ArtPlus
COMPOSITION: Heather Brunton/ArtPlus Limited
COVER DESIGN: Sarah Orr/ArtPlus Limited
COVER PHOTO: © Maria Wachala | Dreamstime.com
PRINTER: CTPS

Library and Archives Canada Cataloguing in Publication Data

Sayre, John E., 1942–
    Principles of microeconomics / John E. Sayre, Alan J. Morris.—7th ed.

Includes index.
ISBN 978-0-07-038546-7

1. Microeconomics—Textbooks. I. Morris, Alan J. (Alan James) II. Title.

HB172.S354 2012   338.5   C2011-906986-5

To Daria: may the
blessings be
(JES)

———— A N D ————

To the ones I love:
Wakako, Daniel and Erika, and Christian
(AJM)

ABOUT THE AUTHORS

John E. Sayre earned a BSBA at the University of Denver and an MA from Boston University. He began teaching principles of economics while in the Peace Corps in Malawi. He came to Vancouver to do PhD studies at Simon Fraser University and ended up teaching at Capilano University for the next thirty-nine years. Now retired from Capilano, John is an avid golfer who also enjoys walking with his dog and listening to a wide range of music.

Alan Morris, though loath to admit it, first worked as an accountant in England, where he became an Associate of the Chartered Institute of Secretaries and obtained his first degree in 1971 in Manchester, U.K. He subsequently obtained his Master's degree at Simon Fraser University, B.C., in 1973. He worked on his doctorate at Leicester University, U.K., and returned to work in business in Vancouver, B.C., until his appointment at Capilano University in 1988. He currently lives in North Vancouver with his wife and one of his two sons, and is an avid devotee of classical music, birding, soccer, and beer. To his knowledge, he has never been an adviser to the Canadian government.

BRIEF CONTENTS

CONTENTS

To the Students

So, you may well ask, why take a course in economics? For many of you, the obvious answer to this question is: "Because it is a requirement for the program or educational goal that I have chosen." Fair enough. But there are other reasons. It is a simple truth that if you want to understand the world around you, then you have to understand some basic economics. Much of what goes on in the world today is driven by economic considerations, and those who know nothing of economics often simply cannot understand why things are the way they are. In this age of globalization, we are all citizens of the world and we need to function effectively in the midst of the enormous changes that are sweeping across almost every aspect of the social/political/economic landscape. You can either be part of this, and all the opportunities that come with it, or not be part of it because you cannot make any sense of it.

It is quite possible that you feel a little apprehensive because you have heard that economics is a difficult subject. Though there may be a grain of truth in this, we are convinced that almost any student can succeed in economics. But it will require some real work and effort on your part. Here are some tips on the general approach to this course that you might find helpful. First, read the **Economics Toolkit** that appears at the beginning of the book. The section titled "Canadian Reality" offers basic information on Canada and its economic picture. "Graphing Reality" gives a quick lesson on graphs, which are an essential part of economics. These two sections will give you a solid foundation on which to build your knowledge of economics.

Second, before each lecture, quickly look over the chapter that will be covered. In this preliminary survey you do not need to worry about the glossary boxes, the self-test questions, or the integrated Study Guide. Third, take notes as much as you can during the lecture because the process of forcing yourself to express ideas *in your own words* is a crucial stage in the learning process. Fourth, re-read the chapter, again taking notes and using your own words (do not just copy everything word for word from the text). While doing this, refer to your classroom notes and try to integrate them into your reading notes. After you finish this, you will be ready to take on the Study Guide. As painful as it may be for you to hear this, we want to say loud and clear that you should do *all* of the answered questions and problems in the Study Guide. You may be slow at first, but you will be surprised at how much faster you become in later chapters. This is a natural aspect of the learning process. It might be helpful for you to get together with one or two other students and form a study group that meets once or twice a week to do economics Study Guide questions. You will be amazed at how explaining an answer to a fellow student is one of the most effective learning techniques. If you ever come across a question that you simply cannot understand, this is a sure sign that you need to approach your instructor (or teaching assistant) for help. Do not get discouraged when this happens, and realize that it will probably happen more at the beginning of your process of learning economics than later on in the term. We are convinced that if you follow this process consistently, beginning in the very first week of class, you will succeed in the course—and not only succeed, but most likely do well. All it takes is effort, good time management, and consistent organization.

Finally, an enormous part of becoming educated involves gaining self-confidence and a sense of accomplishment. Getting an A in a "tough" economics course can be a great step in this direction. We wish you all the best.

To the Instructors

GENERAL PHILOSOPHY

Over the years, we have become increasingly convinced that most economics textbooks are written to impress other economists rather than to enlighten beginning students. Such books tend to be encyclopedic in scope and intimidating in appearance. Small wonder, then, that students often emerge from an economics course feeling that the discipline really is daunting and unapproachable. We agree that the study of economics is challenging, but our experience is that students can also see it as intriguing and enjoyable if the right approach is taken. It is our belief that this right approach starts with a really good textbook that is concise without sacrificing either clarity or accepted standards of rigour.

In writing this text, we attempted to stay focused on four guiding principles. The first is to achieve a well-written text. We have tried to write as clearly as possible, to avoid unnecessary jargon, to speak directly to the student, and to avoid unnecessary abstraction and repetition.

Of equal importance, our second principle is a focused emphasis on student learning. Many years of teaching the principles courses have convinced us that students *learn* economics by *doing* economics. To this end, self-test questions are positioned throughout each chapter. This encourages students to apply what they have just read and gives them continuous feedback on their comprehension of the material being presented. Further, we feel that we offer the most comprehensive and carefully crafted Study Guide on the market, which has evolved over the years as a result of continued use in our own classes. In addition, each chapter's Study Guide contains a Chapter Summary as well as Study Tips for students.

Our third principle has been to avoid an encyclopedic text. It seems that in an effort to please everyone, textbook authors sometimes include bits and pieces of almost everything. The result is that students are often overwhelmed and find it difficult to sort out the more important material from what is less important.

The fourth principle is to avoid problems of discontinuity that can occur when different groups of authors do separate parts of a total package. To this end, we are the sole authors of the text, instructor's manual, and integrated Study Guide. We also carefully supervise the development of the test bank. We have tried to ensure that as much care and attention goes into the ancillary materials as goes into the writing of the text.

Few things are more satisfying than witnessing a student's zest for learning. We hope that this textbook adds a little to this process.

SEVENTH EDITION CHANGES

There are no changes to the basic organizational structure of this edition from the previous one. Please note that the Unanswered Questions in each chapter's Study Guide have been removed and placed online in Connect and into the Instructor's Manual along with the answers to these questions.

The more specific changes to each particular chapter are largely a result of feedback provided by our many users and reviewers. The important changes to the individual chapters are as follows:

- In **Chapter 1**, we eliminated the section on underlying values and replaced it with a new section titled "The Importance of Efficiency" in which the ideas of productive and allocative efficiency are explained. We brought forward the discussion of factors of production to the section on scarcity. Controversy Three on organ donations was replaced with one on road pricing, and we sharpened the definition of positive and normative statements while placing emphasis on the difference between these two terms. We added a new section of shifts in the production possibilities curve and added new problems on deriving PP tables and graphing the results.

- In **Chapter 2**, we improved the economic conversation about demand and supply, and formally defined the terms "shortage" and "surplus" in glossary boxes. We re-wrote the AD box entitled "The Famous Scissors Analogy" and improved the graph in the next AD box, "Sales Always Equal Purchases."

- **Chapter 3**'s AD boxes on the minimum wage in Canada and Giffen goods were re-worked for more clarity. We explained that the term "wage" can be thought of as the price of labour with individuals being the source of supply while demand comes from those who hire workers.

- In **Chapter 4**, we added graphs to illustrate price elasticity in the opening section and expanded the section on elasticity and total revenue to include a graph showing the loss or gain from a price change. We introduced the idea of unitary elasticity in the opening section. We changed the section on the effect of an excise tax by adding a table to show its impact on the supply of a good. We simplified the material on the effect that increasing the excise tax on a product will have on the government's tax revenue. We added two new Study Guide questions on calculating total revenue from a graph.

- In **Chapter 5**, we re-wrote the AD box entitled "Extracting Consumer Surplus."

- In **Chapter 6**, we moved the short run/long run distinction forward to the beginning of the chapter and expanded on the term "wages paid to self." We added an AD box explaining how urbanization drives up the implicit costs of farming and better explained the "kink" in the TP curve in Figure 6.1. We added material establishing the link between costs and profits, and thereby set up the full discussion that follows in Chapter 8.

- In **Chapter 7**, we re-worked the AD box on "Increased Rates of Productivity Growth." We also added information on real-world firms and scale of operations, and removed references to General Motors as a "successful" firm.

- In **Chapter 8**, we added a table showing MC and MR to more clearly demonstrate the idea of profit maximization and then added a graph emphasizing the importance of this equality. We better integrated the figures used in our tables with those used in the graphs to add to the flow of the chapter. Self Test questions 5 and 9 were replaced, to better reflect the material in the chapter.

- In **Chapter 9**, we added a full discussion of producers' surplus and economic surplus to complement the material on consumers' surplus in Chapter 5. The term "costless" was explained in context of allocative efficiency. We added material on the theory of second best under the section on "Market Failures." Under the section on "The Forces of Uncompetition" we explained why imperfect competition reduces the amount of economic surplus. We completely replaced the material under "Marketing Permits to Limit Pollution" with new material entitled "Cap and Trade Policies to Address Pollution."

- In **Chapter 10**, we changed the wording in the introductory section to highlight a major criticism of monopolies—the misallocation of resources—and expressly stated that our analysis is of single-price monopolist. We added a new section discussing the loss of economic surplus (the dead weight loss) that results from monopolies.

- We better emphasized the fact that product differentiation is the main distinguishing feature of monopolistic competition in **Chapter 11**. We better explained the negative implications of collusion in the oligopoly section, and redrew the figure on the OPEC cartel to more clearly show the gain in revenue achieved by the organization's pricing action. We added an AD box explaining why many corporations sell multiple brands of the same product.

- In **Chapter 12**, we added a section explaining the dead-weight loss that results from common property resources and added a Self Test question on this material. We beefed up the section on monopsony, explaining why a monopsonist will pay less and hire fewer workers than a firm that hires in a competitive environment, and added two Study Guide questions on this material.

- In **Chapter 13**, we updated the AD box on "Canada, the Great Trader." We also added a discussion about how low wages do not necessarily imply an advantage to the exporter, and material on the softwood lumber dispute.

Textbook Features

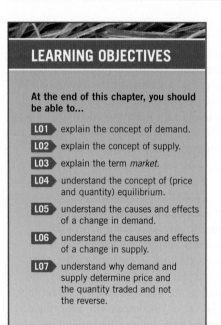

As an initial review and an ongoing resource, the book opens with the **Economics Toolkit**. The first section, "Canadian Reality," offers basic information on Canada and its economy. The second section, "Graphing Reality," provides the student with a primer on how to interpret and create tables and graphs. We have provided a number of features to help the student come to grips with the subject matter.

Learning Objectives, listed at the beginning of each chapter, form a learning framework throughout the text, with each learning objective repeated in the margin at the appropriate place in the main body of the chapter. Each chapter opens with a vignette that provides context and an overview.

Glossary items indicate the first use of any term that is part of the language of economics. The term itself is in bold print and the definition is provided in the margin. The page number where the definition appears is supplied at the end of the chapter for quick and easy reference, and a complete glossary of terms appears at the end of the book.

Self-Test question boxes appear at important points throughout the main body of each chapter. They give students immediate feedback on how well they have understood the more abstract concept(s) discussed. In doing this, we have tried to establish a minimum standard of comprehension that all students should strive to achieve. Students can check their own progress by comparing their answers with those in the Student Answer Key, which is available for download at Connect.

Added Dimension boxes identify general information and supplementary material that we hope adds a little colour to the student's reading.

> **ADDED DIMENSION**   Re-inventing the Market
>
> Modern capitalism first emerged and began to spread about 250 years ago, as commerce moved out of the village markets of Europe into the age of factory-centred manufacturing, which was later combined with widespread systems of wholesale and retail. However, this transformation also introduced a less predictable chain of supply and demand. While the seller in the village market was in direct contact with the buyer, the evolution of capitalism's mass markets and mass production techniques imposed vast gulfs in time and space between buyer and seller. Producers became much less sure of what the demand for their product was, and buyers were never sure there wasn't a better deal somewhere else. In response to this, sellers used the blunt tool of a fixed price list and adjusted output accordingly, while buyers just did the best they could. The phenomenon of the Internet is re-inventing commerce as the seller's market horizon expands, buyers have more information, real-time sales become routine, and the need to stockpile inventory diminishes. In short, supply-chain bottlenecks are being eradicated. What is emerging is far *more efficient markets* and the rise of dynamic pricing based on constantly fluctuating demand and supply.

Highlighted Concepts are important ideas that are pulled out and presented in a separate box—signalling to students that this material is particularly relevant and crucial to their understanding.

> An increase in price will lead to an *increase in the quantity supplied* and is illustrated as a movement up the supply curve.

> A decrease in price will cause a *decrease in the quantity supplied* and is illustrated as a movement down the supply curve.

Simple, clear, and uncomplicated visuals are found throughout the text. These are supported by captions that thoroughly explain the concepts involved.

FIGURE 2.5   **Changes in the Quantity Supplied**

A price change will lead to a movement along the supply curve. An increase in the price from, say, P_1 to P_2 will cause an increase in the quantity supplied from Q_1 to Q_2. A decrease in the price from P_3 to P_4 will lead to a decrease in the quantity supplied from Q_3 to Q_4. The supply curve itself, however, does not change.

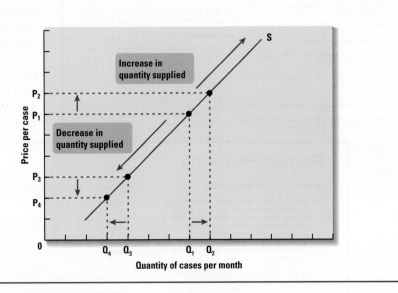

Integrated Study Guide Features

As expressed earlier, we believe that answering questions and doing problems should be an *active part of the students' learning process*. For this reason, we chose to integrate a complete Study Guide within the covers of this text. A **Study Guide** section, with pages screened in colour, immediately follows each chapter. We were careful to write the questions in the Study Guide to cover all the material, but only the material, found in the text itself. We have chosen a colourful, user-friendly design that we hope will encourage significant student participation.

The **Study Guide** has been reorganized into two main sections: a *Review* and a set of *Answered Questions and Problems*.

The Review section contains the *Chapter Summary*, *New Glossary Terms*, and *Key Equations*, as well as *Study Tips*, which are suggestions to help students manage the material in the chapter.

STUDY GUIDE

Review

CHAPTER SUMMARY

The focus of this chapter was elasticity, which is one of the more powerful concepts in microeconomics. Price elasticity of demand is the responsiveness of the quantity demanded to a change in price. Elasticity determines whether the consumer's total expenditure, and more importantly, the seller's total revenue rises or falls as price changes. The chapter presented four specific applications of this concept to illustrate its relevance and importance in microeconomic analysis. We saw how the concept of elasticity can be applied to supply, income, and price changes of related products.

An increase in price will raise the seller's total revenue if demand is inelastic but lower total revenue if it is elastic. A decrease in price will have the opposite effect. Total revenue is unaffected if the demand is unitary elastic.

4.4 The *four applications* of the concept of price elasticity of demand show that:
- the more inelastic the demand curve, the larger is the proportion of a sales tax consumers pay
- governments raise a great deal of revenue from excise taxes on products with high inelastic demand,

Answered Questions

These questions can also be found online on Connect.

Indicate whether the following statements are true or false:

1. **(LO 1) T or F** A firm's total revenue is equal to price times demand.
2. **(LO 1) T or F** The price elasticity of demand coefficient is, technically, always negative, but for convenience economists ignore the minus sign.
3. **(LO 1) T or F** If demand is inelastic and price falls, then total revenue will rise.
4. **(LO 1) T or F** If demand is elastic and price rises, then total revenue will rise.
5. **(LO 1) T or F** If the elasticity of demand is unitary and the price rises, then total revenue will rise.
6. **(LO 3) T or F** A major determinant of price elasticity of demand is the number of complementary products available.
7. **(LO 2) T or F** demand curve
8. **(LO 5) T or F**

9. **(LO 5) T or F** If cross-elasticity of demand is positive, we could conclude that two products are substitutes.
10. **(LO 5) T or F** If income elasticity is positive, we could conclude that the product in question is an inferior good.

Basic (Questions 11–25)

11. **(LO 1)** What is the effect on total revenue if demand is elastic and price rises?
   a) Total revenue will fall.
   b) Total revenue will rise.
   c) Quantity demanded will rise.
   d) Supply will rise.
12. **(LO 5)** What is the effect of a rise in income on the demand for a product?
   a) It will rise if the product is an inferior product.
   b) It will rise if the product is a normal product.
   c) It will fall if the product is a normal product.
   d) It will fall whether it is a normal or inferior product.

The **Answered Questions and Problems** sections include true/false and multiple-choice questions. The multiple-choice questions have been grouped into three learning levels: basic, intermediate, and advanced (available also in Connect for students to practise). In addition, there is a set of problems, each of which has a twin in the Unanswered Parallel Problems section available in Connect (with answers for instructors in the Instructors Manual).

Parallel Problems

ANSWERED PROBLEMS

36A. **(LO 1, 4, 5) Key Problem** Assume that there is only one movie theatre and only one video rental outlet in a small mining town in northern Manitoba. The weekly demand, by all the townspeople, for movies and video rentals is given in Table 4.13.
   a) Fill in the total revenue columns.
   b) What prices would maximize the seller's total revenue?
      Movie price: _____
      Video price: _____
   c) What is the elasticity of demand for movies if the theatre changes the price from $6 to $5, and what is the change in total revenue? What if the price changes from $6 to $7?

As a result, the demand for *movies* increases by 20 at each price. Would the theatre now want to charge the same price for movies?
Yes: _____ No: _____
   f) Given the circumstances in e), what is the cross-elasticity of movies for videos? What does this say about the relationship between the two products?
      Elasticity: _____ ; relationship: _____ .
   g) Referring to the original data in Table 4.13, assume now that the average weekly earnings of the townspeople rise from $500 to $550 with the result that demand for movies increases 20 percent. If the price being charged is $6, what is the income elasticity of demand? What does this suggest about the product, movies?

Students can judge their progress by working through the Answered Questions and Problems, and checking their answers with those in the Student Answer Key available for download at Connect.

Comprehensive Teaching and Learning Package

CONNECT

McGraw-Hill Connect™ is a web-based assignment and assessment platform that gives students the means to better connect with their coursework, with their instructors, and with the important concepts that they will need to know for success now and in the future.

With Connect, instructors can deliver assignments, quizzes, and tests online. Nearly all the questions from the text are presented in an auto-gradeable format and tied to the text's learning objectives. Instructors can edit existing questions and author entirely new problems. Track individual student performance—by question, assignment, or in relation to the class overall—with detailed grade reports. Integrate grade reports easily with Learning Management Systems (LMS) such as WebCT and Blackboard. And much more.

By choosing Connect, instructors are providing their students with a powerful tool for improving academic performance and truly mastering course material. Connect allows students to practise important skills at their own pace and on their own schedule. Importantly, students' assessment results and instructors' feedback are all saved online—so students can continually review their progress and plot their course to success.

Connect also provides 24/7 online access to an eBook—an online edition of the text—to aid them in successfully completing their work, wherever and whenever they choose.

CONNECT FOR STUDENTS

Connect provides students with a powerful tool for improving academic performance and truly mastering course material, plus 24/7 online access to an interactive and searchable eBook. Connect allows students to practise important skills at their own pace and on their own schedule. Importantly, students' assessment results and instructors' feedback are all saved online—so students can continually review their progress and plot their course to success. Answered Questions from the text Study Guide are also available in Connect for students' self study.

INSTRUCTOR'S RESOURCES

INSTRUCTOR'S MANUAL

There are three parts to each chapter of the Instructor's Manual. First is a brief overview of the chapter, with some rationale for the topics included. Second is a description of how we think the material found in the chapter could be presented. Between the two of us, we have taught the microeconomic principles course over two hundred times, and we pass on helpful hints gained from this extensive experience to instructors who may not have been at it so long. More experienced instructors who have found a comfortable groove will simply ignore these suggestions.

The third part contains the answers to the Chapter Self Test questions and all questions and problems in the Study Guide section of the text.

COMPUTERIZED TEST BANK

Barbara Gardner of the Southern Alberta Institute of Technology, put much effort into writing the Computerized Test Bank in order to ensure that the questions cover all topics in the textbook, but only those topics. The Computerized Test Bank is available through EZ Test Online, a flexible and easy-to-use electronic testing program that allows instructors to create tests from book-specific items. EZ Test accommodates a wide range of question types and allows instructors to add their own questions. Test items are also available in Word format (Rich Text Format).

For secure online testing, exams created in EZ Test can be exported to WebCT and Blackboard. EZ Test Online is supported at **www.mhhe.com/eztest**, where users can download a Quick Start Guide, access FAQs, or log a ticket for help with specific issues.

POWERPOINT® PRESENTATIONS

Prepared by Alanna Holowinsky of Red River College, this package includes dynamic slides of the important illustrations in the textbook, along with detailed, chapter-by-chapter reviews of the important ideas presented in the text.

lyryx

LYRYX ASSESSMENT FOR ECONOMICS [LAECON]

Based on *Principles of Microeconomics* by Sayre & Morris, Lyryx Assessment for Economics is a leading edge online assessment system, designed to support both students and instructors.

The assessment takes the form of a homework assignment called a *lab*. The assessments are algorithmically generated and automatically graded so that students get instant grades and feedback. New labs are randomly generated each time, providing the student with unlimited opportunities to try a type of each question. After they submit a lab for marking, students receive extensive feedback on their work, thus promoting their learning experience. Text author Alan Morris collaborated with Lyryx Learning on the 6th edition version of Lyryx to ensure the fullest integration possible between the text and Lyryx lab materials.

FOR THE INSTRUCTOR

The goal of the product is for instructors to use these labs for course marks instead of creating and marking their own labs, saving instructors and teaching assistants valuable time to instead help students directly. After registering their courses with us, instructors can create labs of their choice by selecting problems from our bank of questions and setting a deadline for each one of these labs. The content, marking, and feedback of the problems has been developed and implemented with the help of experienced instructors in economics. Instructors have access to all their students' marks and can view their best labs. At any time, the instructors can download the class grades for their own programs.

FOR THE STUDENT

LAECON offers algorithmically generated and automatically graded assignments. Students get instant grades and instant feedback—no need to wait until the next class to find out how well they did! Grades are instantly recorded in a grade book that the student can view.

Students are motivated to do their Labs for two reasons: first because it can be tied to assessment, and second because they can try the lab as many times as they wish prior to the due date with only their best grade being recorded.

Instructors know from experience that if students are doing their economics homework, they will be successful in the course. Recent research regarding the use of Lyryx has shown that when labs are tied to assessment, even if worth only a small percentage of the total grade for the course, students WILL do their homework—and MORE THAN ONCE!!

Please contact your iLearning Sales Specialist for additional information on the Lyryx Assessment Economics system.

Visit http://laecon.lyryx.com

Other Services and Support

COURSE MANAGEMENT

CourseSmart brings together thousands of textbooks across hundreds of courses in an eTextbook format providing unique benefits to students and faculty. By purchasing an eTextbook, students can save up to 50 percent off the cost of a print textbook, reduce their impact on the environment, and gain access to powerful Web tools for learning—including full text search, notes and highlighting, and e-mail tools for sharing notes between classmates. For faculty, CourseSmart provides instant access to review and compare textbooks and course materials in their discipline area without the time, cost, and environmental impact of mailing print exam copies. For further details contact your *i*Learning Sales Specialist or go to www.coursesmart.com.

McGraw-Hill Ryerson offers a range of flexible integration solutions for Blackboard, WebCT, Desire2Learn, Moodle and other leading learning management platforms. Please contact your local McGraw-Hill Ryerson *i*Learning Sales Specialist for details.

CREATE ONLINE

McGraw-Hill's **Create Online** gives you access to the most abundant resource at your fingertips— literally. With a few mouse clicks, you can create customized learning tools simply and affordably. McGraw-Hill Ryerson has included many of our market-leading textbooks within Create Online for e-book and print customization as well as many licensed readings and cases. For more information, go to www.mcgrawhillcreate.ca.

Your **Integrated Learning Sales Specialist** is a McGraw-Hill Ryerson representative who has the experience, product knowledge, training, and support to help you assess and integrate any of the above-noted products, technology, and services into your course for optimum teaching and learning performance. Whether it's using our test bank software, helping your students improve their grades, or putting your entire course online, your *i*Learning Sales Specialist is there to help you do it. Contact your local *i*Learning Sales Specialist to learn how to maximize all of McGraw-Hill Ryerson's resources.

Acknowledgments

We wish to thank the following economists who participated in the formal review process of the seventh edition:

Hussein Alzyoud, Athabasca University
Charles I. Anaere, Thompson Rivers University
Khyati Antani, Humber College
Sarah E. Arliss, Seneca College
Aurelia Best, Centennial College
Michael Bozzo, Mohawk College
Yolina Denchev, Camosun College School of Business
Carol Derksen, Red River College
Sigrid Ewender, Kwantlen Polytechnic University
Oliver Franke, Concordia University College of Alberta
Barbara Gardner, SAIT School of Business
Ekaterina Gregory, University of Victoria, College of New Caledonia
Darren Howes, Medicine Hat College
Alan Idiens, University of Victoria, College of New Caledonia
Roberto Martínez-Espiñeira, St. Francis Xavier University
Serge Nadeau, Wilfrid Laurier University
Jay Perry, Niagara College
Paul Pieper, Humber College
Don Reddick, Kwantlen Polytechnic University
Terri M. Rizzo, Lakehead University
Chandan Shirvaikar, Red Deer College
Russell Turner, Sir Sandford Fleming College

A very special thank-you must be given to Stephanie Powers, Red Deer College, for her vigilant efforts as the technical reviewer for the text and answers.

We would like to acknowledge our colleagues in the Economics Department of Capilano University—Nigel Amon, Ken Moak, Mahak Yaseri, C.S. Lum, Chieko Tanimura, and Camlon Chau—for their encouragement and vigilance in spotting the errors and omissions in earlier editions. Numerous colleagues in other departments also gave us encouragement, and sometimes praise, which is greatly appreciated.

We would also like to thank our many students, past and present, for their helpful comments (and occasional criticism). Most particularly, we wish to acknowledge the continued help and support of James Booty, our Sponsoring Editor. James continues to take an active interest in the book, and his desire to make it better is always apparent.

We would like to acknowledge Judy Sturrup's editing and Rohini Herbert's proofreading, while Maria Chu, Joanne Limebeer, and Katie McHale at McGraw-Hill Ryerson offered excellent professional skills, which are greatly appreciated.

In the end, of course, whatever errors or confusions remain are our responsibility.

Finally, we wish to acknowledge the continued love and support of our families and those close to us.

PRINCIPLES OF
MICROECONOMICS

ECONOMICS TOOLKIT

Some students take economics because it is a requirement for a program they have chosen or degree that they are working toward. Some are interested in a career in business, and taking economics seems like a natural choice. Some even take it because they think that they might like it. Whatever your reasons for taking economics, we are glad you did and hope you will not be disappointed. Economics is a challenging discipline to learn, but it is also one of the most rewarding courses you will ever take. The logic and analysis used in economics is very powerful, and successfully working your way through the principles of economics over the next term will do for your mind what a serious jogging program will do for your body. Bon voyage!

THE CANADIAN REALITY

The Land

Canada is a huge country—in fact, it is the second-largest country on this planet. It contains seven percent of the world's land mass. It stretches 5600 kilometres from the Atlantic to the Pacific Ocean and encompasses six time zones. Ontario alone, which is the second-largest province (after Quebec), is larger than Pakistan, Turkey, Chile, France, or the United Kingdom. Canada's ten provinces range in size from tiny Prince Edward Island to Quebec, which is nearly 240 times as large. In addition, its three territories—the Northwest Territories, Yukon, and Nunavut—demand that we describe this country's reach as being from sea to sea *to sea*.

Within Canada, there are at least six major mountain ranges: the Torngats, Appalachians, and Laurentians in the east, and the Mackenzie, Rocky, and Coast ranges in the west. Any one of these rivals the European Alps in size and grandeur. In addition, Canada has vast quantities of fresh water—nine percent of the world's total—in tens of thousands of lakes and numerous rivers, of which the St. Lawrence and the Mackenzie are the largest.

Canada is richly endowed with natural resources, including gas, oil, gold, silver, copper, iron, nickel, potash, uranium, zinc, fish, timber, and as mentioned above, water—lots of fresh water. The conclusion is inescapable: Canada is a big, beautiful, and rich country.

The People

The word *Canada* comes from a Huron–Iroquois word meaning *village*. In a sense, this is very appropriate because, big as the nation is geographically, it is small in terms of population. Its 34 million people make up only 0.5 percent of the world's population. In fact, there are more people in California or in greater Tokyo than there are in the whole of Canada. Interestingly, Canada's population growth rate, at 1.2 percent, is the highest among G8 countries, primarily because of Canada's high rate of immigration. Thirty-nine percent of Canadians live in the province of Ontario and 23 percent in

Quebec. On the other hand, Prince Edward Island has a population of only 141 000, less than that of the cities of Sherbrooke, Quebec, or North Vancouver, B.C.

Despite the popular images of small Maritime fishing villages, lonely Prairie grain farmers, or remote B.C. loggers, Canada is, in fact, an urban nation. Over 80 per cent of Canadians live in what Statistics Canada calls "urban" areas. There are six Canadian metropolitan areas with populations of over 1 million: Toronto, with 5.6 million; Montreal, 3.8 million; Vancouver, 2.3 million; Calgary and Edmonton, each with 1.2 million and Ottawa–Gatineau, 1.2 million. It is also true that the vast majority of the 33 million Canadians live in a narrow band stretching along the border with the United States, which, incidentally, is the longest unguarded border in the world.

Approximately half of the Canadian population of 34 million is active in the labour force. The labour-force participation rate is 72 percent for males and 63 percent for females.

Multiculturalism

Within this vast, thinly populated country there is a truly diverse, multicultural mix of people. This reality was officially recognized in 1988 when Parliament passed the *Multiculturalism Act*.

There are two official languages in Canada, yet 18 percent of Canadians speak a language other than English or French. In fact, at least 60 languages are spoken in this country. In each year of the 1990s, more than 200 000 new immigrants arrived in Canada. Over 18 percent of all Canadians are first-generation immigrants. In both Toronto and Vancouver, over half the students in the public school system are from non–English-speaking homes. There are over 100 minority language publications in Toronto, and Vancouver has three daily Chinese-language newspapers.

Canada's First Nations people number 1.1 million (3.8 percent of the total population), and a quarter of them live in Ontario.

Government

Canada is a constitutional monarchy with a democratic parliament made up of the House of Commons, with 308 elected members, and the Senate, with 105 appointed members. In addition to Parliament, the other two decision-making divisions of the federal government are the cabinet, composed of the prime minister and 25 (or so) ministers and their departments, and the judiciary, which includes the Supreme Court as well as the federal and tax courts.

Just as there are two official languages in this country, Canada has two systems of civil law—one uncodified and based on common law in English Canada, and the other as codified civil law in Quebec. Canada's constitution, the first part of which is the *Canadian Charter of Rights and Freedoms*, came into being in 1982, a full 115 years after Confederation created the country in 1867.

The fact that Canada is a confederation means the federal government shares responsibilities with the provinces. For example, while the federal government has jurisdiction in national defence, international trade, immigration, banking, criminal law, fisheries, transportation, and communications, the provinces have responsibility for education, property rights, health, and natural resources. Inevitably, issues arise from time to time that do not fit neatly into any one of these categories, with the result that federal–provincial disputes are a continuous part of the Canadian reality.

Canada the Good

Most Canadians are well aware that they live in a good country. But perhaps many do not realize just how good. The average family after-tax income is currently over $74 000, which puts the Canadian living standard among the highest in the world.

The United Nations maintains a Human Development Index that considers factors in addition to average income levels, including life spans and literacy rates. In 2009, this index ranked Canada as the number four nation in the world in which to live. One reason for this high ranking is that Canadian governments spend over 10 percent of the country's gross domestic product (GDP) on health care.

More than 70 percent of Canadians own their homes, well over 90 percent are literate, and over 80 percent of all Canadians have access to the Internet. All three of these statistics are among the highest in the world.

Canada the Odd

Canada is a good country in which to live; however, it does have its oddities. In 1965—98 years after Confederation—it was decided that Canada really should have a national flag. A parliamentary selection committee was set up to choose one, and received no less than two thousand designs. The flag debate was acrimonious, to say the least, although today most Canadians seem quite comfortable with the Maple Leaf. The English-language lyrics of Canada's national anthem, *O Canada*, were formally approved only in 1975. Canada adopted the metric system of measurement in the 1970s, but the imperial system is still in wide use; for example, Statistics Canada still reports the breadth of this country in miles, we sell sizes of wood in inches (such as 2 × 4s), and football fields are 110 yards long.

In this bilingual country, it is odd to note that there are more Manitobans who speak Cree than British Columbians who speak French. In this affluent country of ours, it also interesting to note that 4 percent of Canadian homes are heated exclusively by burning wood. Canada's official animal is—the beaver.

On a more serious note, it is a sad fact that the trade of many goods, and even some services, between any one province and the United States is freer than trade between provinces. There is an interesting history concerning trade patterns in North America. At the time of Confederation, trade patterns on this continent were mostly north–south. The Maritimes traded with the New England states, Quebec with New York, Ontario with the Great Lakes states to its south, and the West Coast traded with California. Canada's first prime minister, John A. Macdonald, was also elected as its third. During his second administration, he implemented his party's National Policy, which resulted in 1) the building of a railway to the West Coast, which encouraged British Columbia to join Canada; 2) offering free land to new immigrants on the prairies in order to settle this area; and 3) forcing trade patterns into an east–west mode by erecting a tariff wall against American imports. British Columbia did join Confederation; people were enticed to settle in Manitoba, Saskatchewan, and Alberta; and the pattern of trade did become more east–west.

So, was the National Policy a success? Some would argue yes, pointing out that it built a nation and that Canada as we know it might not exist today without it. Others are not so sure and would argue that it set back Canada's development by encouraging and protecting new, less efficient industries through the creation of a branch-plant economy. This occurred because American firms that had previously exported to Canada simply jumped over the tariff walls and established Canadian branch plants. Some believe that the National Policy also promoted Canadian regionalism and aggravated relations between regions because both the West and the Maritimes felt that most of its economic benefits favoured central Canada.

In any case, as a result of the North American Free Trade Agreement (NAFTA) of 1992, trade with the United States (and Mexico) is now mostly without tariffs and north–south trade patterns are re-emerging. Historically, Canadian policy has come full circle. However, the trade barriers between provinces, which were built piece by piece over a century, remain.

The Economy

Canada is among the ten largest economies in the world, despite its small population. In 2008, Canada's GDP was $1600 billion. This figure can be broken down as illustrated in **Table T.1**.

ECONOMICS TOOLKIT

TABLE T.1

Category	Amount ($ billion)
Personal expenditures	891
Investment spending	319
Government spending	365
Exports	564
Less imports	(539)
Total GDP	1 600

Source: Adapted from the Statistics Canada CANSIM database <http://cansim2.statcan.ca>, Table 380-0017, 11 January 2011.

The provincial breakdown of the 2008 GDP figure of $1600 billion is shown in **Table T.2**.

TABLE T.2

Province	Population (millions)	GDP ($ billions)	GDP per capita ($ thousands)
Newfoundland (and Labrador)	0.51	29.2	61.8
Prince Edward Island	0.14	4.5	33.2
Nova Scotia	0.94	32.9	36.5
New Brunswick	0.75	27.0	36.6
Quebec	7.8	297.4	39.0
Ontario	12.9	585.7	45.4
Manitoba	1.2	48.7	42.1
Saskatchewan	1.0	50.8	62.7
Alberta	3.6	256.9	81.0
British Columbia	4.4	191.6	45.2
Yukon	0.3	1.7	57.4
Northwest Territories (pre-Nunavut)	0.4	4.6	116.7
Nunavut	0.3	1.4	50.7

Source: Adapted from the Statistics Canada CANSIM database <http://cansim2.statcan.ca>, Tables 384-0002 and 051-0001, 11 January 2011.

This table illustrates the wide disparity in average incomes between provinces, from a low of $33 200 per person in Prince Edward Island to a high of $81 000 in Alberta (and even higher in the Northwest Territories).

In most years the economy grows and the GDP figure rises. To accurately compare growth in GDP, however, we need to use a common set of prices so that a simple rise in prices is not confused with an actual increase in the output of goods and services. Using *real* GDP figures, which correct for inflation, accomplishes this. **Table T.3** looks at some recent real GDP figures, using 2002 prices.

TABLE T.3

Year	Real GDP ($ billion)	Increase/Decrease ($ billion)	% Increase
2005	1248	—	—
2006	1281	+33	+2.6
2007	1307	+26	+2.0
2008	1304	−3	−0.2
2009	1279	−25	−1.9

Source: Adapted from the Statistics Canada CANSIM database <http://cansim2.statcan.ca>, Table 380-0017, 12 January 2011.

Next, let us look at a breakdown of Canada's GDP by industry in **Table T.4**, presented in order of importance.

TABLE T.4

Industry	Percentage of GDP
Finance	21.0
Manufacturing	12.6
Trade (wholesale & retail)	11.7
Professional & technical	7.6
Health	6.8
Public administration	6.1
Construction	5.8
Education	5.1
Transportation	4.7
Mining/Oil	4.3
Information & cultural	3.8
Other Services	2.7
Utilities	2.5
Accomodation & Food	2.2
Agriculture, fishing & forestry	2.2
Arts & entertainment	0.9

Source: Adapted from the Statistics Canada CANSIM database <http://cansim2.statcan.ca>, Table 379-0027, 12 January 2011.

This information is helpful in many ways. For example, it is certainly time to put to rest the idea that Canada is a resource-based economy and that Canadians are simply "hewers of wood and drawers of water," as many of us were taught in school. In fact, agriculture/fishing/forestry and mining/oil make up less than 7 percent of our economy's GDP. Only 4 percent of working Canadians are employed in primary industries, down dramatically from 13 percent a quarter of a century ago.

In contrast, one can marshal the argument that Canada is quite a sophisticated and technologically advanced economy. For example, it is not generally recognized that Canada was the world's third nation to go into space, with the Alouette I satellite in 1962. Canadian industries pioneered long-distance pipeline technology, and Canada is a world leader in several areas of aviation, including turboprop, turbofan, and firefighting aircraft, not to mention the well-known Canadarm used on space shuttles. Canada is also a world leader in commercial submarine technology, and routinely maintains one of the world's longest and most efficient railway systems.

One can also point to many outstanding Canadian companies that are truly world leaders in technology and performance, including Bombardier in transportation equipment, Ballard Power in fuel cell technology, SNC Lavalin in aluminum plant design, Rio Tinto in mining, Trizec Hahn in real estate development, and Magna International in automobile parts manufacturing.

Exports: The Engine that Drives the Economy

Exports are a fundamental part of the Canadian economy. Almost 40 percent of its GDP is exported, which makes Canada one of the world's greatest trading nations. Exports to the United States alone directly support over 1.5 million Canadian jobs, and a $1 billion increase in exports translates into 11 000 new jobs. Again, contrary to historical wisdom, only 20 percent of Canadian exports are resources—the figure was 40 percent a quarter of a century ago.

Table T.5 breaks down the $439 billion worth of goods Canada exported in 2009 into nine categories in order of size.

TABLE T.5

Export Category	Percentage of Total Exports
Machinery & equipment	18.6
Energy products	18.4
Industrial goods	18.3
Services	15.9
Automotive products	10.1
Agricultural & fishing products	8.6
Forestry products	4.5
Other consumer goods	4.1
Special transactions trade	1.5

Source: Adapted from the Statistics Canada CANSIM database <http://cansim2.statcan.ca>, Tables 228-0043 and 380-0027, 11 January 2011.

A Mixed Economy

At the start of the twenty-first century, the market system dominates most of the world's economies, and Canada is no exception to this. Yet, government also plays a big role in our economy. For example, in 2009, the three levels of government collected $586 billion in tax revenue, which represented over 38 percent of Canada's 2009 GDP. **Table T.6** shows the sources and the use of this revenue.

The largest single source of the government's tax revenue, 32 percent, was personal income taxes. Consumption taxes include, most significantly, the GST (goods and services tax) and the PST (provincial sales tax) as well as gasoline, alcohol, and tobacco taxes, customs taxes, and gaming income. These indirect (consumption) taxes accounted for 18 percent of total revenue. Thus, we can see that the majority of the government's tax revenue comes from individual Canadians in the form of direct income taxes or consumption taxes.

And how does government spend these billions of dollars of tax revenue? The right column of **Table T.6** shows us.

TABLE T.6

Government Revenues	% of Total	Government Expenditures	% of Total
Personal income taxes	32.3	Social services	25.6
Consumption taxes	18.3	Health	20.5
Property taxes	9.4	Education	16.1
Investment income	9.2	Protection of persons & property	8.5
Sales of goods & services	9.2	Debt charges	7.6
Corporate incomes taxes	8.5	Environment	6.3
Social security premiums	6.0	Transportation	5.4
Other taxes	5.3	Government services	3.8

Source: Adapted from the Statistics Canada CANSIM database <http://cansim2.statcan.ca>, Table 385-0001, 12 January 2011.

Here, we see that government's largest single category of spending, 26 percent, was on social service payments to individuals. The lion's share of this expenditure, (approximately two-thirds), was social services (pensions, unemployment benefits, and welfare) payments. Thus, we see that a large percentage of spending by government is an attempt to direct income to poorer Canadians. Since all Canadians pay for most of these expenditures, we can see that government is actively involved in *transferring* income from higher-income to lower-income families and individuals. This income distribution role is seen by many Canadians as an important function of government.

On the other hand, some Canadians take the view that government has gone too far in its interventionist role and yearn for less governmental involvement in the economy. They often point to the United States as an example of an economy in which both welfare, unemployment, and pension payments to individuals and direct government aid to poor regions of the country are lower. The difference in the general approach of the two governments may well lie in historical differences in the attitudes of Canadians and Americans toward government. Over the years, Canadians, by and large, have trusted governments to act in their best interests and have been more tolerant of government attempts at income redistribution. Americans, on the other hand, have a history of being suspicious of big government and have repeatedly rejected attempts to expand its role. The recent controversy in the United States over attempts to implement a national health care policy is an example. Another is the Canadian government's direct aid to cultural endeavours, including the funding of national television and radio networks, while no such efforts exist in the United States.

The next two largest categories of spending are on two essentials, health and education. In 2009, the Canadian government allocated 21 and 16 percent of spending in these two areas. The fourth category, protection of persons and property, includes expenditures on the military, police, fire departments, the court system, and prisons. Interest on the national debt was the fifth biggest item of spending at just under 8 percent. The amount spent in this area has steadily declined in the last few years as Canada has started to get government budget deficits under control. (As recently as 1998, servicing the national debt amounted to as much as 30 percent of total spending). The other categories include a host of such items as culture (the Canada Council), housing, foreign affairs, immigration, labour, and research.

This completes our brief look at the Canadian economic reality. We hope that it has helped fill in some gaps in your knowledge of the country. We are confident that you will come to know your country much better after a thorough grounding in the principles of economics, for, in a very real sense, economics is about understanding and improving on what we already know.

Graphing Reality

Let us face it: a lot of students hate graphs. For them a picture is not worth a thousand words. It may even be true that they seem to understand some economic concepts just fine until the instructor draws a graph on the board. All of a sudden, they lose confidence and start to question what they previously thought they knew. For these students, graphs are not the solution but the problem. This section is designed to help those students overcome this difficulty. For those other, more fortunate, students who can handle graphs and know that they are used to illustrate concepts, a quick reading of this section will help reinforce their understanding.

It is probably true that if an idea can be expressed clearly and precisely with words, then graphs become an unnecessary luxury. The trouble is that, from time to time, economists find themselves at a loss for words and see no way of getting a certain point across except with the use of a graph. On the other hand, by themselves, graphs cannot explain everything; they need to be accompanied by a verbal explanation. In other words, graphs are not a substitute for words but a complement. The words accompanied by a picture can often give us a much richer understanding of economic concepts and happenings.

Graphing a Single Variable

The graphing of a single variable is reasonably straightforward. Often, economists want to concentrate on a single economic variable, such as Canada's exports, or consumers' incomes, or the production of wine in Canada. In some cases, they want to look at the composition of that variable, say, different categories of exports. In other cases, they are interested in seeing how one variable changed over a period of time, such as total exports for each of the years 2005 through 2009. In the first instance, we would be looking at a *cross-section*; in the second instance, we are looking at a *time series*.

Cross-Sectional Graphs

One popular way of showing cross-sectional data is in the form of a pie chart. **Figure T.1**, for instance, shows the composition of Canada's exports for 2009 in terms of the type of goods or services that Canada sells abroad. (This is the same data as presented in **Table T.1**. Which presentation format—table or graph—do you prefer? Which do you find easier to read and understand?)

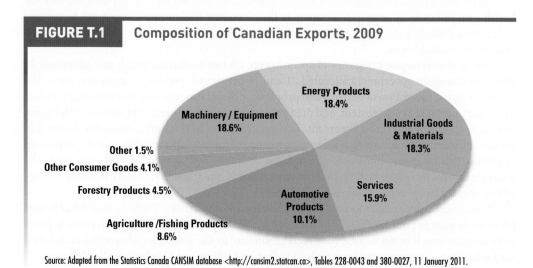

FIGURE T.1 Composition of Canadian Exports, 2009

Energy Products 18.4%

Machinery / Equipment 18.6%

Industrial Goods & Materials 18.3%

Other 1.5%

Other Consumer Goods 4.1%

Forestry Products 4.5%

Agriculture /Fishing Products 8.6%

Automotive Products 10.1%

Services 15.9%

Source: Adapted from the Statistics Canada CANSIM database <http://cansim2.statcan.ca>, Tables 228-0043 and 380-0027, 11 January 2011.

The size of each slice indicates the relative size of each category of exports. But the picture by itself is not always enough. We have added the percentage of total exports that each type represents. Note, however, that there are no dollar amounts for the categories.

Alternatively, the same information could be presented in the form of a bar graph, as in **Figure T.2**.

FIGURE T.2   Composition of Canadian Exports, 2009

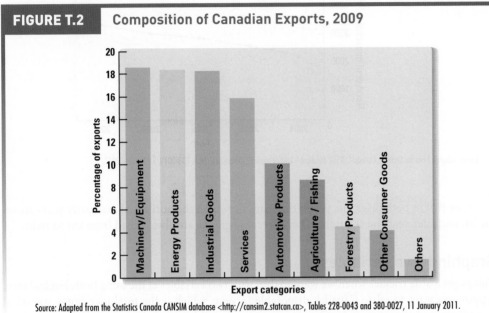

Source: Adapted from the Statistics Canada CANSIM database <http://cansim2.statcan.ca>, Tables 228-0043 and 380-0027, 11 January 2011.

Unlike the pie chart, the bar graph allows us to more easily compare the relative sizes of each category since they are now placed side by side.

Time-Series Graphs

Time-series data can also be presented in the form of a bar graph. **Figure T.3** is a bar graph showing how the number of digital cameras owned by Canadian households has changed over a five-year period.

FIGURE T.3   Ownership of Digital Cameras, 2004–2008

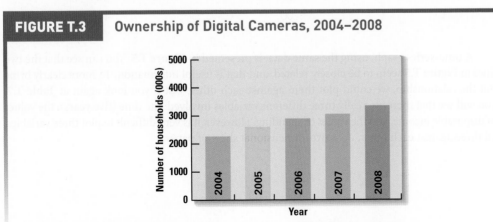

Source: Adapted from the Statistics Canada CANSIM database <http://cansim2.statcan.ca>, Table 203-0010, 12 January 2011.

The same information can be presented in a line graph, as is done in **Figure T.4**.

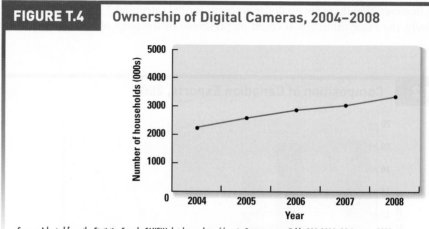

FIGURE T.4   Ownership of Digital Cameras, 2004–2008

Source: Adapted from the Statistics Canada CANSIM database <http://cansim2.statcan.ca>, Table 203-0010, 12 January 2011.

Note that in both cases, the years (time) are shown on the horizontal axis; early years are on the left and later years on the right. This is because graphs are always read from left to right.

Graphing Two Variables

Things get a little trickier when we want to deal with two variables at the same time. For instance, suppose we want to relate Canada's disposable income, which is the total take-home pay of all Canadians, and the amount spent on consumer goods (these numbers are in billions and are hypothetical). One obvious way to do this is with a table, as is done in **Table T.7**.

TABLE T.7

Year	Disposable Income	Spending on Consumer Goods
1	$100	$ 80
2	120	98
3	150	125
4	160	134
5	200	170

A time-series graph, using the same data, is presented in **Figure T.5**. You can see that the two lines in **Figure T.5** seem to be closely related, and that is useful information. To more clearly bring out the relationship, we could plot them against each other. But if you look again at **Table T.7**, you will see that there are really three different variables involved: the time (five years), the values of disposable income, and the values of spending. However, it is very difficult to plot three variables, all three against each other, on a two-dimensional sheet of paper.

FIGURE T.5   Disposable Income and Spending on Consumer Goods (hypothetical numbers)

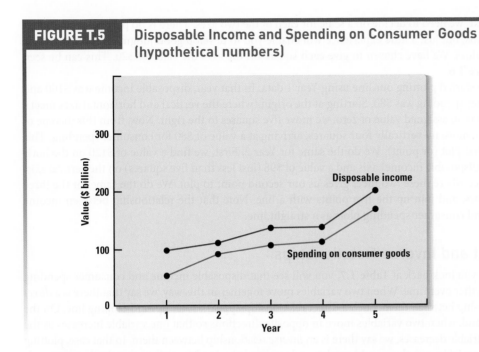

Instead, in **Figure T.6**, we will put disposable income on the horizontal axis (also called the *x*-axis), and consumer spending on the vertical axis (also called the *y*-axis) and indicate time with written notation. There is a rule about which variable goes on which axis, but we will leave that for later chapters.

FIGURE T.6   Spending on Consumer Goods

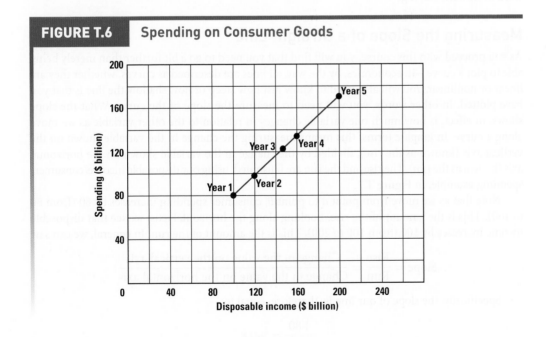

Next, we need to decide on a scale for each of the two axes. There is no particular rule about doing this, but just a little experience will enable you to develop good judgment about selecting these values. We have chosen to give each square on the axes the value of $20. This can be seen in **Figure T.6**.

We started plotting our line using Year 1 data. In that year, disposable income was $100 and consumer spending was $80. Starting at the origin (where the vertical and horizontal axes meet), which has an assigned value of zero, we move five squares to the right. Now, from this income of $100, we move up vertically four squares, arriving at a value of $80 for consumer spending. This is our first plot (or point). We do the same for Year 2. First, we find a value of $120 on the horizontal (disposable income) axis and a value of $98 (just less than five squares) on the vertical axis. The place where these two meet gives us our second point to plot. We do the same for the three next years, and join up the five points with a line. Note that the relationship between income levels and consumer spending plots as a straight line.

Direct and Inverse Relationships

Next, if you look back at **Table T.7**, you will see that disposable income and consumer spending rise together over time. When two variables move together in this way, we say that there is a *direct* relationship between them. Such a direct relationship appears as an upward-sloping line. On the other hand, when two variables move in opposite directions so that one variable increases as the other variable decreases, we say there is an *inverse* relationship between them. In that case, plotting the two variables together would result in a downward-sloping line. (When we talk about upward-sloping and downward-sloping, remember that we are reading the graphs from left to right.)

One last point: the income–consumer-spending line in **Figure T.6** is a straight line. There is no reason that this has to always be the case. Some data might plot as a straight line, and other data might be nonlinear when plotted (as in **Figure T.5**). Either, of course, could still be downward or upward sloping.

Measuring the Slope of a Straight Line

As you proceed with this course, you will find that you need to go a bit further than merely being able to plot a curve—in economics, by the way, all lines are described as curves, whether they are linear or nonlinear. You will also need to know just how steep or how shallow the line is that you have plotted. In other words, you will need to measure the slope of the curve. What the slope shows, in effect, is how much one variable changes in relation to the other variable as we move along a curve. In graphic terms, this means measuring the change in the variable shown on the vertical axis (known as the *rise*), divided by the change in the variable shown on the horizontal axis (known as the *run*). The rise and the run are illustrated, using our disposable income/consumer-spending example, in **Figure T.7**.

Note that as we move from point *a* to point *b*, consumer spending increases by 80 (from 80 to 160). This is the amount of the rise. Looking along the horizontal axis, we see that disposable income increases by 100 (from 100 to 200). This is the amount of the run. In general, we can say:

$$\text{Slope} = \frac{\text{Rise}}{\text{Run}} = \frac{\text{Change in the value on the vertical axis}}{\text{Change in the value on the horizontal axis}}$$

Specifically, the slope of our line is, therefore, equal to:

$$\frac{+80}{+100} = +0.8$$

FIGURE T.7   Rise over Run

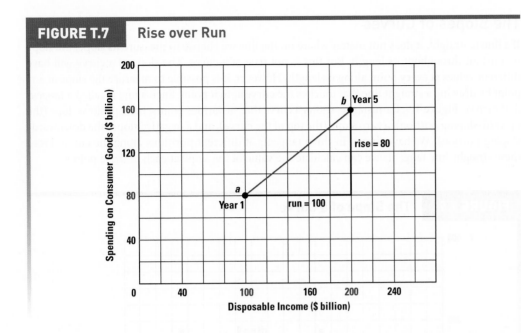

Figure T.8 shows four other curves, two upward-sloping and two downward-sloping, with an indication for each as to how to calculate the various slopes. In each case, we measure the slope by moving from point *a* to point *b*.

FIGURE T.8   Four Different Slopes

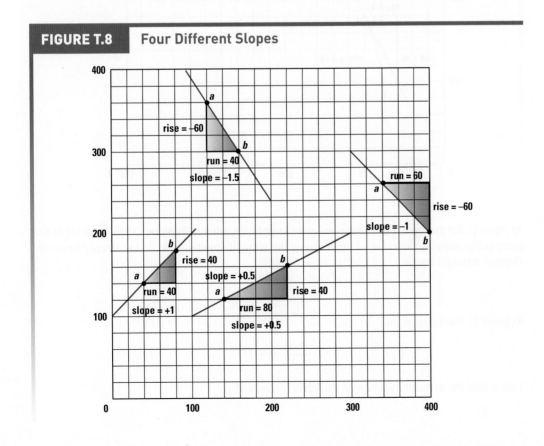

The Slopes of Curves

If a line is straight, it does not matter where on the line we choose to measure its slope; the slope is constant throughout its length. But this is not true of a curve. The slope of a curve will have different values at every point along its length. However, it is possible to measure the slope at any point by drawing a straight line that touches the curve at that point. Such a line is called a *tangent to the curve*. **Figure T.9**, for instance, shows a curve that, at various points, has a positive slope (the upward-sloping portion), a zero slope (the top of the curve), and a negative slope (the downward-sloping portion). We have drawn in three tangents at different positions along the curve. From these straight-line tangents we can calculate the value of the slope at each of these points.

FIGURE T.9	The Slope of a Curve

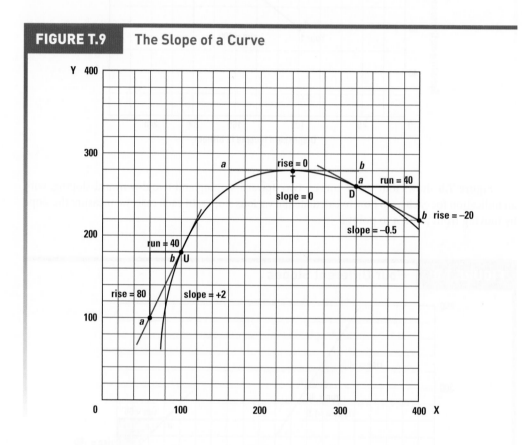

At point U, for example, the curve rises quite steeply. So, what is its slope? Well, its slope at this point is the same as the value of the slope of the straight-line tangent. As we already know the slope of astraight line is:

$$\frac{\text{Rise}}{\text{Run}}$$

At point U, this is equal to:

$$\frac{+80}{+40} = +2$$

This is also the value of the slope of the curve at point U.

At point T, the tangent is a horizontal line, which, by definition, does not rise or fall. The rise/run at this point, therefore, is equal to zero. Finally, at point D, both the curve and the tangent are downward-sloping, indicating a negative slope. Its value is calculated, as before, as rise/run, which equals −20/40 or −0.5.

Equations for a Straight Line

In economics, graphs are a very important and useful way to present information. Thus, you will find the pages of most economics books liberally sprinkled with graphs. But there are other, equally useful, ways of presenting the same data. One of these is an algebraic equation. You will often find it very useful to be able to translate a graph into algebra. In this short section, we will show you how to do this. To keep things simple, we will restrict our attention to straight-line graphs.

In order to find the equation for any straight line, you need only two pieces of information: the slope of the line and the value of the Y-intercept. You already know how to calculate the value of the slope. The value of the Y-intercept is simply the value at which the line crosses the vertical axis. In general, the algebraic expression for a straight line is given as

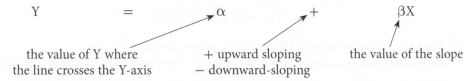

Y   =   α   +   βX

the value of Y where   + upward sloping   the value of the slope
the line crosses the Y-axis   − downward-sloping

For instance, in **Figure T.10**, line 1 has a slope of +1 (the line is upward-sloping and therefore has a positive slope and rises by 10 units for every run of 10 units). The line crosses the *y*-axis at a value of 50. The equation for line 1, therefore, is:

$$Y = 50 + (1)X$$

FIGURE T.10   **Equations for Straight Lines**

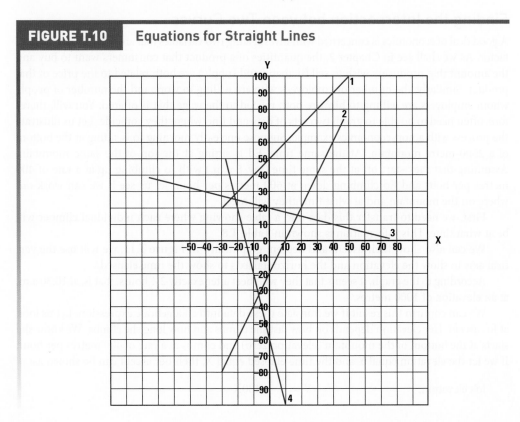

Armed with this equation, we could figure out the value of Y for any value of X. For example, when X (along the horizontal axis) has a value of 40, Y must be equal to:

$$Y = 50 + 40 = 90$$

You can verify this in **Figure T.10**. In addition, we can work out values of X and Y that are not shown on the graph. For example, when X equals 200, Y equals $50 + 200 = 250$.

Let us work out the equations for the other lines shown in **Figure T.10**. Line 2 is also upward-sloping, but it is steeper than line 1 and has a slope of +2 (it rises by 20 for every run of 10).

Its intercept, however, is in the negative area of the y-axis and crosses at the value of −20. The equation for line 2, then, is:

$$Y = -20 + 2X$$

Again, you can check that this is correct by putting in a value for X, finding the corresponding value of Y, and looking on the graph to see if it is correct. For instance, when X has a value of 40, the equation tells us that:

$$Y = -20 + 2(40) = 60$$

You can confirm in **Figure T.10** that this is, indeed, the case.

In contrast, line 3 has a negative slope of 0.25 and a Y-intercept at 20. Its equation, therefore, is:

$$Y = 20 - 0.25X$$

Finally, line 4 has the equation:

$$Y = -60 - 4X$$

Finding the Intersection between Two Curves

A good deal of economics is concerned with investigating two variables that are related to a common factor. As we shall see in Chapter 2, the quantities of a product that consumers want to buy and the amount that producers wish to sell (demand and supply) are both related to the price of that product. Similarly, the number of employees who are willing to work and the number of people whom employers are willing to hire are both related to the wage that is offered. You will, therefore, often need to be able to graph two sets of data and find where they coincide. Let us illustrate the process with a non-economics example. Suppose one early morning Jo is sitting at the bottom of a 2500-metre mountain. At the same time, Ed is sitting at the top of the same mountain. Assuming that they start off at the same time (say, 8 a.m.) with Jo climbing up at a rate of 400 metres per hour and Ed climbing down at 600 metres per hour, let us see if we can work out where on the mountain and at what time they will meet.

First, we need to transfer this data into a table showing where each individual climber will be at what time. This information is shown in **Table T.8**.

We can also show their ascent and descent graphically. In **Figure T.11**, we will use the vertical axis to show the elevation and the horizontal axis to show the time elapsed.

According to the graph, it seems that they will meet after exactly 2½ hours, that is, at 10:30 a.m. at an elevation of 1000 metres.

We can confirm this result if we translate these data into an algebraic expression. Let us look at Jo's ascent. Her elevation depends on how fast she climbs and how long she climbs. We know she starts at the bottom of the mountain (elevation zero) and climbs at a rate of 400 metres per hour. If we let the elevation equal Y and the time elapsed equal X, then her ascent can be shown as:

Jo's elevation: $Y = 0 + 400X$

TABLE T.8

Jo's Ascent			Ed's Descent		
Elapsed/Time		Elevation (metres)	Elapsed/Time		Elevation (metres)
0	(8 a.m.)	0	0	(8 a.m.)	2500
1	(9 a.m.)	400	1	(9 a.m.)	1900
2	(10 a.m.)	800	2	(10 a.m.)	1300
3	(11 a.m.)	1200	3	(11 a.m.)	700
4	(12 noon)	1600	4	(12 noon)	100
5	(1 p.m.)	2000	4:10	(12:10 p.m.)	0
6	(2 p.m.)	2400			
6:15	(2:15 p.m.)	2500			

FIGURE T.11

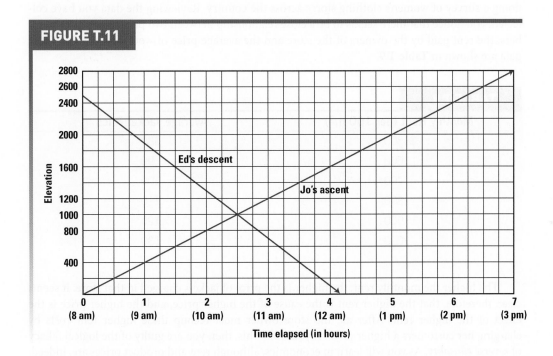

In contrast, Ed starts at an elevation of 2500 metres and his elevation falls as he climbs down. His descent can, therefore, be shown as:

Ed's elevation: $Y = 2500 - 600X$

To find out when and where they will meet is to recognize that whatever this point is, it occurs on the mountain is the same point for the two of them. In other words, Jo and Ed's elevation will be the same. Algebraically, we make the two equations equal and solve. Thus:

$$400X = 2500 - 600X$$

$$1000X = 2500$$

$$X = 2.5$$

So, they will meet after 2.5 hours (2 hours and 30 minutes), or at 10:30 a.m. To find out where they will meet, simply replace X with 2.5 in Jo's and/or Ed's elevation equation:

Jo: $\qquad\qquad 400(2.5) = 1000$ (metres)

Ed: $\qquad\qquad 2400 - 600(2.5) = 1000$

Graphs and Logic

Now, let us look at some potential problems in illustrating data with graphs. For example, the relationship between income and consumer spending in **Table T.7** is hypothetical, since we created it so that it would plot well on a graph. However, any real-world relationship between two variables may not be as neat and simple as this. Data does not always plot into a nice straight line.

Even more seriously, we can never be totally certain of the *nature* of the relationship between the variables being graphed. There is often a great danger of implying something that is not there. You, therefore, need to be on guard against logical fallacies. Suppose, for instance, that you were doing a survey of women's clothing stores across the country. Reviewing the data you have collected, you notice that there seems to be a close relationship between two particular sets of numbers: the rent paid by the owners of the store and the average price of wool jackets sold. These data are shown in **Table T.9**.

TABLE T.9

Monthly Rent (per 100 m²)	Average Jacket Price
$1500	$80
1600	90
1700	100
1800	110
1900	120
2000	130

The higher the monthly rent, the higher is the price of jackets charged in that store. It seems clear, therefore, that the higher rent is the cause of the higher price, and the higher price is the effect of the higher rent. After all, the store owner must recoup these higher rent costs by charging her customers a higher price. If you think this, then you are guilty of the logical fallacy of *reverse causality*. As you will learn in economics, although rent and product prices are, indeed, related, the causality is in fact the other way around. This is because stores in certain areas can charge higher product prices because of their trendy location, and landlords charge those stores higher rents for the same reason—it is a desirable location. Higher prices, therefore, are the cause and high rents the effect. This is not obvious and illustrates how using raw economic data without sound economic theory can lead to serious error.

A second logical fallacy is that of the *omitted variable*, which can also lead to confusion over cause and effect. **Table T.10** highlights this error. Here, we see hypothetical data on rates of alcoholism and the annual income levels of individuals.

There certainly seems to be a very close relationship between these two variables. Presented in this form, without any commentary, one is left to wonder if low income causes alcoholism or if alcoholism is the cause of low income. Perhaps some people with low incomes drink in order to try to escape the effects of poverty. Or perhaps instead it implies that people who drink to excess have great difficulty in finding or keeping a good job. In truth, it is possible that neither of

TABLE T.10

Average Income Levels ($)	Alcoholism (per thousand of population)
5 000	40
15 000	35
25 000	30
35 000	25
45 000	20
55 000	15

these views is true. Simply because two sets of data seem closely related does not necessarily mean that one is the cause of the other. In fact, it may well be that both are caused by an omitted variable. In the above example, it is possible, for instance, that both high alcoholism and low income levels are the result of low educational attainment.

A third fallacy can occur when people see a cause and effect relationship that does not really exist. This is known as the fallacy of *post hoc, ergo propter hoc*, which literally means "after this, therefore because of this." That is to say, it is a fallacy to believe that just because one thing follows another, that one is the result of the other. For example, just because my favourite soccer team always loses whenever I go to see them, that does not mean I am the cause of their losing!

There is a final fallacy you should guard against, a fallacy, unfortunately, that even the best economists commit from time to time. This is the *fallacy of composition*, which is the belief that because something is true for a part, it is true for the whole. You may have noticed, for instance, that fights occasionally break out in hockey games. These fights often occur in the corners of the rink, which makes them difficult to see. The best way for individuals to get a better view is by standing, and, of course, when everybody stands, then most people cannot see. Thus, what is true for a single fan—standing up to see better—is not true for the whole crowd. Similarly, a teacher who suggests that in order to get good grades students should sit at the front of the class is guilty of the same kind of logical fallacy!

We hope that this little primer on Canada and on graphing has been helpful. It is now time to move on to the study of economics.

Answered Questions

Indicate whether the following statements are true or false:

1. **T or F** Canada is the world's largest country in area and has 1 percent of the world's population.

2. **T or F** Ontario has the largest provincial economy, and the largest provincial population, and it is Canada's largest province in area.

3. **T or F** Over 50 percent of Canada's exports are resources.

4. **T or F** The largest single source of government tax revenue is personal income taxes.

5. **T or F** Spending on social services is the largest category of spending by (all) governments in Canada.

6. **T or F** Three popular types of graphs are pie charts, bar graphs, and line graphs.

7. **T or F** Since disposable income and consumer spending both rise together over time, there is a direct relationship between the two.

8. **T or F** The slope of a straight line is measured by dividing the run by the rise.

9. **T or F** If the equation $Y = 5 + 2X$ were plotted, the slope of the line would be equal to 1/2.

10. **T or F** The logic fallacy, *post hoc, ergo propter hoc* means "after this, therefore because of this."

Simple Calculations

11. **Table T.11** shows the dollar value of commercial sea fishing in Canada for 2002.
    a) From these data, construct a bar chart.
    b) Construct a pie chart showing the percentage of the total that each species represents.

TABLE T.11

	$ millions
Groundfish (including cod, halibut, etc.)	288
Pelagic Fish (including salmon and herring)	185
Lobster	594
Crab	505
Shrimps	294
Other shellfish	254
Total Value	**2 120**

12. Complete the following schedules, and plot the following equations:

a) $Y = -200 + 2X$

Y	X
	0
	100
	200
	300
	400

b) $Y = 500 - 4X$

Y	X
	0
	100
	200
	300
	400

13. Given the lines shown in **Figure T.12**, complete the following tables, and calculate the equations for the lines:

a)

Y	X
	0
	20
	40
	60
	80
	100

b)

Y	X
	0
	20
	40
	60
	80
	100

FIGURE T.12

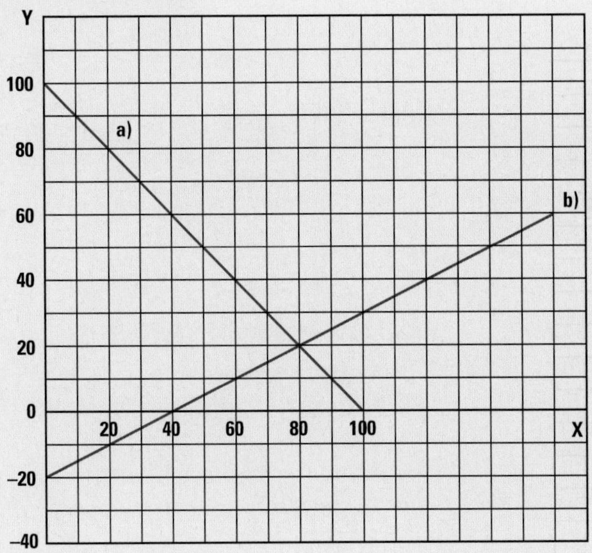

14. The data in **Table T.12** show the results of market research done on the latest Guns' n' Butter album. The numbers indicate the total quantity of albums that fans would purchase at the various prices.

TABLE T.12

Price per CD ($s)	Quantity (hundreds of thousands)
$20	20
19	30
18	40
17	50
16	60
15	70
14	80

a) Graph the table with the price on the vertical (y) axis and the quantity on the horizontal (x) axis.
b) What is the slope of the line?
c) What is the value of the Y-intercept?
d) What is the equation for this line?

15. What are the values of the slopes of the four lines shown in **Figure T.13**?

16. What are the equations that correspond to the four lines shown in **Figure T.14**?

17. Graph the following equations on a single graph, using the same scale for each axis, with the horizontal axis to 120 and the vertical axis to 200, both in squares of 10.
a) $Y = \frac{1}{2}X$
b) $Y = 40 + X$
c) $Y = 160 - \frac{1}{2}X$
d) $Y = -10 + 2X$

FIGURE T.13

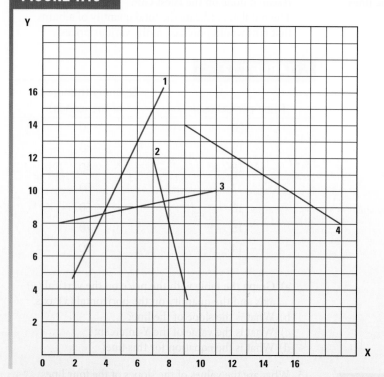

FIGURE T.14

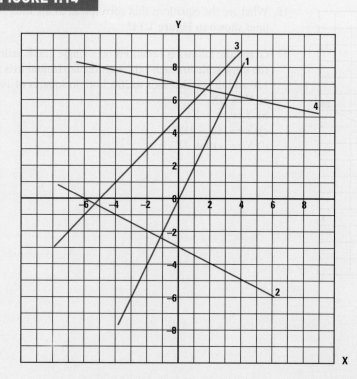

CHAPTER 1

THE ECONOMIC PROBLEM

LEARNING OBJECTIVES

At the end of this chapter, you should be able to...

LO1 understand why economics is a very relevant discipline and why so many of the controversies in our society have a distinct economic flavour.

LO2 define economics, make a distinction between microeconomics and macroeconomics, and understand the importance of the scientific method within the discipline.

LO3 realize that scarcity, choice, and opportunity cost are at the heart of economics and that efficiency, both productive and allocative, provides a major cornerstone.

LO4 understand why greater trade results in more productive economies.

LO5 explain the three fundamental questions that all societies must address and understand the four different ways that economic societies can be organized.

LO6 use the model of the production possibilities as a way to illustrate choice and opportunity cost, and efficiency and unemployment.

WHAT'S AHEAD...

In this first chapter, we introduce you to the study of economics and hope to arouse your curiosity about this fascinating discipline. First, we present six controversial statements to illustrate how relevant economics really is. Next, we discuss the nature of the discipline. From this, we derive a formal definition of economics. Then, we examine what efficiency means and why it is so important. Following this, we look at three of the fundamental questions that all societies face and see how four different types of economies address them. Finally, we introduce the model of production possibilities, which enables us to illustrate many of these concepts.

A Question of Relevance...

Jon and Ashok are both avid soccer fans and play for local teams. They both like old movies, chess, and *Star Trek*. They are both 17 years of age, neither has a steady girlfriend, and both are vegetarians. The other thing they have in common is that their fathers are in banking. Jon's father is the executive vice president of customer relations for the Royal Bank in Toronto. Ashok's father is a night janitor at a branch of the Bank of India in the dock area of Bombay. All of these points are relevant in forming a mental picture of a person, but you will probably agree that a person's economic circumstances are the most relevant of all. In truth, economics is one of the most relevant subjects you will study.

What might you expect from a course in economics? Well, it will probably not help you balance your chequebook and may not be directly helpful in your choice of the right shares to buy. But the study of economics will give you a broad understanding of how a modern market economy operates and what relationships are important within it. If you see yourself as a budding businessperson, the study of economics can offer some general insights that will be helpful. However, you will not find specific tools or instructions here. Economics is an academic discipline, not a self-help or how-to course. The common conception that economics is about money is only partly true. Economists do study money, but more in the sense of what it is, and the effects of different central-bank money policies, than in the sense of how to make it. The study of economics may not help you function better in the world, but it will help you understand better how the world functions.

1.1   THE RELEVANCE OF ECONOMICS

LO1 Understand why economics is a very relevant discipline and why so many of the controversies in our society have a distinct economic flavour.

Furthermore, both of your authors believe that an introductory course in economics will be one of the most important and relevant courses that you will take in your college/university career. Unfortunately, economics has acquired the reputation of being both dull and overly theoretical. Nothing could be further from the truth. In fact, it is at the centre of some of the most vital controversies that engage us all. One of the most effective ways of demonstrating this is to look at six important issues that provoke public opinion today and create debate within the discipline.

Controversy One

> • **Economic growth is something that we should applaud and always strive to achieve.**

PRO: In real terms (removing the effects of inflation), the economic well-being of the average Canadian has more than doubled in the last two generations. This has meant a huge improvement in people's lives and has come about not because the world has become fairer but because of economic growth. As a result of this growth, the individual choices available to Canadians—ranging from education and career choices to lifestyle choices—have increased significantly. In addition, economic growth contributes a great deal to social and political stability simply because finding ways to divide up a growing pie is much easier than trying to divide one that is shrinking, or even one that is stable. Over just the last few generations, economic growth has reduced the birth rate, which has meant lower population growth rates. This provides some welcome relief from threats to the environment.

CON: Continued economic growth simply means buying more of the same things but bigger, such as bigger houses, bigger cars, and holidays to more distant places, all of which adds little to human happiness. Economic growth also means greater environmental damage at a time when it is crucial we become more careful about the way we treat Mother Earth. It has also led to more daily stress in our lives because of things like increased traffic and living congestion. Growth puts too much focus on material things at the expense of things that are far more important for our overall well-being, such as greater contentment with our lives, more job satisfaction, and a stronger sense of community.

Controversy Two

> • **Government should use its income redistribution tools—such as Employment Insurance, welfare payments, and pensions—to channel more income from the rich to the poor.**

PRO: There is too much poverty in this country, and the gap between the rich and poor is growing. In 2000, 53 percent of Canadians earned less than $20 000, and 9.6 percent earned more than $75 000; in 2004, 57 percent of Canadians were low-income earners, and 13.5 percent were high-income earners. The economic pie should be more evenly divided. Failure to do so is a recipe for social unrest and disharmony.

CON: The solution to the problem of poverty is not higher taxes paid by the affluent for the benefit of the less fortunate. Higher taxes are a disincentive to work hard and to take on the risks of more investment. Instead, polices that stimulate more growth will ultimately benefit all Canadians. This means lower, not higher, taxes. The answer is to have the same proportionately-sized slice of a *larger* pie. Income distribution patterns of the rich countries of the world compared with the poor ones show that income is more evenly distributed in the rich countries.

Controversy Three

- The time has come to introduce road pricing in congested Canadian cities to reduce traffic during peak "rush hours."

PRO: Economists know that people respond to financial incentives and charging drivers more for using highways and bridges (which are very expensive to build) during rush hours and less for off-peak times will spread out road usage and thereby reduce congestion. This would also raise needed revenue for more road construction and save lives through reduced accident rates.

CON: Our system of unrestricted and free road usage has worked for generations, and road pricing would simply be another government tax grab and an unfair burden on Canadian drivers. It would also mean that low-income drivers would be paying proportionately more of their incomes than high-income drivers.

Controversy Four

- Globalization benefits large multinational corporations, not ordinary people.

PRO: Globalization means large corporations moving jobs from the rich countries to the poor countries. This creates a race to the bottom among poor countries that are willing to weaken environmental- and labour-standards regulations to appease the corporation. This lowers the cost of production for the corporation at the expense of ordinary people.

CON: Globalization leads to increased world trade, and economic theory clearly demonstrates that more trade means more benefits to those who trade. In fact, UN statistics demonstrate that within the last fifteen years 750 million people in the world have been pulled up out of the category of "abject poverty" (less than $1 a day income) into higher-income categories. Much of this is the direct result of increased trade. While this reduction in the amount of world poverty is encouraging, the causes of poverty are complex, and much remains to be done.

Controversy Five

- Canadians must insist that free-market elements are never allowed to creep into our health care system.

PRO: An egalitarian society cannot allow the rich to buy access to better and quicker health care than that which is available to all. The only fair way to allocate limited health care resources is our current system of first come, first served. Proponents of private, fee-paying medical services suggest that this system will reduce waiting lists in the public health care sector. What is forgotten is that it will also shift resources (doctors, nurses, and medical equipment) from the public to the private sector.

CON: Our health care system already has free-market elements—witness the family doctor's private practice. In addition, the rich are currently able to "jump the queue" by simply flying out of the country to buy medical services privately in another country. Several other systems in the world—France being a classic example—demonstrate that a judicious mixture of public and private health care can be quite effective. This option needs to be explored because wait lists in Canada are too long.

Controversy Six

- The most effective way of dealing with the serious problem of global warming is by establishing a carbon trading system.

PRO: Since the electricity generation industry is the largest single source of carbon emissions, which is the main cause of global warming, let us put our focus there. In a carbon trading system, the government passes the necessary laws and regulations to put a maximum "cap" on the total amount of *net* carbon emissions that each electricity generation firm will be allowed and also creates a carbon trading market. A carbon trading system would provide an economic incentive for entrepreneurial firms to start growing trees on a large scale—much like wheat or oats are now grown. Regulations would provide a mechanism for these tree-growing firms to earn "carbon credits," which recognize the fact that the trees continually suck carbon out of the atmosphere as they grow. These credits would then be sold to the carbon-polluting companies, which must get their net emissions (the amount of carbon dumped into the air less the number of credits they have purchased) down to the capped level imposed by the government.

CON: Global warming is just one more example of the very serious damage the market system does to our environment. To suggest that the same market system be used to solve the problem misses the mark. The solution should be higher taxes on the use of dirty fuels used to generate electricity, along with government subsidies to firms that use "green" fuels such as wind power. In addition, stricter government regulations to limit the amount of carbon emissions allowed is the most direct and effective way of reducing those emissions.

We have put these sample controversies right up front, not because economists have the right answers to any of them, but to demonstrate that almost any issue that faces us today as a society—and thus also as individuals—has an economic dimension. In short, economics is one of the most relevant courses you will ever take. We sincerely hope that this text will help you understand your world a little bit better.

1.2   WHAT IS ECONOMICS?

L02 Define economics, make a distinction between microeconomics and macroeconomics, and understand the importance of the scientific method within the discipline.

From our discussion of controversies, are we to conclude that a person's position on these issues is just a matter of opinion? No, we do not believe that. Economics, as you will discover, provides a unique way of approaching controversies like these, thereby helping each of us to reach reasoned positions on all issues. Generally in the social sciences, including economics, theories are absolutely vital in order to make sense of the world.

All of us ask questions to try to make sense of our existence: what? when? where? The answers to these questions are reasonably straightforward because they involve questions of fact. But the most important question of all, and often the most difficult to answer, is: why? "Why" always involves cause and effect, and it addresses the relationship between facts. Few people believe that things occur randomly in our world; we recognize that actions are related. A road is covered in ice, and a car crashes; a person smokes heavily for 40 years and dies of lung cancer; an army of beetles bores into a tree trunk, and the tree falls. Explaining why these things happen is a matter of uncovering the links between phenomena. That is what theory is all about: explaining *why* things happen.

But in order to begin an explanation, we first need to know *what* happened. In other words, theory must be based on solid facts. Theory is NOT just a matter of opinion; it is built on the solid foundation of facts, or what are termed **positive statements**. Positive statements are assertions about the world that can be verified by using empirical data. "Alexander Ovechkin scored 30 goals last year" or "the unemployment rate in Canada is presently 6.2 percent" are both positive statements because their truth can be verified by finding the appropriate data. But "Alexander Ovechkin should score more goals" or "the unemployment rate in Canada is far too high" are both what are termed **normative statements**. They are based on a person's beliefs or value systems and cannot be verified by appealing to facts. Note, however, that positive statements may not always be easily or readily verified. For instance, "it will rain tomorrow" is a positive statement despite the fact that it cannot be verified until tomorrow.

positive statement: a statement of fact that can be verified.

normative statement: a statement of opinion or belief that cannot be verified.

Economic theory is an attempt to relate positive statements. For instance, the price of apples decreases; people buy more apples. Economic theory looks at how the two things are related. In order to build a theory about, say, apple prices and apple purchases, we need to set up a simple *hypothesis*: for example, the lower the price of a product, the greater will be the quantity sold. But along with the hypothesis, we need to define the terms involved. For instance, what types of apples are we talking about—Granny Smiths, Galas, or all apples? And what price are we considering—wholesale? retail? Vancouver prices? Ottawa prices? Besides this, we need to spell out the assumptions (conditions) under which the hypothesis is true: people will buy more apples when the price falls, as long as the economy does not hit a recession or *as long as the prices of other fruits remain the same*, and so on. The hypothesis is now ready for testing by gathering actual data, and as a result, accepting, rejecting, or possibly modifying the theory.

This is what is termed the *scientific method*. It implies, among other things, that the results that the theory predicts should be valid regardless of who does the testing and that different people should be able to repeat the tests and obtain the same results.

However, some people say that there is no way that economics can ever be considered a true science, even though the discipline does use the scientific method. In some sense, this is true. Economics can never approach the pure sciences in terms of universality. For instance, it can never predict how every (or any one) consumer will react to the drop in the price of apples. But it can predict how the average consumer will react: that is, it deals in *generalities*. It is also true that the lag (delay) between the cause and the effect is often far longer in the social sciences than it is in the pure sciences, which makes the job of theorizing a lot more difficult. But to criticize economics because it is too abstract and unrealistic is not really fair. In fact, it could be suggested that the more realistic economic theory becomes, the less valuable it is. For example, no one would expect a map to be "realistic" because if it were, then every tree, house, and road would have to be drawn to scale. And what would the scale be? 1:1! So, while a map can capture a great deal of reality, trying to make it even more realistic can also make it useless.

At some point in the past, you may have heard jokes about economists, such as, "What do you get when you put five economists in the same room? Six opinions." Economists do often disagree with one another as is easily seen in the popular media. This is a natural by-product of a discipline that is part science and part art. An important reason for such disagreement is that economists, just like all other people, have a particular set of values that they have accumulated

ADDED DIMENSION

To illustrate the point that there is a great deal of agreement among economists, here are five sample issues and the percentage of economists who agree with the statement:

1. A ceiling on rents reduces the quantity and quality of housing available. (93%)
2. Tariffs and quotas generally reduce economic welfare. (93%)

3. A tax cut or an increase in government expenditure has a stimulative effect on a less than fully employed economy. (90%)
4. Government should restructure the social assistance system along the lines of a negative income tax. (79%)
5. Effluent taxes and marketable pollution permits represent a better approach to pollution control than the imposition of pollution ceilings. (78%)

SOURCE: Richard M. Alston, J. R. Kearl, and Michael B. Vaughn, "Is There Consensus among Economists in the 1990s?" *American Economic Review,* May 1992, 230–239.

over a lifetime, and these values vary, sometimes radically, from person to person. Nonetheless, if each of us uses the scientific method in developing our arguments, then lively debate can be fruitful, despite the different value systems with which we started.

It is also true, however, that there is wide agreement among economists on many questions, and this is remarkable given that economists ask a wide variety of questions, many of which do not get asked in other disciplines. For example, why do firms produce some goods internally and buy others in the market? Why do nations sometimes both export and import similar goods? Why does society provide some things to children without charge (education) but not other things (food)?

Trying to understand economic theory can be challenging and certainly does not come easily, but the rewards, in terms of a better understanding of the world we live in, are great. Economics is the study of ideas, and in a very real way this is the most important thing that you can study. One of the most famous of twentieth-century economists, John Maynard Keynes, said: "The ideas of economists, both when they are right and when they are wrong, are more powerful than is commonly understood. Sooner or later, it is ideas, not vested interests, which are dangerous, for good or evil."[1]

There are any number of definitions of economics but most of them agree that it is about how best to use the resources we have available. For instance:

> Economics studies the ways that humans and societies organize themselves to make choices about the use of scarce resources, which are used to produce the goods and services necessary to satisfy human wants and needs.

This gives us the essence of the discipline. We need, then, to understand how societies attempt to satisfy seemingly unlimited human wants in the face of limited resources. As we shall see in the next section, it means that we humans are faced with some very difficult choices.

Finally, we need to make the distinction between macroeconomics and microeconomics. **Macroeconomics** is the study of how the major components of the economy—such as consumer spending, investment spending, government policies, and exports—interact. It includes most of the topics a beginning student would expect to find in an economics course: unemployment, inflation, interest rates, taxation and spending policies of governments, and national income determination.

macroeconomics the study of how the major components of an economy interact; it considers unemployment, inflation, interest rate policy, and the spending and taxation policies of government.

---

[1] John Maynard Keynes, *The General Theory* (1936).

Microeconomics studies the outcomes of decisions made by people and firms and includes such topics as supply and demand, the study of costs, and the nature of market structures. This distinction can be described metaphorically as a comparison between the use of the wide-angle lens and the telephoto lens of a camera. In the first instance (macroeconomics), we see the big picture. In the second instance (microeconomics), a very small part of that big picture appears in much more detail. Many colleges and universities offer a separate course for each of these fields of study, but this is not always the case.

microeconomics the study of the outcomes of decisions by people and firms; it focuses on the supply and demand of goods, the costs of production, and market structures.

 SELF-TEST

1. Identify each of the following statements as either positive (P) or normative (N).

   a) The federal government's budget this year is the largest in history.

   b) The national debt is at a manageable level and therefore is nothing to worry about.

   c) The price of gasoline is higher than it needs to be.

   d) Rising Canadian exports are creating many new jobs in the country.

2. Identify which of the following topics would likely appear in a microeconomics course (Mi) and which in a macroeconomics course (Ma).

   a) The price of iPods

   b) Unemployment rates

   c) The presence of monopolies

   d) The rate of economic growth

1.3 SCARCITY, CHOICE, COST, AND THE IMPORTANCE OF EFFICIENCY

L03 Realize that scarcity, choice, and opportunity cost are at the heart of economics and that efficiency, both productive and allocative, provides a major cornerstone.

Economists put a great deal of emphasis on scarcity and the need to economize. Individual households face income limitations and therefore must allocate income among alternative uses. Most individuals also face a scarcity of time and must somehow decide where to spend time and where to conserve it. In the same sense, an economy as a whole has limited resources and must allocate those resources among competing uses.

Thus, economists see **resources** (the **factors of production** or **inputs**) as *scarce* in the sense that no economy has sufficient resources to be able to produce all the goods and services everyone wants. Even though there may be some people who say they have all they want, there are millions of people who possess a seemingly endless list of wants, with millions more like them waiting to be born. Since the economy cannot produce all that everyone wants, the resources available for production are scarce.

And exactly what constitutes a resource? Well, of the myriad different resources that are or have been used to produce goods and services, economists generally agree that there are, in fact, four categories: labour, capital, land, and enterprise. **Labour** refers to a broad spectrum of human effort, ranging from the work of a skilled naturopathic physician to that of a construction labourer. **Capital** is made up of the tools, equipment, factories, and buildings used in the production process and is not to be confused with financial capital, such as money, stocks or bonds. **Land** is defined as any natural resource, such as fertile soil, forests, fishing grounds, or minerals in the ground. Finally, **enterprise** (some economists prefer the term *entrepreneurship*) is that very special human talent that is able to apply abstract ideas in a practical way. Entrepreneurs are innovators who invent new products or devise new forms of organization and are willing to take the risks to see such projects through to successful completion.

resources (or **factors of production** or **inputs**): physical or virtual entities that can be used to produce goods and services

labour: human physical and mental effort that can be used to produce goods and services.

capital: human-made goods that are used to produce other products.

land: any natural resource that can be used to produce goods and services.

enterprise: the human resource that innovates and takes risks.

wages: the payment made and the income received for the use of labour.

interest: the payment made and the income received for the use of capital.

rent: the payment made and the income received for the use of land.

profit: the income received from the activity of enterprise.

In a market economy, incomes are earned through the payment of wages, interest, rent, and profits to the private owners of the factors of production: labour, capital, land, and enterprise. The general term "**wages**" includes all forms of payment to the various kinds of labour services such as salaries, stock bonuses, gratuities, commissions, and various employee benefits. "**Interest**" means payments to the factor of real capital. "**Rent**" is the income received for the use of the factor of land, such as royalty payments for a stand of timber. Finally, "**profit**" is the return to entrepreneurial effort.

Now, the way that these four factors of production are combined is what economists mean by a **technology**. A technology does not necessarily imply the use of machines or computers; it simply means a method of production. However, whatever technology we use to produce goods and services, the fact remains that we are not capable of producing everything that people want.

Therefore, some kind of mechanism must be put into place to choose what will be produced, and by implication, what will not be produced. This is why economics is sometimes called the *science of choice*.

In short:

> In the face of people's unlimited wants and society's limited productive resources, choice becomes a forced necessity. Because of these choices, the decision to produce one thing means that some other thing will not be produced.

technology: a method of production; the way in which resources are combined to produce goods and services.

This last point is so fundamental that economists have coined a special term to identify it: **opportunity cost**. For instance, suppose that government is considering the purchase of new military aircraft with a price tag of $5 billion. In the conventional sense, that is their cost. However, economists would argue that it is more revealing to measure the cost of the helicopters in terms of, say, ten hospitals that will not be built because purchasing the helicopters was chosen instead. Opportunity costs can thus be defined as what must be given up as a result of making a particular choice: in this case, the hospitals are given up for the aircraft. In addition, we should recognize that the $5 billion could be spent on other things besides hospitals—say, schools, roads, or mass-transit systems. At this point, society would have to choose what it considers to be its next-best alternative: hospitals, schools, roads, or mass transit. Understanding this concept allows us to make a formal definition of opportunity cost: the next-best alternative that is given up as a result of making a particular choice. In conclusion, the making of any decision always involves a trade-off with the next-best alternative that is sacrificed.

A classic example of this trade-off in economics is sacrificing consumer goods to produce more capital goods. Nations that wish to grow more quickly can achieve this if they produce more factories, tools, and equipment—more capital goods—that are used to make other goods. But, of course, an increase in capital goods production necessarily means a reduction in the output of **consumer goods and services**, which are defined as products that are used by consumers to satisfy their wants and needs.

opportunity cost the value of the next-best alternative that is given up as a result of making a particular choice.

consumer goods and services products that are used by consumers to satisfy their wants and needs.

Why is it better to think of cost in terms of opportunity cost rather than simply as money payments? Economists argue that using the concept of opportunity costs captures the true measure of any decision. If we use money payments as the measure, then we have seemingly unlimited means to produce goods, since governments can always print more money. But no matter what any government might wish, any society has only a limited amount of resources. When we understand this, we begin to realize that nothing in life is truly "free"—any decision (to produce military aircraft, for example) necessarily involves the use of scarce resources which could have been used alternatively to produce something else (hospitals).

Recognizing that there are opportunity costs involved also forces us to rethink our idea of what we mean by "free." Simply because money does not change hands does not mean that a product is free. The concept of opportunity cost can be applied not only at the level of the overall society, as we just saw, but also at the individual level. For the individual, the constraint is not the limited quantity of resources but the limited amount of income and time. For example, you could think of the cost of going to two movies on the weekend as the sacrifice of a haircut. If you want to think of both these choices (two movies or one haircut) as each costing about $20, that is fine. But thinking of the one as costing the other is often more effective. In general, your income will not allow you to have everything you may want, and so you are forced to make choices about what you buy. And the cost of these choices can be measured in terms of what must be given up as a result of making the choice.

Another application of opportunity costs is the one that many students face in choosing between taking more courses at college or continuing to work in a part-time job. If a student is presently taking three courses and working twenty hours a week and feels that this is a full-time load, then taking five courses next semester may well mean giving up the job. Thus, the opportunity cost of the two extra courses is the income that is sacrificed as a result of no longer working at the part-time job. We should also point out that there must be some benefit to be gained from the alternative that you do choose. For instance, returning to our example above, if you chose the two movies, the benefit from that choice, must, in your view, exceed (or at least equal) the opportunity cost of the haircut. In the same sense, a society faces a similar set of choices imposed not by limited income but by a constraint on the quantity and quality of the factors of production available.

Scarcity → forces → Choice → which involves → Opportunity Costs

3. Below is a list of economic goods. Decide whether each is a consumer good (C), or a capital good (K), or possibly both (B), depending on the context in which it is used.

a) A jackhammer

b) A carton of cigarettes

c) An office building

d) A tooth brush

e) A hammer

f) A farm tractor

4. Below is a list of resources. Indicate whether the resource in question is labour (L), capital (K), land (N), or enterprise (E):

a) A bar-code scanner in a supermarket

b) Fresh drinking water

c) Copper deposits in a mine

d) The work of a systems analyst

e) The first application of CD-ROM technology to an economics textbook

f) An office building

The Importance of Efficiency

Perhaps not surprisingly, economists (like any other group of people) do not agree on the most important economic goals that an economy should pursue. Nor are they necessarily in agreement on the best methods to achieve those goals. However, they are generally in agreement on the importance of *efficiency*. In fact, this term crops up with great regularity in economic literature. As a result, it is important to have some initial understanding of what the term means and why economists attach so much importance to it.

One of the simplest ways of expressing efficiency is to suggest that it implies getting the most for the least. For example, a technology that requires the use of 10 units of inputs in order to produce an output of 100 units of goods and services would be preferable to one that uses 20 units of inputs to produce those same 100 units of output. Similarly, that same technology that uses 10 inputs to produce 100 units of output would be considered inferior to another technology that uses those same inputs but could produce an output of 150 units. In other words, economists define **productive efficiency** in terms of the ratio of outputs produced to inputs used. Those technologies that produce at a lower ratio will result in lower costs of production.

When you hear the term "productivity" used in the popular press it is usually referring to productive efficiency and is often measured in terms of the amount of output per hour of labour (or machine) input. If we want to be careful in our use of resources, then it is of great importance that every one of us should try to be efficient. However, productive efficiency does not take us far enough. It is all right to produce things at low cost, but it is of little use if people simply are not interested in buying those products. For instance, what would be the point of producing big-screen TVs at $50 each if they could only broadcast in black and white? It is just as important to be efficient in what we produce as how we produce it. Societies therefore need to ensure that the right type of products are produced, those that match the demands of the public. This is what economists mean by **allocative efficiency**.

Allocative efficiency, then, puts the emphasis on the production of the right type of products. However, since all of us have different tastes, what might be the right products for you may not be the right products for me. So, it is important that products are allocated efficiently among people. In *Filthy Lucre*, Joseph Heath gives an amusing example illustrating this idea.

productive efficiency: the production of an output at the lowest possible average cost.

allocative efficiency: the production of the combination of products that best satisfies consumers' demands.

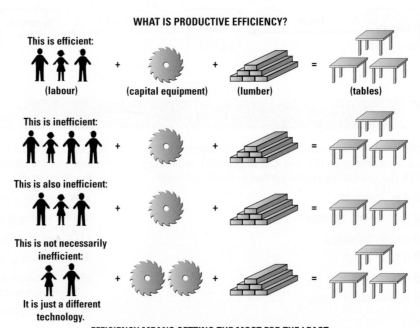

WHAT IS PRODUCTIVE EFFICIENCY?

This is efficient:

(labour)   +   (capital equipment)   +   (lumber)   =   (tables)

This is inefficient:

This is also inefficient:

This is not necessarily inefficient:

It is just a different technology.

EFFICIENCY MEANS GETTING THE MOST FOR THE LEAST.

Imagine that you have been given the task of allocating candies to a group of children at a birthday party. Trying to be fair, you count out the different types of candies so that each child gets an equal number of each. But you discover that some of the kids are not too happy. One child is most upset because he has been given a peanut brittle, and the poor boy is allergic to peanuts! One girl positively detests raisins; some of them hate dark chocolate, while others detest milk chocolate. You can see that, without increasing the overall quantity of candies, you could increase the general happiness of these children just by redistributing the candies. The kids might easily handle this allocation themselves by trading, something that children tend to do quite naturally.

1.4   THE POWER OF TRADE

The final quarter of the twentieth century revealed something very significant: economies that put an emphasis on the market system and international trade—Canada, South Korea, and Ireland, for example—continued to enjoy economic growth and a rising standard of living for their citizens, while economies that rely more on centrally controlled systems and self-sufficiency— the former USSR, or today's Kirghizia and Myanmar, for example—faltered.

L04 Understand why greater trade results in more productive economies.

Adam Smith, the father of economics, gave us a simple but elegant idea that goes a long way toward explaining why, throughout history, some economies have prospered, while others have not. This is the recognition that *voluntary trade* always benefits both parties to the trade. If two peasants voluntarily trade a sack of rice for two bags of carrots, then we can assume that they both must feel that they have benefited, as otherwise they would not have done it. If you buy a slice of pizza and a pop for lunch for $3.50, then we must assume that you feel you have gained by giving up the money and receiving the lunch—otherwise, why did you do it? Likewise, the owner of the business that sold you the lunch must feel that she gained, or she would not have been willing to offer the lunch for sale. There is a gain to both parties engaged in voluntary trade.

It then follows that: *the more trade there is, the greater are the overall benefits that accrue to those engaged in the trade.* It comes as a surprise to many people that the same principle that applies to individuals in this regard also applies to nations. We can demonstrate that this is true by using the concept of opportunity costs to construct a simple example of two hypothetical countries—Athens and Sparta—each of which produces only two goods: bread (a consumer good) and plows (a capital good).

Suppose that the maximum quantities that can be produced of each product are (in thousands of units):

Athens	20 bread	or	10 plows
Sparta	10 bread	or	20 plows

If each country is self-sufficient (no trade between them) and each devotes half its resources to producing the two products, the output in each country would be:

Athens	10 bread	and	5 plows
Sparta	5 bread	and	10 plows

Clearly, the combined output of the two economies is 15 units of bread and 15 plows. It is also clear that Athens is far better at producing bread and Sparta is much better at producing plows. Thus, if the two countries could overcome their sense of rivalry, and if Athens concentrated on producing bread and Sparta on producing plows, then the total combined production of the two countries would be:

Athens	20 bread	(no plows)
Sparta	20 plows	(no bread)

With specialization, the two countries can produce a combined total that is five more of each product (20 units of bread and 20 plows) than when each was self-sufficient. This illustrates why specialization is so important—countries enjoy more output when they do what they do best (produce only the products with the lowest opportunity costs) rather than trying to produce both products. For Athens, the opportunity cost of producing plows is a large sacrifice in bread production, while in Sparta the opportunity cost of producing bread is a large sacrifice in plow production. However, when they both specialize in what they do best, big benefits can be gained. But to reap the benefits of specialization, trade becomes imperative unless, of course, the countries are happy just consuming one product (which is most unlikely). In our example, if Athens were to trade 10 bread for 10 plows from Sparta, then both countries would finish up with 10 units of bread and 10 plows—an improvement for them both.

Returning to our original point about market economies versus planned economies, we know that specialization and trade are maximized when markets are used extensively. This simple illustration helps us understand that every economy faces important choices about what to produce. Let us expand on this point by turning to the three fundamental economic questions faced by every economy.

1.5 THREE FUNDAMENTAL QUESTIONS AND FOUR TYPES OF ECONOMIES

LO5 Explain the three fundamental questions that all societies must address and understand the four different ways that economic societies can be organized.

A broad perspective on the discipline of economics can be obtained by focusing on what might be called the three fundamental questions of economics: *what? how?* and *for whom?* That is, economics is about what and how much gets produced, how it is produced, and who gets it.

What to Produce?

As we have just seen, underlying the question of *what* should be produced is the reality of scarcity. Any society has only a fixed amount of resources at its disposal. Therefore, it must have a system in place to make an endless number of decisions about production, from big decisions—such as should the government buy more military aircraft or build more hospitals?—down to more mundane decisions, such as how many brands of breakfast cereal should be produced.

If we decide to produce hospitals, should we produce ten without research facilities for the study of genetics, or eight without and two with such facilities? Should society exploit natural resources faster to create more jobs and more tax revenue, or slower to conserve these resources for the future? Should our resources be directed toward more preschool day-care facilities so that parents are not so tied to the home? Or, instead, should those same resources be directed toward increasing the number of graduate students studying science and technology so that the Canadian economy can win the competitive international race in the twenty-first century?

Let us once again emphasize that no economist would claim to have the *right* answer to any of these questions. That is no more the role of an economist than it is of any other member of society. What the economist can do, however, is identify and measure both the benefits and the costs of any one answer—of any one choice.

How to Produce?

Let us move on to the second fundamental economic question that every society must somehow answer: what is the most appropriate technology to employ? We could reword this question by asking *how* we should produce what we choose to produce.

For example, there are many ways to produce ten kilometres of highway. At one extreme, a labour-intensive method of production could be used involving rock crushed with hammers, roadbed carved from the landscape with shovels, and material moved in wheelbarrows.

The capital equipment used in this method is minimal. The labour used is enormous, and the time it will take is considerable. At the other extreme, a capital-intensive method could be used involving large earthmoving and tarmac-laying machines, surveying equipment, and relatively little but highly skilled labour. In between these two extremes is a large variety of capital–labour mixes that could also produce the new highway.

The answer to the question of how best to build the highway involves, among other things, knowing the costs of the various resources that might be used. Remember that technology means the way the various factors of production are combined to obtain output. The most appropriate technology for a society to use (the best way to combine resources) depends, in general, on the opportunity costs of these resources. Thus, in the example above, the best way to build a highway depends on the opportunity costs of labour and of capital as well as the productivity of each factor.

Capital intensive technologies using heavy equipment are the most appropriate methods in most countries because they are the cheapest.

For Whom?

We are now ready to move to the third fundamental economic question that every society must somehow answer: *for whom?* Here we are asking how the total output of a society should be shared among its citizens. In the end, we are really asking how the total income in a society should be distributed. Should it involve an equal share for all, or should it, perhaps, be based on people's needs? Alternatively, should it be based on the contribution of each member of society? If so, how should this contribution be measured—in numbers of hours, or in skill level, or in some other way? Further, how should we define what constitutes an important skill and which ones are less important?

Wrapped up in all this is the question of the ownership of resources and whether it is better that certain resources (such as land and capital) be owned by society as a whole or by private individuals. In short, the *for whom* question (as well as the *what* and *how* questions) cannot be adequately addressed unless we look at society's attitude toward the private ownership of resources and the question of who has the power to make crucial decisions.

You can see that in addressing the *for whom* question, other questions about the fairness of income distribution, incentives, and the ownership of resources all come into play. John Stuart Mill pointed out, nearly 150 years ago, that once an economy's goods are produced and the initial market distribution of income has occurred, society can intervene in any fashion it wishes in order to redistribute such income; that is, there are no laws of distribution other than the ones that society wants to impose. Whether this observation by Mill gives enough consideration to the incentive for productive effort remains an open question to this day.

 ADDED DIMENSION   John Stuart Mill: Economist and Philosopher

John Stuart Mill (1806–73) is considered the last great economist of the classical school. His *Principles of Political Economy*, first published in England in 1848, was the leading textbook in economics for 40 years. Raised by a strict disciplinarian father (James), John Stuart began to learn Greek at the age of three, authored a history of Roman government by 11, and studied calculus at 12—but did not take up economics until age 13.

Not surprisingly, this unusual childhood later led to a mental crisis. Mill credited his decision to put his analytical pursuits on hold and take up an appreciation of poetry as the primary reason for his recovery. He was a true humanitarian, who held a great faith in human progress, had a love of liberty, and was an advocate of extended rights for women.

How these fundamental questions actually get answered depends, to a large extent, on the way that different societies organize themselves. Let us now look at the four types of economic organization.

Types of Economies: The Four Cs

Societies have, throughout history, developed systems to co-ordinate their economies in order to answer the fundamental questions of what to produce, how, and for whom. Each of the numerous systems possible have used some blend of the four Cs: cooperation, command, custom, and competition. Whatever blend was used, it was a reflection of who owns and who controls the important resources of that economy.

In the foraging societies of pre-history, the few tools, weapons, and cooking items they possessed were commonly owned: belonging to the band as a whole and not to any one individual. Since these bands were nomadic, they did not preserve or store food, since carrying it around was difficult and undesirable. They lived very much a hand-to-mouth existence. This meant that these societies did not produce a surplus above subsistence that could be used to support non-producers. Consequently, they had no armies, no leaders, no priests, and no ruling hierarchy. The result was a society where decision making was democratic and egalitarian. In short, the members of foraging bands relied on *co-operation* with one another in order to survive the dual threats of starvation and predators.

As we shift our focus to the later command economies of ancient Egypt and Rome, we see that the most important resource was slaves, and whoever owned slaves was almost, by definition, rich and powerful. Decisions were made, and laws were ruthlessly enforced, by an elite group headed by a pharaoh or emperor. The fundamental questions were answered by using *command*.

In the age of feudalism in Europe, which filled the vacuum left by the fall of the Roman Empire, we see power centred on the ownership of land. The landowners—royalty, the aristocracy, and the Church—were very powerful, and everyone else knew his or her place within this rigidly hierarchical system. This was the age of *custom*, which dictated who performed which task—sons followed the work of their fathers, and daughters followed the roles of their mothers—and traditional technology was superior to new ways of doing things, since it had been tried and tested and could therefore be trusted. Above all, custom required that serfs turn over a portion of their produce to the feudal lords.

Then, beginning in Britain towards the end of the eighteenth century, the Industrial Revolution effectively brought feudalism to an end and ushered in the machine age. It is here that capital, in the form of factories, machines, and railroads became the economy's most important resource, and the industrial capitalists became very rich and powerful, while the ordinary people, the land-less, capital-less working class, were left with nothing but their labour to sell. This marks the birth of the market system with its emphasis on *competition* as the coordinating mechanism and the private ownership of resources as a main characteristic. Many people are surprised to learn how modern an invention this form of economic organization really is. What today we call the market economy did not begin to emerge until approximately 250 years ago, although, of course, *markets* have existed for thousands of years.

So what do we see today as we look at the world in which we live? Well, custom is very much alive in a number of Islamic Republics such as Iran, where traditional values, enforced by religion, dominate most aspects of people's lives. But we also see that custom has a part to play in our own society. For instance, movie theatres provide expensive washrooms free of charge while charging for popcorn and soft drinks rather than the reverse. A much more significant example is the custom in our market economy of allowing people to pass wealth on

Source: Marion Bull/GetStock.com

Tradition plays a big role in the lives of many people in Muslim countries.

to their children in the form of inheritance so that the income of the future generation is often based less on what they contribute to the economy and more on who their parents were.

As far as co-operation is concerned, it is impossible to find an example of a country where the economic decisions are made co-operatively by all the citizens. However, we can find many examples of small, self-contained communes where there is an emphasis on common ownership and consensus decision making. Included would be the kibbutzim of Israel, or religious communities such as the Hutterites in the Canadian Prairies or the Doukhobors of British Columbia. Even the internal decision-making process in today's large corporations that stresses the use of team play and group consensus is a form of co-operative behaviour. This same point can be made in reference to most family units within our society. Further, what, if not co-operation, would one call the fact that nearly half of all adults in our society engage (at some point in their lives) in voluntary unpaid activities, such as coaching soccer or helping out at a local hospital or community centre?

To find examples of command economies in the modern world, we need look no further than the brutal totalitarian regimes of the twentieth century: fascism in Italy, Nazism in Germany, and communism in the Soviet Union. In all three examples, the complete command of the economy was in the hands of the leaders who also controlled most aspects of life and dictated what would be produced, how it would be produced, and who earned what.

Finally, competition is the main feature of today's capitalistic, or market, economies. Here, the forces of demand and supply determine most of what is produced, as well as what technology is used and how much people earn. In a pure market economy, government plays no role whatsoever. This means, for instance, that corporations would be totally unregulated, schools and hospitals would all charge fees, and those unable to work would simply receive no income or support from the government at all.

It is clear that in our modern age, there are no examples of countries organized using only one of the Four Cs. Instead, all modern economies use a combination of all four, with competition and command being the dominant ones. Perhaps this is due to the rise in the importance of knowledge as the most important resource in today's fast-changing world; it is difficult to monopolize ownership of this particular resource. At the same time, today, we see only a single example of purely command economy: North Korea. Even "communist" China and Cuba have opened up their economies to private ownership and enterprise.

This blend of competition and command includes the large role played by governments through the provision of, for example, health care and education, leaving the private sector to provide the majority of consumer goods for personal use. The role of government in our economy represents the command function in the sense that the taxes needed to finance government activities are not voluntary, and in the same sense, the various laws governing human conduct and behaviour must be adhered to. This recognition of the role of both market and government in our society is what we mean by the term a *mixed economy*. On the one hand, few of us would wish to live in a pure market economy where, for example, young children from dysfunctional families with no income would be left to starve, or where there was no standardization of weights and measures. and no "rules of the game" concerning the way business is conducted. On the other hand, few of us would want to live in a society where every decision about our lives was made by government. Some blend of the market, and the efficiencies achieved from its use, combined with the order and fairness imposed by government does seem to be the right way to go. However, exactly what constitutes the right amount of government intervention imposed upon the market is, of course, an issue of endless debate.

You have no doubt heard the terms "capitalism" and "socialism" used in the media and in conversation. Just what do these terms mean to an economist? Basically, they distinguish different degrees in the competition–command mix used by society to organize its economic affairs and answer the three fundamental questions. In "socialist" Sweden, for example, the state (government) plays a much larger role in the economy than in the "capitalist" United States. While Sweden does not have central planning as found in the former Soviet Union and does have private property, it also has high taxes and high levels of social spending. Eighty percent of the work force is unionized.

Everyone receives a generous number of paid vacation days per year and generous sick leave benefits at nearly full pay. Sweden has a wide-ranging unemployment insurance plan, which also includes mandatory retraining for those laid off from their jobs. Until very recently, the Swedish government mandated an investment fund which required that corporations give a percentage of their profits to the central bank, which would then release these funds back to the companies in times of recession, with stipulations on how they were to be spent. By contrast, the United States has almost none of this and relies, instead, on a policy of *laissez-faire*, which minimizes the role of government and emphasizes the role of the market in the economy. Canada, France, and the United Kingdom lie somewhere between these extremes.

1.6 PRODUCTION POSSIBILITIES

L06 ▸ Use the model of the production possibilities as a way to illustrate choice and opportunity cost, and efficiency and unemployment.

Economists often use economic models when trying to explain the world in which we live. Let us explain what we mean by a "model" and look at one example. Imagine walking into the sales office of a condominium project under construction. Part of the sales presentation is a model of the entire project sitting on a table. You would have no trouble recognizing the model as an *abstraction*, a representation of what the building will eventually look like. This is true despite the fact that many of the details, such as the elevators, furniture, and appliances, are absent from the model.

So, too, in making their models, economists abstract from reality only the features that are relevant, ignoring extraneous material. Clearly, economists cannot construct a physical model of the economic world. Instead, the level of abstraction is greater in that the model is all on paper and often in the form of numbers, equations, and graphs. But for all that, the aim is not to make the simple and straightforward seem unnecessarily complicated. Just the opposite: the goal is to make the complexities of reality as clear and simple as possible.

Let us now construct a very simple model of a country's production possibilities. This allows us to return to a point that we made earlier: that every economy is faced with the constraint of limited resources. Imagine a society that produces only two products—cars and wheat. Let us then figure out what this economy is capable of producing if it works at maximum potential. This would mean that it is making use of all of its resources: the labour force is fully employed, and all of its factories, machines, and farms are fully operational. But it means more than this. It also means that the society is making use of the best technology and, as a result, overall efficiency is being achieved. Given all of this, and since it can produce either cars or wheat, the exact output of each depends on how much of its resources it devotes to the production of cars and wheat. **Table 1.1** shows six possible output combinations, as well as the percentage of the economy's resources used in producing each combination. These possible outputs are labelled A through F.

The finite resources available to this economy allow it to produce up to a maximum of 20 tonnes of wheat per year if 100 percent of its resources are used in wheat production. Note that this can be done only if no cars are produced (combination A). At the other extreme, a maximum of 30 cars per year can be produced, if all available resources are used in car production. This, of course, would mean that no wheat is produced (combination F). There are many other possible combinations in between these two extremes, and **Table 1.1** identifies four of these (B, C, D, and E).

Since we want to focus on what is produced (the outputs) rather than on what resources are used to produce them (the inputs), we can present **Table 1.1** in the form of a production possibilities table, as is shown in **Table 1.2**.

Further, we can take the data from **Table 1.2** and use it to graph what is called a **production possibilities curve**, which is a visual representation of the various outputs that can be produced. What appears in **Figure 1.1** is simply another way of presenting the data in **Table 1.2**.

Now, recall that:

production possibilities curve: a graphical representation of the various combinations of maximum output that can be produced from the available resources and technology.

> The three assumptions that lie behind the production possibilities curve are: full employment, the use of the best technology, and productive efficiency.

TABLE 1.1	Production of Cars and Tonnes of Wheat (millions of units)			
	CARS		**WHEAT**	
Possible Outputs	% of Resources Used	Output	% of Resources Used	Output
A	0	0	100	20
B	20	10	80	19
C	40	18	60	17
D	60	24	40	13
E	80	28	20	8
F	100	30	0	0

TABLE 1.2	Production Possibilities for Cars and Wheat					
	A	**B**	**C**	**D**	**E**	**F**
Cars	0	10	18	24	28	30
Wheat	20	19	17	13	8	0

FIGURE 1.1   Production Possibilities Curve I

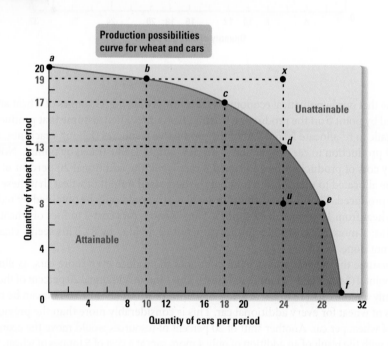

This society's limited resources allow for the production of a maximum of 20 tonnes of wheat if no cars are produced, as represented by point *a*. Moving down the curve from point *a*, we find other combinations of fewer tonnes of wheat and more cars until we reach point *f*, where 30 cars and no wheat are produced. Point *u* indicates either the underemployment of resources, inefficiency in resource use, or the use of inappropriate technology. Point *x* is unattainable.

On the one hand, if any one of these three assumptions does not hold, then the economy will be operating somewhere inside the production possibilities curve, as illustrated by point *u*, which is 24 cars and 8 tonnes of wheat. On the other hand, point *x* represents an output of 24 cars and 19 tonnes of wheat, which, given this economy's current resources and technology, is unattainable.

The Law of Increasing Costs

Next, let us consider the actual shape of the curve. Why is it bowed out this way? We need to understand the implication of this particular shape. **Figure 1.2** will help.

FIGURE 1.2   Production Possibilities Curve II

At point *b*, 19 tonnes of wheat and 10 cars are being produced. If this society decided that it wanted 8 more cars (point *c*), then 2 tonnes of wheat would have to be sacrificed. Thus, 1 more car would cost 0.25 tonnes of wheat. Moving from point *c* to *d* would increase car production by 6 (18 to 24) at a sacrifice of 4 tonnes of wheat (from 17 to 13). In this instance, 1 more car costs 0.67 tonnes of wheat. Moving from point *d* to *e* would increase car production by only 4 (from 24 to 28), while wheat production would drop by 5 (from 13 to 8). Thus, the cost of 1 more car rises to 1.25 tonnes of wheat.

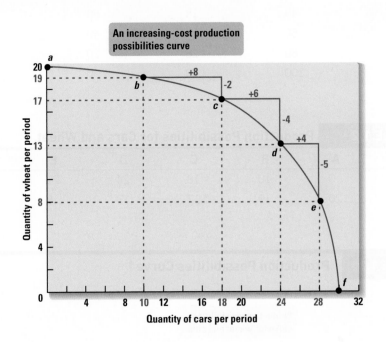

Assume that our hypothetical economy is currently producing 19 tonnes of wheat and 10 cars, as illustrated by point *b* on the production possibilities curve. Then, assume that production decisions are made to re-allocate 20 percent of the productive resources (labour, machines, materials) from wheat production to car production. This new output is illustrated by point *c*. Note that the opportunity cost of producing the additional 8 cars is *not* the additional 20 percent of resources that must be allocated to their production but the decreased output of wheat that these resources could have produced. That is to say, the additional 8 cars could only be obtained by reducing the output of wheat from 19 tonnes to 17 tonnes. Thus, 8 more cars cost 2 tonnes of wheat. This can be restated as: 1 more car costs 0.25 tonnes of wheat (2 divided by 8). This seems clear enough, but we are not done.

Next, assume that society, still at point c, decides to produce even more cars, as illustrated by moving to point *d* (24 cars and 13 tonnes of wheat). This time an additional 20 percent of the resources produces only 6 more cars (18 to 24) at a cost of 4 units of wheat (17 to 13). This can be restated as: 0.67 tonnes of wheat for every additional car. This is considerably more than the previous cost of 0.25 units of wheat per car. Another shift of 20 percent of resources would move the economy from point *d* to *e*, with the result of an addition of only 4 more cars at a cost of 5 tonnes of wheat. Now, each additional car costs 1.25 (5 divided by 4) units of wheat. **Table 1.3** summarizes all the figures above.

law of increasing costs: as an economy's production level of any particular item increases, its *per-unit* cost of production rises.

We have just identified what economists call the **law of increasing costs**. This law states that as the production of any single item increases, the per-unit cost of producing additional units of that item will rise. Note that this law is developed in the context of a whole economy and, as we will see in later chapters, need not apply to the situation of an individual firm.

TABLE 1.3	Opportunity Cost Per Car		
Graphical Movement	Gain in Cars	Opportunity Costs in Wheat	Opportunity Cost per Car
a to b	10	1	0.10
b to c	8	2	0.25
c to d	6	4	0.67
d to e	4	5	1.25
e to f	2	8	4.00

Thus, you can see that as the total production of cars is increased, the rising per-unit cost of cars gives the production possibilities curve its bowed-out shape.

But why does the per unit cost of cars increase—what is the reason behind the law of increasing costs? The answer is that not all resources are equally suitable for the production of different products. Our hypothetical society has a fixed amount of resources that are used to produce different combinations of both wheat and cars. However, some of these resources would be better suited to producing cars, whereas others would be better suited to producing wheat. An increase in the production of cars requires that some of the resources currently producing wheat would need to be re-allocated to the production of cars. It is only reasonable to assume that the resources that are re-allocated first are the ones that are relatively well suited to the production of cars, whereas those resources less well suited to the production of cars would continue to produce wheat. (Perhaps some of the farm workers are immigrants and have manufacturing experience in the old country; or maybe some of them are allergic to working in the sun.) After all this has taken place, if even *more* cars are to be produced, the only resources left to re-allocate will be ones that are not very well suited for the production of cars. Therefore, a larger quantity of less well suited resources will have to be re-allocated to obtain the desired increase in car production. This will increase the per-unit cost of cars because a larger sacrifice of wheat production will be required.

 SELF-TEST

5. Given the accompanying figure:

   a) If society produces 1000 units of butter, what is the maximum number of guns it can produce?

   b) Suppose that society produces the combination shown as point *b* on the production possibilities curve; what is the cost of 1000 additional units of butter?

   c) Would the opportunity cost of 1000 additional units of butter be greater, the same, or smaller as society moves from point *c* to *d*, compared with a move from point *b* to *c*?

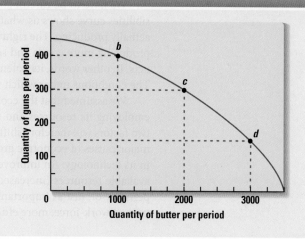

Shifts in the Production Possibilities Curve: The Causes of Economic Growth

A production possibility curve is like a snapshot of an economy: it shows in one quick diagram what an economy is capable of producing at a particular moment. But economies change from year to year, usually—although not always—for the better. The sources of economic growth have been debated for centuries, but our simple model is able to explain some of the important aspects of growth. **Figure 1.3**, for instance, illustrates what economic growth looks like diagrammatically. Here, we see that the maximums of both wheat and car production have increased; the PP curve has shifted out along both axes. Previously, the maximum amount of wheat the country could produce was 80. This has now increased to 100. Similarly, before the change, it could produce a maximum of 80 cars; now it is capable of producing 100 cars.

FIGURE 1.3   The Effect of Economic Growth

The production possibilities curve has shifted from PP1 to PP2, which shows that this economy is now capable of producing more cars *and* more wheat.

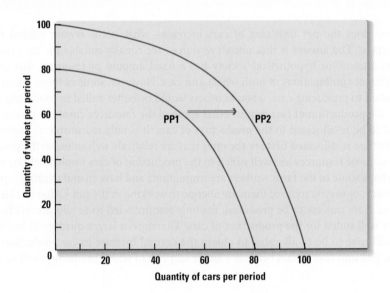

We have to be careful about how we interpret this shift. Remember that a production possibilities curve shows us what an economy is capable of producing; it does not show us what it is actually producing. The rightward shift from PP1 to PP2 does not say that this is economy is now producing more goods and services; it simply shows that it is capable of producing more products. In other words, its potential has improved. And what could have brought about this change? The conditions under which we constructed the production possibilities curve provide a clue.

We assumed that the economy was operating at maximum efficiency, that is to say, it is fully employing its resources and using the best technology. An improvement in either of those last two factors will therefore shift the production possibilities curve to the right. So, here, we have the major causes of economic growth: an improvement in a country's resources or an improvement in its technology. An improvement in resources could mean either an increase in the amount of available resources (increased population, discovery of new oil fields, improved infrastructure, perhaps) or, just as importantly, an increase in the quality of its resources (a better educated or trained work-force, more efficient machines, rather than simply more machines, and so on).

The other factor that has wrought significant change over the last few centuries is technological improvement. To illustrate the effects of technological change, imagine a society that produces capital goods and consumer goods and services. You will recall that consumer goods and services are those products used by consumers to satisfy their wants and needs. In contrast, capital goods, such as machines and factories, do not directly satisfy wants and needs but do help produce consumer goods and services.

Let us start, in **Figure 1.4**, with the economy operating efficiently on the production possibilities curve PP1 at point *a*. Now, let us assume that a new technology becomes available that has application *only* in the consumer goods and services industry. This is represented by a shift outward in the curve, with the new production possibilities curve becoming PP2. There are three possible results. First, the same quantity of capital goods, but more consumer goods and services, can be produced as represented by *b*. Second, more of *both* goods can be produced, as represented by point *c*. And third, this economy could now increase the production of capital goods if the same number of consumer goods and services were produced (point *d*) *despite* the fact that this new technology could only be applied to the consumer goods and services industry.

This emphasizes the important role of technological change. It widens the choices (that word again!) available to society and is often seen in a positive light. Alas, technological change also has costs, and this is a subject that will receive our attention later.

Now, look at **Figure 1.4** and ask yourself the following question: which of the three new possible combinations is preferable? If the choice had been between two consumer goods and services, such as wheat and cars, then we could not give a definitive answer to this question without knowing something about the preferences of the country's consumers. But the choices illustrated in this figure are between capital goods and consumer goods and services, and choosing combination *d* —more capital goods—leads to significantly different effects from those of choosing combination *b*.

FIGURE 1.4   **The Effect of Technological Change on the Production Possibilities Curve**

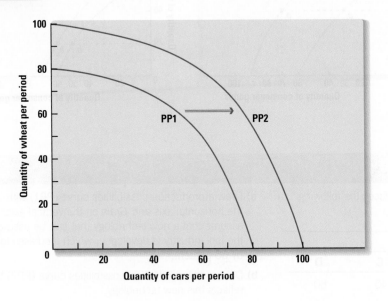

Start at point a, which is a point of efficient production on PP1. An improvement in technology in the consumer goods and services industry shifts the production possibilities curve to PP2. This creates three possible results. First, the same quantity of capital goods and services and more consumer goods and services can now be produced, as represented by point *b*. Alternatively, more of consumer goods and services as well as capital goods and services can be produced, as represented by point *c*. Point *d* represents the third possible result, which is more capital goods and services and the same quantity of consumer goods and services *despite* the fact that the technological change was in the consumer goods and services industry.

This point is illustrated in **Figure 1.5**, in which we show two different economies. Atlantis places greater emphasis on the production of capital goods than Mu does. This can be seen by comparing point a_1 (40 units of capital goods) with point b_1 (20 units of capital goods). This emphasis on capital goods production also means a lower production of consumer goods (30 units in Atlantis, compared with 50 in Mu). The emphasis on capital goods production in Atlantis means that it will experience more economic growth in the future. This faster growth is illustrated by the production possibilities curve shifting, over time, more to the right in the case of Atlantis than in the case of Mu. After the increase in production possibilities, Atlantis can continue producing 40 units of capital goods but now can produce 70 units of consumer goods (a_2). Mu, by contrast, can produce only 60 units of consumer goods and services while maintaining capital goods production at the original 20 units (b_2). All of this is a result of a different emphasis on the output choices by the two economies.

A sage of some bygone age said that there is no such thing as a free lunch. We can now make some sense out of this idea. Producing more of anything—a lunch, for example, since it involves the use of scarce resources—necessarily means producing less of something else. The lunch might be provided free to the people who eat it, but from the point of view of society as a whole, it took scarce resources to produce it, and therefore the lunch is *not* free.

FIGURE 1.5   **Different Growth Rates for Two Economies**

We begin with Atlantis and Mu being the same size, as indicated by the same PP1 curves. However, since Atlantis chooses to emphasize the production of capital goods (point a_1), while Mu emphasizes the production of consumer goods and services (point b_1), Atlantis will grow faster. The result of this faster growth is that over time PP2 shifts out further in the case of Atlantis than it does in the case of Mu.

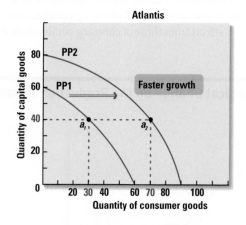

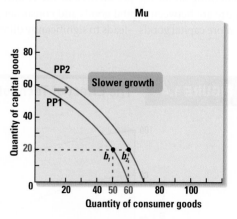

 SELF-TEST

6. Assume that the economy of Finhorn faces the following production possibilities:

Quantities per Year			
	A	**B**	**C**	**D**
Grain	0	25	40	50
Tools	12	8	4	0

a) Draw a production possibilities curve (PP1) with *Tools* on the horizontal axis and *Grain* on the vertical axis. Now, assume that a new technology that can be used only in the tool industry is developed, which increases tool output by 50 percent.

b) Draw a new production possibilities curve (PP2) that reflects this new technology.

c) If Finhorn produced 12 units of tools per year, how many units of grain could be produced after the introduction of the new technology?

Review

CHAPTER SUMMARY

In this introductory chapter, you gained an insight into the scope and depth of economics. You learned that economists are very focused on the choices that individuals, corporations, and governments face when making decisions and the related costs of those choices.

1.1 Topical controversies can easily be used to illustrate the relevance of economics.

1.2a Distinguishing between positive and normative statements is part of the scientific method, which is used extensively by economists in their attempt to better understand the world.

1.2b The discipline of economics is subdivided into:

- microeconomics, which studies the decisions made by people and firms and their outcomes; and
- macroeconomics, which studies how the major components of the whole economy interact and how well an economy achieves economic goals, such as full employment and economic growth.

1.3a Scarcity forces choice (for society, government, and the individual), and choice involves an (opportunity) cost.

1.3b Efficiency implies that economies make the best use of their resources and technology. There are two major

types of efficiency: productive efficiency and allocative efficiency, and both are important.

1.4 Greater specialization and trade can make economies more productive.

1.5a The three fundamental questions that all societies must somehow answer are:

- *What* is the right combination of consumer goods to produce, and what is the right balance between consumer goods and capital goods?
- *How* should these various goods be produced?
- *Who* is to receive what share of these goods once they are produced?

1.5b There are four fundamental ways to organize society: co-operation, command, custom, and competition.

1.6 The production possibilities model is an abstraction and simplification that helps illustrate:

- the opportunity cost involved in making a choice,
- the necessity of choice in deciding what to produce,
- inefficient production and the consequences of unemployed resources, and
- economic growth.

NEW GLOSSARY TERMS

allocative efficiency   10
capital   7
consumer goods and services   8
enterprise   7
factors of production   7
inputs   7
interest   8
labour   7

land   7
law of increasing costs   18
macroeconomics   7
microeconomics   6
normative statements   5
opportunity cost   5
positive statements   8

production possibilities curve   16
productive efficiency   10
profit   8
rent   8
resources   7
technology   8
wages   8

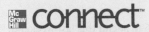

Practise and learn online with Connect, where you can find the Answered Questions and the Unanswered Problems for all chapters of this textbook's Study Guide section.

STUDY TIPS

1. Since this is the first chapter, do not be concerned if it seemed to contain so much new terminology that it was overwhelming. Mastering the principles of economics requires that you first learn the language of economics, and the best way to do this is to use it over and over. Let this Study Guide help you do this. Conscientiously work through all of the answered questions before proceeding to the next chapter.

2. Developing a knack for inventing useful acronyms for yourself can be helpful. For example, wages, interest, rents, and profits could be remembered as "WIRP."

3. Opportunity cost is one of the most important concepts in economics. As a start, make sure that you understand the basic idea that cost can be measured not just in dollars and cents but also in what has to be given up as a result of making a particular decision.

4. This chapter introduces you to the use of graphs with the production possibilities curve. If you have any difficulty understanding graphs, you might return to the Tool Kit at the beginning of the book and review that section.

5. For many of you, economics will be one of the more difficult courses that you will encounter in your undergraduate studies. Yet it can be mastered, and doing so can be very rewarding. You will probably be much more successful if you work a little on economics several times a week rather than have one long session a week. This way, you will gain mastery over the language more quickly through repetition and thereby gain confidence. You might consider buying a pack of 3" × 5" index cards and writing two or three definitions or simple ideas on each card. Carry several cards around with you so that you can glance at them several times a day. The authors found this technique helpful when (oh, so many years ago) they started to learn the discipline.

Answered Questions

These questions can also be found online on Connect.

Indicate whether the following statements are true or false.

1. **(LO 3) T or F**   An economy as a whole faces scarcity because of limited national income.

2. **(LO 3) T or F**   The three fundamental questions in economics are what, how, and how many.

3. **(LO 3) T or F**   Opportunity cost is the value of the next-best alternative that is given up as a result of making a particular choice.

4. **(LO 5) T or F**   There are only three Cs that humankind has used to coordinate its economies: co-operation, custom, and competition.

5. **(LO 3) T or F**   Wages, interest, rent, and profits are the four factors of production.

6. **(LO 6) T or F**   A production possibility curve is a graphical representation of the various combinations of output that are wanted.

7. **(LO 2) T or F**   Macroeconomics focuses on the outcomes of decisions by people and firms, whereas microeconomics is a study of how the major components of an economy interact.

8. **(LO 6) T or F**   Technological improvement can be illustrated graphically by a rightward shift in the production possibilities curve.

9. **(LO 6) T or F**   A point inside the production possibilities curve for an economy illustrates unemployment.

10. **(LO 6) T or F**   The straight-line production possibilities curve illustrates the law of increasing cost.

Basic (Questions 11–23)

11. **(LO 3)** All of the following statements, *except one*, are valid examples of the way economists use the term "scarcity." Which is the exception?
    a) Households face a scarcity of income.
    b) Individuals face a scarcity of time.
    c) Economies face a scarcity of resources.
    d) The world faces a scarcity of ideas.

12. **(LO 2)** All of the following, *except one*, are topics found in microeconomics. Which one is the exception?
    a) Supply and demand analysis
    b) Cost analysis
    c) Individual firm behaviour
    d) What causes inflation

13. **(LO 3)** Meridith had only $16 to spend this last weekend. She was, at first, uncertain about whether to go to two movies she wanted to see, or to buy a new CD she had recently listened to. In the end, she went to the movies.

Which of the following statements is correct?
a) The choice of the two movies and not the CD is an example of increasing costs.
b) The opportunity cost of the two movies is one CD.
c) The opportunity cost of the two movies is $16.
d) The choice of two movies rather than one CD was a bad one.

14. **(LO 4)** In reference to voluntary trade, what was Adam Smith the first to recognize?
a) It does not happen very often.
b) It may or may not benefit one or both of the parties to the trade.
c) It benefits one party to the trade but only at the expense of the other.
d) It benefits both parties to the trade.

15. **(LO 5)** What are the three fundamental questions in economics?
a) What to produce, how to produce it, and for whom is it produced.
b) Is it necessary, is it right, and is it valuable?
c) Who should produce, what is the right way to produce, and how should we decide?
d) What to produce, how to produce it, and who should produce it.

16. **(LO 5)** When, in time, did the market system first emerge?
a) In the early years of the twentieth century.
b) About 200 years ago.
c) Around the twelfth century.
d) The market system is as old as humankind.

17. **(LO 3)** Resources is a term that can be used interchangeably with:
a) Models
b) Consumer goods
c) Either factors of production or inputs
d) Technologies

18. **(LO 3)** What are the factors of production?
a) Land, labour, money, and enterprise
b) Land, labour, money, and capital
c) Land, labour, capital, and enterprise
d) Competition, command, custom, and co-operation

19. **(LO 3)** What are the names of the factor payments?
a) Consumption spending and investment spending
b) Wages and profits
c) Wages, interest, and profits
d) Wages, interest, rent, and profits

20. **(LO 2, 6)** What is an example of an economic model?
a) Opportunity costs and comparative advantage
b) Scarcity of resources and unlimited wants

c) Positive statements and normative statements
d) The production possibilities curve

21. **(LO 3)** All of the following, *except one*, are capital goods. Which is the exception?
a) An office building
b) A boiler in a pulp mill
c) A householder's garden shed
d) An airport runway

22. **(LO 3)** What is the definition of opportunity cost?
a) The amount of money spent on a good
b) The value of the next-best alternative that is given up as a result of making a particular choice
c) The value of all the alternatives given up as result of making a particular decision
d) The cost incurred in producing a good

23. **(LO 3)** What is meant by allocative efficiency?
a) Ensuring that goods and services are distributed equally to people
b) Producing goods and services at the least cost
c) Maximizing the amount of output for a given input
d) The production of the combination of products that best satisfies consumers' demands

Intermediate (Questions 24–30)

24. **(LO 5)** Which of the following refers to the concept of specialization?
a) Different individuals value goods differently
b) Some individuals are richer than others
c) Different nations have different opportunity costs of producing goods
d) Some nations are richer than others

25. **(LO 6)** All of the following, *except one*, are causes of economic growth. Which is the exception?
a) The discovery of new oilfields
b) Unemployed workers find jobs
c) A number of effective new training schemes for young people are introduced
d) An improved fuel-cell is invented

26. **(LO 5)** What are the four basic ways in which society can organize its economic affairs?
a) With consumer goods, capital goods, models, and positive statements
b) Using cooperation, command, custom, or competition
c) Using plentiful resources, opportunity costs, technology, and specialization
d) Using capitalism, communism, innovation, and technology

27. **(LO 2)** What is the distinction between a positive statement and a normative statement?
    a) Positive statements are assertions that can be tested with data, whereas normative statements are based on a value system of beliefs.
    b) Normative statements are assertions that can be tested with data, whereas positive statements are based on a value system of beliefs.
    c) The distinction depends on the context in which each statement is used.
    d) Positive statements are correct statements of fact, whereas normative statements are incorrect.

Figure 1.6 shows Mendork's production possibility curve for the only two goods that it produces—guns and butter. Refer to this figure to answer questions 28 to 32.

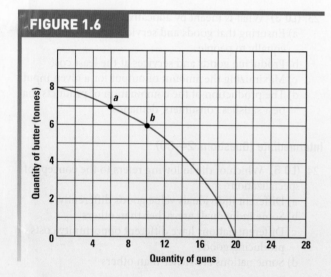

FIGURE 1.6

28. **(LO 6)** Refer to **Figure 1.6** to answer this question. If Mendork's production is currently that indicated by point *a*, what is the cost of producing four more guns?
    a) 1 tonne of butter
    b) 2 tonnes of butter
    c) 6 tonnes of butter
    d) 10 tonnes of butter

29. **(LO 6)** Refer to **Figure 1.6** to answer this question. What is the opportunity cost of 1 more tonne of butter as output changes from point *b* to *a*?
    a) 2 guns
    b) 4 guns
    c) 10 guns
    d) 6 guns

30. **(LO 6)** Refer to **Figure 1.6** to answer this question. Which of the following statements is correct if Mendork is currently producing 5 tonnes of butter and 8 guns?
    a) This society is using competition to coordinate its economic activities.
    b) This society is experiencing either unemployment or inefficiency.
    c) This economy is experiencing full employment.
    d) This society is not adequately answering the "for whom" question.
    e) This economy is growing quickly.

Advanced (Questions 31–35)

31. **(LO 6)** Refer to **Figure 1.6** to answer this question. What is the total opportunity cost of producing the first 2 tonnes of butter?
    a) 2 guns
    b) 18 guns
    c) 20 guns
    d) The answer cannot be determined from the information given

32. **(LO 6)** Refer to **Figure 1.6** to answer this question. If new technology increased the output of guns by 50 percent, how many guns could be produced if 6 tonnes of butter were produced?
    a) 18 guns
    b) 20 guns
    c) 15 guns
    d) 10 guns
    e) 0 guns

33. **(LO 6)** Which of the following statements is implied by a straight-line production possibilities curve?
    a) The law of increasing cost does not apply.
    b) The resources being used are homogeneous.
    c) The two goods being produced are very similar.
    d) The opportunity cost of both goods is constant.
    e) All of the above are correct.

34. **(LO 6)** Which of the following statements describes the law of increasing costs as it relates to the whole economy?
    a) As the quantity produced of any particular item decreases, its per-unit cost of production rises.
    b) As the quantity produced of any particular item increases, its per-unit cost of production rises.
    c) The prices of consumer goods and services always rise and never fall.

d) If you wait to make a purchase, you will pay a higher price.

e) The total cost of production rises as output goes up.

35. **(LO 6)** Which of the following statements is correct for a society that emphasizes the production of capital goods over that of consumer goods?

a) The society could enjoy the same quantity of capital goods and a larger quantity of consumer goods in the future.

b) The society will have to save more now, compared with a society that did not emphasize the production of capital goods.

c) The society could enjoy the same quantity of consumer goods and a larger quantity of capital goods in the future.

d) The society will grow faster than a society that emphasizes the production of consumer goods.

e) All of the above are correct.

Parallel Problems

ANSWERED PROBLEMS

36A. **(LO 6)** **Key Problem Table 1.4** contains the production possibilities data for capital goods and consumer goods in the economy of New Harmony.

TABLE 1.4

	A	B	C	D	E
Capital goods	0	8	14	18	20
Consumer goods	30	27	21	12	0

a) Use the grid in **Figure 1.7** to draw the production possibilities curve for New Harmony, and label it PPI. Label each of the five output combinations with the letters *a* through *e*.

b) Assume that the people of New Harmony have decided to produce 12 units of consumer goods. How many units of capital goods could be produced?
Answer: _____

c) Assume that the people of New Harmony have decided to produce 11 units of capital goods. Approximately how many units of consumer oods could be produced?
Answer: _____

d) What is the total cost of (the first) 14 capital goods produced?
Answer: _____

e) Assuming the economy is producing combination C, what is the total cost of 6 additional consumer goods?
Answer: _____

f) Assuming the economy is producing combination B, what is the approximate per-unit cost of an additional capital good?
Answer: _____

FIGURE 1.7

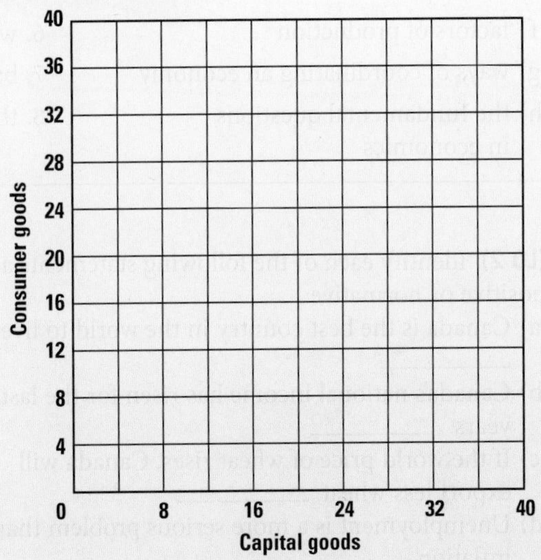

g) Assuming the economy is producing combination C, what is the approximate per unit cost of an additional capital good?
Answer: _____

h) What law is illustrated in your answers to f) and g)?

i) Fill in **Table 1.5** assuming that, 10 years later, the output potential of capital goods has increased by 50 percent, while the output potential for consumer goods has risen by 6 units for each combination A through D.

j) Using the data from this table, draw in PP2 in **Figure 1.7**.

k) As a result of the economic growth, can New Harmony now produce 24 capital goods and 26 consumer goods?
Answer: _____

TABLE 1.5

	V	W	X	Y	Z
Capital goods	___	___	___	___	___
Consumer goods and services	___	___	___	___	___

l) What are three possible explanations for the shift from PP1 to PP2?

Answer: _____

Basic (Problems 37A–45A)

37A. **(LO 1, 2, 3, 4, 5, 6)** Match the letters on the left with the numbers on the right. Place the correct letter in the blank.

a) capital good

b) recession

c) exports and imports

d) labour

e) enterprise

f) factors of production

g) ways of coordinating an economy

h) the fundamental questions in economics

1. cooperation, custom, command, and competition _____
2. the service of a brain surgeon _____
3. high unemployment _____
4. a satellite _____
5. labour, capital, land, and enterprise _____
6. what, how, and for whom _____
7. balance of trade _____
8. the original marketing of a new power cell _____

38A. **(LO 2)** Identify each of the following statements as positive or normative:

a) Canada is the best country in the world to live in. _____

b) Canada's national income has risen for the last five years. _____

c) If the world price of wheat rises, Canada will export less wheat. _____

d) Unemployment is a more serious problem than inflation. _____

39A. **(LO 6)** Answer the questions below based on **Figure 1.8** which is for the country of the planet Quantz. How much tea is gained and what is the cost in coffee:

a) in moving from U to V? _____ tea is gained at the cost of _____.

b) in moving from V to W? _____ tea is gained at the cost of _____.

c) in moving from W to X? _____ tea is gained at the cost of _____.

d) in moving from X to Y? _____ tea is gained at the cost of _____.

e) in moving from Y to Z? _____ tea is gained at the cost of _____.

40A. **(LO 3)** Below is a list of resources. Indicate whether each is labour (L), capital (K), land (N) or enterprise (E).

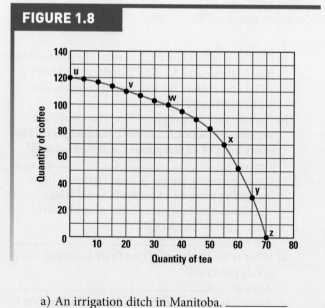

FIGURE 1.8

a) An irrigation ditch in Manitoba. _____

b) The work done by Jim Plum, a labourer who helped dig the irrigation ditch. _____

c) A lake. _____

d) The air we breathe. _____

e) The efforts of the founder and primary innovator of a successful new software company. _____

41A. (LO 3) Below is a list of economic goods You are to decide whether each is a consumer good, or a capital good (K), or possibly both (B), depending on the context in which it is used.
  a) A pair of socks
  b) A golf course
  c) A Big Mac hamburger
  d) A wheelbarrow

42A. (LO 6) Table 1.6 shows the production possibilities for the country of Emilon.

TABLE 1.6

	A	B	C	D	E
Rice	0	50	90	120	140
Beef	50	45	35	20	0

Complete the following (approximate) possibilities for Emilon: _____
  a) 130 rice and _____ beef
  b) 100 rice and _____ beef
  c) _____ rice and 5 beef
  d) _____ rice and 47 beef

Which of the following possibilities is Emilon capable of producing:
  e) 100 rice and 35 beef _____
  f) 100 rice and 40 beef _____
  g) 70 rice and 35 beef _____
  h) 100 rice and 5 beef _____

43A. (LO 6) Table 1.7 shows the production possibilities for the country of Emilon.

TABLE 1.7

	A	B	C	D	E
Rice	0	50	90	120	140
Beef	50	45	35	20	0

  a) What is the total cost of producing 90 rice?
    Answer: _____ beef
  b) What is the total cost of producing 45 beef?
    Answer: _____ rice
  c) What is the total cost of going from possibility C to possibility D?
    Answer: _____ (rice/beef)
  d) What is the approximate per-unit cost of going from possibility C to possibility D?
    Answer: _____ (rice/beef)

  e) What is the total cost of going from possibility D to possibility C?
    Answer: _____ (rice/beef)
  f) What is the approximate per unit cost of going from possibility D to possibility C?
    Answer: _____ (rice/beef)

44A. (LO 2) Explain why economics is sometimes called the *science of choice*.

45A. (LO 5) Identify and explain the four factors of production and the names given to payments received by each.

Intermediate (Problems 46A–50A)

46A. (LO 6) Utopia produces only two products: cheese and wine. The production levels are shown in **Table 1.8**.
  a) From these data, complete Utopia's production possibilities table in **Table 1.9**

TABLE 1.8

CHEESE		WINE	
% Inputs	Output	% Inputs	Output
0	0	0	0
20	30	20	40
40	50	40	70
60	65	60	95
80	75	80	105
100	80	100	110

TABLE 1.9

Possibility	A	B	C	D	E	F
Cheese	0	__	__	__	__	__
Wine	__	__	__	__	__	0

  b) Can Utopia produce 65 cheese and 95 wine?
    Answer: _____
  c) Can Utopia produce 75 cheese and 40 wine?
    Answer: _____
  d) If Utopia is at D, what is the total cost of 10 more cheese?
    Answer: _____
  e) If Utopia is at D, what is the total cost of 25 more wine?
    Answer: _____

47A. **(LO 6)** **Table 1.10** shows Lanark's production possibilities:

TABLE 1.10

	A	B	C	D	E	F
Wheat	0	20	35	45	50	52
Cars	21	20	18	14	8	0

a) If Lanark is producing 16 cars, approximately how much wheat can it produce?
Answer: _____

b) If Lanark is currently producing combination C, what is the cost of 10 more wheat?
Answer: _____

c) If Lanark is currently producing combination C, what is the cost of 2 more cars?
Answer: _____

d) If Lanark is currently producing combination D, what is the approximate unit cost of an additional car?
Answer: _____

e) If Lanark is currently producing combination D, what is the approximate unit cost of an additional wheat?
Answer: _____

48A. **(LO 6)** Shangri-La produces only two goods: bats and balls. Each worker comes with a fixed quantity of material and capital, and the economy's labour force is fixed at 50 workers. **Table 1.11** indicates the amounts of bats and balls that can be produced daily with various quantities of labour.

TABLE 1.11

Number of Workers	Daily Production of Balls	Number of Workers	Daily Production of Bats
0	0	0	0
10	150	10	20
20	250	20	36
30	325	30	46
40	375	40	52
50	400	50	55

a) What is the opportunity cost of increasing the output of bats from 46 to 52 units per day? _____

b) What is the opportunity cost of increasing the output of balls from 325 to 375 units per day? _____

c) Suppose that a central planning office dictates an output of 250 balls and 61 bats per day. Is this output combination possible? _____

d) Assume that a new technology is introduced in the production of bats so each worker can produce half a bat more per day. Can the planning office's goal of 250 balls and 61 bats now be met? _____

49A. **(LO 5)** The data below show the total production (in millions) of the only two goods produced in Kitchener and Waterloo, two small planets in deep space.

| **Kitchener** | 16 kiwis | or | 12 trucks |
| **Waterloo** | 8 kiwis | or | 14 trucks |

a) What is the opportunity cost of a kiwi in Kitchener? _____

b) What is the opportunity cost of a kiwi in Waterloo? _____

c) What is the opportunity cost of a truck in Kitchener? _____

d) What is the opportunity cost of a truck in Waterloo? _____

e) Which planet is best at producing kiwis? _____

f) Which planet is best at producing trucks? _____

g) If, before trade, each planet was devoting half its resources to producing each product, what is the total amount that both were producing? _____

h) If the two planets were to specialize in producing the product they do best, what would be the total amount they could produce? _____

i) What are the total gains as a result of specialization? _____

50A. **(LO 2, 6)** Write down a normative statement that relates to economics. Next, change your statement to make it a positive one.

51A. **(LO 6)** Illustrate economic growth using a production possibilities curve (remember to label the axes). What are two possible causes of economic growth?

52A. **(LO 6)** Suppose the country of Catalona produces leather shirts and leather moccasins whose production requires the same amount of leather and the same tools. Further suppose that workers in Catalona are equally capable of producing either product. Draw a production possibilities curve for Catalona, and comment on its shape.

Advanced (Problems 53A–57A)

53A. **(LO 2)** Explain the analogy between the use of theory and the use of a map.

54A. **(LO 6)** The data in **Table 1.12** are for the small country of Xanadu. Assume that the economy is producing combination C, but technological change occurs that enables it to produce 60 percent more capital goods.

TABLE 1.12

	A	B	C	D	E	F
Capital goods	0	25	40	50	55	58
Consumer goods	50	40	30	20	10	0

a) If the economy wants to continue with the same quantity of consumer goods, how many more capital goods can it now have as a result of the technological improvement? _____
b) If, instead, the economy wants to continue with the same quantity of capital goods, how many more consumer goods can it now have as a result of the technological improvement? _____
c) Before the technological change, what was the opportunity cost of the first 40 consumer goods? _____
d) After the technological change, what was the opportunity cost of the first 40 consumer goods? _____

55A. **(LO 6)** Jennifer is planning how to spend a particularly rainy Sunday, and the choice is between watching video movies (each lasting 2 hours) or studying her economics textbook. She has 10 hours available to her. If she decides to study, she could read the number of pages as shown in **Table 1.13**:

TABLE 1.13

Hours	Pages
2	80
4	130
6	160
8	175
10	180

a) Given this information, draw Jennifer's production possibilities curve between movies watched and pages studied on the grid in **Figure 1.9**.

b) What is the opportunity cost of watching 2 movies? _____

c) Could Jennifer watch 3 movies and study 150 pages of her textbook? _____

d) If Jennifer has already watched 4 movies, what is the opportunity cost of watching the fifth movie? _____

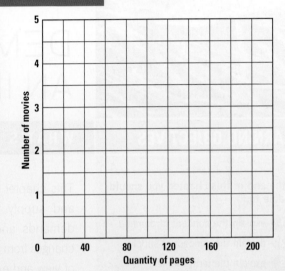

FIGURE 1.9

56A. **(LO 5)** To what extent is the organization of a family based on the four Cs? Give examples of how each of the four Cs is used to assign household chores to its members. What blend of the four Cs do you think is preferable, and why?

57A. **(LO 3)** Kant Skatte is a professional player in the National Hockey League. Because he loved the game so much, Kant dropped out of high school and worked very hard to develop his physical strength and overcome his limitations. Eventually he made it to the NHL. What data are needed to estimate Kant's annual opportunity costs, in dollars, of continuing to play in the NHL?

58A. **(LO 6)** Assume that an economy can produce either 300 tonnes of coffee and no rubber or 100 tonnes of rubber and no coffee. You may further assume that this 3:1 coffee/rubber ratio is constant. Draw a production possibilities curve for this economy with coffee on the vertical axis. Next, indicate with the letters a and b an increase in rubber production. Finally, illustrate with a triangle the cost of this additional rubber.

DEMAND AND SUPPLY: AN INTRODUCTION

At the end of this chapter, you should be able to...

LO1 explain the concept of demand.

LO2 explain the concept of supply.

LO3 explain the term *market*.

LO4 understand the concept of (price and quantity) equilibrium.

LO5 understand the causes and effects of a change in demand.

LO6 understand the causes and effects of a change in supply.

LO7 understand why demand and supply determine price and the quantity traded and not the reverse.

WHAT'S AHEAD...

This chapter introduces you to the fundamental economic ideas of demand and supply. It explains the distinction between individual and market demands and looks at the various reasons that the demand for products changes from time to time. We then take a look at things from the producers' point of view and explain what determines the amounts that they put on the market. Next, we explain how markets are able to reconcile the wishes of the two groups and we introduce the concept of equilibrium. Finally, we look at how the market price and the quantity traded adjust to changes in demand or supply.

A Question of Relevance...

Have you ever wondered why the prices of some products, such as computers or DVD players, tend to fall over time, while the prices of other products, such as cars or auto insurance, tend to rise? Or perhaps you wonder how the price of a house can fluctuate tens of thousands of dollars from year to year. Why does a poor orange harvest in Florida cause the price of apple juice made in Ontario to rise? And why do sales of fax machines continue to fall despite their lower prices? This chapter will give you insights into questions such as these.

If the average person were to think about the subject matter of economics, it is unlikely that she would immediately think of choice or opportunity costs, which was a principal topic of Chapter 1. More likely, she would think in terms of money or interest rates, and almost certainly demand and supply. Most people realize, without studying the topic, that demand and supply are central to economics. In our own ways, and as a result of our experiences in life, most of us feel that we know quite a lot about the subject. After all, who are better experts on the reaction of consumers to changes in the market than consumers themselves? However, as we will see shortly, the way that economists define and use the terms "demand" and "supply" differs from the everyday usage of these terms. To make matters worse, there does not seem to be a consensus among non-economists about the meaning of either of these two words: there is a range of meanings. This is often the case with language, but it does lead to a great deal of confusion, which can be illustrated in the following exchange between two observers of the consumer electronic goods market:

Justine: "Have you noticed that the price of big-screen TVs has dropped quite a bit recently?"

Eric: "Well, yes, but that is just supply and demand."

Justine: Are you saying that the supply has gone up?"

Eric: "Sure, must have."

Justine: "But why would supply go up if the price is going down?"

Eric: "Well, I don't know—maybe it is because demand has gone up as well."

There is much confusion here. While Eric's belief that the price has fallen because supply went up is probably correct in this context, we see that price will also fall if demand decreases. Justine's second question about why supply would go up if the price goes down reveals a common confusion over cause and effect. And Eric's final response is confused because he is not aware that demand and supply factors are separate and not inter-related.

We hope to soon clarify all of this type of confusion. It is probably clear to you already that economists are very fussy about defining and using economic terms correctly, and this is particularly true in a discussion about demand and supply. As we shall see in this chapter, demand does not simply mean what people want to buy, nor is supply just the amount being produced.

Another source of confusion in the above discussion is a misunderstanding of cause and effect: is the change in TV prices the effect of changing demand, or is it the cause? This chapter will clear up some of the confusion and give us a basis upon which to analyze and clarify some real, practical problems. First, let us take a look at the concept of demand.

2.1   DEMAND

Individual Demand

 L01 Explain the concept of demand.

There are several dimensions to **demand**. First, economists use the word in the sense of wanting something, not in the sense of commanding or ordering. However, this "want" also involves the ability to buy. In other words, demand refers to both the *desire* and the *ability* to purchase a good or service. This means that although I may well have a desire for a new top-of-the-line BMW, I unfortunately do not have the ability to buy one at current prices, and therefore my quantity demanded is zero. Similarly, I might have the income to buy only expensive, upmarket wines but no desire to do so.

demand: the quantities that consumers are willing and able to buy per period of time at various prices.

Second, even though many factors determine what products and what quantities a consumer purchases, economists would suggest that price is usually the most important. For this reason, they look at how consumers might react to a change in the price, assuming that all other factors remain unchanged. The Latin phrase for this perspective is ***ceteris paribus***, which literally means "other things being equal." However, it is usually interpreted by economists to mean "other things remaining the same." In other words, demand is the relationship between the price of a product and the quantities demanded, *ceteris paribus*.

ceteris paribus: other things being equal, or other things remaining the same.

Third, demand is a hypothetical construct that expresses this desire and ability to purchase, not at a single price, but over a *range of* hypothetical prices. Finally, demand is also a flow concept in that it measures quantities over a period of time. In summary, demand:

- involves both the desire and the ability of consumers to purchase,
- assumes that other things are held constant,
- refers to a range of prices, and
- measures quantities over time.

demand schedule: a table showing the various quantities demanded per period of time at different prices.

All of these aspects of demand are captured in **Table 2.1**, which shows the **demand schedule** for an enthusiastic beer drinker named Tomiko.

TABLE 2.1	Individual Demand
Price per Case	**Quantity Demanded (Number of Cases per Month)**
$17	7
18	6
19	5
20	4
21	3
22	2

Once again, what we mean by demand is the entire relationship between the various prices and the quantities that people are willing and able to purchase. This relationship can be laid out in the form of a demand schedule. The above schedule shows the amounts per week that Tomiko is willing and able to purchase at the various prices shown. Note that there is an inverse relationship between the price and quantity. This simply means that at higher prices, Tomiko would not be willing to buy as much as at lower prices. In other words:

> The higher the price, the lower will be the quantity demanded; and the lower the price, the higher will be the quantity demanded.

Another less obvious statement of this law of demand is to say that in order to induce Tomiko to buy a greater quantity of beer, the price must be lower. Tomiko's demand schedule is graphed in **Figure 2.1**.

In **Figure 2.1**, at a price of $21 per case, the quantity demanded by Tomiko is 3 cases per month, while at a lower price of $18 per case, she would be willing to buy 6 cases. The demand is therefore plotted as a downward-sloping curve by connecting these two price/quantity coordinates and then extending a straight line. (To economists, curves include straight lines!) Once again, note that when we say "demand," or "demand schedule," or "demand curve," we are referring to a whole array of different prices and quantities.

It is very important for you to note that since the price of any product is part of what we call the "demand" for that product, a change in the price cannot change the demand. It can, however, affect the amounts we are willing to purchase, and we express this by saying that:

change in the quantity demanded: the change in quantity that results from a price change. It is illustrated by a movement along a demand curve.

> A change in the price of a product results in a **change in the quantity demanded** for that product.

FIGURE 2.1   Individual Demand Curve

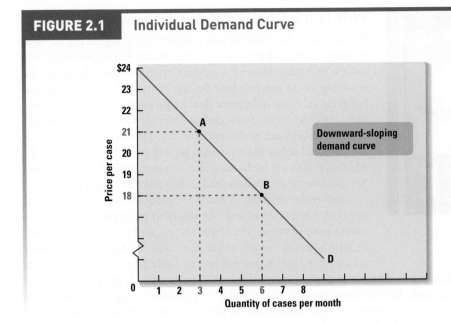

At a price of $18 per case, Tomiko is willing and able to buy 6 cases per month (point B). At a higher price, $21 per case, the amount she is willing and able to buy falls to 3 cases (point A). The higher the price, then, the lower is the quantity demanded. (Note that the vertical axis contains a "broken" portion. In general, an axis is often broken in this manner whenever the information about, say, low prices, is unavailable or unimportant.)

In other words, point A in **Figure 2.1** represents a price of $21 and a quantity demanded of 3 cases. Point B shows another possible combination: at a price of $18, the quantity demanded is 6 cases. The *quantity demanded*, then, is a single point on the demand curve whereas the *demand* is the entire collection of points.

This is illustrated in **Figure 2.2**. Graphically, as we move the demand curve, from $18 to $17, the quantity demanded increases from 6 to 7 cases; as we move up the demand curve, from $21 to $22, the quantity demanded decreases from 3 cases to 2 cases.

FIGURE 2.2   Changes in the Quantity Demanded

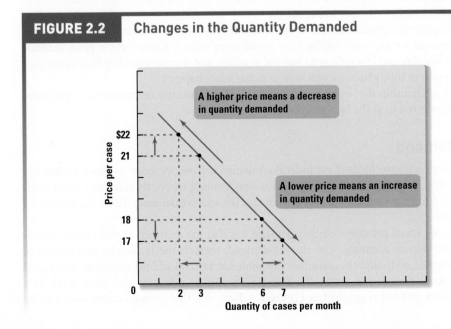

Whenever the price changes, there is a movement along the demand curve. An increase in the price from, say, $21 to $22, causes a decrease in the quantity demanded from 3 to 2. A decrease in the price from $18 to $17 leads to an increase in the quantity demanded from 6 to 7. Neither the demand nor the demand curve, however, changes.

A SALE sign is often all it takes to attract consumers.

Why Is the Demand Curve Downward Sloping?

People tend to buy more at lower, rather than at higher prices. Most of us can confirm from our own experiences that a lower price will induce us to buy more of a product or to buy something that we would or could not purchase before. Witness the big crowds that are attracted to nothing more than a sign saying SALE. In addition, most microeconomic research done over the years tends to confirm this law of demand, and theories of consumer behaviour (such as the marginal utility theory, which we will study in Chapter 5) lend additional support to the idea. But is it that simple? Let us explore the question of why people tend to buy more at lower prices.

Remember that our demand for products is a combination of our desire to purchase and our ability to purchase. A lower price affects both of these. The lower the price of a product, the more income a person has left to purchase additional products. Assume, for instance, that the price of beer in **Table 2.1** was $20, and Tomiko was buying 4 cases per month, for a total expenditure of $80 per month. If the price decreases to $18, Tomiko could buy the same quantity for an outlay of $72, thus saving a total of $8. It is almost as if Tomiko had received a pay raise of $8. In fact, in terms of its effect on Tomiko's pocketbook, it is exactly the same. Or, as economists would express it, her **real income** has increased. A decrease in price means that people can afford to buy more of a product (or more of other products) if they wish. This is referred to as the **income effect** of a price change, and it affects people's *ability* to purchase. This is because a lower price means a higher real income, so people will tend to buy more of a product. (Conversely, an increase in the price effectively reduces a person's real income.)

In addition to this, a price change also affects people's *desire* to purchase. We are naturally driven to buy the cheaper of competing products, and a drop in the price of one of them increases our desire to substitute it for a relatively more expensive product. If the price of wine were to drop (or if the price of beer were to increase), then some beer drinkers might well switch to what they regard as a cheaper substitute. In general, there are substitutes for most products, and people will tend to substitute a relatively cheap product for a more expensive one. This is called the **substitution effect**. A higher price, however, tends to make the product less attractive to us than its substitutes, and so we buy less of it.

When the price of a product drops, we buy more of it because we are *more able* (the income effect) and because we are *more willing* (the substitution effect). Conversely, a price increase means we are less able and less willing to buy the product, and therefore we buy less. (There is a possible exception to this, which we will look at in the next chapter.)

The close relationship that exists between price and the quantity demanded is so pervasive that it is often referred to as the *law of demand*.

Market Demand

Up to this point, we have focused on individual demand. Now, we want to move to **market demand** (or total demand). Conceptually, this is easy enough to do. By summing every individual's demand for a product, we are able to obtain the market demand. **Table 2.2** provides a simple example.

Let us say we know not only Tomiko's demand but also the demands of three other friends in a small, four-person economy. The market demand, then, is the horizontal summation of individual demands, so to find the quantities demanded at $18, we add the quantities demanded by each individual: $6 + 3 + 4 + 9 = 22$. The same would be done for each price level. This particular market demand is graphed in **Figure 2.3**. Note that this demand curve, which is the

---

real income: income measured in terms of the amount of goods and services that it will buy. Real income will increase if either actual income increases or prices fall.

income effect: the effect that a price change has on real income and therefore on the quantity demanded of a product.

substitution effect: the substitution of one product for another as a result of a change in their relative prices.

market demand: the total demand for a product by all consumers.

TABLE 2.2	Deriving the Market Demand				
NUMBER OF CASES PER MONTH					
Price per Case	Tomiko's Quantity Demanded	Meridith's Quantity Demanded	Abdi's Quantity Demanded	Jan's Quantity Demanded	Market Quantity Demanded
$18	6	3	4	9	22
19	5	2	4	7	18
20	4	2	4	6	16
21	3	0	3	3	9
22	2	0	3	1	6

FIGURE 2.3	The Market Demand Curve

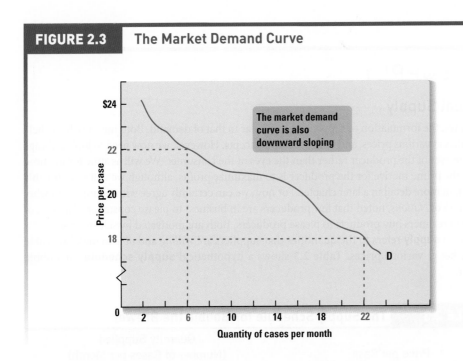

The market demand curve is also downward sloping

At a price of $18, the total or market quantity demanded equals 22 cases. As with individual demand, when the price increases to $22, the quantity demanded will drop, in this case to 6. This is because at a higher price, each individual buys less, and there are fewer people who can afford to or are willing to buy any at all. (Meridith has dropped out of the market.)

summation of the specific numbers of the four people in **Table 2.2**, is not a straight line. Yet it is still downward sloping and so conforms to the law of demand. For the most part, we will work with straight-line demand curves, although there is no reason to assume that all real-life demand curves plot as straight lines.

Note that, as with the individual demand curve, the market demand curve also slopes downward. This is because people buy more as the price drops—and more people buy. In our example, Meredith is not willing to buy any beer at a price of $22. Only if the price is $20 or lower will all four people buy beer.

Finally, before we look at the supply side of the market, note again that our demand schedule tells us only what people *might* buy; it tells us nothing about what they are actually buying. To know this, we also need to know the actual price. And to find out what the price of beer should be, we need to know…yes, the supply.

SELF-TEST

1. The data in the table indicate the weekly demand for litres of soy milk by Al, Bo, and Cole (the only three people in a very small market).

a) Fill in the blanks in the table.

b) What is the basic shape of the demand curve in this market?

c) What is the highest price at which all three will buy at least one litre of milk?

Price	Quantity Demanded: Al	Quantity Demanded: Bo	Quantity Demanded: Cole	Total (market) Quantity Demanded:
$4.00	1	0	0	_____
3.50	1	1	0	_____
3.00	1	1	1	_____
2.50	2	1	1	_____
2.00	2	2	1	_____

2.2 SUPPLY

L02 Explain the concept of supply.

Individual Supply

In many ways, the formulation of supply is very similar to that of demand. Both measure hypothetical quantities at various prices, and both are flow concepts. However, we now need to look at things through the eyes of the producer rather than the eyes of the consumer. We will assume for the time being that the prime motive for the producer is to maximize profits, although we will examine this assumption in more detail in a later chapter. For now, we can certainly agree with Adam Smith who, in *The Wealth of Nations*, noted that few producers are in business to please consumers. Neither, of course, do consumers buy products to please producers. Both are motivated by self-interest.

The term **supply** refers to the quantities that suppliers are *willing* and *able* to make available to the market at various prices. **Table 2.3** shows a hypothetical **supply schedule** for Bobbie the brewer.

supply: the quantities that producers are willing and able to sell per period of time at various prices.

supply schedule: a table showing the various quantities supplied per period of time at different prices.

TABLE 2.3	The Supply Schedule for Bobbie the Brewer
Price per Case	**Quantity Supplied (Number of Cases per Month)**
$18	2
19	3
20	4
21	5
22	6

Note that there is a *direct* relationship between the price and the quantity supplied, which means that a higher price will induce Bobbie to produce more. Remember that Bobbie's reason for being in business is to make as much profit as possible. How much would Bobbie, hypothetically, be prepared to supply if the beer could be sold at $18 per case? Knowing what her costs are likely to be, she figures that she could make the most profit if she produces two cases. At a higher price, there is a likelihood of greater profits, and therefore she is willing to produce more. Also, as we shall see in Chapter 6, when firms produce more, the cost per unit tends to rise. Therefore, a

ADDED DIMENSION   Adam Smith: The Father of Economics

Adam Smith (1723–90) is generally regarded as the founding father of economics. In his brilliant work, *The Wealth of Nations*, Smith posed so many interesting questions and provided such illuminating answers that later economists often felt that they were merely picking at the scraps he left behind. Smith was born and brought up in Scotland, and educated at Glasgow and Oxford. He held the Chair of Moral Philosophy at Glasgow College for many years. He was a lifelong bachelor and had a kind but absent-minded disposition.

Smith was the first scholar to analyze the business of "getting and spending" in a detailed and systematic manner. In doing this, he gave useful social dignity to the professions of business and trading. Besides introducing the important idea of the *invisible hand*, which was his way of describing the coordinating mechanism of capitalism, he examined the division of labour, the role of government, the function of money, the advantages and disadvantages of free trade, what constitutes good and bad taxation, and a host of other ideas. For Smith, economic life was not merely a peripheral adventure for people but their central motivating force.

producer needs the incentive of a higher price *in order to* increase production. For the time being, however, we can rely on the proposition that a higher price means higher profits and therefore will lead to higher quantities produced. This is illustrated in **Figure 2.4**.

Joining the individual points from the supply schedule in **Table 2.3** gives us the upward-sloping supply curve shown in **Figure 2.4**. Again, we emphasize the fact that as with the term "demand," the term "supply" does not refer to a single price and quantity but to the whole array of hypothetical price and quantity combinations contained in the supply schedule and illustrated by the supply curve.

Since price is part of what we mean by the term *supply*, a change in the price level cannot change the supply. A change in price does, of course, lead to a change in the quantity that a producer is willing and able to make available. Thus, the effect of a change in price we call a **change in the quantity supplied**. This is illustrated in **Figure 2.5**.

change in the quantity supplied: the change in the amounts that will be produced as a result of a price change. This is shown as a movement along a supply curve.

FIGURE 2.4	**Individual Supply Curve**

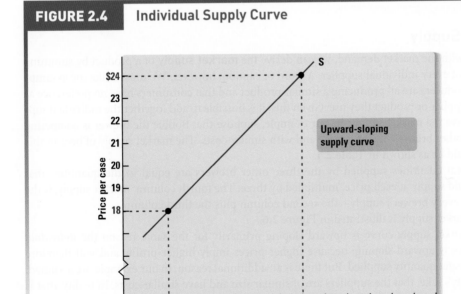

At a low price of $18, the most profitable output for Bobbie is 2 cases. If the price increased, she would be willing and able to produce more, since she would be able to make greater profits. At $24, for instance, the quantity she would produce increases to 8 cases.

| FIGURE 2.5 | Changes in the Quantity Supplied |

A price change will lead to a movement along the supply curve. An increase in the price from, say, P_1 to P_2 will cause an increase in the quantity supplied from Q_1 to Q_2. A decrease in the price from P_3 to P_4 will lead to a decrease in the quantity supplied from Q_3 to Q_4. The supply curve itself, however, does not change.

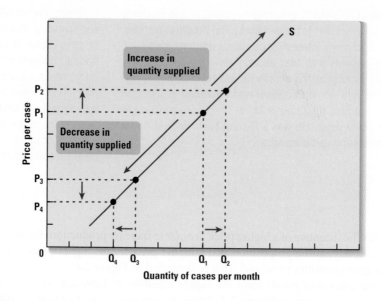

To summarize:

An increase in price will lead to an *increase in the quantity supplied* and is illustrated as a movement up the supply curve.

A decrease in price will cause a *decrease in the quantity supplied* and is illustrated as a movement down the supply curve.

Market Supply

market supply: the total supply of a product offered by all producers.

As we did with the market demand, we can derive the **market supply** of a product by summing the supply of every individual supplier. A word of caution, however. We must make the assumption that producers are all producing a similar product and that consumers have no preference as to which supplier or product they use. Given this, it is possible to add together the individual supplies to derive the market supply. In our example, suppose that Bobbie the brewer is competing with three other brewers of similar size and with similar costs. The market supply of beer in this market would be as shown in **Table 2.4**.

The total quantities supplied by the three other brewers are equal to the quantities that Bobbie would supply at each price, multiplied by three. The fourth column, market supply, is the addition of every brewer's supply—the second column plus the third column.

The market supply is illustrated in **Figure 2.6**.

The *market* supply curve is upward sloping primarily for the same reason the *individual* supply curve is upward-sloping: because higher prices imply higher profits and will therefore induce a greater quantity supplied. But there is an additional reason. In our example, we assumed, for simplicity's sake, that the suppliers are of similar size and have similar costs. In reality, that is unlikely; costs and size probably differ, so a price that generates a profit for one firm may mean a loss for another. As the price of a product increases, however, some firms that were previously

TABLE 2.4	Deriving the Market Supply		
NUMBER OF CASES PER MONTH			
Price per Case	Bobbie the Brewer's Quantity Supplied	Quantity Supplied of Other Brewers	Market Quantity Supplied
$18	2	6	8
19	3	9	12
20	4	12	16
21	5	15	20
22	6	18	24

FIGURE 2.6   The Market Supply

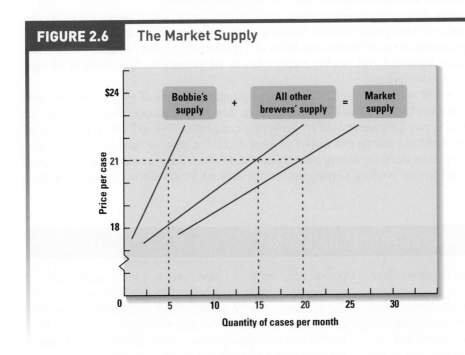

The market supply is the horizontal summation of each individual producer's supply curve. For instance, at a price of $21, Bobbie would supply 5 cases; the other brewers combined would supply 15 cases. The market quantity supplied, therefore, is the total quantity supplied of 20 cases. In short, to derive the market supply curve, we add the totals of each supplier at each price level.

unable to produce will now find that they can successfully operate at a profit. Thus, as the price of the product increases, currently operating firms will produce more, and other firms not previously producing will enter the market and start to produce.

In summary, a higher price, which deters consumers from buying more, is an incentive for suppliers to produce more. Conversely, a lower price induces consumers to buy more but is a reason for suppliers to cut back their output.

The motives of consumers and producers are very different: consumers wish to obtain the lowest price possible, and producers want to sell at the highest. How can their wishes converge? How is trade possible at all in these circumstances? Certainly, it is not possible for *all* prospective consumers and suppliers to be satisfied. But it is almost always possible for *some* of these people to be satisfied. Of course, this will require that they be able, in some sense, to meet and get together. A market enables them to do just that.

2.3   THE MARKET

market: a mechanism that brings buyers and sellers together and assists them in negotiating the exchange of products.

Most people are able to understand the terms *market price* and *market demand*, but many are not clear as to what constitutes a **market**. Certainly, the term includes places that have a physical location, such as a local produce or fish market. But in broader terms, a market really refers to any exchange mechanism that brings buyers and sellers of a product together. There may be times when we need to inspect or get further on-the-spot information about a product before we buy it, and this is the purpose of the retail market. But there are other times when we possess sufficient information about a product or a producer, and it is not necessary to actually see either of them before we purchase. This applies, for instance, if you wish to buy stocks and bonds or make a purchase on the Internet. Increasingly, in these days of higher costs of personal service and greater availability of electronic communication, markets are becoming both wider and more accessible. The market for commodities, such as copper, gold, and rubber, for instance, is both worldwide and anonymous in that the buyers and sellers seldom meet in person.

By a market, then, we mean any relatively open environment in which buyers and sellers can communicate, and that operates without preference. When we talk of the market price, then, we mean the price available to *all* buyers and sellers of a product. By market demand, we mean the total quantities demanded. And market supply refers to the quantity made available by all suppliers at each possible price.

Later, you will encounter several different types of markets, some of which work very well and others that work poorly, if at all. The analysis in this chapter assumes that the market we are looking at is very (economists call it "perfectly") competitive. We will devote the whole of Chapter 8 to examining this type of market in more detail. For now, we need to mention that a perfectly competitive market is, among other things, one in which there are many small producers, each selling an identical product. Keeping this caution in mind, let us see how this market works.

▶ ADDED DIMENSION   Re-inventing the Market

Modern capitalism first emerged and began to spread about 250 years ago, as commerce moved out of the village markets of Europe into the age of factory-centred manufacturing, which was later combined with widespread systems of wholesale and retail. However, this transformation also introduced a less predictable chain of supply and demand. While the seller in the village market was in direct contact with the buyer, the evolution of capitalism's mass markets and mass production techniques imposed vast gulfs in time and space between buyer and seller. Producers became much less sure of what the demand for their product was, and buyers were never sure there wasn't a better deal somewhere else. In response to this, sellers used the blunt tool of a fixed price list and adjusted output accordingly, while buyers just did the best they could. The phenomenon of the Internet is re-inventing commerce as the seller's market horizon expands, buyers have more information, real-time sales become routine, and the need to stockpile inventory diminishes. In short, supply-chain bottlenecks are being eradicated. What is emerging is far *more efficient markets* and the rise of dynamic pricing based on constantly fluctuating demand and supply.

2.4   MARKET EQUILIBRIUM

We now examine the point at which the wishes of buyers and sellers coincide by combining the market demand and supply for beer in **Table 2.5**.

L04 Understand the concept of (price and quantity) equilibrium.

TABLE 2.5	Market Supply and Demand		
	NUMBER OF CASES PER MONTH		
Price per Case	Market Quantity Demanded	Market Quantity Supplied	Surplus (+)/ Shortage (−)
$18	22	8	−14
19	18	12	−6
20	**16**	**16**	**0**
21	9	20	+11
22	6	24	+18

You can see from this table that there is only one price, $20, at which the wishes of consumers and producers coincide. Only if the price is $20 will the quantity demanded and quantity supplied be equal. This price level is referred to as the **equilibrium price**. Equilibrium, in general, means that there is balance between opposing forces; here, those opposing forces are demand and supply. The word *equilibrium* also implies a condition of stability. If this stability is disturbed, there will be a tendency to automatically find a new equilibrium.

To understand this point, refer to **Table 2.5** and note that if the price were, say, $18, then the amount being demanded, 22, would exceed the amount being supplied, which is 8. At this price, there is an excess demand, or more simply, a shortage of beer, to the tune of 14 cases. This amount is shown in the last column and marked with a minus sign. In this situation, there would be a lot of unhappy beer drinkers. Faced with the prospect of going beer-less, many of them will be prepared to pay a higher price for their suds and will therefore bid the price up. As the price of beer starts to rise, the reaction of consumers and producers will differ. Some beer drinkers will not be able to afford the higher prices so the quantity demanded will drop. On the supply side, producers will be delighted with the higher price and will start to produce more—and the quantity supplied will increase. Both these tendencies will combine to reduce the shortage as the price goes up. Eventually, when the price has reached the equilibrium price of $20, the shortage will have disappeared, and the price will no longer increase. Part of the law of demand suggests, then, that:

equilibrium price: the price at which the quantity demanded equals the quantity supplied such that there is neither a surplus nor a shortage.

Shortages cause prices to rise.

This is illustrated in **Figure 2.7**.

Now, again using **Table 2.5**, let us see what will happen if the price happens to be above equilibrium, at $22 a case. At this price, the quantity demanded is 6 cases, and the quantity supplied is 24 cases. There is insufficient demand from the producers' point of view, or more simply, there is a surplus (or excess supply) of 18 cases. This is shown in the last column of **Table 2.5** as +18. This is not a stable situation because firms cannot continue producing a product that they cannot sell. They will be forced to lower the price in an attempt to sell more. As the price starts to drop, two things happen concurrently. Consumers will be happy to consume more, or to use economic terms, there will be an increase in the quantity demanded.

FIGURE 2.7   How the Market Reacts to a Shortage

At a price of $18, the quantity supplied of 8 is far below the quantity demanded of 22. The horizontal distance between the two shows the amount of the shortage, which is 14. As a result of the shortage, price bidding between consumers will force up the price. As the price increases, the quantity demanded will drop, but the quantity supplied will rise until these two are equal at a quantity of 16.

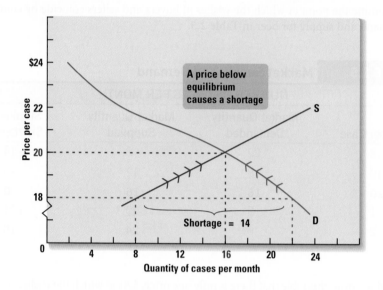

In **Figure 2.8**, note that as the price falls, the quantity demanded increases, and this increase is depicted as a movement down the demand curve. At the same time, faced with a falling price, producers will be forced to cut back production—decreasing the quantity supplied. In the same figure, this is shown as a movement along (down) the supply curve. The net result of this will be the eventual elimination of the surplus as the price moves toward equilibrium. In other words:

Surpluses cause prices to fall.

FIGURE 2.8   How the Market Reacts to a Surplus

A price above equilibrium will produce a surplus. At $22, the quantity supplied of 24 exceeds the quantity demanded of 6. The horizontal distance of 18 represents the amount of the surplus. The surplus will result in producers dropping the price in an attempt to increase sales. As the price drops, the quantity demanded increases, while the quantity supplied falls. The equilibrium quantity is 16.

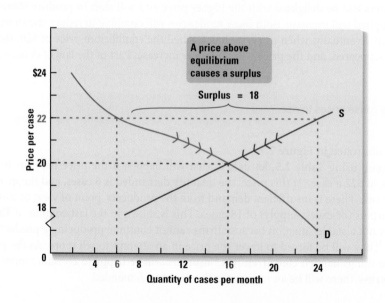

Only if the price is $14 will there be no surplus or shortage, and the quantity produced will be equal to the quantity demanded. This is the equilibrium price. The quantity prevailing at the equilibrium price is known as the **equilibrium quantity**, in this case 16 cases. This equilibrium quantity is the quantity both demanded and supplied (since they are equal).

equilibrium quantity: the quantity that prevails at the equilibrium price.

 SELF-TEST

2. What effect does a surplus have on the price of a product? What about a shortage?

3. The following table shows the demand and supply of eggs (in hundreds of thousands per day).

   a) What are the equilibrium price and the equilibrium quantity?

   b) Complete the surplus/shortage column. Using this column, explain why your answer to question A must be correct.

   c) What would be the surplus/shortage at a price of $2.50? What would happen to the price and the quantity traded?

   d) What would be the surplus/shortage at a price of $4? What would happen to the price and the quantity traded?

Price	Quantity Demanded	Quantity Supplied	Surplus/ Shortage
$2.00	60	30	_____
2.50	56	36	_____
3.00	52	42	_____
3.50	48	48	_____
4.00	44	54	_____

2.5 CHANGE IN DEMAND

Recall from the definition of demand that the concept refers to the *relationship* between various prices and quantities. In other words, both price and quantity make up what is known as demand. Thus, a change in price cannot cause a change in demand but does cause a change in the quantity demanded. That said, we must now ask: what are the other determinants, besides price, that influence how much of any particular product consumers will buy? Or, once equilibrium price and quantity have been established, what might disturb that equilibrium? One general answer to this question is a **change in demand**. Table 2.6 shows such a change in the demand for beer.

Here, we will introduce new figures for demand in order to revert to straight-line demand curves. Let us say that D_1 is the demand for beer that existed last month and D_2 is the demand this month. Demand has increased by 6 cases per week at each price, so whatever the price, consumers are willing and able to consume an additional 6 cases. Thus, there has been an increase in the demand. **Figure 2.9** graphically illustrates an increase in demand.

LO5 Understand the causes and effects of a change in demand.

change in demand: a change in the quantities demanded at every price, caused by a change in the determinants of demand.

TABLE 2.6	An Increase in Demand	
NUMBER OF CASES PER MONTH		
Price per Case of Beer	**Quantity Demanded 1**	**Quantity Demanded 2**
$18	16	22
19	15	21
20	14	20
21	13	19
22	12	18

FIGURE 2.9   An Increase in Demand

At each price, the quantities demanded have increased. In this example, the increase is by a constant amount of 6, thus producing a parallel shift in the demand curve. For example, at $20 the quantity demanded has increased from 14 to 20 (by 6).

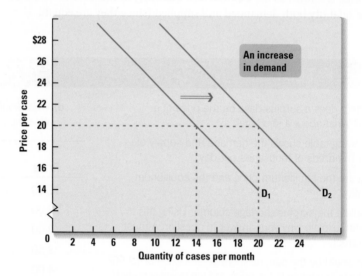

An increase in demand, then, means an increase in the quantities demanded *at each price*, that is, a total increase in the demand schedule, which is illustrated by a rightward shift in the demand curve. Similarly, a decrease in demand means a reduction in the quantities demanded at each price—a decrease in the demand schedule—and this is illustrated by a leftward shift in the demand curve.

Determinants of a Change in Demand

Now that we know what an increase in demand looks like, we need to look at the factors that could bring about such a change. Some of these determinants of demand affect people's willingness to purchase, others affect their ability to purchase, and still others affect both.

The first factor that affects our willingness to purchase a product is our own *preference*. An increase in demand as shown in **Table 2.6** could simply have been caused by a change in consumer preferences: consumers now prefer more beer.

But many things could affect our preferences. Tastes change over time and are influenced by the weather, advertising, articles and reports in books and magazines, opinions of friends, special events, and much more. Specific examples would include decreased demand for steak as the summer barbeque season passes, increased demand for a book that has won a prestigious literary award, or the increase in demand for hotel rooms in the host city of the Olympics.

The second factor affecting the demand for a product is the *income* of consumers. This affects their ability to consume. Generally speaking, you would expect that an increase in income leads most people to increase their purchases of most products and that a decrease in income generally causes a drop in demand—that is, there is a direct relationship between income and demand. This is true for most products that we buy, and these products are called **normal products** such as sushi, soda pop, cars, and movies.

But it is certainly not true for all people and all products. For instance, as the incomes of most people increase, these consumers tend to buy less of such things as low-quality hamburger meats, boxes of macaroni and cheese, cheap toilet paper, and so on. Instead, they start to substitute higher-quality and higher-priced articles that they could not previously afford. When income is low, we buy lower-quality staple products that economists call **inferior products**. There is an inverse relationship between income and the demand for inferior products: as income

normal products: products for which demand will increase as a result of an increase in income, and decrease as a result of a decrease in income.

inferior products: products for which demand will decrease as a result of an increase in income, and increase as a result of a decrease in income.

levels go up, the demand goes down. It also means that as incomes fall, demand for these inferior products will rise. In our beer example from **Table 2.6**, the increase in market demand could have been caused by an increase in incomes because beer is a normal product.

A third important determinant of demand is the *prices of related products*. A change in the price of related products will affect people's willingness and ability to purchase a particular good. Products are related if a change in the price of one causes a change in the demand for the other. For instance, if the price of Pepsi were to increase, a number of Pepsi drinkers might well switch over to Coke.

There are, in fact, two ways in which products may be related. They may be related as substitutes, or they may be related as complements. **Substitute products** (also known as *competitive products*) are those that are so similar in the eyes of most consumers that price is the main distinguishing feature. Pepsi and Coke, therefore, are substitute products because an increase in the price of one will cause an increase in the demand for the other. The relationship between the price of a product and the demand for its substitute is therefore a direct one. It also means that if the price of a product falls, then the demand for its substitute will also fall, since many consumers are now buying a cheaper product.

Complementary products tend to be purchased together, and their demands are interrelated. Skis and ski boots are complementary products, as are cars and gasoline or beer and pretzels. If the price of one product increases, causing a decrease in the quantity demanded, then people will also purchase less of the complement. If the price of greens fees were to increase so that people were buying fewer rounds of golf, then we would also expect a decrease in the demand for complementary products such as golf balls and golf tees.

There is, in this case, an inverse relationship between the price of a product and the demand for its complement: an increase in price of the one product leads to a decline in the demand for the complementary product. Similarly, a decrease in the price of a product will lead to an increase in the demand for a complement.

A fourth determinant of demand is consumers' *expectations of the future*. There are many ways that our feelings about the future influence our present behaviour. Future expected prices and incomes can affect our present demand for a product, as can the prospect of a shortage. If consumers think that the price of their favourite beverage is likely to increase in the near future, they may well stock up, just in case. The present demand for the product will therefore increase. Conversely, expected future price declines cause people to hold off their current purchases while awaiting the hoped-for lower prices.

An anticipated pay increase may cause some people to spend more now as they adjust to their expected higher standard of living. People who fear a layoff or other cause of a loss of income may cut down spending in advance of the fateful date. Finally, the possibility of future shortages, such as those caused by an impending strike, may cause a frantic rush to the stores by anxious customers trying to stock up in advance.

These four determinants of demand—preferences, income, prices of related products, and future expectations—affect individual demand to varying degrees. If we shift our attention to the market demand, these four factors still apply. In addition, a few other factors need to be mentioned. The *size of the market population* will affect the demand for all products. An increase in the size of the population, for example, leads to an increase in the demand for everything from houses and cars to sports equipment and credit cards. In addition, a *change in the distribution of incomes* leads to an increase in the demand for some products and a decrease in the demand for others. For example, if the percentage of total income earned by those over 65 years of age rises, while the percentage going to those under the age of 24 falls, then we would expect to see an increase in the demand for holiday cruises and a decrease in the demand for entry into popular night clubs.

The same will also be true for the *age composition of the population*. An aging population increases the demand for products that largely appeal to older people (Anne Murray recordings) and decrease the demand for those that appeal only to the young (Justine Bieber recordings).

substitute products: any products for which demand varies directly in relation to a change in the price of a similar product.

complementary products: products that tend to be purchased jointly and for which demand is therefore related.

Statistics Canada reports that annual per capita beer sales fell to 84.7 litres in 2002 from 92 litres a decade earlier. The decline in beer drinking is probably due to an aging population, lifestyle changes, and higher taxes.

Note that one factor is *not* included on this list of determinants of demand, and that is supply. Economists are scrupulous in their attempts to separate the forces of demand and supply. Remember that the demand formulation is a hypothetical construct based on the quantities that consumers are willing and able to purchase at various prices. There is an implied assumption that the consumer will be able to obtain these quantities, otherwise the demand schedule itself would not be relevant. In other words, when specifying demand, we assume that the supply will be available, just as when formulating supply, we make the assumption that there will be sufficient demand.

In summary, the determinants of demand are as follows:

- consumer preferences
- consumer incomes
- prices of related goods
- expectations of future prices, incomes, or availability
- population size, or income and age distribution

✓ SELF-TEST

4. The accompanying table shows the initial weekly demand (D_1) and the new demand (D_2) for packets of pretzels (a bar snack).

To explain the change in demand from D_1 to D_2, what might have happened to the price of a complementary product, such as beer? Alternatively, what might have happened to the price of a substitute product, such as nuts?

Price	Quantity Demanded (D_1)	Quantity Demanded (D_2)
$2.00	10 000	11 000
3.00	9 600	10 600
4.00	9 200	10 200

The Effects of an Increase in Demand

We have just seen that the demand for any product is affected by many different factors. A change in any of these factors will cause a change in demand, which, as we shall see, leads to a change in price and production levels. Let us first consider the effects of an *increase* in the demand for a product. Any one of the following could cause such an increase in the market demand:

- a change in preferences toward the product
- an increase in incomes if the product is a normal product or a decrease in incomes if the product is an inferior product
- an increase in the price of a substitute product
- a decrease in the price of a complementary product
- the expectation that future prices or incomes will be higher or that there will be a future shortage of the product
- an increase in the population or a change in its income or age distribution

Any of these changes could cause people to buy more of a product, regardless of its price. As an example, let us combine supply and demand data in **Table 2.7**.

You can see that at the old demand (Demand 1) and supply, the equilibrium price was $20 and the quantity traded was 14 cases. Assume now that the demand for beer increases (Demand 2). Since consumers do not usually signal their intentions to producers in advance, producers are not aware that the demand has changed until they have evidence. The evidence will probably take

TABLE 2.7	The Effects of an Increase in Demand on the Market		
NUMBER OF CASES PER MONTH			
Price per Case	Quantity Supplied	Quantity Demanded 1	Quantity Demanded 2
$18	10	16	22
19	12	15	21
20	14	14	20
21	16	13	19
22	18	12	18

the form of unsatisfied customers. At a price of $20 a case, the producers in total have produced 14 cases. At this price, the new quantity demanded is 20 cases. There is a **shortage** of 6 cases, and some customers will go home disappointed because there is not sufficient beer, at a price of $20, to satisfy all customers. Will these brewers now increase production to satisfy the higher demand? The surprising answer is no—at least not at the present price. Brewers are not in the business of satisfying customers, they are in the business of making profits. As Adam Smith wrote over 200 years ago:

shortage: at the prevailing price, the quantity supplied is smaller than the quantity demanded.

It is not from the benevolence of the butcher, the brewer, or the baker that we expect our dinner but from regard to their own self-interest.[1]

You may say that unless firms are responsive to the demands of customers, they will soon go out of business. And you are right. But a firm that is *solely* responsive to its customers will go out of business even faster. Look again at the supply schedule in **Table 2.7**. At a price of $20, the brewers are prepared to produce 14 cases. They are not prepared to produce 20 cases, the amount that consumers now want. Why is that? It may be because they can make more profits from producing 14 cases than from producing 20 cases; otherwise, they would have produced 20 in the first place. In fact, it may well be that if they produced 20 cases at the current price of $20, they would end up incurring a loss. Does this mean that the shortage of beer will persist? No. As we saw earlier, *shortages drive prices up* until the shortage disappears and the new quantity demanded is equal to the quantity supplied. This will occur at a price of $22, where the quantity demanded and the quantity supplied are equal at the equilibrium quantity of 18. This adjustment process can be seen in **Figure 2.10**.

You can see in the graph that at the old price of $20, the new quantity demanded exceeds the quantity supplied. This shortage causes the price to rise. As it does so, the quantity of beer that producers make also rises; that is, there will be an increase *in the quantity supplied*. Producers will produce more, not because there is a shortage but because the shortage causes a rise in price. Note also that the increase in price causes some customers to reduce their purchases of beer; that is, there is a decrease *in the quantity demanded*. The price of beer will continue to increase as long as there is a shortage and will stop as soon as the shortage disappears. This occurs when the price has increased to $22. At the new equilibrium price, the quantity demanded will again equal the quantity supplied but at a higher quantity traded of 18 cases.

An increase in demand causes an increase in both price and the quantity traded.

[1] Adam Smith, *Wealth of Nations* (Edwin Cannan edition, 1877), pp. 26–27.

FIGURE 2.10	Adjustment to an Increase in Demand

The increase in demand from D_1 to D_2 creates an immediate shortage of 6. This will cause an increase in the price of beer. The increase affects both producers, who will now increase the quantity supplied, and consumers, who will reduce the quantity demanded. Eventually, the price will reach a new equilibrium at $22, where the equilibrium quantity is 18, and there is no longer a shortage.

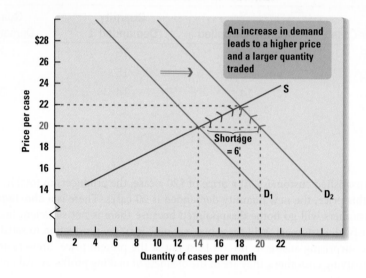

The Effects of a Decrease in Demand

Now, let us see what happens when there is a decrease in demand. Remember that a decrease in demand cannot be caused by an increase in price but is caused by a change in any of the nonprice determinants, including:

- a decrease in preferences for the product
- a decrease in incomes if the product is a normal product, or an increase in incomes if the product is an inferior product
- a decrease in the price of a substitute product
- an increase in the price of a complementary product
- the expectation that future prices or incomes will be lower
- a decrease in the population or a change in its income or age distribution

A decrease in demand is shown in **Table 2.8** and illustrated in **Figure 2.11**.

The initial equilibrium price is $14, and the quantity traded is 14. Assume that the demand now decreases to Demand 3 in the table and D3 in **Figure 2.11**. At a price of $14, producers will continue to produce 14 cases, yet consumers now wish to purchase only 8 cases. A **surplus** is immediately created in the market. Mounting unsold inventories and more intensive competition between suppliers will eventually push down the price. Note in **Figure 2.11** that as the price

surplus: at the prevailing price, the quantity demanded is smaller than the quantity supplied.

TABLE 2.8	The Effects of a Decrease in Demand on the Market

NUMBER OF CASES PER MONTH			
Price per Case	Quantity Supplied	Quantity Demanded 1	Quantity Demanded 3
$18	10	16	10
19	12	15	9
20	14	14	8
21	16	13	7
22	18	12	6

FIGURE 2.11   Adjustment to a Decrease in Demand

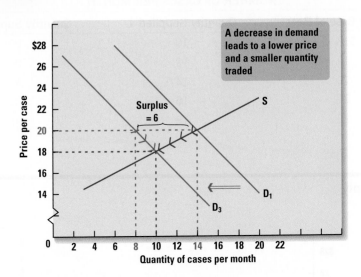

The drop in demand from D_1 to D_3 will cause an immediate surplus of 6, since the quantity supplied remains at 14, but the quantity demanded drops to 8. This surplus will cause the price to fall, and as it does, the quantity demanded will increase, while the quantity supplied will fall. This process will continue until the surplus is eliminated. This occurs at a new equilibrium price of $18 and an equilibrium quantity of 10.

decreases, the quantity supplied also starts to decrease, and the quantity demanded begins to increase. Both these factors will cause the surplus to disappear. The price will eventually drop to a new equilibrium of $18, where the quantity demanded and the quantity supplied are equal at 10 cases. In short:

A decrease in demand will cause both the price and the quantity traded to fall.

✓ SELF-TEST

5. What effect will the following changes have upon (i) the demand for, (ii) the price of, and (iii) the quantity traded of commercially brewed beer?

a) A new medical report affirming the beneficial health effects of drinking beer (in moderation, of course)

b) A big decrease in the price of home-brewing kits

c) A rapid increase in population

d) Talk of a strike by brewery workers

e) A possible future recession

2.6   CHANGE IN SUPPLY

Let us reiterate what we mean by supply: it is the relationship between the price of the product and the quantities producers are willing and able to supply. Price is *part* of what economists call supply. In other words, supply does not mean a single quantity. We now need to address what could cause a **change in supply**. What factors will cause producers to offer a different quantity on the market, even though the price has not changed—what will cause a change in supply? We begin with **Table 2.9**, where an increase in supply is illustrated. For reasons we will soon investigate, suppliers are now willing to supply an extra 6 cases of beer at every possible price. This is illustrated in **Figure 2.12**.

L06 Understand the causes and effects of a change in supply.

change in supply: a change in the quantities supplied at every price, caused by a change in the determinants of supply.

TABLE 2.9	An Increase in Supply	
NUMBER OF CASES PER MONTH		
Price per Case of Beer	Quantity Supplied 1	Quantity Supplied 2
$18	10	16
19	12	18
20	14	20
21	16	22
22	18	24

FIGURE 2.12   An Increase in Supply

At each price, the quantities supplied have now increased, that is, the supply curve has shifted right, from S₁ to S₂. For example, at a price of $20, the original quantity was 14 and has now increased to 20. Similarly, at a price of $16, the quantity supplied has increased from 6 to 12. In this example, the quantities supplied have increased by 6 units at every price level, thus causing a parallel shift in the supply curve.

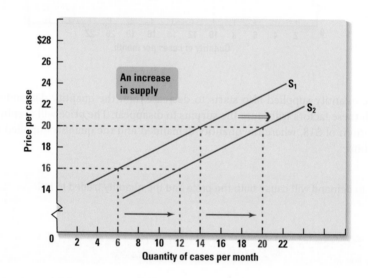

An increase in supply causes the whole supply curve to shift right. (Do not be tempted to describe it as a downward shift because then you would be saying that as the supply goes up, the supply curve goes down, which could make things very confusing! It would be better to talk about a rightward shift.) This means that at each and every price, producers are now willing to produce more.

Determinants of a Change in Supply

What could have happened in the brewers' world to make them wish to produce more, even though the price is unchanged? Since we are assuming that the prime motivation for the supplier is profit, then something must have happened to make brewing more profitable, which is inducing a higher supply. Profit is the difference between revenue and cost, and since the price (and therefore revenue) is unchanged, then something must have affected the cost of producing beer.

First, we will look at the *price of resources*. For brewers, this includes the price of yeast, hops, malt, and other ingredients, as well as the cost of brewing vats, bottles, and so on. If any of these should drop in price, then the cost for the brewers will fall, and profits will rise. Under these circumstances, since they are now making a bigger profit on each case of beer, they will be very willing to produce more. A fall in the price of resources will lead to an increase in supply. Conversely, an increase in the price of resources will cause a decrease in supply.

Another way of looking at the increase in supply, as shown in **Figure 2.12**, is to say that rather than firms being willing to produce more at a given price, they are willing to accept lower prices to produce any given quantity. For instance, previously, in order to induce the brewers to supply a total of 20 cases per week, the price needed to be $17. Now that the costs of production have dropped, these same brewers are able to make the same profits by producing the 20 cases at a lower price of $14: the brewers are now willing to produce the same quantities as before at lower prices. Again, this would produce a rightward shift in the supply curve.

It is often suggested that the availability of resources is a major determinant of the supply of a product. A poor grape harvest—grapes being the key input in the making of wine—will obviously have an impact on the supply of wine. However, it is not really the difficulty in obtaining grapes that causes a decrease in the wine supply, since most things can be obtained *at a price*. But there's the rub. A poor grape harvest will cause the price of grapes to increase, and this increase will reduce the profitability and production of wine producers.

A poor grape harvest is likely to cause the price of grapes to rise.

A second major determinant of supply is the *business taxes* levied by the various levels of government. They are similar to the other costs of doing business, and a decrease in them (or an increase in a subsidy) will lead firms to make higher profits and encourage them to increase the supply. An increase in business taxes, conversely, will cause a decrease in supply.

A third determinant of supply is the *technology* used in production. An improvement in technology means nothing more than an improvement in the method of production. This will enable a firm to produce more with the same quantity of resources (or to produce the same output with fewer resources). An improvement in technology will not affect the actual price of the resources, but because more can now be done with less, it will lead to a fall in the per-unit cost of production. This means that an improvement in technology will lead to an increase in supply.

The price of related products also affects supply, just as it affected demand. But we must be careful, since we are looking at things from a producer's point of view and not a consumer's. What a producer regards as related will usually differ from what a consumer regards as related. A fourth determinant of supply, then, is the *price of substitutes in production*. To a wheat farmer, the price of other grains, such as rye and barley, will be of great interest because the production of all grain crops are related in terms of production methods and equipment. A significant increase in the price of rye may well tempt the wheat farmer to grow rye in the future instead of wheat. In other words, an increase in the price of one product will cause a drop in the supply of products that are substitutes in production. A decrease will have the opposite effect.

A fifth determinant of supply is the *future expectations of producers*. This is also analogous to the demand side of the market, but with a difference. While consumers eagerly look forward to a drop in the price of products, producers view the same prospect with great anxiety. Producers who feel that the market is going to be depressed in the future, and that prices are likely to be lower, may be inclined to change production now, before the anticipated collapse. Lower expected future prices therefore tend to increase the present supply of a product. Anticipating higher prices has the opposite effect; producers hold off selling all of their present production hoping to make greater profits from the future higher prices, assuming the product is something like oil, which is not perishable.

Finally, market supply will also be affected by the *number of suppliers*. An increase in the number of suppliers will cause an increase in market supply, whereas a decrease in the number of suppliers will reduce overall market supply.

Again, note that one thing omitted from this list of supply determinants is any mention of demand. At the risk of repetition, firms are not in business to satisfy demand but to make profits. Increased demand for a product does not mean that producers will immediately increase production to satisfy the higher demand. However, the higher demand will cause the price to increase, and this increase induces firms to supply more. But this is an increase in the quantity supplied and *does not* imply an increase in supply—the supply curve remains unchanged.

In summary, the determinants of market supply are as follows:

- prices of resources
- business taxes
- technology
- prices of substitutes in production
- future expectations of suppliers
- number of suppliers

The Effects of an Increase in Supply

We have just discussed six different factors that could affect the supply of a product. Let us be more specific and look at what can cause an *increase* in supply:

- a decrease in the price of resources
- a decrease in business taxes (or increase in subsidies)
- an improvement in technology
- a decrease in the price of a productively related product
- the expectation of a decline in the future price of the product
- an increase in the number of suppliers

Let us see the effects of an increase in supply using the original demand for beer and the increase in supply in **Table 2.10**.

TABLE 2.10	The Effect of an Increase in Supply on the Market		
NUMBER OF CASES PER MONTH			
Price per Case of Beer	Quantity Demanded 1	Quantity Supplied 1	Quantity Supplied 2
$18	16	10	16
19	15	12	18
20	14	14	20
21	13	16	22
22	12	18	24

At the original demand (Quantity Demanded 1) and supply (Quantity Supplied 1), the equilibrium price was $20 per case, and the quantity traded was 14 cases. Assume that the supply now increases to Quantity Supplied 2. At the present price of $20, there will be an immediate surplus of 6 cases.

Before we look at the implications of this surplus, we ought to address a couple of possible qualms that some students might have. The first is this: won't customers take up this excess of beer? It is easy to see that at this price, consumers have already given their response. They want to buy 14 cases, not 20 cases, or any other number. In other words, consumers are buying beer to satisfy their own tastes, not to satisfy the brewers. A second question is this: why would producers produce 20 cases, knowing that the demand at this price is only 14 cases? The answer is that they do not know. Producers knows the circumstances in their own breweries and knows that until now, they have been able to sell everything they have produced. With the prospect of higher profits coming from, say, a decrease in costs, a brewer wants to produce more. If all producers do the same, there will be a surplus of beer. **Figure 2.13** shows what happens as a result of this surplus.

Faced with a surplus of beer, market price will be forced down. As price falls, the quantity demanded increases, and the quantity supplied falls. Production increased initially, but is now dropping slightly because of the resulting drop in price. The price will continue to drop until it reaches $18. **Table 2.10** shows that at this price, the quantity demanded and the quantity supplied are now equal at 16 cases. The effect of the increase in supply, then, is a lower price and a higher quantity traded.

We leave it to you to confirm that a decrease in supply will cause a shortage that will eventually raise the price of the product. (The factors that cause such a decrease in supply are exactly the same as those mentioned above that cause an increase—except they move in the opposite direction.) The net result will be a higher price but a lower quantity traded.

FIGURE 2.13   Adjustment to an Increase in Supply

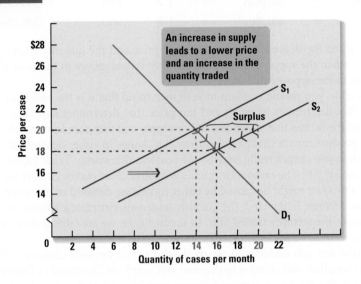

The increase in the supply has the immediate effect of causing a surplus because the demand has remained unchanged. In this figure, at a price of $20, the quantity supplied has increased from 14 to 20, causing a surplus of 6. This will cause the price to drop, and as it does, the quantity demanded increases, and the quantity supplied decreases, until a new equilibrium is reached at a new equilibrium price of $18 and quantity of 16.

 SELF-TEST

6. Suppose that the demand and supply for strawberries in Corona are as follows (the quantities are in thousands of kilos per week):

| | QUANTITY | | |
Price	Demanded	Supplied 1	Supplied 2
$4.00	140	60	_____
4.50	120	80	_____
5.00	100	100	_____
5.50	80	120	_____

a) What are the present equilibrium price and equilibrium quantity? Graph the demand and supply curves, labelling them D_1 and S_1, and indicate equilibrium.

b) Suppose that the supply of strawberries were to increase by 50 percent. Show the new quantities in the Supply 2 column. What will be the new equilibrium price and quantity? Draw in S_2 on your graph, and indicate the new equilibrium.

7. What effect will the following changes have on the supply, price, and quantity traded of wine?

a) A poor harvest in the grape industry results in a big decrease in the supply of grapes.

b) The number of wineries increases.

c) The sales tax on wine increases.

d) The introduction of a new fermentation method reduces the time needed for the wine to ferment.

e) Government introduces a subsidy for each bottle of wine produced domestically.

f) Government introduces a quota limiting the amount of foreign-made wine entering Canada.

g) There is a big increase in wages for the workers in the wine industry.

h) A big increase occurs in the prices of wine coolers (an industry that is similar in technology to the wine industry).

2.7   FINAL WORDS

To complete this introduction to demand and supply, let us use the following chart as a summary:

↑ Demand	→	shortage	→	↑ P	and	↑ Q traded
↓ Supply	→	shortage	→	↑ P	and	↓ Q traded
↓ Demand	→	surplus	→	↓ P	and	↓ Q traded
↑ Supply	→	surplus	→	↓ P	and	↑ Q traded

Note that when the demand changes, both the price and the quantity traded move in the same direction; when the supply changes, the quantity traded moves in the same direction, but the price moves in the opposite direction.

From this table, you should confirm in your own mind that it is the supply of and demand for a product that determines its price, and not price that determines supply and demand. A change in any of the factors that affect demand or supply will therefore lead to a change in price. The price of a product *cannot* change *unless* there is a change in either demand or supply. It follows therefore that you cannot really analyze any problem that starts: "What happens if the price increases (decreases)…?" The reason for this, as the above chart makes clear, is that an increase in the price of a product might be caused by either increasing demand or decreasing supply. But in the case of an increase in demand, the quantity traded also increases, whereas in the case of a decrease in supply, the quantity traded falls. In the first case, we are talking about an expanding industry; in the second, we are looking at a contracting industry.

Finally, make sure you understand clearly the distinction between changes in the quantities demanded and supplied, and changes in demand and supply as illustrated in **Figure 2.14**.

To close this chapter, let us ponder a simple example and make some final observations. Looking back over the past decade or so, what has happened to the prices of laptops? Generally speaking, even allowing for inflation, prices have decreased. And what about the quantity of laptops that are bought and sold now, compared with the situation a decade ago? Definitely, the quantity has increased. So, according to our chart above, what could have produced this result in the marketplace? Well, there is only one thing that could lead to a decrease in price and an increase in the quantity traded, and that is an increase in supply. And what in the computer world over the past years could have caused an increase in supply? At first glance, we might credit an improvement in technology that has significantly reduced the costs of producing computers as well as the continuously falling price of silicon chips used in computer hard drives. However, we should mention a number of themes that we will take up in Chapter 8. In the modern world, competitive markets are few and far between, since many markets are dominated by big corporations, big trade unions, and consumer associations, and are affected by government intervention. In addition, even when they are competitive, markets do not provide any guarantee that there will not be future periods of recession or inflation. Further, competitive markets cannot ensure that the type of products produced meet external standards, such as being environmentally sound or healthy, or that the distribution of incomes and wealth in a country is fair.

Finally, let us look back at the discussion that started this chapter and see if we can make sense of it. Justine made an observation about the price of big-screen TVs falling, and Eric responded rather flippantly, "But that is just supply and demand." We now know that price can fall because either supply increased or demand decreased. Justine asked if Eric thinks that the price fall was due to increase in supply and Eric said, "Sure." Then came the really hard question: why would supply go up if price was falling? Eric once again responded that this was just supply and demand. Of course, we now know that Eric should have said that the supply had gone up—perhaps because of increased technology—and that increased supply caused the price to fall. That is, changes in supply cause changes in price, not the other way around.

All of this is summarized in **Figure 2.14**. In graph A, we see a movement from point *a* to *b*, which is an increase in the quantity demanded resulting from the fall in price caused by an increase in supply (S_1 to S_2). Graph B shows an increase in demand, which causes an increase in

ADDED DIMENSION   The Famous Scissors Analogy

Since the time of Adam Smith, economists have emphasized the importance of understanding the role of price determination. Toward the end of the nineteenth century, there were two schools of thought about what determined price. The first was made up of those who believed that the cost of production was the main determinant—the supply-side view. The second was made up of those, including the famous economist Alfred Marshall, who believed that consumer demand was the main determinant—the demand-side view.

Marshall, writing at the end of that century, was the first to present a lucid synthesis of the two views and suggest that

neither demand nor supply alone can provide the answer to the determination of price. His famous analogy of the scissors says, "We might as reasonably dispute whether it is the upper or the under blade of scissors that cuts a piece of paper as whether value [price] is governed by utility or cost of production. It is true that when one blade is held still, and the cutting is effected by moving the other, we may say with careless brevity that the cutting is done by the second; but the statement is not strictly accurate and is to be excused only so long as it claims to be merely a popular and not a strictly scientific account of what happens."[2]

FIGURE 2.14 **Changes in the Quantity Demanded and Demand**

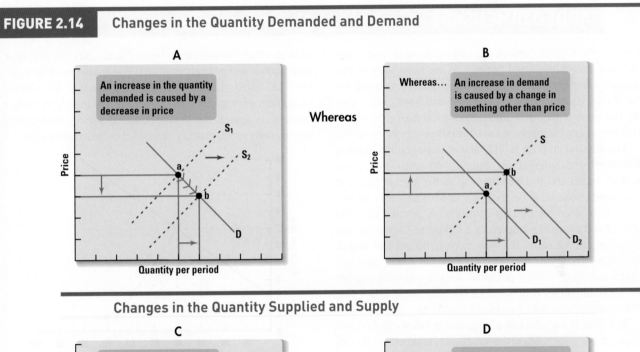

Changes in the Quantity Supplied and Supply

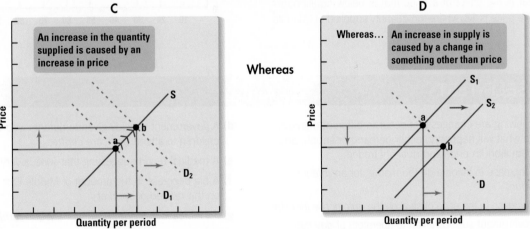

[2] Alfred Marshall, *Principles of Economics*, 8th edition, Macmillan (1920). Reproduced with permission of Palgrave Macmillan.

price and in the quantity supplied (*a* to *b*). Graph C shows an increase in the quantity supplied (*a* to *b*), which follows an increase in price caused by an increase in demand (D_1 to D_2). Finally, in graph D, we see an increase in supply (S_1 to S_2) resulting in a fall in price and an increase in the quantity demanded (*a* to *b*). This allows us to conclude that:

> An increase in the quantity demanded results when an increase in supply pushes price down (A). An increase in demand increases price, and thus the quantity supplied increases (B).

> An increase in the quantity supplied results when an increase in demand pushes price up (C). An increase in supply decreases the price and thus the quantity demanded increases (D).

You now know what an important and versatile tool supply-and-demand analysis can be— but, like all tools, you must use it properly, and clean it after every use!

▶ ADDED DIMENSION   Sales Always Equal Purchases

It is important not to confuse the terms "demand" and "supply" with "purchases" and "sales." As we have seen in this chapter, the quantity demanded and the quantity supplied are not always equal. However, purchases and sales, since they are two sides of the same transaction, must always be equal. The accompanying graph explains the differences in the terms.

The equilibrium price is $12, and at this price the quantity demanded and supplied are equal at 40 units—this is the amount traded and is the same thing as the amount sold and purchased. However, if the price happened to be above equilibrium—$16—then the quantity demanded is denoted by *a* (30 units) and the quantity supplied by *b* (60 units). Clearly, the two quantities are not equal. But how much is bought and sold at this price? The answer is quantity *a* (30 units). It really does not matter how much is being produced, since at this price quantity *a* is the maximum amount that consumers are willing to buy. The difference *ab* represents the amount unsold, or a surplus of 30.

But what is the effect of a price that is below equilibrium? Suppose the price is $8, where the quantity supplied of 20 units

(*c*) is less than the quantity demanded of 50 units (*d*)? This time, how much is being bought and sold? The answer must be quantity *c* (20 units). It does not matter how much of this product consumers want to buy if producers are only making quantity *c* available. In general, the amount bought and sold is always equal to the smaller of the quantity demanded or the quantity supplied.

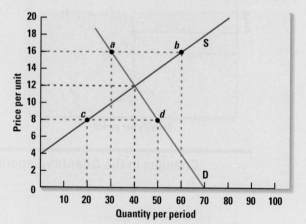

✓ SELF-TEST

8. The following are changes that occur in different markets. Explain what will happen to either demand or supply, and to the equilibrium price and quantity traded.

   a) An increase in income on the market for an *inferior product*

   b) A decrease in the price of steel on the *automobile industry*

   c) A government subsidy given to operators of *day-care centres*

   d) A government subsidy given to parents who want their children to attend *day-care centres*

   e) A medical report suggesting that *wine* is very fattening

   f) A big decrease in the amount of Middle East oil exports on the *refined-oil market*

   g) An increase in the popularity of *antique furniture*

   h) An increase in the price of coffee on the *tea market*

Review

CHAPTER SUMMARY

In this chapter, you learned that in competitive markets, the price and quantity traded of any product depend on both the demand for and the supply of that product. Once equilibrium is achieved, price and quantity will not change unless either supply or demand changes. In order to fully understand this, you must also understand the following:

2.1a *Demand* is the price–quantity relationship of a product that consumers are willing and able to buy per period of time.

2.1b The demand curve is *downward sloping* because of the:
- substitution effect
- income effect

2.1c Products can be *related* in two ways:
- complements
- substitutes

2.1d *Market demand* is the conceptual summation of each individual's demand within a given market.

2.2a *Supply* is the price–quantity relationship of a product that producers are willing and able to sell per period of time.

2.2b *Market supply* is the conceptual summation of each firm's supply within a given market.

2.3 A market is a mechanism that brings buyers and sellers together.

2.4 Market equilibrium occurs when the quantity demanded and the quantity supplied are equal at a particular price.

2.5a All products are *either*:
- normal products, or
- inferior products

2.5b Market demand *changes* if there is a change in:
- consumers' preferences
- consumers' incomes
- the price of related products
- expectations of future prices, incomes, or availability
- the size of the market, or income and age distribution

2.5c An *increase in demand* will cause a shortage and result in both price and the quantity traded rising.

2.5d A *decrease in demand* will cause a surplus and result in both price and the quantity traded falling.

2.6a Market supply *changes* if there is a change in:
- the price of resources
- business taxes
- technology
- prices of substitutes in production
- future expectations of suppliers
- the number of suppliers

2.6b An i*ncrease in supply* causes a surplus and results in the price falling and the quantity traded rising.

2.6c A *decrease in supply* causes a shortage and results in the price rising and the quantity traded falling.

2.7 It is the demand for, and the supply of, a product that determines price and not price that determines demand and supply.

Practise and learn online with Connect, where you can find the Answered Questions and the Unanswered Problems for all chapters of this textbook's Study Guide section.

NEW GLOSSARY TERMS

ceteris paribus   33
change in demand   45
change in supply   51
change in the quantity demanded   34
change in the quantity supplied   39
complementary products   47
demand   33
demand schedule   34

equilibrium price   43
equilibrium quantity   45
income effect   36
inferior products   46
market   42
market demand   36
market supply   40
normal products   46

real income   36
shortage   49
substitute products   47
substitution effect   36
supply   38
supply schedule   38
surplus   50

STUDY TIPS

1. It is with this chapter that you will learn to appreciate the need for precision in the use of economic terms. For instance, the terms *demand* and *supply* have very clear definitions. "Demand" does *not* mean the amount a person wishes to buy or the amount bought. Demand is not a single quantity but a combination of different prices and quantities. Similarly, you cannot use the term "supply" synonymously with output, production, or quantity supplied. It is *not* a single quantity but a range of different quantities and prices.

2. If you have understood the first point, then this next one should make sense. A change in price cannot affect the demand, since price is part of what we mean by demand. That does not mean that a change in price does not affect consumers; generally, people change the amounts they purchase as a result of a price change. But this is a change in the quantity demanded, *not* a change in demand. Similarly, a change in price leaves the supply unaffected. But it definitely affects the *quantity supplied*. These points are illustrated in the way that the demand and supply curves are affected. A change in price causes no change in the demand and supply curves but results in a movement *along* the curves. Only changes in other determinants, besides price, will cause a shift in the curves.

3. It is important for you to keep the concepts of demand and supply separate in your mind. A change in demand does *not* have any effect on supply. This means that the supply curve will not shift when the demand curve changes. Similarly, you must disconnect demand from supply. A change in supply has no impact on demand.

4. There is no alternative to learning the factors that do affect demand and supply. Memorize the five determinants of market demand and the six determinants of market supply. Note that, with the exception of expectations of future price changes, the factors that affect demand have no impact on supply, and vice versa. Try not to be too "cute" when trying to figure out the way in which various changes in determinants affect markets. It is possible to give a convoluted explanation of why, for example, a change in the number of suppliers can affect preferences and therefore the demand of customers of that product. While remotely possible, the effect would be of minor significance. Instead, use common sense and focus on the main effects. Remember that a change in one determinant will usually affect only demand or only supply but seldom both.

5. Do not skip the basics in this chapter, even if at times they seem a little obvious. For example, you need to know that if the price of good A increases, then the demand for the complement good B decreases. Similarly, if income increases, the demand for a normal good increases and the demand for an inferior good decreases.

6. Finally, the most important lesson to learn from this chapter is that the price of a product is determined by both demand and supply. Price is the effect and not the cause. This means that equilibrium price cannot change in a free market unless there has been a change in either demand or supply.

Answered Questions

These questions can also be found online on Connect.

Indicate whether the following statements are true or false:

1. **(LO 1) T or F**   The term "demand" means the quantities that people would like to purchase at various prices.

2. **(LO 4) T or F**   A change in the price of a product has no effect on the demand for the same product.

3. **(LO 1) T or F**   An increase in the price of a product causes a decrease in the real income of consumers.

4. **(LO 4) T or F**   An increase in the price of a product leads to an increase in the supply.

5. **(LO 4) T or F**   Equilibrium price implies that everyone who would like to purchase a product is able to.

6. **(LO 4) T or F**   Surpluses drive prices up; shortages drive prices down.

7. **(LO 5) T or F**   An increase in incomes will lead to a decrease in the demand for an inferior product.

8. **(LO 7) T or F**   A decrease in the demand for a product will lead to a decrease in both price and the quantity traded.

9. **(LO 6) T or F**   An increase in business taxes causes the supply curve to shift left.

10. **(LO 6) T or F**   A decrease in supply causes price to fall and quantity traded to increase.

Basic (Questions 11–22)

11. **(LO 1)** What does the term "demand" refer to?
    a) The amounts that consumers are either willing or able to purchase at various prices
    b) The amounts that consumers are both willing and able to purchase at various prices
    c) The quantity purchased at the equilibrium price
    d) The price consumers are willing to pay for a certain quantity of a product

12. **(LO 6)** What will a surplus of a product lead to?
    a) A reduction in supply
    b) A reduction in price
    c) An increase in price
    d) An increase in supply

13. **(LO 1)** What is the effect of a decrease in the price of a product?
    a) It will increase consumers' real income while leaving their actual income unchanged.
    b) It will increase consumers' actual income while leaving their real income unchanged.
    c) It will decrease demand.
    d) It will have no effect on income.

14. **(LO 5)** What is the effect of an increase in the price of coffee?
    a) It will lead to an increase in the demand for tea.
    b) It will lead to a decrease in the demand for tea.
    c) It will have no effect on the tea market.
    d) It will decrease the demand for coffee.

15. **(LO 1)** What is the slope of the demand curve?
    a) It is downward sloping because when the price of a product falls, consumers are willing and able to buy more.
    b) It is upward sloping because when the price of a product falls, consumers are willing and able to buy more.
    c) It is upward sloping because when the price of a product increases, consumers are willing and able to buy more.
    d) It is downward sloping because higher prices are associated with larger quantities.

16. **(LO 6)** What is the effect of an increase in the price of a productive resource?
    a) It will cause a decrease in the supply of the product.
    b) It will cause an increase in the supply of the product.
    c) It will cause a decrease in the demand for the product.
    d) It will cause an increase in the demand for the product.

17. **(LO 5)** In what way are Pepsi-Cola and Coca-Cola related?
    a) They are substitute products.
    b) They are complementary products.
    c) They are inferior products.
    d) They are unrelated products.

18. **(LO 6)** Which of the following could cause an increase in the supply of wheat?
    a) A decrease in the price of oats
    b) An imposition of a sales tax on wheat
    c) An increase in the price of fertilizer
    d) A decrease in the price of wheat

19. **(LO 5)** All of the following, *except one*, would cause an increase in the demand for a normal product. Which is the exception?
    a) An increase in consumers' incomes
    b) An increase in the price of a substitute product
    c) An increase in the size of the market
    d) Consumer expectations of a lower future price for the product

20. **(LO 5)** Which of the following pairs of goods are complementary?
    a) Coffee and tea
    b) Skis and ski boots
    c) Bread and crackers
    d) Popcorn and pretzels

21. **(LO 6)** All of the following, *except one*, would cause a decrease in the supply of product A. Which is the exception?
    a) An increase in the price of resources used to make product A
    b) An increase in business taxes
    c) An improvement in technology
    d) The expectation by suppliers that future prices of product A will be higher

22. **(LO 5)** Which of the following best describes a normal product?
    a) A product that people both need and like
    b) A product whose demand increases if incomes increases
    c) A product whose demand increases if incomes decreases
    d) A staple product that everyone needs

Intermediate (Questions 23–32)

23. **(LO 5)** How will a change in income affect the demand for an inferior product?
    a) The demand will increase if the incomes of consumers increases.
    b) The demand will increase if the incomes of consumers decreases.
    c) The demand for an inferior product is not affected by consumer incomes.
    d) The demand will remain the same, but the quantity demanded will increase if incomes decrease.

24. **(LO 5)** Which of the following factors will shift the demand curve left?
    a) An increase in the price of a substitute product
    b) A decrease in the price of a complementary product
    c) An increase in incomes if the product is an inferior product
    d) The expectation that future prices of the product will be higher

25. **(LO 6)** A rightward shift in the supply curve for a product could be caused by all of the following *except one*. Which is the exception?
    a) The expectation by suppliers that the future price of the product will be higher

b) A decrease in the price of a productive resource used in its manufacture
    c) A decrease in the price of a product that is a substitute in production
    d) A technological improvement in manufacturing methods

26. **(LO 6)** What is the effect of a decrease in the supply of a product?
    a) It will cause an increase in both the price and the quantity traded.
    b) It will cause an increase in the price but a decrease in the quantity traded.
    c) It will cause a decrease in both the price and in the quantity traded.
    d) It will cause a decrease in the price but an increase in the quantity traded.

Table 2.11 depicts the market for mushrooms (in thousands of kilograms per month). Use this table to answer questions 27 and 28.

TABLE 2.11

Price ($)	2.50	3.00	3.50	4.00	4.50	5.00	5.50	6.00
Quantity Demanded	64	62	60	58	56	54	52	50
Quantity Supplied	40	44	48	52	56	60	64	68

27. **(LO 4)** Refer to **Table 2.11** to answer this question. What are the values of equilibrium price and quantity traded?
    a) $3 and 52
    b) $3 and 62
    c) $4 and 58
    d) $4.50 and 56
    e) They cannot be determined from the data.

28. **(LO 4)** Refer to **Table 2.11** to answer this question. What will happen if the price of the product is $3?
    a) There would be a surplus of 18, which would lead to a decrease in price.
    b) There would be a shortage of 18, which would lead to an increase in price.
    c) There would be a shortage of 18, which would lead to a decrease in price.
    d) There would be a surplus of 18, which would lead to an increase in price.
    e) There would be neither a surplus nor a shortage.

29. **(LO 5)** In what way are products A and B related if an increase in the price of product A leads to a decrease in the demand for product B?
    a) Product A must be a resource used in the manufacture of product B.
    b) Product B must be a resource used in the manufacture of product A.
    c) The two products must be complements.
    d) The two products must be substitutes.
    e) The two products must be inferior products.

30. **(LO 3)** What is the effect of a shortage?
    a) It will cause a decrease in price, leading to an increase in the quantity supplied and a decrease in the quantity demanded.
    b) It will cause a decrease in price, leading to a decrease in the quantity supplied and an increase in the quantity demanded.
    c) It will cause an increase in price, leading to an increase in the quantity supplied and a decrease in the quantity demanded.
    d) It will cause an increase in price, leading to a decrease in the quantity supplied and an increase in the quantity demanded.

31. **(LO 7)** What is the effect of an increase in demand for a product?
    a) Its price will rise, and quantity traded will decrease.
    b) Its price will rise, and quantity traded will increase.
    c) Its price will fall, and quantity traded will decrease.
    d) Its price will fall, and quantity traded will increase.

32. **(LO 7)** Refer to **Figure 2.15** to answer this question. What will be the effect if the price is now $1200?
    a) There would be a surplus of 30.
    b) There would be a shortage of 30.
    c) 160 would be purchased.
    d) There would be a surplus of 60.
    e) The price will increase.

Advanced (Questions 33–35)

33. **(LO 7)** Refer to **Figure 2.15** to answer this question. Assume that there is a shortage of 60 units. What does this mean?
    a) Purchasers would be willing to pay an additional $600 for the quantity they are now purchasing.
    b) The price must be above equilibrium.

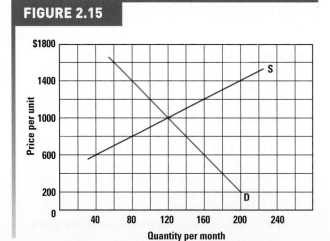

FIGURE 2.15

c) The price must be $1200.
d) The price must be $600.
e) None of the above is correct.

34. **(LO 7)** Refer to **Figure 2.15** to answer this question. Suppose that initially the market was in equilibrium and that demand increased by 60. What will be the new equilibrium as a result?
    a) A price of $1000 and quantity traded of 120
    b) A price of $1000 and quantity traded of 160
    c) A price of $1200 and quantity traded of 160
    d) A price of $1400 and quantity traded of 160
    e) A price of $1400 and quantity traded of 240

35. **(LO 7)** How will the demand and supply of a product be affected if both producers and consumers expect the price of a product to increase?
    a) It will cause an increase in demand but a decrease in supply.
    b) It will cause an increase in both the demand and supply.
    c) It will cause a decrease in both the demand and supply.
    d) It will cause an increase in supply but will have no effect on demand.
    e) It will cause an increase in supply but a decrease in demand.

Parallel Problems

ANSWERED PROBLEMS

36A. (LO 1, 2, 4, 5, 6) Key Problem Table 2.12 shows the market for wool in the economy of Odessa (the quantities are in tonnes per year).

a) Plot the demand and supply curves on **Figure 2.16**, and label them D_1 and S_1. Mark the equilibrium as e_1 on the graph.

b) What are the values of equilibrium price and quantity?
equilibrium price: _____
equilibrium quantity: _____

c) If the price of wool were $600, would there be a surplus or shortage?
Surplus/shortage _____ of _____.
Indicate the amount of the surplus or shortage on the graph.

d) Suppose that the demand were to increase by 60. Draw and label the new demand curve as D_2. What are the new values of equilibrium price and quantity?
equilibrium price: _____
equilibrium quantity: _____
Mark the new equilibrium as e_2 on the graph.

e) Following the change in d), suppose that the supply were to increase by 50 percent. Draw and label the new supply curve as S_2. What are the new values of equilibrium price and quantity?
equilibrium price: _____
equilibrium quantity: _____
Mark the new equilibrium as e_3 on the graph.

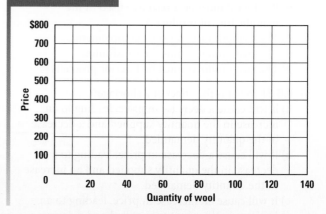

FIGURE 2.16

d) An increase in the price of apple juice

e) An increase in consumers' average income

f) An improvement in the juicing process that lowers the cost of producing cranberry juice

38A. (LO 3, 4, 6) Table 2.13 shows the market demand and supply for Fuji apples in Peterborough.

a) What is the equilibrium price and quantity traded?
price: _____ quantity: _____

b) Suppose that supply increases by 30. What would be the price and quantity traded at the new equilibrium?
price: _____ quantity: _____

c) After the increase in supply, what would be the surplus/shortage at a price of $8?
Surplus/shortage _____ of _____.

Price ($)	100	200	300	400	500	600	700
Quantity demanded	130	110	90	70	50	30	10
Quantity supplied	10	20	30	40	50	60	70

TABLE 2.12

Basic (Problems 37A–44A)

37A. (LO 5) Circle which of the following factors will lead to an increase in the demand for cranberry juice (which is a normal good).

a) A decrease in the price of cranberry juice

b) A decrease in the price of cranberries

c) The expectation by consumers that the price of cranberry juice is likely to increase

TABLE 2.13

Price	Quality Demanded	Quantity Supplied
0	180	90
2	170	110
4	160	130
6	150	150
8	140	170
10	130	190

39A. (LO 1, 2, 5, 6) In each of the two graphs in **Figure 2.17**, explain the change in equilibrium from a to b in terms of

a) an increase or decrease in demand or supply

b) an increase or decrease in the quantity demanded or supplied

FIGURE 2.17

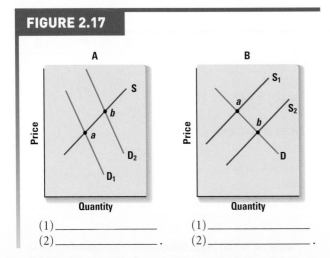

A

B

(1)_____   (1)_____
(2)_____ .   (2)_____ .

40A. (LO 4)
a) Given the data in **Table 2.14**, draw the demand curve on **Figure 2.18**.
b) What is the equilibrium price and quantity?
   price: _____ quantity: _____

TABLE 2.14

Price	Quantity Demanded
1	80
2	70
3	60
4	50
5	40
6	30

FIGURE 2.18

Price (vertical axis: 1-7)

Quantity of copy paper (horizontal axis: 0, 20, 40, 60, 80, 100, 120, 140)

S

41A. (LO 4, 5, 6) Suppose that new medical research strongly indicates that the consumption of coffee can cause cancer of the colon. What effect will this news have on the equilibrium price and quantity traded of the following products?
a) Coffee beans.
   price: _____ quantity traded: _____
b) Tea, a substitute for coffee.
   price: _____ quantity traded: _____
c) Danish pastries, a complement to coffee.
   price: _____ quantity traded: _____
d) Teapots, a complement to tea.
   price: _____ quantity traded: _____

42A. (LO 5, 6) What must have happened to demand or supply to cause the following changes?
a) The price of guitars falls, but the quantity traded increases.
   Demand/supply _____ must have _____.
b) The price and quantity traded of saxophones decrease.
   Demand/supply_____ must have _____.
c) The price of trombones increases, while the quantity traded falls.
   Demand/supply _____ must have _____.
d) The price and quantity traded of clarinets increases.
   Demand/supply _____ must have _____.

43A. (LO 1, 5) What is the distinction between demand and quantity demanded?

44A. (LO 1, 4) Explain the effect of a shortage on prices.

Intermediate (Problems 45A–49A)

45A. (LO 4, 5, 6) Consider the effects of each of the events outlined in **Table 2.15** on the market indicated. Place a (↑), (↓) or (−) under the appropriate heading to indicate whether there will be an increase, decrease, or no change in demand (D), supply (S), equilibrium price (P), and the quantity traded (Q).

46A. (LO 4) Figure 2.19 shows the market for the new Guns and Butter album, "Live at Saskatoon."
a) Suppose that the album producers put it on sale for $8 each. How much will be the surplus or shortage? How many will be sold?
   Surplus/shortage _____ of _____.
   quantity sold: _____
b) What is the maximum price at which the quantity actually sold in a) could have been sold?
   Maximum price: _____
c) If the album producers had actually put the album on the market at the price mentioned in b), what would have been the resulting surplus/shortage?
   Surplus/shortage _____ of _____.

TABLE 2.15

Market	Event	D	S	P	Q
a) DVDs	A technological improvement reduces the cost of producing DVD players.				
b) Butter	New medical evidence suggests that margarine causes migraines.				
c) Newspapers	Because of worldwide shortages, the prices of pulp and paper increase dramatically.				
d) Low-quality toilet paper	Consumer incomes rise significantly.				
e) Movie rentals	Movie theatres halve their admission prices.				
f) Beef	World price of lamb increases.				

FIGURE 2.19

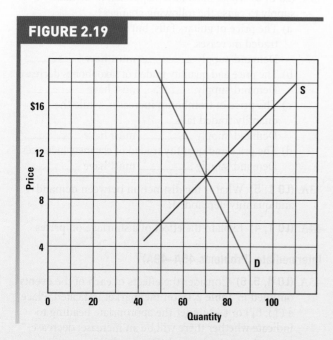

47A. **(LO 1, 5)** "The prices of houses rise when the demand increases. The demand for houses decreases when prices increase." Change one of these statements so that the two are consistent with each other.

48A. **(LO 5)** Briefly explain the five determinants of market demand.

49A. **(LO 4, 5)** Explain, step by step, how an increase in demand eventually affects both price and quantity traded.

Advanced (Problems 50A–52A)

50A. **(LO 1, 4)** In Kirin, at a market price of $1 per kilo, there is a shortage of 60 kilos of avocados. For each 50-cent increase in the price, the quantity demanded drops by 5 kilos, while the quantity supplied increases by 10 kilos.
  a) What will be the equilibrium price? _____.
  b) What will be the surplus/shortage at a price of $4.50? Surplus/shortage _____ of _____ kilos.

51A. **(LO 4, 5, 6)** Identify any two possible causes and five specific effects involved in the movement from point *a* to *b* to *c* in **Figure 2.20**.

FIGURE 2.20

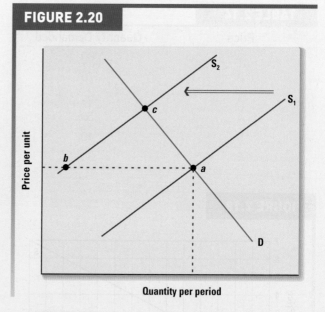

52A. **(LO 6)** Suppose that in response to the high rent and low supply of affordable rental accommodation in the Toronto market, the city constructed 5000 additional rental units and put them on the market at below-equilibrium rents. Draw a supply-and-demand graph showing the effects on the rental market.

THE ALGEBRA OF DEMAND AND SUPPLY

THE ALGEBRA OF THE MARKET

We have described the marketplace in both tables and graphs. This appendix explains how we can also analyze demand and supply algebraically. Suppose that **Figure A1** shows the demand for soy milk in Canada.

FIGURE A1

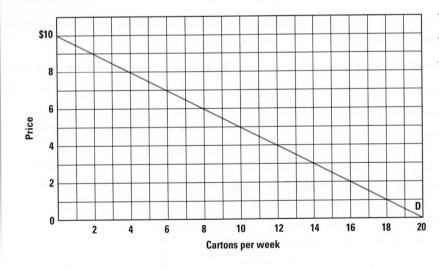

Number of Cartons per Week	
Price ($)	Quantity
0	20
1	18
2	16
3	14
4	12
5	10
6	8
7	6
8	4
9	2
10	0

You will remember from the Toolkit that, in general, the algebraic expression for a straight line is:

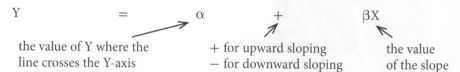

$$Y = \alpha + \beta X$$

the value of Y where the
line crosses the Y-axis

+ for upward sloping
− for downward sloping

the value
of the slope

On our graph, price is shown on the vertical (Y) axis and the quantity demanded on the horizontal (X) axis. Therefore, the general expression for the demand curve is given as:

$$p = \alpha + \beta Q^d$$

Here, the value of α is equal to ($)10. This is where the demand curve crosses the price axis; that is, it is the highest price payable. The value of the slope is the ratio of change or rise over run. In terms of the demand curve, the slope shows by how much the quantity changes as the price changes.

$$\text{the slope} = \frac{\Delta \text{ (change in) } P}{\Delta \text{ (change in) } Q}$$

For our demand curve, that value equals

$$\frac{1}{-2}$$

This means that each time the price changes by $1, quantity changes (in the opposite direction) by 2 units. The equation for this demand curve, then, is:

$$P = 10 + \frac{1}{-2} Q^d \text{ or } P = 10 - \frac{1}{2} Q^d$$

Though this is graphically the correct way to express it, in terms of economic logic, the quantity demanded is dependent on price rather than the other way around, so let us rearrange the terms, as follows:

$$Q^d = 20 - 2P$$

Now, let us look at the supply side of things. The table and graph in **Figure A2** show the supply of soy milk in the market.

FIGURE A2

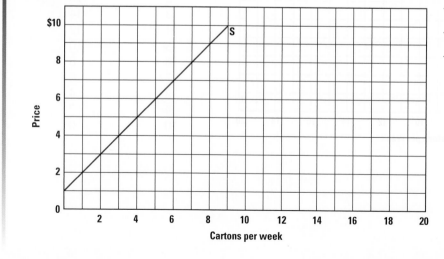

Number of Cartons per Week	
Price ($)	Quantity
0	—
1	0
2	1
3	2
4	3
5	4
6	5
7	6
8	7
9	8
10	9

The general equation for the supply curve is:

$$p = \alpha + \beta Q^s$$

As with the demand curve, α shows the value where the curve crosses the vertical (price) axis. This happens at a price of $1. The value of the slope is, again, the same as for the demand curve.

$$\frac{\Delta \text{ (change in) P}}{\Delta \text{ (change in) Q}}$$

For this supply curve, it equals:

$$\frac{1}{+1}$$

A $1 change in price causes a change of 1 unit in the quantity supplied. The equation for this supply curve, then, is:

$$P = 1 + Q^s$$

As we did with the demand curve, let us rearrange this equation in terms of Qs; thus:

$$Q^s = -1 + P$$

Bringing demand and supply together, in **Figure A3**, allows us to find the equilibrium values. From either the table or the graph, it is easy to see that the equilibrium price is equal to $7. At this price, the quantity demanded and the quantity supplied are both 6 units. Finding equilibrium algebraically is also straightforward. We want to find the price at which the quantity demanded equals the quantity supplied. We know the equations for each, and so we simply set them equal.

$$Q^d = Q^s$$

$$20 - 2P = -1 + P$$

That gives us:

$$3P = 21$$

Therefore,

$$P = 7$$

FIGURE A3

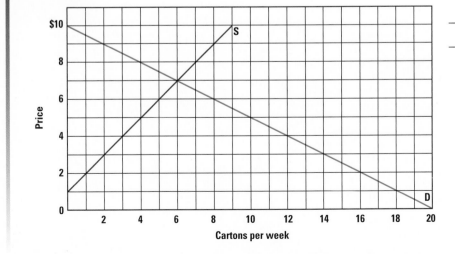

	Number of Cartons per Week		
Price ($)	Q^d	Q^s
0	20	—
1	18	0
2	16	1
3	14	2
4	12	3
5	10	4
6	8	5
7	6	6
8	4	7
9	2	8
10	0	9

Substituting in either equation (and it is best to do both to make sure you are correct) gives us:

$$Q^d = 20 - 2(7) = 6$$
$$Q^s = -1 + (7) = 6$$

Doing things algebraically sometimes makes things easier. For instance, suppose the market demand increased by 3 units; that is, the quantities demanded increased by 3 units at every price. What effect would this have on the equilibrium price and quantity? Algebraically, this is quite straightforward to calculate. The increase in demand means that the value of the (quantity) intercept increases by 3 and gives us a new demand equation:

$$Q^d{}_2 = 23 - 2P$$

The supply has not changed, and so we can calculate the new equilibrium as

$$(Q^d{}_2 = Q^s) : 23 - 2P = -1 + P$$

This gives us:

$$3P = 24$$

Therefore,
$$P = 8$$

The new equilibrium quantity becomes 7. We can obtain this quantity by inserting the price of $8 into both equations, thus:

$$Q^d{}_2 = 23 - 2(8) = 7 \text{ and } Q^s - 1 + (8) = 7$$

Questions for Appendix to Chapter 2

ANSWERED PROBLEMS

1. If $Q^d = 40 - 2P$ and $Q^s = 10 + 3P$, what are the equilibrium values of price and quantity?

2. a) If $Q^d = 100 - 5P$ and $Q^s = 10 + P$, what are the equilibrium values of price and quantity?
   b) If demand increases by 12 and price remains the same as in a), will there be a surplus or a shortage? How much?
   c) If demand increases by 12, what will be the new equilibrium price and quantity?

3. a) If $P = 11 - 0.25Q^d$, what is the algebraic expression for Q^d?
   b) If $P = 16 + 2Q^s$, what is the algebraic expression for Q^s?
   c) What are the equilibrium values of price and quantity?

4. The following table shows the demand and supply of kiwi fruit in Montreal:
   a) What is the algebraic expression for the demand curve?
   b) What is the algebraic expression for the supply curve?
   c) Find algebraically the values of equilibrium price and quantity.

5. Suppose that the demand equation is $Q^d = 230 - 3P$ and the supply equation is $Q^s = -10 + 9P$.
   a) If the price is 15, will there be a surplus or a shortage? How much?
   b) If the price is 22, will there be a surplus or a shortage? How much?

6. Suppose that the demand equation is: $Q^d = 520 - 3P$ and the supply equation is $Q^s = 100 + 4P$.
   a) If the quantity presently supplied is 380, what is the price?
   b) At the price in a), what is the quantity demanded?
   c) At the price in a), is there a surplus or a shortage?

Price per Kilo	Quantity Demanded	Price per Kilo	Quantity Supplied
0	675	0	0
$1	575	$1	50
2	475	2	100
3	375	3	150
4	275	4	200
5	175	5	250

DEMAND AND SUPPLY: AN ELABORATION

LEARNING OBJECTIVES

At the end of this chapter, you should be able to...

LO1 explain the effects of simultaneous changes in supply and demand on equilibrium price and quantity traded.

LO2 explain why markets do not always work well.

LO3 understand why price ceilings cause shortages.

LO4 understand that price floors cause surpluses.

LO5 ask some interesting "what if" questions concerning the shape of demand and supply curves.

WHAT'S AHEAD...

We start this chapter by looking at circumstances that could cause simultaneous changes in demand and supply. We then ask how well markets operate and why governments often intervene. We next look at why governments sometimes introduce various types of price controls, and then we try to identify the costs and benefits of such intervention. Finally, we explore a number of variations of demand and supply, and explain the situations that could cause the demand and supply to deviate from normal.

A Question of Relevance...

You are probably aware that every province in Canada has legislated a minimum wage for hired labour. Do you think that this benefits you as a student looking for work to help pay for your education? Do you think that farmers should be guaranteed minimum prices for the products they sell? Are you living in a province that has rent controls? If so, who do you think benefits from such a policy? These are questions that sometimes generate a lot of debate. Make a mental note of your answers now, and see if they change as a result of studying this chapter.

When we look at the way that markets operate, there is a great danger in believing that the laws of demand and supply are immutable scientific laws that are an integral part of the natural universe. Nothing could be farther from the truth. As Oser and Brue wrote, commenting on the approach of the economist Alfred Marshall:

> Economic laws are social laws—statements of tendencies, more or less certain, more or less definite.[1]

The collective behaviour of consumers and producers in the marketplace is a result of the society in which we live. Each society has its own history, economic structure, and political structure. The tools of demand and supply are versatile and powerful aids for economists, but while they demonstrate general tendencies, they also have certain limitations. For example, in the previous chapter, we suggested that the price of a product is determined by demand and supply. This is only true under certain conditions. In many cases, the price of products we buy is set by the manufacturers and retailers, not by consumers and producers somehow coming together to form an agreement. Similarly, government determines the price of a number of goods and services that it provides, and as we shall see later in this chapter, it also stipulates the minimum and maximum prices of a number of other products provided by the private sector.

Under what circumstances do the forces of demand and supply determine the price of products? Strictly speaking, they do so only in what economists term a "perfectly competitive" market, a market in which there are no big dominant firms and no interference by government. (Chapter 8 will look at this type of market in some detail.) It is important to be aware that competitive markets as described in Chapter 2 only work well if they are truly competitive. The existence of bigness in the marketplace, whether it is in the form of big corporations, big trade unions, or big government, limits the efficient working of the market. In essence, whenever there is a powerful participant or a group of participants buying or selling in the market, the benefits of competition will be seriously reduced.

But does this also mean that if there are big firms operating, they can then ignore the market and charge whatever prices they like? Well, from one point of view, yes they can—but only at their own peril. **Figure 3.1** makes this clear.

ADDED DIMENSION   Alfred Marshall: The Neoclassical Giant

Alfred Marshall (1842–1924) was the son of a tyrannical father who was a cashier at the Bank of England. His father wanted him to put away such frivolous pastimes as chess and mathematics, and instead devote himself to higher pursuits. To this end, he decided that Alfred would train for the church. However, Alfred rebelled, and instead of taking up a scholarship to study divinity at Oxford University, he studied mathematics, physics, and later economics at Cambridge University with financial help from an uncle. Later, as professor of economics at the same school, he influenced a whole generation of economists.

His fame was sealed with the publication of his *Principles of Economics* in 1890. Marshall was a precise and painstaking scholar, and his book was the result of years of study and research. In this text, Marshall established himself as the intellectual leader of "neoclassical economics" and provided a synthesis of the classical ideas of Smith and Ricardo, with the new ideas of marginal analysis (which we introduce in Chapter 5).

Despite the fact that Marshall was an expert mathematician, he believed that mathematics should be regarded merely as a useful tool for economists rather than as the provider of fundamental economic truths. He also thought that the "laws of demand" suggest what possible outcomes may result under certain circumstances and that those results may be desirable but not imperative. Students of economics also owe a debt to Marshall for introducing graphical analysis into the discipline.

[1] J. Oser and S. L. Brue, *The evolution of economic thought*, 4th ed. (New York: Harcourt Brace), p. 273.

FIGURE 3.1   An Overpriced Product

Although an SUV manufacturer can price its SUVs at whatever level it wishes, this graph shows that if it wants to sell *all* of its output of SUVs, then it must sell this particular model at a price of $20 000 or less. If it overprices it at, say, $25 000, the result will be a surplus of 20 000 unsold vehicles.

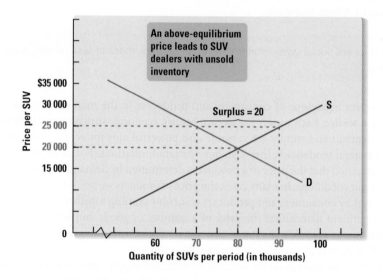

This figure illustrates the market for a particular type of SUV. The demand curve, as usual, shows the market demand for this vehicle at various prices. The supply curve shows the outputs that provide the greatest profit for the SUV manufacturer at each different selling price. For information, the graph also shows what would be the equilibrium price. But this manufacturer can, if it wishes, charge any price it wants. Let us say it charges a price of $25 000 and produces 90 000 SUVs, since this is the quantity that will produce the greatest profit for the firm at this price.

Unfortunately, the manufacturer will soon discover that consumers are not as excited about this vehicle as it had hoped. At a price of $25 000, it is only able to sell 70 000 units, leaving it with a surplus of 20 000. Obviously, it will eventually have no choice but to drop the price perhaps by offering dealer's rebates. If it does not, the manufacturer could end up with huge losses. The market can be a stern taskmaster.

What this example demonstrates is that even powerful producers (or for that matter, consumers or governments) must heed market forces because the market embodies the simple maxim that people cannot be forced to buy something they do not want. Similarly, producers cannot be forced to produce products that do not earn them sufficient profits.

This chapter will look at situations in which the market works well and at other situations where government sees the need to intervene and correct what it perceives to be deficiencies in the market system. As we shall see, markets do not always produce the "right" results for a number of reasons, but in other cases, interference by government may do more harm than good. How well and how fairly markets operate is a central theme in microeconomics, one we will examine from various angles throughout this book. This chapter is a preliminary exploration into the efficiency of the market system and will help you understand the power of demand and supply analysis. First, however, we need to dig a little deeper into these concepts.

3.1 SIMULTANEOUS CHANGES IN DEMAND AND SUPPLY

L01 Explain the effects of simultaneous changes in supply and demand on equilibrium price and quantity traded.

In the last chapter, we looked at the causes of changes in demand and supply, and how they affect both the price and quantity traded of a product. However, in order to deepen our understanding, we need to be able to explain what will happen if *both* demand and supply change simultaneously, since this may well happen in a dynamic, ever-changing economy.

In this next example, we look at the factor market rather than the product market, but the approach remains the same. In particular, let us examine possible changes in the supply of computer programmers. The supply of computer programmers is definitely increasing these days, since a career in computers is an attractive proposition for many students, and colleges and universities offer a wide range of computer courses. In addition, the demand for programmers by software companies as well as by other businesses and government is steadily increasing. Since both the demand and the supply are increasing at the same time, what can we say about the wage of programmers and about future job opportunities in the industry? Here it is helpful to think of the wage as the price of labour, with the supply coming from individuals in the labour market and the demand coming from firms that hire programmers. **Figure 3.2** shows the effect of a simultaneous increase in both demand and supply.

We see that the result is a definite increase in the number of employed programmers from Q_1 to Q_2; however, the wage level W_1 seems not to have changed. In contrast, **Figures 3.3A** and **3.3B** give different results.

JobServe.ca is a leading web-based employment company catering to those seeking or offering experience in a multitude of industries including IT, engineering, finance, accounting, and many more.

Courtesy of www.jobserve.ca

FIGURE 3.2   The Demand for and Supply of Computer Programmers

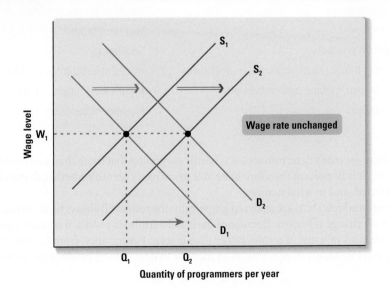

A simultaneous increase in both the demand for and supply of computer programmers will lead to an increase in the number of programmers employed, Q_1 to Q_2, and in this example the wage rate, W_1, is unchanged. However, it is uncertain what will happen to the wage level without knowing exactly how much demand increases in comparison to the increase in supply.

FIGURE 3.3	Simultaneous Increases in Demand and Supply, and the Effect on Wages

In Figure A, the increase in demand, from D_1 to D_2, is greater than the increase in supply, from S_1 to S_2. The result is an increase in the wage level, from W_1 to W_2. In Figure B, in contrast, the increase in supply, from S_1 to S_2, exceeds the increase in demand, from D_1 to D_2. The result, in this case, is a drop in the wage level, from W_1 to W_2.

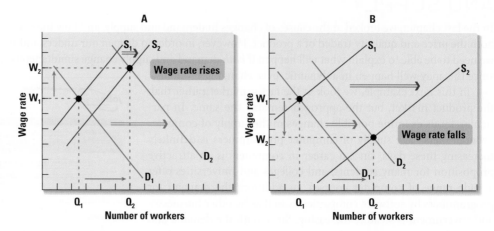

In **Figure 3.3A**, the shift in the demand curve is greater than the shift in the supply curve, and since demand increases more than supply, the wage level increases from W_1 to W_2. **Figure 3.3B** shows, in contrast, a situation in which the supply increase exceeds the demand increase, resulting in a lower wage level. Both graphs show, as does the graph in **Figure 3.2**, that the number of programmers employed will increase, but what happens to the wage level depends on the comparative magnitude of the change in demand and supply. In other words, to find out what will happen to the wage level, we need to know the amounts by which demand and supply increase, otherwise the effect is inconclusive (or indeterminate, as economists say).

It is important to remember that many factors can affect the demand for and supply of a product. To refresh your memory of these determinants, **Table 3.1** might be helpful.

TABLE 3.1	Determinants of Demand and Supply
Determinants of Demand	**Determinants of Supply**
Consumer preferences	Prices of productive resources
Consumer incomes	Business taxes
Prices of related products	Technology
Expectations of future prices, incomes, or availability	Prices of substitutes in production
Population: its size, income distribution, and	Future expectations of suppliers
age distribution	Number of suppliers

Since there are many determinants, it is hardly surprising that more than one could change at the same time. It is important therefore to be able to correctly identify whether demand or supply has been affected, and in what manner.

Whenever multiple shifts are analyzed graphically, the result will always be uncertain unless the amount of each change is known. Because of these indeterminate results, it is often a good idea to analyze the changes in terms of arrows rather than graphs. For instance, from Chapter 2, we know that if the market is initially in equilibrium an increase in demand will produce the following result:

$$\uparrow D \rightarrow \uparrow P \uparrow Q$$

On the other hand, an increase in supply will lead to:

$$\uparrow S \rightarrow \downarrow P \uparrow Q$$

As you can see, both changes will tend to push up the quantity traded. However, the increase in demand will push the price up, whereas the increase in supply will push the price down. So, if both changes happen at the same time, the net result on the price is indeterminate. It follows that:

$$\left. \begin{array}{l} \uparrow D \\ \\ \uparrow S \end{array} \right\} \rightarrow\; ?\; P \uparrow Q$$

Similarly, we can analyze the effects of a decrease in both demand and supply:

$$\left. \begin{array}{l} \downarrow D \;\}\; \rightarrow\; \downarrow P \downarrow Q \\ \\ \downarrow S \;\}\; \rightarrow\; \uparrow P \downarrow Q \end{array} \right.$$

The net result is: $? \; P \downarrow Q$

In this case, the quantity will definitely decrease; however, the effect on price, as in our last example, is indeterminate.

Next, let us look at what happens when demand and supply move in opposite directions. Suppose that the demand for a product were to increase, while supply decreases—what effect would this have on the market? In terms of arrows, the result is clear, though, as usual, the net result is indeterminate:

$$\left. \begin{array}{l} \uparrow D \;\}\; \rightarrow\; \uparrow P \uparrow Q \\ \\ \downarrow S \;\}\; \rightarrow\; \uparrow P \downarrow Q \end{array} \right.$$

$$\uparrow P\; ?\; Q$$

It is the change in the quantity this time that is indeterminate; price will definitely increase.

Finally, let us take a look at the last combination: a decrease in demand accompanied by an increase in supply:

$$\left. \begin{array}{l} \downarrow D \;\}\; \rightarrow\; \downarrow P \downarrow Q \\ \\ \downarrow S \;\}\; \rightarrow\; \downarrow P \uparrow Q \end{array} \right.$$

$$\downarrow P\; ?\; Q$$

As in the previous case, the effect on the quantity is indeterminate; price, however, will definitely decrease.

Returning to our market for computer programmers, we can now pose a practical problem that many students have to address: what are the prospects for a good job or a decent salary, given the present trends? The answer depends to a great extent on the number of graduating students and the number of new jobs being created in industry. Suppose, in **Figure 3.4**, that the increase in the supply of graduates exceeds the increased demand.

FIGURE 3.4   When the Increase in Supply Exceeds the Increase in Demand

The original wage is W_1, and the number of employed programmers is equal to *a*. Demand and supply now simultaneously increase, from D_1 to D_2 and from S_1 to S_2, respectively. As a result, the number of programmers wanting jobs (*c*) exceeds the number of jobs available (*b*). The surplus of programmers, *bc*, will cause the wage to drop to W_2, and the new equilibrium number of programmers will be quantity *d*.

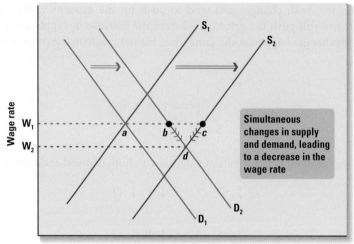

The initial wage level is W_1, and the quantity of programmers employed is shown as quantity *a*. Suppose that there is a simultaneous increase in demand from D_1 to D_2, and in supply from S_1 to S_2. The increase in the supply of programmers, however, exceeds the increase in demand from the industry. At the present wage level of W_1, the number of new programmers wanted by the industry is represented by the increased quantity *b*; the number of qualified programmers, however, has now increased to quantity *c*. There are a number of unemployed programmers (a surplus of programmers) in the amount *bc*. The competition among programmers for jobs may cause the wage level to eventually drop to a lower wage level, W_2. This lower wage level has eliminated the unemployed programmers, some of whom presumably gave up trying to find a job in computers and started looking for other types of work. The workings of the marketplace, therefore, do not ensure that everyone will be happy with the results. The number of employed programmers, however, has definitely increased from quantity a to the new equilibrium quantity *d*.

What this programmer example shows is the way markets operate and how, by changing the price (the wage level, in this case), surpluses and shortages are eliminated. Does this describe how markets always work? Well, not entirely. Certainly it is true that if the number of graduates exceeds the number of new jobs created, many of these graduates are going to be unemployed. The market's cure for this would be a reduction in wage levels. However, the market solution is not always a popular solution. Throughout the centuries, people have often attempted to circumvent or impede the workings of the market because they have either doubted the efficiency of the marketplace or not liked the results it produces. The rest of this chapter investigates this interference.

SELF-TEST

1. In each of the following cases, explain what effect the changes will have on the equilibrium price and quantity in each market.

Market	Change
a) Day-care services	More mothers with small children are returning to the labour force; at the same time, government decides to introduce subsidies for day-care operators.
b) Marijuana	Government severely increases the penalties for both buying and selling marijuana.
c) DVDs	A new processing method significantly reduces the costs of producing DVDs; at the same time, more consumers download video content directly onto their computers.
d) Organic vegetables	Vegetarianism increases as a result of medical reports extolling its health benefits; at the same time, tighter regulations on the definition of organically grown products are introduced.

2. If the demand for a product were to decrease more than the supply decreases, will the result be a surplus or a shortage at the original equilibrium price? What will happen to the price level and the quantity traded as a result?

3.2 HOW WELL DO MARKETS WORK?

Suppose that a devastating tidal wave hit a major North American coastal city, resulting in the total destruction of half of its housing stock. Let us assume that this was a particularly benign tidal wave in that nobody was actually killed; however, half the residents find themselves without a place to live. The situation is illustrated in **Figure** 3.5.

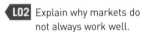 **L02** Explain why markets do not always work well.

FIGURE 3.5   Market Adjustment to a Decrease in Supply

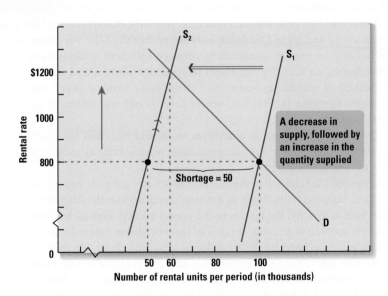

The initial equilibrium rental value was $800, and the number of rental units occupied was 100 000. A tidal wave demolishes half the units, which is reflected in the supply curve shifting left from S_1 to S_2. With a resulting shortage of 50 000 units, rents are forced up, and in time, a new equilibrium is reached at a rent of $1200 and with 60 000 units now occupied.

Before the tidal wave struck, the average monthly value of the housing stock (rented and owned, houses and apartments) was $800 per month, and the number of occupied units was 100 000. The effect of the tidal wave has been to reduce the supply of housing units to 50 000, leading to a shortage of 50 000 units at the present monthly value of $800. What we now want to look at is the way in which the market addresses these kinds of changes in supply. The severe shortage of accommodation is definitely going to cause rents to increase appreciably because many families left homeless are only too willing to pay more than $800 per month for housing. As the monthly value starts to increase, the quantity supplied will also go up.

This will happen in a variety of ways. Many homeowners will be willing to rent out their basements; some shopkeepers may be willing to convert their shops into rented accommodation; many landlords and tenants will be very happy to subdivide their premises; and at the low end of the accommodation scale, warehouses, stables, sheds, and garages will become available—all at a price. As rents continue to skyrocket, the quantity demanded will fall, since many people will simply be unable to afford the higher rents. (These people will have to find someone to live with, such as a parent or room-mate, or live on the streets, or leave the city.) Rents will continue to rise as long as there is a shortage and will stop rising when the market has eliminated that shortage. This occurs, in **Figure 3.5**, when the average value of accommodation has increased to the new equilibrium price of $1200. At this figure, the number of units now occupied has increased to 60 000.

Yet, this is not the end of the story. This adjustment process probably occurs over a short period, maybe a few weeks. In the long run, more lasting change will come about in the market. The high value of rents and of property in general will encourage developers to start building more units. As new units are built, the supply of housing will increase, which we could have shown as a rightward shift in the supply curve. In time, as a result of the increased supply, the price of accommodation will drop and the number of housing units on the market will increase. It could well be that eventually the number of units will return to 100 000, and the price of accommodation will revert to $800.

Now, consider the question that faces government. Should it sit back and allow the market to cure the problem of the shortage, or should it step in and effect its own cure? Certainly, the competitive market can eliminate shortages, but since it works through economic incentives and disincentives on a voluntary basis, it may not always work fast enough for society's liking. In emergency situations, governments can effect change far more quickly than can the marketplace. In the case of large-scale disasters, such as floods or earthquakes, we expect government to step in immediately and take charge to alleviate suffering. Similarly, in wartime, we take it for granted that government would and should mobilize industry on behalf of the war effort. Governments generally will not rely on market incentives to produce sufficient armaments or military personnel. In other words, we expect government to conscript workers and factories because this is the fastest method of mobilizing resources. On the other hand, it is certainly possible that governments might intervene in situations where they should not, or might use inappropriate methods of intervention.

Markets do not always adjust as quickly as we would like, and this can be a problem. Furthermore, markets do not always produce equitable results, as far as society or government is concerned. Let us look at this aspect.

In our example of the tidal wave, the market's short-run solution was to increase the price of accommodation. Suppose (admittedly an extreme scenario) that the destroyed houses were all in the richer section of the city; the houses in the poorer section were all left intact. As the price of accommodation starts to increase, a number of tenants will no longer be able to afford to rent their homes and will be evicted by their landlords, who will gladly see them replaced by new tenants from the rich side of the town. In time, we may well find that the rich now totally inhabit the poor side of the town and that the former tenants are now homeless, forced to double up or relocate. Note in **Figure 3.5** that when the price of accommodation reaches $1200, there is no longer a shortage despite the fact that there are now only 60 000 units occupied, compared with the 100 000 prior to the tidal wave. There is technically no shortage of housing despite the fact that 40 000 families have had their lives disrupted. Remember that a shortage means insufficient supply at a particular price. There is sufficient supply at $1200. The fact that many people cannot afford accommodation at $1200 is a different point and is true of many products in our society.

In a sense, the market, like justice, is blind. Resources and products are allocated according to the forces of demand and supply. Whether the results are desirable or not is not the concern of the market. The fact that most people cannot afford everything they would like is a fact of economic life. A number of things are unavailable to most of us, from luxury yachts to summer cabins, from the latest computer to this year's new car model. The market allocates these products according to supply conditions and according to people's desire *and ability* to purchase. The market does not allocate on the basis of who should or who should not get things. That is not the function of markets. However, most people believe that it is the job of governments to see that a certain amount of fairness prevails in society. Throughout history, governments have attempted to correct what they perceive to be inequities in the market. In addition, they often intervene where a competitive market just does not exist.

The problem here is not so much the goals of government (which are obviously a matter of some debate) but the methods used to achieve those goals. It is these methods to which we now turn.

3.3   PRICE CEILINGS

A favourite method chosen by governments to correct what they see as undesirable market prices is the introduction of **price controls**. These are legally imposed minimum or maximum prices on various types of privately produced goods and services. Failure to observe these controls usually carries fines or imposes other punishments on the buyer or seller.

> A price ceiling is a maximum price at which a product can be sold legally; a price floor is a minimum price at which a product can legally be sold.

In both cases, government is establishing limits, not a fixed price. Let us start by looking at price ceilings.

Governments introduce a **price ceiling** primarily when they believe that the present market price of a particular product—usually something thought to be a necessity—is too high for many buyers. One example is rental accommodation. **Figure 3.6** shows the market for apartment rentals in a major Canadian city. Given the demand and the supply, the market rental is presently $600 and the number of rental units is 100 000. However, government believes that this rent is too high, causing a great deal of financial stress for many poor people. As a result, government decides to impose a form of price ceiling known as **rent control**, which establishes a maximum rent of $400, though, in reality, there could be a number of ceilings, depending on the size of the accommodation, the number of bedrooms, and so on. (For a price ceiling to be effective, it has to be below the equilibrium price.) Landlords are not allowed to charge a higher rent, though they may charge less, if they wish. However, at a rent of $400, the number of rented apartments demanded has now increased to 120 000 units, since at this lower rate, renting has become a more popular choice than buying.

The lower rent is good news for renters but decidedly bad news for landlords who will find it difficult to make a profit at this lower rent. Many of them might well decide to sell off their apartments or convert them into condominiums rather than rent them. Or they may convert the apartments into shops or warehouses, if possible, or do what many landlords do in New York and other cities that have introduced rent controls—simply board up their properties and leave them empty because this alternative is more attractive than renting them out. The result, in our example, is that the number of apartments available to rent has decreased to 90 000 units. And the consequence of this is a 30 000 unit shortage of apartments.

L03 Understand why price ceilings cause shortages.

price controls: government regulations to set either a maximum or minimum price for a product.

price ceiling: a government regulation stipulating the maximum price that can be charged for a product.

rent control: a government regulation making it illegal to rent out accomodation above a stipulated level.

FIGURE 3.6   The Effect of a Price Ceiling on Rented Accommodation

The initial market equilibrium is a rent of $600 and 100 000 rental units. Establishing a price ceiling of $400 causes the quantity demanded to rise to 120 000 and the quantity supplied to fall to 90 000 units. The result is a shortage of 30 000 units.

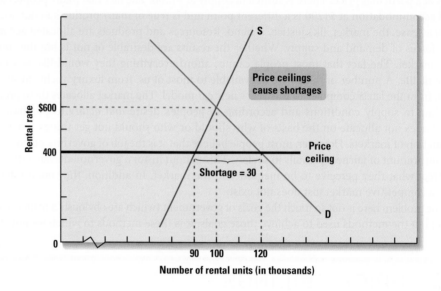

Price ceilings cause shortages

Price ceiling

Shortage = 30

Rental rate

$600

400

S

D

0   90 100   120

Number of rental units (in thousands)

With rent control, abandoning a building may be a better economic option than renting it.

This leads to an important conclusion:

Price ceilings cause shortages.

If all this is not bad enough, there is another serious problem with rent controls. The people who are currently renting are the people who benefit from rent controls because they are paying below-market rents. In addition to those in need, this might also include many professionals who could easily afford to pay the market rate. Landlords are in a very strong position because many people are desperate to find accommodation, but single mothers, members of visible minorities, low-income students, and other disadvantaged groups will find themselves in a very vulnerable position because landlords can now pick and choose the types of tenants they want. This leads to a great deal of unfairness and discrimination. In Canada, there is no federal legislation covering rent controls. The province of Ontario had rent controls between 1944 and 1994. Alberta has never had rent controls but does limit landlords to one rent increase per year.

Another situation in which price ceilings are introduced is during national emergencies, such as wartime. During World War II, most of the belligerent nations felt it necessary to introduce price controls. War-time economies have to be mobilized for the war effort, which means that productive resources are conscripted by government away from their peacetime activities: certain factories are either taken over directly by government or ordered to start producing armaments and other military requirements; workers are redirected into certain industries or directly into the military. This reduces the amount of resources available to produce civilian goods and services.

The result of this sudden reduction in the supply will be an increase in the prices of most civilian products, including the prices of most foods. Under these circumstances, government may well feel obligated to introduce price ceilings so as to keep prices affordable for most people. The effect of a price ceiling, any price ceiling, will be to cause a shortage, as **Figure 3.7** shows.

| FIGURE 3.7 | The Effects of a Price Ceiling on Butter |

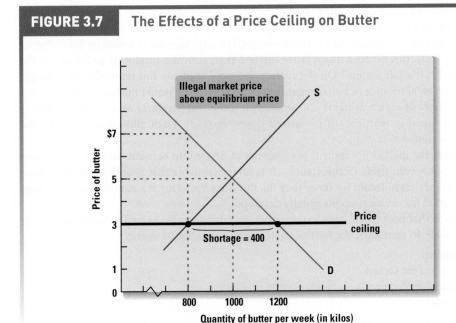

Equilibrium is at a price of $5 per kilo and a quantity of 1000 kilos. If government introduces a price ceiling at $3, the result is a shortage of 400 kilos. The dashed line, at quantity 800, shows the maximum (illegal market) price at which the quantity supplied could be sold. In this case, it is $7 per kilo.

Assume that the graph illustrates the market for butter. The equilibrium price is $5 per kilo, and the quantity being traded is 1000 kilos per week. Let us suppose that the price is unfortunately far higher than the peacetime price of $3, so government decides to establish a price ceiling for butter at this former price. This lower price is looked on very favourably by consumers, and the quantity demanded rises to 1200 kilos. For many farmers, however, the lower price spells disaster: a number of them are forced to cut back production, and some are forced out of the business of producing butter. At $3, the quantity supplied falls to 800 kilos. The price ceiling, therefore, has caused a shortage of 400 kilos of butter per week.

Shortages, whether or not they are caused by price ceilings, often produce illegal markets. This means that some people who can get their hands on commodities that are in great demand will be willing to risk the fines and penalties from breaking the law and will sell these items above the price ceiling. **Figure 3.7** shows that if illegal marketeers could get their hands on the total supply of 800 kilos, they could sell this quantity for as high as $7 per kilo—which is above both the price ceiling *and* the equilibrium price.

The butter example demonstrates that if the market is not allowed to allocate goods and services in the normal manner, then someone or something else must perform that task. At the price ceiling of $3 per kilo, the supply of 800 kilos must somehow be allocated to consumers who are demanding 1200 kilos. One way of allocating this short supply is on the basis of "first come, first served." But this is not a fair system, since people who have time on their hands will be able to line up more easily than, say, a parent with young children to look after. Another method is to leave the allocation decision to **producers' preference**, that is, leave it to the seller to decide which customers get what amount of butter and which customers go without. Unfortunately, this method opens itself up to the possibility of favouritism, bribery, and corruption. For instance, sellers may demand extra payments or services from customers before selling, decide to sell only to favourites, refuse to sell to anyone they do not like, and so on.

For this reason, governments are usually forced to undertake the allocation process themselves through the introduction of a **rationing** scheme. This means that butter, for instance, would be distributed equally among all families, each family being given ration coupons that allow it to

producers' preference: an allocation system in which sellers are allowed to determine the method of allocation on the basis of their own preferences.

rationing: allocating products that are in short supply using coupons issued by government, guaranteeing a certain quantity of something per family.

purchase a specified quantity. In our example, each family would get ration coupons entitling it to 2/3 kilo of butter per week. (We are assuming that at $3 per kilo there would be 1200 families each wanting to buy one kilo of butter. Therefore, each family's allocation would be 800/1200, or 2/3 kilo.) Certainly, this seems a much fairer method than allowing producers to decide on the allocation. But is it a fair system? On the surface, it would seem so. But remember that people are being given an allowance of butter regardless of whether they would normally buy it or not. Imagine the plight of coffee drinkers and smokers if those two products were rationed (beer is not usually rationed in wartime—it is watered down, instead). Their allowance would be the same as that of nonaddicts.

In contrast, the market normally takes intensity of desire into account, whereas a rationing system does not. Given these circumstances, it is understandable that people might well trade away coupons they do not want for those they do. But since bartering is a cumbersome exchange method, a market for ration coupons usually develops.

This means that people will have to pay to obtain extra coupons as well as having to pay for the product itself. In summary, the four possible methods of allocation are:

- the market
- first come, first served
- producers' preferences
- rationing

From this, you can see that with its faults, the market system usually works better than any alternative. Price ceilings are usually introduced when supplies of a product are limited, and prices consequently are high. But ceilings only address one problem—high prices, and they usually cause the limited supply to shrink even further. Many economists suggest that if the problem is affordability, then it might be better attacked by giving direct income relief to those in need rather than helping rich and poor alike by artificially depressing the price.

Let us now see what happens when government introduces price controls, not to depress prices but to increase them.

 SELF-TEST

3. The following graph shows the demand for and supply of milk in the land of Apollo (the quantities are in thousands of litres per day).

a) Suppose that the government of Apollo introduces an effective price ceiling that is 20 cents below the present equilibrium price. Would the result be a surplus or a shortage? Of what quantity?

b) If an illegal market were to develop as a result of the price ceiling, what would be the maximum illegal market price?

4. Given the demand and supply shown in the previous question, suppose that the government of Apollo imposed a price ceiling of $1.20 per litre of milk. What impact would this have?

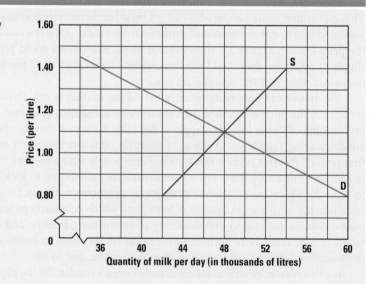

3.4   PRICE FLOORS

Figure 3.8 shows a market in which government believes that the price is, in fact, too low. It has, therefore, introduced a **price floor** above equilibrium. The price floor represents a minimum price. Sellers may sell at a higher price if they wish, but it is illegal to sell at a lower price. In order to be effective, a price floor must be set above the equilibrium price.

It is obvious in this situation that by imposing a price above equilibrium, government is assisting the producers and not the consumers. A higher price is going to mean a higher income for the producers. Which type of producers would government help in this way, and why? The answer is often farmers, because farming has always been regarded as a special type of industry. Agriculture is different from other types of production for a number of reasons. First, unlike, say, manufacturing, supply cannot be totally controlled by farmers. The size of the harvest can fluctuate greatly from year to year, and with it the price and income of farmers. Second, farmers produce a very basic and important commodity: food. Throughout history, countries have tried to ensure that they are not totally dependent on others for their food supply. If they were so dependent and the supply were interrupted because of war, civil unrest, drought, or other disaster, then their position would become precarious. Finally, governments have often been reluctant to allow agricultural land to be traded freely in the marketplace. It is felt that this particular resource is very precious because once it is used for other purposes, such as a housing development or shopping mall, reconverting it to farming is virtually impossible. For these and other reasons, governments in most countries have tried to protect and encourage their agricultural communities. One way of doing this is a price floor on agricultural products, which will guarantee farmers a minimum price.

Figure 3.8 illustrates a basic principle:

Price floors cause surpluses.

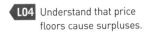 **L04** Understand that price floors cause surpluses.

price floor: a government regulation stipulating the minimum price that can be charged for a product.

FIGURE 3.8   The Effects of a Price Floor on the Wheat Market

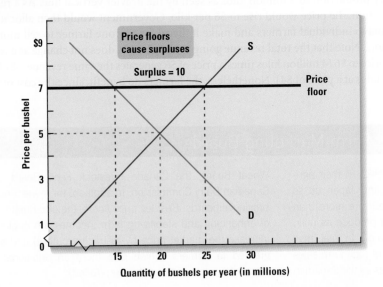

A price above equilibrium will always produce a surplus. In this figure, the price floor of $7 causes a drop in the quantity demanded from the original 20 down to 15; it also causes the quantity supplied to increase from 20 to 25. The result is a surplus of 10 million bushels.

The graph shows the market for wheat where the equilibrium price is $5 per bushel and the quantity traded is 20 million bushels per year. Suppose that government now introduces a price floor of $7 per bushel. At this higher price, the quantity demanded drops to 15 million bushels. The higher price will induce present farmers to produce more, and others to start up new wheat farms. As a result, the quantity supplied increases to 25 million bushels, so now there is a surplus of 10 million bushels of wheat. This surplus belongs to government; by introducing the price floor it must take responsibility for any surplus thus created.

Now government's problem is how to get rid of the surplus that a price floor will inevitably produce. A number of possibilities exist. If the surplus is storable, which is true of most grains, then it could be stored in grain elevators and used in the future, when the supply may be lower. In this way, the grain elevators are used as reservoirs, taking in grain whenever there is a surplus and releasing it whenever it is in short supply. If the agricultural surplus is perishable, as in the case of milk or eggs or produce, then government may be able to convert it into other foods or freeze, dry, or can it. But all such methods are likely to be expensive. Failing this, government will have to dispose of the surplus. But this is more difficult than it sounds. Selling it to other countries may not be feasible, since in order to do so, the price may have to be reduced. But this is **dumping**, and it is forbidden by many international conventions. Donating the grain to countries in need is similarly difficult, except in times of natural disasters, because doing so will undermine the receiving country's own agricultural industry or disturb its present trading arrangements. The last option may be simply to destroy the surplus by burning it, burying it, or literally dumping it in the ocean. Understandably, this last alternative is politically embarrassing to governments and is also unacceptable to many people. In summary, there are five ways to deal with a surplus:

dumping: the sale of a product abroad for a lower price than is being charged in the domestic market or for a price below the cost of production.

- store it
- convert it
- sell it abroad at a reduced price (dump)
- donate it
- destroy it

An alternative method, which has been tried by some governments, is to get farmers to stop producing a surplus! This can be accomplished by imposing a government-determined quota on total production. In **Figure 3.9**, the equilibrium price and quantity produced for raspberries is $4 per pound and 6 million kilos. If government wanted to improve the lot of the berry farmers by increasing the price *without generating a surplus*, it could impose a quota limiting the overall level of berry production to 4 million kilos as seen by the heavier vertical line. As a result of this lower production, the price would rise to $6 per kilo. Government would then allocate this production quota to individual farmers and make it illegal for any one farmer to sell more than the assigned quota. Note that the total revenue going to the growers does not change as a result of the increase in price to $6 (4 million kilos times a price of $6 generates the same revenue—$24 million— as 6 million kilos at a price of $4). Nonetheless, the farmers do benefit, since the cost of producing

ADDED DIMENSION   Farm Marketing Boards

Most countries' governments involve themselves in their agricultural sectors; the European Community and Japan do so more extensively than most. In Canada, there are more than 100 farm marketing boards regulating such produce as milk, eggs, wheat, peanuts, grains, poultry, and so on. In total, they exercise control over more than 50 percent of total farm sales in the country and include such federal bodies as the Canadian Wheat Board, the Canada Livestock Feed Board, and the Canadian Dairy Commission. In addition, there are a number of provincial boards. Besides price floors, the other main methods of enhancing and stabilizing farm incomes are quotas (which increase the market price by restricting output) and subsidies granted to farmers (which give them an additional sum of money for each unit of output produced).

FIGURE 3.9	The Imposition of a Production Quota

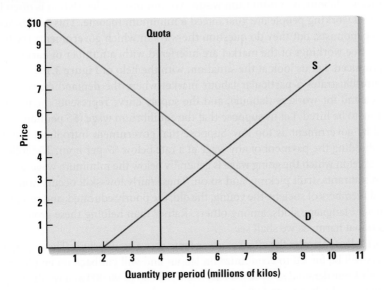

Equilibrium price is $4, and quantity produced is 6 million kilos. Imposing a quota of 4 million will raise price to $6.

4 million kilos is lower than producing 6 million kilos. The obvious shortcoming of this scheme is the politics involved in allocating the overall quota to individual farmers. Many are likely to think that their quota is too low and their neighbour's too high.

It should be clear from this that price floors in agriculture can lead to serious problems. Again, many economists would suggest that rather than interfering with the market, governments might be better advised to address the problem through direct income assistance to farmers. After all, this is the main problem that they are trying to correct.

✓ SELF-TEST

5. The market for corn is described in the accompanying figure.

   a) In equilibrium, what is the total sales revenue being received by producers?

   b) Suppose that government now imposes a price floor of $4 per kilo. What quantity will now be demanded? What quantity will the farmers produce? What quantity will government purchase?

   c) How much will it cost government to purchase the surplus?

6. Given the same graph, what is the effect of a government-imposed price ceiling of $4?

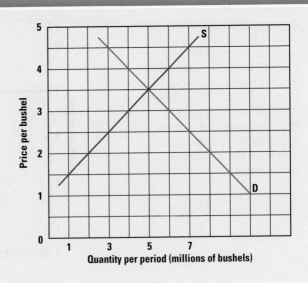

The Minimum Wage

minimum wage: the lowest
legal rate of pay per hour for
workers, as set by government.

Finally, we will take a look at another type of price floor that is used in many countries—a minimum price for labour, or a **minimum wage**. Minimum-wage legislation is often introduced to ensure that all working people are guaranteed a minimum income. This goal is generally not criticized by economists, but they do question the ways in which governments try to achieve it. Whenever the free workings of the market are interfered with, a number of harmful side effects are usually produced. Let us look at the situation, with the help of **Figure 3.10**.

This figure illustrates a particular labour market where the demand curve represents the employers' demand for workers (labour), and the supply curve represents the number of individuals wanting to be hired. Let us suppose that the equilibrium wage ($5 per hour in our graph) is considered by government as too low. Suppose that government introduces minimum-wage legislation forbidding the payment of any wage at a rate below $7 per hour. The following graph describes a market in which the going wage is generally below the minimum wage, as, for instance, in fast-food restaurants, fruit picking, and so on. These fairly low-skill occupations often attract disadvantaged members of society: the young, the old, the poorly educated, and recent immigrants without sufficient language skills, among others. Rather than helping these groups, may well be to cause additional harm, as we shall see.

Figure 3.10 demonstrates the effect of a wage rate above equilibrium. The higher wage means that employers will be forced to economize on labour and will cut back on employment; that is, the quantity of labour demanded by firms falls from 100 000 to 90 000 as a result of layoffs. At the same time, the now higher wage will attract more workers to this market and the quantity of labour supplied will increase from 100 000 to 110 000. The net result is that there will be a surplus of labour, that is, unemployment to the tune of 20 000 workers. The 90 000 workers who have retained their jobs are obviously helped by the minimum-wage legislation, though it is possible that they are required to work harder now that the number of employees has been reduced.

However, minimum-wage legislation has resulted in an increase in unemployment. It is this aspect of minimum wages that has been seriously criticized by some economists, who feel that the poor may be better assisted by income relief that is channelled to them directly rather

---

FIGURE 3.10   **Labour Markets and Minimum Wages**

As a result of the minimum wage of $7 per hour, the quantity demanded will drop from 100 000 to 90 000 and the quantity supplied increases from 100 000 to 110 000. The result will be a surplus of 20 000 workers. That is, there will be 20 000 unemployed workers in this particular labour market.

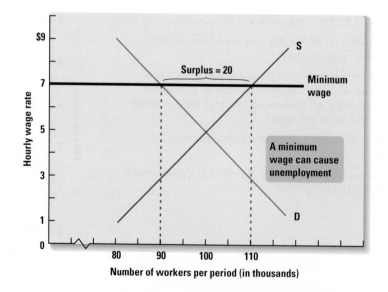

ADDED DIMENSION   The Minimum Wage in Canada

The minimum wage rate in Canada falls under provincial juris-diction. As of late in 2010, it ranged from $8.75 in British Columbia to $10.25 in Ontario, with the other provinces' rates falling between those two. There are, however, some exceptions. For example, in Ontario, the rate is $9.60 for students and $8.90 for those who serve alcohol. In Quebec, those who receive gratuities are paid $8 per hour, while others get $9.50. Approx-imately 5 percent of wage earners in Canada earn only the minimum wage. Provincially, this figure ranges from 6.5 percent in Newfoundland to 0.9 percent in Alberta. The federal minimum wage in the United States is $7.25 U.S.

than indirectly through the marketplace. It is also highly likely that since employers now have a big pool of unemployed workers from which to choose, some of them may be inclined to discriminate on the basis of age, gender, race, religion, or other non–work-related grounds. As an example of the effects of such discrimination, a recent study in the United States found that over half of the minimum-wage workers in that country came from families with *above*-average incomes. This astounding statistic makes more sense when one thinks of the thousands of teenagers, mostly from higher-income homes, who work for minimum wages at restaurants, gas stations, and retail shops.

A number of supporters of minimum-wage legislation, however, consider that the benefits far exceed the costs. They suggest that many workers are not paid low wages because they are unproductive, but that they are unproduc-tive because they are paid such low wages. If this is so, then the imposition of a minimum wage would increase productivity, lead to an increase in the demand for labour by firms, and reduce the amount of unemployment.

No matter who is right, the point of this analysis is that the allocation imposes costs, whether it is done by government or by the market, and these costs are not always obvious. Economic analysis helps us identify and understand these costs.

Young people eating at a fast food restaurant, a place where some of their friends probably work.

ADDED DIMENSION   Do Increases in the Minimum Wage Really Increase Unemployment?

For years, economists took it for granted that a legislated minimum wage set above equilibrium would increase unem-ployment. This supposition was challenged by two economists whose study of the results of New Jersey's 1992 increase in the minimum wage indicated that this may not be true. The discus-sion was further complicated when another study by two differ-ent economists concluded that the conventional view was valid. Both groups went back and redid their work, with the result that the difference between the two studies was narrowed.

The different results were partly the result of perspective: do we look at the total number of people employed in an industry or the total number of hours that are worked? Since many minimum-wage workers are part-timers, it is possible that the total number of hours does fall, as conventional theory predicts, even if the total number of individuals employed does not.

3.5 SOME ELABORATIONS

A great deal of economic analysis and theorizing is the result of observing the real world. However, much progress has been made as a result of economists abstracting from reality rather than merely reporting on it. In the context of demand and supply, economists are forever speculating on scenarios that do not exist. They ask, theoretically, what would happen if…? Having worked out the consequences of their analysis, they may even discover that their conclusions have applications to real world considerations.

Therefore, in the final section of this chapter we will look a little more closely at the shape and position of the demand and supply curves. In doing this, we are exploring possibilities—it may help give you a deeper understanding of demand and supply.

Do All Demand Curves Slope Downward?

The law of demand suggests that a lower price will produce a higher quantity demanded than will a higher price, but is this always true? Can the law of demand be broken? **Figure 3.11**, for instance, shows a vertical demand curve. Is such a construct a figment of some economist's imagination, or can it really exist?

The demand curve in **Figure 3.11** seems to suggest that for these particular consumers or in this particular market, the price of the product is irrelevant—the quantity remains the same, regardless of the price. It says that the quantity demanded remains constant at $Q_{1,2}$ whether the price is P_1 or P_2—or any price, for that matter. It would seem that this product is an "ultra" necessity so that no matter how high the price goes, the same quantity would still be purchased. Perhaps it describes the demand for cigarettes by smokers or for gasoline by drivers? But does it not seem ludicrous to suggest that they would not reduce consumption even a little if the price got astronomically high? Or, for that matter, that they would not consume more if the price

---

FIGURE 3.11   **A Vertical Demand Curve**

Whether the price is P_1 or P_2, the quantity demanded is the same: $Q_{1,2}$.

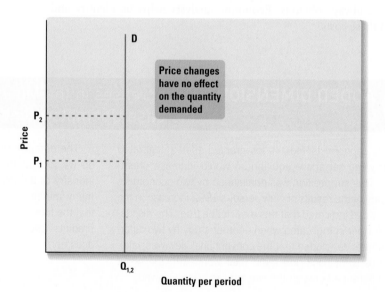

Price changes have no effect on the quantity demanded

were zero? What about drugs, then—either life-preserving drugs, such as insulin, or life-taking drugs, such as cocaine? Isn't the demand for these products unlimited because people have to have them, regardless of price? Again, need alone does not determine demand. Consider the unfortunate fact that even though humans need to eat food to stay alive, many millions die of starvation every year. In other words, our demand is limited by our income, by our ability to purchase. There is a maximum price for all of us, whether we are rich or poor. Therefore, although our demand for certain products may remain constant over a range of prices, eventually, above a certain price the quantity demanded will decrease, which means that the demand curve must eventually slope backward.

The next example seems even more perverse and totally contradicts the law of demand. **Figure 3.12** shows an upward-sloping demand curve.

This demand curve suggests that as the price increases, from, say, P_1 to P_2, the quantity that consumers purchase *increases* from Q_1 to Q_2. Surely, this is nonsensical? Well, certainly, it is unlikely that the *whole* market would buy increasing quantities at increasing prices. However, it may be true for *some individuals* over a limited range of prices. There are certain products whose values to some people are determined by their prices. The higher the price, the more attractive such products as jewellery, furs, and perfumes may become for some people, simply because the price is now higher. A higher price means that only an exclusive few people can now afford to buy such products. It is this exclusivity that makes such products attractive and invites these customers to "conspicuously consume," to use a phrase made popular by the iconoclastic American economist Thorstein Veblen. But, again, there is still a limit to this conspicuous consumption; eventually, at some high price, one would imagine, even for the few individuals involved, the quantity demanded will start to fall so that the demand curve again becomes downward sloping.

FIGURE 3.12   **An Upward-Sloping Demand Curve**

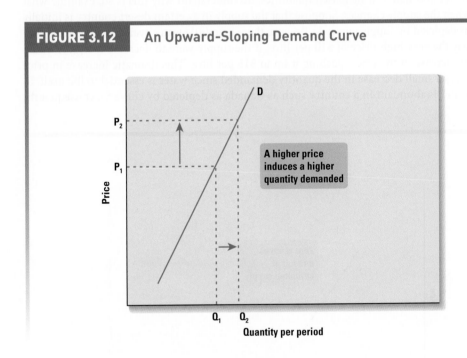

At price P_1, the quantity demanded is Q_1. At the higher price of P_2, the quantity demanded *increases* to Q_2.

ADDED DIMENSION   Giffen Goods: Are They for Real?

Another explanation sometimes given for an upward-sloping demand curve relates to what are termed *Giffen goods*. In the nineteenth century, economist Sir Robert Giffen, as the result of research he had done into the quantity demanded of potatoes in Ireland following the 1856 famine, discovered an interesting paradox. As the price of potatoes rose, the quantity demanded of potatoes actually increased, instead of falling. The reason for this is that purchases of potatoes in those days represented a

big portion of the average working person's food budget. The increase in price meant a sharp drop in real incomes, which meant that for many families the purchase of meat or vegetables was out of the question. Thus, instead of buying any meat, they bought even more potatoes, which at least guaranteed a full stomach. Not all economists, however, trust Giffen's data, and few believe that there is much other evidence of an upward-sloping market demand curve.

Economics is generally concerned with products that have a positive (above-zero) price. **Figure 3.13**, in contrast, illustrates a market for a free good. The reason it is a free good is that the supply is so great that it does not require the inducement of a higher price in order to elicit a higher quantity. It might describe the supply of air, perhaps, or certain types of goods called *public goods*, which we will look at in a later chapter. For these types of products, the equilibrium price is zero, and for that reason, it is not worthwhile for a private company to produce them. Note, however, that free availability does not imply that the quantity demanded is unlimited. There is a maximum quantity demanded for most things in life.

The graph in **Figure 3.14** is straightforward, though the interpretation of the slope is a little more difficult. It describes the demand for water. Note that the demand curve starts very steep and gets flatter and flatter at increased quantities. To understand why this is so, examine what happens when the supply changes. Suppose that the supply in a certain desert country is initially very low as depicted by supply curve S_1. Because there is so little water available, people are prepared to pay the very high price of $10 per litre. If the supply were to decrease to S_{1A}, it would cause a big increase in the price, pushing it up to $15 per litre. This dramatic increase in price results in only a small decrease in the quantity demanded since water is essential to life itself. In contrast, water is abundant in a country such as Canada as depicted by curve S_2; consequently,

FIGURE 3.13   A Free Product

At a price of zero, the supply is unlimited. Regardless of the position of the demand curve, this must be a free good: that is, demand plays no part in determining the price. However, the quantity demanded is still limited—in this case to a quantity Q_1.

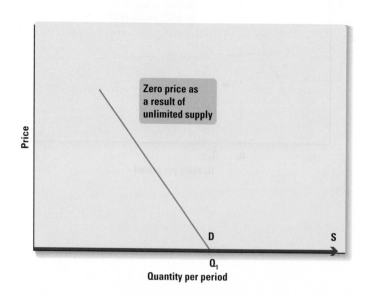

FIGURE 3.14   **The Demand for Water**

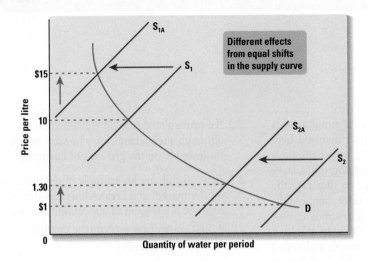

If the supply decreases from S_1 to S_{1A} and because the demand curve is so steep, the price increases from $10 to $15. The same decrease in supply where the demand is flat, from S_2 to S_{2A}, only causes the price to increase from $1 to $1.30.

the price is very low—$1 per litre, in our example. If the supply were to fall to S_{2A}, the effect on the price would be minimal, increasing it by only 30 cents to $1.30. In other words, the effect of a change in supply depends very much on the shape of the demand curve. We will continue this theme in the next chapter.

This completes our look at various aspects of demand and supply. However, as you may have become aware in this chapter, demand/supply analysis can be used, and is used, in so many different situations that it would be presumptuous to suggest that this is the end of the discussion. The tool of demand/supply analysis is so powerful and its application is so pervasive that, to an extent, much of economics is merely an elaboration and amplification of its basic principles.

 SELF-TEST

7. a) Under what circumstances would an increase in supply have no effect on the price of a product?

b) Under what circumstances would it have no effect on the quantity traded of a product?

Review

CHAPTER SUMMARY

In this chapter, we first explored the effects of simultaneous changes in supply and demand. The analysis involved here is simply an extension of what you learned in the previous chapter. Next, the example of a disaster wiping out a large portion of a city's housing stock was used to illustrate the fact that a market will reach equilibrium under any conditions, although many may feel that the equilibrium is arrived at too slowly and the results may be objectionable. We then looked at three specific examples of price controls and ended the chapter by speculating on some "what if" questions in reference to the shape of demand and supply curves.

3.1a In a noncompetitive market, a seller is able to set any price desired, but if a price above equilibrium is chosen, then a surplus will result, and sellers will have to either reduce the price to the equilibrium level, or sell less than they would like.

3.1b The four possible combinations of *simultaneous changes in demand and supply* are:

- an increase in both demand and supply that results in an increased quantity traded but an indeterminate change in price

- a decrease in both demand and supply that results in a decrease in the quantity traded but an indeterminate change in price

- an increase in demand with a decrease in supply that results in an increase in price but an indeterminate change in the quantity traded

- a decrease in demand with an increase in supply that results in a decrease in price but an indeterminate change in the quantity traded

3.2 An unregulated market will always find *equilibrium*, although such a result may be seen by some as undesirable on the grounds of fairness.

3.3 *Rent controls* are an example of *price ceilings* imposed on the market and create shortages that force the use of some other form of allocation, such as:

- first come, first served (the queue)
- sellers' preferences
- rationing

3.4a *Price controls* on agriculture products imposed on the market are an example of *price floors* and create surpluses that must then be:

- stored
- converted to another product
- sold abroad
- given away
- destroyed

3.4b The *minimum wage* is another example of a price floor. It is controversial because many economists believe that although it does benefit those who remain working, it creates unemployment that works against those it is mainly intended to help.

3.5a It is possible to conceive of a perfectly vertical demand curve and even an upward-sloping one, and we can think of examples where the supply of a good is so abundant that its equilibrium price is zero.

3.5b The *shape of the demand curve* for a product, such as water, probably changes significantly as the quantity in question increases.

NEW GLOSSARY TERMS

dumping   86
minimum wage   88
price ceiling   81

price controls   81
price floor   85
producers' preference   83

rationing   83
rent control   81

STUDY TIPS

1. In the first part of the chapter, we take some of the principles from the last chapter and apply them to real-world examples; the last part deals with abstractions and may not necessarily describe a real-life situation. However, you need to become familiar with the process of abstraction. This simply means exploring various possibilities. (What if the demand curve looked like this, or if the supply curve took this shape?) This process often uncovers interesting insights, so do not be afraid of abstractions. And do not try to immediately find practical uses—they may not always exist.

2. The chapter does not really introduce any new ideas, it simply extends the ideas developed in the last chapter. This means that even though the analysis, especially when we are dealing with multiple curve shifts, might seem forbidding at first, you are already familiar with the principles.

3. Many students confuse the terms *scarcity* (or short supply) and *shortage*. Remember that although all products and resources are "scarce," the markets for them may well be in equilibrium in that the quantity demanded and the quantity supplied are equal. A shortage, on the other hand, describes a disequilibrium situation, in which the quantity demanded exceeds the quantity supplied.

4. Remember that a price ceiling is a *maximum price* and when it is imposed *below* the equilibrium price, it results in a *shortage*. On the other hand, a price floor is a *minimum* price and when it is imposed *above* the equilibrium price, it results in a *surplus*.

Answered Questions

These questions can also be found online on Connect.

Indicate whether the following statements are true or false:

1. **(LO 1) T or F**   Economic laws are social laws—statements of tendencies, more or less certain, more or less definite.

2. **(LO 1) T or F**   If both demand and supply increase, it is impossible to say whether price will rise or fall.

3. **(LO 1) T or F**   If demand increases and supply decreases, it is impossible to say what will happen to price.

4. **(LO 1) T or F**   A shortage is caused by either a decrease in demand or an increase in supply.

5. **(LO 4) T or F**   A price floor, to be effective, must be set below the equilibrium price.

6. **(LO 3) T or F**   A price ceiling is a government regulation stipulating the maximum price that can be charged for a product.

7. **(LO 3) T or F**   Imposing a price ceiling often results in illegal markets and rationing schemes.

8. **(LO 4) T or F**   Invariably, price floors cause shortages and price ceilings cause surpluses.

9. **(LO 5) T or F**   If the demand curve is vertical, then an increase in supply will have no effect on the price.

10. **(LO 5) T or F**   Since water is a necessity, its demand is unlimited.

Basic (Questions 11–26)

11. **(LO 4)** A minimum wage is an example of a:
    a) Price floor
    b) Price ceiling
    c) A market in equilibrium
    d) Producers' preference

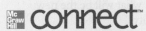

12. **(LO 3)** Rent control is an example of a:
   a) Price floor
   b) Price ceiling
   c) Market in equilibrium
   d) Producers' preference

13. **(LO 1)** What will happen if both the demand for and supply of a product increase simultaneously?
   a) The effect on the price is indeterminate.
   b) The price will increase.
   c) The price will decrease.
   d) The effect on quantity traded is indeterminate.

14. **(LO 1)** What will happen if both the demand for and supply of a product decrease simultaneously?
   a) The effect on the price is indeterminate.
   b) The price will increase.
   c) The price will decrease.
   d) The effect on quantity traded is indeterminate.

15. **(LO 1)** What will happen if both the demand for and supply of a product increase simultaneously?
   a) The effect on the quantity traded is indeterminate.
   b) The quantity traded will increase.
   c) The quantity traded will decrease.
   d) The price will rise.

16. **(LO 1)** What will happen if both the demand for and the supply of a product decrease simultaneously?
   a) The effect on the quantity traded is indeterminate.
   b) The quantity traded will increase.
   c) The quantity traded will decrease.
   d) The price will fall.

17. **(LO 3)** All of the following, except one, are examples of price ceilings. Which is the exception?
   a) Minimum-wage legislation
   b) Rent controls
   c) Wartime price controls on the price of consumer necessities
   d) A freeze on credit card interest rates

18. **(LO 4)** Which of the following types of firm would be most affected by minimum-wage legislation?
   a) A company of management consultants
   b) An airline company
   c) A fast-food restaurant
   d) A hospital

19. **(LO 3)** Which of the following is an example of a price ceiling?
   a) Minimum-wage legislation
   b) Dumping
   c) Rent controls
   d) Agricultural price supports

20. **(LO 5)** What does a vertical demand curve suggest?
   a) That producers are unable to adjust the quantity they produce
   b) That the price is not a determinant of the quantity demanded
   c) That consumers will not buy the product unless it is free
   d) That a change in supply has no effect on the price

21. **(LO 5)** What term is used to describe certain goods whose demand curve is upward sloping?
   a) Inferior goods
   b) Giffen goods
   c) Complementary goods
   d) Substitute goods

Refer to **Figure 3.15** when answering questions 22 and 23.

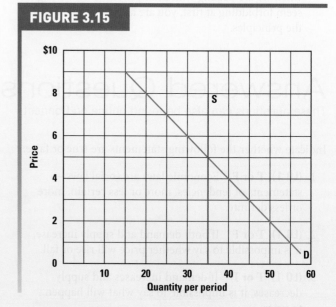

FIGURE 3.15

22. **(LO 1)** If this market is originally in equilibrium and demand increases by 10, what will be the new equilibrium price and quantity?
   a) $3 and 45 units
   b) $5 and 35 units
   c) $5 and 45 units
   d) $7 and 35 units

23. **(LO 1)** If the market is originally in equilibrium and supply increases by 10 units, what will be the new equilibrium price and quantity?
   a) $3 and 35 units
   b) $3 and 45 units
   c) $5 and 35 units
   d) $5 and 45 units

24. **(LO 1)** Under what circumstances would an increase in the supply of a product have no effect on the price?
   a) If the demand curve is vertical
   b) If the supply curve is vertical
   c) If the demand curve is horizontal
   d) If both the demand and supply curves are vertical
   e) If the demand curve is upward-sloping

Table 3.2 describes the market for day-care workers in the city of Vishna (quantity of workers in hundreds). Refer to this table to answer questions 25–27.

TABLE 3.2

Hourly Wage ($)	5.00	5.50	6.00	6.50	7.00	7.50
Quantity demanded	17	16	15	14	13	12
Quantity supplied	13	14	15	16	17	18

25. **(LO 1)** What is the result if this market is in equilibrium?
   a) The wage rate would be $5 an hour, and there would be 400 unemployed workers.
   b) The wage rate would be $5.50 an hour, and there would be 200 unemployed workers.
   c) The wage rate would be $6 an hour, and there would be no unemployed workers.
   d) The wage rate would be $6.50 an hour, and there would be 200 unemployed workers.
   e) The wage rate would be $5 an hour, and there would be 1,300 unemployed workers.

26. **(LO 4)** What would happen if government established a minimum wage of $6.50 an hour?
   a) The wage would stay at $6, and there would be no unemployment.
   b) The equilibrium wage would rise to $6.50, and there would be no unemployment.
   c) The number employed would increase by 100.
   d) There would be 200 day-care workers unemployed.
   e) The day-care centres would have difficulty finding sufficient workers.

Intermediate (Questions 27–32)

27. **(LO 4)** Suppose that after the imposition of a minimum wage of $6.50, a number of new day-care centres open up, increasing the demand for workers by 400. In what way would this market be affected?
   a) The wage would increase to $7, and there would be no unemployment.
   b) The wage would remain at $6.50, but there would now be no unemployment.

   c) The wage would remain at $6.50, and there would now be 200 unemployed day-care workers.
   d) The wage would remain at $6.50, and there would now be 200 job vacancies.
   e) The wage would drop to $5, and there would be no unemployment.

28. **(LO 3, 4)** Under what circumstances might an illegal market exist?
   a) When a price ceiling is imposed
   b) When a price floor is imposed
   c) When price is not at equilibrium
   d) When there is a big surplus of a product

Refer to **Figure 3.16** when answering questions 29 and 30.

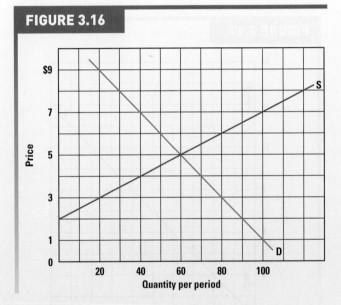

FIGURE 3.16

29. **(LO 4)** What would be the result if an effective price floor is set that is $2 different from the equilibrium price?
   a) The price would be above equilibrium, and a surplus of 60 would be produced.
   b) The price would be below equilibrium, and a shortage of 60 would be produced.
   c) The price would be above equilibrium, and a shortage of 60 would be produced.
   d) The price would be below equilibrium, and a surplus of 60 would be produced.

30. **(LO 3)** What would be the result if an effective price ceiling is set that is $2 different from the equilibrium price?
   a) The price would be above equilibrium, and a surplus of 60 would be produced.

b) The price would be below equilibrium, and a shortage of 60 would be produced.
c) The price would be above equilibrium, and a shortage of 60 would be produced.
d) The price would be below equilibrium, and a surplus of 60 would be produced.

31. **(LO 3)** Refer to **Figure 3.17** to answer this question. What will the price and revenue received by farmers be if a quota of 400 kilos is imposed?
    a) $6 and $2400
    b) $6 and $3600
    c) $8 and $4800
    d) $8 and $3200
    e) $9 and $3600

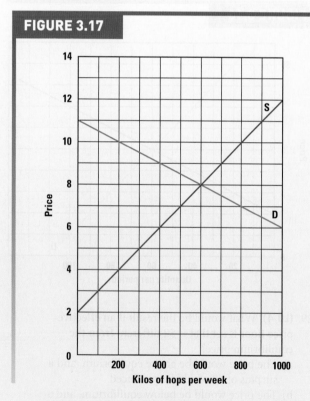

FIGURE 3.17

Kilos of hops per week

32. **(LO 3, 4)** Why is the market's allocation of products preferable to that of either the producers or government?
    a) Because it ensures that even the poor will be able to afford to buy everything
    b) Because it ensures that only people who really need certain products will be able to afford them
    c) Because it ensures that both demand and supply factors are taken into consideration

d) Because it will mean that scarce resources are available at low prices
e) Because it ensures that the income distribution of the population is ignored

Advanced (Questions 33–35)

Use **Table 3.3** to answer questions 33 to 35.

TABLE 3.3

Price per Litre ($)	Quantity Demanded	Quantity Supplied
1.80	160	142
1.90	156	144
2.00	152	146
2.10	148	148
2.20	144	150
2.30	140	152
2.40	136	154

33. **(LO 4)** Suppose that government introduces an effective price floor that is $0.20 different from the equilibrium price. What will be the result?
    a) 140 units will be sold.
    b) The quantity traded will be 156.
    c) There will be a shortage.
    d) The price will be $1.90 and quantity sold will be 156.

34. **(LO 3)** Suppose that government introduces an effective price ceiling that is $0.20 different from the equilibrium price and as a result an illegal market develops. What will be the illegal market price?
    a) $2.10
    b) $2.20
    c) $2.30
    d) $2.40
    e) Cannot be determined

35. **(LO 3)** Suppose that government introduces an effective price ceiling that is $0.20 different from the equilibrium price and at the same time supply increases by 12 units. What will be the result?
    a) Price will be $2.30, and quantity traded will be 164.
    b) Price will be $2.30, and quantity traded will be 152.
    c) Price will be $1.90, and quantity traded will be 156.
    d) Price will be $1.90, and quantity sold will be 144.

Parallel Problems

ANSWERED PROBLEMS

36A. **(LO 1, 3, 4)** **Key Problem** **Figure 3.18** depicts the market for rice in the country of Shiva.

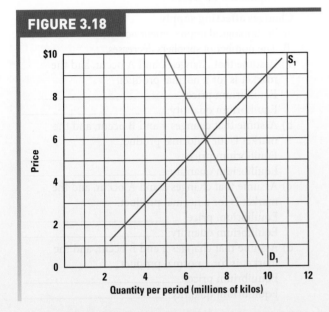

FIGURE 3.18

a) What is the present equilibrium price and quantity traded in this market? Price: _____ ; quantity traded: _____

b) How much, in total, are rice buyers paying for this quantity? Total spending: _____

c) Suppose that government introduces a price floor of $8 per kilo. How much in total will rice buyers now be paying? Total spending: _____

d) As a result of the price floor, what will be the total amount of the surplus? What will be the dollar amount of this surplus? Who will be responsible for buying this surplus? Surplus: _____ kilos of rice; dollar amount of surplus: $ _____ ; surplus is responsibility of: _____

e) Suppose that after the imposition of the price floor, the demand in Shiva increases by 1.5 million kilos. Draw the new demand on **Figure 3.18**, and label it D_2. Now, how much in total will rice buyers be paying? Price: _____ ; quantity traded: _____ ; total spending: _____

f) What will be the total amount of the new surplus? What will be the dollar amount of this surplus? Surplus: _____ kilos of rice; dollar amount of surplus: $ _____

g) After the change in demand, what would happen if, as a result of a bad harvest, the supply now drops by three million kilos? Draw the new supply curve on **Figure 3.18**, and label it S_2. What will be the new price, the quantity traded, the total spending of buyers, the surplus and the dollar amount of the surplus?
Price: _____ ; quantity traded: _____ ;
total spending: _____ ;
surplus: _____ kilos;
dollar amount of surplus: _____

Basic (Problems 37A–45A)

37A. **(LO 1)** **Figure 3.19** shows the market for mandarin oranges in Odin for the month of November (in thousands of kilos).

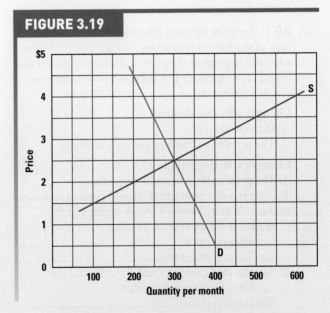

FIGURE 3.19

Suppose that in December the supply of mandarin oranges increases by 350 while the demand increases by 100.

a) Draw and label the new curves D_2 and S_2.

b) What will be the new equilibrium price and quantity? price: _____ ; quantity: _____

38A. **(LO 1)** **Table 3.4** shows Osiris's market for olive oil (in thousands of litres per month). Suppose that olive oil increases in popularity, and Osiris's buyers are willing to buy an additional 10 units at each of the eight prices in **Table 3.4**. At the same time, as the result

TABLE 3.4

Price ($)	Quantity Demanded	Quantity Supplied
1	70	10
2	60	20
3	50	30
4	40	40
5	30	50
6	20	60
7	10	70
8	0	80

of improved technology, oil producers are willing to produce 30 more units at each of the eight prices. What will be the new equilibrium price and quantity?
New equilibrium price: _____
Equilibrium quantity: _____

39A. **(LO 1)** Suppose that two concurrent changes occur in each of the following markets. In each case, indicate what will happen to the price and quantity traded as a result. (↑ = increase; ↓ = decrease; 0 = no change; ? = indeterminate)

Changes affecting demand
1. Incomes increase.
2. The price of a substitute product increases.

Changes affecting supply
A. The price of inputs (resources) falls.
B. The price of a productively related product increases.
a) Assume that changes 1 and A occur, and the market is for an inferior product.
   Equilibrium price: _____
   Equilibrium quantity: _____
b) Assume that changes 1 and B occur, and the market is for a normal product.
   Equilibrium price: _____
   Equilibrium quantity: _____
c) Assume that changes 2 and A occur, and the market is for a normal product.
   Equilibrium price: _____
   Equilibrium quantity: _____
d) Assume that changes 2 and B occur, and the market is for a normal product.
   Equilibrium price: _____
   Equilibrium quantity: _____

40A. **(LO 1)** Suppose that two concurrent changes occur in each of the following markets. In each case, indicate what will happen to the price and quantity traded as a result. (↑ = increase; ↓ = decrease; 0 = no change; ? = indeterminate)

Changes affecting demand
1. The price of a complementary product increases.
2. Population increases.

Changes affecting supply
A. Technological improvement occurs.
B. The number of suppliers decreases.
a) Assume that changes 1 and A occur, and the market is for a normal product.
   Equilibrium price: _____
   Equilibrium quantity: _____
b) Assume that changes 1 and B occur, and the market is for a normal product.
   Equilibrium price: _____
   Equilibrium quantity: _____
c) Assume that changes 2 and A occur, and the market is for a normal product.
   Equilibrium price: _____
   Equilibrium quantity: _____
d) Assume that changes 2 and B occur, and the market is for a normal product.
   Equilibrium price: _____
   Equilibrium quantity: _____

41A. **(LO 1)** In **Figure 3.20**, show graphically how a change in the *same direction* of both the demand and supply curves can produce the following results.
a) Price decreases, quantity traded decreases.
b) Price is unchanged, quantity traded decreases.
c) Price increases, quantity traded decreases.

42A. **(LO 1)** Table 3.5 shows the demand and supply per year for freezers in Antarctica.
a) In **Figure 3.21**, graph and label the curves.
b) What quantity will be bought and sold?
   Answer: _____.
c) Explain your results.

TABLE 3.5

Price	Quantity Demanded	Price	Quantity Supplied
$200	30	$500	0
300	20	600	10
400	10	700	20
500	0	800	30
600	0	900	40

FIGURE 3.20

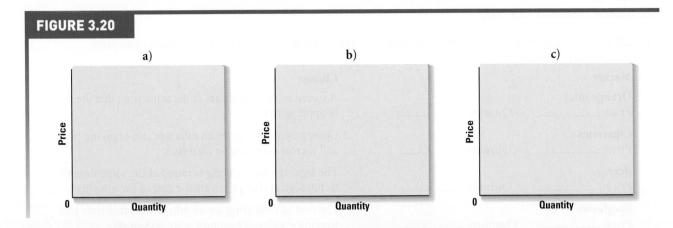

a)   b)   c)

FIGURE 3.21

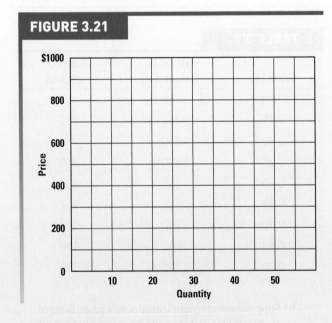

FIGURE 3.22

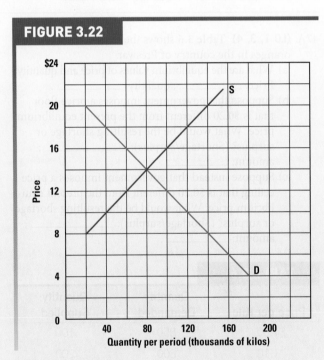

43A. **(LO 1)** **Figure 3.22** depicts the market for New York steaks.
   a) If government were to impose a price floor of $18 per kilo, what would be the result?
   Shortage / surplus of _____ kilos
   b) If government were to impose a price ceiling of $12 per kilo, what would be the result?
   Shortage / surplus of _____ kilos

44A. **(LO 1)** What will be the effect on equilibrium price and quantity if demand for a product increases at the same time that the supply decreases?

45A. **(LO 3, 4)** What is price control? Explain.

Intermediate (Problems 46A–51A)

46A. (LO 1) In each of the following markets, explain what effect the change will have on the equilibrium price and quantity traded.

Market	Change
Orange juice Price: _____ Quantity: _____	A freeze in Florida occurs at the same time that the price of apple juice rises.
Cigarettes Price: _____ Quantity: _____	Government introduces an effective anti-smoking policy and increases the tax on cigarettes.
Beer Price: _____ Quantity: _____	The legal age for drinking is raised at the same time that technological change lowers the cost of brewing beer.
Eyeglasses Price: _____ Quantity: _____	The cost of producing lenses falls at the same time that wearing eyeglasses becomes quite fashionable.

47A. (LO 1, 3, 4) Table 3.6 shows the market for mandarin oranges in the country of Preswar.
  a) What are the equilibrium values of price and quantity? Price: _____ ; quantity: _____ .
  b) Suppose that government imposes a price floor that is $0.20 different from the present equilibrium price. What would be the resulting shortage or surplus? (Shortage/surplus): _____ ; amount: _____ .
  c) Suppose instead that government imposes a price ceiling that is $0.20 different from the present equilibrium price. What would be the resulting shortage or surplus? (Shortage/surplus): _____ ; amount: _____ .

TABLE 3.6

Price per Kilo	Quantity Demanded	Quantity Supplied
$1.00	850	100
1.10	800	200
1.20	750	300
1.30	700	400
1.40	650	500
1.50	600	600
1.60	550	700
1.70	500	800

48A. (LO 1, 4) Table 3.7 shows the market for goat's milk in the country of Pegasus (in thousands of litres).
  a) What is the present equilibrium price and quantity traded? Price: _____ ; quantity: _____ .

TABLE 3.7

Price ($)	Quantity Demanded	Quantity Supplied
0.10	520	200
0.15	480	240
0.20	440	280
0.25	400	320
0.30	360	360
0.35	320	400
0.40	280	440
0.45	240	480
0.50	200	520

  b) Suppose government introduces a price floor of $0.40 per litre. What would be the resulting shortage or surplus? (Shortage/surplus) of _____ .
  c) What would be the result if, after the introduction of the price floor, both the quantity demanded and the quantity supplied were to increase by 20 percent? Answer: _____ .
  d) What would happen if, instead, the quantity demanded and quantity supplied were to decrease by 20 percent? Answer: _____ .

49A. (LO 4) Figure 3.23 depicts the international market for the Canadian dollar (price in terms of the U.S. dollar).
  a) Assuming that the market is in equilibrium, suppose that the demand increased by $20 (billion), while the supply of dollars increased by $10 (billion). What is the new equilibrium price of the dollar and the new quantity traded? Price: _____ ; quantity: _____ .

FIGURE 3.23

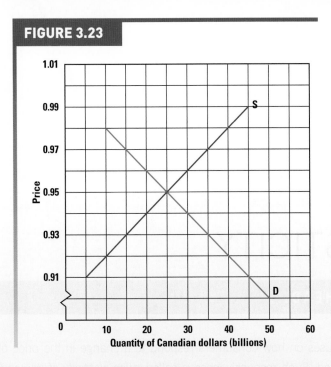

Price

Quantity of Canadian dollars (billions)

FIGURE 3.24

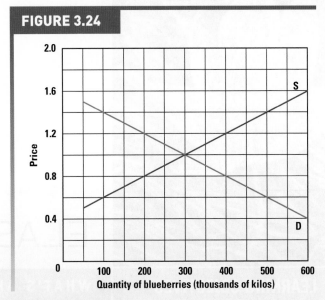

Price

Quantity of blueberries (thousands of kilos)

FIGURE 3.25

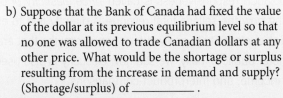
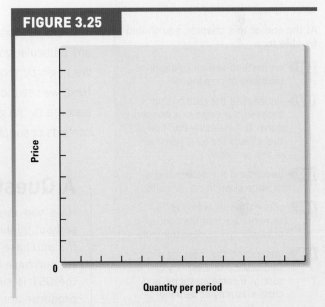

Price

Quantity per period

b) Suppose that the Bank of Canada had fixed the value of the dollar at its previous equilibrium level so that no one was allowed to trade Canadian dollars at any other price. What would be the shortage or surplus resulting from the increase in demand and supply? (Shortage/surplus) of _____ .

50A. **(LO 4)** Explain how the imposition of minimum-wage legislation might cause unemployment.

51A. **(LO 5)** Is it possible for a demand curve to be upward sloping? Explain.

Advanced (Problems 52A–54A)

52A. **(LO 1, 4)** Figure 3.24 depicts the market for blueberries in the country of Roni.
  a) Suppose that in an attempt to boost the price of blueberries for its farmers, the government of Roni introduces a quota that limits the total amount that farmers can sell to 200 000 kilos. What is the maximum price at which this quantity could be sold? Answer: _____ .
  b) What would be the result if this government decides, instead of using a quota, to introduce a price floor of $1.20 per kilo? What difference, if any, is there between the two schemes?
    Result of price floor: _____ Difference: _____

53A. **(LO 1)** "Technological improvements over the last ten years have so reduced the costs of producing DVD players that, although they have greatly increased in popularity, the average price has dropped." Illustrate the changes in the DVD market on the graph in Figure 3.25.

54A. **(LO 5)** Suppose that both the quantities demanded and supplied of an exclusive French perfume called "Eau de Biere" increase with its price.
  a) If a price above equilibrium results in a surplus, what can you say about the slope of the two curves? Answer: _____ .
  b) What will happen to price if it is currently above equilibrium? Answer: _____ .
  c) What will happen to the surplus? Answer: _____ .

ELASTICITY

At the end of this chapter, you should be able to...

LO1 understand and calculate price elasticity of demand.

LO2 understand the relationship between the slope of a demand curve and elasticity and how this affects the total revenue of the producer.

LO3 understand the determinants of price elasticity of demand.

LO4 use real-world examples to demonstrate that the concept of elasticity is a powerful tool.

LO5 understand the meaning and significance of elasticity of supply, income elasticity, and cross-elasticity of demand.

WHAT'S AHEAD...

This chapter focuses on how consumers respond to a change in the price of any particular good. Such responsiveness is called *price elasticity of demand*. We begin by showing how the seller's total revenue is directly tied to elasticity. Next, we use the idea of elasticity to analyze four popular myths that are widely believed by the general public. Finally, we see how elasticity is also used in the contexts of supply, income, and interproduct comparisons.

A Question of Relevance...

Have you ever noticed that people appear to make some purchases without thinking about them and yet agonize, sometimes for days, over the purchase of other things? We are all aware that almost everything we purchase in Canada is taxed. It may seem clear that an increase in the GST is simply passed on to the consumer, while the retailer and producer are nothing more than disinterested bystanders. But is this really the case? Do the ticket scalpers you see outside the venues of high-profile events, such as playoff hockey games or a Lady Gaga concert, always make a profit from the resale of the tickets they hold? Although these questions seem unrelated, they have a common link that we will explore in this chapter.

If a business drops the price of its product, will its revenue also fall? Most people would instinctively answer *yes*. However, such an answer is correct only under certain conditions. You will recall that Chapter 2 introduced the law of demand and established the inverse relationship between price and quantity. Thus, we know that a decrease in the price of, say, an airline ticket from Toronto to Montreal would result in an increase in the quantity of tickets sold. Obviously, this would be beneficial to consumers, but what we have not yet discussed is whether this would or would not be beneficial to the airline company selling the tickets. Would the airline receive more or less total revenue as a result of selling more tickets at a lower price per ticket? **Total revenue** (TR), not to be confused with total profit, is simply the total dollar value of some quantity of an item sold at a certain price. Formally, it is:

$$TR = P \times Q \qquad \text{[4.1]}$$

total revenue: the total receipts of a firm from its sales; formally, it is price multiplied by the quantity of the product sold.

Here, P stands for the price of the product, and Q stands for the quantity sold. The effect of lowering price, if nothing else is changed, would be to decrease total revenue. At the same time, however, the lower price will result in the quantity sold going up, and this will tend to increase total revenue. So, what will be the net effect of these opposing pressures? The answer to this question depends on the concept economists call **price elasticity of demand**. The dictionary defines elasticity as "the state of being elastic or flexible," and our focus is on the flexibility of consumers' reactions to a change in price.

price elasticity of demand: a measure of the percentage change of quantity demanded relative to a change in price.

4.1   PRICE ELASTICITY OF DEMAND

Price elasticity of demand can be defined as a measure of how much the quantity demanded changes as a result of a change in price. The measurement of elasticity is obtained by taking the percentage change in quantity and dividing it by the percentage change in price. Note that we use percentage changes because price is expressed in dollars and quantity is measured in units, so using just the absolute change in quantity divided by the absolute change in price would not work. Also, showing elasticity in percentage terms means that we can ignore the units in which the price and quantity are measured. Let us look at some hypothetical data, shown in **Table 4.1**.

LO1 Understand and calculate price elasticity of demand.

Suppose the price of an airline ticket from Vancouver to Edmonton is $650 and the quantity of tickets sold per day is 1000. This would yield total revenue to the airline of $650 × 1000 = $650 000. Next, assume that the price of a ticket falls to $550. As a result, the quantity of tickets sold rises to 1100. Total revenue, however, actually *drops* to $550 × 1100 = $605 000. Although the Vancouver to Calgary flight experiences the same price change, from $650 to $550, and also results in quantity rising, this time the quantity increases a lot more from 1000 to 1250. As a result, total revenue also *rises* to: $550 × 1250 = $687 500. From these examples, we can conclude that the effect on total revenue can vary greatly, depending on how quantity responds to a price change. It also means that one cannot predict the effect on total revenue of a price decrease without knowing how responsive the quantity demanded will be. This is what is meant by the concept of elasticity.

TABLE 4.1	**Demand for Airline Tickets I**				
Vancouver to Edmonton			Vancouver to Calgary		
Price	Quantity of Tickets	Total Revenue	Price	Quantity of Tickets	Total Revenue
$650	1000	$650 000	$650	1000	$650 000
550	1100	605 000	550	1250	687 500

elasticity coefficient: a number that measures the responsiveness of quantity demanded to a change in price.

Let us use the information in **Table 4.1** to do some calculations of elasticity. To obtain what is called the **elasticity coefficient**, we use a general equation, where elasticity is symbolized by the Greek uppercase letter epsilon, the subscript p indicates that it is the *price* elasticity of demand that is being referred to, and Δ means "change in."

$$\epsilon_p = \frac{\%\Delta \text{ quantity demanded}}{\%\Delta \text{ price}} \qquad \text{[4.2]}$$

This basic equation can be expanded as follows:

$$\epsilon_p = \frac{\dfrac{\Delta Q_d}{\text{average } Q_d} \times 100}{\dfrac{\Delta P}{\text{average } P} \times 100} \qquad \text{[4.3]}$$

To obtain the elasticity coefficient in the Vancouver to Edmonton example, we first need to determine the percentage change in quantity as the quantity changes from 1000 to the new quantity of 1100. The absolute increase is 100, and we need to put this 100 over a base to get the percentage increase. This raises the question of whether that base should be the original 1000 or the new 1100. Since $100 \div 1000$ is 0.1 and $100 \div 1100$ is 0.09, it clearly does make a difference which base is chosen. To resolve this question, we take the *average* of the original base and the new base, which, in this case, is:

$$\frac{1000 + 1100}{2} = 1050$$

(Using averages ensures that we get the same result if the quantity goes down from 1100 to 1000 or up from 1000 to 1100.) Thus, the percentage change in quantity is the absolute change of 100 divided by the average base of 1050 multiplied by 100. Let us show this explicitly:

$$\%\Delta\, Q_d = \frac{100}{1050} \times 100 = 9.5\%$$

The result of 9.5 percent is the numerator in equation 4.3 above. Next, we calculate the percentage change in price by dividing the absolute change of $100 by the average of the original and new prices. The percentage change in the price is:

$$\%\Delta\, \text{Price} = \frac{\$100}{\$600} \times 100 = 16.7\%$$

Technically, the answer is −16.7 percent, but since we know it is always negative, we simply ignore the minus sign. The reason economists do this is that price and quantity always move in opposite directions, and thus, *any* calculation of price elasticity of demand would result in a negative coefficient. We can now obtain the elasticity coefficient:

$$\epsilon_p = \frac{\%\Delta Q}{\%\Delta P} = \frac{9.5\%}{16.7\%} = 0.57$$

inelastic demand: quantity demanded that is not very responsive to a change in price (coefficient of elasticity is less than 1).

So, the Vancouver to Edmonton market has an elasticity coefficient of 0.57, which is less than one and is referred to as **inelastic demand**. This means that the quantity demanded is not very responsive to a price change. Specifically, a 1-percent change in price leads to a change of just 0.57 percent in quantity. Note that because the demand is inelastic, total revenue will fall as a result of the decrease in price. In the calculation above, we saw that total revenue decreases from the original $650 000 to $605 000. We are now able to make our first generalization involving elasticity:

If demand is inelastic and price falls, then total revenue will also fall.

Let us make the same calculation using the figures in the Vancouver to Calgary example. Here, the absolute change in quantity is 250 and the average quantity is:

$$\frac{1000 + 1250}{2} = 1125$$

So, the percentage change in quantity is:

$$\frac{250}{1125} \times 100 = 22.2\%$$

To obtain the denominator, we again put the absolute change in price, $100, over the average price of:

$$\frac{\$650 + \$550}{2} = \$600$$

This gives us the same denominator of:

$$\frac{100}{600} \times 100 = 16.7\%$$

Thus, the elasticity coefficient is:

$$\frac{22.2\%}{16.7\%} = 1.32$$

The Vancouver to Calgary market, therefore, has an elasticity coefficient of 1.32, which is greater than one and is referred to as **elastic demand**. Here, the quantity demanded is much more responsive to a change in price. A one percent change in price leads to a 1.32-percent change in quantity demanded. Since the increase in quantity, which pushes total revenue up, is stronger than the decrease in price, which pushes total revenue down, we would expect that the net effect will be an increase in total revenue and this is verified by our earlier calculation where total revenue increased from $650 000 to $687 500. We can now make our second generalization about elasticity:

elastic demand: quantity demanded that is quite responsive to a change in price (coefficient of elasticity is greater than 1).

> If demand is elastic and price falls, then total revenue will rise.

Do we get the same kind of result if the price increases instead of decreasing? Let us examine this by going to **Table 4.2**, in which we see the price increasing from the original $650 to $750.

We see from **Table 4.2** that a $100 price increase in each market ($650 to $750) results in a decrease in the number of tickets sold: for Vancouver-to-Edmonton flights, ticket sales decrease by only 100, but they decrease by 250 for the Vancouver-to-Calgary flights.

You should be able to verify that the elasticity coefficient in the Vancouver-to-Edmonton market is 0.74 and in the Vancouver-to-Calgary market is 2. These figures are different from the coefficients calculated previously, and there is a lesson in this. Moving up or down a demand curve results in the elasticity coefficient changing because the average base changes. Recall that the elasticity coefficient in the Vancouver-to-Edmonton example was 0.57 in the $550–$650 price range (see **Table 4.1**), whereas it is 0.74 in the $650–$750 price range (see **Table 4.2**).

TABLE 4.2	Demand for Airline Tickets II				
Vancouver to Edmonton			**Vancouver to Calgary**		
Price	Quantity	Total Revenue	Price	Quantity	Total Revenue
$650	1000	$650 000	$650	1000	$650 000
750	900	675 000	750	750	562 500

This is so despite the fact that the absolute change in price is $100 and the absolute change in quantity is 100 tickets in both cases. However, the two average bases are not the same. The average quantity in the first instance is 1050 but only 950 in the second. Similarly, the average price is $600 in the first instance but $700 in the second.

Despite the difference in elasticity coefficients at different prices, one thing remains consistent (at least in this example): the Vancouver-to-Edmonton market is an example of inelastic demand, and the Vancouver-to-Calgary market is an example of elastic demand. We saw earlier that if price decreases and demand is inelastic, then total revenue would fall. Thus, if price were to rise, we would expect the opposite, a rise in total revenue, and this is exactly what we get as total revenue increases from $650 000 to $675 000.

Similarly, **Table 4.1** indicated that if price *falls* and demand is elastic, we would experience an increase in total revenue. Thus, we would expect that a price rise in combination with elastic demand would cause a decrease in total revenue, and this is exactly what happens in **Table 4.2**, as total revenue falls from $650 000 to $562 500.

unitary elasticity: the point where the percentage change in quantity is exactly equal to the percentage change in price; that is where the elasticity coefficient is equal to 1.

Finally, we should look at the curious case of **unitary elasticity**. This is where the percentage change in price and quantity are exactly equal. For instance, suppose that the fare from Edmonton to Calgary was increased from $225 to $275, a $50 or 20 percent increase ($50/250 \times 100$) and this resulted in a drop in the number of tickets sold from 550 to 450. This fall in quantity also happens to equal 20 percent ($100/500 \times 100$). The elasticity coefficient is, therefore, equal to one (or unitary): (20 percent divided by 20 percent). Because the percentage increase in price is identical to the percentage fall in the quantity of tickets sold, the total revenue of the airline remains the same. Before the change, the total revenue was $123 750 (550 tickets at $225 each). After the price increase, total revenue is still $123 750 (450 tickets at $275 each).

If the demand is unitary elastic, then a change in price has no effect on total revenue.

Table 4.3 summarizes the effect of elasticity on total revenue as a result of a price change. We could also summarize the effects of a price change by saying that:

> If the demand is inelastic, price and total revenue move in the same direction. If the demand is elastic, price and total revenue move in opposite directions. If the demand is unitary elastic, total revenue is unaffected by a price change.

TABLE 4.3	Relationship between Price and Total Revenue	
If Demand is:	**and Price …**	**then Total Revenue …**
inelastic (<1)	falls	falls
inelastic (<1)	rises	rises
elastic (>1)	falls	rises
elastic (>1)	rises	falls
unitary elastic (=1)	falls	stays the same
unitary elastic (=1)	rises	stays the same

SELF-TEST

1. This table shows three sets of prices and their related quantities. Calculate the elasticity coefficients for each set.

	Price	Quantity
Set I	$1.50	200
	2.00	100
Set II	120.00	1600
	100.00	1800
Set III	18.50	37
	21.50	43

2. Here are two sets of prices and their related quantities:

	Price	Quantity
Set I	$9	1
	8	2
Set II	2	8
	1	9

a) Calculate the elasticity coefficients for each set.

b) In each set the change in price is $1 and the change in quantity is one unit. Why aren't the coefficients the same?

3. What would happen to total revenue in each of the circumstances below?

a) $\varepsilon > 1$ and price falls

b) $\varepsilon < 1$ and price rise

c) $\varepsilon < 1$ and price falls

d) $\varepsilon > 1$ and price rises

e) $\varepsilon = 1$ and price rises

4. Suppose that the price of four different products all increased by 20 percent. Given the elasticity coefficients shown below, what is the percentage change in the quantity of each product?

a) $\varepsilon = 4$

b) $\varepsilon = 0.5$

c) $\varepsilon = 1$

d) $\varepsilon = 0$

4.2   PRICE ELASTICITY GRAPHICALLY

What we need to do next is to take this concept of elasticity and give it graphical representation. We will start with **Figure 4.1**.

Figure 4.1 shows us graphs of three different products, each with a different elasticity. In all three cases, the price drops from $6 to $5 so that, both the absolute change ($1) and the percentage change (18.18 percent, (1/5.5 × 100) is the same. However, the impact on quantity demanded is very different in each case.

In the case of **Figure 4.1A**, the quantity demanded has only changed by 9.52 percent (5/52.5 × 100), just over a half of the price change in percentage terms. This means that the demand is inelastic with a coefficient equal to 0.52 (9.52/18.18) As a result, the demand curve plots as a fairly steep demand curve.

With **Figure 4.1B**, the percentage change in quantity of 18.18 percent (10/55 × 100) is exactly equal to the percentage change in price. The result is an elasticity coefficient of 1 and is, therefore, unitary elastic. (Note that the resulting demand curve is not a 45–degree line but a rectangular parabola.)

Finally, the curve in **Figure 4.1C** is fairly flat and illustrates the fact that the demand here is elastic. In the case of this third product, the percentage change in quantity of 46.15 percent (30/65 × 100) far exceeds the 18.18 percent change in the price. Its coefficient is equal to 2.54.

L02 Understand the relationship between the slope of a demand curve and elasticity and how this affects the total revenue of the producer.

FIGURE 4.1   Three Different Elasticities

Figure A

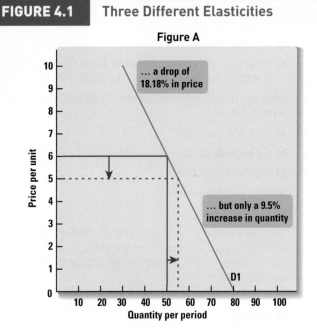

Figure B

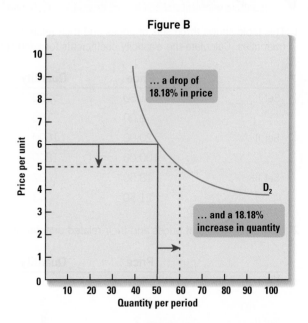

Figure A depicts an inelastic (steep) demand curve showing that the percentage change in quantity is far smaller the percentage change in price. In Figure B, the price and quantity change by equal percentages and the elasticity is equal to 1 (unitary). Figure C depicts an elastic (flat) demand curve. In this case, the percentage change in quantity is greater than the percentage change in price.

Figure C

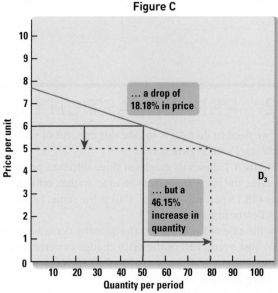

Although it is possible to identify the elasticity of demand in terms of the slope, we must be very careful here, since the slope of a demand curve is not the same thing as elasticity. Let us explain this important point using the example in **Table 4.4**.

Note how total revenue *rises* as price decreases from $10 to a price of $5. Since price is falling and total revenue is rising, we know this means that demand must be elastic. This is confirmed by the elasticity coefficients in the last column. Further, as price continues to fall from $5 to $0, total revenue *falls*, indicating that demand is inelastic in this range of the demand curve. The price/quantity combination of $5 and 5 units is also of particular interest because total revenue is at its maximum.

It is also evident that this $5 price is the midpoint of the demand curve. This is no coincidence. If total revenue ceases to rise as price falls, we can no longer be on the elastic portion of the demand curve. If total revenue has not yet begun to fall as price decreases, we cannot yet be

TABLE 4.4		Demand, Total Revenue, and Elasticity Schedule		
Price	Quantity	Total Revenue (price × quantity)	Elasticity	
$10	0	0		
9	1	9	19.0	Elastic
8	2	16		
7	3	21	3.0	
6	4	24		
5	5	25	1.0	Unitary
4	6	24		
3	7	21		
2	8	16	0.33	Inelastic
1	9	9		
0	10	0	0.05	

on the inelastic portion of the demand curve. Thus, if demand is no longer >1 and not yet <1, then it can only be exactly equal to 1. From this we can conclude that:

The upper half of any straight-line demand curve is elastic and the lower half is inelastic.

Furthermore, the midpoint is where we experience unitary elasticity. You will recall that this means that the percentage change in quantity is exactly equal to percentage change in price, and thus, total revenue does not change. As we can see, it also means that at this point total revenue is at a maximum.

These ideas are graphed in **Figure 4.2**.

Here, we see that at the top of the demand curve, the demand is very elastic (at its extreme, infinite). As the price drops, so, too, does the elasticity. And as the bottom graph shows, as the price drops, total revenue rises. At the midpoint of the demand curve, elasticity is one (unitary elasticity) and total revenue is at its maximum. Thereafter, as the price drops, both elasticity and total revenue fall until they are equal to zero at price zero.

It is clear, then, that the slope of the demand curve is not the same thing as its elasticity, and as we have seen, elasticity itself has different values at different points on the demand curve. Given that, you might ask why we earlier suggested that a product with an elastic demand curve has a flat demand curve and one with an inelastic demand has a steep curve. The answer is that when we look at a shallow-sloped demand curve, such as D_1 in **Figure 4.3**, what we are looking at is the upper half of what would be a much longer curve if it were extended all the way to the horizontal axis of the graph.

Since the upper half of any straight-line demand curve is the elastic portion, we can look at D_1 and say that it is an elastic demand curve because we know that the lower half of the curve (most of which we do not see) is the inelastic portion. Similarly, when we look at D_2, we are looking at the lower portion of a much longer demand curve, and this lower portion is inelastic.

Let us finish off this section by looking at the full range of price elasticities in **Figure 4.4**. The perfectly inelastic demand plots as a vertical line which shows that a change in price has zero effect upon quantity demanded. Demands with elasticities between zero and 1 are inelastic. A unitary elastic demand, that is, with an elasticity of one, plots as a curve called a rectangular hyperbola. The essence of this curve is that every price/quantity combination produces the same total revenue. The demands for products with elasticities above one are elastic. At its extreme of infinite elasticity, the demand is said to be perfectly elastic. Such a demand plots as a horizontal straight line which shows that even a small change in price produces an infinite change in quantity.

FIGURE 4.2   Elasticity and Total Revenue

In Figure A, at the top half of the demand curve, the demand is elastic. Figure B shows that as the price drops from $10 to $5, total revenue increases. At the midpoint, at a price of $5, demand is unitary and total revenue is maximum. As prices are reduced below $5, Figure A shows that demand is inelastic, and Figure B shows that total revenue falls.

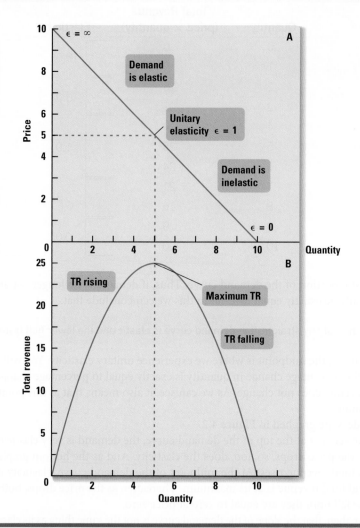

FIGURE 4.3   Elastic and Inelastic Demand Curves

Demand curve D₁ is the elastic (upper) portion of a curve that could be extended downward, and D₂ is the inelastic (lower) portion of a demand curve that could be extended upward.

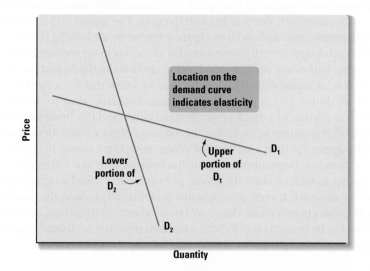

FIGURE 4.4	**Range of Elasticities**

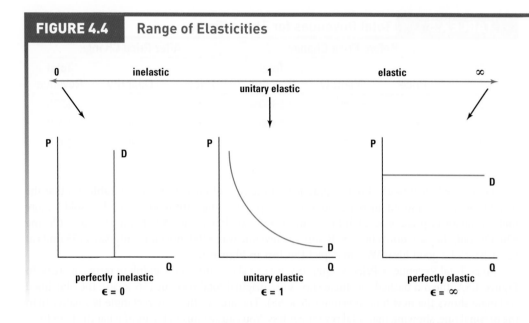

A vertical demand curve illustrates a perfectly inelastic demand. The centre graph shows a rectangular hyperbola illustrating unitary elasticity. The right graph shows a horizontal line illustrating a perfectly elastic demand.

✓ SELF-TEST

5. a) Graph a demand curve using the data from the accompanying demand schedule (make each square on both axes equal to 2).

b) What is the slope of this demand curve?

c) How could you demonstrate that the elasticity of demand was not the same as the slope?

Price	Quantity
1	18
2	16
3	14
4	12
5	10
6	8
7	6
8	4
9	2

Elasticity and Total Revenue, Graphically

We have seen the importance of price elasticity to business. Whether a firm's total revenue will increase or decrease as the result of a price change depends solely on the elasticity of demand of the product. We can graphically show this impact. Let us revisit our earlier **Figure 4.1** graph. In this example, we looked at three totally different products made by three different firms, as shown in **Table 4.5**.

The only things that the firms have in common is the fact the price of each of their products happens to be $6 and they are each selling 50 units of their products. In other words, the initial total revenues of the three firms is $300 each ($6 × 50). Now, suppose that each firm decides to decrease the price of its product to $5 in an effort to increase sales. Each firm is willing, in effect, to lose $1 on the sale of all its units (it must sell them all at the same lower price) in order to sell more units. Each firm is gambling that the loss of $50 ($1 each on the 50 units they normally sell) will be more than offset by the gain in revenue from selling more units.

TABLE 4.5	Total Revenues for Three Firms					
	Before Price Change			**After Price Change**		
	Price	Quantity	Total Revenue	Price	Quantity	Total Revenue
Firm 1	$6	50	$300	$5	55	$275
Firm 2	$6	50	$300	$5	60	$300
Firm 3	$6	50	$300	$5	80	$400

Let us see how it worked out in practice. In the case of Firm 1, we see in **Table 4.5** that the quantity sold does, indeed, increase, but only by a paltry 5 units, from 50 to 55. They sold 5 more units at the lower price of $5 each for a gain of $25. So, they gained $25 but at the cost of losing $50. Overall, they are down by $25. Before, its revenue was $300; now it is only $275 (55 units at $5 each). Not a good idea! We can depict this loss in **Figure 4.5**.

Since Total Revenue = Price × Quantity, we can show this on the graph in terms of areas. In **Figure 4.5A**, the red dashed rectangle shows the original total revenue ($6 × 50); the blue lined rectangle shows the new total revenue ($5 × 55). The area of the new rectangle is smaller than the original one, showing that total revenue is less. You can see this in terms of what the firm loses in revenue and what it gains as a result of lowering the price. In **Figure 4.5A**, the top wedge shows the loss in revenue as a result of dropping the price; the amount is $1 × 50, or $50. The gain is the vertical wedge and is equal to $5 × 5, or $25. The gain of $25 is less than the loss of $50. Overall the firm loses $25 in total revenue.

Figure 4.5B illustrates the gain and loss in revenue when the elasticity of demand is unitary. Here, we see that the loss in total revenue of $50 ($1 × 50) is exactly equal to the gain in total revenue of $50 (10 × $5). The area lost is exactly equal to the area gained. The result is no change in total revenue.

In the final graph, **Figure 4.5C**, the gain in total revenue of $150 (30 × $5) far exceeds the loss of $50 ($1 × 50). The overall gain, therefore, is $100. This illustrates an elastic demand. In summary then:

> A drop in price will decrease total revenue if the demand is inelastic, increase total revenue if the demand is elastic, and leave it unchanged if the demand is unitary elastic.

Conversely:

> An increase in price will increase total revenue if the demand is inelastic, decrease total revenue if the demand is elastic, and leave it unchanged if the demand is unitary elastic.

FIGURE 4.5   Loss and Gain in Total Revenue

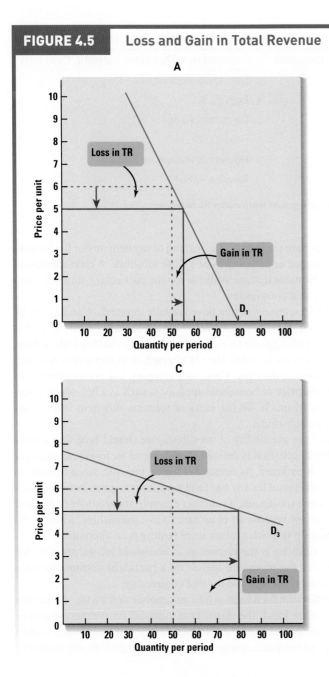

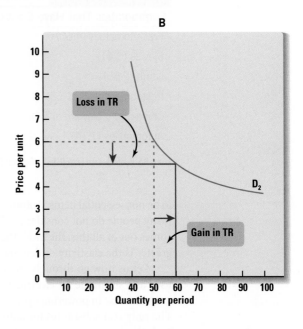

Figure A shows an inelastic demand. The loss in TR from the price fall is greater than the gain. In Figure B, the demand is unitary and the gain and loss are equal. In Figure C, an elastic demand, the gain is greater than the loss.

4.3   DETERMINANTS OF PRICE ELASTICITY

Before we examine the determinants of elasticity, let us look at **Table 4.6**, which identifies some commodities that typically have elastic demands and some that typically have inelastic demands.

A major determinant of price elasticity is the *availability of close substitutes*. For example, in most people's eyes, almost any other vegetable is a substitute for tomatoes. Home videos and other forms of entertainment are substitutes for movies, whereas pork and beef are close substitutes for lamb. The substitute for a restaurant meal is one cooked at home. Many households find that the substitute for furniture or china and tableware is to simply make do with less of what many consider

L03 Understand the determinants of price elasticity of demand.

TABLE 4.6	Examples of Products with Different Elasticities of Demand
Commodities That Have Elastic Demands	**Commodities That Have Inelastic Demands**
Fresh tomatoes (4.60)	Household electricity (0.13)
Movies (3.41)	Eggs (0.32)
Lamb (2.65)	Car repairs (0.36)
Restaurant meals (1.63)	Food (0.58)
China and tableware (1.54)	Household appliances (0.63)
Automobiles (1.14)	Tobacco (0.86)

Source: H.S. Houthakker and Lester D. Taylor, *Consumer Demand in the United States* (Cambridge, MA: Harvard University Press, 1970).

to be non-essential items. Automobiles have the least elastic demand of any item on our list because many people do not consider public transit or bicycling to be a close substitute. A clear conclusion comes out of all this: the more the substitutes that are available for any particular commodity, the greater is the elasticity of demand for that commodity.

Let us now go through the list of commodities that have inelastic demands. Candles can be used as a substitute for electric light, but this is not an attractive option to most people. (And it is not much use in powering up a computer!) Eggs are an essential ingredient in baking and cooking. The only real substitutes for auto repairs are to repair the car yourself or to buy a new one, and both these options are impractical most of the time. Food, as a category, has no substitutes. To most families, significant swings in the price of household appliances such as a hot-water heater will not change the quantity demanded much. To the users of tobacco, this item involves an addiction for which there is simply no substitute.

Before leaving this discussion of the availability of substitutes, we should note that a great deal depends on how the commodity in question is defined. The demand for food is an example of a broadly defined category and as mentioned, its demand is highly inelastic, since there is no substitute for food. Yet, the elasticity of demand for any one food item, such as green beans, is much more elastic because there are many close substitutes. As another example, the elasticity of demand for accommodation is generally quite low because all of us have to live somewhere, whereas the elasticity of demand for home ownership is much greater, since renting is an alternative.

A second determinant of price elasticity is the *percentage of household income spent on the commodity*. In general, we can say that the more one spends on a particular commodity (as a percentage of income), the more elastic is the demand for that commodity.

For this reason, the elasticity of demand for a high-priced automobile or for a top-of-the-line stereo system will be high. On the other hand, the elasticity of demand for ordinary spices or hand soap will tend to be inelastic, simply because the total percentage of a household's budget that is spent on such items is small and the price change will have little impact on our budgets.

 ADDED DIMENSION   What Is a Necessity?

It is not uncommon for people to think of products as either luxuries or necessities, so it is tempting to conclude that luxury products are elastic in demand, and necessities must be inelastic. While there is undoubtedly validity in this rule of thumb, we must be careful. To some, wine with a meal is an absolute necessity, whereas to others, it is a seldom-bought luxury. What really matters when we are talking about the elasticity of demand is

that we are looking at market demand, that is, the preferences of the majority of people.

We must also be careful in assessing products such as cigarettes. We know that the price elasticity of demand for cigarettes is very low. Does this mean that they must be a necessity? No, of course not. The low price elasticity simply reflects that fact that there are no close substitutes for cigarettes.

The third determinant of price elasticity involves the *amount of time that has elapsed since the price change.* The classic example here is that of oil. When the Organization of Petroleum Exporting Countries (OPEC) oil embargo of 1973 resulted in the halting of (most) oil shipments to North America, the price of oil increased fourfold in just eighteen months. Measurements of elasticity made over this period of time indicated a very inelastic demand. This was because in the immediate aftermath of such a price shock, very few close substitutes for oil were available. But North Americans (as well as most people around the world) soon became far more energy-conscious and began to find ways to conserve fuel by turning down thermostats and water temperatures in the home and becoming less dependent on the automobile by finding other ways to commute, shop, and take holidays.

When it became apparent that high oil prices were becoming a permanent fact of life, alternative energy sources, such as coal, nuclear, and solar, were explored, and in some countries, windmills started to dot the landscape. As well, oil drilling was embarked upon in some of the less accessible regions of the world, such as the North Atlantic Ocean and the Canadian Arctic. Finally, the North American love affair with big, gas-guzzling automobiles came to an end as smaller, more fuel-efficient cars were introduced. Subsequent measurements of the elasticity of demand for oil ten years after the price shock showed elasticity coefficients that were much higher than those taken in the first eighteen months. All of this can lead us to conclude that the longer the period that is involved, the greater the elasticity of demand tends to be. In summary, the more elastic the demand for a product:

- the more similar and the more available are the number of available substitutes
- the larger is the percentage of one's income that is spent on the product
- the longer is the period involved

 SELF-TEST

6. Imagine that elasticity coefficients were recently measured in Canada over a period of one year for the following products. Indicate whether you think such a measurement would be elastic (>1) or inelastic (<1).

a) Sugar

b) Gasoline

c) Ocean cruises

d) Restaurant meals

e) Women's hats

f) Alcohol

4.4 APPLICATIONS OF PRICE ELASTICITY

Who Pays Sales Taxes?

Sales taxes can take the form of a tax imposed by (federal or provincial) governments on a *specific* product, such as alcohol, gasoline, or cigarettes (these are often referred to as **excise taxes**). Sales taxes can also take the form of a *general* tax on a wide category of goods, as in the case of the Goods and Services Tax (GST) and the Harmonized Sales Tax (HST) recently introduced in five Canadian Provinces. In all cases, the tax is calculated as a percentage of the sales price of the product. It is the seller who is, by law, responsible for collecting these taxes and actually sending the money to government. But who really pays these taxes—the seller or the consumer? Most people believe it is the consumer because they assume that the seller simply adds whatever amount the tax might be on to the price of the product and thus passes the tax on to the buyer. But is this correct?

L04 Use real-world examples to demonstrate that the concept of elasticity is a powerful tool.

excise tax: a sales tax imposed on a particular product.

		Quantity Supplied	Quantity Supplied
Price	Quantity Demanded	(before tax)	(after tax)
5	8	2	0
6	7	3	1
7	6	4	2
8	**5**	**5**	**3**
9	**4**	6	**4**
10	3	7	5
11	2	8	6

TABLE 4.7   Demand and Supply of Movie Tickets, before and after Tax

We can use basic supply-and-demand analysis and the concept of price elasticity of demand to answer this question. The first three columns of **Table 4.7** show the supply and demand for movie tickets before the imposition of an excise tax. The equilibrium price is initially $8 and the equilibrium quantity is five million tickets.

These are plotted in **Figure 4.6**, where the intersection of D and S_1 shows the initial equilibrium.

Now, suppose that government imposes an excise tax of $2 on each movie ticket. How will the movie theatre market be affected? Well, initially, the ticket price will increase from $8 to $10. Now, how many movie tickets would theatre owners be prepared to sell at $10? Since the theatre owners will have to remit $2 to the government, they will still only receive revenue of $8. The answer then is that they will supply the same number of tickets (and seats)—5 million, at the after-tax price of $10, as they did when the price was $8 and there was no tax. In **Table 4.7**, therefore, we have added a fourth column showing the supply of tickets if the price now includes the $2 tax. We can see there that if the price is $10 and there is no tax, 7 million tickets would be offered; but if the price is $10 but this includes the $2 tax, then they would only offer 5 million tickets. Effectively then, the quantities supplied in the table shift down by two rows ($2) after the imposition of the tax. In graphical terms, as we see in **Figure 4.6**, the new supply curve (supply$_{+ tax}$) shifts upward or to the left. This says that at a price of $10 the theatre owners will make five million tickets available, just as they did when the price was $8 with no tax.

FIGURE 4.6   The Effect of an Excise Tax on the Price and Quantity of Movie Tickets

The effect of a $2 per ticket excise tax is to shift the supply curve up from S_1 to S_{+tax}. The result is that equilibrium price increases from $8 to $9 and equilibrium quantity decreases from 5 million to 4 million tickets per month.

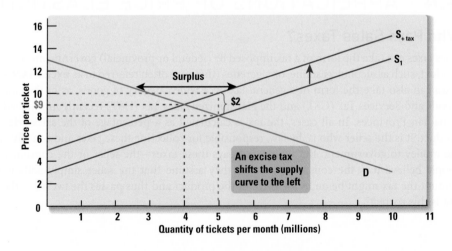

In summary, then, the imposition of a tax will shift the supply curve to the left (or up) by the amount of the tax. But what about the demand? How is that affected by the imposition of the tax? It is not, in the sense that there is no shift in the demand curve. But customers will certainly react—and none too favourably—to the $2 increase in ticket prices caused by the new tax. According to both the table and the graph, the quantity demanded at $10 will be only 3 million tickets, leaving a surplus of 2 million tickets (and 2 million empty seats). This will eventually cause the theatre owners to reduce prices, and in our example, they will continue to drop prices until the price is $9. At this new equilibrium price, the quantity demanded and supplied will be 4 million tickets.

So, who ended up paying the $2 tax? In this case, and almost always, the answer is that it is shared between the buyers and the sellers. Movie goers are now paying an extra dollar as a result of the tax. And what about theatre owners? Well, previously they were receiving $8 in revenue for each ticket. Now they receive $9 (the new equilibrium price), but of this, they have to send $2 to the tax department. So, they end up with only $7—$1 less than before. It, therefore, "costs" movie goers $1 and theatre owners $1. They share the tax 50/50.

But is it always the case that they end up each paying a half? Not at all. We obtained this particular result because we assumed that the demand for movie tickets is elastic and drew our demand curve accordingly. If demand was inelastic, we would have obtained a different result. We can see this in **Figure 4.7**. In both graphs, the shift in supply, S_1 to S_{+tax}, is the same. However, the demand D_1 in graph A is inelastic, whereas demand D_2 in graph B is elastic. The initial price in both instances is the same. But note how much more price increases in the circumstances illustrated in graph A compared with that in graph B. Since the price increase is a result of the sales tax, consumers are paying a larger percentage of the tax in graph A than they are in graph B. It follows that the larger the percentage paid by the consumers, the smaller the percentage of the tax paid by the sellers of the product.

Thus, we can generalize to say:

> The more inelastic the demand for a product, the larger is the percentage of a sales (or excise) tax the consumer will pay.

Another way to look at this is that since there are few substitutes for products with inelastic demand, the higher price will not have a big effect on consumers and they will be more willing to pay a larger percentage of the tax and a higher price.

FIGURE 4.7   The Effect of an Excise Tax on Two Different Demand Curves

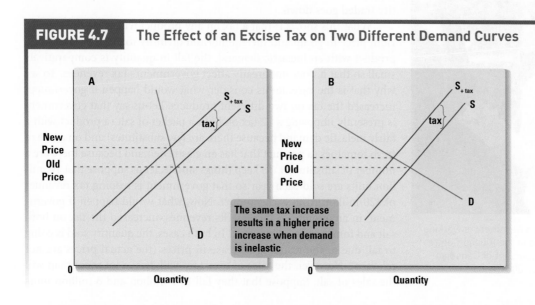

Here, the supply curve shifts by the same amount, from S to S_{+tax}, in both graph A and graph B as a result of the imposition of a sales tax. The two demands, however, are quite different—inelastic in the case of graph A and elastic in the case of graph B. The resulting increase in price is much greater in graph A than in graph B.

✓ SELF-TEST

7. The accompanying graph shows the demand and supply for headphones.

a) What are equilibrium price and quantity, assuming demand schedule D and supply schedule S?

b) Suppose that a $30-per-unit excise tax was placed on this product. Draw in the new supply curve labelled S_{+tax}.

c) What are the new equilibrium price and quantity?

d) What proportion of the tax is paid by the consumer, and what proportion is paid by the seller in this case?

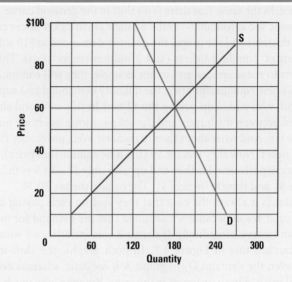

Why do Governments Impose "Sin Taxes"?

The price of cigarettes in Canada today ranges from $5 to nearly $10 per pack—the price varies because both the federal and provincial governments impose taxes and the rate of taxation varies from province to province. Generally, the tax on a pack of cigarettes is between $4 and $5. In addition, about 80 percent of the price of beer, wine, and other types of alcohol is tax.

The reason for these high "sin taxes," as they are called, is not complicated. Both these products have very inelastic demand, and governments discovered, a long time ago, that they could raise their tax revenues by simply raising the tax rate.

A block from Parliament, where government is working on antismoking legislation, teens in the Rideau Centre shopping mall light up. Thirteen percent of Canadian teenagers smoke, according to a 2009 Canadian Tobacco Use Monitoring Survey.

The graphical effect of increasing the tax rate on a product with an inelastic demand is illustrated in **Figure 4.8**. A higher tax rate shifts the supply curve to the left, and the price goes up much more than the quantity traded goes down.

What this shows is that a tax on any product will cause the equilibrium price to go up and the equilibrium quantity to fall. However, for a product with an inelastic demand, the fall in quantity is comparatively small so that it does not greatly affect government's tax revenues. To see why that is the case, let us consider what would happen if government increased the tax on two different products. Let us say that government is presently imposing a $2 tax on both a packet of salt (a product with a fairly inelastic demand because there are few substitutes) and on a kilo of fresh tomatoes (a product that has an elastic demand because there are a number of substitutes). To keep things simple, let us suppose that 10 million units are sold each year so that government is reaping tax revenues of $20 million from each product. Now, what would happen if government, in an attempt to increase its revenues, increased the tax on both salt and tomatoes by $1 per unit? In both cases, the quantity sold is going to fall due to the resulting increase in prices (the actual prices are not relevant). However, the sales of tomatoes will drop a lot more than will the sales of salt. Suppose that they fall to 9 million and 6 million units

FIGURE 4.8	The Effect of an Increase in the Tax on Cigarettes

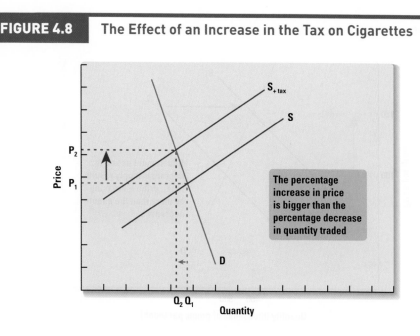

The percentage increase in price is bigger than the percentage decrease in quantity traded

An increase in the tax on cigarettes has the effect of shifting the supply curve to the left, from S to S_{+tax}. Since the demand for cigarettes is inelastic, the resulting increase in price, P_1 to P_2, is greater than the decrease in the quantity demanded, Q_1 to Q_2.

respectively. The result is an increase in the tax revenue of $7 million ($20 to $27 million) in the case of the salt, but a drop in tax revenue of $2 million (from $20 to $18 million) in the case of the tomatoes. We can summarise the results in **Table 4.8.**

TABLE 4.8	The Effect of a $1 Increase in the Tax on Salt and Tomatoes

Tax Revenues before the Tax Increase:	
Salt	**Tomatoes**
10 million units @ $2 each = $20 million	10 million units @ $2 each = $20 million
Tax Revenues after the Tax Increase:	
9 million units @ $3 each = $27 million	6 million units @ $3 each = $18 million

It is clear, then, that if a government wants to maximize its tax revenues, it is better to impose taxes on those products that have inelastic demands: cigarettes, alcohol, and gasoline. (They seldom tax salt these days, though Britain infamously taxed salt during its colonial rule of India.)

In summary, we can conclude that although some members of government may have a genuine concern for people's health, the main reason governments put "sin" taxes on goods with inelastic demands is because they can increase their tax revenues.

Why Might a War on Drugs Increase Crime Rates?

Most people feel that crime rates in North American society are high and seem to rise year after year. Furthermore, the effects of crime appear to be spreading into the middle class and are no longer confined to the underworld. The mood of the general public is becoming more intolerant of all this, and some politicians are responding by calling for tougher laws against criminal activity. The criminal activity that often gets targeted in any get-tough-on-crime campaign is the selling of illegal drugs, such as cocaine and heroin.

What is ignored in any such anticrime policy is the fact that heroin and cocaine have highly inelastic demands. This has serious consequences when we consider that even if the anticrime policy is effective, the supply of illegal drugs will not be eliminated. This is illustrated in **Figure 4.9.**

FIGURE 4.9   The Cocaine Market

If D_1 and S_1 are the demand and supply curves for cocaine, the equilibrium price and quantity will be $100 per gram and 500 000 grams per week. A campaign against the drug trade will reduce the supply of cocaine: that is, the supply curve will shift to the left, as in S_2. This will greatly increase the price to $180.

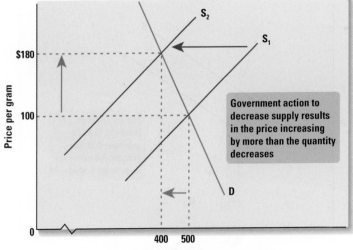

Government action to decrease supply results in the price increasing by more than the quantity decreases

Drug paraphernalia, including cocaine on a mirror, a razor, marijuana, and a pipe.

Let us assume that D_1 is the (inelastic) demand for cocaine and that S_1 is the original supply that results in a price of $100 per gram and a quantity traded of 500 000 grams per week. Next, let us assume that government launches a campaign to crack down on drug imports with the result that the supply decreases, as illustrated by the curve shifting back to S_2. This causes the price of cocaine to rise to $180 per gram, while the quantity demanded decreases to 400 000 grams per week.

So, the quantity of heroin on the streets is reduced a little. However, what is important in all this is the amount that is spent by the consumers of cocaine in the two instances. When the price is $100 per gram, a total of $50 million per week is spent ($100 × 500 000), while $72 million is spent after the rise in price caused by the decrease in supply ($180 × 400 000). A large percentage of this money is obtained by the users of cocaine through various types of crime, such as robberies, car thefts, muggings, and holdups, as well as white-collar crimes such as embezzlement and fraud. In our example, $22 million more per week is spent on cocaine than before the decrease in supply. We would have to conclude that it is highly likely that more crime will be committed to obtain these additional funds.

What we are left with is the seeming paradox that this policy aimed at reducing crime, in fact, increases the incidence of crime. This provides an insight into why some types of crime seem to continue to rise despite (or because of?) our anticrime policies and the efforts of our police forces.

When Is a Good Harvest Bad for Farmers?

A good harvest is one in which crop yields are high and farmers are able to bring large quantities of what they grow to market. For example, a typical wheat farmer might harvest 20 000 bushels in an average year, whereas in a good year, he might harvest 25 000 bushels. Would not a good harvest then be cause for celebration on the part of the farmer? Not necessarily, and the reason involves the price elasticity of demand.

FIGURE 4.10   The Effect of a Good Harvest on the Wheat Market

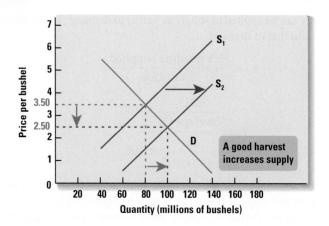

A good harvest increases the supply of wheat and shifts the supply curve from S_1 to S_2. Given the inelastic demand for wheat, the decrease in price is substantial and the total revenue going to farmers as a group decreases.

The elasticity of demand for some agricultural products is certainly elastic—tomatoes, lettuce, and plums, for example—since there are many close substitutes available. However, the elasticity of demand for the more basic commodities, such as wheat, is more inelastic.

If we combine an inelastic demand with the fact that a good harvest would increase supply and shift the supply curve to the right and thus decrease price, the total revenue that would flow to the farmers as a group would decline. This is illustrated in **Figure 4.10**. Here, we see that the equilibrium price and quantity in a normal year is $3.50 per bushel and 80 million bushels. This would give wheat farmers total revenue of $280 million (the red dashed rectangle). In a good harvest year, the supply curve shifts to the right, and the new equilibrium price and quantity are $2.50 and 100 million bushels (the blue lined rectangle). This results in price dropping far more than the quantity increases so that the total revenue decreases to $250 million. The good harvest results in farmers losing $30 million in revenue. This illustrates the old adage that farmers ask the gods for a poor harvest—for everyone except themselves.

 ## SELF-TEST

8. The data on the right are for economy-line bicycles.

a) What are the equilibrium price and quantity?

b) What is the total expenditure (= total revenue) at equilibrium?

c) If the supply were increased by 50 percent, what would be the new equilibrium price and quantity?

d) What is the total expenditure (= total revenue) at this new equilibrium?

e) What is the price elasticity of demand between these two equilibrium points?

Quantity Demanded (D_1) per Week	Price per Unit	Quantity Supplied (S_1) per Week
2 000 000	$260	800 000
1 800 000	320	1 200 000
1 600 000	380	1 600 000
1 400 000	440	2 000 000
1 200 000	500	2 400 000

4.5 OTHER ELASTICITY MEASURES

L05 Understand the meaning and significance of elasticity of supply, income elasticity, and cross-elasticity of demand.

elasticity of supply: the responsiveness of quantity supplied to a change in price.

The concept of elasticity can be applied to supply as well as to demand. The definition of **elasticity of supply** is analogous to that of demand.

$$\epsilon_s = \frac{\%\Delta \text{ quantity supplied}}{\%\Delta \text{ price}} \qquad [4.4]$$

$$\epsilon_s = \frac{\dfrac{\Delta Q_s}{\text{average } Q_s} \times 100}{\dfrac{\Delta P}{\text{average } P} \times 100} \qquad [4.5]$$

As we did with the demand curve, we can make some generalizations about the elasticity of supply from the position and slope of the curve as seen in **Figure 4.11**.

Here, we have two supply curves, S_1 and S_2, and a common price change from \$2 to \$3. In the case of supply curve S_1, the quantity supplied rises from 400 to 500, and in the case of supply curve S_2, the quantity supplied almost doubles from 800 to 1400. We can, therefore, legitimately conclude that the elasticity of supply of S_2 must be larger than that in S_1. In the case of S_1, the supply elasticity equals:

$$\frac{\dfrac{100}{450} \times 100}{\dfrac{1}{2.5} \times 100} = \frac{+22.2\%}{+40\%} = +0.55$$

And for S_2, its supply elasticity is:

$$\frac{\dfrac{600}{1100} \times 100}{\dfrac{1}{2.5} \times 100} = \frac{+54.5\%}{+40\%} = +1.36$$

FIGURE 4.11	**Elasticity of Supply**

Supply curve S_1 is inelastic, as can be seen from the fact that only a small quantity change (from 400 to 500) results from the price increasing from \$2 to \$3. S_2, on the other hand, is an elastic supply curve, since quantity increases from 800 to 1400 as a result of the same price increase.

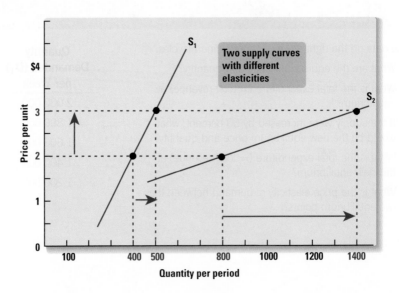

This allows us to generalize that the elasticity of supply of more shallow curves is greater than that of steeper curves, although we again caution that elasticity does change as we move along any supply curve, just as it did in the case of the demand curve. Given that producers would like to increase the quantity they supply as much as they can in response to an increase in price, what might explain the kind of difference in response indicated by S_1 and S_2? The first possible explanation involves the *level of technology* in use. If it is a sophisticated technology, such as one that requires complicated tool and die making, then S_1 is probably more representative. The use of a very simple technology, such as in cardboard carton production, would more likely be represented by S_2. Implied in this explanation, however, is an even more important determinant of supply elasticity, and that is the *time involved.*

Alfred Marshall recognized the importance of time in the determination of supply elasticity with his famous fish market example. In **Figure 4.12A** we see a perfectly inelastic supply curve. This represents what Marshall called the *momentary market period*; it is now usually referred to simply as the *market period*. As an example, he talked about the day's catch of fish, in the quantity of Q_1, having been landed at the docks. This is all the fish that will be supplied until the next day (momentary supply), no matter how high the price might go. Marshall called the supply curve S_2 in **Figure 4.13B** the *short-run supply curve*; it is more elastic than S_1 and is reflective of the various responses that fishers might be able to make in the short run to a higher price. This might include hiring extra crew, staying out longer, or using more nets. The supply curve in **Figure 4.13C** is the *long-run supply curve*, reflecting long-term adjustments to higher price, such as training additional crew and building more boats, which could take a number of months to accomplish.

FIGURE 4.12   **Supply Elasticity in Three Periods**

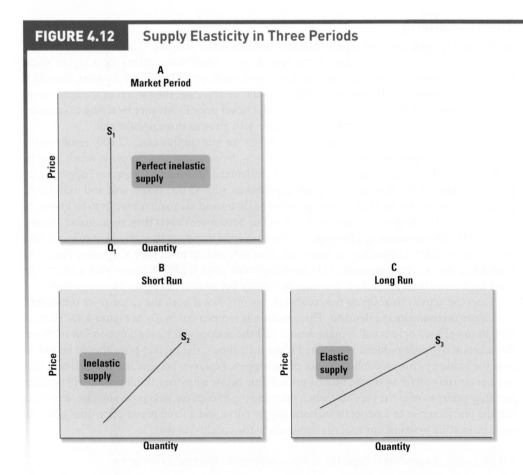

Supply is perfectly inelastic in graph A. Marshall called this the *momentary or market period.* In graph B, the short run, supply is still inelastic but not perfectly inelastic. In graph C, the long run, supply is elastic.

ADDED DIMENSION   Supply Elasticity for Milk

The *International Farm Comparison Network* released a study of supply elasticities in various countries in 2005. The data collected covered a three-year period and included the following:

U.S.	0.86
U.K.	0.70
Netherlands	0.37
Canada	0.34
Poland	0.27

You will notice that all five of these elasticity measures are less than one, which means that the supply elasticity of milk is generally inelastic.

From Marshall's fish market example, we can conclude that:

> The longer the time frame involved, the more elastic will be the supply.

 SELF-TEST

9. Calculate the price elasticity of supply in the $2 to $3 range if the quantity supplied increases from 35 to 45.

Ticket Scalping

An interesting application of supply elasticity involves ticket scalping. This occurs when individuals who have purchased tickets at the regular price resell those tickets for a higher price. Consider any popular event, such as a hockey playoff game or a high-profile concert, for which only a limited number of tickets are available for sale. In this case, the owners of the home team (or the promoters of the event) must set the regular ticket price in advance by trying to estimate, as best they can, the demand for the event. **Figure 4.13** gives us three possibilities.

The fact that there is a limited number of tickets for sale (in this case, 17 000) results in the supply curve being perfectly inelastic, as reflected by S_1. Now, assume that the price, which must be fixed before the tickets go on sale, is set at $40. If the demand for tickets to this event happens to be that represented by D_1, then we would have equilibrium with 17 000 tickets sold and would congratulate the promoters for their correct guesstimate. If, instead, demand turns out to be higher, as represented by D_2, the general public will wish to buy 5000 more tickets than are available for sale. These are the circumstances of a shortage that ticket scalpers thrive on; they get in line to buy tickets as early as possible and then buy as many tickets as they can, to resell later at a higher price. (As **Figure 4.13** shows, with a demand of D_2, the equilibrium price is $80.) Whether such activity is or is not legal varies from province to province in Canada but undoubtedly goes on everywhere.

Does the activity of scalping tickets always pay off? Not if both the ticket-price setters and the scalper overestimate the demand. This situation is represented by D_3 in **Figure 4.13**. Here, at the $40 price, 3000 tickets will remain unsold and the scalper will have no option but to dump the tickets at a greatly reduced price. (As **Figure 4.13** shows, the market price should be $15 to clear the market.) This probably does not often happen, however, because there is evidence that event organizers prefer to set the official price a little below what they think people will actually pay; they prefer to reap the publicity when there are big lineups for tickets. In any case, it is clear that the phenomenon of a perfectly inelastic supply curve and a fixed preset price does generate some interesting twists in our analysis and leads to the conclusion that:

> If the supply of a product is fixed, the demand determines the equilibrium price.

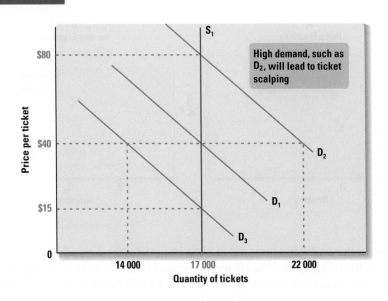

FIGURE 4.13   Perfectly Inelastic Supply

High demand, such as D₂, will lead to ticket scalping

A concert hall or hockey rink has a fixed number of seats, which gives us the perfectly inelastic supply curve. Here, the price per seat is preset at $40. If demand turns out to be exactly as indicated by D_1, this $40 price will be equilibrium. If, however, demand turns out to be higher than anticipated, D_2, 5000 people who wanted tickets will have to do without. Finally, if demand proves to be that represented by D_3, there will be unsold seats for the event.

 SELF-TEST

10. Leonard Cohen is scheduled to perform at Centennial Hall, which seats 5000. Ticket prices for this one-night concert are set at $50 each and go on sale two weeks in advance.

a) Suppose that many more than 5000 people want a ticket at the set price. Draw a graph showing both the supply curve and the demand curve.

b) Is the ticket price above or below the equilibrium price?

Income Elasticity

As we have seen, the concept of price elasticity of demand involves the responsiveness of the quantity demanded to a change in price. Another important idea is the responsiveness of quantity demanded to a change in income (with the price being held constant), which is called **income elasticity** (of demand). In the case of price elasticity, our measurement involves moving up or down on a single demand curve as illustrated in **Figure 4.14A**; with income elasticity, the whole demand curve shifts, since, as you recall from Chapter 2, a change in income causes a change in demand.

The increase in the quantity demanded in **Figure 4.14B** is a result of the shift in the demand curve from D_1 to D_2, and the higher the income elasticity, the greater this shift will be.

Measuring the coefficient of income elasticity is much like measuring the coefficient of price elasticity.

income elasticity: the responsiveness of quantity demanded to a change in income.

$$\epsilon_Y = \frac{\%\Delta \text{ quantity demanded } (Q_d)}{\%\Delta \text{ income } (Y)} \qquad [4.6]$$

$$\epsilon_Y = \frac{\dfrac{\Delta Q_d}{\text{average } Q_d} \times 100}{\dfrac{\Delta Y}{\text{average } Y} \times 100} \qquad [4.7]$$

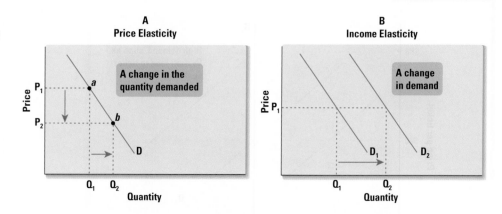

FIGURE 4.14   Price Elasticity and Income Elasticity

In Figure A, the movement along the demand curve from point *a* to point *b* involves the price elasticity of demand. In contrast, income elasticity of demand involves a shift in the demand curve, such as D_1 to D_2 in Figure B.

Once again, if this coefficient turns out to be greater than 1, the demand is said to be *income elastic*; if it is less than 1 but greater than 0, we say demand is *income inelastic*. Examples of products that tend to be income elastic are air travel, restaurant meals, hairstyling services, and private swimming pools. Examples of products that tend to be income inelastic are tobacco, food, newspapers, and telephone hookups.

If these examples suggest to you that the distinction between products that are income elastic and income inelastic is one of luxuries and necessities, you are correct. Households with limited income tend to buy only necessities. If the household's income rises, almost all of that additional income would be spent on the luxuries that previously could not be purchased. An undeniable characteristic of a post-industrial economy is that as income rises the percentage of total consumption of services rises, while that of physical goods declines. This is a reflection of the fact that most people consider such services as travel, dining out, and hiring a gardener as little ways that they might give themselves a treat, and this kind of expenditure undoubtedly becomes a greater part of one's total expenditures as income rises.

Most products, whether income elastic or inelastic, have an income elasticity coefficient that is greater than zero and are, therefore, the *normal* products that were defined in Chapter 2. However, for *inferior* products, the quantity demanded of the product actually declines in response to an increase in income, and therefore, the income elasticity is negative. Staple foods, such as rice, flour, and potatoes, are the most likely examples of inferior goods. Imagine a family so poor that it eats rice three times a day. This family then experiences a rise in income. It is feasible that this family may, in fact, consume less rice (and greater quantities of more expensive foods) as a result. If the experience of this hypothetical family was typical of the families in society generally, rice would be an inferior good and conform to our definition of negative income elasticity.

Table 4.9 shows how the proportion of income spent on different categories of goods varied from one income group to another in Canada in 1996. It is a truism that rich people spend more on almost everything than poor people do, but the proportion that they devote to the necessities of life is smaller, while the proportion they spend on luxury items is much greater.

All the items on the left are income inelastic. For instance, 54.7 percent of total spending by the poorest income groups went to food and shelter (20.1 percent on food and 34.6 percent on shelter). For the richest group, food and shelter represented 37.8 percent of total spending (15.9 percent on food and 21.9 percent on shelter). The items on the right are all income elastic, which means that higher income groups spend more in absolute terms and also proportionately more on such things as private transport, clothing, and recreation.

TABLE 4.9	Differences in Spending between the Richest and Poorest Groups in Canada, 2009					
	Income Inelastic			**Income Elastic**		
Category	Lowest Income Percentile	Highest Income Percentile	Category	Lowest Income Percentile	Highest Income Percentile	
Food	16.3%	8.0%	Furniture	2.5%	3.0%	
Shelter	31.4	16.0	Recreation	4.6	6.0	
Health care	4.2	2.0	Insurance & pension contributions	1.8	6.0	
Household operation	6.2	4.0				
Education	2.6	2.0				
Tobacco and alcohol	3.5	1.0				

Source: Based on Statistics Canada, *Spending Patterns in Canada*, 2009. Catalogue No. 62-202-X, December 2010. http://www.statcan.gc.ca/bsolc/olc-cel/olc-cel?lang=eng&catno=62-202-X.

 SELF-TEST

11. You are given the following data and may assume that the prices of X and Y do not change:

a) Calculate the income elasticity for products X and Y.

b) Are products X and Y normal goods?

Income	Quantity Demanded of X	Quantity Demanded of Y
$10 000	200	50
15 000	350	54

Cross-Elasticity of Demand

Finally, in addition to price elasticity of demand, elasticity of supply, and income elasticity, we also need to understand the concept of **cross-elasticity of demand**. Here, we are comparing how the quantity demanded of one product, A, responds to a change in the price of another product, B. The formal definition is:

cross-elasticity of demand: how the quantity demanded of product A responds to a change in the price of product B.

$$\epsilon_{AB} = \frac{\%\Delta \text{ quantity demanded of product A}}{\%\Delta \text{ price of product B}} \qquad [4.8]$$

$$\epsilon_{AB} = \frac{\dfrac{\Delta Q_d^A}{\text{average } Q_d^A} \times 100}{\dfrac{\Delta P^B}{\text{average } P^B} \times 100} \qquad [4.9]$$

Consider butter and margarine. An increase in the price of margarine will lead to an increase in the demand for butter, as indicated in **Table 4.10**.

TABLE 4.10	Cross-Elasticity of Margarine and Butter		
Margarine		**Butter**	
Price	Quantity Demanded per Week (lb.)	Price	Quantity Demanded per Week (lb.)
$1.50	5000	$3.00	1000
2.10	3200	3.00	2000

Given the data in **Table 4.10**, it seems clear that the increase in the demand for butter is the result of the change in the price of margarine, since the price of butter remains unchanged. The cross-elasticity of demand of butter for margarine, therefore, is:

$$\epsilon_{AB} = \frac{\dfrac{+1000}{1500} \times 100}{\dfrac{+0.60}{1.80} \times 100} = \frac{+67\%}{+33\%} = +2$$

When we are looking at cross-elasticity, the sign of the coefficient is important. The fact that the coefficient is a positive number verifies that these two goods are substitutes and reinforces something that we learned in Chapter 2: a rise in the price of a product (margarine) will increase the demand of a substitute product (butter).

It stands to reason that if substitute products have a positive cross-elasticity, then complementary products will have a negative cross-elasticity. We can easily verify this. What would happen to the demand for computer games as a result of a *decrease* in the price of computers? Surely, it would increase, and as a result the cross-elasticity calculation between the two would have a negative sign, as we would expect in the case of complementary products.

As we have seen, elasticity is a concept with wide application and one that extends our understanding of supply/demand analysis in many useful ways. You may find the following graphical summary of the various elasticity measures helpful.

PRICE ELASTICITY OF DEMAND AND SUPPLY

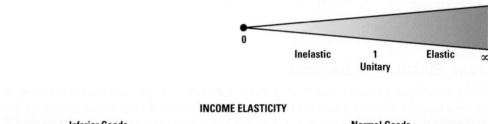

INCOME ELASTICITY

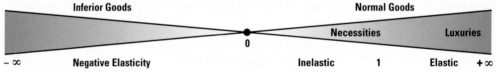

CROSS-ELASTICITY

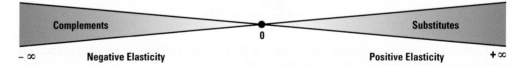

12. Think of a Mars bar and a Snickers bar. Do you think the cross-elasticity of these two products is positive or negative? Do you think the coefficient would be high or low? Next, think of beer and beer nuts. Do your answers to the two questions change, and, if so, how?

Review

CHAPTER SUMMARY

The focus of this chapter was elasticity, which is one of the more powerful concepts in microeconomics. Price elasticity of demand is the responsiveness of the quantity demanded to a change in price. Elasticity determines whether the consumer's total expenditure, and more importantly, the seller's total revenue rises or falls as price changes. The chapter presented four specific applications of this concept to illustrate its relevance and importance in microeconomic analysis. We saw how the concept of elasticity can be applied to supply, income, and price changes of related products.

4.1a Price elasticity of demand is defined as a measure of how much the quantity demanded changes as a result of a change in price. A standard formula relates the percentage change in quantity demanded to the percentage change in price. Using this formula yields a number called the elasticity coefficient.

4.1b The price elasticity of demand is *inelastic* if the coefficient is less than 1, it is *elastic* ifthe coefficient is greater than 1, it is *unitary elastic* if the coefficient is exactly 1.

4.1c If the price elasticity of demand is *inelastic*, price and the firm's total revenue move in the same direction. If it is *elastic*, price and the firm's total revenue move in opposite directions. If it is *unitary elastic*, then a change in price does not affect total revenue.

4.2 The *determinants* of the price elasticity of demand are:
- the number of substitutes available
- the percentage of income that is spent on the product
- the time involved in the measurement

4.3 While it can be easily demonstrated that the *slope of a demand curve* and its elasticity are not the same thing, we can, nonetheless, generalize and say that:
- a relatively steep demand curve is mostly inelastic
- a relatively shallow demand curve is mostly elastic

An increase in price will raise the seller's total revenue if demand is inelastic but lower total revenue if it is elastic. A decrease in price will have the opposite effect. Total revenue is unaffected if the demand is unitary elastic.

4.4 The *four applications* of the concept of price elasticity of demand show that:
- the more inelastic the demand curve, the larger is the proportion of a sales tax consumers pay
- governments raise a great deal of revenue from excise taxes on products with high inelastic demand, such as cigarettes
- any attempt to crack down on crime by focusing on the supply of illegal drugs will likely increase crime
- a good harvest is not always good news for farmers

4.5a The *elasticity of supply* depends primarily on the time involved, so:
- supply is perfectly inelastic in the market period
- supply is inelastic, but not perfectly so, in the short run
- supply is elastic in the long run

4.5b The case of *ticket scalping* is a classic application of the concept of supply elasticity.

4.5c *Income elasticity* involves a shift in the demand curve as a result of a change in income (rather than a movement along the demand curve as in the case of price elasticity of demand).
- A negative coefficient indicates an inferior product.
- A positive coefficient that is less than 1 indicates a necessity.
- A positive coefficient that is more than 1 indicates a luxury product.

4.5d Cross-elasticity of demand involves the percentage change in the quantity demanded of one product as a result of a percentage change in the price of another product. A positive elasticity coefficient indicates a substitute product. A negative coefficient indicates a complementary product.

NEW GLOSSARY TERMS AND KEY EQUATIONS

Equations:

[4.1] $TR = P \times Q$

[4.2] $\epsilon_p = \dfrac{\%\Delta \text{ quantity demanded}}{\%\Delta \text{ price}}$

[4.3] $\epsilon_p = \dfrac{\dfrac{\Delta Q_d}{\text{average } Q_d} \times 100}{\dfrac{\Delta P}{\text{average } P} \times 100}$

[4.4] $\epsilon_s = \dfrac{\%\Delta \text{ quantity supplied}}{\%\Delta \text{ price}}$

[4.5] $\epsilon_s = \dfrac{\dfrac{\Delta Q_s}{\text{average } Q_s} \times 100}{\dfrac{\Delta P}{\text{average } P} \times 100}$

[4.6] $\epsilon_Y = \dfrac{\%\Delta \text{ quantity demanded } (Q_d)}{\%\Delta \text{ income } (Y)}$

[4.7] $\epsilon_Y = \dfrac{\dfrac{\Delta Q_d}{\text{average } Q_d} \times 100}{\dfrac{\Delta Y}{\text{average } Y} \times 100}$

[4.8] $\epsilon_{AB} = \dfrac{\%\Delta \text{ quantity demanded of product A}}{\%\Delta \text{ price of product B}}$

[4.9] $\epsilon_{AB} = \dfrac{\dfrac{\Delta Q_d^A}{\text{average } Q_d^A} \times 100}{\dfrac{\Delta P^B}{\text{average } P^B} \times 100}$

STUDY TIPS

1. It may be helpful to think of elasticity as a concept that measures the responsiveness of one variable to a change in a related variable. To summarize, the most common application is the responsiveness of quantity demanded to a change in price, which is called price elasticity of demand or, simply, demand elasticity.

2. The concept of elasticity can also be applied to the ways that a change in income or a change in the price of a related good affects the quantity demanded of a particular product. Similarly, it can be applied to the way a change in price affects quantity supplied. These applications are called income elasticity, cross-elasticity (of demand), and supply elasticity.

3. Learn the formulas for calculating elasticities the same way you learned your phone number—use them until they stick. The index-card suggestion made earlier would really work here. Note that the various formulas are similar, and once you learn one, the others follow easily.

4. Since price elasticity involves price and quantity, it also directly relates to a seller's total revenue. The effect of a price increase on total revenue will be to either increase it or decrease it, depending on elasticity. The same can be said for a price decrease. The exact relationships are, again, something you simply have to memorize.

5. The power of the concept of elasticity is illustrated in the analysis of the four applications presented in the chapter. If you follow the arguments in each of these, you can be reasonably assured that you have grasped the basic ideas of elasticity.

Answered Questions

These questions can also be found online on Connect.

Indicate whether the following statements are true or false:

1. **(LO 1) T or F**   A firm's total revenue is equal to price times demand.

2. **(LO 1) T or F**   The price elasticity of demand coefficient is, technically, always negative, but for convenience economists ignore the minus sign.

3. **(LO 1) T or F**   If demand is inelastic and price falls, then total revenue will rise.

4. **(LO 1) T or F**   If demand is elastic and price rises, then total revenue will rise.

5. **(LO 1) T or F**   If the elasticity of demand is unitary and the price rises, then total revenue will rise.

6. **(LO 3) T or F**   A major determinant of price elasticity of demand is the number of complementary products available.

7. **(LO 2) T or F**   A straight-line (constant-sloped) demand curve does not imply constant elasticity.

8. **(LO 5) T or F**   Supply elasticity is measured by percentage change in quantity supplied divided by percentage change in quantity demanded.

9. **(LO 5) T or F**   If cross-elasticity of demand is positive, we could conclude that two products are substitutes.

10. **(LO 5) T or F**   If income elasticity is positive, we could conclude that the product in question is an inferior good.

Basic (Questions 11–25)

11. **(LO 1)** What is the effect on total revenue if demand is elastic and price rises?
    a) Total revenue will fall.
    b) Total revenue will rise.
    c) Quantity demanded will rise.
    d) Supply will rise.

12. **(LO 5)** What is the effect of a rise in income on the demand for a product?
    a) It will rise if the product is an inferior product.
    b) It will rise if the product is a normal product.
    c) It will fall if the product is a normal product.
    d) It will fall whether it is a normal or inferior product.

13. **(LO 4)** What is the effect of the imposition of a sales tax?
    a) The supply curve will shift to the left.
    b) The supply curve will shift to the right.
    c) The demand curve will shift to the left.
    d) The demand curve will shift to the right.

14. **(LO 5)** What is the elasticity of supply of seats for a one-night concert in an auditorium?
    a) It is elastic.
    b) It is inelastic.
    c) It is perfectly inelastic.
    d) It is perfectly elastic.

15. **(LO 4)** What is the effect if government increases the excise tax on a product that has an inelastic demand?
    a) Tax revenue will rise.
    b) Tax revenue will fall.
    c) The price of the product will rise, but the quantity traded will remain unchanged.
    d) The price of the product will rise, and the quantity traded will rise.

16. **(LO 5)** What is a normal good?
    a) It is a good whose income elasticity of demand is less than zero.
    b) It is a good whose demand will rise as income rises.
    c) It is a good that has many substitutes.
    d) It is a necessity.

17. **(LO 1)** Under which of the following situations will total revenue rise?
    a) If elasticity is >1 and price falls
    b) If elasticity is >1 and price rises
    c) If elasticity is <1 and price falls
    d) If elasticity = 1 and price falls

18. **(LO 3)** If a product has many substitutes, which of the following statements is correct?
    a) Its income elasticity is high.
    b) It is likely that it is an inferior product.
    c) Its supply elasticity is high.
    d) Its price elasticity of demand is high.

19. **(LO 3)** If people spend a large percentage of their income on a particular product, which of the following statements is true?
    a) The product has a large number of substitutes.
    b) The price elasticity of demand for the product is high.
    c) The income elasticity of demand for the product is low.
    d) The elasticity of supply for the product is low.

20. **(LO 3)** What will cause the price elasticity of demand for a product to be high?
    a) A low percentage of income is spent on the product.
    b) There are a small number of available substitutes.
    c) The elasticity of supply for the product is high.
    d) A long period is used to measure elasticity.

21. **(LO 1)** How is a firm's total revenue calculated?
    a) Price times average revenue
    b) Price times quantity sold
    c) Average revenue times quantity produced
    d) Quantity demanded times quantity supplied

22. **(LO 1)** What is the price elasticity of demand coefficient?
    a) A number that measures the responsiveness of quantity demanded to a change in price
    b) A number that measures the responsiveness of quantity demanded to a change in demand
    c) A number that measures the responsiveness of price to a change in the quantity demanded
    d) A number that measures the responsiveness of price to a change in demand

Refer to **Table 4.11** to answer questions 23 and 24. Below are two sets of prices and their related quantities demanded:

TABLE 4.11

	Price	Quantity Demanded
Set I	$8.50	2000
	9.35	1600
Set II	$200	16
	150	24

23. **(LO 1)** What is the price elasticity for the product represented by Set I?
    a) 0.002
    b) 0.5
    c) 2.33
    d) 400

24. **(LO 1)** What is the price elasticity for the product represented by Set II?
    a) 0.16
    b) 0.71
    c) 1.4
    d) 6.25

25. **(LO 5)** How is the cross-elasticity of demand calculated?
    a) By dividing the change in the quantity demanded of product A by the change in the price of product B
    b) By dividing the percentage change in the quantity demanded of product A by the percentage change in the price of product B
    c) By dividing the change in the price of product A by the change in the quantity demanded of product B

d) By dividing the percentage change in the price of product A by the percentage change in the quantity demanded of product B

Intermediate (Questions 26–32)

26. **(LO 5)** What is the elasticity of Marshall's short-run supply curve?
    a) It is perfectly elastic.
    b) It is elastic.
    c) It is inelastic.
    d) It is perfectly inelastic.

27. **(LO 1)** A local transit authority has just applied to its regulatory board for a fare increase on its rail-transit system, arguing that the increase is needed to cover rising costs. A citizens' committee is opposed to the proposed increase, arguing that the company could increase its revenue by decreasing fares. Which of the statements below is correct?
    a) The company thinks that the demand is inelastic, whereas the committee thinks it is elastic.
    b) The company thinks that the demand is elastic, whereas the committee thinks it is inelastic.
    c) Both the company and the committee think that elasticity is unitary.
    d) It is possible that both the company and the committee are correct.

28. **(LO 4)** Graphically, what is the effect of imposing an excise tax on a product?
    a) It will shift both supply and demand curves for the product to the left.
    b) It will shift the supply curve for the product to the left.
    c) It will shift the supply curve for the product to the right.
    d) It will shift both supply and demand curves for the product to the right.
    e) It will shift the supply curve for the product to the left and the demand curve to the right.

29. **(LO 4)** What is the likely effect of government reducing the supply of illegal drugs?
    a) The total amount spent on drugs will decrease.
    b) The total amount spent on drugs will increase.
    c) The quantity of drugs consumed will remain unchanged.
    d) The demand for drugs will fall.
    e) The demand for drugs will increase.

Refer to **Table 4.12** to answer questions 30, 31, and 32.

TABLE 4.12

Income	Quantity of K Demanded	Quantity of L Demanded	Quantity of M Demanded
$50 000	200	40	80
60 000	260	50	85

30. **(LO 5)** What is the income elasticity of product K?
    a) 1.5
    b) 15
    c) Approximately 14
    d) Approximately 1.4
    e) Approximately 0.7

31. **(LO 5)** What is the income elasticity of product L?
    a) Approximately 12
    b) Approximately 1.2
    c) Greater than the income elasticity of product K
    d) Approximately 0.8
    e) 8

32. **(LO 5)** Which of the following is correct about product M?
    a) It has an income elasticity of approximately 6.7.
    b) It has an income elasticity of approximately 0.2.
    c) It has an income elasticity of approximately 0.6.
    d) It is a normal good.
    e) It is an inferior good.

Advanced (Questions 33–35)

33. **(LO 2)** What will happen to the quantity demanded if the price elasticity of demand is 2 and the price increases by 10 percent?
    a) It will increase by 10 percent.
    b) It will decrease by 10 percent.
    c) It will decrease by 20 percent.
    d) It will increase by 20 percent.

34. **(LO 4)** If government puts a $2 excise tax on a product, causing the price to rise by $0.75, which of the following statements is correct?
    a) The sellers pay more of the tax than do the buyers.
    b) The buyers pay more of the tax than do the sellers.
    c) Government's tax revenue falls.
    d) The quantity demanded of the product falls by 37.5 percent.

35. **(LO 5)** Which of the following circumstances will raise the total revenue of oat farmers?
    a) A good harvest, combined with inelastic demand
    b) A poor harvest, combined with inelastic demand
    c) A poor harvest, combined with elastic demand
    d) A good wheat and oat harvest, combined with inelastic demand
    e) A poor wheat and oat harvest, combined with elastic demand

Parallel Problems

ANSWERED PROBLEMS

36A. **(LO 1, 4, 5) Key Problem** Assume that there is only one movie theatre and only one video rental outlet in a small mining town in northern Manitoba. The weekly demand, by all the townspeople, for movies and video rentals is given in **Table 4.13**.
   a) Fill in the total revenue columns.
   b) What prices would maximize the seller's total revenue?
      Movie price: _____
      Video price: _____
   c) What is the elasticity of demand for movies if the theatre changes the price from $6 to $5, and what is the change in total revenue? What if the price changes from $6 to $7?
      From $6 to $5: _____
      Change in revenue: _____
      From $6 to $7: _____
      Change in revenue: _____
   d) What conclusions can you draw from your answers in c)? _____
      _____
      _____

   e) Suppose that the video store was charging the price that maximized total revenue, but the city government imposes an excise tax on *videos* that resulted in the price of videos rising to $4.50.

As a result, the demand for *movies* increases by 20 at each price. Would the theatre now want to charge the same price for movies?
      Yes: _____ No: _____
   f) Given the circumstances in e), what is the cross-elasticity of movies for videos? What does this say about the relationship between the two products?
      Elasticity: _____ ; relationship: _____ .
   g) Referring to the original data in **Table 4.13**, assume now that the average weekly earnings of the townspeople rise from $500 to $550 with the result that demand for movies increases 20 percent. If the price being charged is $6, what is the income elasticity of demand? What does this suggest about the product, movies?
      Elasticity: _____ ; it suggests: _____ .

Basic (Problems 37A–45A)

37A. **(LO 1)** Suppose that the price of a kilo of bananas drops from $4.50 to $3.50, and as a result, the quantity sold increases from 85 to 115 kilos.
   a) What is the value of total revenue before and after the price change?
      _____
      _____
   b) What is the percentage change in the price?
      _____

TABLE 4.13

Prices of Movies	Quantity of Movies Demanded	Total Revenue	Prices of Videos	Quantity of Videos Demanded	Total Revenue
$3	450	_____	$2.00	950	_____
4	400	_____	2.50	900	_____
5	350	_____	3.00	825	_____
6	300	_____	3.50	750	_____
7	250	_____	4.00	650	_____
8	200	_____	4.50	550	_____
9	150	_____	5.00	425	_____

c) What is the percentage change in the quantity?
_____

d) What is the value of the price elasticity of demand?
_____

e) Is the demand elastic or inelastic?
_____

38A. (LO 5) If the quantity of bread supplied increased by 12 percent when the price increased by 10 percent, what is the value of the elasticity of supply?
_____

39A. (LO 5) Suppose that household incomes in Sherbrooke rose from $48 000 to $52 000, and assuming no change in price, the quantity of Kraft macaroni and cheese rose from 156 to 164 cases per week.
a) What is the value of the income elasticity of demand for Kraft macaroni and cheese?
_____

b) What does this suggest about this product?
_____

40A. (LO 5) Suppose that the price of President's Choice macaroni and cheese decreased from $9 to $7 per case, and at the same time, the quantity of Kraft macaroni and cheese dropped from 192 to 128 cases.
a) What is the cross-elasticity of demand between the two products?
_____

b) What is the relationship between the two products?
_____

41A. (LO 2) Given the demand curve in **Figure 4.15**:
a) What can you say about the slope of the demand curve?
b) What is the elasticity of demand between points *a* and *b*, and between points *c* and *d*?
a and *b*: _____
c and *d*: _____
c) At what price is the elasticity of demand equal to one? Price: _____
d) At what price would consumers spend the most on this product? Price: _____
e) Between what prices is demand inelastic?
Between _____ and _____

42A. (LO 2) **Table 4.14** is the demand schedule for poetry booklets in the town of Never Ending.
a) On **Figure 4.16A**, draw the demand curve and indicate the point of unitary elasticity.
b) From **Table 4.14**, calculate the total revenue of the seller at each quantity.

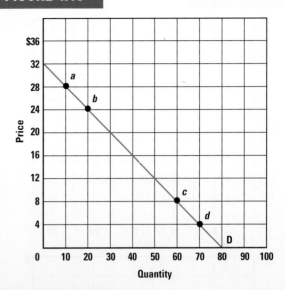

FIGURE 4.15

TABLE 4.14

Price	Quantity	TR
$20	0	_____
18	3	_____
16	6	_____
4	9	_____
2	12	_____
10	15	_____
8	18	_____
6	21	_____
4	24	_____

c) On **Figure 4.16B**, draw the total revenue curve.
d) At what quantity and price is total revenue maximized, and how does this relate to the price elasticity of demand?

43A. (LO 1) Define the term *price elasticity of demand*. What does it mean if a calculation of the price elasticity of demand turns out to be less than one?

44A. (LO 3) Why is the price elasticity of demand for carrots so different from that for cigarettes?

45A. (LO 3) Below is a list of six products. Do you think each product's income elasticity is high, low, or negative?
a) Skiing holidays _____
b) Postage stamps _____

FIGURE 4.16

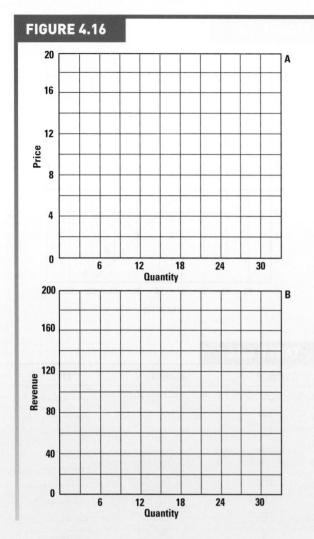

FIGURE 4.17

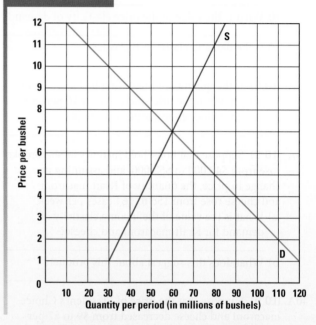

c) Potatoes _____

d) Scuba diving equipment _____

e) Prescription drugs _____

f) Low-priced, single-ply toilet paper _____

Intermediate (Problems 46A–53A)

46A. **(LO 4)** Figure 4.17 shows the market for oats.
  a) At the present equilibrium, what is the total revenue received by farmers (in millions of dollars)?
     $ _____
  b) Suppose that the oat industry had a very good harvest and the supply increased by 30 million bushels. Draw the new supply curve in Figure 4.17.
  c) What will be the new total revenue received by farmers (in millions of dollars)? $ _____
  d) What does this suggest about the elasticity of demand for oats? Answer: _____

47A. **(LO 5)** Table 4.15 relates to a particular market.
  a) What is the price elasticity of demand for product M?
     _____
  b) What is the price elasticity of demand for product N?
     _____
  c) What is the income elasticity of demand for product M? _____
  d) What is the income elasticity of demand for product N? _____
  e) What is the cross-elasticity of demand of product M for a change in the price of product N?
     _____

48A. **(LO 1, 2, 3)** Table 4.16 shows the demand for haircuts from seniors and other customers on an average weekday in the local hairdressing shop.
  a) Between the prices of $16 and $20, which of the two demands is more elastic? Explain.
     _____
     _____
  b) What is the price that would give the shop the greatest sales revenue? Price: _____

49A. **(LO 1)** Adam makes specialized garden figurines out of a small shop on his property, and his monthly sales average is $800 when he charges $20 for each figurine. One month, he tried lowering his price to $18, and his sales that month dropped to $756. On the basis of these data, what is the price elasticity of demand for Adam's product? Answer: _____

TABLE 4.15

Year	Average Income	Price of M	Quantity of M	Price of N	Quantity of N
1	$50 000	$2.50	100	$20	800
2	50 000	2.80	90	20	750
3	50 000	2.80	80	30	700
4	55 000	2.80	90	30	720

TABLE 4.16

Price of Haircut	Quantity Demanded by Seniors	Quantity Demanded by Other Customers
$20	1	9
18	4	10
16	7	11
14	10	12
12	13	13
10	16	14
8	19	15
6	22	16
4	25	17
2	28	18

50A. **(LO 2)** The data in **Table 4.17** are for electricity, measured in megawatts.
   a) At what price is the total expenditure by consumers at a maximum? Answer: _____

TABLE 4.17

Price	Quantity Demanded
$ 97	103
98	102
99	101
100	100
101	99
102	98

b) What is the price elasticity of demand at this price?
Answer: _____
_____

51A. **(LO 2)** Trader Tom delivers boxes of tomatoes (and sometimes other perishable items) to two remote towns in northern Alberta. The demand schedules for tomatoes in each of the towns are shown in **Table 4.18**.
   a) If during a particular week Tom has only four boxes to deliver, how many boxes should he deliver to each town if he wishes to maximize his total revenue? _____

b) What would be your answer if Tom had six boxes the next week? _____
c) How many boxes should Tom deliver to each town—if available—to maximize his total revenue? _____

52A. **(LO 4)** The data in **Table 4.19** are for five-kilo boxes of lobsters.
   a) Before the tax, what are the equilibrium price and quantity? Price: _____ ; quantity: _____ .
   b) Fill in the Quantity Supplied (after tax) column, assuming that a $20-per-unit excise tax is put on the product.
   c) What are the new equilibrium price and quantity? Price: _____ ; quantity: _____ .
   d) What portion of the $20-per-unit excise tax is paid by the seller, and what portion is paid by the consumer? Paid by seller: _____ % Paid by consumer: _____ %

TABLE 4.18

	Town A			Town B	
Price	Quantity Demanded	Total Revenue	Price	Quantity Demanded	Total Revenue
$5	15	___	$5	11	___
10	14	___	10	10	___
15	13	___	15	9	___
20	12	___	20	8	___
25	11	___	25	7	___
30	10	___	30	6	___
35	9	___	35	5	___
40	8	___	40	4	___
45	7	___	45	3	___
50	6	___	50	2	___
55	5	___	55	1	___
60	4	___	60	0	___
65	3	___	65		___
70	2	___	70		
75	1	___	75		

TABLE 4.19

Price	Quantity Demanded	Quantity Supplied (before tax)	Quantity Supplied (after tax)
$100	900	820	___
110	880	840	___
120	860	860	___
130	840	880	___
140	820	900	___
150	800	920	___

53A. **(LO 4)** Table 4.20 contains data for the demand for a box of blueberries in two different markets.
   a) What is the equilibrium price and quantity in each market?
   Market 1: price _____ quantity _____
   Market 2: price _____ quantity _____
   b) What is the total revenue earned by suppliers in each market? Market 1: _____
   Market 2: _____

   Now, assume that government has imposed a quota of 560 in both markets.
   c) In which market would the blueberry growers be happier? Answer: _____
   d) Explain your answer in terms of total revenue and elasticity of demand. _____
   _____

TABLE 4.20

	Market 1		Market 2	
Price	Quantity Supplied	Quantity Demanded	Quantity Supplied	Quantity Demanded
$9.50	800	560	800	480
9.00	760	580	760	520
8.50	720	600	720	560
8.00	680	620	680	600
7.50	640	640	640	640
7.00	600	660	600	680

Advanced (Problems 54A–57A)

54A. **(LO 4)** Under what conditions will the consumer pay all of the excise tax placed on a particular product?

55A. **(LO 2)** Which of the demand curves in Figure 4.18, D_1 or D_2, is more elastic at price P_1? At price P_2?
At price P_1: _____ % At price P_2: _____ %

FIGURE 4.18

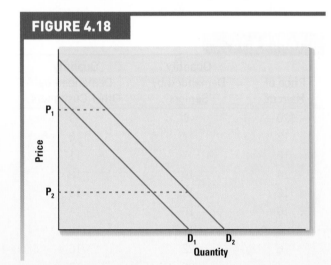

56A. **(LO 1, 5)** The dean of arts at a large university recently said she felt that the demand for postsecondary education must be very inelastic because enrolment has decreased very little despite a doubling in tuition fees (after inflationary effects have been removed) over the last ten years.
Do you agree with the dean? Why, or why not?
_____
_____
_____
_____

57A. **(LO 5)** Suppose you are a researcher attempting to calculate the price elasticity of demand for products A and B. Your research associate has collected the data in Table 4.21 to assist you. Suppose you use these data to calculate the price elasticities of demand for products A and B. Comment on the validity of your calculations.
_____
_____
_____
_____

TABLE 4.21

Year	Price of Product A	Quantity Traded of Product A	Price of Product B	Quantity Traded of Product B	Average Consumer Income
1	$8	1000	$25	300	$32 000
2	10	1100	22	350	34 000

CONSUMER CHOICE

WHAT'S AHEAD...

This chapter looks at the approach to consumer behaviour known as *marginal utility theory*. This theory helps us better understand how the rational consumer allocates income toward the purchase of various products. It also provides a deeper understanding of demand and why consumers are willing and able to purchase more at lower prices. We explain the idea of consumer surplus and look at attempts by producers to acquire this surplus through price discrimination.

A Question of Relevance...

Suppose the government of Canada gave a $200 bonus to every citizen of the country, with the proviso that it must be spent immediately. What are the odds that any two individuals would buy exactly the same products? One in a thousand? One in a million? Probably more like one in twenty million. Each individual is unique, and this uniqueness is reflected in each person's tastes and spending behaviour. What determines individual tastes is more a subject for the psychologist than the economist, but how taste translates into purchases is very much the province of the economist and is the subject of this chapter.

You do not need to be a student of economics to appreciate that people's tastes differ: one person's paradise is another person's prison! And even when people buy the same products, we cannot be sure that they receive the same amount of satisfaction from them. Yet, our formulation of an individual's demand is predicated on the basis that it measures, or at least indicates, their desire and ability to purchase. An increase in either would presumably cause that person to purchase more. Measuring ability to purchase is easy enough: it can be gauged by individuals' income and wealth. But how do we measure intensity of desire? Well, a number of economists in the latter part of the nineteenth century attempted to do just that; in doing so, they introduced the important new idea called the **margin**.

margin: the extra or additional unit (also 'marginal').

The marginal revolution shifted the focus of economists away from totals, such as total profits or total costs or total utility, and toward the margin, which means the extra or additional profit or cost or utility. English economist Alfred Marshall believed that concentrating on people's actions *at the margin* provided a better understanding of their behaviour. If we are trying to understand why a consumer buys one particular basket of goods rather than any other, it is more instructive conceptually to look at each purchase one at a time, rather than trying to evaluate the total result of a morning's shopping. The basket of goods is, after all, the result of a number of individual decisions, not one single decision.

Using this approach, Marshall developed the concept of *marginal utility* and with it the important law of diminishing marginal utility. The theory of consumer behaviour, which uses this concept, is the focus of this chapter. Before we look at it, we should mention that the idea of the margin is not always easy to grasp at first acquaintance. It is definitely worth the effort, however, since it lies at the heart of so much economic analysis and is the basis of many of the ideas contained in later chapters.

5.1 THE LAW OF DIMINISHING MARGINAL UTILITY

LO1 Explain the law of diminishing marginal utility.

Suppose I wished to communicate to you the immense satisfaction I get from my first beverage of the day. I could use words like "greatly" or "fantastically" or even "indescribably" refreshing, but no words could accurately capture the degree of my pleasure, or **utility**, as economists call it. Suppose, instead, that I assign a number to indicate the amount of my utility, say, 100 utils. Does this communicate my pleasure any more accurately? Probably not, since you have no idea what a util is and we have no instrument with which to measure it. However, if I then tell you that the second beverage of the day gives me only 50 utils of pleasure, you have a very clear indication of how I rate these two drinks.

utility: the satisfaction or pleasure derived from the consumption of a product.

On the other hand, my friend Cleo might suggest that she gets 200 and 100 utils from her first two drinks. Since neither of us can objectively measure the amount of utility, we cannot conclude that she derives twice as much utility as I do. In other words, we cannot make interpersonal comparisons of utility. Nevertheless, we can still draw some interesting conclusions about consumer behaviour by pursuing this idea of utility.

For example, assume that a frantic student, Anna, is at her local coffee bar, beginning an all-night cram session for finals. Further assume that Anna keeps score of the amount of pleasure (measured in utils) that she derives from successive lattés that keep her going through the night. (Of course, this is her subjective evaluation, and it might change from time to time.) It seems reasonable to suppose that the very first latté would give her the greatest satisfaction, and each one afterward would give less and less pleasure, as shown in **Table 5.1**.

marginal utility: the amount of additional utility derived from the consumption of an extra unit of a product.

The column headed **marginal utility** shows the amount of pleasure or satisfaction, measured in utils, that Anna derives from each latté consumed. We can express marginal utility in terms of an equation:

$$\text{Marginal utility (MU)} = \frac{\Delta \text{ total utility}}{\Delta \text{ quantity}} \qquad \text{[5.1]}$$

TABLE 5.1	Total Marginal Utility	
Quantity	Marginal Utility (MU)	Total Utility (TU)
1	45	45
2	36	81
3	25	106
4	21	127
5	12	139
6	0	139
7	−6	133

Since **Table 5.1** shows that the quantity changes by one unit each time, the denominator in the above equation is equal to one. It can be seen that Anna derives decreasing MU from each successive latté. Although every latté, at least until the sixth cup, gives her positive marginal utility, each one is less satisfying than the previous one. This is known as the **law of diminishing marginal utility**. It seems reasonable to suppose that this law is applicable to most of us most of the time. Our knowledge of life and our personal experiences alone can validate the law of diminishing utility:

law of diminishing marginal utility: the amount of additional utility decreases as successive units of a product are consumed.

More may be better, but additional units do not give the same degree of pleasure.

Furthermore, in time, there will come a point where more becomes worse. For Anna, that point comes with the seventh cup where her MU is −6. Since the first unit of anything we consume gives us positive utility, and the last one gives us negative utility, MU must be declining with successive amounts.

The last column in **Table 5.1** shows Anna's total utility (TU) derived from consuming the various quantities. TU can be found by summing the marginal utility from each unit. For example, the TU from consuming 5 units is equal to:

$$TU_5 \text{ units} = MU_1 + MU_2 + MU_3 + MU_4 + MU_5 \qquad [5.2]$$

From **Table 5.1**, we can see that the TU from 5 units equals:

$$TU_5 \text{ units} = 45 + 36 + 25 + 21 + 12 = 139$$

You can see, looking at the same table, that Anna's TU increases with the amount consumed, but the rate of increase slows down with increasing quantities. This is the same thing as saying that MU diminishes. **Table 5.1** is illustrated in **Figure 5.1**.

TU increases as more of this product is consumed—at least, up to the sixth unit. However, the rate at which it increases gets smaller and smaller, that is, the slope of the TU curve gets smaller (or the curve gets flatter). The slope of the TU curve is the same thing as the MU. In other words, starting from a high of 45 utils when one unit is consumed, the MU declines with increased consumption until it eventually becomes zero with the consumption of the sixth unit. Note that the TU curve is at a maximum when MU equals zero.

Before we start to develop this theory of utility a bit further, it is important to state the conditions under which it operates. First of all, we take it for granted that the consumers we are describing act rationally. By this, we mean that they will wish to consume more as long as total utility increases. This point bears repeating: a rational consumer will want to consume more, only so long as increased consumption adds to total satisfaction:

The objective of the consumer, it is assumed, is to maximize the pleasure derived from consumption, that is, to maximize total utility.

FIGURE 5.1   Total and Marginal Utilities

The TU curve increases as the quantity consumed increases. But it increases at a declining rate: that is, the slope gets smaller and becomes 0 at a quantity of 6. This is where TU is at a maximum (of 139). Since the slope of the TU curve is equal to the MU, this means that the MU declines as the quantity increases and gets to 0 at 6 units.

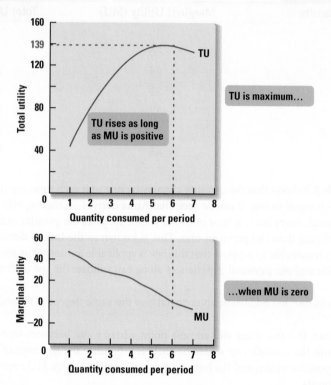

In addition, this idea of diminishing marginal utility makes sense only if we are considering a particular period. If Anna were to consume the seven lattés over seven evenings, then it is likely that her marginal utility would remain constant. Finally, as Alfred Marshall pointed out, certain products are indivisible; thus, a small quantity may be insufficient to meet certain special wants. For example, three automobile tires would not give a great deal of utility without the fourth. In summary, marginal utility theory applies when:

- the consumer is behaving rationally
- the consumer's objective is maximum satisfaction
- purchases and consumption take place over a short period
- the units purchased may sometimes be sets of items

✓ SELF-TEST

1. Complete the table, which shows Michelle's utility for milkshakes.

Quantity	Total Utility (TU)	Marginal Utility (MU)
1	20	
2	35	
3	___	10
4	___	8
5	58	
6	60	___
7	___	0
8	___	−5

5.2 OPTIMAL PURCHASING RULE

From the information contained in **Table 5.1**, it is apparent that even if Anna had unlimited income or if the refreshment were free, there would still be a limit to how much she would drink. She would never drink more than six lattés, since no rational consumer would consume a unit that gives negative marginal utility. In other words, if we wanted to develop some rule of rational consumer behaviour, we might suggest that a person with unlimited income should consume every product to the point of satiation! The problem with this little rule is that it does not apply to any known consumer because all people, no matter how rich or poor, have limited incomes (not to mention limited time) and therefore have to make choices.

To derive a more relevant rule of consumer behaviour, let us suppose that Anna has a limited budget of $24 and is choosing between two products: lattés and pieces of pastry, each costing $4. The utility of both products is shown in **Table 5.2**.

L02 Derive a consumers' purchasing rule that ensures satisfaction is maximized.

Brand X/Getty Images

TABLE 5.2	Comparison of the Utilities of Lattés and Pieces of Pastry				
	LATTÉ			**PIECES OF PASTRY**	
Quantity	Marginal Utility	Total Utility	Quantity	Marginal Utility	Total Utility
1	45	45	1	64	64
2	36	81	2	52	116
3	25	106	3	40	156
4	21	127	4	26	182
5	12	139	5	10	192
6	0	139	6	0	192
7	−6	133	7	−7	185

The question now is, how should Anna best allocate her evening's budget if she wishes to maximize her total utility? She certainly cannot consume both products to the points of maximum total utility, since that would cost $24 for the 6 cups of latté and $24 for 6 pieces of pastry, a total of $48—double her budget. We need to figure out (on her behalf) what combination of the two goods, costing $24, will produce the maximum total utility. One way to do this would be to work out every possible combination, given the $24 constraint, and see which particular combination maximizes utility. The procedure is a little tedious, but not particularly difficult, as **Table 5.3** shows.

TABLE 5.3	Utility Obtained from Combinations of Lattés and Pastries				
	LATTÉS		**PIECES OF PASTRY**		**BOTH**
Quantity	Total Utility	Quantity	Total Utility		Total Utility
0	0	6	192		192
1	45	5	192		237
2	**81**	**4**	**182**		**263**
3	106	3	156		262
4	127	2	116		243
5	139	1	64		203
6	139	0	0		139

For instance, one possible combination might be zero lattes and 6 pieces of pastry. This would give Anna a total utility of 192. But another feasible—and better—way of spending $24 would be on one latte and 5 pieces of pastry for a total utility from both products of 237 utils. The table shows every possible combination of the two products costing $24. A glance at the last column of **Table 5.3** shows that the best combination is 2 cups of latté and 4 pieces of pastry because this yields the maximum total utility of 263 utils.

But most of us do not allocate our budget this way. In Anna's case, it is unlikely that she would sit down in advance and try to figure out which combination is the best for her. Instead, she is more likely to make her choices one at a time, that is, marginally. This marginal approach will give us the same results as looking at every single combination as we just did, but it is less tedious and far more instructive.

Suppose that on entering the coffee bar, Anna takes $4 from the $24 out of her purse and walks up to the counter to place an order. What should she buy? **Table 5.2** shows us that a pastry looks more attractive because the marginal utility of the first pastry (64 utils) exceeds that of the first latté (45 utils). Having eaten her pastry, should Anna now buy her *second* pastry or should she buy her *first* latté? Well, the *second* pastry is worth 52 utils to her, while the *first* latté is worth 45 utils, so she should buy a pastry. Now, what about her third purchase? Should it be a *third* pastry or her *first* latté? Since the *first* latté, at 45 utils, is better than the *third* pastry at 40 utils, she should buy her first latté. On to her fourth purchase. Should it be a *second* latté (36) or a *third* pastry (40)? It should be a third pastry. We continue in a similar fashion until Anna's $24 has been exhausted. This is shown in **Table 5.4**.

TABLE 5.4	Successive Purchase Choices			
	Product	**Total Spent**	**Marginal Utility**	**Total Utility**
First purchase	first pastry	$ 4	64	64
Second purchase	second pastry	8	52	116
Third purchase	first latté	12	45	161
Fourth purchase	third pastry	16	40	201
Fifth purchase	second latté	20	36	237
Sixth purchase	fourth pastry	24	26	263

At the end of the evening, Anna will have purchased a total of 2 lattés and 4 pieces of pastry, and in doing so, she will have maximized her utility at 263 utils. We have already seen from **Table 5.3** that this combination will ensure maximum utility.

From this knowledge, we could perhaps adopt a new optimal purchasing rule: in order to maximize total utility, a consumer should allocate spending by comparing the marginal utility of each product and purchase the product that gives the greatest marginal utility. There is, however, a very serious defect in this rule. Suppose that I were to compare the marginal utilities of two following products and, according to this rule, purchase the one that gives the greatest marginal utility:

First bottle of beer: MU = 120 utils

First Porsche car: MU = 10 000 000 utils

So, I would buy the Porsche because it has a higher marginal utility for me! The only problem is that I cannot quite afford it. Our purchasing rule obviously needs a little more refinement, since we need to take the price of products into consideration. In order to make a rational decision, what we really need to compare is not utils but the amount of utils per dollar spent. Or, expressing it more colloquially, we are trying to find out which product gives the most bang for the buck! In terms of a formula, it is:

$$\text{MU per \$ spent} = \frac{\text{MU}}{\text{price}} \qquad \text{[5.3]}$$

For instance, suppose we are trying to decide whether to buy a $2 slice of pizza that gives us 40 utils or a $1.50 pop that gives 36 utils. Figuring out the MU per dollar spent gives us:

$$\text{MU per \$ spent on pizza} = \frac{40}{2} = 20$$

$$\text{MU per \$ spent on pop} = \frac{36}{1.50} = 24$$

Clearly then, buying the pop would be a more sensible decision.

What this suggests is that a rational consumer would continue to purchase a product as long as its marginal utility per dollar spent is greater than that of any other product. Of course, as the consumer increases the consumption of any given product, its marginal utility is going to fall, and so some other product will then become a more attractive proposition. Let us stay with the latté/pastry example but this time, in **Table 5.5**, assume that the management of the coffee bar decides to decrease the price of lattés to $3 but leaves the price of pastry unchanged at $4. Now, how would Anna spend her budget of $24?

TABLE 5.5	Marginal Utility per Dollar Spent				
LATTÉS			**PIECES OF PASTRY**		
Quantity	MU	MU per $ (price = $3)	Quantity	MU	MU per $ (price = $4)
1	45	15	1	64	16
2	36	12	2	52	13
3	25	8.3	3	40	10
4	21	7	4	26	6.5
5	12	4	5	10	2.5
6	0	0	6	0	0

To figure out the optimal allocation of Anna's $24 budget, we will proceed as we did before, by looking at each separate purchase. However, since lattés and pastries have different prices, we need to do some calculations to make them comparable. We do this by dividing the marginal utility of lattés by three and the marginal utility of pastry by four, as shown in **Table 5.5**. To start with, the first pastry gives a higher marginal utility per dollar spent than the first latté (16 compared with 15), so this would be her first purchase. The first latté gives a higher MU per dollar spent (15) than the second pastry (13), so that is her second purchase. We can continue in this fashion, purchase by purchase, and the results are summarized in **Table 5.6**.

TABLE 5.6	Choice of Lattés and Pieces of Pastry, Purchase by Purchase				
	Product	Total Spent	Marginal Utility per $ Spent	Marginal Utility	Total Utility
First purchase	first pastry	$4	$16	64	64
Second purchase	first latté	7	15	45	109
Third purchase	second pastry	11	13	52	161
Fourth purchase	second latté	14	12	36	197
Fifth purchase	third pastry	18	10	40	237
Sixth purchase	third latté	21	8.3	25	262
Seventh purchase	fourth latté	24	7	21	283

The best way for Anna to spend her $24 is to purchase four lattés and three pieces of pastry. This would give her (check back to **Table 5.2**) a total utility of 283 (127 + 156) utils, which is higher than could be produced by any other combination that could be purchased with $24. Note also the effect of this decrease in the price of lattés: the number of lattés purchased increased from two to four, whereas the quantity of the related product, pieces of pastries, dropped from four to three. We will look at this in more detail later.

The optimal spending choice for the rational consumer, then, is that consumers should purchase the product that yields the greatest marginal utility per dollar spent.

optimal purchasing rule:
in order to maximize utility, consumers should allocate their budgets so that marginal utility per dollar spent on all products is equal.

The procedure we have just developed enables us to derive an **optimal purchasing rule**. It suggests that whenever the marginal utility per dollar spent on product A is greater than that for product B, we would buy and consume more of A. As this is done, of course, the marginal utility per dollar spent on product A starts to decline, until we get to the point where other products, B or C, become more attractive, that is:

$$\text{if } \frac{MU_A}{P_A} > \frac{MU_B}{P_B} \Rightarrow \text{consume more A}$$

$$\text{if } \frac{MU_A}{P_A} < \frac{MU_B}{P_B} \Rightarrow \text{consume more B}$$

Our conclusion:

> We should buy and consume products to the point at which the marginal utility per dollar spent on each product is more or less equal for all products.

The optimal purchasing rule, then, is:

$$\frac{MU_A}{P_A} = \frac{MU_B}{P_B} = \text{.......} \frac{MU_Z}{P_Z}$$ [5.4]

If we did not purchase products in this fashion, we would be acting irrationally. For instance, suppose that the marginal utility per dollar spent on the last apple we bought is 15 utils (and it does not matter if this is the first, fifth, or hundredth apple) and an additional pear gives a marginal utility per dollar spent of 25 utils—we would gain 10 utils by giving up one apple and buying an additional pear instead.

✓ SELF-TEST

2. Given the marginal utilities and prices of the four products in the accompanying table, which product would a rational consumer choose as her next purchase?

	Apple	Beer	Ice Cream	Hot Dog
Marginal Utility	120	300	140	150
Price	$1.50	$4.00	$2.00	$3.00

3. Melissa's marginal utility per dollar spent for apples and pears is given in the accompanying table. How many of each kind of fruit would she purchase if she were to make only nine purchases?

Pears	MU per Dollar Spent	Apples	MU per Dollar Spent
1	9	1	18
2	8	2	14
3	7	3	10
4	6	4	6
5	5	5	2
6	4	6	0

5.3 APPLICATIONS OF MARGINAL UTILITY THEORY

Marginal utility theory, as esoteric as it might at first appear, does provide us with some interesting insights into consumer behaviour. It can explain some obvious and some not-so-obvious activities.

L03 Explain how marginal utility theory is applicable to real-world examples.

Why Our Favourite Things Are Not Always Our Favourites

None of us spends all our income on a single product. Even our favourite product is only a favourite *up to a point*. After consuming a certain quantity, its marginal utility per dollar spent drops to the point where other things become more attractive.

What Determines Your Priority Spending?

It is an interesting experiment to imagine how one would spend additional increments of income starting off, say, with a basic $100 per week, and increasing it by increments of $100. Let us say you did have only $100 per week; what would you spend the money on? Presumably, you would spend it on those things that have the greatest marginal utility for you; for most of us, this would mean using our money on food and shelter. Income would need to increase appreciably before any allocations are made for clothes and be higher still before any entertainment dollars are spent.

The way in which we adjust our purchases to higher income levels is what is meant by the concept of income elasticity that we encountered in the last chapter. You can imagine that products with low income elasticities (water, food) have the highest initial marginal utilities and thus will be highest in terms of priority. Similarly, those products with high income elasticities (air travel, movies) will have lower initial marginal utilities and must be of a lower priority. Research has consistently demonstrated that poorer families spend, by far, the largest proportion of their incomes on the basic necessities, such as food and shelter (often well over 50 percent), whereas richer families spend proportionately less (sometimes less than 30 percent).

Don't Some Things Improve with Age?

Another intriguing aspect of marginal utility theory is those situations in which the law of diminishing marginal utility may not apply. The law is applicable to all products and all people, but maybe not at all times. For example, it is certainly possible to think of certain things for which the marginal utility seems to increase the more they are consumed. (Think of a new music album; it often takes repeated hearings before you get full enjoyment from it.) This may be true also of fine wines and paintings and so on. However, Alfred Marshall cautioned his readers that the idea of diminishing marginal utility only makes sense if the product is consumed over a reasonably short period. Furthermore, our rule applies only to the purchasing of the product, not to its repeated "consumption," as is the case with music and artwork.

Shouldn't Incomes Be More Equally Distributed?

Diminishing marginal utility takes another interesting twist when we look at the fascinating subject of money. Is money also subject to the law of diminishing marginal utility? In other words, is it true that the more money you have, the less valuable additional amounts become for you? Since money is just one form of wealth, often the question is amended to ask: does the marginal utility of wealth or income decline as more is obtained? For example, imagine a rich person and a poor person walking toward each other on the street; halfway between them lies a $10 bill.

Which of them would gain the greater utility from its possession—the rich person, for whom it might be the hundred-thousandth $10 bill of the year, or the poor person, for whom it could be the difference between a good week and a bad one? Intuition suggests that the marginal utility of the poor person is likely to be far higher than that of the rich person, for whom the gain (or loss, for that matter) of $10 might well go unnoticed. Here, intuition seems to confirm the law of diminishing marginal utility even for the product money. If this is so, some might argue that this is strong grounds for advocating a more equitable distribution of income and wealth, since the gain in marginal utility by the poor would greatly exceed the loss of marginal utility by the rich so that overall utility (or social welfare) is increased.

Note that the above idea need not imply an equal distribution, only a more equitable or fairer one. The idea would be to take from the rich and give to the poor as long as the marginal utility of the former is smaller than the marginal utility of the latter. This would continue until (figuratively) the screams of the rich person (who may no longer be quite so rich) are equal to the whoops of joy coming from the poor person (who may no longer be quite so poor). It may well be that their marginal utilities become equalized when the rich person now has an income reduced to $5000 per week, while that of the poor person has been increased to $500.

However, you might protest such a scheme. After all, you may well ask, what is fair about a system that takes income from one person, who may have worked extremely hard to earn it, and gives it to another who may have done nothing to deserve it? Nevertheless, modern governments do try to increase the overall well-being of their communities by transferring income from the rich to the poor. It is most likely that those individuals with higher incomes (a lower marginal utility of money) tend to save more and receive, in turn, relatively more of their income from their investment sources. Governments have typically imposed higher taxes on this type of income, which is a de facto acceptance of the argument that these marginal income dollars yield a lower marginal utility for their recipients than the higher marginal utility gained from labour by lower income earners when they sell their labour.

There is, however, another issue in all of this. As pointed out earlier, we simply cannot compare utilities between people. Thus, while we might well be inclined to believe that the rich person's marginal utility is less than the poor person's, there is simply no way of measuring this.

From all of this, however, we should not conclude that the theory of marginal utility is of little use or that it should be discarded. One of its most important uses is to give a strong underpinning to the law of demand, which is the topic of the next section.

 SELF-TEST

4. The table below shows the total utility that two children, Jan and Dean, derive from various amounts of weekly allowance.

As their parent, you can afford to pay them a total allowance of only $10. How would you divide this amount between the two children so as to maximize their combined total utility? What will be the combined total utility?

Amount of Weekly Allowance	Jan's Total Utility	Dean's Total Utility
$ 1	200	400
2	380	500
3	540	595
4	680	685
5	800	770
6	900	850
7	980	925
8	1040	995
9	1080	1060
10	1100	1120

5.4   MARGINAL UTILITY AND DEMAND

We saw earlier, in our latté/pastry example, that marginal utility theory suggests that a decrease in the price of one product leads to an increase in the quantity purchased of that particular product while decreasing the quantity purchased of the competitive product. We need to look at this in more detail.

L04 Provide a theoretical rationale for downward-sloping demand curves.

We know that the particular numbers we assign to utility are quite arbitrary; any set of numbers would do. However, there is one particular measuring unit with which we are all familiar, and that is money. We could, if we wished, measure utility in dollars. For instance, Akio could suggest that his first drink after a hard game of tennis gives him, say, $8 worth of utility. Another way of expressing it would be to say that, irrespective of its actual price, he would be willing to pay $8 for that drink. Let us examine Akio's utility for his favourite drink in terms of *dollar marginal utility* ($MU) in **Table 5.7**.

TABLE 5.7	Akio's Dollar Marginal Utility
Quantity Consumed	**$MU**
1	$ 8
2	5
3	4
4	3
5	2
6	1
7	0

Although they look similar, do not confuse our previous term, marginal utility per dollar spent, which measures the number of utils obtained for each dollar spent, with $MU, which is measuring utility itself in terms of dollars. **Table 5.7** shows that Akio's $MU declines with increasing quantities; this simply reflects the law of diminishing marginal utility. However, with this information, we can work out exactly how much Akio would purchase at different prices. Suppose, for instance, that the price of his drink was $10 a bottle. How much would he purchase? The answer must be zero, since even his first drink of the day is worth only $8 for him. So, why would he pay $10 for the product? We would get the same result if the price was $9. What if the price dropped to $8. How many would he buy now? The answer will be one, since he would surely pay $8 for something he felt was worth $8. However, he would not purchase a second drink, since he rates it at only $5, which is less than the price. Let us continue to drop the price. Say, the price is $7. How many will he purchase now? Presumably, he still would not be prepared to buy more than one, since the price is still higher than his valuation of the second drink. The same is true at $6. Not until the price drops to $5 would Akio be prepared to buy two drinks. Continuing to drop the price by $1 each time would produce the results in **Table 5.8**.

What **Table 5.8** spells out is Akio's demand schedule, which relates the quantities demanded at various different prices. This is graphed in **Figure 5.2**.

The derivation of the demand curve in this manner, while not being particularly ingenuous, does provide a very different perspective on demand. In a sense, it shifts the emphasis away from the price and onto the quantity. Instead of asking, "How many would you buy at this price?" it asks, "What is the maximum price you would pay to buy this quantity?" From Akio's point of view, the price cannot be more than $8 to induce him to buy one drink. In order to get him to buy two drinks, the price of the second drink must drop, simply because we know that the marginal utility of his second drink will be lower. In other words, to induce people to buy increasing quantities of any product that they value less and less, the price must be lower. To get Akio to buy six drinks, the price must be as low as $1. In a sense, it is the value of the last one purchased and not the total value of them all that determines how much is bought.

TABLE 5.8	Demand Curve, Derived
Price of Drinks	**Quantity Demanded**
$ 10	0
9	0
8	1
7	1
6	1
5	2
4	3
3	4
2	5
1	6

FIGURE 5.2	Marginal Utility and the Demand Curve

To induce Akio to buy one drink, the price cannot be higher than $8, since that is how much he values the first drink. To get him to buy a second drink, the price must drop to $5 because that is his evaluation of the second drink. If the price drops to $4, Akio would be prepared to buy three drinks. The price must continue to drop in order to encourage Akio to buy more. His $MU curve is the same thing, then, as his demand curve.

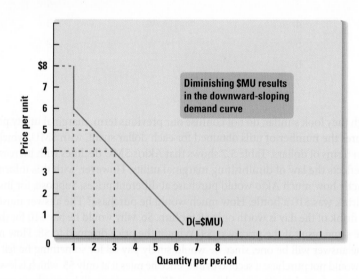

Diminishing $MU results in the downward-sloping demand curve

The fact that it is the marginal utility *of the last unit* purchased that determines the price you are prepared to pay for a product and the quantity you are buying is a very subtle idea, one that is difficult to grasp at first. It does, however, provide a solution to the famous diamond–water paradox, which was first mentioned by Aristotle and introduced by Adam Smith in his 1776 work, *The Wealth of Nations*.

The Famous Diamond–Water Paradox

Smith was interested in finding out what determines the value of products and realized that the rather elusive term "value" is used in two different contexts. It could mean what he termed "value in use," which is what we mean by utility, that is, the amount of satisfaction that individuals derive on the basis of their individual evaluation. Alternatively, the word might mean what Smith termed "value in exchange." This is the value the market places on the product—in exchange for other products or for money. Most things we buy have similar values in use and in exchange. However, a number of products, like water, have a very high value in use but are worth almost nothing in exchange.

Conversely, other products like diamonds have a very high exchange value but quite a low value in use. Smith tried, unsuccessfully, to resolve this seeming paradox. It took almost a century and the introduction of marginal utility theory before economists were able to provide a solution. In the following example, instead of considering diamonds, let us look at the contrast between water and another very precious commodity, oil. Suppose we are comparing the utilities derived from 50-litre drums of each. **Table 5.9** presents the preferences of Karl, an average consumer.

TABLE 5.9		The Utilities of Water and Oil				
WATER			**OIL**		
Quantity	**$MU**	**$TU**	**Quantity**	**$MU**	**$TU**
1	$1000	$1000	1	$30	$30
2	500	1500	2	29	59
3	200	1700	3	28	87
4	100	1800	4	27	114
5	50	1850	5	26	140
6	25	1875	6	25	165
7	10	1885	7	24	189
8	5	1890	8	23	212
9	2	1892	9	22	234
10	1	1893	10	21	255

The first striking observation is how highly valuable water is when compared with oil. Its total utility (value in use) far exceeds that of oil. Suppose that you literally had no water. How much would you be prepared to pay for it? Karl would pay almost anything—$1000 for the first drum of water. This may be his whole income, but he would pay it to stay alive. But note how dramatically the $MU of water drops. After nine drums Karl not only has enough to drink, but enough to wash his clothes, his body, and his house, and still have plenty left over to water the garden. The value of a tenth drum of water to Karl is only $1. In contrast, though, note how gradually the $MU of oil drops.

Now, suppose that Karl has a budget of $300 and that the price of both oil and water is $25 so that he is able to make a total of 12 purchases. How much of each would he purchase? You can see that his first $125 would be spent on 5 drums of water, but the next $125 would go on 5 drums of oil. Then, he would buy one of each, for a total of 6 drums of water and 6 drums of oil. After

 ADDED DIMENSION The Marginal Revolution

In the 1870s, three economists independently developed the concept of marginal utility. The work of Stanley Jevons in Manchester, England; Leon Walras in Lausanne, Switzerland; and Carl Menger in Vienna, Austria, led to what is today known as the marginal revolution. They wanted to improve on the classical view concerning the determination of a product's value that could be traced back to Adam Smith and Karl Marx. This classical view held that the value of a product is derived from the labour used to produce it—or, more generally, from the cost of producing the product.

Each of these three economists argued that a product's value was determined by the marginal utility gained by each individual consumer. Given this, and the idea that consumers will maximize their utility by equating marginal utility with price, we are left to conclude that value can simply be thought of as price. This is now known as the neoclassical view. Menger also came to be known as the father of the Austrian School of economics, which produced many great economists over the years. Walras was one of the first economists to develop a theory of general equilibrium.

spending $300, he values the oil and water equally despite the fact that 6 drums of water gives him a total dollar utility of $1875 compared with only $165 for oil—over 11 times as much. But the total utility is irrelevant when deciding on the next purchase, and Smith's idea of *value in exchange* centres on the marginal and not the total utility. Thus, we can see that the answer to Smith's paradox is as follows:

Value in use is reflected in the *total utility* of a product, whereas the value in exchange (the price) is determined by its *marginal utility*.

In conclusion, we reiterate that it is the marginal utility of a product that determines just how much of a product we will buy.

5.5 CONSUMER SURPLUS

L05 Understand why consumers generally value a product more than the price they pay.

consumer surplus: the difference between what a customer is willing to pay and the actual price of the product.

Our water–oil paradox showed that the total value a consumer derives from consuming products usually exceeds the total expenditure on them. **Table 5.9** shows, for instance, that if the price of water is $25 a drum, Karl would consume 6 drums at a cost of $150. Karl's total dollar utility of those 6 drums, however, is $1875. In dollar terms, then, Karl obtains a bonus amounting to the difference of $1725. This bonus is called **consumer surplus**. This surplus is not a sum of money received but the additional satisfaction that we receive for free. It comes about from the fact that normally we can obtain as much or as little of a product as we want at a single constant price. Karl could obtain one drum or 5 drums or 100 drums, and they would still have cost him $25 each. However, except for the last one, every unit he buys is worth more than the price. He obtains a consumer surplus on each one, as **Table 5.10** shows.

The marginal consumer surplus is the difference between the dollar marginal utility of a unit and the price paid for that product, that is:

$$\text{marginal consumer surplus (MCS)} = \$MU - \text{price} \qquad \textbf{[5.5]}$$

And total consumer surplus is the sum of the marginal consumer surplus derived from each successive unit consumed (5 units in this case):

$$\text{total consumer surplus}_{5 \text{ units}} = MCS_1 + MCS_2 + MCS_3 + MCS_4 + MCS_5 \qquad \textbf{[5.6]}$$

Since all of us derive consumer surplus from our purchases, we can illustrate the idea in terms of the market demand. **Figure 5.3** shows the demand curve for CDs.

The demand curve shows the maximum price that could be charged at various different quantities; for example, 10 000 CDs could be sold at a price of $30, while 20 000 CDs could be sold at $28

TABLE 5.10	Marginal and Total Consumer Surplus			
Drums of Water	**$MU**	**Price**	**Marginal Consumer Surplus**	**Total Consumer Surplus**
First	$1000	$25	$975	$ 975
Second	500	25	475	1450
Third	200	25	175	1625
Fourth	100	25	75	1700
Fifth	50	25	25	1725
Sixth	25	25	0	1725

FIGURE 5.3	**Consumer Surplus, Graphically**

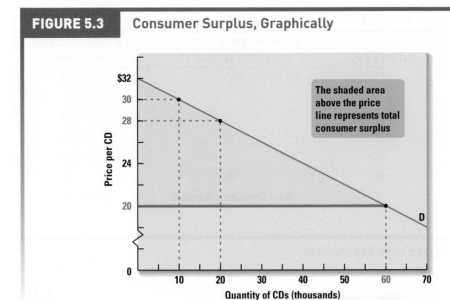

For each quantity, the vertical distance between the price line and the demand curve represents the amount of (marginal) consumer surplus. For instance, at a quantity of 10 (thousands) the price is $20, but customers would be prepared to pay $30, and so the difference of $10 is the marginal consumer surplus. At a quantity of 20, the price is $20, and the customers are willing to pay $28, and so the marginal consumer surplus is $8. Adding all the marginal consumer surpluses gives the total consumer surplus (the shaded area).

each, and so on. The demand curve, therefore, represents how much people would be willing to pay. Let us assume that the price is $20. The vertical distance between the price line and the demand curve represents the amount of consumer surplus at each quantity. For instance, 10 000 people would have been prepared to pay $30 for this CD. The fact that they only have to pay $20 means that each of them obtains a consumer surplus of $10. If, instead, the price had been $28, then 20 000 people would have bought the CD. But we already know that 10 000 of those 20 000 would have paid $30; the other 10 000 were not prepared to pay $30, but they are willing to pay $28. Members of this latter group, then, are enjoying a consumer surplus of $8 each. If we continue this exercise down to the $20 price level, we will discover that the total consumer surplus is $300 000, as shown in **Table 5.11.** (Theoretically, if purchases could be made in any quantities, including partial units, and if they could be sold at any price, even fractions of a cent, then we could calculate the total consumer surplus as the area of the triangle between the demand curve and the price line. In our example, that area amounts to $1/2 \times 60\ 000 \times \$12 = \$360\ 000$).

This consumer surplus, then, can be represented by the triangular area below the demand curve and above the price line, as shown in **Figure 5.3.** A higher price will, of course, mean that consumers will enjoy a smaller total consumer surplus; a lower price means a higher total consumer surplus from that product. In addition, **Figure 5.4** shows that consumers enjoy a bigger consumer surplus from products with inelastic demands than from those that have elastic demands.

If the price is P_1, then the quantity purchased of each of the two products is quantity Q_1. At lower quantities, however, buyers of product 1 (demand curve D_1) in **Figure 5.4A** would be prepared to pay higher prices than would buyers of product 2 (demand curve D_2) in **Figure 5.4B.** The area between the price line and the demand curves represents the total amount of consumer surplus. The graph shows that this area is much greater in the case of the inelastic demand curve, D_1, than it is with the elastic demand curve, D_2.

The idea that consumers derive a greater surplus from products with inelastic demands conforms to our idea of what is meant by inelastic, which is that buyers are not particularly affected by a price change, presumably because they think that the value of the product far exceeds its market price the product than is represented by the price of the product. For example, the benefit that most smokers get from cigarettes usually far exceeds even the very high prices they have to pay for them.

Ryan McVay/Getty Images

For the average consumer, the price of many CDs is below what he or she would be prepared to pay.

TABLE 5.11   Calculating Consumer Surplus

Consumers	would have paid:	but only pay:	therefore get a marginal consumer surplus of:	for a total consumer surplus of:
1st 10 000	$30	$20	$10	$100 000
2nd 10 000	28	20	8	80 000
3rd 10 000	26	20	6	60 000
4th 10 000	24	20	4	40 000
5th 10 000	22	20	2	20 000
6th 10 000	20	20	0	0
			Total Consumer Surplus	$300 000

FIGURE 5.4   Consumer Surplus Varies with Elasticities

The demand curves in graphs A and B both have the same price (P_1) and quantities (Q_1). However, demand curve D_1 is steeper (the demand is more inelastic) than D_2 (the demand is elastic). As a result, the total consumer surplus (the shaded area) is bigger in A than in B.

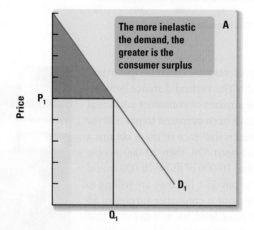

The more inelastic the demand, the greater is the consumer surplus

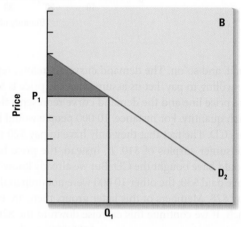

It is easy to see why producers would like, if they could, to capture this consumer's surplus for themselves. At the present price of $20 per CD, producers in our last example (see **Figure 5.3**) are deriving revenues of 60 000 × $20 = $1 200 000 from the sales. However, as **Table 5.11** shows, consumers are enjoying an additional psychological benefit, or consumer surplus, of $300 000. The temptation for sellers to try to capture this surplus is great. Let us examine the ways in which sellers might try to do this.

One way sellers capture the consumer surplus is to figure out just how much individual consumers are prepared to pay for the product. This can be done through consumer question-naires, as well as through auctions, such as those on eBay. In an auction, customers bid up the price to the point where (ideally from the seller's point of view) the sole remaining customer is being forced to pay what she really thinks it is worth. An example of this are the e-commerce Web sites. A "Dutch auction" works even better from the seller's point of view and captures even more of the consumer surplus. Here, the auctioneer starts the bidding at a very high price, which is then lowered, step by step, until someone indicates she is willing to pay the last price mentioned. In order to avoid missing out on a purchase, customers may well end up paying the maximum they are prepared to go. For instance, suppose that I want to bid on an ornament at an auction and I happen to be the keenest buyer. In fact, I would be prepared to go as high as $500, whereas the next keenest bidder would not go higher than $300. At a regular auction, I could buy the ornament for $301, but at a Dutch auction, I would likely bid my maximum of $500.

In addition, note that an auctioneer with four identical items to sell will sell them one at a time, so as to get the maximum consumer surplus from each. Another way of capturing this consumer surplus is to recognize that consumers value the first item purchased far more than they do subsequent purchases. A seller of CDs, then, might charge $25 for a single CD but sell two for $40 and three for $50, and so on. You might think of this as receiving a discount from bulk buying, but you could also look on it as having to pay a premium for buying small quantities.

✓ SELF-TEST

5. Given Akio's utility for beverages as shown in **Table 5.7**, what quantity would he purchase if the price was $2, and what would his total consumer surplus be as a result?

6. The demand for chocolate-covered kumquats is quite small and is shown below:

Price	Quantity
$10	1
9	2
8	3
7	4
6	5

Assuming partial units cannot be bought, what is the marginal consumer surplus for each unit bought, and what is the total consumer surplus if the price is $6?

5.6 PRICE DISCRIMINATION

A final example of the way in which producers attempt to capture the consumer surplus is through **price discrimination**. Price discrimination means that the same product, with the same costs of production, is being sold to different consumers at different prices. It recognizes the fact that consumers have different demands for the same product and are, therefore, prepared to pay different prices in order to obtain the product. As we shall see, in order for sellers to practice price discrimination, they must be able to recognize that there are different groups of buyers with different demand elasticities, and somehow be able to separate those groups. Furthermore, if people are being charged different prices, then the seller must try to find a way of preventing resales of the product. In addition, the sellers must have control over the price they charge.

Suppose that you are the owner of an independent movie theatre and you estimate that the demand for movie tickets is as shown in **Table 5.12**. At present you are charging $12 admission and receiving a daily revenue of $2400. Of course, you would like to increase your revenue by attracting more customers. You realize, however, that a number of people are not willing to pay $12 on a regular basis and that the only way to attract them is to reduce the price. The trouble is that if you do reduce the price, your total sales revenue will fall to $2250 at $9 (that is, $9 × 250) and to $1800 at $6 ($6 × 300). This is so because if you do reduce the price, you will have to reduce the price for everyone.

Or do you? What if you could charge different prices to different groups of people? But first, you need to identify the people who are reluctant to pay $12 but would be willing to pay, say, $6. (There are 300 people prepared to pay $6 but only 200 prepared to pay $12. Thus, there are 100 people not prepared to pay this extra $6.) Included in this group are low-income people, many of whom would happily visit the theatre for $6 but are unable to afford a price of $12. However, you have no way of recognizing such people. But there are identifiable groups who are generally, though not always, poor. This includes young people and retired people.

 LO6 Understand why some sellers charge different prices to different consumers for the same product.

price discrimination: the selling of an identical product at a different price to different customers for reasons other than differences in the cost of production.

TABLE 5.12	Demand for Movie Tickets	
Price of Admission	Number of Daily Tickets Sold	Total Revenue
$12	200	$2400
9	250	2250
6	300	1800

FIGURE 5.5	Price Discrimination and Consumer Surplus

The blue area shows the total revenue received if the owner wishes to have 300 clients at a single price. By practising price discrimination he can still have 300 clients, but 200 of those now pay $12 each. The result will be extra income as a result of capturing some of the consumer surplus, shown as the pink area.

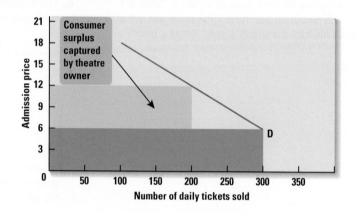

So, what you would do is charge a lower price for these groups but continue the high price for your regular patrons. In this way, you can increase your revenue appreciably. Your regular 200 patrons continue to pay $12, but you attract an additional 100 patrons who each pay $6. Your total revenue increases by $600 per day as a result. On the surface, it looks as though you are offering discount prices to certain identifiable groups and, of course, that is how you would probably advertise it. The truth of the matter is that you are charging a premium price to the other identifiable group (the higher income group).

Figure 5.5 shows how the movie theatre owner is able to capture some of the consumer surplus by practising price discrimination. The blue rectangle shows the total revenue received if a single price of $6 is charged to all the moviegoers. With two-tier pricing, the total revenue is increased by the pink area. The pink area is the part of the consumer surplus captured by the theatre owner.

In order to practice price discrimination, then, it is necessary to:

- identify groups of customers with different demand elasticities
- separate them from the others
- ensure that those obtaining the lower prices cannot resell the product
- ensure that the seller has control over the price

These features exist for theatre admissions because a young person cannot resell the seat to an older person. For this reason, price discrimination is mostly practised with personal services rather than goods. Other examples of discrimination on the basis of age occur in the area of transportation, where, in most countries and cities, seniors and students travel at reduced fares on buses, trains, and planes.

Price discrimination is also practiced on the basis of *time*. Suppose I own a coffee shop and I have no trouble attracting customers between 7 and 10 o' clock in the morning, the time when most people are desperate for coffee. However, business falls off considerably after 10 o'clock. In order to attract more customers in the off-peak periods, I would have to drop my prices, but why should I give everyone the benefit of lower prices when they are quite happy to pay my regular prices?

The answer, of course, is to have two-tiered prices: a higher price in peak periods than in off-peak periods. Again, this method is practised by many transport companies and other businesses, such as hairdressers and movie theatres, that have times of the day or the week when sales are sluggish. Similarly, many telephone and hydro companies have different rates at different times of the day. Other examples would be airlines that give discounts to travellers who spend weekends away from home and long-distance phone companies who charge lower prices for calls at certain hours.

Another case in which customers are charged different prices for the same item is that of bulk-buying. This is discrimination on the basis of the *volume of purchases*. As we saw earlier, it is typical for a single item to cost more than the per-item cost for, say, a dozen. However, this practice may not always be price discrimination, since the costs per unit in terms of packaging, storing, and merchandising are often much higher for single items than for bulk. In a sense, when you buy in bulk, the costs are lower per item for the seller, and as a result the savings are passed on to the buyers (witness the success of warehouse-style stores opening up in many countries). On the other hand, it is certainly true that big customers often get charged lower fees for many services, such as banking and legal services, than do small customers, who use these services infrequently or not extensively. These are almost certainly examples of price discrimination. To sum up, price discrimination is typically practiced on the basis of:

The prices for coffee may vary before and after 10 o'clock in the morning.

- age
- time
- volume of purchases

It is important to understand what price discrimination involves, since as we shall see in Chapter 10, many monopolists can, and do, discriminate on the basis of price.

✓ SELF-TEST

7. The following table shows the demand for haircuts on an average weekday in your hairdressing salon. Investigation into the market has revealed to you that the demand from seniors differs greatly from that from your other customers.

Price of Haircut	Quantity Demanded by Seniors	Quantity Demanded by Other Customers
$20	1	9
18	4	10
16	7	11
14	10	12
12	13	13
10	16	14
8	19	15

a) If you could only charge one price to all customers, which price would give you the greatest sales revenue?

b) Suppose that you charged seniors a different price compared with your other customers. What prices would you charge each group in order to maximize your sales revenue?

Review

CHAPTER SUMMARY

This chapter examined the theory of consumer behaviour using the concept of marginal utility. You learned that given a fixed income or budget, consumers will maximize their total utility (satisfaction) by equating the marginal utility per dollar spent on each product purchased with the marginal utility per dollar spent on every other product. You then learned that the law of diminishing marginal utility can be used to explain downward-sloping demand curves, and this opened the discussion of consumer surplus and price discrimination.

5.1a *Marginal utility* is the amount of extra satisfaction derived from the consumption of one more unit of a product. It can be expressed as:

$$MU = \frac{\Delta \text{ total utility}}{\Delta \text{ quantity}}$$

It can be measured in hypothetical numbers of utils or actual dollars.

5.1b The *law of diminishing marginal utility* states that the extra satisfaction derived from one more unit of a product declines as more of that product is consumed.

5.2 The *optimal purchasing rule* can be expressed as:

$$\frac{MU_A}{P_A} = \frac{MU_B}{P_B} = \text{.......} \frac{MU_Z}{P_Z}$$

5.3 Marginal utility theory helps us understand why we do not spend all of our income on our single favourite product and why we have priorities in our purchasing decisions.

5.4a The law of diminishing marginal utility explains why individual consumers are willing to buy more of a product only if its price is lower. This, in turn, explains why *demand curves* are downward sloping.

5.4b The realization that consumers' purchasing decisions are based on marginal utility and not total utility can be used to explain why *water*, essential to life itself, has a low price but *diamonds* have a high price.

5.5 The fact that consumers are able to buy all they want of most products at a fixed price but base their decisions on how much to buy on marginal utility, leads to the concept of *consumer surplus*, which is the difference between the consumer's evaluation of a product and the price paid for it.

5.6 If sellers could *price discriminate* by charging a higher price to certain groups and a lower price to others, then most (all) consumer surplus would be exploited. In order to do this, the seller would have to identify customers with different demands, separate them from the other customers, and ensure that those obtaining the lower prices cannot resell the product.

NEW GLOSSARY TERMS AND KEY EQUATIONS

consumer surplus   154
law of diminishing marginal utility   143
margin(al)   142

marginal utility   142
optimal purchasing rule   148

price discrimination   157
utility   142

Equations:

[5.1]   Marginal utility (MU) $= \dfrac{\Delta \text{ total utility}}{\Delta \text{ quantity}}$ **page 142**

[5.2] $TU_n \text{ units} = MU_1 + MU_2 + MU_3 + \ldots MU_n$ **page 143**

[5.3]   MU per \$ spent $= \dfrac{MU}{\text{price}}$ **page 146**

[5.4] $\dfrac{MU_A}{P_A} = \dfrac{MU_B}{P_B} = \ldots \dfrac{MU_Z}{P_Z}$ **page 148**

[5.5]   marginal consumer surplus (MCS) $= \$MU - \text{price}$ **page 154**

[5.6]   total consumer surplus$_{n \text{ units}} = MCS_1 + MCS_2 + MCS_3 + MCS_4 + MCS_n$ **page 154**

STUDY TIPS

1. Do not be discouraged if, on first reading, you are dismayed by the level of abstraction in this chapter. It may seem to you that all economists do is to make the commonplace seem unnecessarily esoteric and complicated. But think of the level of abstraction that a physicist brings to her job. Imagine that you are trying to find out how a five-year-old successfully negotiates a steep curve without falling off his bike. The boy might give you a very graphic and comical description of his achievement. A physicist, on the other hand, is likely to enter into a serious and pedantic discourse involving such factors as centrifugal force, the velocity of the bike, the weight of the child, angle of declension, and so on. Both are describing the same phenomenon: the child's description is likely to be more interesting, but the physicist's will be more illuminating and helpful in the long run—once you understand it. In a sense, this is what an economist is trying to do with the mundane tasks of buying and selling. We are not dealing in abstractions to make things incomprehensible but to make them, eventually, more comprehensible.

2. If, initially, you have difficulty grasping the optimal purchasing rule, try working through a number of problems. You may find, in this case, actually "doing" economics is preferable to simply reading it.

3. One of the most important lessons in this chapter is that it is the marginal utility and not the total utility that determines consumer behaviour. This simply means that asking a person to name his favourite product does not make sense except in context. In other words, my favourite product at any moment depends on how much of it I have recently consumed. If I have recently consumed very little, I am likely to rate it highly (it has a high marginal utility); if I have consumed a great deal recently, then I am not likely to rate it as highly (its marginal utility is small) and will likely prefer other products.

4. Bear in mind that economic theories of consumer behaviour try to explain people's actions and do not try to figure out the reasons for that behaviour; this, after all, is the role of the psychologist. It is sufficient for economists to conclude that faced with identical prices, a consumer who buys product A rather than product B does so because it possesses a higher marginal utility, that is, because the consumer prefers it. This is not a particularly profound observation; however, its implications are reasonably fruitful.

Answered Questions

These questions can also be found online on Connect.

Indicate whether the following statements are true or false:

1. **(LO 1) T or F**   The term "marginal" means the difference between averages.

2. **(LO 1) T or F**   Utility is defined as the satisfaction or pleasure derived from the consumption of a product.

3. **(LO 1) T or F**   Marginal utility is the additional utility derived from the consumption of one more unit of a product.

4. **(LO 1) T or F**   The law of diminishing marginal utility suggests that as successive units of a product are consumed, total utility declines.

5. **(LO 2) T or F**   If the marginal utility per dollar spent on product A is greater than that of product B, then a rational consumer should consume more of product B to compensate.

6. **(LO 5) T or F**   It is the marginal utility of the *last* unit consumed that determines how much a consumer is prepared to pay for a product.

7. **(LO 5) T or F**   Consumer surplus is the additional amount that consumers have to pay if they really need a particular product.

8. **(LO 5) T or F**   The consumer surplus derived from products that have an inelastic demand is greater than that from products with an elastic demand.

9. **(LO 6) T or F**   Price discrimination is the practice of charging different prices for different products.

10. **(LO 6) T or F**   Price discrimination cannot be practised if consumers are able to resell the product.

Basic (Questions 11–25)

11. **(LO 1)** What is marginal utility?
    a) It is the total satisfaction resulting from consuming a product.
    b) It is the total satisfaction resulting from consuming all products.
    c) It is the additional satisfaction resulting from consuming one more unit of all products.
    d) It is the additional satisfaction resulting from consuming one more unit of a product.

12. **(LO 2)** When is total utility at a maximum?
    a) When marginal utility is maximum
    b) When marginal utility is zero
    c) When marginal utility is increasing
    d) When marginal utility is decreasing

13. **(LO 1)** What is the law of diminishing marginal utility?
    a) The amount of additional utility decreases as successive units of a product are consumed.
    b) Marginal utility increases quickly at first but more slowly later.
    c) Total utility declines at first but starts to increase after some point.
    d) Whereas total utility rises with the consumption of additional units, marginal utility is always constant.

14. **(LO 2)** Which of the following is a correct statement of the optimal purchasing rule?
    a) $MU_A/MU_B = P_B/P_A$
    b) $MU_A/P_A = MU_B/P_B$
    c) $P_A/MU_B = P_B/MU_A$
    d) $P_A/P_B = MU_B/MU_A$

15. **(LO 2)** What will happen if $MU_A/P_A > MU_B/P_B$?
    a) The price of A will be forced to drop.
    b) The price of B will be forced to drop.
    c) The consumer will purchase more of product A.
    d) The consumer will purchase more of product B.

Refer to **Table 5.13** when answering questions 16 and 17.

TABLE 5.13

Quantity Consumed	Total Utility
1	30
2	55
3	75
4	90
5	100
6	105
7	105
8	100

16. **(LO 1)** What is the marginal utility of the fifth unit?
    a) 10
    b) 20
    c) 100
    d) Cannot be answered from this information

17. **(LO 1)** With the consumption of what quantity is marginal utility equal to zero?
    a) 1
    b) 5
    c) 7
    d) 8

18. **(LO 6)** In order for price discrimination to work, three conditions must be fulfilled. Which of the following is not one of those conditions?
    a) The seller must be able to identify and separate different groups of buyers.
    b) The different groups of buyers must have different elasticities of demand.
    c) The product must be a necessity.
    d) It must be impossible to resell the product.

19. **(LO 2)** Suppose that, for a certain consumer, the marginal utility of product A is equal to 40 and its price is $42, while the marginal utility of product B is 30 and its price is $40. What conclusion can be inferred from this?
    a) This consumer should buy more of product A and less of product B.
    b) This consumer should buy more of product B and less of product A.
    c) This consumer should buy more of product B because it is cheaper.
    d) This consumer should buy neither product, since the prices exceed the marginal utilities.
    e) This consumer should buy more of product B because it gives greater value for money.

Refer to **Table 5.14** when answering questions 20 and 21.

TABLE 5.14

Quantity	TU	MU
1	100	_____
2	_____	90
3	270	_____
4	_____	90
5	400	_____
6	_____	50

20. **(LO 1)** What are the missing numbers in the total utility column?
    a) 135, 305, and 435
    b) 90, 340, and 450
    c) 190, 340, and 450
    d) Cannot be determined from the information given

21. **(LO 1)** What are the missing numbers in the marginal utility column?
    a) 0, 80, and 60
    b) 100, 80, and 60
    c) 100, 90, and 82
    d) Cannot be determined from the information given

22. **(LO 5)** Under which of the following circumstances will total consumer surplus be greatest?
    a) When price is high and demand is elastic
    b) When price is low and demand is inelastic
    c) When price is low and demand is elastic
    d) When price is high and demand is inelastic

23. **(LO 6)** Which of the following statements is true about price discrimination?
    a) It is practised on the basis of age, time, and the volume of purchases.
    b) It is illegal in Canada.
    c) It works with luxury goods but not with necessities.
    d) It works with necessities but not with luxury goods.

Refer to **Table 5.15** when answering questions 24 and 25.

TABLE 5.15

Quantity Consumed	MU Apples	MU Bananas
1	20	18
2	18	17
3	16	14
4	14	11
5	12	8
6	10	5
7	8	2
8	6	0

24. **(LO 2)** Suppose that apples and bananas cost $1 each and this consumer has $8 to spend. In order to maximize her total utility, how many of each should she purchase?
    a) 3 apples and 5 bananas
    b) 4 apples and 4 bananas
    c) 5 apples and 3 bananas
    d) 8 apples
    e) 8 bananas

25. **(LO 2)** Suppose that an apple costs $2 and a banana costs $1 and this consumer has $8 to spend. In order to maximize her total utility, how many of each should she purchase?
    a) 1 apple and 6 bananas
    b) 2 apples and 4 bananas
    c) 3 apples and 2 bananas
    d) 4 apples
    e) 8 bananas

Intermediate (Questions 26–32)

26. **(LO 5)** What does the diamond–water paradox refer to?
    a) The fact that water is far more plentiful than diamonds, even though people need more diamonds.
    b) The fact that water is far more valuable than diamonds, and yet its price tends to be far lower.
    c) The fact that although people do not necessarily want diamonds, they are prepared to pay a high price for them.
    d) The fact that diamonds are more plentiful than water in some countries.

27. **(LO 5)** Which of the following products are likely to yield the greatest amount of consumer surplus?
    a) Water
    b) Diamonds
    c) Ice cream
    d) A Persian carpet

Refer to **Figure 5.6** when answering questions 28 and 29.

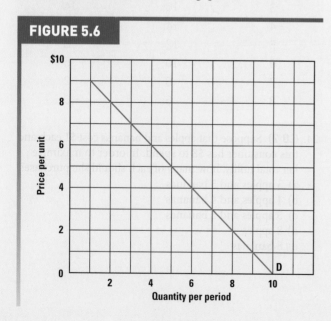

FIGURE 5.6

28. **(LO 5)** If partial units cannot be purchased, what is the value of total consumer surplus at a unit price of $5?
    a) $10
    b) $12
    c) $20
    d) $35

29. **(LO 5)** If partial units cannot be purchased, at what unit price is the total consumer surplus equal to $21?
    a) $3
    b) $4
    c) $5
    d) $6
    e) $9

30. **(LO 2)** Suppose that Jon is purchasing the optimal amounts of apples and oranges. The marginal utility of the last apple is 8 and of the last orange is 6. If the price of an apple is $1, what must be the price of an orange?
    a) 50 cents
    b) 75 cents
    c) $1.33
    d) $1.40
    e) Cannot be determined from this information

Refer to **Table 5.16** when answering questions 31 and 32. The following table shows Ketta's total utility for coffee and croissants:

TABLE 5.16

Quantity	Coffee Total Utility	Croissants Total Utility
1	10	11
2	18	20
3	24	27
4	28	32
5	30	35

31. **(LO 2)** If Ketta has a budget of $15, and the price of both are coffees and croissants are $3 each, what will be her optimal purchase?
    a) 5 croissants
    b) 1 coffee and 4 croissants
    c) 2 coffees and 3 croissants
    d) 3 coffees and 2 croissants
    e) 4 coffees and 1 croissant

32. **(LO 2)** If Ketta has a budget of $15 and the price of croissants is $3, but the price of a coffee is $2, what will be her optimal purchase?
    a) 5 croissants
    b) 3 coffees and 2 croissants
    c) 3 coffees and 3 croissants
    d) 4 coffees and 3 croissants
    e) 6 coffees and 1 croissant

Advanced (Questions 33–35)

33. **(LO X)** Suppose that the price of a plate of sushi is $10 and that Jan's marginal utility is 8, while Jin's marginal utility is 12. What can be deduced from this information?
    a) Jin should buy the sushi, but Jan should not.
    b) Jin likes sushi better than Jan does.
    c) Jan's MU per $ spent on sushi is greater than Jin's.
    d) No deductions can be made from this information.

Refer to **Table 5.17** when answering questions 34 and 35.

34. **(LO 2)** Assume that pastries cost $4 each. What are the missing numbers in the MU column for pastries?
    a) 15, 6.25, 2.92, 1.31, 0.80, 0.42, 0
    b) 15, 25, 26.25, 21, 20, 15, 0
    c) 120, 90, 65, 45, 25, 23, 10
    d) 60, 50, 35, 21, 16, 10, 0

35. **(LO 2, 4)** Assume that the price of a latté is $5 and pieces of pastry are $4 each. If Kyle has $36 to spend, how many units of each will he buy in order to maximize his TU?
    a) 2 lattés and 6 pieces of pastry
    b) 3 lattés and 5 pieces of pastry
    c) 4 lattés and 4 pieces of pastry
    d) 5 lattés and 3 pieces of pastry

TABLE 5.17

	LATTÉS			PIECES OF PASTRY	
Quantity	MU	MU per Dollar Spent	Quantity	MU	MU per Dollar Spent
1	120	_____	1	_____	15
2	90	_____	2	_____	12.5
3	65	_____	3	_____	8.75
4	45	_____	4	_____	5.25
5	25	_____	5	_____	4
6	23	_____	6	_____	2.5
7	10	_____	7	_____	0

Parallel Problems

ANSWERED PROBLEMS

36A. **(LO 2) Key Problem** Suppose that you are vacationing at a resort in the Caribbean and you are trying to determine how to spend your time and money on two activities, windsurfing and snorkelling, which both cost $10 per hour. The marginal utility of the activities are shown in **Table 5.18**.
   a) Complete the columns of total utilities.
   b) Assume that you have a budget of $60. To maximize your total utility, how would you allocate your spending between the two activities? What is the resulting total utility?

   $ _____ (_____ hours) on windsurfing, and $ _____ (_____ hours) on snorkelling. Total utility: _____ utils.
   c) At the end of the day, you dig deep into your pocket and discover an extra $20. How would you allocate this additional spending between the two activities so as to maximize your total utility? What is the resulting total utility?
   $ _____ (_____ hours) on windsurfing, and $ _____ (_____ hours) on snorkelling. Total utility: _____ utils.
   d) Suppose that your utility from the two activities remains unchanged the next day, when you arrive

TABLE 5.18

| No. of Hours | WINDSURFING | | | SNORKELLING | |
	Marginal Utility	Total Utility		Marginal Utility	Total Utility
1	85	_____		100	_____
2	80	_____		90	_____
3	65	_____		75	_____
4	60	_____		70	_____
5	55	_____		50	_____
6	40	_____		25	_____
7	30	_____		20	_____
8	5	_____		10	_____

with $80 in you pocket. Unfortunately, you discover that the hourly charge for snorkelling has increased to $15. How will you now allocate your expenditures to maximize your total utility, assuming that partial hours cannot be purchased? (Completing the columns in **Table 5.19** marked "Marginal Utility per Dollar Spent" will be helpful.)

$ _____ (_____ hours) on windsurfing, and $ _____ (_____ hours) on snorkelling. Total utility: _____ utils.

e) Show the effects of the change in the price of snorkelling in **Figure 5.7**.

f) What has happened to the demand for windsurfing?

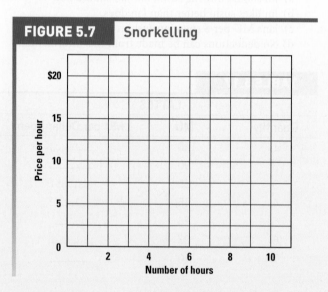

FIGURE 5.7   Snorkelling

TABLE 5.19

| No. of Hours | WINDSURFING | | | | SNORKELLING | | |
	Marginal Utility	Total Utility	Marginal Utility per Dollar Spent		Marginal Utility	Total Utility	Marginal Utility per Dollar Spent
1	85	_____	_____		100	_____	_____
2	80	_____	_____		90	_____	_____
3	65	_____	_____		75	_____	_____
4	60	_____	_____		70	_____	_____
5	55	_____	_____		50	_____	_____
6	40	_____	_____		25	_____	_____
7	30	_____	_____		20	_____	_____
8	5	_____	_____		10	_____	_____

Basic (Problems 37A–44A)

37A. (LO 1) Given Jan's total utility from consuming packets of potato chips in **Table 5.20**, calculate her marginal utility for each unit.

TABLE 5.20

Quantity	Total Utility	Marginal Utility
1	60	_____
2	110	_____
3	140	_____
4	155	_____
5	167	_____
6	177	_____
7	186	_____
8	192	_____
9	195	_____
10	196	_____

38A. (LO 2) Given Jon's marginal utility from consuming packets of potato chips in **Table 5.21**, calculate his total utility for each quantity.

TABLE 5.21

Quantity	Total Utility	Marginal Utility
1	_____	38
2	_____	26
3	_____	22
4	_____	18
5	_____	14
6	_____	10
7	_____	8
8	_____	5
9	_____	3
10	_____	2

39A. (LO 2) Elina cannot decide whether to buy a packet of potato chips, cheese whirls, or nacho chips, whose marginal utilities are 50, 36, and 42, respectively. The prices of the snacks are $1.25, $0.80, and $1.20, respectively.
  a) Calculate the MU per dollar spent for each of the three products. _____ ; _____ ; _____
  b) If Elina can afford to buy only one packet, which should she buy? _____

40A. (LO 2) Erika's evaluation of packets of nacho chips in terms of $MU is as follows: 1st packet, $3; 2nd packet, $2.50; 3rd packet, $1.80; 4th packet, $1.50; and the 5th packet, $1.25. If the price of nacho chips is $1.20, and June buys five packets, calculate her marginal consumer surplus for each packet and the total consumer surplus from all five.
Consumer Surplus: _____ ; _____ ; _____ ; _____ ; _____ ; total: _____ .

41A. (LO 4)
  a) Suppose that Daniel is willing to pay a maximum of $5 for his first slice of pizza. For each additional slice, he would be prepared to pay up to 50 cents less. If Daniel could obtain the pizza for free, how many slices would he eat?
Number of slices: _____
  b) If the price of a slice of pizza happened to be $2, how many slices would he purchase (assuming his budget allowed it)? What would be his total consumer surplus as a result?
Number of slices: _____ ; consumer surplus $ _____

42A. (LO 4) **Table 5.22** shows Juanita's demand for rented videos.
  a) Complete the above table.
  b) At what quantity is total utility maximized? _____
  c) What is marginal utility at this quantity? _____

43A. (LO 1) What does *marginal utility* mean, and what is the law of *diminishing marginal utility*?

44A. (LO 3) Explain why a rational consumer does not spend all of his income buying only his favourite product.

TABLE 5.22

Quantity	MU	TU
1	50	_____
2	_____	90
3	_____	125
4	25	_____
5	20	_____
6	_____	188
7	_____	200
8	6	_____
9	_____	206
10	_____	200

Intermediate (Problems 45A–51A)

45A. **(LO 4)** **Figure 5.8** depicts Christian's $MU for ice creams and for giant chocolate cookies.
   a) If Christian's budget only allowed him to make a total of six purchases, how many of each product would he buy?
   _____ ice creams, and _____ cookies.
   b) If he found he could afford 10, how many of each product would he buy?
   _____ ice creams, and _____ cookies.

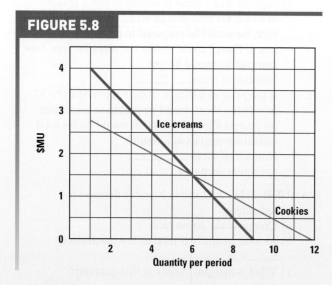

FIGURE 5.8

46A. **(LO 2)**
   a) Chika has calculated the marginal utility that she derives from her paid employment and from leisure. This is presented in **Table 5.23**. In her ideal world,

TABLE 5.23

Hours	MU Paid Employment	MU Leisure
1	100	80
2	90	75
3	80	70
4	70	65
5	60	60
6	50	55
7	40	50
8	30	45
9	20	40
10	10	35

where she could work as few or as many hours as she wished, how would she allocate her 16 waking hours? (She does need to sleep.)
   _____ working hours, and _____ leisure hours
   b) Unfortunately, Chika begins to realize that unless she gets an education she will not enjoy a high salary and therefore will not be able to afford more leisure time. She therefore decides to spend six hours each day studying (in addition to her eight hours' sleep). How will she now devote the remaining hours between work and leisure?
   _____ working hours, and _____ leisure hours

47A. **(LO 2)** Maria has $7 to spend on breakfast. Unfortunately, the snack bar in the building where she works has only three items: muffins at $1 each; soup at $1.50; and cappuccinos at $2 each. Given her utility figures in **Table 5.24**, how should she allocate her budget? _____ muffin(s); _____ soup(s); _____ cappuccino(s)

TABLE 5.24

Quantity	Muffins TU	Soup TU	Cappuccinos TU
1	60	120	70
2	110	186	130
3	140	234	160
4	160	273	170
5	162	291	175

48A. **(LO 6)** Sam's drive-in movie theatre attracts two main groups of customers: teenagers and parents with young children. The demand of the two groups is shown in **Table 5.25**.
   a) If Sam charges a single admission price and wants to maximize his total revenue, what price should he charge, and what will be his total revenue?
   Price: $ _____ ; total revenue: $ _____
   b) Suppose, instead, that Sam is able to price discriminate between the two groups and charge different prices to each. How much would he charge each, and what would be his total revenue now?
   Price to teenagers: $ _____
   Price to parents: $ _____
   Total revenue: $ _____

49A. **(LO 2)** Jeremy loves eating toast and drinking cans of pop. **Table 5.26** shows his marginal utility measured in terms of dollars, that is, in $MU.

TABLE 5.25

	TEENAGERS			PARENTS		BOTH
Admission Price ($)	Quantity Demanded	Total Revenue ($)		Quantity Demanded	Total Revenue ($)	Total Revenue ($)
8	100	_____		0	_____	_____
7	150	_____		5	_____	_____
6	180	_____		15	_____	_____
5	200	_____		30	_____	_____
4	210	_____		55	_____	_____
3	215	_____		80	_____	_____
2	218	_____		100	_____	_____
1	220	_____		150	_____	_____

TABLE 5.26

PIECES OF TOAST		POPS	
Pieces	$MU	Cans	$MU
1	3	1	1.50
2	2.50	2	1.40
3	2	3	1.00
4	1.20	4	0.60
5	0.20	5	0.20
6	−0.50	6	−0.20

Suppose that Jeremy has a budget of $7 and the price of both the toast and the pop is $1.

a) How many of each item will Jeremy buy to maximize his total utility? Pieces of toast: _____ Cans of pop: _____

b) How much $ total utility will he derive? Answer: _____

c) How much total consumer surplus will he obtain from each item? Toast: _____ Pop: _____

Now, suppose that Jeremy moves back to his parents' home, where he considers eating to be a free activity.

d) How much of each item will he now consume? Pieces of toast: _____ Cans of pop: _____

e) How much total consumer surplus will he now obtain from each item? Toast: _____ Pop: _____

50A. **(LO 1, 4)** Explain the relationship between the marginal utility of a product and the demand for it.

51A. **(LO 6)** What does price discrimination mean? Give three examples of price discrimination.

Advanced (Problems 52A–58A)

52A. **(LO 2)** Christina has decided to spend her evening eating sushi and watching videos. Each piece of sushi and each video costs $2. Her total utility for the two products is shown in **Table 5.27**.

a) How should Christina allocate a budget of $10 to achieve utility maximization, and what will be her total utility? _____ videos and _____ pieces of sushi. Total utility _____ .

b) Suppose that the sushi shop offered a deal whereby Christina can buy a four-piece pack for $6. How will Christina allocate her budget now, and what will be her total utility now? _____ videos and _____ pieces of sushi and _____ sushi packs. Total utility _____ .

TABLE 5.27

VIDEO MOVIES		SUSHI PIECES	
Number	Total Utility	Number	Total Utility
1	48	1	45
2	86	2	85
3	112	3	115
4	130	4	134
5	142	5	150
6	150	6	158

53A. **(LO 6)** In Mt. Pleasant, the consumption of green tea seems to be related to political party membership. The demand for kilograms of tea per month by party affiliation is shown in **Table 5.28**.

TABLE 5.28

Kilograms of Tea Price	Liberals Quantity	Conservatives Quantity	NDPs Quantity
$6.00	4	6	8
5.40	5	7	9
4.80	6	8	10
4.20	7	9	11
3.60	8	10	12
3.00	9	11	13

A single firm supplies green tea in Mt. Pleasant.
a) What single price should the firm charge everyone if it wants to maximize its total sales revenue?
Price: _____
b) What will be its resulting total revenue?
Answer: _____
c) Suppose that the government of Mt. Pleasant allows the firm to price-discriminate on the basis of political affiliation. If the firm wishes to maximize its total sales revenue, how much should it charge each group?
Liberal price: _____
Conservative price: _____
NDP price: _____
d) What is the firm's total sales revenue now?
Answer: _____
e) What is the price elasticity of demand for these three groups between the prices of $6 and $5.40?
Liberal: _____ Conservative: _____
NDP: _____
f) What is the relationship between elasticity and the prices charged? Answer: _____

54A. **(LO 5)** **Figure 5.9** indicates Alberto's demand for tickets for the amusement park ride called the Twisted Bender.
a) What is Alberto's total consumer surplus if the price per ticket is $6? Answer: _____
b) What is Alberto's total consumer surplus if the price per ticket is $2? Answer: _____

55A. **(LO 2)** **Figure 5.10** indicates Marshall's marginal utility for two products, A and B.
a) If $P_A = P_B = \$1$, what quantity of each good would Marshall purchase if his budget was $8?
Quantity of A: _____
Quantity of B: _____

FIGURE 5.9

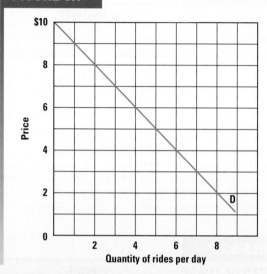

FIGURE 5.10

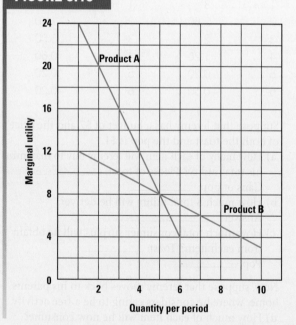

b) Suppose that P_A increases to $2. If Marshall's budget remained the same, what quantities of each good would he now purchase?
Quantity of A: _____
Quantity of B: _____

56A. **(LO 5)** Suppose that that **Figure 5.11** depicts the demand for grape oil, which can be purchased in any quantities and sold at any price.
   a) What is the total consumer surplus if the price per litre is $4? Answer: _____
   b) What is the total consumer surplus if the price per litre is $2? (*Hint:* Area of a triangle?) Answer: _____

57A. **(LO 4)** **Figure 5.12** shows the demand for haircuts at the Uppercuts Hairdressing Salon.
   a) If the salon charges a single price of $9, what will its total daily revenue be? Answer: _____
   b) Suppose, instead, that the salon practises price discrimination and now charges $15 for haircuts to regulars but only $9 to retirees and economics instructors. What will its new total daily revenue be? Answer: _____
   c) What is the value of consumer surplus that the salon has captured as a result of price discriminating? Answer: _____
   d) Show in **Figure 5.12** the area that represents the value of consumer surplus captured.

58A. **(LO 1)** "If marginal utility is decreasing, then total utility must also be decreasing." Is this correct?

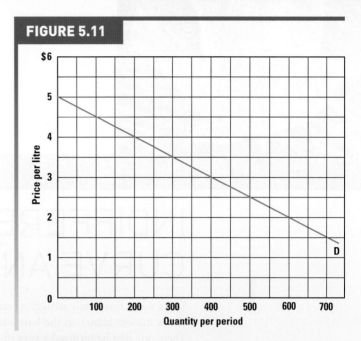

FIGURE 5.11

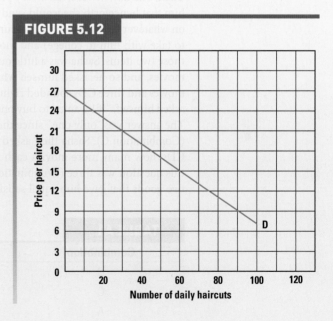

FIGURE 5.12

INDIFFERENCE CURVE ANALYSIS

Sasha was a financially struggling student who spent all his hard-earned savings (plus the proceeds of his student loans) on the bare essentials of life—food, rent, tuition, books, bus pass, and so on. Then, one day, he received a very pleasant surprise in the mail. An understanding aunt wrote to tell him that henceforth she would send him $64 per month on the condition that he spend all of it only on whatever gave him a little pleasure. Since Sasha loved both music (he had been given a CD player to take with him to college) and movies, he decided that he would spend this monthly gift on only those two items. Sasha was a little out of touch with prices but he did know that CDs cost more than movies, and so he asked himself what would be his ideal combination to purchase. He felt that five movies and three CDs sounded right (Combination B). But then he thought a little more about it and asked himself, "If I wanted to buy one more CD, how many movies would I be prepared to sacrifice?" The answer was "only one," since the prospect of fewer than 4 movies per month was not appealing (Combination C). Sasha then asked the same question in reverse: "If I had to sacrifice one of these CDs, how many more movies each month would compensate me?" He decided that the answer to this question was three (Combination A). In effect, Sasha now identified three combinations of the two goods that gave him equal satisfaction (or pleasure) as summarized in **Table A1**.

TABLE A1		
Combination	CDs	Movies
B	3	5
C	4	4
A	2	8

THE INDIFFERENCE CURVE

indifference curve:
shows the combinations of goods that would give the same satisfaction (or total utility) to an individual (or household).

An economist, observing Sasha's thought process, would say that Sasha was attempting to maximize total utility from his spending on entertainment and had identified three points on his **indifference curve**.

Figure A1 illustrates this indifference curve.

There are two important aspects to this indifference curve that we need to emphasize. First, it is downward sloping, which is to say that Sasha will be willing to give up CDs only if he gets more movies, and vice versa. This seems eminently reasonable. Second, the rate at which he is willing to

FIGURE A1

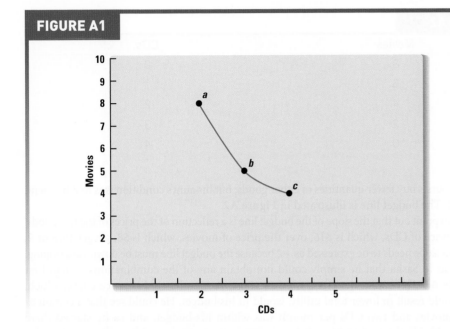

Sasha's preferences for movies and CDs are such that he is indifferent among the three possible combinations indicated by points *a*, *b*, and *c*. Connecting these points yields an indifference curve.

give up movies for a CD or CDs for a movie is crucial. Economists call this the **marginal rate of substitution**, or, as we will call it, the MRS.

If we focus on point *a* in **Figure A1**, we see that this is the combination of eight movies and two CDs. If we move from point *a* to point *b*, we see that Sasha is willing to give up three movies (eight down to five) to gain one more CD (two up to three). Between these two points, the value of Sasha's MRS of a CD for movies is 3/1 or 3. Note, however, what happens as we move from point *b* to *c*. Here, Sasha is willing to give up only one movie (five down to four) to gain one more CD (three up to four). Thus, here, the value of his MRS of CDs for movies is only 1/1 or 1. What we have just identified is the **law of diminishing marginal rate of substitution**. This is quite analogous to the law of diminishing marginal utility that we encountered in Chapter 5 and reflects the fact that the more CDs that Sasha already has, the fewer movies he is willing to give up to gain yet another CD. Again, this seems reasonable because we know that Sasha loves both CDs and movies.

The effect of the law of diminishing MRS is that the indifference curve will be "bowed in" (convex), and because we have already established that it is downward sloping, we now have the basic shape of all indifference curves. Furthermore, we can point out two more things about the indifference curve: its slope is equal to the MRS, and this slope becomes less steep as we move down the curve, since the MRS of CDs for movies diminishes the more CDs Sasha has. We, thus, know that Sasha's indifference curve in **Figure A1** would become less steep to the right of point *c* and more steep to the left of point *a*.

THE BUDGET LINE

Let us now return to Sasha's story to report that he has just made a trip downtown to price out both CDs and movies (remember his previous financial situation had made him a little out of touch). He was surprised, and more than a little disappointed, to learn that movies were now $8 and the type of CDs that he wanted averaged $16. He then returned to his dorm and made **Table A2**, which lists the combinations of the two goods that he could *afford to buy* with his budget of $64 per month.

We can now graph the data in **Table A2** and obtain what economists call the budget line (BL) or budget constraint line, since Sasha's limited budget constrains him to only these combinations

marginal rate of substitution: the amount of one good a consumer is willing to give up to get one more unit of another good and still maintain the same level of satisfaction.

law of diminishing marginal rate of substitution: the more of one good a person has, the less of another good he will be willing to give up to gain an additional unit of the first good.

TABLE A2

Movies	CDs
8	0
6	1
4	2
2	3
0	4

(he could, of course, buy fewer quantities of either goods, but his aunt's condition was that he spend all of the $64). The budget line is illustrated in **Figure A2**.

We need to point out that the slope of the budget line is a reflection of the prices of the two goods. If we put the price of CDs, which is $16, over the price of movies, which is $8, we get 16/8 or 2. Technically, this slope needs to be expressed as −2 because the budget line must be downward sloping.

It was clear to Sasha that he simply could not obtain any of the combinations he had first listed in **Table A1**. He would, therefore, need to construct another indifference curve, which, although it would result in lower total utility, would fit his budget. He could see that a combination of four movies and two CDs per month was within his budget, and so he started there (Combination E). He then asked himself how many more movies would compensate him for reducing the number of CDs from two to one. He decided that this would be three movies, giving him a second combination of seven movies and one CD (Combination D). He then asked himself, alternatively, how many movies would he sacrifice in order to have three, rather than two CDs. The answer is only one, which gives him a third combination (F) of three movies and three CDs. These new combinations are summarized in **Table A3**.

Since Sasha is indifferent among these three (new) combinations, we can take this information and plot a new indifference curve (I_2) on **Figure A3**.

Let us examine what **Figure A3** is telling us. First, points d, e, and f are all combinations of the two goods to which Sasha is indifferent, since they are all on the same indifference curve, I_2, and give him equal utility. Second, Sasha would prefer any combination of the two goods on indifference

FIGURE A2

The budget line, BL, identifies the various combinations of movies and CDs that Sasha is able to afford given his financial constraint of $64. The budget line begins with the combination of 8 movies and zero CDs and has a slope of −2. Any combination of the two goods in the pink-shaded area is unobtainable.

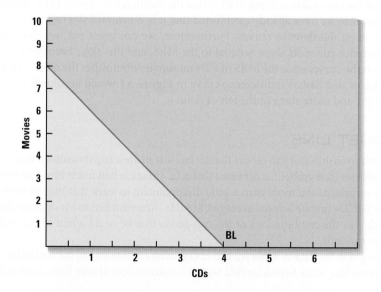

TABLE A3

Combination	Movies	CDs
d	7	1
e	4	2
f	3	3

FIGURE A3

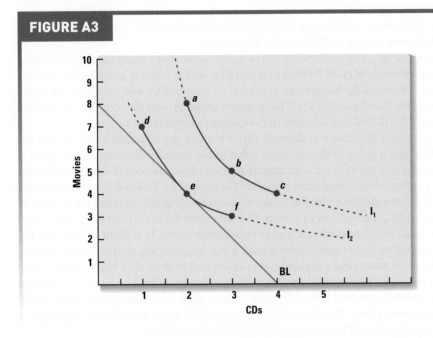

Sasha is indifferent to the combinations represented by points *d, e,* and *f* because they all are on the same indifference curve, I_2.
Given his budget line, BL, only combination *e* is affordable.

curve I_1 since it higher than (or is to the right of) I_2. Third, he is limited by his budget to the points, that lie on the budget line, BL. And finally, of all these points only *e* is within Sasha's budget, and this will, then, be his obvious choice.

UTILITY MAXIMIZATION

There is something very fundamental about point *e* that you need to fully understand. At this point, the indifference curve and the budget line are tangent, and this means that their slopes are the same. Since we know that this slope is −2 and since we have established that the budget line is equal to the relative prices of the two goods and that the slope of the indifference curve is equal to the MRS, we have:

$$\frac{P_{CDs}}{P_M} = MRS$$

Furthermore, we know that the MRS is a reflection of Sasha's marginal utility for the two goods. Therefore, the above equation can be expressed as:

$$\frac{P_{CDs}}{P_M} = \frac{MU_{CD}}{MU_M}$$

This second equation can be rewritten as:

$$\frac{MU_M}{P_M} = \frac{MU_{CD}}{P_{CD}}$$

You will recognize that this is the optimal purchasing rule that we obtained in Chapter 5. Sasha will maximize his utility, given a budget constraint, by equating the marginal utility per dollar spent on movies with the marginal utility per dollar spent on CDs. What is different about the indifference curve approach, however, is that we got here without having to assign values for the marginal utilities of either good. Interesting, isn't it?

THE INCOME AND SUBSTITUTION EFFECT

In Chapter 2, we learned that if the price of a particular good increases, then the quantity demanded will decrease for two reasons—the income effect and the substitution effect. This can be illustrated nicely using indifference curves, as illustrated in **Figure A4**.

Given budget line BL_1 and indifference curve I_2, the consumer's maximization point is a, which results in quantity Q_1 of good B being purchased (as well as some of good A). An increase in the price of good B pivots the budget line to the left, as seen in BL_2, and the consumer's purchases change to point b and quantity Q_3. This is quite consistent with the idea that an increase in the price of good B will lead to a decrease in the quantity demanded.

But how much of the decrease (Q_1 down to Q_3) is because the consumer's real income has decreased, and how much is due to the consumer substituting the now relatively cheaper good A for good B? To answer this question, we conceptually give the consumer enough additional income to enable her to purchase the original combination of the two goods. This is illustrated by budget line BL_3, which has been shifted right and passes through the original combination at point a. You should note that BL_3 is parallel to BL_2, since BL_3 represents the same price level as BL_2 with a higher income level. BL_3 is tangent to a higher indifference curve, I_3 at point c. Note that the consumer could purchase the original combination a but has, instead, chosen combination c. This latter combination must yield a higher level of utility and is, thus, on a higher indifference curve. The point of tangency between BL_3 and I_3, point c, yields quantity Q_2. Thus, this consumer has decreased her purchases of good B from Q_1 to Q_2 because she is substituting good A for good B, which is the substitution effect. The decrease in the quantity of good B purchased, Q_2 to Q_3, is the result of the decrease in real income and, thus, is the income effect.

This completes our brief discussion of indifference curve analysis.

FIGURE A4

Point a illustrates the original maximization of utility, which results in the consumer purchasing quantity Q_1 of good B. An increase in the price of good B results in the budget pivoting from BL_1 to BL_2 and a new maximization illustrated by b. Budget line BL_3 passes through the original combination a but is now tangent to a higher indifference curve, I_3, at point c and quantity purchased of Q_2. Thus, Q_1 to Q_2 is the substitution effect, and Q_2 to Q_3 is the income effect.

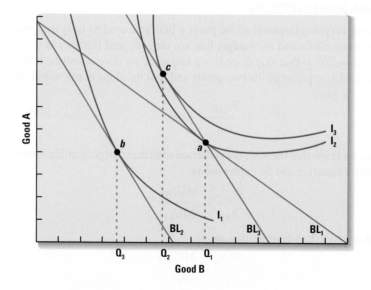

Review

NEW GLOSSARY TERMS

indifference curve   172

law of diminishing marginal rate of substitution   173

marginal rate of substitution   173

Answered Questions

These questions can also be found online on Connect.

Indicate whether the following statements are true or false. If false, indicate why they are false.

1. The budget line is bowed out from the origin.
   T or F If false: _____
   _____

2. An increase in the price of the product on the vertical axis will make the BL steeper.
   T or F If false: _____
   _____

3. It is logically inconsistent for any two indifference curves to cross.
   T or F If false: _____
   _____

4. Lower indifference curves represent lower levels of income.
   T or F If false: _____
   _____

5. The point at which the budget line is tangent to the indifference curve is where the consumer derives equal utility from both products.
   T or F If false: _____
   _____

6. Suppose that a consumer has a budget of $30. The price of a can of pop is $2, while pizza slices are $3. Which of the following combinations is on the budget line?
   a) 15 cans of pop and 10 slices of pizza
   b) 6 cans of pop and 6 slices of pizza
   c) 0 can of pop and 15 slices of pizza

Table A4 shows combinations of CDs and movies that give a consumer equal amounts of total utility.

TABLE A4		
Combination	CDs	Movies
A	0	16
B	1	9
C	2	5
D	3	3
E	4	2

7. Refer to Table A4 to answer this question. How many movies is the consumer prepared to give up in order to obtain a second CD?
   a) 3
   b) 4
   c) 5

8. Suppose that John's budget doubles and the prices of both of the goods he spends this budget on also double. What will happen to his budget line?
   a) It will shift out but not change slope.
   b) It will shift in but not change slope.
   c) It will remain unchanged.

9. If the price of one good changes but the price of a second good does not, how can the income and substitution effects be identified graphically?
   a) By drawing in a third budget line, parallel to the original one, which is tangent to the original indifference curve
   b) By drawing in a third budget line, parallel to the original one, which passes through the original point of utility maximization

c) By drawing in a third budget line, parallel to the second one, which is tangent to the original indifference curve
d) By drawing in a third budget line, parallel to the second one, which passes through the original point of utility maximization

10. Suppose that a consumer has a budget of $64 and the price of a CD is $16, while a movie costs $8. If CDs are measured on the vertical axis, what is the slope of the budget line?
   a) 4
   b) 2
   c) −4
   d) −2
   e) −1/2

Parallel Problems

ANSWERED PROBLEMS

11A. **Table A5** shows three indifference schedules for Barbara. The price of each fruit is $1, and Barbara's budget is $12.
   a) Draw the three indifference curves and the budget line on **Figure A5**.
   b) What quantities of each will maximize Barbara's total utility if she spends all of her budget?
      _____ apples;
      _____ bananas

   Suppose that the price of apples increases to $1.50.
   c) Draw the new budget line in **Figure A5**.
   d) What quantities of each will now maximize Barbara's total utility if she spends all of her budget?
      _____ apples;
      _____ bananas

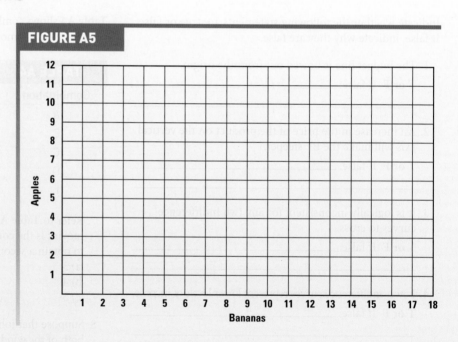

FIGURE A5

(vertical axis: Apples, from 1 to 12; horizontal axis: Bananas, from 1 to 18)

TABLE A5

INDIFFERENCE CURVE 1		INDIFFERENCE CURVE 2		INDIFFERENCE CURVE 3	
Apples	Bananas	Apples	Bananas	Apples	Bananas
9	2	10	4	12	6
6	3	6	6	8	7
5	5	5	9	6	8
4	9	4	13	5	11
3	14	3	18	4	16

12A. **Figure A6** shows an indifference map for Alan.
   A's cost $3, and B's cost $2.
   Alan has a budget of $30.
   a) Draw Alan's budget line in **Figure A6**.
   b) What quantities of each product will maximize
      Alan's total utility if he spends all of his budget?
      _____ A's; _____ B's
   Suppose that the price of B's increases to $3.
   c) Draw in the new budget line in **Figure A6**.
   d) What quantities of each will maximize Alan's
      total utility if he spends all of his $30 budget?
      _____ A's; _____ B's

   e) In **Figure A6**, draw a budget line (BL$_3$) which
      reflects the new price but with the same real income
      as before the price change. _____ A's;
      _____ B's
   f) How much does the quantity of B decline due to:
      the substitution effect _____; the income
      effect _____

FIGURE A6

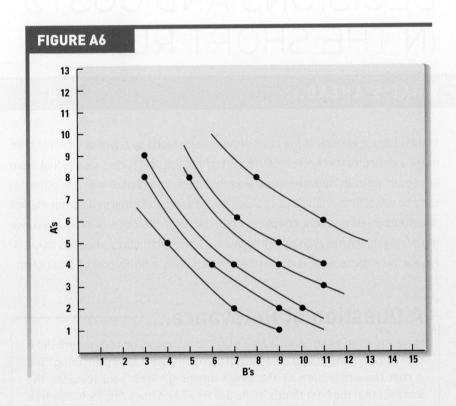

CHAPTER 6

A FIRM'S PRODUCTION DECISIONS AND COSTS IN THE SHORT RUN

WHAT'S AHEAD...

In this chapter, we look at the costs of production faced by a typical firm. First, we make a distinction between explicit cost and implicit cost. Later, we see that there are seven ways to measure costs and that each interrelates with the others in specific ways. This enables us to study the behaviour of firms in different market structures in subsequent chapters. To understand the costs of production, we must first understand *productivity* because a firm's productivity underlies its costs. Finally, we explore what is meant by a reduction in a firm's cost of production.

A Question of Relevance...

Have you even been given a free ticket to a concert or ball game? Did it cost you anything? Did it cost the person who gave it to you anything? Did it cost the organizers of the event anything? Who said (besides the Beatles) that the best things in life are free? And does this include a free lunch? In this chapter, we will discuss how to identify free goods and economic goods and how to measure the cost of economic goods.

Chapters 4 and 5 looked in some detail behind the demand curve. In this chapter and the next, we will explore the derivation of the supply curve, so our focus shifts from the behaviour of consumers to that of producers, and to an analysis of the business organization—what economists call "the firm."

We will discuss the firm and its behaviour in the next five chapters. As a general introduction to the study of the firm, consider some of the types of decisions the typical firm must make:

- What is the right product(s) to produce?
- What is the right level of production for now, and how might this change in the future?
- What methods of distribution and marketing approaches are the most appropriate?
- What is the right price to charge?

Out of this come two fundamental questions that economists ask about the behaviour of firms. First, how do firms decide on the price of their products? Second, how do they determine the level of production? In the process of answering these questions, we will look (in Chapters 8 through 11) at what economists call market structure. But first, we need to understand all that falls under the general topic called the *costs of production*. We will look at short-run costs in this chapter and long-run costs in the next chapter. The difference between the short run and the long run will be explained below.

Production is the activity of a business organization or firm using inputs to obtain output of some product. We see examples of production every day. For example, think of sand, gravel, cement, water, machines, and labour (inputs) that are used to produce concrete (the output). Of course, the inputs used in production have to be paid for, and this payment becomes the firm's cost.

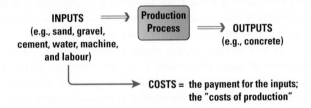

When most students hear the word "costs," they think of the dollars and cents actually paid out by the firm. Many costs can be thought of in just this way, but this is by no means the whole story. For example, a firm may buy a machine for $200 000 that it expects to be able to use for eight years. What is the cost of this machine in the first year of its use? Surely, the answer is not the full $200 000. Instead, could the cost could be thought of as the portion of the machine that is used up or worn out during that year. The annual amount of this wear is called **depreciation**. In this example, the cost of depreciation could be equal to, say, one-eighth of $200 000, or $25 000.

depreciation: the annual cost of any asset that is expected to be in use for more than one year.

 ADDED DIMENSION   Why Do Firms Exist? The Coase Answer

One of the truly intriguing questions in economics is: why do firms exist? Ronald Coase (1910–), a Nobel laureate who taught for many years at the University of Chicago, offered an elegant answer in the late 1930s. Consider this situation: I want a new house. I could find a lot and arrange to buy it. Then I could hire someone to prepare the lot for construction, locate and hire someone to dig a hole for the basement, hire still someone else to prepare and pour the concrete foundation, hire others to frame the building (after someone else has been found to design the structure), and hire still others to do the roofing, plumbing, electrical, and finishing work.

At each stage, I would have to seek bids, negotiate prices, decide on product types and schedules, and hope that everyone delivered on what they promised. All of this would take a lot of time and money—that is, it has *transactions costs*.

Alternatively, I could simply buy a house that some firm has put on the market. In putting a house up for sale, the firm has absorbed all the transactions costs, and since it has produced dozens (hundreds) of houses, including the one I buy, it has been able to reduce the per-house transactions costs. That is why a firm exists—it is more efficient.

6.1 EXPLICIT AND IMPLICIT COSTS

L01 Understand how and why economists measure costs differently from how accountants do and distinguish between the accountants' and economists' views of profits.

Let us take another example, this time the case of smaller firms of the mom-and-pop variety, in which the owners often contribute their own money and time to the firm. Is the contribution of money to the firm free? Should we consider the time put into the firm by its owners as having no costs? The answer to both questions is no, and this once again raises the concept of opportunity costs, which was introduced in Chapter 1.

Let us say that two hypothetical owners, Otto and Melissa, inherit $96 000 and put it into their tote bag company, Total Totes. The costs to the firm, economists would argue, must include what this couple could have done with the $96 000 instead of putting it into their own business. One clear alternative would be to buy some mutual funds, from which they could earn, let us say, 10 percent per year. Therefore, the cost to the firm of using this $96 000 is the sacrifice of the lost return of $9600 per year (or $800 per month).

Similarly, we could ask what Otto and Melissa could do instead of putting sixteen hours a day (eight hours each) of work into their own business. Well, both of them could hire their labour out to someone else in a similar business who wanted the skills that Otto and Melissa possess. Let us assume that the going market wage for this type of labour is $100 per day. We should then assign to the firm a cost of this couple putting their time into the business of $4000 per month (two people times $100 per day times twenty days). The important thing for you to note is that neither the $9600 in interest per year nor the $4000 per month in wages need necessarily be actually paid out by the firm, but each is a legitimate cost of doing business using the concept of opportunity cost. In other words, to an economist, there is a cost involved—even if no payment is made—if an activity involves the use of productive resources, since those resources could have been used elsewhere.

We can see that there are two distinct types of costs in our example of Total Totes. **Explicit costs** are the costs paid to non-owners, such as wages to employees and payments to suppliers. **Implicit costs** are the costs of using the owners' resources when no payment is made. If the owners did choose to take a payment for their implicit wage costs, we could think of this as "wages paid to self" and this would change the implicit cost into an explicit cost.

Table 6.1 shows a typical month's accounting of the business activity for Total Totes.

explicit cost: a cost that is actually paid out in money.

implicit cost: a cost that does not require an actual expenditure of money.

TABLE 6.1	Total Totes: Profit and Loss Statement (for a typical month)		
Total Revenue:	Cash sales (excluding sales tax)		$20 000
Explicit Costs:	Rent	$ 1 500	
	Materials and supplies	4 200	
	Utilities	1 000	
	Hired labour	10 000	
	Depreciation on equipment	500	
Total Explicit Costs:			17 200
Accounting Profit:			2 800
Implicit Costs:	Opportunity costs of the $96 000 put into business	800	
	Labour put in by owners	4 000	
Total Implicit Costs:			4 800
Total Explicit and Implicit Costs:			22 000
Economic Profit or (Loss):			(2 000)

We should mention that an accountant and an economist calculate the depreciation on equipment differently. Let us assume that the $500 depreciation expense is the maximum amount that the tax laws allow monthly, and this is the figure used by the accountant. The economist would argue, however, that the actual cost of equipment this year is the decline in its market value that results from it being one year older. This might or might not be equal to $500, but for expediency, we will assume that it is.

As you can see from **Table 6.1**, if we considered only direct out-of-pocket expenses (explicit costs) we would conclude that Otto and Melissa had made a profit of $2800 in this month. In fact, this is the way that an accountant would report the month's activities:

Total accounting profit = total revenue − total explicit costs   **[6.1]**

Economists, however, recognizing the concept of opportunity costs, would calculate that rather than making a $2000 profit, Total Totes lost $2000 in this month:

Total economic profit = total revenue − total costs (implicit and explicit)   **[6.2]**

In other words, if Otto and Melissa had put their money into a mutual fund and hired themselves out at the going market wage rate, they would have received an income of $4800 rather than the "profit" of $2800 that they did receive. In other words, they are $2000 worse off. What this means is that the two of them need to earn at least $4800 per month to make it all worth while. This is what economists refer to as a **normal profit**: the amount that has to be earned in order to keep an entrepreneur in that line of business. In other words—and as strange as it sounds—economists regard this normal profit as a cost, no different from any other cost. You can perhaps work out that Total Totes needs to have sales of at least $22 000 (assuming no change in costs) in order for Otto and Melissa to make a normal profit.

normal profit: the minimum profit that must be earned to keep the entrepreneur in that type of business.

Now, let us suppose that business really picks up (and, for simplicity's sake, costs remain the same) and sales increase to $25 000. With explicit costs of $17 200 plus implicit costs (or normal profits) of $4800, there would now be a surplus of $3000. This surplus is what economists refer to as **economic profit**. As you can see, this surplus is over and above the normal profits and is sometimes referred to as *supernormal profit* (normal profit is a necessary cost of production and must be earned in order for the entrepreneur to stay in business). Economic profit, on the other hand, is unnecessary (though desirable) in the sense that it does not have to be earned to keep

economic profit: revenue over and above all costs, including normal profits.

the entrepreneur in business. It can be regarded as the reward for the risk that the entrepreneur takes. This means that even if Otto and Melissa earned zero economic profit, they will still be happy to stay in the tote bag business as long as they can earn a normal profit.

The graphic on the right illustrates these ideas.

There is another aspect of opportunity cost that is also interesting. Consider the following scenario. While you are walking through the local mall, you come upon the food court and decide to buy something to eat. At first, you cannot decide between a taco platter for $4.99 or a soup-and-sandwich combo for the same price. You understand (from Chapter 1) that the opportunity cost of the one is the sacrifice you make by not

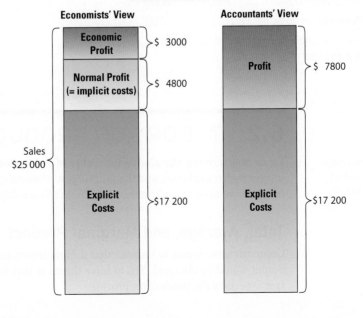

Different Views of Profit

ADDED DIMENSION   Urban Encroachment on Agricultural Land

An interesting application of the concept of implicit cost involves the phenomenon of the growing pressure of urbanization on our nation's farmland. As our population continues to grow, our cities have spread out into land that is used for farming. This drives up the implicit costs of agricultural activities, since land used for housing or urban support activities, such as gas stations or golf courses, carries a far higher price than land used for farming. This increased implicit cost intensifies the pressure on farmers to sell out to developers.

---

sunk cost: costs that are unrecoverable.

buying the other, but there is more. Let us assume that you decide on the taco platter and sit down to enjoy your purchase. After a single bite, you realize that you made the wrong choice and you really do not want to eat even another bite. What is the cost of leaving the platter uneaten and simply walking away? To an economist, the answer is zero because the $4.99 you spent on the taco platter is a **sunk cost**, the amount you spent to purchase something that has no current resale value. Sunk costs are absolutely irrelevant to decision making. Even if a firm has spent millions of dollars on equipment, if that money has already been spent and the equipment has no resale value, then throwing it away has no cost. What we are really saying here is that if an asset is a sunk cost, it no longer carries any opportunity cost. Other examples of sunk costs would be fees paid to a consultant or money spent on market research.

 SELF-TEST

1. Judy is presently working as an activities facilitator at a local community centre, where she earns $1000 per month after tax. However, she is not happy with her job and is thinking of returning to college to do a two-year programme to upgrade her skills. She has estimated the costs as follows:

Annual costs of tuition and textbooks	$2800
Annual cost of board and lodging (same as her present costs)	8000
Additional transportation costs per year	700

What would be an economist's estimate of the cost of Judy taking the two-year programme?

2. Abdi recently gave up a job that paid $1500 a month after tax to open up his own convenience store. He works full time in the store, which had a total revenue of $105 000 last year. His total (explicit) costs amounted to $65 000. He reckons his store is now worth $200 000 and if he were to sell it and invest the proceeds in his dad's supermarket he would earn himself an 8-percent annual return. What is Abdi's economic profit during the year?

6.2   THEORY OF PRODUCTION

LO2 Understand the crucial relationship between productivity and costs.

Let us now turn our attention to the theory of production. It is clear that increased production will involve higher total costs, and this output/cost relationship is one that we need to explore fully. First, however, we need to understand some basic relationships *within* the concept of production itself.

Total, Average, and Marginal Product

Common sense seems to indicate that if more inputs are added to the production process, more output would be obtained. Yet, to leave things at that would skirt over some of the most important aspects of the production process.

Not all inputs can be increased at the same time. For example, a farmer can add more variable inputs, such as water and fertilizer, to his fields this season, but he cannot increase the size of his fields. Thus, we need to recognize that, within any given period, some inputs will be fixed. This leads us to the very important point that as long as any one input is fixed, we are in what economists call the short run. This chapter will be entirely in the context of the **short run**. The next chapter will look at the long run, in which all inputs are considered variable. What we mean by variable, then, is that the amount of inputs varies with the amount of output. Simply put, the more that is produced, the greater will be the number of variable inputs that are required.

short run: any period of time in which at least one input in the production process is fixed (cannot be increased or decreased).

Different amounts of LABOUR added ⟹ A fixed amount of LAND ⟹ Different OUTPUT levels of grain

Let us now look at a simple model of production. In **Table 6.2**, we show what happens to the number of tote bags Otto and Melissa can produce each day in their small factory when they employ different amounts of labour. In this case, the fixed factor is the size of their premises. The variable factor is labour (which we assume is provided with the necessary materials). **Table 6.2** shows what happens as Total Totes employs an increasing number of employees.

The right-hand column in **Table 6.2** indicates the output, which is what economists call **total product** (TP). Here, we see what happens to total product as we add successive units of labour. It is important to note that total product does not rise proportionately with the increase in labour. Economists call this concept **marginal product** (MP), and define it as the change in total product caused by adding one more unit of input, in this case labour. Practically speaking, the marginal product is simply the extra output from each additional worker. Formally, then, the marginal product of *labour* is:

total product: the total output of any productive process.

marginal product: the increase in total product as a result of adding one more unit of input.

$$MP_L = \frac{\Delta TP}{\Delta L}$$ [6.3]

Do not confuse marginal product with **average product** (AP), which is nothing more than total product divided by the number of inputs. Average product is often called *productivity per worker*, or the average product of the average worker. Formally, the average product of labour is:

average product: total product (or total output) divided by the quantity of inputs used to produce that total.

$$AP_L = \frac{TP}{L}$$ [6.4]

Let us go to **Table 6.3** to examine these new concepts in detail.

TABLE 6.2	Total Product Data
Units of Labour (L)	Total Product (TP), Number of Tote Bags
0	0
1	8
2	20
3	45
4	75
5	100
6	120
7	130
8	135
9	135
10	130

TABLE 6.3	Marginal and Average Product Data		
Units of Labour	**Total Product (TP)**	**Marginal Product (MP)**	**Average Product (AP)**
0	0	—	—
1	8	8	8
2	20	12	10
3	45	25	15
4	75	30	18.8
5	100	25	20
6	120	20	20
7	130	10	18.6
8	135	5	16.9
9	135	0	15
10	130	−5	13

The data in the third column of **Table 6.3** indicate that the marginal product of the first unit of production is eight, whereas that of the second production unit rises to twelve. Why might the marginal product of labour rise? Does it mean that the second worker is better than the first? No, because we assume that each worker is equally good. So, what is the explanation?

An analogy may help here. Can you imagine trying to build a fence by yourself? It could be done, but it would be slow and awkward. You would have to set each post temporarily with a stake and support and then step back to see if it was straight, then readjust the support and step back again and so on and so on. It is likely that two people (each with tools and material) could build a fence at a rate that is *more than* twice as fast as one person could. That is to say, the marginal product of the second person would be higher than that of the first person due to the rewards of specialization.

division of labour: the dividing of the production process into a series of specialized tasks, each done by a different worker.

law of diminishing returns: as more of a variable input is added to a fixed input in the production process, the resulting increase in output will, at some point, begin to diminish.

Adam Smith referred to this phenomenon as the **division of labour** in his famous example of the pin factory. Smith marvelled at the fact that a state-of-the-art factory in eighteenth-century England, which employed only ten workers, was able to produce 48 000 ordinary straight pins in a single day by dividing the process of pin-making into ten distinct functions in which each worker performed only one task. The emphasis here is on the word *process*, as distinct from the situation where each worker separately and independently would make a whole pin from start to finish. In Smith's estimation, if each worker made complete pins, the factory would produce fewer than 1000 pins in a day.

We can now see how the marginal product of labour will, at first, increase as more labour is added to a production process. Next, we need to ask why, after a point, does marginal product decline? (We see this in **Table 6.3**, beginning with the addition of the fifth unit of labour.) In a similar vein, we could ask why the benefits of specialization do not continue indefinitely?

The answer to both of these questions raises one of the most important concepts in all of microeconomics: the **law of diminishing returns**, a concept first developed by David Ricardo. This law states that as more and more units of a variable resource (in this case, labour) are added to a production process, at some point, the resulting increase in output (MP) begins to decrease, assuming that at least one other input (in this case, the factory size) is fixed. The reason for the decreasing marginal product of labour is simply that the fixed size of factory will eventually become overly crowded ("too many cooks spoil the broth") with additional workers. A more accurate term would be the *law of diminishing marginal productivity*, but in this chapter, we will stick with the more commonly used *law of diminishing returns*.

John A. Rizzo/Getty Images

This production line is a modern-day example of Adam Smith's division of labour.

ADDED DIMENSION   Division of Labour: The Key to the Industrial Revolution

Adam Smith saw five distinct reasons for the productive power of the division of labour.

a) the ability to fit the best person to the right job

b) the increased dexterity achieved when the worker specializes in a single operation

c) the time saved when workers do not have to change tools

d) the time saved that would otherwise be lost in moving from one operation to another (what we would today call "assembly-line production")

e) the machine specialization that can be developed around specific, discrete operations

This last aspect is a vital step in the industrial process. Without the division of labour, the extensive use of machines that has occurred over the past two centuries simply would not have been possible.

The law of diminishing returns is a technological reality that must be valid; otherwise, we could grow the world's food in a flowerpot by simply adding more and more variable inputs until production rose to the necessary level. We cannot do this, and the reason we cannot is the law of diminishing returns.

We now need to make four points of clarification. First, while the fixed input in our example above happens to be the size of the factory, it could have been *any* input—the only necessity for the law of diminishing returns to apply is that at least one input be fixed. Second, our example had only one variable input—labour—and we illustrated the law of diminishing returns by showing that the marginal product of labour declines. However, if there had been two variable inputs instead of one, both would have manifested diminishing returns. Third, any discussion of the law of diminishing returns assumes that technology is unchanging. If technological change does occur, we get a new set of output numbers, but those numbers are still subject to diminishing returns. Finally, while our example is in the context of manufacturing, the law of diminishing returns applies in all productive activities, including agriculture.

It is very important to note that even when diminishing returns set in, the total product *continues to rise*. However, the *rate of increase* in the total product begins to fall. Those of you who have taken calculus will recognize that marginal product is the first derivative of total product. Everyone else need only realize that total product can continue to rise even though marginal

 ADDED DIMENSION   David Ricardo: The Businessman Economist

Regarded in his time as the natural heir to Adam Smith, David Ricardo (1772–1823) was the acknowledged leader of classical economics. The third of 17 children born to Jewish immigrants to England, he trained in his father's successful brokerage firm. When he was 21, he fell in love with a Quaker woman and left his faith to become a Unitarian. His father disowned him, but Ricardo married her and, supported by friends, entered the brokerage business on his own. By the time he was 25, his personal fortune had surpassed his father's. He retired at age 43 and devoted himself full time to his real love—the study of economics.

Though he was a hardheaded businessman, his contributions to economics were the result of abstract reasoning rather than experience and observation. He is known for his theories of trade, rent, and income distribution, and for elegantly stating the law of diminishing returns, which he developed. His *Principles of Economy and Taxation* (1817) quickly replaced Smith's *Wealth of Nations* as the standard text in economics.

FIGURE 6.1   The Total, Average, and Marginal Product Curves

As more units of the variable input labour are used (up to 9 units), total product rises, but the rate of increase slows with the use of the fifth unit of labour. This is the point of diminishing returns. Maximum *total* product of 135 is reached when 9 units of labour are employed (where MP = 0). When the marginal product curve is above the average product curve, the latter rises. Similarly, when the marginal product curve is below the average product curve, the average declines. At the point where the marginal product curve intersects the average product curve, the average is at its maximum, which is 20 tote bags per unit of labour.

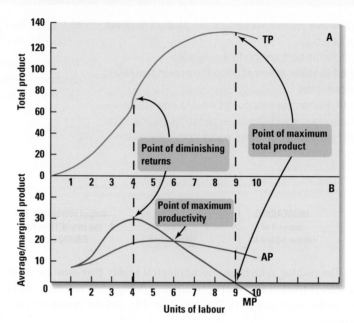

product has started to decline. As you can see from **Table 6.3**, after the ninth worker is added, the total product declines, indicating that the marginal product of additional workers is negative.

The data in **Table 6.3** can also be put into graphical form. This is illustrated in **Figure 6.1A**.

Note three things about the TP curve. First, total product rises quickly at first because of the advantages gained from the division of labour. Second, at the point of diminishing returns (after the use of the fourth unit of labour), the rate of increase in the curve decreases, Third, the rise in total product continues despite having passed the point of diminishing returns. You may also notice that there is a small "kink" in the TP curve when the fourth unit of labour is added. This reflects the fact that the MP curve has reached its maximum with the use of four units of labour and declines thereafter.

Let us now turn to a discussion of average product. There is a marginal/average relationship reflected in the data in **Table 6.3** that needs to be emphasized. All students intuitively know what this relationship is without being aware of it. Imagine that you are taking a course in which your class mark is made up of ten quizzes worth ten points each. You know that if you got four points on the first quiz and six points on the second quiz, your average quiz score is, at that point, five. You also know that in order to raise your average test score, you will have to get a mark on the third quiz that is above five. The mark on the third quiz is the marginal mark, and if the marginal is above the average, the average will rise. If, however, your third test mark is less than five, your average of all three quizzes would fall; that is, if the marginal is below the average, the average will fall.

Let us take this marginal/average relationship and look back at the data in **Table 6.3**. Note that the third, fourth, and fifth units of labour all have a marginal product that is above the average product, and therefore, average product rises. The addition of the sixth unit of labour, which has a marginal product that is exactly the same as the previous average (20), results in the average product neither increasing nor decreasing but remaining constant at 20. The seventh unit of labour has a marginal product of 10, which is below the average, and therefore average product falls to 18.6. We can generalize as follows:

Average product will rise if marginal product exceeds it and will fall if marginal product is less than it.

Figure 6.1B illustrates this relationship graphically. In this figure, you can see that marginal product is at a maximum when four units of labour are used. Further, when marginal product equals average product, average product is at its maximum. Because of the way these particular sets of numbers work out, this maximum average product *appears* (see **Table 6.3**) to occur with the addition of the fifth unit of labour. But we must be careful here because, technically speaking, it is with the sixth unit that average product is maximized, since this is where average product is equal to marginal product.

We have now identified three maximums: of total product, which was achieved with the addition of the ninth unit of labour; of marginal product, which was achieved with the addition of the fourth unit of labour; and of average product, which is at a maximum with the sixth unit of labour. So, which is the most productive point? When economists use the term *most productive* or mention *highest productivity*, they are referring to maximum *average* product. This is an engineering concept that refers to the point where the most output *per unit of input* is achieved.

A similar question is: what is the best output to produce? But we cannot answer that question without knowledge of the costs of the inputs and the price of the output. We will leave discussion of the price of output for later and take up discussion of the costs of production next.

 SELF-TEST

3. Assume that the amount of capital is fixed.

   a) Fill in the blanks in the table.

   b) With the addition of which unit of labour do diminishing returns begin?

   c) How many units of labour are used in the average product of labour at a maximum?

   d) What is the value of marginal product when total product is at a maximum?

4. Given the data in the table, calculate both the MPL and the APL for each unit of labour used.

Units of Labour	TP_L	MP_L	AP_L
0	0	/	/
1	80	___	___
2	170	___	___
3	___	80	___
4	310	___	___
5	___	___	70
6	370	___	___
7	370	___	___

Quantity of Labour	Total Output
1	400
2	1000
3	1500
4	1800
5	1900

6.3 MARGINAL AND VARIABLE COSTS

We now want to forge a link between the quantity of output produced and the cost of producing it. While production relates the number of units produced to the amount of labour used, costs relate dollars to the number of units produced. One of the important questions Otto and Melissa want to address in their company is: how much does it cost us to produce a tote bag? As we shall see, the answer is not a single figure but depends on the level of production; that is, it depends on how many workers they employ and the level of total product.

Table 6.4 reproduces the first four columns from **Table 6.3** and adds a fifth column, **total variable cost** (TVC), which is the sum of all costs that vary directly with the level of output. Variable costs

L03 Understand the important difference between fixed costs and variable costs.

total variable cost: the total of all costs that vary with the level of output.

would normally include the cost of variable inputs, such as materials, power, and labour. However, in our simplified example, we have assumed that labour is the only variable cost. Suppose that Otto and Melissa can obtain labour for $100 per unit per day. The figures in the total variable costs column are then obtained by simply multiplying the number of units of labour by $100.

The sixth column introduces the very important concept of the **marginal cost** (MC). Marginal cost is the increase in total variable cost as a result of producing one more unit of output. Ignore the seventh column for the moment.

To obtain the value for marginal cost, we need to remember that the definition of marginal cost involves the cost of each additional *unit* of output produced. Therefore, we need to divide the $100 increase in total variable cost, which results from using one more unit of labour, by *marginal product* in order to find the cost of an additional *unit of output* produced. For example, the first unit of labour can produce 8 units of output at a cost of $100. Each unit, therefore, costs $100 divided by 8, or $12.50 per unit.

Similarly, the second unit of labour increases total product by (has a marginal product of) 12 at a cost of $100. This yields a marginal cost of $8.33 ($100 divided by 12). The third unit of labour has a marginal product of 25, and therefore, the marginal cost of production when 3 inputs are employed is $4, and so on.

In summary, each unit of labour that is hired costs an identical $100. However, the amount of additional output that each unit produces (MP) is different. The cost of producing additional units of output (the marginal cost), therefore, will also vary.

We will see later, in this and subsequent chapters, that this concept of marginal cost is at the centre of a great deal of microeconomics analysis. The formal definition of marginal cost can be expressed as:

marginal cost: the increase in total variable costs as a result of producing one more unit of output.

$$MC = \frac{\Delta TVC}{\Delta \text{ total output}}$$ [6.5]

average variable cost: total variable cost divided by total output.

Let us now look at the seventh column of our data in **Table 6.4**. Here, we have **average variable cost** (AVC), which is simply the total variable cost divided by the total output. Formally, this is:

$$AVC = \frac{TVC}{\text{total output}}$$ [6.6]

TABLE 6.4	Cost Data for a Firm					
(1)	(2)	(3)	(4)	(5)	(6)	(7)
Units of Labour	TP	MP	AP	TVC	MC	AVC
0	0	/	/	0	/	/
1	8	8	8	$ 100	$12.50	$12.50
2	20	12	10	200	8.33	10.00
3	45	25	15	300	4.00	6.67
4	75	30	18.8	400	3.33	5.33
5	100	25	20	500	4.00	5.00
6	120	20	20	600	5.00	5.00
7	130	10	18.6	700	10.00	5.38
8	135	5	16.9	800	20.00	5.93
9	135	0	15	900	____	6.67
10	130	−5	13	1000	____	7.69

To illustrate this calculation, assume, in **Table 6.4**, that 8 units of labour were being used, which result in an output of 135 and total variable cost of $800. Dividing the $800 by 135 yields an average variable cost of (approximately) $5.93.

We should point out that the same marginal/average relationship we discussed in reference to the marginal and average products also applies to marginal and average costs. Thus, just as the average product was at a *maximum* when it was equal to marginal product, average variable cost will be at a *minimum* when it is equal to marginal cost. **Figure 6.2**, which uses the data from **Table 6.4**, will help you understand this.

In **Figure 6.2A**, you see the marginal product and average product curves. They are, roughly, two inverse U-shaped curves with the marginal product curve intersecting the average product curve at the latter's *maximum* point. This occurs when six units of labour are being used and is the firm's *most productive* point for this size of plant. Next, look at the graphing of the marginal cost and average variable cost curves in **Figure 6.2B**. What you see there are two U-shaped curves, with marginal cost intersecting average variable cost at the latter's *minimum* point. This is at an output of 120, which is the output that 6 units of labour are able to produce. In short, when the average product of the variable *input* is at a maximum, the average variable cost of *output* will be at its minimum. It is also true that when the marginal product is at a maximum, marginal costs will be at a minimum.

FIGURE 6.2	**The Marginal Cost and Average Variable Cost Curves**

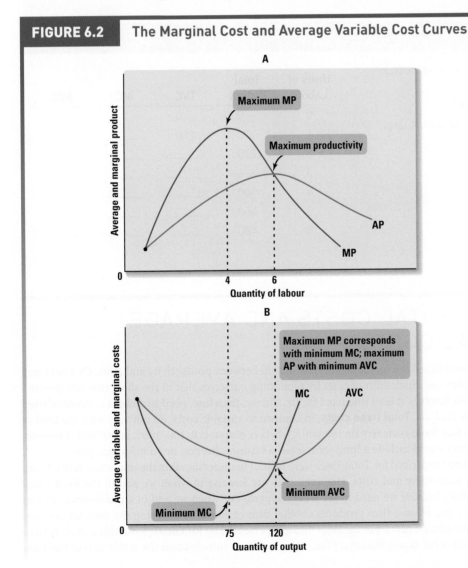

In Figure A, the MP curve intersects the AP curve at its maximum point when 6 units of labour are being used.
In Figure B, the MC curve intersects the AVC curve at its minimum, which occurs at an output of 120. This is the output that 6 units of labour can produce.

As mentioned above, this is not a coincidence. Average variable cost and marginal cost are upside-down images of average product and marginal product. That is:

> Variable costs of production are a reflection of productivity.

This is what lies behind the observation that an increase in productivity is equivalent to a decrease in costs.

This relationship bears repeating. We can see in either **Table 6.4** or in **Figure 6.2** that as marginal product (MP) initially *increases*, marginal cost (MC) *decreases*. Similarly, as average product (AP) increases, average variable cost (AVC) declines. This is a result of the division of labour. However, after a certain point, diminishing returns sets in. When this happens, marginal product (and average product) starts to *decrease*. As a result, marginal cost (and average variable cost) starts to *increase*. Perhaps a summary might be useful:

$$\text{division of labour} \Rightarrow \text{MP and AP} \uparrow \text{ and MC and AVC} \downarrow$$

$$\text{diminishing returns} \Rightarrow \text{MP and AP} \downarrow \text{ and MC and AVC} \uparrow$$

✓ SELF-TEST

5. a) Assuming that all units of labour cost the same, fill in the blanks in the table.

b) When is marginal cost at a minimum?

c) What is the marginal product of labour when 4 units of labour are used?

Units of Labour	Total Output	TVC	MC	AVC
0	0	0	/	/
1	100	200	___	___
2	220	___	___	___
3	320	___	___	___
4	400	___	___	___
5	460	___	___	___
6	480	___	___	___

6.4 TOTAL COSTS AND AVERAGE TOTAL COSTS

LO4 List and graph the seven specific cost definitions used by economists.

total fixed costs: costs that do not vary with the level of output.

We have established the fundamental relationship between productivity and costs. Our next step is to complete our discussion of costs by reminding ourselves that in the short run, any production process involves at least one fixed factor, and we, therefore, need to add the concept of fixed cost to our analysis. **Total fixed costs**, in contrast to variable costs, do not vary with the level of output. In fact, fixed costs remain the same, whether output is 0, 100, 1000, or 100 000. Examples of fixed costs would include a long-term lease, a business licence, or an insurance policy.

The data we derived for Total Totes were helpful in understanding the important relationship between productivity and costs. However, they are less useful when we add in the fixed costs. This is simply because we need to see what happens, not when we add in an additional amount of an *input*, but when a firm produces another unit of *output*. That being the case, we are now going to introduce a new set of figures,—those experienced by Rosemary, who runs a small pottery business out of her home. Rosemary faces very low fixed costs because she is able to rent kiln time

TABLE 6.5	The Complete Table of Costs						
Output (per week)	TVC	AVC	MC	TFC	AFC	TC	ATC
0	0	/	/	$30	/	$ 30	/
1	$ 20	$20.00	$20	30	$30.00	50	$50.00
2	28	14.00	8	30	15.00	58	29.00
3	42	14.00	14	30	10.00	72	24.00
4	60	15.00	18	30	7.50	90	22.50
5	82	16.40	22	30	6.00	112	22.40
6	110	18.33	28	30	5.00	140	23.33
7	148	21.14	38	30	4.28	178	25.43
8	198	24.75	50	30	3.75	228	28.50

at the local school. Note that the new data in **Table 6.5** (unlike **Table 6.4**) show what happens to costs as we increase *output* one unit at a time rather than investigating the effects of increasing *inputs* one unit at a time. This will make our calculations much easier.

The first column is simply the output (or total product) per week of the large vases that Rosemary specializes in. Columns two, three, and four have been explained. The fifth column is the total fixed cost. In this example, we assume it to be $30 per week. Next, we have **average fixed costs** (AFC), which are, simply:

$$AFC = \frac{TFC}{total\ output} \qquad [6.7]$$

average fixed cost: total fixed cost divided by the quantity of output.

Note that average fixed cost declines continuously as output rises. To obtain **total cost** (TC), we simply do a summation:

$$TC = TVC + TFC \qquad [6.8]$$

total cost: the sum of both total variable cost and total fixed cost.

Total cost rises continuously as output rises, and the *rate* of rise also begins to increase once diminishing returns set in.

Finally, **average total cost** (ATC) is:

$$ATC = \frac{TC}{total\ output} \qquad [6.9]$$

average total cost: total cost divided by quantity of output.

We know that:

$$TC = TVC + TFC$$

As a result, we also know that:

$$ATC = AVC + AFC \qquad [6.10]$$

There is one more equation that is useful to know. Since marginal cost is the change in total variable cost, it follows that:

$$\Sigma MC = TVC \qquad [6.11]$$

(Σ means "the summation of").

The relationship between marginal cost and *average variable cost* that we stressed earlier in this chapter also applies to the interaction between marginal cost and *average total cost*. As long as marginal cost is below average total cost, average total cost will fall (as it does for the first units of

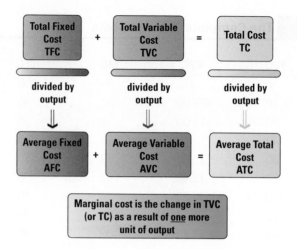

output in **Table 6.5**). But as soon as marginal cost rises above average total cost, the latter will begin to rise. Given this basic relationship, it is also true that the marginal cost curve will intersect the average total cost curve at the latter's minimum point. This can be seen at point *b* in **Figure 6.3**, where we now put the quantity of output on the horizontal axis and dollar costs on the vertical.

Using this figure as a visual representation, let us pull things together.

- Both the U-shaped marginal cost curve and the saucer-shaped AVC curve reflect the advantages of the division of labour as it declines and then, as it rises, the law of diminishing returns.
- Marginal cost is initially below the average variable cost curve and the average total cost curve but then rises above each of these, which explains their basic saucer shape.
- The marginal cost curve intersects the average variable cost curve at its minimum point and the average total cost curve at its minimum point.
- The average fixed cost curve continuously declines.

Let us now focus on point *a*, the minimum point of the average variable cost curve. Note that this occurs at an output of three vases. Since the average variable cost curve is an upside-down image of the average product curve, we know that the average product curve must be at its maximum.

FIGURE 6.3   The MC, ATC, AVC, and AFC Curves

The U-shaped marginal cost curve intersects the average variable cost curve at its minimum point (*a*), which is an output of 3 units and a cost of $14. It also intersects the average total cost curve at its minimum point (*b*), which is 5 units and $22.40. The average fixed cost curve declines continuously.

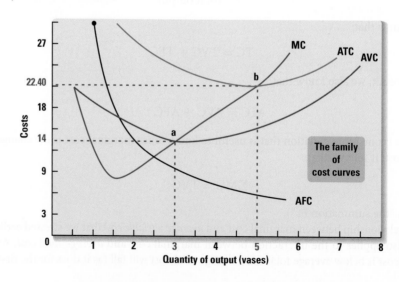

FIGURE 6.4   Three Important Cost Curves

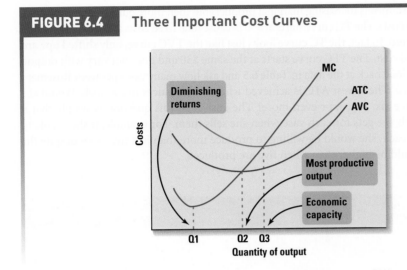

Q$_1$ is the point of diminishing returns where MC is lowest (and where MP is highest). The most productive output is Q$_2$ where AVC is lowest (AP is highest). Q$_3$ is economic capacity where ATC is lowest.

Next, note that the minimum point on the average total cost curve is at an output of five vases (point *b*). Such an output level is defined by economists as **economic capacity**. Graphically, this simply means the lowest point on the average total cost curve. This level of output does not, however, imply maximum physical capacity. This is because most production processes probably reach minimum average total cost at about 75 to 80 percent of physical capacity. Comparing points *a* and *b* enables us to emphasize that the most productive point (point *a* on the graph), where average product is at a maximum, is *not* the lowest-cost point (point *b* on the graph), where average total cost is at a minimum. This is simply a reflection of the fact that fixed costs are part of average total costs, but they are not part of average variable costs.

economic capacity: that output at which average total cost is at a minimum

To help you get a good grasp of these various points, **Figure 6.4** shows a classic version of the three most important curves. Can we conclude that a firm would always want to produce the output that minimizes ATC? The answer is "not necessarily," since we have no information, at this point, about the price the firm receives when it sells the product. We will sort this out in Chapters 8 through 11.

Let us now look at the corresponding total curves. **Figure 6.5** graphs the total cost (TC), total variable cost (TVC), and total fixed cost (TFC) curves. The TVC curve starts at the origin because variable costs are zero when output is zero and rises slowly at first (reflecting declining average

FIGURE 6.5   The TC, TVC, and TFC Curves

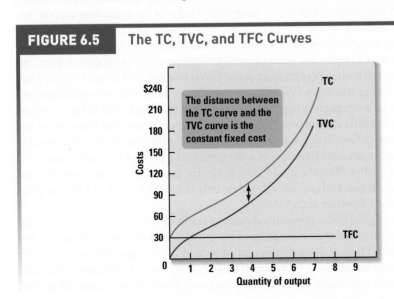

The total cost curve begins at $30 (the amount of fixed cost) and rises from there. The total variable cost curve starts at the origin, since variable cost is zero when there is no output. The total fixed cost curve is horizontal, reflecting the fact that the fixed cost of $30 does not vary with output. The difference between the TC and TVC is this constant $30.

variable cost, which also means increasing marginal product) but then more quickly later (reflecting rising average variable cost). The TC curve starts at $30 because total fixed costs are equal to this level even when output is zero. In fact, the TC curve looks just like the TVC curve, only shifted upward by the amount of fixed cost. The TFC curve starts at the same $30 and does not vary with output.

Let us now take a look back at the data in **Table 6.5** and ask how many vases per week Rosemary would want to produce. The lowest ATC is achieved when she produces five a week. Would she ever choose to produce six, seven, or even more? The answer to this question is simply that it depends on how much she gets for each vase when she sells them. For example, if she is able to sell her vases for $30 each, she would be willing to produce more than just five vases despite the fact that her ATC would be higher than when five are produced.

✓ SELF-TEST

6. Fill in the blanks in the table below:

Output (per day)	TC	TVC	AVC	TFC	AFC	ATC	MC
0	$200	0	/	____	/	/	/
1	280	____	____	____	____	____	____
2	340	____	____	____	____	____	____
3	420	____	____	____	____	____	____
4	520	____	____	____	____	____	____
5	640	____	____	____	____	____	____
6	780	____	____	____	____	____	____

6.5 HOW CAN A FIRM CUT COSTS?

L05 Explain the meaning of *increasing productivity* and *cutting costs*.

There is a great deal of discussion in the media about the need for firms to "cut costs." Unfortunately, this phrase is, by itself, ambiguous. A firm can always cut *total* cost by decreasing output. But surely, this is not what is meant by the urgent calls for reductions in costs. It seems likely that when firms are planning to cut costs, what they intend is a reduction in *average* costs rather than total costs. But first, we need to make one point clear. So far, our presentation of costs is based on the assumption that the firm is already producing at the lowest possible cost *for each output level*. In other words, it is producing efficiently. (We will have more to say about efficiency in Chapter 9.) Given this, is it possible for average costs to get any lower? Yes, if the firm is able to buy its inputs cheaper. The firm often has little control over the prices of the inputs it buys, but these prices can and do change from time to time. It is possible that the price of either the fixed or the variable inputs might change. Let us consider the effect of a decrease in the price of a variable input.

In graphical terms, such a decrease would shift down the marginal, average variable, and average total cost curves. In our analysis, we will isolate only the average total and the marginal cost curves in **Figure 6.6** to illustrate such a shift.

In **Figure 6.6**, the marginal cost curve shifts down as a result of a decrease in the input price of the variable input such that the minimum point of the curve occurs at a lower dollar cost but at the same level of output. There is also a corresponding shift in the average total cost curve. We have not shown the average variable cost curve, but if we had, it, too, would shift down. The basic shapes of the curves remain unchanged, however, since the law of diminishing returns still applies.

| **FIGURE 6.6** | A Shift in the Marginal and Average Total Cost Curves |

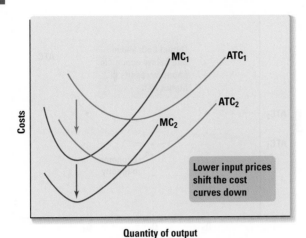

The shift down in the marginal cost curve—MC_1 to MC_2—and in the accompanying average total cost curve—ATC_1 to ATC_2—is the result of input prices decreasing.

Would the average fixed cost curve also shift down? Only if the price of the fixed input(s) decreased. Similarly, the curves would shift up if input prices increased.

There is another possibility that we need to mention. Recall that the marginal cost of output is determined by the marginal product of the factor inputs. What if marginal product were to increase? This would decrease marginal cost, which would pull both average variable and average total cost down as well. And what might cause this increase in productivity leading to a decrease in costs? It might be as simple as a firm replacing, within the same plant, older inefficient machines with newer, more efficient ones. Even something as simple as a new photocopier might make the small staff in a law firm more productive.

We do need to be careful with this analysis, however, since we are getting very close to a discussion of technological change and applying new technology often involves a new size of plant. That takes us to the subject of the long run, which we deal with in the next chapter. We can say, however, that if the marginal product of a productive process increases, then the cost of production will decrease, even in the short run.

If neither resource prices nor productivity change, is there any other way that a firm can reduce average costs? Certainly, this will *not* be possible if the firm is already producing the output that results in the lowest average cost, that is, it is at economic capacity.

Would firms ever want to operate at an output that is less than economic capacity output? No, they would not want to, but firms are sometimes forced to reduce output because of market conditions. The consequences of this are illustrated in **Figure 6.7**. In **Figure 6.7**, we assume that market conditions have forced this firm to choose an output of Q_2 with average total costs of ATC_2, which are higher than they would be at economic capacity (ATC_1). This is what economists describe as **excess capacity**, defined as the situation in which the firm's output is less than economic capacity. Excess capacity is inefficient in the sense that average total costs are not at a minimum. In summary, if a firm has excess capacity, average costs could be cut by *increasing* output. However, this option may not be available to the firm if it does not have sufficient orders for its product. We will refer to this concept again in Chapter 11.

Conversely, would firms want to operate at an output level above this capacity, say, output Q_3, despite the higher average cost? Perhaps in the short run they would, if demand and prices were particularly high, but no firm wants to produce above economic capacity indefinitely. The cost in terms of overtime pay and the wear and tear on machinery can become prohibitive. Given this, it is likely that the firm will soon be looking to move into larger premises. (This is what we mean by the long run, the subject of the next chapter.)

excess capacity: the situation in which a firm's output is below economic capacity.

FIGURE 6.7   A Firm Experiencing Excess Capacity

If market conditions force a firm to operate at output level Q_2, then its average total costs (ATC_2) will be higher than they would be if the firm operated at economic capacity (Q_1). Similarly, a firm will have a higher average cost, if it is operating above economic capacity, such as Q_3.

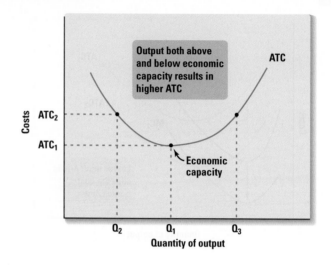

✓ SELF-TEST

Inputs	Total Output	TC_1	MC_1	ATC_1	TC_2	MC_2	ATC_2
0	0	$150	/	/	____	/	/
1	10	175	____	____	____	____	____
2	25	200	____	____	____	____	____
3	35	225	____	____	____	____	____
4	40	250	____	____	____	____	____
5	42	275	____	____	____	____	____

7. a) Fill in the blanks in the MC_1 and ATC_1 columns above.

   b) Assuming that the price of the variable inputs decrease by $5, fill in the TC_2, MC_2, and ATC_2 columns.

8. Given the accompanying graph:

   a) At what output do diminishing returns begin?

   b) What is the most productive output?

   c) What output is economic capacity?

   d) When output is 250, what does *ab* represent?

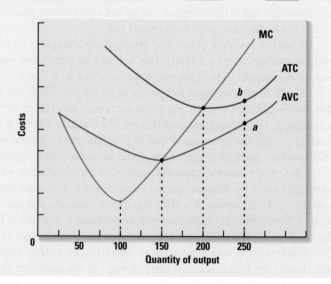

Review

CHAPTER SUMMARY

The focus of this chapter was on the crucial relationship between the productivity of the factors of production (inputs) and the costs of production. Productivity involves the output of the final product that results from using various amounts of factor inputs. Costs involve the dollar amount that is incurred in producing that output.

6.1 The chapter begins by distinguishing between explicit cost and implicit cost, and this distinction leads to the definitions of normal profit and economic profit.

6.2a Total product (output) is the end result of *adding inputs* to the production process, and from this we get:

$$MP_L = \frac{\Delta TP}{\Delta L}$$

$$AP_L = \frac{TP}{L}$$

6.2b Advantages gained from the *division of labour* (specialization) explains why MP initially rises as more inputs are used; the *law of diminishing returns* explains why MP eventually declines as more units of input are used.

6.2c AP will:
- rise if MP is above it
- fall if MP is below it

6.3a *Total variable cost* is the dollar amount of variable inputs incurred in producing output, and from this we get:

$$MC = \frac{\Delta TVC}{\Delta \text{ total output}}$$

$$AVC = \frac{TVC}{\text{total output}}$$

6.3b Two very important *relationships* are:
- MP is at a maximum when (the number of inputs being used are able to produce an output where) MC is at a minimum.
- AP is at a maximum when (the number of inputs being used are able to produce an output where) AVC is at a minimum.

6.4a *Total cost* is:

$$TC = TVC + TFC$$

From this, we get:

$$AFC = \frac{TFC}{\text{total output}}; \; ATC = \frac{TC}{\text{total output}}$$

and:

$$ATC = AVC + AFC$$

6.4b Graphically, the *MC curve* is U-shaped and intersects:
- the AVC curve at its minimum, indicating the most productive output
- the ATC curve at its minimum, indicating economic capacity

6.4c MC, AVC, and ATC decrease (and, graphically, their respective curves shift down) if input prices fall and productivity increases.

6.5 Economic capacity is always below physical capacity and occurs when ATC is at a minimum.

Mc Graw Hill connect™

Practise and learn online with Connect, where you can find the Answered Questions and the Unanswered Problems for all chapters of this textbook's Study Guide section.

NEW GLOSSARY TERMS AND KEY EQUATIONS

average fixed cost   193
average product   185
average total cost   193
average variable cost   190
depreciation   181
division of labour   186
economic capacity   195

economic profit   183
excess capacity   197
explicit cost   182
implicit cost   182
law of diminishing returns   186
marginal cost   190
marginal product   185

normal profit   183
short run   185
sunk cost   184
total cost   193
total fixed costs   192
total product   185
total variable cost   189

Equations:

[6.1]   Total accounting profit = total revenue − total explicit costs   **page 183**

[6.2]   Total economic profit = total revenue − total costs   **page 183**

[6.3] $MP_L = \dfrac{\Delta TP}{\Delta L}$ **page 185**

[6.4] $AP_L = \dfrac{TP}{L}$ **page 185**

[6.5] $MC = \dfrac{\Delta TVC}{\Delta \text{ total output}} = \dfrac{\Delta TVC}{MP}$ **page 190**

[6.6] $AVC = \dfrac{TVC}{\text{total output}}$ **page 190**

[6.7] $AFC = \dfrac{TFC}{\text{total output}}$ **page 193**

[6.8] $TC = TVC + TFC$ **page 193**

[6.9] $ATC = \dfrac{TC}{\text{total output}}$ **page 193**

[6.10] $ATC = AVC + AFC$ **page 193**

[6.11] $\Sigma MC = TVC$ **page 193**

STUDY TIPS

1. There are many new terms and definitions for you to learn in this chapter—probably more than in any other chapter. None of the terms is complex, however, so you should be able to handle them if you simply learn a few at a time.

2. Students usually find the distinction between explicit costs and implicit costs quite straightforward but get a little puzzled over how these concepts tie in with normal and economic profits. Simply remember that if both explicit and implicit costs are being covered, then the

firm is earning a normal profit. Revenues in excess of explicit and implicit costs result in economic profits.

3. Two of the most important concepts in microeconomics are the division of labour and the law of diminishing returns. They are used in this chapter to explain the relationship between the use of factors of production and their productivity. Once you understand marginal and average productivity, you can understand marginal and average variable costs. This is crucial and is, therefore, the focus of **Key Problem 36**.

4. Adding fixed cost and average total cost to the analysis is quite straightforward. Once this is done, a graph, such as that found in **Figure 6.3**, can be constructed. Here is a prime example of the phrase "a picture is worth a thousand words."

5. Always remember that the amount of total cost when output is zero is the total fixed cost that the firm faces.

6. We hear a great deal about the importance of firms cutting their costs. Just what is meant by this phrase is ambiguous. A firm can always cut its total cost by reducing output, and it might be able to decrease its average cost by changing its output level. The only unambiguous way "cutting costs" makes sense is as a reduction of marginal and average cost *at each level of output*. This is illustrated graphically by a downward shift in the two curves.

7. The introduction of the concepts of economic capacity and excess capacity in this chapter provide a springboard into the discussion of long-run costs, which is the focus of the next chapter.

Answered Questions
These questions can also be found online on Connect.

Indicate whether the following statements are true or false:

1. **(LO 3) T or F**   Marginal cost equals average variable cost when the latter is at a minimum.

2. **(LO 1) T or F**   Depreciation is the annual cost of any asset that is expected to be in use for more than one year.

3. **(LO 1) T or F**   Implicit costs are the amounts actually paid out in money.

4. **(LO 1) T or F**   Sunk costs are the historical costs of an asset that has no current resale value.

5. **(LO 1) T or F**   If a firm is making economic profits, then it must also be making normal profits.

6. **(LO 4) T or F**   The short run is any period of time in which at least two inputs are fixed.

7. **(LO 2) T or F**   Marginal product is the increase in total product as a result of adding one more unit of output.

8. **(LO 2) T or F**   Total product and total output are the same thing.

9. **(LO 2) T or F**   The division of labour is the dividing of the production process into a series of specialized tasks, each done by a different worker.

10. **(LO 4) T or F**   The short run is a period in which the output is fixed.

Basic (Questions 11–23)

11. **(LO 2)** Which of the following statements about the MP of labour is correct?
    a) It may either rise or fall as more labour is used.
    b) It always falls as more labour is used.
    c) It always rises as more labour is used.
    d) It is always constant.

12. **(LO 3)** Which of the following statements about marginal cost is correct?
    a) It is always below average total costs.
    b) It can be either above or below average total costs.
    c) It is always below average variable costs.
    d) It is always above average variable costs.

13. **(LO 2)** Which of the following statements is true about the average product of labour?
    a) It is equal to total output divided by the quantity of labour inputs used.
    b) It is equal to the increase in total output divided by the quantity of labour used.
    c) It is equal to the change in the marginal product of labour.
    d) It is equal to the quantity of labour inputs used divided by total output.

14. **(LO 2)** Which of the statements below is true about the marginal product of labour?
    a) It is total output divided by the quantity of labour used.
    b) It is the increase in total output resulting from the use of one more unit of labour.
    c) It is the increase in total output divided by the quantity of labour used.
    d) It is always constant.

15. **(LO 4)** What is the sum of the marginal costs of all of the units produced?
    a) Total cost
    b) Average cost
    c) Total variable cost
    d) Total fixed costs

16. **(LO 4)** What is average fixed cost?
    a) All the costs that do not vary with the level of output
    b) Total cost less total variable cost
    c) Total fixed cost divided by the level of output
    d) Total fixed costs less total variable costs

17. **(LO 4)** What is the sum of total variable costs and total fixed costs?
    a) The sum of average product and marginal product
    b) The sum of all marginal costs
    c) Total cost
    d) AVC times the quantity of output

18. **(LO 1)** All of the following items, except one, are explicit costs. Which is the exception?
    a) The weekly cost of a lease on a building
    b) The total wages paid each week
    c) The monthly hydro bill
    d) Money withdrawn from the business by the owner

19. **(LO 1)** Which of the following conditions is necessary in order to consider a cost a sunk cost?
    a) It must have occurred over six months ago.
    b) It must have occurred as a result of the purchase of a fixed asset.
    c) It must have occurred as a result of the purchase of a fixed asset and have no resale value.
    d) It must have occurred as a result of the purchase of a fixed asset and be fully paid for.

20. **(LO 4)** How do economists define economic capacity?
    a) The maximum physical output possible
    b) The output that maximizes total cost
    c) The output that maximizes total product
    d) The output that minimizes marginal cost
    e) The output that minimizes average total cost

21. **(LO 2)** What is true at the point of maximum productivity?
    a) The marginal product of labour is at a maximum.
    b) The marginal costs of production is at a minimum.
    c) The average product of labour is at a maximum.
    d) The average total costs of production is at a minimum.

22. **(LO 4)** All of the following curves, *except one*, form a U shape when graphed. Which is the exception?
    a) The marginal cost curve
    b) The average variable cost curve
    c) The average total cost curve
    d) The average fixed cost curve

23. **(LO 4)** Which of the following pairs are related?
    a) Maximum average product and minimum marginal cost
    b) Maximum average product and minimum average variable cost
    c) Maximum marginal product and minimum average variable cost
    d) Maximum marginal product and minimum average total cost

Intermediate (Questions 24–31)

24. **(LO 2)** Which of the following statements is true about the division of labour?
    a) It causes the marginal product of labour to increase, but it has no effect on the average product of labour.
    b) It was first thought of by David Ricardo in his example of a hat factory.
    c) It is an idea that has little application in the real world.
    d) Its application results in both the marginal and average products of labour increasing.

25. **(LO 2)** What is significant about the level of output at which marginal product begins to decline?
    a) It is the point of maximum average product.
    b) It is the point of minimum average cost.
    c) It is the point at which the division of labour begins.
    d) It is the point at which diminishing returns begins.

26. **(LO 2)** What will happen to total product after the point of diminishing returns has been reached?
    a) It will continue to rise until marginal product becomes zero.
    b) It will continue to rise until marginal product begins to decline.
    c) It will begin to fall.
    d) It will start to rise for the first time.

27. **(LO 4)** What do economists mean by the term "the most productive output"?
    a) The output where total product is at a maximum
    b) The output where average product is at a maximum
    c) The output where marginal product is at a maximum
    d) The output where marginal cost is at a minimum
    e) The output where average total cost is at a minimum

28. **(LO 4)** Which of the following statements regarding total fixed costs is correct?
   a) When total fixed costs are graphed, the curve will rise from the origin at a constant rate.
   b) When total fixed costs are graphed, the curve will be horizontal.
   c) Total fixed costs equal total variable costs less total average costs.
   d) Total fixed costs rise slowly at first but then more quickly as output increases.
   e) Total fixed costs equal total marginal costs plus total variable costs.

29. **(LO 4)** If we assume that the level of output remains unchanged, which of the following could cause a decrease in average total, average variable, and marginal costs?
   a) A decrease in the price of resources
   b) An increase in the price of resources
   c) An increase in the firm's capacity output
   d) A decrease in the firm's capacity output
   e) A decrease in the firm's fixed cost

Use **Table 6.6** to answer questions 30 and 31.

TABLE 6.6

Units of Labour	Total Output	TC	MC	ATC
0	0	$ 80	/	/
1	8	120	___	___
2	18		___	___
3	25		___	___
4	28		___	___

30. **(LO 3)** Assuming that the only variable input is labour and all units of labour cost the same, what is the value of marginal cost when it is at a minimum?
   a) $4
   b) $5
   c) $15
   d) $40

31. **(LO 3)** Assuming that the only variable input is labour and all units of labour cost the same, what is the value of average variable cost when it is at a minimum?
   a) $4
   b) $4.44
   c) $15
   d) $40

Advanced (Questions 32–35)

32. **(LO 2)** What is the significance of the maximum point on the total product curve?
   a) It is the point where the increase in output begins to slow down.
   b) It is the point where diminishing returns sets in.
   c) It is the point of maximum marginal product.
   d) It is the point where marginal product becomes zero.

33. **(LO 2)** If marginal product is declining, which of the following statements is correct?
   a) Average product must be falling.
   b) Average product could be rising or falling.
   c) Marginal cost must be falling.
   d) Average variable cost must be rising.
   e) Average variable cost must be falling.

34. **(LO 2, 4, 5)** All of the following statements, except one, are correct. Which is the exception?
   a) If the marginal cost curve shifts down, then the average total cost curve will also shift down.
   b) If the marginal cost curve shifts down, then the average variable cost curve will also shift down.
   c) The average fixed cost curve will be unaffected by a shift in the marginal cost curve.
   d) If the marginal product curve shifts up, then the marginal cost curve will shift up.
   e) If the marginal product curve shifts up, then the average product curve will shift up.

35. **(LO 5)** Which of the following statements would be true about a firm that is operating under conditions of excess capacity?
   a) The firm's average total cost would be at a minimum.
   b) The firm's average total cost would not be at a minimum.
   c) The firm's average total cost may or may not be at a minimum, but the firm would not be at capacity output.
   d) The firm would not be at capacity output, but its average total cost would be at a minimum.
   e) The firm would need to reduce output to achieve minimum average total cost.

Parallel Problems

ANSWERED PROBLEMS

36A. **(LO 2, 3)** **Key Problem** Last summer Daniel started the Custom Made Fencing Company, which specializes in building fences to meet the specific needs of his customers. Since Daniel works out of his parents' basement, uses an old pickup, and needs only a few simple tools, his fixed costs are minimal. He measures the firm's output in terms of the number of feet per day of fence that is built. Experience has shown Daniel that different crew sizes can build fences as shown in **Table 6.7**.

TABLE 6.7

Number of Workers in Crew	TP$_L$ (feet per day)	MP$_L$ (feet per day)	AP$_L$ (feet per day)
1	20	_____	_____
2	80	_____	_____
3	150	_____	_____
4	200	_____	_____
5	230	_____	_____
6	246	_____	_____

a) Fill in the marginal and average product of labour columns in the table above.

b) On the graph in **Figure 6.8**, draw the two curves.

c) Assuming that each worker costs $240 a day (wages and materials), fill in **Table 6.8**.

d) On the graph in **Figure 6.9**, draw the average variable and marginal cost curves.

e) Looking back at **Figure 6.8**, determine how many workers are used to achieve maximum average product. (Remember that the definition of maximum AP is where it equals MP.)
Answer: _____

f) What output can this number of workers produce?
Answer: _____

g) Now, from **Figure 6.9**, what is true at the output level you gave as your answer in f)?
Answer: _____

h) Return to **Table 6.7**, and this time, determine how many workers are used to achieve maximum marginal product. Answer: _____

i) What output can this number of workers produce?
Answer: _____

FIGURE 6.8

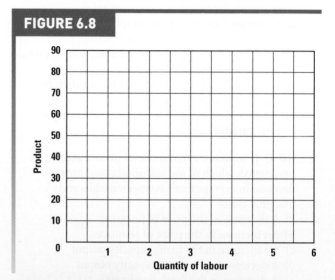

TABLE 6.8

Number of Workers in Crew	TP (feet per day)	TVC	AVC	MC
1	20	_____	_____	_____
2	80	_____	_____	_____
3	150	_____	_____	_____
4	200	_____	_____	_____
5	230	_____	_____	_____
6	246	_____	_____	_____

FIGURE 6.9

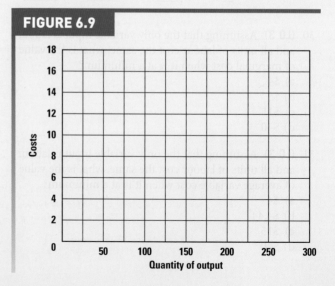

j) Look at **Figure 6.9** again, and determine what is true at the output level you gave as your answer in i).
Answer: _____

k) What conclusion can you make from your answers in e) through j)? Answer: _____

Basic (Problems 37A–44A)

37A. **(LO 2)** Table 6.9 shows the total product for a firm. Complete the average and marginal products.

TABLE 6.9

Units of labour	Total product	Average product	Marginal product
0	0	_____	_____
1	12	_____	_____
2	30	_____	_____
3	54	_____	_____
4	68	_____	_____
5	80	_____	_____
6	84	_____	_____
7	77	_____	_____

38A. **(LO 4)** Table 6.10 shows the total fixed and variable costs of a firm. Complete the table.

39A. **(LO 3, 4)** Which of the following are fixed costs (F), and which are variable costs (V)?
a) A business licence _____
b) The setup costs for a computerized payroll accounting system _____
c) Production cost for materials and supplies _____
d) Production staff wages _____

e) Leasehold costs for the firm's land and buildings _____

40A. **(LO 1)** Emily recently graduated with a B.A. in Economics and was offered a job with a small but growing company for $38 400 per year. About the same time, Emily inherited $60 000. She decided to pass up the job and use her inheritance to purchase a video rental shop rather than put the money into a bond fund (as her uncle suggested), which would have paid 5 percent per year interest. Emily works full-time at her new business, and in the typical month of October, she has revenues of $6750 and total explicit costs of $3500.
a) What was Emily's accounting profit for the month? _____
b) What was her economic profit or loss for the month? _____

41A. **(LO 2)**
a) Complete **Table 6.11** for Bannister Inc.
b) How many workers are being used when the point of diminishing returns is first apparent? _____

TABLE 6.11

Number of Workers	Total Product	Average Product	Marginal Product
1	2	_____	_____
2	5	_____	_____
3	_____	3	_____
4	_____	_____	3
5	14	_____	_____
6	_____	_____	1
7	15	_____	_____

TABLE 6.10

Output	TFC	TVC	TC	AFC	AVC	ATC	MC
1	1200	400	_____	_____	_____	_____	_____
2	1200	600	_____	_____	_____	_____	_____
3	1200	720	_____	_____	_____	_____	_____
4	1200	800	_____	_____	_____	_____	_____
5	1200	1500	_____	_____	_____	_____	_____
6	1200	3000	_____	_____	_____	_____	_____
7	1200	5250	_____	_____	_____	_____	_____
8	1200	8000	_____	_____	_____	_____	_____

TABLE 6.12

Output	TFC	TVC	TC	MC	AFC	AVC	ATC
0	$210	0	___	/	/	/	/
1	___	___	___	$100	___	___	___
2	___	___	___	60	___	___	___
3	___	___	___	50	___	___	___
4	___	___	___	80	___	___	___
5	___	___	___	100	___	___	___
6	___	___	___	126	___	___	___
7	___	___	___	156	___	___	___
8	___	___	___	190	___	___	___
9	___	___	___	242	___	___	___
10	___	___	___	296	___	___	___
11	___	___	___	381	___	___	___
12	___	___	___	529	___	___	___

c) How many workers are being used when total product is at a maximum?

_____

d) What is the most productive output?

_____

42A. **(LO 4)** Table 6.12 shows data for Big Bob's Brewing Company. The quantities are for large vats of beer.
a) Fill in the blanks in the table.
b) At what level of output is average product at a maximum? Answer: _____
c) What is the value of average total cost at this output level? Answer: $ _____
d) What is the output at economic capacity? Answer: _____
e) If fixed costs were to double, what would be the marginal cost of the fifth unit of output? Answer: $ _____

43A. **(LO 1)** Distinguish between explicit cost and implicit cost.

44A. **(LO 2)** Identify and define the terms total products, average products, and marginal products.

Intermediate (Problems 45A–50A)

45A. **(LO 3, 4)** Table 6.13 gives data for a firm named Crystal Clear Speech Writing Services. Fill in the blanks in the table.

46A. **(LO 4)** The data in Table 6.14 are for the Quite Small Blueberry Farm. The quantities are for the number of tonnes of berries per year.

TABLE 6.13

Output	AFC	AVC	ATC	MC	TVC	TC
1	___	___	___	40	___	___
2	___	___	___	___	70	___
3	___	___	90	___	___	___
4	40	___	___	___	___	320
5	___	___	___	70	___	___
6	___	55	___	___	___	___
7	___	___	___	___	480	___
8	___	___	___	___	___	840

TABLE 6.14

Quantity	Total Cost
0	$2000
1	2400
2	2700
3	2800
4	2860
5	3000

a) What is the amount of TFC? _____
b) What is the MC of the third tonne produced?

_____

c) What is the TVC of producing 4 tonnes?

_____

d) What is the ATC of producing 2 tonnes?

_____

TABLE 6.15

Output	TVC_1	TVC_2	AVC_1	AVC_2	MC_1	MC_2
1	$ 44	_____	$44.00	_____	$44.00	_____
2	64	_____	32.00	_____	20.00	_____
3	78	_____	26.00	_____	14.00	_____
4	88	_____	22.00	_____	10.00	_____
5	100	_____	20.00	_____	12.00	_____
6	120	_____	20.00	_____	20.00	_____
7	150	_____	21.42	_____	30.00	_____
8	200	_____	25.00	_____	50.00	_____

47A. (LO 4)
a) Fill in the blank columns in **Table 6.15** for the firm Bannister Railings, assuming that the cost of variable inputs decreases by 50 percent.
b) Draw AVC_1, MC_1, AVC_2, and MC_2 on the grid in **Figure 6.10**.

FIGURE 6.10

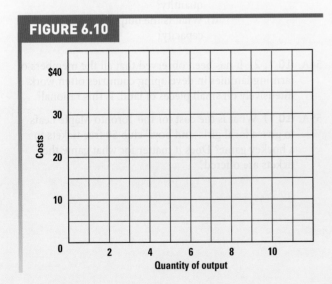

48A. (LO 2) **Figure 6.11** is for the Grow 'Em Right Nursery company.
a) Calculate Grow 'Em Right's total product and average product.
b) Add the AP curve to the graph.
c) What is the value of maximum AP? _____

49A. (LO 2) What is the relationship between the AP/MP curves and the AVC/MC curves?

50A. (LO 2) What is excess capacity?

FIGURE 6.11

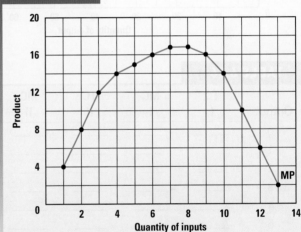

Advanced (Problems 51A–55A)

51A. (LO 3)
a) On **Figure 6.12**, draw AVC, AFC, and ATC curves that have the following characteristics: AVC is $30 and AFC is $20 when output is 10; AVC declines $5 for every increase in output of 10, up to an output of 50; above output levels of 50, AVC rises $5 for every increase in output of 10.
b) What is the level of output at economic capacity? Answer: _____
c) What is the most productive output? Answer: _____

52A. (LO 5) A firm has a choice of two different technologies to produce its product. The first technology has a total fixed cost of $1200 and a constant marginal cost of $200. The second has a total fixed cost of $2000 and a constant marginal cost of $60.

FIGURE 6.12

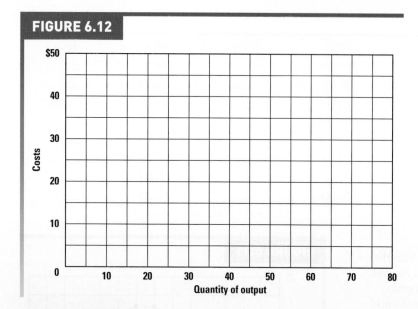

TABLE 6.16

Output	TC I	MC I	TC II	MC II
0	___	___	___	___
1	___	___	___	___
2	___	___	___	___
3	___	___	___	___
4	___	___	___	___
5	___	___	___	___
6	___	___	___	___
7	___	___	___	___
8	___	___	___	___
9	___	___	___	___
10	___	___	___	___

Use **Table 6.16** to gather the information needed to determine the output levels where Technology I would give the lowest total cost and those output levels where Technology II would give the lowest total cost.

a) It is best to use Technology I between output levels _____ and _____ .

b) It is best to use Technology II between output levels _____ and _____ .

53A. **(LO 2, 3, 4)** Table 6.17 shows the cost data of a furniture manufacturer named Cindy's Custom Made.

a) Complete the table, assuming that labour (and materials) costs $12 an hour.

b) What is the most productive output?

c) What are AVC and ATC at this quantity?

d) What is the output at economic capacity?

54A. **(LO 1, 2)** It has been observed that all the members of farming families in developing countries often work intensively on small pieces of land. Is this rational?

55A. **(LO 1)** What is the cost for the Toronto Maple Leafs to give a local girls' and boys' club 50 free tickets to a hockey game? Does it matter for what game the tickets are offered?

TABLE 6.17

Output of Chairs	Total Hours	Average Hours per Chair	Marginal Hours per Chair	TVC	AVC	TFC	TC	ATC	MC
1	5	___	___	___	___	180	___	___	___
2	9	___	___	___	___		___	___	___
3	12	___	___	___	___		___	___	___
4	18	___	___	___	___		___	___	___
5	25	___	___	___	___		___	___	___
6	36	___	___	___	___		___	___	___

CHAPTER 7

COSTS IN THE LONG RUN

At the end of this chapter, you should be able to...

L01 distinguish between the short run and the long run.

L02 understand why medium-sized firms are sometimes just as efficient as big firms.

L03 understand why big firms sometimes enjoy great cost advantages.

L04 understand why firms can sometimes be too big.

L05 understand the effect of technological change on a firm's cost.

L06 explain what is meant by the right size of firm.

L07 explain why markets can sometimes be too small.

In this chapter, we continue discussing costs but shift the focus from the short run to the long run. We define what economists mean by the long run and explain how it relates to the size of the firm. We show why there are great advantages for a firm to be big, but also look at what happens when firms get too big. Finally, we discuss the idea of the right size of firm by looking at the concept of minimum efficient scale.

A Question of Relevance...

If we think of all the different products that you and I purchase, it is apparent that we could produce some of them for ourselves—tomatoes, cookies, and even a birdhouse. So, why do we buy the things we could make ourselves? And why is it that something as comparatively simple to make as a cardboard box is produced in giant factories, whereas highly complex computers are produced in small workshops that dot the countrysides of Asian countries? Why, for that matter, aren't furniture factories as big as car assembly plants, and why aren't aluminum smelters as small as dairy plants? The answers to these questions involve the concept of economies of scale, the central theme of this chapter.

7.1 THE LONG RUN

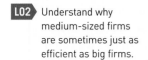 **LO1** Distinguish between the short run and the long run.

long run: the period in which all inputs are variable.

In the discussion about the costs of production in the previous chapter, we made the assumption that at least one factor of production was fixed. This is what we referred to as the short run. In contrast, economists define the **long run** as a period in which the producing firm has the option of changing all of its inputs. In other words, in the long run, there are no fixed factors and all inputs are variable.

There is a technique to thinking about the long run. You should recognize that at any *one point in time*, the firm must always be in the short run. Imagine a factory manager as he steps out of his office onto the shop floor. Are any of the factor inputs used in production fixed? The answer is yes, of course. At least one input, and probably several, would be fixed—the square footage of the plant, or the number of machines, or the quantity of some crucial raw material. Firms are always operating in the short run and, as a result, the reality of diminishing marginal product is present.

Now, imagine our factory manager walking back into his office and closing the door as he sits down to ask himself: where do we want to be in five years? As he proceeds to answer this question, he is able to treat all inputs as variable. He is able to conceptualize the long run. It is in this sense that economists describe the long run as a planning horizon:

> All production processes operate in the short run, and diminishing marginal productivity is an unavoidable reality.

> In the long run, there are no fixed factors, and diminishing marginal productivity does not apply. All costs are variable.

long-run average cost curve: a graphical representation of the per-unit costs of production in the long run.

We now need to elaborate on this very important short-run/long-run distinction by carefully developing the **long-run average cost curve** (LRAC). (Note that for the balance of this chapter we will use the term "average cost" to refer to the short run and "long-run average cost" for the long run.)

7.2 CONSTANT RETURNS TO SCALE

LO2 Understand why medium-sized firms are sometimes just as efficient as big firms.

We begin this discussion by imagining a firm, Rising Sun Products Limited, that produces high-quality DVDs and operates in a small-sized plant, which we shall call plant 1. Further, we will assume that there are also three other plant sizes available to Rising Sun: plant 2, which is exactly twice the size of plant 1; plant 3, which is exactly three times the size of plant 1; and plant 4, which is exactly four times the size of plant 1. Some short-run average cost data are presented in **Table 7.1**.

Remember from the previous chapter that economic capacity is defined as the output at which (short-run) average costs are at a minimum. From **Table 7.1**, we can see that in plant 1 (the present plant), economic capacity is achieved with an output of 200 DVDs per day. However, Rising Sun's reputation for producing a quality product has been steadily growing within the industry, and it has had to increase production to 400 a day for the last couple of months just to meet customers' orders. The consequence of this strong demand, which the firm welcomes, is that its average costs have been running at $8 per unit, which is far above the minimum average cost level of $5. Something has to be done. Rising Sun must either refuse some customers' orders, which is undesirable; raise prices, which might have negative long-run consequences; or build a bigger plant that can handle the 400 per day output and still maintain average costs of $5.

Suppose the firm decides to build a larger plant. This decision leads to a management debate about the size of the new plant. One option is to go conservative and opt for plant 2, which achieves

TABLE 7.1	Rising Sun's Plant Size Alternatives			
Output of DVDs per Day	AC in Plant 1	AC in Plant 2	AC in Plant 3	AC in Plant 4
100	$ 6.00	$ 7.00	$7.50	$8.00
200	5.00	6.00	6.50	7.10
300	6.00	5.50	6.00	6.50
400	8.00	5.00	5.70	6.00
500	11.00	5.50	5.30	5.80
600	15.00	6.00	5.00	5.50
700	20.00	7.00	5.30	5.20
800	26.00	8.00	5.70	5.00
900	33.00	9.50	6.00	5.20
1000	41.00	11.00	6.50	5.50

minimum average costs of $5 at the current output level of 400 units per day. The second option is to anticipate even more growth in the future and opt for plant 3, which would require an output of 600 units a day to achieve the desired minimum average costs of $5. There are, however, two drawbacks associated with plant 3. The first is that it is more expensive to build, and the second is that if plant 3 is chosen, the current rate of production of 400 per day would only lower average costs to $5.70. Thus, building plant 3 would prove to be the right decision only if orders increase sufficiently to justify a production run that is higher than the current level. Since no one can predict the future with certainty, let us assume that a conservative decision is made to build plant 2.

In time the new plant is ready, and Rising Sun is able to handle the runs of 400 units per day at a reduced average total cost of $5. But the story does not end here. Our firm's fortunes continue to grow, and sales rise to the point that production runs of 600 units a day are needed to keep up with commitments made to customers. As we can see in **Table 7.1** (plant 2 column), this raises average cost to $6 in new plant 2, and Rising Sun is again faced with a major decision about the correct plant size for its operations. Now, it could upgrade to plant 3 and reduce average costs (at current rates of output) to $5, or it could make the bold decision to build a new plant—plant 4—in anticipation of even more sales growth in the future. If Rising Sun does this, it faces the risk that future sales might decline, and it could again face high average costs.

As you can see, the long run involves planning—firms must try to anticipate the future. This is, by its very nature, risky. Businesspeople do not always like taking risks, but doing so is often unavoidable.

Figure 7.1 is a graphical presentation of the average costs data from **Table 7.1**. Points *a*, *b*, *c*, and *d* in **Figure 7.1** identify economic capacity in each of the four plant sizes, that is, where (short-run) average costs are at a minimum. By connecting these four points, can we obtain a long-run average cost curve? Technically, the answer is no, if these four different-sized plants are the *only* options. This is because the LRAC curve would be the curve up to output 200 and the curve between outputs 200 and 400. However, if we assume that there are many other possible plant sizes, then there would exist many other AC curves that have not been shown. Each of these unseen cost curves would have a minimum point, and connecting these many minimum points would give us something close to a horizontal LRAC curve, as shown in **Figure 7.1**. Let us make this assumption and proceed with our focus remaining on the four mentioned plant sizes.

Inventory is just one of the costs of production.

FIGURE 7.1   Average Costs of Production in Four Plant Sizes

Points *a*, *b*, *c*, and *d* are each points of minimum average costs in four different plant sizes. By connecting these four points, we obtain the long-run average cost curve.

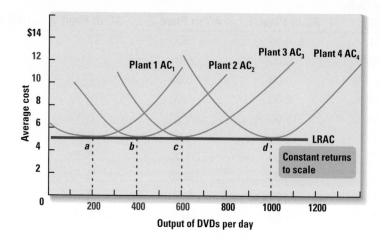

In its long-run planning, Rising Sun must choose one of these four points as its daily production target. Which of the four it chooses would, of course, depend on its estimates of its long-run production requirements, and that would depend on its estimates of its future sales. However, once a decision is made, be it plant 1, 2, 3, or 4, the firm finds itself on one of the four (short-run) average cost curves. That is, the firm finds itself in the short run where, at output levels above economic capacity, average cost rises. Thus, we say, once again:

A firm can *plan* as if it is in the long run, but it always *operates* in the short run.

constant returns to scale: a firm's output increases by the same percentage as the increase in its inputs.

Let us return to **Figure 7.1** and point out that the horizontal long-run average cost curve shown there is a reflection of the concept of **constant returns to scale**. This term is used only in the context of the long run and refers to the situation in which output increases in exact proportion to an increase in inputs.

You will recall that in this example, we assumed that plant 2 was exactly twice as large as plant 1. If we also assume that the amount of labour and materials being used in plant 2 is also exactly twice the quantity used in plant 1, and if we assume that the prices of these inputs do not change, then the total cost of producing 400 units per day would be exactly twice the total costs of producing 200 units per day. This means that the average costs will be the same in both cases. You can verify that this is so by looking back at **Table 7.1**. Here, you can see that the minimum average cost for all the plants is the same—$5. These are the conditions that result in a horizontal long-run average cost curve, that is, constant returns to scale.

✓ SELF-TEST

1. The accompanying table shows the average costs associated with three different plant sizes.

   a) Which plant is best suited to produce an output of 4 units?

   b) What is the value of long-run average cost?

Output	Plant 1 Average Cost	Plant 2 Average Cost	Plant 3 Average Cost
1	$45	$62	$80
2	36	47	63
3	42	36	49
4	55	44	36
5	70	68	52

7.3 ECONOMIES OF SCALE

To take our discussion of long-run costs one step further, we introduce a new firm, Deep Sea Concrete, which is currently producing 1000 cubic metres of concrete a day in plant 1. We will assume that the total cost of doing this is $40 000, which means that Deep Sea's average cost of production is currently $40 per metre.

Now, let us assume that Deep Sea builds a larger plant that is exactly double its present size and consequently has experienced a doubling in its total cost. What will happen to the average costs of production as a result? The answer very much depends on what happens to the level of output. With our last example, Rising Sun, a doubling of inputs led simply to a doubling of output. But in reality, this may not be true. In fact, in many cases, output could more than double and cause average costs to fall. This is what economists term **economies of scale**. Let us see how this works out in the case of Deep Sea.

Let us assume that as a result of doubling its inputs, Deep Sea's output level increased from the original 1000 cubic metres up to 2500 cubic metres per day. Remember that total costs have doubled from $40 000 to $80 000. If we divide the new output level of 2500 cubic metres into $80 000, we obtain a new per cubic metre cost of $32, well below the original average cost of $40. This is illustrated in **Figure 7.2**. The original plant's average costs are shown as AC$_1$. At its original output, it was producing an output of 1000 cubic metres at an average cost of $40 per metre. Plant 2 is exactly double the size of plant 1, and yet it achieves certain economies of scale enabling it to produce an output of 2500 at a lower cost of $32.

Firms in industries characterized by assembly-line production of standardized products, such as automobiles, television sets, refrigerators, or railway cars, are likely to experience declining long-run average cost. In these cases, such firms become formidable competitors because increased output means lower per-unit costs. As we will discuss in later chapters, this is the reason why these industries are often dominated by a few large firms.

L03 Understand why big firms sometimes enjoy great cost advantages.

economies of scale: cost advantages achieved as a result of large-scale operations.

Economies of scale in production has dramatically increased global trade.

FIGURE 7.2 **Long-Run Average Costs under Conditions of Economies of Scale**

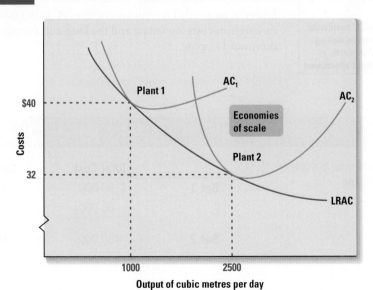

AC$_1$ (plant 1) and AC$_2$ (plant 2) are both short-run average cost curves. We have identified one point on each curve representing two output levels used in our example. Connecting these two points gives us a portion of the long-run average cost curve, which declines as output rises.

Now, we need to understand these economies of scale and why many larger firms are able to produce at lower average costs than smaller firms. First, there are technical economies that are very closely related to the advantages gained from the *division of labour* discussed in the previous chapter. In many contexts, production workers save time if they do not have to switch job functions during the day, or if they develop special skills as a result of performing only one particular operation. Small plants also use division of labour, but big plants are able to exploit it on a far greater scale.

In addition to using the division of labour, large-scale production also encourages *management specialization*. Two examples of this are a supervisor who is just as capable of handling twelve workers as eight, or an accounting department that does not grow in size despite a 30-percent increase in the output of the firm. Further, as a firm grows in size, rather than increasing the number of general managers, it makes sense for the firm to hire specialized managers, such as controllers, marketing managers, production managers, and so on.

A third type of technical specialization, *machine specialization*, is also possible. A classic example is the use of robots on an expensive assembly line, something that would probably not be an option for a firm with a small output. These technical economies mean that when the physical inputs are increased by a certain percentage, outputs will increase by a larger percentage. For this reason, they are often referred to as **increasing returns to scale**.

increasing returns to scale: a firm's output increases by a greater percentage than the increase in its inputs.

But big firms also enjoy other advantages in the form of pecuniary economies of scale. These come in four forms.

- Large firms with large output often need, and are able, to borrow large sums of money, and their *cost of borrowing* (the interest rate they have to pay) is often lower than the rate charged when smaller amounts are borrowed.
- High-volume firms can also *buy inputs in bulk*, which also often means at a lower per-unit price. In addition, bulk selling lowers their per-unit sales cost.
- A large volume of output often means that previously wasted *by-products can be sold*—think of wood chips from a lumber mill that can be used to make particle board.
- Large firms have economies of scale in *marketing and advertising*. A thirty-second national television advertisement costs the big firm no more than it does the small firm, but the per-unit output cost of the advertisement is much lower.

In summary, think of Rising Sun Products, which experiences constant returns to scale. This means that there must have been no economies of scale present. When we think of Deep Sea Concrete, however, we see that it enjoys economies of scale, which means that its long-run costs are falling and the long-run average cost curve is downward sloping.

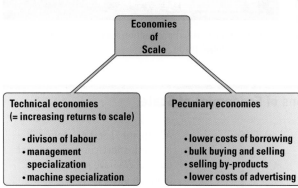

✓ SELF-TEST

2. Indicate the presence of either constant returns to scale or increasing returns to scale in each set of data.

		Total Cost	Output
Set 1		$ 30 000	175
		60 000	375
Set 2		450 000	100
		900 000	200

7.4   DISECONOMIES OF SCALE

The Deep Sea Concrete example illustrated economies of scale. It is also possible for **diseconomies of scale** to exist. When diseconomies of scale are present, average costs of production will increase rather than decrease as output is increased. When this is so, big firms are at a serious disadvantage. Assume that Deep Sea, as in our previous example, doubled its plant size with a consequent doubling in its total costs from $40 000 to $80 000. However, suppose that its output was unable to keep pace and, instead, increased only by 60 percent from 1000 cubic metres to 1600 metres. The result would be an increase in its average costs from $40 ($40 000 divided by 1000) to $50 ($80 000 divided by 1600). This is illustrated in **Figure 7.3**. Here, we see the original output of 1000 cubic metres in plant 1 resulted in an average cost of $40. Plant 2 is twice as big. However, the output has only increased to 1600 cubic metres resulting in an average cost curve which is higher than that of plant 1. As a result, the average cost has increased to $50. Since output increased by less than inputs, diseconomies of scale are present. These can also be referred to as **decreasing returns to scale**.

But why might productivity fall and average costs increase as a result of a firm's growth? The answer lies in the bureaucratic inefficiencies in management that all larger firms (as well as nonprofit organizations and governments) experience. This is due to size and does not necessarily imply incompetence. Such diseconomies can result because communication must pass through more channels becoming subject to interpretation by many more people. Since the lines of communication increase exponentially with the number of personnel, the cost of communication can increase dramatically. Misinterpretation also becomes more likely, especially if the information is complicated and technical in nature. Further, as the management organization within the firm becomes larger, the points of responsibility and decision making become blurred. If the problem of miscommunication and uncertain responsibility become serious enough, diseconomies of scale occur.

If such technical diseconomies of scale outweigh the pecuniary economies of scale that might be present, then diseconomies of scale result and the long-run average cost curve begins to rise. The following illustrates what might happen to physical output when inputs are doubled.

L04 Understand why firms can sometimes be too big.

diseconomies of scale: bureaucratic inefficiencies in management that result in decreasing returns to scale.

decreasing returns to scale: the situation in which a firm's output increases by a smaller percentage than the increase its inputs.

| **FIGURE 7.3** | **The LRAC Curve under Conditions of Diseconomies of Scale** |

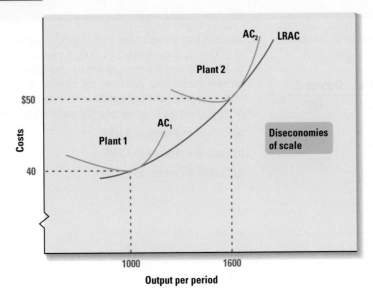

Plant 2 is twice the size of plant 1. However, because of diseconomies of scale, output only increases from 1000 to 1600 cubic metres. The result is an increase in average cost from $40 to $50.

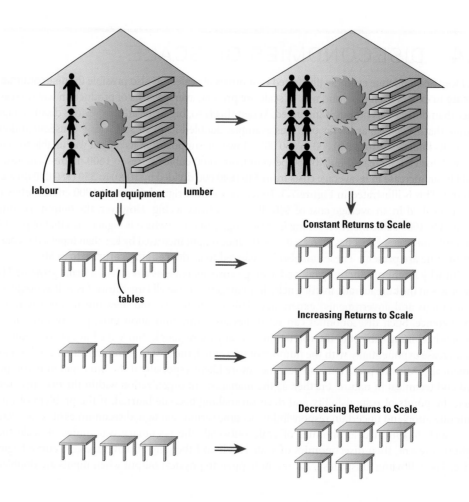

labour   capital equipment   lumber

tables

Constant Returns to Scale

Increasing Returns to Scale

Decreasing Returns to Scale

 SELF-TEST

3. Decide in each of the following cases (A–D) whether constant returns to, economies of, or diseconomies of scale exist:

	Inputs 1	Inputs 2	Output 1	Output 2
A	6	12	240	480
B	46	92	275	650
C	18	27	500	800
D	260	540	1240	2480

4. Assume that a firm's total cost of producing an output of 600 units is currently $24 000. If total cost increases to $48 000 and the price of inputs and technology remain unchanged, calculate the change in average cost, and state whether constant returns and economies or diseconomies of scale exist for each of the three cases.

a) Output increases to 1100

b) Output increases to 1250

c) Output increases to 1200

7.5 CHANGES IN SHORT- AND LONG-RUN COSTS

We pointed out at the end of Chapter 6 that if the price of factor inputs decreases, then short-run average cost, as well as marginal cost, would decrease. This would result in the average cost curves shifting down. Such a shift in the short-run average cost curve would result in a corresponding shift in the long-run average cost curve. Recall that the long-run average cost curve is derived from a family of short-run cost curves. If these short-run cost curves shift down, so will the long-run average cost curve. As well as a decrease in input prices, costs can also decrease at all levels of output and thus cause the average and marginal cost curves to shift down. Improvements in technology have this effect. In fact, one of the possible definitions of **technological improvement** is *change that reduces the costs of production at all output levels*. This emphasizes the importance of technological improvement for the firm in this modern, competitive world. Improved technology (in the economic sense) means lower costs of production, and lower costs of production means more success.

L05 Understand the effect of technological change on a firm's cost.

technological improvement: changes in production techniques that reduce the costs of production.

We can add one more point to the discussion of reducing costs. As you are aware, corporate takeovers and mergers between firms are quite prevalent these days. Why is this? One explanation involves fixed costs. If the new, larger firm that results from a takeover or merger can keep its fixed cost below the *combined* fixed costs of the original two firms, then average costs of production will have been reduced and the profitability of the new firm will be enhanced.

ADDED DIMENSION   Increased Rates of Productivity Growth

One of the truly phenomenal trends in the years just before the recession of 2008 was the impressive growth rates in output per capita in the United States. Underlying this trend were increases in labour productivity in the 2.5–3 percent range, something that has not been seen for decades. Such statements as "productivity growth is the cornerstone of economic growth and wealth creation" were found in popular publications as well as in academic journals.

Most economists agree that at the root of these productivity increases is the *technological change* associated with the computer and information "revolution." Nonetheless, Canada's rates of productivity increases have consistently lagged behind those of the United States. In 2009, research by John Baldwin and Wulong Gu (both with Statistics Canada) concluded that Canada's lagging productivity rates had three causes: reluctance of Canadian firms to meet foreign competition head-on, inadequate spending on new capital equipment, and a failure of firms to grow large enough to capture minimum efficient scale (see Section 7.7 of this chapter).

7.6 WHAT IS THE RIGHT SIZE OF FIRM?

In the previous chapter, when we looked at a firm's operations in the short run, we pointed out that it is crucial for firms to decide their best output level. Similarly:

L06 Explain what is meant by the right size of firm.

In the long run, what is the best size of firm?

Can a firm be too small? Can it be too big? Our discussion of economies and diseconomies of scale allows us to answer questions like these. **Figure 7.4** will help.

Firms in many industries do not necessarily experience constant returns to scale, *or* economies of scale, *or* diseconomies of scale; all three may be present over different output ranges. **Figure 7.4** illustrates a situation in which economies of scale exist for any output level up to quantity Q_1. Output levels that are greater than Q_1 but less than Q_2 are subject to constant returns to scale, and any output level above quantity Q_2 is subject to diseconomies of scale.

If this long-run average cost curve were typical for a particular industry, we would conclude that any firm that has an output level below quantity Q_1 is probably too small. Output levels below Q_1 would put any firm at a cost disadvantage compared with its competitors. Similarly, we would also conclude that any firm whose output level was above quantity Q_2 was probably too big and could lower its average cost of production by scaling down the size of its operations.

Note that the long-run average cost curve in **Figure 7.4** has the same general U-shape as the short-run average cost curve found in the previous chapter. The similar shapes of the two curves, however, are the result of quite different reasons. In the case of the short-run average cost curve, the reasons involve the division of labour and diminishing marginal productivity. The long-run average cost curve, on the other hand, takes on this shape because of economies and diseconomies of scale and constant returns to scale.

Another important way to view the issue of the right size of firm is to ask: is bigger better? We will see that it really depends on the industry in question. Appropriate-sized firms are able to take advantage of any economies of scale that exist, without becoming too big and experiencing diseconomies.

Figure 7.5 shows three possible LRAC curves for different industries, each resulting in the appropriate-sized firm being different.

Figure 7.5A illustrates the case in which a firm would have to be quite large to capture all of the economies of scale available. In this type of industry, small- and medium-sized firms, because of their comparatively higher average costs, are simply not able to compete with larger firms. Thus, this type of industry tends to be dominated by large firms. Examples are the automobile, pipeline, satellite data transmission, cable distribution, television transmission, and petrochemical industries.

In **Figure 7.5B**, we can imagine a variety of different-sized firms, all of which are able to capture economies of scale. This is because costs remain constant over a wide range of outputs, and therefore, an appropriate-sized firm could be either relatively small or large. Examples here would be such industries as computer software, real estate services, and meat packing.

Finally, **Figure 7.5C** illustrates an industry in which only relatively small firms would be appropriate. This is the case with vegetable farming and small-scale retailing, such as the corner convenience store.

FIGURE 7.4   The Complete Long-Run Average Cost Curve

Economies of scale exist for output levels up to Q_1. Constant returns to scale prevail for output levels between Q_1 and Q_2. Finally, diseconomies of scale prevail for output levels above Q_2.

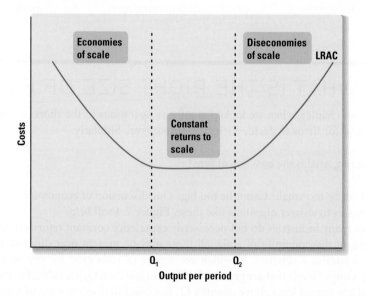

| FIGURE 7.5 | Three Possible LRAC Curves |

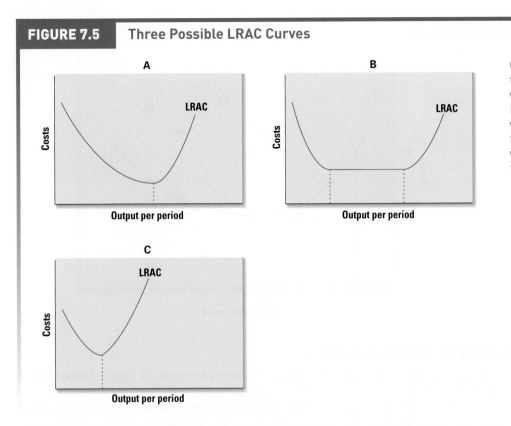

Given the LRAC curve in Figure A, the appropriately sized firm would need to be large. In Figure B, a variety of firm sizes would be appropriate. However, the LRAC curve in Figure C would indicate that only small firms would be appropriate.

7.7   CAN A MARKET BE TOO SMALL?

Adam Smith observed, over 200 years ago, that the division of labour was limited by the size of the market. Is it possible that a limited size of market can restrict the extent to which firms enjoy economies of scale? This is the case in Canada, with its small population and correspondingly small market, at least for some industries.

This leads us to the concept of **minimum efficient scale** (MES), which refers to the smallest size that a firm can be and yet be able to minimize its long-run average costs. If a small market means firms cannot achieve minimum efficient scale, then inefficiency can become widespread throughout the industry. The Canadian economy has historically faced this problem. Its domestic market is too small for those industries in which the MES dictates that a large output is necessary to minimize average cost. As a result, such firms are inefficient by world standards. This situation is illustrated in **Figure 7.6**.

A small market may force a firm to limit its output to Q_1 and experience average total cost of AC_1 as illustrated in **Figure 7.6**. This is above the level of minimum long-run average cost. A larger market would allow the firm to build a larger plant, as represented by the AC_2 curve, and thereby achieve minimum long-run average costs.

Thus, we can see that Adam Smith was correct in his observation that the division of labour can be limited by the size of the market in both the short run and the long run. In the short run, a limited-sized market can force a firm to produce at an output below economic capacity. More significantly, a limited-sized market can prevent firms from building large-scale plants and capturing available economies of scale through increased output levels. This inability to increase output levels limits the firm's ability to gain all of the possible advantages of the division of labour.

 L07 Explain why markets can sometimes be too small.

minimum efficient scale:
the smallest-sized plant capable of achieving the lowest long-run average cost of production.

FIGURE 7.6	Minimum Efficient Scale

If a small market limits the firm's output to Q_1, then its average cost, AC_1, is not able to achieve minimum efficient scale. A larger market that allowed an output of Q_2, and thus a larger firm as represented by AC_2, would enable that firm to achieve its minimum efficient scale.

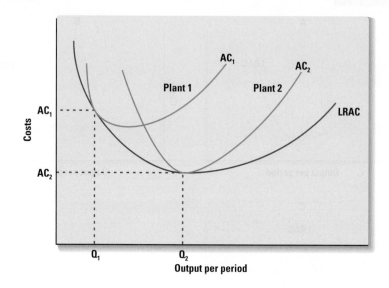

Does Size Matter Anymore?

Let us consider what is probably the economist's favourite example of technical economies of scale. The cost of a pipeline is roughly proportional to its circumference—the larger the circumference, the more steel is needed to build it. However, the carrying capacity of a pipeline is determined by its area, which means that larger pipelines have disproportionately increased capacity and thus lower per-unit costs. For instance, a twelve-inch-diameter pipe requires twice the steel of a six-inch pipe but can carry *four* times the volume. This illustrates the classic relationship between bigger volume and lower long-run average cost.

For most of the twentieth century, conventional wisdom suggested that the bigger a firm became, the more likely it was that it would be successful. The Royal Bank, Barrick Gold, Imperial Oil, and IBM are big and successful and are likely to remain so. But recently things have started to change. The specialty channels like CNN and ESPN broke the strangle-hold that the big three American TV networks held for decades. Small mini-mill companies in the steel industry are more profitable than the large mainstream firms. Large multi-national corporations are making deals with small Ballard Power to hedge their bets on the future. What is happening here? Don't economies of scale count any more?

 ADDED DIMENSION   Free Trade Agreements and MES

Proponents of both the Canada–United States Free Trade Agreement and the North American Free Trade Agreement (NAFTA) argued in the late 1980s that a failure to achieve minimum efficient scale was hindering the success of many Canadian firms. The logical extension of this argument was that both agreements would extend the size of the market considerably for Canadian producers, and this would allow these firms to increase output and achieve minimum efficient scale. For this to happen, Canadian exports would have to rise substantially. In fact, Canadian exports to the United States and, to a lesser extent, Mexico, increased significantly in the last twenty years. Exports of goods from Canada to the United States increased a whopping 250 percent (from $117 billion to $409 billion) between 1988 and 2008. (The figure was lower in 2009 and 2010, but this was simply a reflection of the recession).

Does this mean that more Canadian firms have achieved minimum efficient scale? We cannot answer yes on the evidence of increased exports alone, but greater exports and lower long-run average costs following an expansion in the size of the market are certainly consistent with one another.

In many cases, they still do, but that is not the whole story. For new firms, changing technology is lowering the barriers to entry into some industries despite the presence of economies of scale. Financial capital is much more mobile and, therefore, more available to small firms. In addition, as technology advances, smaller and smaller computers can do what could previously only be done with a room-sized mainframe. As a result, increased efficiency comes from *reductions* in the size of the means of production. This new concept, that smaller is better, fits well with emerging evidence that market demand for many products is shifting away from standardized products toward customized products. More and more, consumers are demanding unique products that meet highly specialized needs. Thus production must become much more flexible, and the emphasis is shifting to customized products.

Next, consider the fact that networks of small computers can quickly be expanded or scaled back. Thus, firms can deploy *many* assembly lines, each one turning out a customized variant of the same basic product rather than only *one* huge assembly line that stamps out a standardized product in massive volumes.

An interesting example of the trend toward smaller-scale production is the rise in the use of bio-energy. Burning wood to produce heat and electricity is an old idea gaining new ground as the price of oil reaches new highs. This new approach to electricity generation involves using marginal agricultural land to grow what are known as "short rotation coppice" (SRC) trees that have been developed to grow very quickly. The crop can be harvested every four years, dried and then fed into relatively small wood-pellet mills. The resulting pellets can match coal in terms of heat generation when burned to produced electricity. In addition to the environmental advantage of this method—it is carbon neutral (the carbon released in the burning of the wood is exactly equal to that sequestered from the atmosphere as the trees grew)—it is likely to be cheaper than burning oil or natural gas to generate electricity. The future may well see scores of relatively small-scale pellet-mill plants scattered across the nation's agricultural regions.

This raises a fundamental question: will this new technology alter the scale of the firm that uses it? In other words, as production becomes more customized and computers become more sophisticated, will efficient production mean smaller firms? These days, it seems that huge corporations are finding it cheaper to farm out work to lower-cost specialists, which are often more flexible, rather than retain the bureaucratic organizational structure necessary to manage the entire process within a single operation. In addition, unions have a much greater presence in large manufacturing companies; this often leads to higher labour costs as a result of better wages and benefits than are found in small companies.

Computer chips like these are getting smaller and more powerful every year.

Evidence for such downsizing comes from the fact that small automotive-parts firms have been growing in the last decade, while large automobile manufacturers have been laying off workers. This leads some economists to argue that as production becomes significantly more specialized and products more customized, the growth in the numbers of efficient small firms will come at the expense of giant firms.

Not all economists agree that this is the trend. They point out that what can be done efficiently in a small firm can also be done in the corner of a General Motors plant. However, if the trend of "smaller is better" does prove valid, then a great deal will change, and this chapter on long-run average cost and the related advantages of economies of scale will have to be rewritten.

 SELF-TEST

5. Draw a graph showing short-run and long-run average costs curves that illustrates a firm producing both below economic capacity and at less than minimum efficient scale.

STUDY GUIDE

Review

CHAPTER SUMMARY

In this chapter, you focused on the long-run average costs and on the three types of "returns to scale" that are associated with them. This opened the door for a discussion of two questions. What is the right size of firm? And can a market be too small?

7.1a Firms always operate in the *short run* where at least one factor of production (input) is fixed and diminishing marginal productivity is inevitable.

7.1b Firms can plan as if they are in the *long run* where, conceptually, there are no fixed factors of production and diminishing marginal productivity does not apply.

7.2 Constant returns to scale exist when an increase in a firm's inputs result in a proportional increase in output. In these cases, a medium-sized firm can be as efficient as a big firm.

7.3 *Technical economies* of scale (resulting in increasing returns to scale) occur as a result of:
- division of labour
- management specialization
- machine specialization

Pecuniary economics of scale (in which large firms have a significant advantage) include:
- lower cost of borrowing
- bulk buying and selling
- the selling of by-products
- lower costs of advertising

7.4 *Diseconomies of scale* can occur if bureaucratic inefficiencies within large firms are significant.

7.5 Both short-run and long-run average costs can *decrease* if:
- the price of factor inputs decreases
- technological improvement occurs
- mergers reduce the average fixed costs of the new firm

7.6 A firm can be considered to be of the *right* size only if it is big enough to capture economies of scale but not so big as to suffer diseconomies. The right size is called the *minimum efficient scale*.

7.7 A market can be *too small* if it limits the size of the firm to an output level that is:
- below economic capacity in the short run
- below minimum efficient scale in the long run

NEW GLOSSARY TERMS

STUDY TIPS

1. Students who come to understand the law of diminishing returns (or diminishing marginal product) wonder what explains the often observed phenomenon of both rising output levels and falling prices for such things as VCRs, computers, and DVD players. Surely, if the law of diminishing returns applies, then higher output would be associated with higher marginal and average costs and therefore higher prices. Yet, we actually see prices for these products fall as output increases *over time*. An understanding of the long run, where diminishing MP does not apply but economies of scale often do, reconciles this apparent contradiction.

2. Many students are thrown by the word "pecuniary." It simply means *pertaining to money*.

3. Remember that, for the sake of convenience, we often refer to average total cost in the short run as "average cost," or AC, and to average total costs in the long run as "long-run average cost" or LRAC.

4. The value of graphical analysis to understanding economic concepts is especially apparent in this chapter. Do take the time to draw the graphs in the questions where you are asked to, and keep in mind the concept being illustrated. You will find yourself beginning to "think in graphs" as well as in words.

Answered Questions

These questions can also be found online on Connect.

Indicate whether the following statements are true or false:

1. **(LO 1) T or F**   The long run is the circumstance in which at least one input is variable.

2. **(LO 1) T or F**   While a firm can plan for the long run, it must always operate in the short run.

3. **(LO 2) T or F**   Constant returns to scale means a firm's output increases by the same percentage as the increase in its inputs.

4. **(LO 3) T or F**   Economies of scale means average costs increase as a firm grows in size.

5. **(LO 3) T or F**   The long-run average cost curve declines continuously as output levels increase.

6. **(LO 3) T or F**   Labour, management, and machine specialization are examples of pecuniary economies of scale.

7. **(LO 3) T or F**   Economies of scale are divided into those cost advantages that are technical and those that are pecuniary.

8. **(LO 6) T or F**   A firm's economic capacity and its most productive output level are the same.

9. **(LO 4) T or F**   Bureaucracy is the main cause of diseconomies of scale.

10. **(LO 6) T or F**   The right size of firm is determined by the minimum point on its short-run average cost curve.

Basic (Questions 11–24)

11. **(LO 1)** Which of the following is correct in reference to the long run?
    a) All inputs are variable.
    b) Only one input is variable, and all others are fixed.
    c) Only one input is fixed, and all others are variable.
    d) All inputs are fixed.

12. **(LO 3)** If economies of scale are present, then:
    a) Average variable costs are falling but average fixed costs are constant
    b) Average costs are constant
    c) Average costs are decreasing
    d) Average costs are increasing

13. **(LO 1)** Which of the following statements is correct?
    a) A firm can operate in either the short run or the long run.
    b) While a firm can plan as if it is in the long run, it can operate only in the short run.
    c) The short run is a period of time of less than six months.
    d) The short run is a period of time of less than one year.

14. **(LO 2)** What is meant by the term "economic capacity"?
    a) The output level at which the firm is physically unable to increase output
    b) The output level at which average variable cost is at a minimum
    c) The output level at which average total cost is at a minimum
    d) The output level at which marginal cost is at a minimum

15. **(LO 2)** Which of the following statements is correct if constant returns to scale are present?
    a) A doubling of inputs will lead to output more than doubling.
    b) A doubling of inputs will lead to output also doubling.
    c) A doubling of output will lead to inputs more than doubling.
    d) Output remains constant irrespective of inputs.

16. **(LO 2)** Economies of scale:
    a) Is another term for constant returns to scale
    b) Are cost advantages achieved as a result of large-scale operations
    c) Only come in pecuniary forms
    d) Are the same as decreasing returns to scale

17. **(LO 3)** The ability of a person to supervise twelve workers just as well as eight is an example of:
    a) Division of labour
    b) Labour specialization
    c) Management specialization
    d) Decreasing returns to scale

18. **(LO 3)** All of the following, except one, are examples of pecuniary economies of scale. Which is the exception?
    a) A lower interest rate paid on money borrowed
    b) The ability to sell the by-products of production
    c) The ability to use specialized inputs, such as a robotic assembly line
    d) The ability to obtain lower prices by buying in bulk

19. **(LO 3)** Which of the following illustrates the fact that a one-minute television commercial costs a large firm no more than a small firm?
    a) Increasing returns to scale
    b) Pecuniary economies of scale
    c) Technical economies of scale
    d) Management specialization

20. **(LO 4)** Which of the following is the most likely cause of diseconomies of scale?
    a) Increasing returns to scale
    b) A small scale of operations and output
    c) Low productivity
    d) Bureaucracy

21. **(LO 2, 3, 4)** Which of the following statements is correct if a firm builds a larger plant and, at any particular output, its short-run average cost increases?
    a) Diseconomies of scale must be present.
    b) Economies of scale must be present.
    c) Constant returns to scale must be present.
    d) Economies, diseconomies, and constant returns to scale are all possible.

22. **(LO 7)** What does the term "minimum efficient scale" mean?
    a) The smallest size a firm can be in order to minimize both short-run and long-run average costs
    b) The smallest size a firm can be in order to minimize short-run marginal cost
    c) The smallest size a firm can be in order to minimize short-run average cost
    d) The smallest size a firm can be in order to minimize long-run marginal cost
    e) The smallest size a firm can be in order to minimize both short-run and long-run marginal cost

23. **(LO 3)** Suppose that a firm's total cost of producing an output of 400 units a day is currently $2000. If technology and the price of inputs remain unchanged, what level of output would be produced if total cost rises to $4000 and increasing returns to scale exist?
    a) 5 units
    b) More than 400 but less than 800 units
    c) 800 units
    d) More than 800 units

24. **(LO 4)** Suppose that a firm's total cost of producing an output of 400 units a day is currently $2000. If technology and the price of inputs remain unchanged, what level of output would be produced if total cost rises to $4000 and decreasing returns to scale exist?
    a) 5 units
    b) More than 400 but less than 800 units
    c) 800 units
    d) More than 800 units

Intermediate (Questions 25–33)

25. **(LO 4)** Which of the following statements is correct if a firm's capacity output increases from 400 to 800 and its total costs rise from $60 000 to $110 000?
    a) The firm is experiencing constant returns to scale.
    b) The firm is experiencing diseconomies of scale.
    c) The firm is experiencing economies of scale.
    d) The firm's long-run average cost must have decreased, but its short-run average cost could have either decreased or increased.

26. **(LO 2)** If a firm builds a larger plant and constant returns to scale apply, which of the following statements is correct?
    a) The capacity output of the larger plant has a lower average cost.
    b) The capacity output of the larger plant has the same average cost.
    c) Economies of scale are present.
    d) LRAC will decrease as output increases.

27. **(LO 6)** Which of the following statements is correct if the appropriately sized firm is one with a large output?
   a) Constant returns to scale must begin at low levels of output.
   b) Economies of scale must prevail until high levels of output are reached.
   c) Diseconomies of scale must begin at low levels of output.
   d) Constant returns to scale must be absent.

28. **(LO 5)** Graphically, what is the effect of technological change?
   a) The long-run average cost curve will shift down, but the short-run curves will not change.
   b) Both the long-run and short-run average cost curves will shift down.
   c) The long-run average cost curve will shift up, but the short-run curves will not change.
   d) Both the long-run and short-run average cost curves will shift up.
   e) It will reduce the size of the average firm.

Refer to **Figure 7.7** to answer questions 29 and 30.

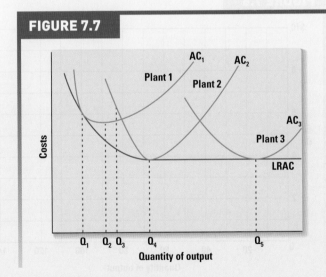

FIGURE 7.7

29. **(LO 6)** All of the following statements, except one, are correct. Which is the exception?
   a) Plant 1 has excess capacity at output level Q_1.
   b) Output level Q_2 is economic capacity for plant 1.
   c) Output level Q_3 can be produced cheaper in plant 2 than in plant 1.
   d) Plant 2 achieves minimum efficient scale.
   e) Economies of scale are experienced when output is increased from Q_1 to Q_4.

30. **(LO 6)** All of the following statements, except one, are correct. Which is the exception?
   a) AC_1, AC_2, and AC_3 are short-run average cost curves.
   b) The long-run average cost curve illustrates both economies of and constant returns to scale.
   c) Constant returns to scale exist between outputs Q_4 and Q_5.
   d) Plant 3 achieves minimum efficient scale.
   e) Both the short run and the long run are illustrated in this graph.

Refer to **Table 7.2**, which gives data for plant size 1, to answer questions 31 and 32.

TABLE 7.2		
Output	Average Cost	Total Cost
0	/	$6000
100	$80	
200	75	
300	70	
400	65	
500	70	
600	75	

31. **(LO 2)** Assume that technology and the price of inputs remain unchanged. If the firm builds a bigger plant and all of its inputs exactly double, what will be its output at economic capacity in the new plant under conditions of constant returns to scale?
   a) Exactly 800
   b) Exactly 1000
   c) More than 500 but less than 1000
   d) More than 1000

32. **(LO 1)** If the firm builds a bigger plant and all of its inputs exactly double, what will be the value of its fixed cost?
   a) $6000
   b) $12 000
   c) $32 000
   d) More information is needed to answer this question

33. **(LO 7)** What does MES refer to?
   a) The marginal efficient size of a firm
   b) The biggest-sized plant that is capable of achieving economies of scale
   c) The biggest-sized plant that is capable of achieving diseconomies of scale
   d) The smallest-sized plant that is capable of achieving diseconomies of scale
   e) The smallest-sized plant capable of achieving the lowest long-run average cost of production

Advanced (Questions 34–35)

34. **(LO 7)** Adam Smith observed that the division of labour is limited by the size of the market. Which one of the following statements is not consistent with this observation?
   a) A limited-sized market can prevent firms from achieving economic capacity.
   b) A limited-sized market can prevent firms from achieving their minimum efficient scale.
   c) A limited-sized market can prevent firms from achieving minimum short-run average cost.
   d) A limited-sized market can prevent firms from achieving minimum long-run average cost.
   e) A limited-sized market can prevent firms from achieving excess capacity.

35. **(LO 7)** All of the following, except one, are possible explanations for why large-scale operations may not be as important for firms in many industries in the future.
   a) Economies of scale are becoming less important in some industries because of new technology.
   b) Financial capital is now more readily available to small firms than it used to be.
   c) Consumer demand is shifting toward more customized products.
   d) Very large, established firms are often less flexible.
   e) Small firms can advertise their products on TV for a per-unit cost that is just as inexpensive as large firms.

Parallel Problems

ANSWERED PROBLEMS

36A. **(LO 3, 4, 5)** **Key Problem** Table 7.3 contains short-run cost data for five different plant sizes for the R2D2 Robotics Company.

TABLE 7.3

Output	Plant 1	Plant 2	Plant 3	Plant 4	Plant 5
10	$ 8.00	$10.50	/	/	/
20	7.00	9.00	/	/	/
30	6.00	7.50	$10.00	/	/
40	6.50	6.00	8.00	/	/
50	7.50	5.00	6.50	$10.30	/
60	9.00	5.80	4.00	8.50	/
70	10.50	7.00	4.90	7.00	/
80	/	8.20	6.00	5.10	$6.50
90	/	10.00	7.80	4.00	6.00
100	/	/	8.50	4.30	5.40
110	/	/	/	5.60	5.00
120	/	/	/	7.70	5.30
130	/	/	/	10.00	6.00
140	/	/	/	/	7.10

a) On the grid in **Figure 7.8**, graph the short-run average cost curves for the five plants.

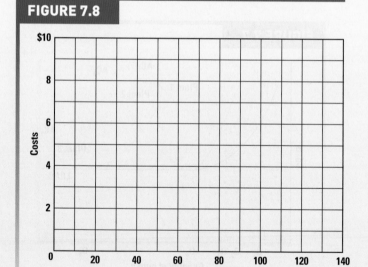

FIGURE 7.8

b) Fill in the blanks, indicating the best size of plant when output is:

30	_____	80	_____
40	_____	90	_____
50	_____	100	_____
60	_____	110	_____
70	_____	120	_____

c) Roughly sketch the long-run average cost curve in **Figure 7.8**.

d) What plant size would the firm need in order to achieve minimum efficient scale (MES)?
Answer: _____

e) What is the output level that achieves MES?
Answer: _____

f) If R2D2 is producing an output of 80 in plant 4, does excess capacity exist?
Answer: _____

g) What would be the economic capacity for plant 5?
Answer: _____

h) Given the LRAC curve in **Figure 7.8**, between what output levels are economies of scale present?
Answer: _____

i) Given the LRAC curve in **Figure 7.8**, between what output levels are constant returns to scale present?
Answer: _____

j) Given the LRAC curve in **Figure 7.8**, between what output levels do diseconomies of scale exist?
Answer: _____

k) If R2D2's sales are limited to 50, for which plant sizes we can say that the market is too small?
Answer: _____

Basic (Problems 37A–43A)

37A. **(LO 3, 4, 5)** Suppose that Jump A Lot Inc. can produce 16 trampolines a day for a total cost of $1920. If technology and input prices remain the same and total cost increases to $3840, what must be the new quantity of output per day under conditions of:
a) constant returns to scale? _____
b) economies of scale? _____
c) diseconomies of scale? _____

38A. **(LO 2, 3, 4, 5, 6)** **Table 7.4** contains average cost data for four different sized plants—1, 2, 3, and 4—which are the only four sizes possible.
a) At what output is economic capacity for each of the four plants?
Plant 1: _____ Plant 2: _____
Plant 3: _____ Plant 4: _____

TABLE 7.4

Output	Plant 1	Plant 2	Plant 3	Plant 4
40	$60	$70	$90	$110
50	55	60	80	95
60	60	50	70	80
70	65	60	60	65
80	70	70	50	55
90	80	80	60	45
100	90	90	70	55

b) In what plant and at what output is minimum long-run average cost achieved?
Plant: _____ ; output: _____

c) What is the right size of plant to produce an output of 60? Plant # _____

d) What is the right size of plant to produce an output of 80? Plant # _____

39A. **(LO 2, 4, 6)** **Figure 7.9** illustrates a series of short-run average cost curves, numbered AC_1 through AC_5, which correspond to five different plant sizes, which are the only sizes possible.

FIGURE 7.9

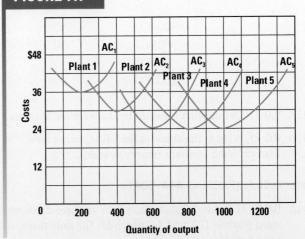

a) What is true about output levels 200, 400, 600, 800, and 1000? Answer: _____

b) What is the right size of a plant to produce an output of 500? Answer: _____

c) Between what output levels do economies of scale prevail? Answer: _____

40A. **(LO 2, 3, 4)** Assuming that technology and the prices of all inputs remain fixed, decide, in each of the four cases (A–D) in **Table 7.5**, whether economies of, diseconomies of, or constant returns to scale exist.
Case A: _____ Case B: _____
Case C: _____ Case D: _____

TABLE 7.5

	Inputs 1	Inputs 2	Output 1	Output 2
A	7	14	21	42
B	26	52	230	420
C	38	57	300	500
D	360	432	2200	2750

41A. **(LO 2, 3, 4)** Assuming that technology and the prices of all inputs remain fixed, decide, in each of the four cases in **Table 7.6**, whether economies of, diseconomies of, or constant returns to scale exist.

Case A: _____ Case B: _____

Case C: _____ Case D: _____

TABLE 7.6

Case	Total Cost	Output
A	$ 12 500	50
	25 000	100
B	6 000	20
	12 000	42
C	450 000	225
	980 000	450
D	80 000	40
	150 000	80

42A. **(LO 1)** Define what is meant by the term *the long run*.

43A. **(LO 2)** What is the shape of the LRAC curve for a firm enjoying constant returns to scale?

Intermediate (Problems 44A–50A)

44A. **(LO 6, 7)** **Table 7.7** shows cost data for three different-sized plants—1, 2, and 3—which are the only three sizes possible.

a) In what plant size is MES achieved?

Answer: _____

b) What is economic capacity for plant 3?

Answer: _____

c) What is the right-sized plant to produce an output of 400?

Answer: _____

TABLE 7.7

Output	Plant 1	Plant 2	Plant 3
100	$12	$15	$19
200	11	12	16
300	10	8	12
400	11	11	9
500	12	15	10

45A. **(LO 2, 3, 5)** **Figure 7.10** illustrates a series of short-run average cost curves, numbered AC_1 through AC_4, which correspond to the only four different automobile plant sizes possible.

FIGURE 7.10

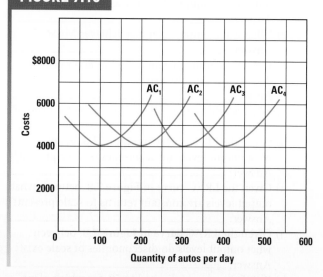

a) What can you say about returns to scale?

Answer: _____

b) Are economies of scale present?

Answer: _____

c) If it takes 40 workers and 100 units of capital to produce 200 automobiles a day, how much labour and capital is involved in producing 600 automobiles a day?

Answer: _____

46A. **(LO 7)** On the graph in **Figure 7.11**, sketch both short- and long-run average cost curves that illustrate a firm producing both below economic capacity and at less than minimum efficient scale. Label the output Q_1.

FIGURE 7.11

Costs

Quantity of output

47A. **(LO 2, 3, 4)** Table 7.8 shows the long-run total costs for three different firms.

Are these three firms experiencing economies, diseconomies, or constant returns to scale?

Jad: _____

Hafiz: _____

Ynari: _____

48A. **(LO 6)** In what sense might a firm be too small?

49A. **(LO 7)** Define the term *minimum efficient scale*.

50A. **(LO 3)** The inputs and outputs for Carbon Credits Inc. are as shown in **Table 7.9**.
   a) If capital costs $50 per unit and labour costs $10 per unit, fill in the blanks in the table.
   b) With what output does increasing returns come to an end? Answer: _____

51A. **(LO 3)** Discuss the distinction between increasing returns to scale and economies of scale.

52A. **(LO 7)** Is the idea of a right-sized firm a short-run or long-run concept?

TABLE 7.8

Jad		Hafiz		Ynari	
Output	Total Cost	Output	Total Cost	Output	Total Cost
10	$ 300	100	$ 60 000	20	$ 4 000
20	600	200	110 000	40	4 800
30	900	300	155 000	60	5 400
40	1200	400	195 000	80	6 800
50	1500	500	200 000	100	8 200
60	1800	600	203 000	120	9 600
70	2100	700	205 000	140	11 200
80	2400	800	245 000	160	12 800
90	2700	900	285 000	180	15 000
100	3000	1000	325 000	200	17 500

TABLE 7.9

Output	Inputs		Total Cost	LRAC ($)
	Capital	Labour		
100	1	5	_____	_____
200	2	8	_____	_____
300	3	11	_____	_____
400	4	12	_____	_____
500	5	22	_____	_____
600	6	37	_____	_____

PERFECT COMPETITION

WHAT'S AHEAD...

In this chapter, we take our first look at market structures using what economists call the perfectly competitive model. After describing some examples of perfect competition, we look at the behaviour of the individual firm, how it decides on its production level, and how profits are affected. We derive rules for determining the output level at which the producer breaks even, the level at which it will make the most profit, and the level at which it might be advised to shut down operations. The rest of the chapter shows how the market and the individual producer react to changes in demand, technology, and input costs.

A Question of Relevance...

Market systems are dynamic and always changing. New industries are born, and established industries die on a fairly regular basis. Are new firms guaranteed a profit? Would you be a fool to look for a job in a declining industry, or would you be an even bigger fool to join the multitudes looking for jobs in the growing industries? Is it possible for a firm caught in the drag of a dying industry to redefine itself and become successful doing something else? Is there some kind of common denominator that we can use to study "the market"? In this chapter, we will find out.

We looked at the firm's revenue side in the demand-focused Chapter 4, and the firm's cost of production (the supply side) in Chapters 6 and 7. We are now ready to put the demand side and the supply side together and focus on two of the firm's most important output decisions. What output will a firm choose to produce? What price will prevail? To answer these questions, we need to know a lot about the firm's costs of production and something about the product itself, as well as about other firms in the industry, and, of course, about the customers who buy the product. In other words, we need to know more about the market in which the product is sold.

Let us clarify some terminology before we go any further: *industry* is the collective name for all the firms producing a similar product. The different firms in the industry may or may not know each other well, they may or may not be members of some sort of common association, and they may or may not agree on various types of collective action. What they have in common is that they produce a similar product, usually using the same technology. A *market*, you will remember from Chapter 2, refers to the interactions of both producers and consumers. In other words:

> An industry is the name for a group of producers; a market refers to the interaction of both producers and consumers.

8.1 CHARACTERISTICS OF DIFFERENT MARKETS

Economists see two main ways in which markets differ. The first is the types of products sold: do all the producers sell an identical product, or are there differences between one firm's product and those of other firms? The second difference reflects the numbers of buyers and sellers: is the market populated by many firms and consumers, or is it dominated by a few big players? The number of competing firms and what they produce indicates just how much power any one firm might have in the marketplace and how easy or difficult it is for a new firm to enter a market.

L01 Distinguish among a firm, an industry, and a market.

For instance, if there are lots of firms and their products are almost identical, then no single firm will have much control over the price, and it will be easy for new firms to join the industry. Economists call this type of market *perfect competition*, something we will study in this chapter. But in other types of markets, there may be very few firms, and each firm may produce an easily identified product that's different from its competitors. **Table 8.1** provides a sort of road map of the different types of markets that we will be studying in this and later chapters. **Table 8.1** shows each of the four markets that we will be studying in this and the next three chapters, including the number of firms in the market and the type of product that is produced.

In essence, then, there are four major types of markets: *perfect competition*, such as commodity markets where many producers all produce an identical product; *monopolistic competition*, where there are also lots of producers but each producer sells a slightly different product—convenience stores for example; *oligopoly* (either *differentiated* or *undifferentiated*), where a few large producers dominate the market, as in the oil refining business; and finally, *monopoly*, where there is a single producer in the market, as in the public utility industries of most provinces. This is further summarized in **Table 8.2**.

TABLE 8.1	**Characteristics of the Four Markets**		
Number of Firms ⟶	**Many**	**A Few**	**One**
Type of Product ⬇			
Identical	Perfect Competition	Undifferentiated Oligopoly	Monopoly
Differentiated	Monopolistic Competition	Differentiated Oligopoly	

TABLE 8.2 The Different Types of Markets

Market	Number of Sellers	Type of Product	Ease of Entry to Market	Seller's Control over Price	Examples
Perfect competition	Numerous	Identical	Easy	None	Commodities, such as wheat
Monopolistic competition	Many	Differentiated	Easy	Low	Convenience stores, restaurants
Oligopoly: undifferentiated	Few	Identical	Difficult	Moderate	Oil refining, lumber
Oligopoly: differentiated	Few	Differentiated	Difficult	Substantial	Automobiles, cigarettes
Monopoly	One	Unique	Very difficult	Substantial	Public utilities, cable companies

 SELF-TEST

1. In what type of market will you find the following types of firms/products?

   a) Hairdressing salons

   b) Industrial chemicals in Canada

   c) Commercial breweries in Canada

   d) World market for coffee

   e) Rogers Cable in Ontario

8.2 PERFECT COMPETITION AND THE MARKET SYSTEM

Features of Perfect Competition

 LO2 Explain what is meant by perfect competition and the market system.

perfect competition:
a market in which all buyers and sellers are price takers.

Markets are said to be in **perfect competition** when no single consumer or producer has any greater power or influence in the market than does any other consumer or producer. In other words, in such a market, no single producer or consumer can affect the price or the quantity produced. A perfectly competitive market, in other words, provides a level playing field for its participants.

This can only happen when four conditions are fulfilled. First, there must be a *large number of buyers and sellers*, and all must be small in relation to the whole market. Since each producer is relatively small, a decision by any particular producer to double its output (or to produce nothing at all) will not have much impact on the market. Similarly, a decision by any particular consumer to increase or decrease her purchases will have no perceptible effect on total sales. Also, a competitive market does not exist if there is any collusion between producers or between consumers, since it is assumed that each person operates separately and independently. Nor is a market considered perfectly competitive if producers or consumers form co-operatives or associations that make decisions on behalf of their members. A competitive market, therefore, is one in which the buyers and sellers all act separately and independently and in which each individual producer and consumer has so little market power that no single one of them can affect the quantity bought and sold. As a result, they have no influence on the price of the product. For each of them, the market price is a given. This last point is particularly relevant to perfectly competitive firms, which have no choice but to accept the going market price; that is, they are price takers.

The second feature of a perfectly competitive market is that it is a market in which *there are no preferences shown*. This means that the consumer neither knows nor cares where the product comes from, since the producers all make identical, or undifferentiated, products. Nor are there any other reasons why a particular producer would be preferred. Similarly, producers show no preference toward any particular consumer. For them, all consumers are the same.

The third defining feature of a competitive market is that *there should be easy entry into and exit from the market*, for both producers and consumers. This is sometimes rephrased to say that there are no significant barriers to entry. For the prospective producer, this implies that it should be reasonably easy to set up in business: the producer does not require a great deal of financial capital or have to pay an unreasonable membership, licence, or entry fee, or have to join any club or organization in order to trade. In this manner, existing firms in an industry have no advantage over newcomers. Easy entry and exit also mean that consumers are not required to belong to a particular organization or to possess particular attributes in order to buy a certain product.

The fourth and final feature of perfectly competitive markets is that *producers have all the market information necessary to make rational production and purchasing decisions*. This condition ensures that no particular participant in the market has any advantage (or competitive edge) over the other participants. It means, for instance, that we do not have a situation in which only a select few customers are aware of a particular sale going on in town or in which a firm introduces a superior technology that is unknown to other firms. In other words, if the knowledge is not equally shared, then some people will have an advantage over others; and unless there is equality in the marketplace, it is not perfectly competitive. In summary, the four conditions for a perfectly competitive market are as follows:

- many small buyers and sellers all of whom are price takers
- no preferences shown by consumers
- easy entry and exit by both buyers and sellers
- the same market information available to all

If these four conditions exist, the marketplace is said to be perfectly competitive. The result will be that the anonymous forces of demand and supply determine both the price of the product and the quantity traded. Conversely, if these conditions do not exist, it will usually mean that one participant is stronger than the others and can, therefore, have some degree of influence over the price and quantity. If markets are perfectly competitive, any change in the demand or supply conditions should affect the price; and since presumably demand and supply are almost always changing, we should expect to see the price change quite frequently. This means, therefore, that whenever the price of a product changes frequently, it is very likely that this market is competitive. Conversely, if the price of a particular product seldom changes, this is *prima facie* evidence that that market is not competitive. Let us try then to find some examples of competitive markets in our economy.

Examples of Perfectly Competitive Markets

In searching for examples of perfectly competitive markets, we should emphasize that the first condition (many small buyers and sellers) does not require every producer to be small in its scale of operations, only *small in relation to the total market*. It is just as possible, then, to have some reasonably big competitive firms as it is to have one single, small monopolist. For example, a 1000 hectare wheat farm in Manitoba could be considered large—say, $400,000 in annual sales—but is not even close to being a monopolist, given the enormous size of the world's wheat market which has annual sales in billions of dollars. On the other hand, a small gas station with only $40,000 in sales could be a monopolist in a remote northern town. The second condition, that no preference be shown by consumers, immediately rules out such examples as travel agents, hairdressers, gas stations, and so on, since customers do show preferences, even though the difference between suppliers may seem small. For instance, economists recognize that, from a chemist's point of view, one brand of gasoline may well be identical to some other brand, but if consumers show a preference for one over the other, then there is a difference between the two, even if it is only the name of the gasoline.

Another important point is that it is not the number of products that makes the market competitive but the number of individual producers. For example, although there are more than a hundred different breakfast cereals on the market, most are produced by just two or three giant firms, which means the market is not perfectly competitive.

Given these cautions, are there good examples of perfectly competitive markets these days? Well, the closest we will come is a situation in which the market is very big and the product is generic—for example, the world markets for such commodities as cotton, rubber, wheat, and so on. These are all examples of homogeneous products; wheat is wheat wherever it is produced. The price of these products often changes hourly in response to changing conditions around the world, and the current prices are available every day on the Internet.

A Canadian producer of a particular commodity, however big it may be in Canada, is unlikely to have much impact on the world supply. In most respects, then, world markets for commodities are reasonably competitive. But what about inside Canada—are there any perfectly competitive markets domestically? The stock market is often cited as an example of a perfect market, in which the prices of products (stocks and bonds) often change minute by minute. However, on closer inspection, it falls short of being perfectly competitive because the action of a single large buyer or seller can and does affect the price of shares. This offends our criterion that no single buyer or seller can affect the market price. In addition, you need to use the services of an agent or broker and pay a commission to buy a particular share, which means that access to the market is not perfectly free.

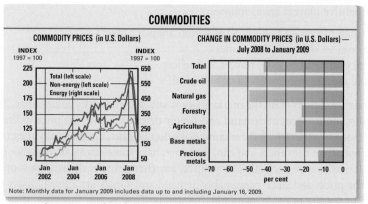

Source: Canada's Economic Action Plan, Budget 2009, Chapter 2: Recent Economic Developments and Prospects, Chart 2.20, Commodities. Department of Finance Canada Commodity Price Index. Reproduced with the permission of the Minister of Public Works and Government Services, 2011.

At first glance, markets for agricultural products in many countries seem to provide a good example of fairly competitive markets. In Canada, for instance, there are thousands of farmers of wheat and other grain crops, and though some prairie farms are very big, they are insignificant in relation to the total market. In addition, the products are identical and consumers do not know, or for that matter care, which particular farmer grew the wheat or the oats or the potatoes that they purchase. So, on the surface it appears that agricultural markets are perfectly competitive. However, as we saw in Chapter 3, the Canadian government has a great deal of involvement in agricultural markets through various marketing boards that regulate price and output levels.

In truth, there are few examples of perfectly competitive markets in the modern world, compared with the situation in the eighteenth century, when Adam Smith first wrote about market characteristics. In Smith's day, all producers were small, and the output of most producers was very similar to that of the competition. This is no longer true. Given this fact, it is reasonable to ask why economists continue to talk about and analyze a market structure that hardly exists. The answer is that economists use the construction of the perfectly competitive market structure as an "ideal structure." Then, once we have figured out how perfectly competitive markets work, we have a benchmark with which to judge and compare "real world" markets.

In this sense, the economist is no different from the physicist who explains what will happen in ideal situations and then revises his conclusions for other circumstances. Galileo, for example, inves-

ADDED DIMENSION   Competition and the Internet

A number of commentators have suggested that the Internet will make the economic system more competitive. For instance, in its March 20, 2000, edition, *The Economist* said that

> "...the Internet cuts costs, increases competition, and improves the functioning of the price mechanism. It thus moves the economy closer to the textbook model of perfect competition."

Economists have identified a number of reasons for this. First, the Internet increases the amount of information about products and prices that is available to buyers. Secondly, it reduces the transactions cost for consumers to obtain this information because it cuts out the traditional middlemen, who hamper economic efficiency. Thirdly, it increases the transparency of markets (everything is open to public scrutiny) and so intensifies the amount of competition. Finally, it reduces the technical barriers to entry for new firms, since setting up a Web site and accessing the market is much easier and cheaper than using traditional methods.

However, there are many who believe that the competitive benefits of the Internet are overrated. They suggest that while the amount of information is, indeed, vast, consumers' resources to handle it are limited. Because of this, consumers respond by restricting their searches to the big "brand name" sites, such as Amazon and eBay, which account for immeasurably more hits than their closest rivals. Furthermore, not all sellers are treated equally, and when doing a search for products, most customers will visit the sites that come at the top of the list or the site with the most links to other sites. Getting to that enviable position usually involves a significant marketing expenditure, which smaller firms cannot afford. Finally, they point out that if e-commerce is actually making markets more competitive, the result should be a uniformity of prices for the same product, but empirical studies suggest that the opposite is happening and that the amount of price dispersion may well have increased in recent years.

tigated the behaviour of falling bodies and concluded that they all fall at identical rates of acceleration. It is surprising that many people have learned this snippet of theory, forgetting that it is true only in the idealized situation of a vacuum. They will argue vigorously that a kilo bag of feathers and a kilo bag of lead, if thrown from a high building will both hit the ground at the same time. (They do not, as a matter of fact! A kilo bag of feathers is far bigger than a kilo of lead and encounters more air resistance.) In short, the physicists' vacuum is like the economists' "perfectly competitive" market.

Finally, it should be said that the economists' definition of perfect competition differs greatly from the everyday understanding of the term *competition*. Most people, asked to give examples of "vigorous" competition, would cite Pepsi-Cola and Coca-Cola or Reebok and Nike or the competition in the automobile industry. To economists, however, this is about as uncompetitive as you can get, since each of these producers is very powerful and exerts a great deal of influence in its own markets. In other words, though the rivalry between Pepsi and Coke might be intense, the competition is weak. In economics, true competition exists between a wheat farmer in Alberta and another farmer she has never met in Manitoba, hundreds of kilometres away.

Perfect Competition and the Market System

A perfectly competitive market system is part of what economists refer to as the *market economy* and what others refer to as *free enterprise*. Much has been written on the benefits and defects of the market system, and we will look at many of these ideas in the next chapter. But, first, we need to understand that competition is only one aspect of the *market system*. Besides competition, the market economy also implies that specialization and trade are practised, that resources are privately owned, and that a sound legal and social foundation is in place. Let us take a brief look at each of these four aspects.

Specialization and trade within a market economy involves the exchange of products and services and is one of the cornerstones of wealth creation. As we mentioned in Chapter 1, voluntary trade between people is a win–win situation, in that each participant receives something preferable to what they already have—otherwise they would not trade. But in order to trade, an individual must have a surplus of something and, in order to have that surplus, must have produced more than that individual wishes to consume. In other words, the economy and its people must practise specialization. And specialization can increase productivity enormously and help make a country wealthy.

Put another way, if a self-sufficient country or individual does not trade, then an efficient market system is not necessary. But there are few, if any, historical examples of countries that become wealthy through self-sufficiency. Specialization is the key to high levels of productivity, and specialization requires trade. Therefore, the bigger the market, the more specialization and trading that goes on, and the wealthier a nation will become.

However, some people believe that trade, rather than being a win–win situation, produces winners and losers. But since people are not forced to trade, or to buy or sell anything, if they voluntarily decide to make a transaction they must be gaining—otherwise, why do it? But given that, it is certainly true that one person in the transaction might gain more than the other does. For instance, imagine that, while on vacation, you decide to buy an alpaca rug in the local bazaar. The only trader selling the item wants $500, which you decide is a little steep. After an hour of bargaining, you talk him down to $300 and successfully make the purchase. On leaving the bazaar, you glance back to see the trader laughing uproariously with his friends. You have been burned! You definitely think the rug is worth $300, otherwise, you would not have bought it. On the other hand, you definitely feel that you could have gotten it a lot cheaper. And the reason you did not was that there was a lack of competition, with only one trader in the bazaar. Competition involves not only bargaining between buyer and seller but also between seller and seller. The absence of competition will certainly reduce the amount of trading that takes place and will also give more power to the sellers than to the buyers. We will look at other aspects of "imperfect" competition in Chapters 10 and 11.

The third aspect of a market economy is the institution of private property. The desire for increased wealth provides a big incentive for people to work hard and be innovative, and the risk of losing what they already have is usually a sufficient deterrent to laziness and incompetence. Put another way, without private property, government itself must provide rewards and penalties in order to promote economic efficiency. But leaving this up to the whim of government officials opens up the system to all sorts of abuse and corruption.

The final requirement of a successful market system is what Adam Smith called "a legal and social foundation," that is, rules of good conduct must be present so that people have trust in the system. The market system has often been compared with sports, where individuals (and producers) need a certain amount of hard work, skill, and good luck in order to come out on top and beat the competition. And competition requires that contestants are all treated equally—that there is a level playing field.

The basic requirement for all contests is that there are rules, and that they are applied consistently and impartially by officials. Without rules and without officials, there is no sport. A true superstar in any sport (or industry), the one who earns the big salary and endorsements, is the one who does things differently from anyone that has ever played that sport before. But this originality cannot extend to breaking the rules of the game. A soccer player who, in the name of innovation, decides that instead of kicking the ball he will pick it up and throw it into the goal would not be mobbed for his originality but would get red-carded instead! Soccer without rules would be a totally pointless endeavour. Similarly, free enterprise without regulation would simply descend into anarchy and lawlessness.

Pushing the analogy one step further, the best sports tend to be those that have a small number of simple, easy to understand rules. And within the sport, games are most enjoyable when there are few stoppages for infringements, thus allowing the players to exercise their skills and imaginations to the fullest. The same is true for the economy. Government's role is to lay out simple, basic regulations within which firms must operate—and governments must be ready to prosecute firms that infringe the rules.

In short, for the market system to work effectively, there must be:

- extensive specialization and trade
- perfect competition
- private ownership of productive resources
- a legal and social foundation

ADDED DIMENSION Russia and Free Enterprise: The Rush to Transform

The history of Russia since the breakup of the Soviet Union in 1991 provides us with a real-life lesson of what can go wrong when all four conditions for the market system are not in place. Commentators, such as Economics Nobel Prize winner Joseph Stiglitz and others, have suggested that Boris Yeltsin and the new Russian government were in too much of a hurry to convert the economy into a free enterprise market system. After 70 years of communism, public ownership, and state planning, the results were calamitous.

In an article in the *Guardian* (a British newspaper), Stiglitz noted that between 1991 and 1998, the Russian output fell by almost a half, while poverty had increased from 2 percent of the population to over 40 percent. Although things improved after 1998, by 2003 GDP remained almost 30 percent below what it had been in 1990. In addition to criticizing the role of the World Bank (which, incidentally, fired him for airing his objections to its attitude toward Russia's transition to capitalism), Stiglitz clearly

understood that privatization will not, by itself, lead to a market system and all its attendant benefits. As he makes clear in his book, *Globalization and Its Discontents*, so eager was the Russian leadership to introduce capitalism that it gave scant attention to ensuring that a proper "legal and social foundation" was in place. He emphasized the "importance of the institutional infra-structures that make a financial system work" and "fostering competition, rather than just privatizing state-owned industries."

Because these things were ignored, the transition failed to produce prosperity for all. Instead, it created corruption and fraud, and fostered increases in crime and the size of the under-ground economy. It also created a class of instant super-rich, with Moscow boasting more billionaires (33 of them) than any other city in the world. The Putin years of 1999–2008 were kinder to the economy's overall size and stability. By 2007, Russia's GDP equalled that of 1990 and its growth rate remained robust through 2010.

✓ **SELF-TEST**

2. In what way(s) is the stock market a good example of perfect competition? In what way(s) is it a bad example?

8.3 THE COMPETITIVE INDUSTRY AND FIRM

As we have seen, in perfectly competitive markets, individual producers (and consumers) have no control over the price at which the product is bought and sold. The price is determined by the collective action of thousands, if not millions, of separate participants in the market. The forces of demand and supply determine the price, and once the price is established, it becomes a "take it or leave it" proposition for each individual. Using grommet manufacturing as an example, assuming no intervention from the government, this is illustrated in **Figure 8.1**.

In **Figure 8.1A**, given the market demand and supply curves for grommets, the equilibrium price is $20 per unit. This is the market price and is the only price at which grommets will be bought and sold. From the individual manufacturer's point of view, shown in **Figure 8.1B**, the price will remain at $20, irrespective of how much or how little this manufacturer decides to produce. In a sense, as far as the manufacturer (we will call her Wallis) is concerned, this price line represents the (perfectly elastic) demand curve, D*, for her grommets. She cannot sell the grommets for a higher price because nobody will buy them if they can purchase grommets elsewhere for $20; nor would she want to sell them at a lower price because she can sell as much as she wants at $20 anyway. Wallis is very much at the mercy of the market, and should the demand for grommets increase, she will benefit from a higher price. On the other hand, if more manufacturers are attracted to the grommet industry, the supply of grommets will increase, and the individual manu-facturer will lose out because of the lower price. Since the individual manufacturer cannot affect the price, the only decision is to figure out what quantity will provide the greatest profit. Before we do this, however, we need to look a bit deeper at the possible sales revenue for the manufacturer.

 L03 Use two approaches to explain how a firm might maximize its profits.

FIGURE 8.1 | The Competitive Industry and Firm

The market demand, D_1, shown in Figure A, is the total demand from the many buyers of grommets, and the supply of grommets, S_1, comes from thousands of individual manufacturers. The individual manufacturer depicted in Figure B produces a tiny part of the supply, S_1. The market price of $20 applies to all buyers and sellers, including this particular manufacturer, who can then sell as much or as little as she wishes at this price.

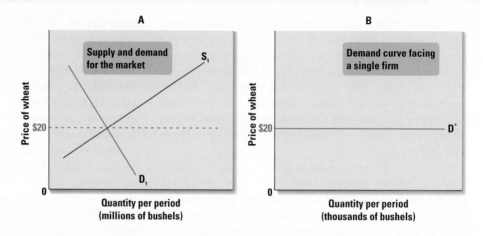

A — Supply and demand for the market. Price of wheat vs. Quantity per period (millions of bushels). S_1, D_1, price $20.

B — Demand curve facing a single firm. Price of wheat vs. Quantity per period (thousands of bushels). D^* at $20.

Total, Average, and Marginal Revenues

Suppose that the market price for grommets is $20 per unit and Wallis is trying to decide how much to produce. **Table 8.3** shows what sales revenues she will receive for different quantities sold.

The total (sales) revenue Wallis receives depends on the quantity she sells and the price at which she sells it, that is:

$$\text{Total Revenue (TR)} = \text{Output (Q)} \times \text{Price (P)} \qquad [8.1]$$

average revenue: the amount of revenue received per unit sold.

The **average revenue** she receives per unit is simply the total revenue divided by the quantity sold:

$$\text{Average Revenue (AR)} = \frac{\text{Total Revenue (TR)}}{\text{Output (Q)}} \text{ or } \frac{Q \times P}{Q} = P \qquad [8.2]$$

TABLE 8.3 | Deriving Average and Marginal Revenue

Output	Price	Total Revenue (TR)	Average Revenue (AR)	Marginal Revenue (MR)
0	$20	$ 0	$ /	$ /
1	20	20	20	20
2	20	40	20	20
3	20	60	20	20
4	20	80	20	20
5	20	100	20	20
6	20	120	20	20
7	20	140	20	20
8	20	160	20	20
9	20	180	20	20
10	20	200	20	20

Finally, the **marginal revenue** is the additional total revenue derived from the sale of an additional unit:

marginal revenue: the extra revenue derived from the sale of one more unit.

$$\text{Marginal Revenue} = \frac{\Delta \text{Total Revenue (TR)}}{\Delta \text{Output (Q)}} \text{ or } \frac{\Delta Q \times P}{\Delta Q} = P \qquad \text{[8.3]}$$

The concept of the marginal is of great importance in economics so we need to clearly understand what is meant by marginal revenue. This refers to the amount that total revenue changes as a result of selling an additional unit of the product. In the case of a perfectly competitive firm, how much it receives from selling another unit is simply the price of the product but, as we shall see in later chapters, this is not true for firms in other types of markets.

In **Table 8.3**, you can see that the price, average revenue, and marginal revenue all equal $20. The equality of these three measures of revenue holds for all competitive firms. Stated in the form of an equation, **Table 8.3** says that, given a perfectly elastic demand curve:

$$\text{Price} = \text{Average Revenue} = \text{Marginal Revenue}$$

This simply says that the average amount Wallis receives for selling a unit of grommets is the price she sells it for, and this remains a constant $20. Similarly, the marginal revenue (the amount she receives for selling an additional unit) is also a constant $20, that is, the same as the price. Although this might all seem unnecessarily complicated, the concept of the marginal lies at the heart of economic analysis. In addition, as we shall also see in later chapters, price and marginal revenue are not the same in other market situations.

Let us look at these variables graphically in **Figure 8.2**. The total revenue curve is a straight, upward-sloping curve; its steepness depends on the marginal revenue (or price) of the product. The greater the price, the steeper will be the slope of the total revenue curve. Since average and marginal revenues are equal, they are represented by a single curve, as we already saw in **Figure 8.1B**. This curve is horizontal to the output axis.

Price, Profit, and Output under Perfect Competition

We have seen that the price at which the manufacturer can sell her grommets is a given; she has no control over it. She has only one decision to make: what output level will produce the maximum profit? (Economists generally assume that profit maximization is the prime goal of the firm. Whether this is a legitimate assumption, and what other goals might be considered, is a discussion we will leave until Chapter 11.)

Profit maximization depends on both the revenue and the costs of production. **Table 8.4** repeats the revenue information from **Table 8.3** and adds to it the costs of production in Wallis's workshop.

Total profit is the difference between total revenue and total costs:

$$T\pi = TR - TC \qquad \text{[8.4]}$$

The amount of profit—we are talking about economic profit—varies with the output level. When Wallis produces no grommets, she still has to contend with fixed costs of $30 and so would make a loss of $30 at zero output. If she produces an output of one unit of grommets, she would still make a loss (of $28), though it is less than when she produces nothing at all. If she produces three units, she will make zero profit, since her total costs and revenue are equal. This level of output is referred to by economists as the **break-even output**. Remember, though, that economists regard a normal profit as being part of costs so that although Wallis is making zero economic profit when she produces three units, she is still making normal profit and would, therefore, remain a producer rather than go out of business. If she were to produce an output of more than three units, she would be making not only normal profit but also the economic profit shown in the table. She would make maximum economic profit of $30 at an output of six units. As Wallis tries to increase production above an output of six units, her total costs start to rise faster than the revenue,

break-even output: the level of output at which the sales revenue of the firm just covers fixed and variable costs, including normal profit.

FIGURE 8.2   Revenue Curves

The total revenue curve is upward sloping, which means that the more grommets sold, the greater is the total revenue. It also has a constant slope (it is a straight line) because each additional unit sold increases the total revenue by the same amount, in this example, by $20.

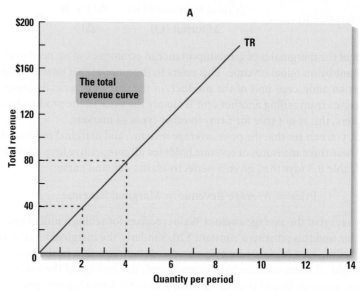

The average revenue, the marginal revenue, and the price are all equal to $20, and all remain constant, regardless of the quantity sold. This horizontal line is also the demand curve faced by the individual firm.

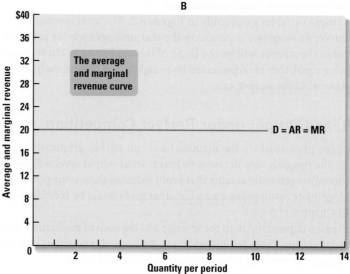

and so the total profits start to decline. At an output of eight she would again be breaking even, and at outputs above eight she would start to encounter losses.

A firm will maximize profit, therefore, when (Total Revenue − Total Cost) is greatest. This idea is illustrated in **Figure 8.3**.

Because of fixed costs, total costs are always higher than revenues at low output levels. Until break-even is reached at an output of three bushels, the total cost curve is above the total revenue curve, and Wallis would be making a loss; this is shown in the total profit curve at the bottom of the graph. Break-even occurs where the two curves intersect, at outputs of three and eight units, and where the total profit curve crosses the horizontal axis. At these two output levels, total profit is zero. At outputs above eight units, Wallis would again be making a loss, but any output between three and eight would produce a profit. Graphically, the distance between the two curves shows the amount of profit or loss, and the greatest profit is realized when the gap between the two

TABLE 8.4	Total Revenue, Cost, and Profit for a Perfectly Competitive Producer			
Output (Q)	Price (AR = MR)	Total Revenue (TR)	Total Cost (TC)	Total Profit (Tπ)
0	$20	$ 0	$ 30	$ −30
1	20	20	48	−28
2	20	40	58	−18
3	20	60	60	0
4	20	80	63	17
5	20	100	70	30
6	20	120	90	30
7	20	140	120	20
8	20	160	160	0
9	20	180	220	−40
10	20	200	300	−100

curves is greatest, and this occurs at an output of six units. (It also occurs at an output of five units but for reasons we will soon explain, six units is the "real" maximum profit point.) This is shown explicitly in the total profit curve.

Now, let us see what happens if the price of grommets increases. In that case, Wallis will enjoy a higher total revenue at every price. This means that at every output level total profit will be higher (or total losses lower). In addition, as **Table 8.5** shows, the range of outputs where she can make a profit is greater.

If the price increases to $30, it is possible for her to make a profit at any output between two and nine, and the amount of profit is higher at every output level than when the price was $20. Her profit-maximizing output level is now at the higher level of seven.

FIGURE 8.3   Total Revenue, Costs, and Profits

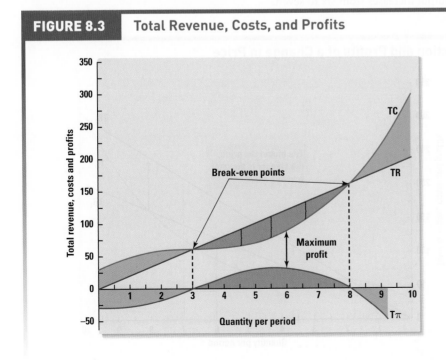

If Wallis produces either 0, 1, or 2 units, she will make an economic loss, illustrated as the distance between the TR curve and the TC curve and shown explicitly at the bottom in the total profit curve. At an output of 3 and 8 units, the two curves intersect, which are the break-even outputs. Any output between 3 and 8 will produce an economic profit. Maximum profits occur at the point where the distance between the two curves is greatest—at an output of 6 units. Outputs greater than 8 would result in a loss, since the TR curve is below the TC curve.

TABLE 8.5	Total Profit at a Price of $30		
Output	Total Revenue (TR)	Total Cost (TC)	Total Profit (Tπ)
0	$ 0	$ 30	−$30
1	30	48	−18
2	60	58	2
3	90	60	30
4	120	63	57
5	150	70	80
6	180	90	90
7	**210**	**120**	**90**
8	240	160	80
9	270	220	50
10	300	300	0

In summary:

> A higher price implies a wider range of profitable outputs, increased production, and greater profit.

In contrast, a lower price reduces the range of profitable outputs and results in lower production and smaller profit (or bigger losses) for the producers. These general points are illustrated in **Figure 8.4**. A higher price level pivots the total revenue curve to the left (it gets steeper) from TR_1 to TR_2. This means that profits are higher (or losses are lower) at every output level. In addition, a firm will produce a higher output because it can make more profit by doing so. The profit-maximizing output increases from six to seven.

FIGURE 8.4   The Effect on Production and Profits of a Change in Price

The higher the price of a product, the greater is the total revenue at each output. An increase in price will shift the total revenue curve from TR_1 to TR_2. The result will be greater profits and an increase in the profit-maximizing output from 6 to 7 units.

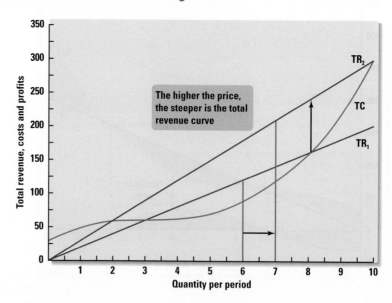

The Marginal Approach to Profitability

An alternative method of finding the maximum profit level for the producer is in terms of marginals. This marginal approach, though at first glance slightly more daunting than the total approach, is a far more revealing way of looking at profit and also highlights other interesting facets. Instead of looking at every possible output that Wallis could produce, let us begin by imagining her increasing production of grommets by one unit at a time, that is, marginally. However, before producing that first unit Wallis is aware that she has fixed costs of $30. If she does not produce anything at all, she will make a loss of $30. So she starts producing the first unit, which will require her to pay for supplies, wages, and so on (not forgetting a normal profit for herself).

Starting from **Table 8.4**, where the price of a grommet was $20, let us work out the marginal cost of each unit which we do in **Table 8.6**. Here we see that the marginal cost of the first unit is $18. But since she can sell this unit for $20, it is certainly worth producing it, since she can make a surplus of $2 on it. What about the second unit? Its marginal cost, at $10, is less than the first unit. Again, if Wallis can sell this grommet for $20, she will make a surplus of $10, so it is definitely worthwhile. **Table 8.6** shows the marginal cost of each unit and the surplus that could be made on each.

Wallis will continue to produce as long as the price can cover the marginal cost of each unit. **Table 8.6** therefore tells us that she will continue to produce up to an output of six units. That is because each unit up to six has more than covered its marginal cost. She would never produce the seventh unit because its marginal cost ($30) exceeds its marginal revenue (price) of $20.

This result confirms what we already know from **Table 8.4**—but puts it in a very different light and suggests that:

$$\text{if marginal revenue } > \text{ marginal cost } \rightarrow \text{ produce more}$$
$$\text{if marginal revenue } < \text{ marginal cost } \rightarrow \text{ produce less}$$

Therefore, to maximize its total profit, the firm should increase production to the point at which:

$$\text{marginal revenue} = \text{marginal cost}$$

We can illustrate this important point in **Figure 8.5**, which shows the marginal revenue (price) for Wallis, the grommet maker.

Now, let us add the rest of the average costs for Wallis, in **Table 8.7**.

TABLE 8.6	Marginal Cost and Marginal Revenue			
Output (Q)	Marginal Cost	Marginal Revenue = Price	Marginal Surplus/Deficit	Total Profit/Loss
0				−30
1	$18	$20	$2	−28
2	10	20	10	−18
3	2	20	18	0
4	3	20	17	17
5	7	20	13	30
6	**20**	**20**	**0**	**30**
7	30	20	−10	20
8	40	20	−20	0
9	60	20	−40	−40
10	80	20	−60	−100

FIGURE 8.5   Marginal Revenue and Marginal Cost

A firm will continue to increase production as long as the MR (price) is greater than (above) the MC. Here, production will increase to 6 units. Although this last unit makes no surplus, all previous units have. The producer would not produce a seventh unit since that unit would make a loss.

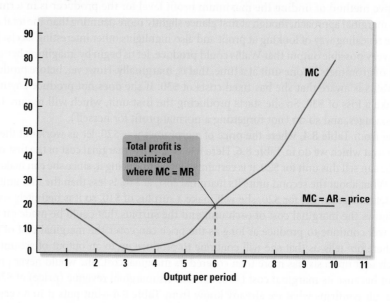

Total profit is maximized where MC = MR

MC = AR = price

Output per period

If we graph these curves and contrast them with the total curves, we see that the break-even outputs occur at quantities of three and eight, where TR = TC in **Figure 8.6A** and where Price (= AR = MR) = ATC in **Figure 8.6B**. Similarly, the profit-maximizing output is at an output of six where the difference between TR and TC is greatest in **Figure 8.6A** and where MC = MR in **Figure 8.6B**.

Finally, in **Figure 8.7** we are able to show the actual amount of total profit that Wallis is making at an output of six units. **Table 8.7** has shown us that at that output the average cost of a unit of grommets is $15. We know that the price is $20. So the **average profit** is $5 which is shown as the distance *ab*.

average profit: the profit per unit produced; that is, the total profit divided by the output.

TABLE 8.7   Average and Marginal Costs

Output (Q)	AVC	ATC	Price = AR = MR	MC
0	/	/	$20	/
1	$18	$48	20	$18
2	14	29	20	10
3	10	20	20	2
4	8.25	15.75	20	3
5	8	14	20	7
6	10	15	20	20
7	12.8	17.1	20	30
8	16.25	20	20	40
9	21.3	24.6	20	60
10	27	30	20	80

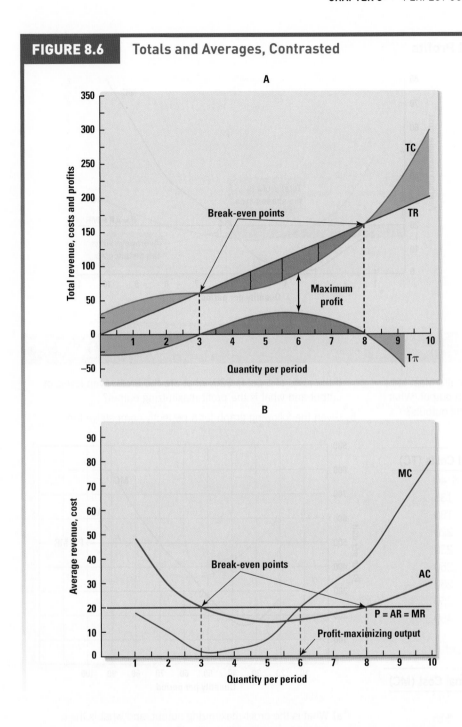

FIGURE 8.6 Totals and Averages, Contrasted

Break-even outputs occur at ouputs of 3 and 8 units where TR and TC are equal (in Figure A) and where the price (AR) is equal to AC (in Figure B). Profit-maximizing output occurs at an output of 6 units where the difference between TR and TC is greatest (in Figure A) and where MC = MR (in Figure B)

The average or per unit profit is simply the difference between the average revenue (price) and the average cost, that is:

$$A\pi = P\ (=AR) - AC \text{ or } \frac{T\pi}{Q} \qquad \text{[8.5]}$$

If we multiply the average profit of $5 by the output of six, it gives us a total profit of $30, which we know is the maximum total profit that Wallis can make. Graphically, this is shown as the shaded area in **Figure 8.7**.

| **FIGURE 8.7** | **Average and Total Profits** |

At an output of 6 units, the average cost is $15 and the average profit is $5 — the distance *ab*. The total profit is equal to the average profit times the quantity produced. This is represented graphically by the shaded area.

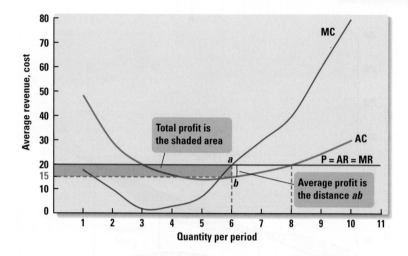

 SELF-TEST

3. Given the accompanying data for Marshall's Meat Ltd., calculate the level of total profits at each output. What are the break-even and profit-maximizing outputs?

Marshall's Meat Ltd.

Output (Q)	Price (P)	Total Costs (TC)
0	$50	$ 40
1	50	135
2	50	180
3	50	220
4	50	230
5	50	250
6	50	280
7	50	350
8	50	450

4. The following data are for Garden Pots Ltd.:

Output (Q)	Average Cost (AC)	Marginal Cost (MC)
0	/	/
1	$45	$15
2	25	5
3	20	10
4	18.75	15
5	19	20
6	20	25
7	22	34
8	25	46

If the price of a pot is $20, what are the break-even levels of output and what is the profit-maximizing output?

5. Given the following graph for a perfectly competitive firm:

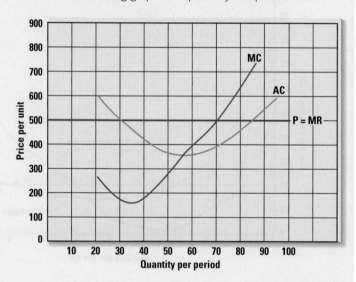

a) What is the profit-maximizing output, and what is the amount of profit at that output?

b) On the graph, shade in the area depicting the firm's total profit.

8.4 BREAK-EVEN PRICE AND SHUTDOWN PRICE

If the demand for a product increases, then the price at which it is sold will rise for all the competitive firms. You can perhaps work out for yourself in **Figure 8.7** that the effect of an increased price will be that the intersection with the marginal cost curve will now occur at a higher level of output and will result in a higher profit for the firm.

But what if the price should drop? Then, the firm will be forced to cut production and accept a lower profit. What we now need to establish is the lowest level to which the price can fall before the firm is producing at a loss. To find this, we need to realize that as long as the price is above the average cost, the firm can be profitable. If it is below, then it does not matter where the firm produces; it will be making a loss. The **break-even price** is, therefore, the price that is just equal to the minimum average total cost.

If you look back at **Table 8.7** you can see that the lowest average total cost that Wallis can produce at is $14. Her break-even price then is $14. This is depicted in **Figure 8.8**.

We can now state that any price above the break-even price of $14 in **Figure 8.8** will enable Wallis to make an economic profit, and any price below $14 will result in a loss. But would Wallis or any firm ever willingly produce at a loss? In many cases, yes. In the *short run*, given that the size of its operations is fixed, and faced with a *price that is less than average cost*, the competitive firm has only two choices: continue to produce, but at a loss, or temporarily shut down. In either case, the firm will continue to exist, hoping that the market will eventually pick up. (If it does not, in the *long run*, it may have little choice but to shut down permanently). So, if the price is below the break-even price, what should it do? Produce or shut down? The answer will depend on whether the loss from producing is bigger or smaller than the loss from shutting down. And what loss will be incurred if the firm decides to shut down? This would be the amount of its total fixed costs. We can thus conclude that:

> As long as the losses from production are less than its total fixed costs, the firm would be advised to produce.

LO4 Explain what is meant by break-even price and shutdown price.

break-even price: the price at which the firm makes only normal profits; that is, makes zero economic profits

---

FIGURE 8.8   **Break-Even Price and Shutdown Price for the Competitive Firm**

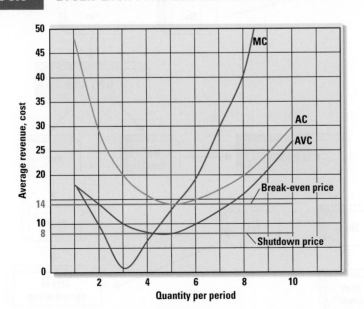

The break-even price is located at the point of minimum average total cost. For Wallis, this is equal to $14. If the price is above $14, the firm can make a profit; below this, it will make a loss. The shutdown price is located at the minimum of the average variable cost curve. In this case it is equal to $8. If the price is above $8, the firm will produce; below this, it will (temporarily) shut down.

shutdown price: the price that is just sufficient to cover a firm's variable costs.

If the total fixed costs of a firm are $10 000 per week, then the worst loss that the firm can incur is $10 000, which will result from shutting down and producing zero. What this says, in terms of an operational rule, is that since the firm can do little about its fixed costs because these costs are sunk costs that have already been incurred, it should at least try to ensure that it can cover its variable costs, such as wages, materials, and so on. If the firm is unable to cover even its variable costs, let alone its fixed costs, it would be foolish to produce at all because this will just make its loss even bigger. However, if it can at least cover the variable costs with a little surplus left over, then this surplus can help pay for some of the fixed costs.

All of this suggests that the aim of the firm must always be to cover its variable costs (at minimum), and if it cannot, then it should shut down. In **Figure 8.8**, this means that the **shutdown price** is $8 and is located at the lowest point of the average variable cost curve. If the price is above $8, Wallis will produce even if it entails a loss because she can more than cover her variable costs. And the best output to produce will be the amount at which the price is equal to the marginal cost. This will at least ensure the smallest loss. If the price falls below the shutdown price, then Wallis should shut down temporarily and absorb the loss, which will be equal to her total fixed costs.

A decision to temporarily close its doors and cease operations is not a decision a firm will make lightly and how long it can stay closed will depend on a number of factors, particularly its ability to finance its losses. If it becomes unable to finance its losses, then the temporary closure may well become permanent.

You can now see that the firm needs to make different decisions and that different cost curves are used to make these decisions. The average variable cost curve is used to decide whether to produce at all or shut down, the marginal cost curve is used to decide the best output, and the average cost curve is used to determine the level of profit or loss.

Since some of these ideas can seem a little confusing on first acquaintance, let us summarize what we have said so far in the following graphic:

The Decisions Facing the Firm

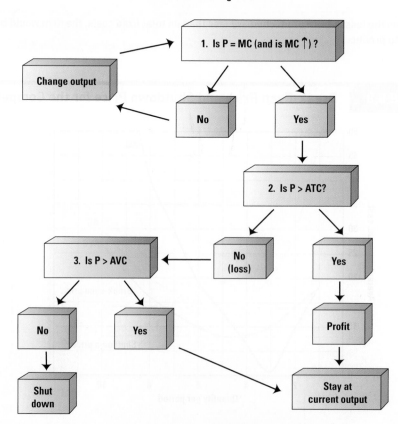

ADDED DIMENSION Marginal Pricing in Action

The concepts of marginal costs and marginal revenue, far from being esoteric ideas that have no relevance in the business world, play a very important part in determining prices and total profits for many major companies. For example, fixed costs are very high for most airlines. To fly a 747 from Toronto to Los Angeles is an expensive proposition, costing tens of thousands of dollars in terms of flight crew, fuel, insurance, landing fees, and so on. The increased variable cost—the marginal costs per passenger—

on the other hand, is very low because it consists of a prepackaged meal, perhaps a drink or two, the cost of cleaning a headset, and a little more fuel because of the extra weight. Rather than cancel a flight, which an airline cannot do anyway if it is a scheduled flight, it is entirely reasonable for the airline to offer seats below their full costs to at least cover the marginal costs. In other words, as long as the price is above the marginal costs, it will be worthwhile to take on one more passenger.

 SELF-TEST

6. The accompanying graph shows the costs of production for Smith Industries, a perfectly competitive firm.

   a) What is the break-even price?

   b) What is the shutdown price?

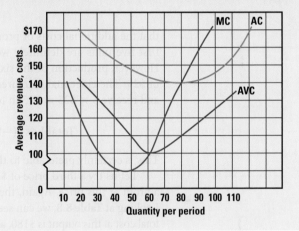

8.5 THE FIRM'S SUPPLY CURVE

Let us now put some flesh on these ideas by working through an example, and in doing so help derive a supply curve for the firm. For a change of pace, let us look at some of the costs of an apple cider producer, as shown in **Table 8.8**. Assume that the output is in quantities of 10-litre jugs.

L05 Explain how a firm's supply curve is derived.

First of all, let us confirm some important benchmarks for this producer. The lowest average total cost is $29, and this is the value of the break-even price. If the price is higher than this, he can make a profit; if it is lower, he will make a loss. The lowest average variable cost is $20, and this is the value of the shutdown price. If the price is between $20, and $29, the producer will make a loss but the cider is still worth producing; below $20, the producer should, at least temporarily, shut down operations. Given this basic information, let us figure out the supply curve for this producer, relating the quantities he would like to produce at different prices.

Suppose that the price is $15. We have already decided that he would not produce at this price. By not producing at all, his loss will be equal to his total fixed costs of $40. (This is the value of total fixed costs when output is zero.) Now, let us see what happens at a price of, say, $25. We know he will make a loss at this price, but let us confirm the best output and the size of the loss. To do this, we look down the MC column. As long as the price the cider producer receives can cover the cost of each additional unit, it will be worthwhile producing the cider. Bear in mind

TABLE 8.8	Deriving the Firm's Supply Curve			
Output (Q)	Total Costs (TC)	Marginal Costs (MC)	Average Variable Costs (AVC)	Average Total Costs (ATC)
0	$ 40	/	/	/
1	65	$25.00	$25.00	$65.00
2	85	20.00	22.50	42.50
3	100	15.00	20.00	33.33
4	120	20.00	20.00	30.00
5	145	25.00	21.00	29.00
6	180	35.00	23.33	30.00
7	225	45.00	26.43	32.14
8	280	55.00	30.00	35.00

that the additional costs of producing each unit involve variable costs only. Given this, then, the first five units are definitely worthwhile, since the marginal cost of each unit is less than $25. However, production of the sixth unit results in a marginal cost of $35, which exceeds the price of $25. The cider manufacturer should therefore produce only five units at a total cost of $145 and receive 5 × $25 = 125 in total revenue, thereby making a loss of $20, that is:

$$\text{Total Loss} (-\$20) = \text{TR} (5 \times \$25 = \$125) - \text{TC} (\$145)$$

This is certainly preferable to the shutdown loss of $40.

Let us try a third price of $35. We know in advance that the producer should be able to make a profit at this price. Again, the profit-maximizing output is where the price is equal to the MC. Looking at **Table 8.8**, we can see that this occurs at an output of six, where the MC is also $35. The total cost at this output is $180, and total revenue is equal to 6 × $35 = $210. The profit, therefore, is:

$$\text{T}\pi (\$30) = \text{TR} (\$210) - \text{TC} (\$180)$$

We could continue in similar fashion for other prices, say, $45 and $55. The results are tabulated in **Table 8.9**.

You can see from this table that the higher the price of the cider, the higher is the chosen level of production and the more profitable is production. This table relates the various quantities that the producer would produce at different prices; in other words, this is the producer's supply schedule. Since the producer will always equate the price with the MC, the supply curve of the firm is, in fact, identical to its MC curve, as **Figure 8.9** makes clear. Here, we see that the profit-maximizing (or loss-minimizing) output occurs where the MR (or price) equals the MC.

TABLE 8.9	The Firm's Supply Schedule	
Price (P)	Output (Q)	Profit/Loss
$15	0	$ −40
25	5	−20
35	6	+30
45	7	+90
55	8	+160

| FIGURE 8.9 | The Firm's Supply Curve |

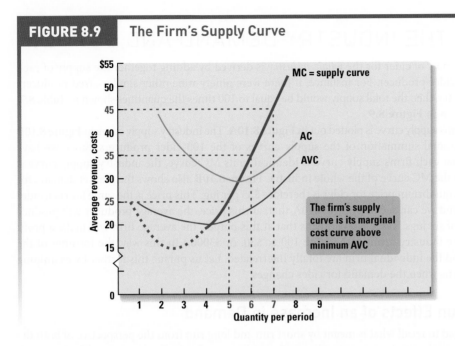

To maximize profits, the firm equates the price with MC. Therefore, if the price is $25, it is equal to MC at a quantity of 5. At a price of $35, they are equal at a quantity of 6; at $45, an output of 7 and so on. Below $20, the quantity is zero because this is the shutdown price.

The firm's supply curve is its marginal cost curve above minimum AVC

At a price of $25, profit maximization is at an output of five; at $35, it is at an output of six; at $45, an output of seven, and so on. These points all occur along the MC curve, which is, therefore, synonymous with the firm's supply curve; that is, the MC curve is the supply curve. However, if the price is below $20, the firm could not cover its AVC. It would, therefore, shut down and produce zero. The supply curve is therefore not the whole of the MC curve, but that portion above the AVC curve. Because of the equality between the price and MC:

> The supply curve for the firm is that portion of its MC curve that lies above its average variable cost curve.

As we noted before, if the price is lower than the minimum AVC, then the firm would simply not produce.

 SELF-TEST

7. Given the accompanying data for a competitive firm, what quantities will the firm produce at prices of $25, $35, $45, $55, $65, and $75?

Output	Marginal Costs	Average Variable Costs
0	—	—
1	$40	$40
2	20	30
3	30	30
4	40	32.5
5	50	36
6	60	40
7	70	44.3
8	80	48

8.6   THE INDUSTRY DEMAND AND SUPPLY

LO6 Explain the effect of a change in market demand or market supply on both the industry and the firm.

The total supply of cider for the *whole industry* is derived by adding together the supply of each individual cider producer. For instance, if there were ninety-nine other similar-sized producers in the industry, then the total supply would be equal to 100 times the quantities shown in **Table 8.7**. This is shown in **Figure 8.9**.

The firm's supply curve is plotted out in **Figure 8.10A**. The industry supply curve in **Figure 8.10B** is the horizontal summation of the supply curves of the 100 cider producers. Since we have assumed that each firm's supply curve is identical to its MC curve, the industry supply curve is identical to the MC curve of the whole industry. **Figure 8.10B** also shows the market demand for cider. The equilibrium price for cider is therefore $35 per jug. This price is the same for each cider producer, and we can see in **Figure 8.10A** that, at this price, the average producer will produce an output of six jugs. **Table 8.9** confirms that at this output, the average firm will make a profit of $30. (The industry profit is therefore 100 × $30, or $3000.) In this way, the fortunes of the industry and the individual firm are totally interrelated. Let us pursue this further by examining what happens when the demand for cider changes.

Long-Run Effects of an Increase in Demand

We now need to recall what is meant by short run and long run from the perspective of both the firm and the industry. As we saw in Chapter 7, the short run for the firm is a period during which it can do nothing to affect the size of its premises: the capacity of the firm is, therefore, fixed. From the industry's point of view, the short run also means that the size of the industry is fixed (because the number of firms in the industry is fixed and the size of each firm is fixed). From the firm's point of view, the long run is the amount of time it takes to change the size of its premises, whereas for the industry the long run is the amount of time it takes for present firms to quit or new firms to join the industry. In summary:

> The short run is a period in which the sizes of both the firm and the industry are fixed; in the long run, they are variable.

FIGURE 8.10   **Industry Supply and Market Equilibrium**

The supply of the firm shown in Figure A is based on Table 8.9. If the industry consists of 10 identical firms, the market supply would be that shown in Figure B. Given the demand curve shown in that figure, the equilibrium quantity is 600 and the market equilibrium price will be $35. Figure A shows that at a price of $35, this average firm will produce 6 units, and since there are 100 firms in total, this confirms the industry output of 600.

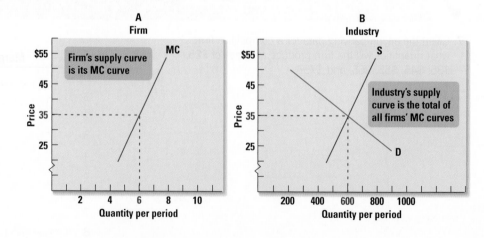

Let us now work through the effects of an increase in the demand for cider in both the short run and the long run. Suppose that new medical evidence suggests that cider reduces cholesterol levels and the result of this information is a big increase in the demand for cider. From the industry point of view, the effect of this good news is an increase in the price of cider.

Figure 8.11A shows that the increase in demand leads to an increase in price and an increase in the quantity produced—a movement from point *a* to point *b*. Suppose that the firm shown in **Figure 8.11B** is a representative cider producer and is initially breaking even, that is, making only normal profit. As the price of cider starts to rise, this firm and the other producers realize they can increase profit by increasing production. The increased production in the industry (from point *a* to *b* in **Figure 8.11A**) is the result of the present firms producing more (from point *a* to *b* in **Figure 8.11B**) with their present facilities. Each producer, previously making only normal profit, now finds itself making economic profit.

This situation is unlikely to last indefinitely. New firms will be attracted by the high profit being made in the cider industry and will enter the industry, thus increasing the number of firms. This is shown by a shift in the supply curve from S_1 to S_2 in **Figure 8.11A**. The effect of this increased competition in the industry will be a fall in the price of cider and a new equilibrium being established at point *c*. For the older firms, this drop in the price of cider will force a cutback in production and profit until they are back where they started at point *a* in **Figure 8.11B**. Although in the long run, the price, profitability, and production levels for the average firm have remained the same, there is one significant difference: the industry is now much bigger, and the larger number of firms means increased industry production.

There may well be an additional change to consider. The first effect of the increase in demand was an increase in price, which stimulated firms to produce more. However, the maximum production of each firm was limited by the size of its premises and by the fact that costs would increase significantly as the firm approached its physical limits. If the average firm believed that the higher demand was likely to be maintained in the future, it would have every incentive in the long run to increase the size of its facilities. In other words, in the long run, the capacity of the industry may increase not only because there are more firms but also because firms are larger. The chain of events is diagrammed below.

FIGURE 8.11   The Effects of an Increase in Demand on the Industry and Firm

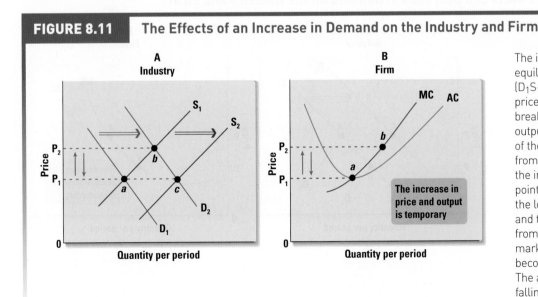

The industry was initially in equilibrium at point *a* in Figure A (D_1S_1), and at the equilibrium price, P_1, the average firm was breaking even and producing an output of *a* in Figure B. As a result of the increase in the demand from D_1 to D_2, both the price and the industry output increase to point *b* in Figure A. However, in the long run, new firms enter, and the market supply increases from S_1 to S_2. As a result, the market price drops, and point *c* becomes the new equilibrium. The average firm finds the price falling and reduces its output back to point *a* in Figure B.

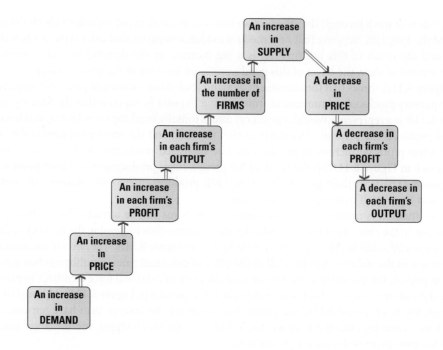

Long-Run Effects of a Decrease in Demand

As in the last example, we will assume that initially the average cider producer is just making normal profit. Suppose that new medical evidence suggests that while cider may reduce cholesterol levels, it also causes tooth decay and constipation. Faced with this new information, consumers drastically reduce their purchases of cider. The decrease in demand is shown in **Figure 8.12A**.

FIGURE 8.12   The Effects of a Decrease in Demand on the Industry and Firm

The drop in demand from D₁ to D₂ reduces the output level and the price from point *a* to point *b* in Figure A. Output drops because the average firm is forced to cut back production as the price falls. This is shown in the movement from *a* to *b* in Figure B. Since the average firm is now producing at a loss, in the long run, some firms will be forced out of business. This is shown by a leftward shift in the supply curve from S₁ to S₂ in Figure A, which will cause the price to recover to point *c*. From the existing firm's point of view, the higher price will cause it to return to point *a* in Figure B, where it again will be breaking even.

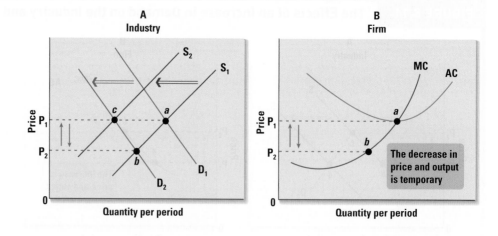

The fall in demand will cause a drop in the price and quantity traded in the industry, as shown in the movement from point *a* to point *b* in **Figure 8.12A**. This reduction is the result of changes forced on the average cider producer, as shown in **Figure 8.12B**. Here, the drop in price causes a fall in profit and a fall in production from point *a* to *b*. The average firm is now being forced to produce at a loss.

This is an untenable situation in the long run. There is a limit to how long firms can continue to incur losses. In the long run, some firms will be forced to close down permanently. The more inefficient ones with higher costs will presumably be forced out of business first.

The effect of this exodus from the industry is shown as a decrease in the industry supply in **Figure 8.12A**. The supply curve shifts left from S₁ to S₂. The effect of this will be fewer firms serving the industry, with the result that the price will be forced up until the industry losses disappear. This will occur when the representative firm is no longer making a loss, that is to say, when the price level returns to its original level at point *c*. From the firm's viewpoint, **Figure 8.12B** shows that as the price starts to recover, production and prices will follow suit, and so eventually the firm is back at production level *a*.

The representative firm in the long run is back where it started, having suffered lower production and profit in the meantime. However, in the long run, the size of the industry shrank following the exit of a number of firms.

Canadian Auto Worker union members create a picket line blocking access to the General Motors Canada head office in Oshawa, Ontario, on June 4, 2008, in protest of the announced closing of the Oshawa truck plant.

✓ SELF-TEST

8. The following graphs show the market demand and supply for orange swizzlers (A) and the costs for a single firm in the industry (B).

   a) What is the equilibrium price and what quantity will the firm produce? Show the price line on graphs A and B.

   Suppose that the demand for orange swizzlers increases by 600.

   b) What will be the new price and quantity in the market, and how many will the representative firm produce? Show the new demand and price on graph A and the price and quantity on graph B.

   c) Suppose that, as a result of the increase in demand, the supply increases with the result that the price returns to its original level. Show the new supply on graph A and the resulting changes on graph B.

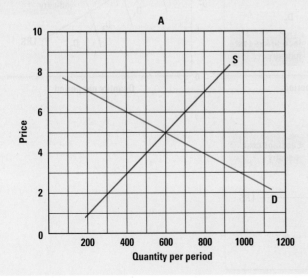

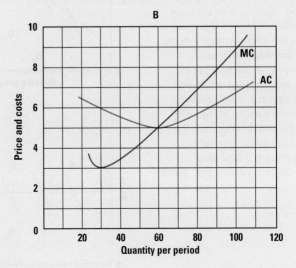

8.7 LONG-RUN SUPPLY OF THE INDUSTRY

This analysis of the long-run effects of a change in the demand for a product suggests that, although a change in demand may have an impact on the size of the industry and on levels of production, it leaves the price level unchanged. However, this may or may not be true depending on whether or not changes in the industry size affect the costs of production. For instance, as the industry grows in size with the entrance of new firms, its demand for all sorts of resources, including labour, will similarly grow. The result may be that the price of these resources, and therefore, the costs of production for the representative firm, will increase. If that happens, the marginal cost will be higher as the industry grows. Graphically, it results in the marginal cost curve shifting upward. The result will mean a higher price being charged for the product.

If costs of production tend to rise as an industry expands, it is known as an **increasing-cost industry**, and its *long-run supply curve* will look like the one in **Figure 8.13A**. If, on the other hand, costs of production fall as an industry expands in size, then we have a **decreasing-cost industry**, and the resulting downward-sloping supply curve is illustrated in **Figure 8.13B**. Finally, the type of industry we have supposed so far—a **constant-cost industry** with a perfectly elastic long-run supply curve—is shown in **Figure 8.13C**.

But why would the costs change as an industry expands? The answer, as we suggested, lies in the effect that such an expansion has on the price of resources. If the cider industry consumes a big proportion of all apples sold in the market, then it is likely that as the cider industry grows, and with it the demand for apples, the price of apples and therefore, the industry's own costs of production will start to rise.

If that were the case, the cider industry would be regarded as an increasing-cost industry. The long-run supply curve in that case would be upward sloping, which means that an increase

increasing-cost industry: an industry in which the prices of resources and products both rise as the industry expands.

decreasing-cost industry: an industry in which the prices of resources and products both fall as the industry expands.

constant-cost industry: an industry in which the prices of resources and products remain unchanged as the industry expands.

FIGURE 8.13   Increasing-Cost, Decreasing-Cost, and Constant-Cost Industries

In all three cases, A, B, and C, the increases in demand from D_1 to D_2 to D_3 are accompanied in the long run by increases in supply from S_1 to S_2 to S_3. If this expansion has no impact on the costs in the industry, as in Figure C, then the price is unaffected, with the result that the long-run supply curve is horizontal. In Figure A, however, costs increase as the industry expands so that the long-run supply curve is upward sloping. In Figure B, as the industry expands, the costs of production falls, resulting in a downward-sloping, long-run supply curve.

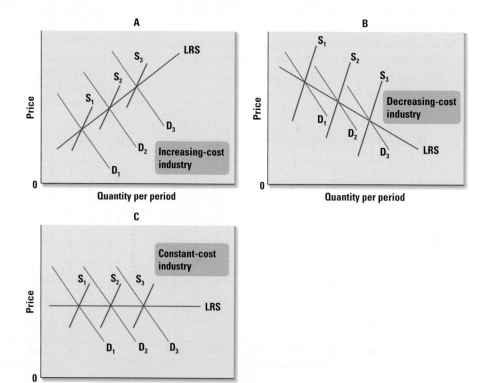

in the size of the industry is accompanied by an increase in the price of cider. If, on the other hand, the cider industry purchased only a very small fraction of the output of the apple industry (or if in general the cost of apples was only a tiny fraction of the total costs of producing cider), then the cider industry could grow without having any impact on apple prices. It would then be categorized as a constant-cost industry, and its supply curve would be horizontal.

But what about decreasing costs in the long run? This could happen if, say, the expansion of both the cider and apple industries caused the latter to start to enjoy economies of scale; it could then start to offer apples at a lower price to the cider industry. The cider industry would then be a decreasing-cost industry, with a corresponding downward-sloping long-run supply curve.

We can find a number of examples of each type of industry in the real world. Perhaps the classic example of a decreasing cost industry is the computer industry, which originated in Silicon Valley south of San Francisco. As the market for computers (particularly personal computers) grew rapidly, the demand for components—chips, boards and so on—grew apace. Whole industries developed to serve manufacturers of computers, and the increased competition among these suppliers led to a dramatic decrease in the costs of inputs to the computer industry.

An example of an industry where costs and therefore prices have *increased* over the years is that of the National Hockey League. As the sport developed rapidly, particularly with the expansion of franchises to new American cities in the 1990s, the demand for NHL players grew along with it. The result was an escalation of players' salaries—by far the largest expense for hockey clubs. The result has been an increase in both the costs of operating an NHL team and the prices to attend games.

Finally, a constant cost industry would be one where the major input was content (music, books, information) that is available at a more or less constant price. A radio station or a book publisher would be examples.

In summary, we can see from these examples that competitive markets are dynamic, inter-related, and self-adjusting. A change in demand gets translated into price changes, which affects production, profitability, and the size of the industry. Needless to say, each of these changes will also affect employment and the purchase of resources, which, in turn, will bring about changes to the suppliers of both complementary and competing industries. Changes in costs and technology will also affect the profitability of firms and cause the exit or entry of firms, which will, in turn, affect the production and profitability of the industry, and the price.

In this way, perfectly competitive markets could be called perfectly sensitive markets because they respond quickly and efficiently to the smallest of changes. As Chapter 9 will show, they also produce a number of other significant benefits. But that chapter will also point out the ways in which a perfect market can sometimes fail to respond to change, and ways in which responding to change might produce unfavourable results.

 SELF-TEST

9. Suppose that initially the market demand and supply for a product are as shown in the accompanying graph.

a) Now assume that the demand increases by 30 units at every price and, as a result, new firms enter, causing the supply to increase by a similar 30 units. Label the new curves D_2 and S_2. Identify the new equilibrium. What are the new price and quantity?

b) Assume that, as a result of the industry expansion, the costs of production increase by $6 per unit. (The supply curve shifts up by $6). Label the new supply curve S_3. What are the new price and quantity? Identify the equilibrium, and draw in the industry's long-run supply curve.

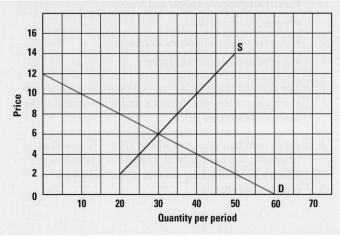

Review

CHAPTER SUMMARY

In this chapter, you looked at market structures, focusing on what economists call perfect competition. This market structure enabled you to understand and measure the concepts of marginal, average, and total revenue. You then learned to compute a firm's profitability using both the total approach and the marginal approach. Finally, you learned to assess how an increase or a decrease in demand, and thus market price, cause adjustments for both the firm and the industry.

8.1a *Firms* make up an *industry*, and this industry operates within the context of a *market*, where both producers and consumers interact.

8.1b Markets are differentiated by:

- the number of firms
- the type of product

There are four types of markets: perfect competition, monopolistic competition, oligopoly, and monopoly.

8.2a The four conditions that must exist for an industry to be *perfectly competitive* are:

- many small sellers and buyers all of whom are price takers
- no preferences shown by either buyers or sellers
- easy entry and exit by both buyers and sellers
- the same market information available to all

8.2b To work effectively, the market system must possess:

- extensive specialization and trade
- perfect competition
- private ownership of resources
- a legal and social foundation

8.3a The *demand curve* for a firm in a perfectly competitive environment is perfectly elastic and is horizontal at the market-determined price.

8.3b *Break-even* output occurs where TR = TC as well as where AC = price (or MR), and this is a situation in which a firm is making normal profits only, with no economic profits.

8.3c A firm will *maximize* its economic profits where MC = MR or TR − TC is greatest.

8.3d A firm should *increase* its output if:

- MR > MC

  A firm shoud *decrease* its output if:

- MR < MC

To maximize total profit, a firm should produce an output where MR = MC.

8.4a The break-even price is equal to the lowest minimum ATC. If the price is above this, the firm will make a profit; below it, the firm will make a loss.

8.4b The *minimum point* of the AVC curve is significant for two reasons:

- if the market-determined price is below this, the firm should shut down and limit its losses to TFC
- the portion of the MC curve that lies above this point is the firm's supply curve

8.5 When an industry, which is initially in equilibrium, experiences an *increase in market demand*, the following will occur:

- market price will increase
- each firm's profit will increase
- output of each firm will increase
- new firms will enter the industry
- market supply will increase

8.6 The *long-run* supply curve for an industry can be one of the following:

- upward sloping, which is called an increasing-cost industry
- downward sloping, which is called a decreasing-cost industry
- horizontal, which is a constant-cost industry

NEW GLOSSARY TERMS AND KEY EQUATIONS

average profit   244
average revenue   238
break-even output   239
break-even price   247

constant-cost industry   256
decreasing-cost industry   256
increasing-cost industry   256

marginal revenue   239
perfect competition   232
shutdown price   248

Equations

[8.1] $TR = Q \times P$ page 238

[8.2] $AR = \dfrac{TR}{Q}$ page 238

[8.3] $MR = \dfrac{\Delta TR}{\Delta Q}$ page 239

[8.4] $T\pi = TR - TC$ page 239

[8.5] $A\pi = \dfrac{T\pi}{Q}$ page 245

STUDY TIPS

1. Probably the most difficult part of this chapter, for most students, is the derivation of the firm's profit maximizing output using the marginal approach. Remember, if all else fails, it is always possible to find this output level by using the total approach; that is, for each different price, compare the total revenue and total cost for every output level and see which gives the greatest profit. However, it is worth the effort to understand the marginal approach because it is a far more efficient and more revealing method.

2. When looking at the marginal approach, bear in mind two things: first, the fixed costs play no part in the decision making, since these costs have already been incurred. Think of them as the amount of the firm's maximum possible loss in the short run. The second thing to remember is that the marginal costs are changes in variable costs and do not need to be incurred, since the firm is not obliged to incur them if it decides not to produce. Given these two facts, you can think of the production process as involving a number of separate, discrete decisions. The owner awakes each day to ask: shall we produce or not today? If not, the fixed costs will still have to be paid, and that will be the total loss. On the other hand, producing and selling just one unit produces both cost (the marginal

cost) and revenue (the price). As long as the price exceeds the marginal cost, it pays to produce it, since the excess will help go against the fixed costs. What about a second unit, or a third unit? Are they worthwhile? Yes, as long as the (same constant) price exceeds the marginal cost. That is how we derive the rule that a firm should produce as long as the price exceeds the marginal cost.

3. Another point of confusion for many students is the idea of breaking even. They wonder why a firm would ever produce if it is merely breaking even and not making profits. But the firm is making profits. It is making enough to keep the owners in business; that is, it is making normal profits, which economists include in, and regard as, a cost of production. However, at break-even, it is true that the firm will not be making economic profits. These are an added bonus and are not necessary to the continued existence of the firm. A similar point of confusion, for some, involves the rule that a firm maximizes its profit by producing at an output at which the price is equal to marginal cost. Some would ask: doesn't this mean that the firm is just breaking even? No. Although the firm does, indeed, break even on the last item it has produced, it has made profits on each unit up until that last one.

Practise and learn online with Connect, where you can find the Answered Questions and the Unanswered Problems for all chapters of this textbook's Study Guide section.

4. Most students can accept the fact that it is often worthwhile for a firm to stay in business in the short run, even though it might be operating at a loss, since the alternative is closing down and possibly incurring even bigger losses. Yet, despite this, they still feel that the rule should be that a firm must only cover its fixed costs to avoid shutdown. This is not true. It does not matter whether the firm produces a little or a lot or whether it produces at all; fixed costs remain the same. What it does have control over are the variable costs. These costs must be covered because if they are not, the firm is in "double trouble," being unable to pay all of either the fixed or the variable costs. In this case, it would definitely be better not to produce at all. Therefore, the rule is: cover the variable costs; ignore the fixed costs.

Answered Questions

These questions can also be found online on Connect.

Indicate whether the following statements are true or false:

1. **(LO 1) T or F**   In a perfectly competitive market, all buyers and sellers are price takers.

2. **(LO 3) T or F**   Marginal revenue is the extra income a firm receives above break-even.

3. **(LO 3) T or F**   Profit maximization occurs at the output where marginal revenue equals zero.

4. **(LO 4) T or F**   A firm will not shut down in the short run so long as it is covering its variable costs.

5. **(LO 3) T or F**   In order to maximize its profits, a firm will produce an output at which the marginal revenue equals the marginal cost.

6. **(LO 3) T or F**   A firm will maximize its total profits at the output at which the difference between its average revenue and average cost is greatest.

7. **(LO 5) T or F**   The supply curve of the firm in perfect competition is that portion of the marginal cost curve above the average variable cost curve.

8. **(LO 6) T or F**   An increase in the demand for a product will cause many firms to leave the industry.

9. **(LO 7) T or F**   The long-run supply curve of an increasing cost industry is upward sloping.

10. **(LO 7) T or F**   The reason why the long-run supply curve is upward or downward sloping is the result of changes in production costs that accompany any change in the size of the industry.

Basic (Questions 11–22)

11. **(LO 1)** What is the name of the type of market that is dominated by a few firms?

    a) Oligopoly
    b) Monopolistic competition
    c) Monopoly
    d) Perfect competition

12. **(LO 1)** Which of the following is true for a perfectly competitive firm?
    a) It can control its price but not its output.
    b) It can control its output but not its price.
    c) It can control both its price and its output.
    d) It cannot control either its price or its output.

13. **(LO 3)** How is average revenue defined?
    a) It is the extra revenue derived from the sale of one more unit.
    b) It is the total revenue divided by the number of units sold.
    c) It is marginal revenue divided by the number of units sold.
    d) It is the sum of the marginal revenue of all units sold.

14. **(LO 2)** What type of product is sold by the representative firm in a perfectly competitive market?
    a) The same as is sold by the other firms
    b) A unique product
    c) A product different from that sold by the other firms
    d) It could be any of the above three types

15. **(LO 4)** What does break-even output mean?
    a) The output at which the price is equal to the average revenue
    b) The output at which the price is equal to the marginal revenue
    c) The output at which the price is equal to the average cost
    d) The output at which the price is equal to marginal cost

16. **(LO 3)** Which of the following conditions means that the competitive firm is maximizing its profits?
    a) The price equals average revenue.
    b) The price is equal to marginal revenue.
    c) The price is equal to marginal cost.
    d) The price is equal to average cost.

17. **(LO 3)** What is the shape of the demand curve facing the perfectly competitive firm?
    a) Downward sloping
    b) Horizontal
    c) Vertical
    d) Upward sloping

18. **(LO 2)** Which of the following industries provides the best example of a perfectly competitive market?
    a) Automobile manufacturing
    b) Restaurants
    c) Oil refining
    d) Wheat farming

19. **(LO 6)** What will happen graphically if a number of firms exit from a perfectly competitive industry?
    a) The market demand curve will shift to the right.
    b) The market demand curve will shift to the left.
    c) The market supply curve will shift to the right.
    d) The market supply curve will shift to the left.

20. **(LO 5)** What is the correct interpretation of the perfectly competitive firm's supply curve?
    a) It is the same as its average variable cost curve.
    b) It is the same as its total variable cost curve.
    c) It is the same as the portion of its marginal cost curve that lies above the average variable cost curve.
    d) It is the same as the portion of its average variable cost curve that lies above the marginal cost curve.

Use **Table 8.10** to answer questions 21 to 23. The data are for a firm operating in perfect competition.

TABLE 8.10

Output	Marginal Costs	Average Variable Costs	Average Costs
1	70	70	200
2	60	65	130
3	50	60	103.3
4	60	60	92.5
5	70	62	88
6	75	64.3	86
7	105	70	88.6
8	120	76.25	92.5

21. **(LO 4)** What is the firm's break-even price?
    a) $60
    b) $70
    c) $86
    d) $200

22. **(LO 4)** What is the firm's shutdown price?
    a) $60
    b) $70
    c) $86
    d) $200

Intermediate (Questions 23–28)

23. **(LO 4)** If the market price is $80, what is the profit-maximizing output, and what will be the firm's profit or loss?
    a) 4 units and a loss of $80
    b) 5 units and a loss of $40
    c) 6 units and a loss of $36
    d) 6 units and zero profit

Use **Table 8.11** to answer questions 24 to 28, which refers to a perfectly competitive firm.

TABLE 8.11

Output	Total Costs	AVC	AC
0	$10	/	/
1	15	5	15
2	18	4	9
3	20	3.33	6.67
4	23	3.25	5.75
5	28	3.60	5.60
6	38	4.67	6.33
7	50	5.71	7.14

24. **(LO 4)** What is the break-even price?
    a) $3.25
    b) $5
    c) $5.60
    d) $18
    e) $28

25. **(LO 4)** What is the shutdown price?
    a) $3.25
    b) $4
    c) $5.60
    d) $13
    e) $23

26. **(LO 4)** What is the profit-maximizing output if the price is $3?
    a) 0
    b) 3
    c) 4
    d) 5
    e) 6

27. **(LO 4)** What is the profit-maximizing output if the price is $10?
    a) 0
    b) 3
    c) 4
    d) 5
    e) 6

28. **(LO 4)** If the price is $10, what profit or loss will this producer earn?
    a) 0
    b) −$4.40
    c) +$4.40
    d) +$22
    e) +$32

Advanced (Questions 29–35)

Use **Figure 8.14** to answer questions 29 to 31, which refer to a perfectly competitive firm.

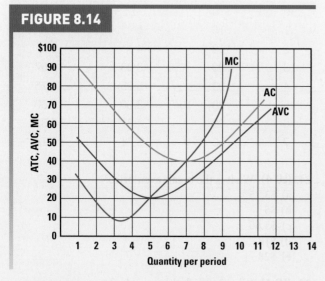

FIGURE 8.14

29. **(LO 4)** What is the value of the break-even price?
    a) $10
    b) $20
    c) $40
    d) $50
    e) Cannot be determined from the information

30. **(LO 4)** What is the value of the shutdown price?
    a) $0
    b) $10
    c) $20
    d) $40
    e) Cannot be determined from the information

31. **(LO 4)** If the price of the product is $70, what is the profit-maximizing output, and what is the amount of economic profits?
    a) 7 and zero
    b) 7 and $10
    c) 7 and $70
    d) 9 and $180
    e) 11 and zero

32. **(LO 3, 4)** What action should a perfectly competitive firm take if, at its present output, MC is equal to price, is increasing, and is less than the average variable cost.
    a) It should shut down.
    b) It should increase its output.
    c) It should decrease its output.
    d) It should increase its price.

33. **(LO 3, 4)** What action should a perfectly competitive firm take if, at its present output, MC is both increasing and is greater than the price, and the price is greater than the average variable cost?
    a) It should shut down.
    b) It should increase its output.
    c) It should decrease its output.
    d) It should increase the price.

34. **(LO 7)** What long-run effect will a decrease in market demand have on a constant-cost industry?
    a) The price will stay the same, and the number of firms in the industry will increase.
    b) The price will stay the same, and the number of firms in the industry will decrease.
    c) The price will decrease, and the number of firms in the industry will increase.
    d) The price will decrease, and the number of firms in the industry will decrease.

35. **(LO 7)** What long-run effect will a decrease in market demand have on a decreasing-cost industry?
    a) The price will increase, and the number of firms in the industry will increase.
    b) The price will increase, and the number of firms in the industry will decrease.
    c) The price will decrease, and the number of firms in the industry will increase.
    d) The price will decrease, and the number of firms in the industry will decrease.

Parallel Problems

ANSWERED PROBLEMS

36A. **(LO 3, 4, 5, 6) Key Problem Table 8.12** shows the cost data for Farmer Mill, a barley farmer.
   a) Complete the table, and graph the MC, AC, and AVC curves in **Figure 8.15**.
   b) What are the values of the break-even and shutdown prices?
      Break-even price: _____
      Shut-down price: _____
   c) Given the prices shown in column 1 of **Table 8.13**, complete columns 2 and 3, indicating how much Farmer Mill would produce and what profit or loss she would make. (Assume that partial units cannot be produced.)
   d) Suppose that there are a total of 100 farms in the barley market, including and identical to Farmer Mills'. Show the total supply in column 4.

   e) If the market demand for barley is as shown in column 5, what will be the equilibrium price and quantity traded?
      Price: _____ ; quantity traded: _____ .
   f) At the equilibrium price, what quantity will Farmer Mill produce, and what will be her profit? Indicate the price and quantity on your graph. What will be the industry profit? Quantity: _____
      Firm profit: $ _____ Industry profit: $ _____
   g) As a result of your answer in e), will firms enter or leave this industry? Answer: _____ .
   h) Suppose that in the long run, the number of firms increases by 50 percent. Show the new totals in column 6 of the table. As a result, what will be the new equilibrium price? What quantity will Farmer Mill produce, and what will be her profit? Again, indicate the new price and quantity on your graph. What will be the industry profit?
      Equilibrium price: $ _____ Quantity: _____
      Firm profit: $ _____ Industry profit: $ _____ .

TABLE 8.12

Quantity	Total Cost ($)	Total Variable Cost ($)	Marginal Cost ($)	Average Cost ($)	Average Variable Cost ($)
0	6	0	/	/	0
1	___	___	4	___	___
2	___	___	2	___	___
3	___	___	4	___	___
4	___	___	6	___	___
5	___	___	8	___	___
6	___	___	10	___	___
7	___	___	12	___	___

TABLE 8.13

(1)	(2)	(3)	(4)	(5)	(6)
Price	Output	Profit(+)/Loss(−)	Total Quantity Supplied 1	Total Quantity Demanded	Total Quantity Supplied 2
$2	___	___	___	800	___
4	___	___	___	700	___
6	___	___	___	600	___
8	___	___	___	500	___
10	___	___	___	400	___

FIGURE 8.15

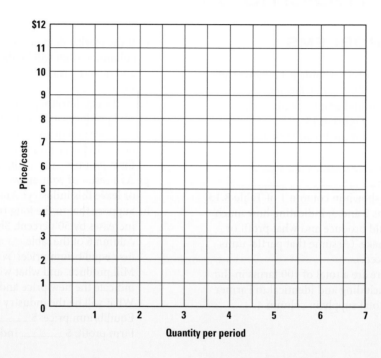

Basic (Problems 37A–44A)

37A. **(LO 3)** If the price of oats is $3 per kilo, calculate the total revenue and the total profit (or loss) at the quantities shown in **Table 8.14**.

TABLE 8.14

Quantity (kilos)	600	700	800	900	1000
Total revenue	___	___	___	___	___
Total cost	$2000	2150	2400	2650	2910
Total profit	___	___	___	___	___

38A. **(LO 3)** A grommet-maker sold 45 grommets last week and received total revenue of $1215. This week, he sold 48 grommets and received total revenue of $1296. What are the average and marginal revenues of grommets? Average: _____ ; marginal: _____ .

39A. **(LO 3)** Complete **Table 8.15**, which shows the total profits from producing grommets.

TABLE 8.15

Quantity	11	12	13	14	15	16
Total profit	$220	$264	$325	$336	$345	$352
Average profit	___	___	___	___	___	___

40A. **(LO 3, 4)** **Figure 8.16** shows the TC and TVC curves of Galbraith's Globes Inc., a perfectly competitive firm.

FIGURE 8.16

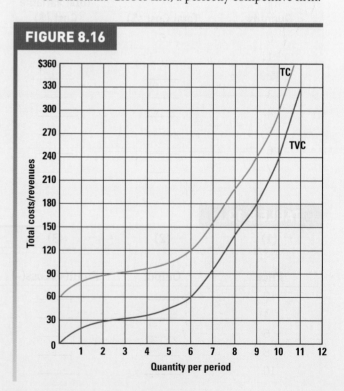

a) If the price is $30, draw in the total revenue curve, and label it TR_1. At this price, what are the break-even output(s), the profit-maximizing output, and the level of profits at that output?
Break-even output(s): _____ P____ ;
profit-maximizing output: _____ T____ ;
total profit: $ _____ .

b) Draw a total revenue curve, labelled TR_2, which results in Galbraith's Globes, at best, breaking even. What is the corresponding break-even price? Price: $ _____ .

c) Draw a total revenue curve, labelled TR_3, which results in Galbraith's Globes, at best, just remaining in operation. What is the corresponding shutdown price? Price: $ _____ .

41A. **(LO 3, 4, 5, 6)** In **Figure 8.17**, graph A shows the *market* demand and supply in a competitive market, and graph B shows the cost curves of a representative *firm* in that industry.

a) What are the market equilibrium price and quantity?
Price: _____ ; quantity traded: _____ .

b) At equilibrium, what quantity is the firm producing? What is its total profit or loss?
Quantity: _____ ;
profit (+)/loss (−): _____ .
Suppose that the market demand increases by 600 units.

c) What are the new equilibrium price and market quantity?
Price: _____ ; quantity traded: _____ .

d) At this new equilibrium, what quantity is the firm producing? What is its total profit or loss?
Quantity: _____ ;
profit (+)/loss (−): _____ .

42A. **(LO 3, 4)** **Figure 8.18** shows the average and marginal cost curves for Kandi Keynes, a perfectly competitive firm.

a) If the price is $60, draw in the marginal revenue curve, and label it MR_1, At this price, what are the break-even output(s), the profit-maximizing output, and the level of total profits at that output?
Break-even output(s): _____ P____ ;
profit maximizing output: _____ T____ ;
total profits: _____ .

b) Draw a marginal revenue curve, labelled MR_2, which ensures that, at best, the firm breaks even. What is the corresponding break-even price?
Break-even price: _____ .

c) Draw a marginal revenue curve, labelled MR_3, which ensures that, at best, the firm just remains in operation. What is the corresponding shutdown price?
Shutdown price: _____ .

43A. **(LO 1)** Explain the difference between an *industry* and a *market*.

44A. **(LO 2)** What are the four main features of perfectly competitive markets? Explain each.

FIGURE 8.17

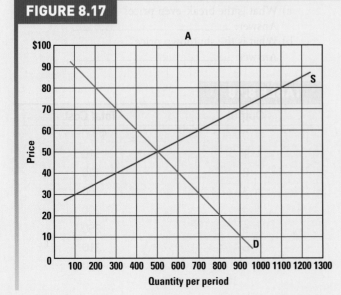

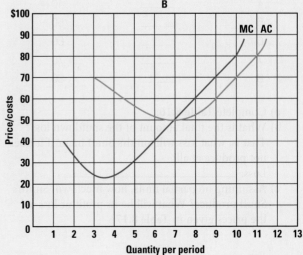

FIGURE 8.18

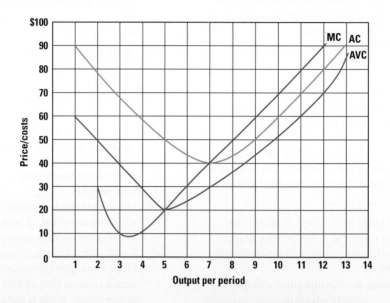

Intermediate (Problems 45A–51A)

45A. **(LO 4)** Table 8.16 shows the cost data for Smith's Snuff, a perfectly competitive firm.

TABLE 8.16

Output	Total Cost	Marginal Cost
0	$120	/
1	_____	$30
2	_____	20
3	_____	30
4	_____	40
5	_____	50
6	_____	60
7	_____	70
8	_____	80

a) Complete Table 8.16.
b) What is the total amount of the shutdown loss? That is, what loss will Smith's Snuff incur if it does not produce at all?
   Loss: _____ .
c) Assuming no partial units, how much will Smith's Snuff produce? What will be its profit or loss at the prices given in Table 8.17?

TABLE 8.17

Price ($)	Output	Profit (+) or Loss (−)
$20	_____	_____
40	_____	_____
60	_____	_____
80	_____	_____

46A. **(LO 4)** The cost data in Table 8.18 are for Marshall's Meats, a perfectly competitive firm.
   a) What is the break-even price?
      Answer: _____ .
   b) What is the shutdown price?
      Answer: _____ .

TABLE 8.18

Output	Total Cost
0	$ 80
1	110
2	130
3	160
4	200
5	250
6	310
7	420

c) If the market price of the product is $50, what quantity will Marshall's Meats produce? What will be its profit or loss?
Quantity: _____ ; profit or loss: _____ .

d) If the market price of the product is $110, what quantity will Marshall's Meats produce? What will be its profit or loss?
Quantity: _____ ; profit or loss: _____ .

47A. **(LO 3)** You are given the following information for Clarke's Cookies, which produces in a perfectly competitive market.

TFC = $12   Market price = $10

The marginal cost of production appears in **Table 8.19**.

TABLE 8.19

Output	MC ($)
1	10
2	8
3	6
4	4
5	6
6	8
7	10
8	12
9	14

a) Draw the MC, AVC, AC, and AR curves in **Figure 8.19**.

b) What is the profit maximizing output? Is the firm making a profit or loss? How much?
Output: _____
Profit/Loss: _____ : _____

48A. **(LO 3, 4, 5, 6)** **Table 8.20** shows information for Hayek's Maps, a perfectly competitive firm.

a) Given the prices in **Table 8.20**, fill in columns 2 and 3 of **Table 8.21** indicating how much the firm would produce and what profit or loss it would make. (Assume that partial units cannot be produced.)

b) Suppose there are 100 firms identical to this one. Show the total supply in column 4 of **Table 8.21**.

c) If the market demand is as shown in column 5 of **Table 8.21**, what will be the equilibrium price? What quantity will be traded in the market?
Price: _____ ; quantity traded: _____ .

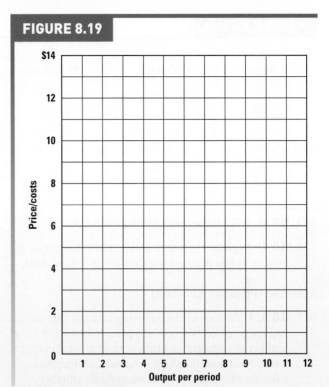

FIGURE 8.19

TABLE 8.20

Output	AVC	AC	MC
1	$100	$200	$100
2	95	145	90
3	90	123.33	80
4	92	117	98
5	95	115	107
6	100	116.67	125
7	110	124.28	170
8	120	132.50	220

d) At equilibrium, what quantity will this firm produce? What will be its profit or loss?
Quantity produced: _____ ;
profit or loss: _____ .

e) As a result of your answer in d), will firms enter or leave this industry?
Answer: _____ .

49A. **(LO 7)** Explain what will happen to the output and price of a constant-cost industry if there is an increase in market demand.

TABLE 8.21

(1) Price	(2) Output	(3) Profit/Loss	(4) Total Supply	(5) Total Demand
$ 89	——	——	——	800
98	——	——	——	700
107	——	——	——	600
116	——	——	——	500
125	——	——	——	400
134	——	——	——	300

50A. (LO 4) What is meant by *break-even price*?

51A. (LO 4) Explain why a firm will continue to operate as long as its loss is no greater than its total fixed costs.

Advanced (Problems 52A–56A)

52A. (LO 3, 4) In each of the following cases, a) through c), you are given certain cost and price information for a number of competitive firms, at their present output levels. Assuming the short run, and that marginal costs are increasing in all cases, indicate whether each firm should
i) produce more
ii) produce less
iii) shut down
iv) cannot be determined without more information
a) Total variable cost exceeds total revenue _____
b) Total fixed cost exceeds total revenue _____
c) Total cost exceeds total revenue _____ .

53A. (LO 3, 4) Suppose that the total fixed cost for a particular competitive firm is $40. The marginal cost for the first unit produced is $12 and decreases by $2 for each of the next three units produced and thereafter marginal cost increases by $2 for each additional unit.

a) What is the shutdown price? What is the break-even price?
Shutdown: _____ ; break-even: _____ .
b) If the market price is $16, what is the firm's profit-maximizing output? What is the firm's total profit or loss?
Output: _____ ; profit or loss: _____ .

54A. (LO 3, 4) You are given the following cost and revenue data for Parkin's Pickles, a perfectly competitive firm at its current output level:
TR = $1430   TFC = $440   MC = $20
AC = $12   AVC = $8
a) Is the firm making a profit or a loss? How much?
Profit or loss: _____ ; amount: _____ .
b) Is the firm producing the optimal output? If not, should it produce more, less, or none at all?
_____ .

55A. (LO 7) What is the long-run supply curve of the industry? How might it be upward-sloping? Downward-sloping? Horizontal?

56A. (LO 2) What four conditions are necessary if the market system is to work effectively? Briefly explain each.

CHAPTER 9

AN EVALUATION OF COMPETITIVE MARKETS

LEARNING OBJECTIVES

At the end of this chapter, you should be able to...

LO1 explain how perfectly competitive markets encourage technological improvement and growth in the size of firms.

LO2 explain the benefits of perfectly competitive markets.

LO3 understand the five reasons perfect competition might fail to achieve desirable results.

LO4 understand how governments try to deal with external costs, such as pollution.

LO5 understand how governments try to deal with external benefits, such as education.

WHAT'S AHEAD...

This chapter examines the successes and the failures of competitive markets and how with such markets the producer is, to use the words of Adam Smith, "led by an invisible hand to promote an end which was no part of his intention."[1] Out of this comes the concept of efficiency, which we define and explain. We look at some of the other benefits of competition and then examine various situations in which competitive markets fail. Finally, we look at the reasons for the failure and explore some of the ways that these problems can be addressed, either through government intervention or by helping the market find its own solutions.

A Question of Relevance...

It is commonly recognized that competition leads to efficiencies and that we all benefit as a result. But these benefits also carry a cost. Canada is one of the richest countries in the world, and yet it has been estimated that over five million Canadians live in poverty. This poverty, as well as the ugliness and deprivation that come with it in the midst of plenty, beauty, and affluence, highlights both the huge success of the market economy and, at the same time, one of its failings. This chapter may better enable you to better understand these issues.

---

[1] Adam Smith, *Wealth of Nations* (Edwin Cannan edition, 1877), p. 354.

We saw, in Chapter 8, how competitive firms react to changes in prices and profitability. Each change causes an adjustment by the firm and by the whole industry as well. This chapter will continue to examine this theme of adjustment and will evaluate the results.

Adam Smith popularized the compelling and (at that time) original idea that an economy, thus a society, functions best if government leaves it alone. The pursuit of self-interest, it seemed to Smith, would lead people, as if directed by an *invisible hand*, to create a harmony of interests. It should be remembered that in Smith's time, interference by governments in the lives of ordinary people was often arbitrary and despotic. Both these points led Smith, along with other writers at the time, to suggest that political and economic interference by the government should be limited. In other words, he advocated the doctrine of **laissez-faire**.

For Smith, political and economic liberties went hand in hand. He argued that people should be free to decide their own economic actions, to work wherever and in whatever firm or location they wish, and to produce, sell, and buy whatever products they desire. He tried to explain that not only was such a doctrine morally correct but, just as importantly for our purposes, that it was also economically sound. An economy works best, he believed, if it is left unplanned, uncoordinated, and undirected. Interference by government is undesirable; if a government tries to direct you to buy certain types of goods that it feels you want, you will probably resent its interest in your welfare. After all, you know better than any government what you want. Such interference is also unnecessary. You certainly do not need any government to persuade you to buy more of a product if it becomes cheaper, you will probably do so anyway. Similarly, entrepreneurs do not need to be told that it is a good idea to open a business in a profitable industry rather than in a declining industry; they already know this. The market works perfectly well, Smith would have suggested, without a manager or a controller or a planning committee to direct it.

Such a doctrine of laissez-faire raises several questions, however. Will the pursuit of self-interest result in the best of all economies? Will it help generate a good society? Might not the result be a society of greedy and selfish individuals who are unconcerned about their neighbours, a society in which one person's gain is at the expense of another? And is it possible that an unplanned economy may result in chaos and anarchy?

The major thrust of this chapter is to look at these questions to see just how effective a perfectly competitive economy (as envisioned by Smith) is, how well it reacts to economic changes, and how desirable the resulting changes are. Thus, what we first need to look at is how changes are accommodated by a perfectly competitive market.

laissez-faire: an economic doctrine asserting that an economy works best with the minimum amount of government intervention.

9.1 HOW COMPETITIVE MARKETS ADJUST TO LONG-RUN CHANGES

LO1 Explain how perfectly competitive markets encourage technological improvement and the growth in the size of firms.

We saw, in the last chapter, how competitive markets adjust to changes, such as an increase or decrease in demand. These are short-run changes. We begin this chapter by looking at how they adjust to long-run changes, such as technological change and the growth in the size of firms.

Technological Improvement and Perfect Competition

If an industry, or an economy, is to grow and prosper, its environment must encourage and stimulate innovation. Let us see how well perfect competition encourages change by looking at how it accommodates the most economically important type of change: technological change.

Suppose that Bobby Brewer discovers an improved brewing method that speeds up the fermentation process by 50 percent so that beer can now be produced more quickly and therefore more cheaply. The result for Bobby will be higher profits. Will the other brewers (assuming there are no patent laws) be inclined to introduce this new process? Some will, and some will not. Regardless of this, as word of the new process spreads, it is likely that a number of new brewers, sensing the prospect of economic profits, will join the industry. The whole industry will start to grow. However, the result of this influx of new brewers is a long-run increase in supply and a resulting decline in price. And what will happen to the older breweries that did not introduce Bobby's new technology? Faced with a fall in the price, they will be forced to introduce it; if not, their accumulating losses will force their exit from the industry. Eventually, only firms that use the new process will survive. Producers in competitive markets are therefore forced to be innovative; if they are not, competition from new, more progressive firms will force them to change or go the way of the dodo.

The Effect of Perfect Competition on the Size of the Firm

In Chapter 8, we observed that in the short run, an increase in demand increases both the price and the profitability of the representative firm. This will stimulate the firm to increase production. If the firm believes that the industry is likely to remain a high-demand and high-profit industry, it will be encouraged to grow in size, especially if this leads to economies of scale. This idea is illustrated in **Figure 9.1**.

If the firm is operating out of plant 1 and the present price is P_1, then the best it can do is break even by producing an output of Q_1. It is not worth trying to produce a higher output than this because the average costs will be higher, and the result will be a loss. If there are economies of scale to be obtained in this industry, however, it will pay the firm to increase the size of its operations in the long run. For instance, if it were to operate out of plant 2, it could now make economic profits because the average costs of production will be lower. In plant 2, profit maximization occurs at an output of Q_2. In time, then, firms will tend to grow in size if there are economies of scale to be enjoyed.

Unfortunately, from the individual firm's point of view, what is true for it will also be true for all firms in this industry: they will all be encouraged to grow in size. The effect on the market would be the same as if new firms entered the industry; that is, the capacity of the industry will expand, which means that market supply increases, and this will result in a reduction in price. The result of this expansion is illustrated in **Figure 9.2**.

FIGURE 9.1   **Long-Run Equilibrium for the Competitive Firm**

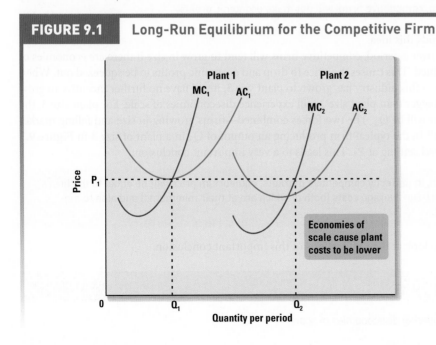

Suppose that a firm is operating out of plant 1 and the present market price is P_1. The profit-maximizing output in this case will be quantity Q_1, where, in fact, the firm is just breaking even. However, if we assume that there are economies of scale to be obtained in this industry, it will pay the firm to move to a bigger plant, such as plant 2, and increase its level of production to Q_2 (where $P = MC$) and thereby earn economic profits.

| **FIGURE 9.2** | **Plant Growth and its Effect on the Market** |

The existence of economies of scale will encourage firms to grow in size. Assume that at present the price is P_1 and the firm is operating out of plant 1 where it is breaking even. In the long run, it will wish to move into a bigger plant, say, plant 2, where it can now enjoy economic profits at Q_2 *if* the price stays the same. However, if all firms do the same, the market supply will increase, causing the price eventually to drop to P_2, where the firm is back again making only normal profits, that is, breaking even.

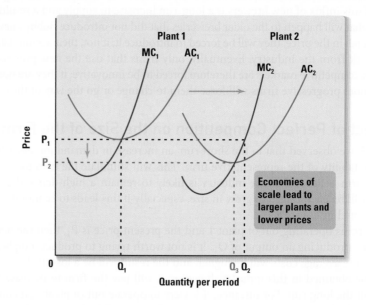

Suppose that the price of the product is initially at P_1 and the average firm's cost curves are shown as AC_1 and MC_1 in **Figure 9.2**. In the short-run, the firm is making only normal profits; that is, it is breaking even. However, higher profits can be made through growth because economies of scale can be obtained. This will cause the representative firm to move into bigger plants, such as plant 2, and since other firms will do the same, the price will drop as the industry supply increases. As this firm and others grow in size, their costs drop—and so does the price. In time, the eventual price of the product will drop to price P_2 in **Figure 9.2**. This is to say:

> In the long run, competitive firms will not make economic profits.

Figure 9.3 extends this idea.

As we saw, over a period, competitive firms will tend to grow in size if there are economies of scale to be obtained. This causes the price to drop and economic profits to be squeezed out. When the typical firm in this industry has grown to plant size 3, it will have no further incentive to grow because plants bigger than plant size 3 will experience diseconomies of scale. For plant size 3, the optimum output will be Q_3. The two forces combined—firms growing in size and falling market price—will result in the typical firm producing an output of Q_3 in a plant of size 3 in **Figure 9.3** and the price level settling at P_3. This leads to a very important conclusion:

> In the long run, in perfectly competitive markets, equilibrium price will be equal to the firm's long- and short-run average costs (both of which are at their minimums) and also to the marginal cost.

We now need to look at the implications of this important conclusion.

 SELF-TEST

1. Exactly why should a firm downsize if it is suffering diseconomies of scale?

| **FIGURE 9.3** | **Price and Long-Run Equilibrium** |

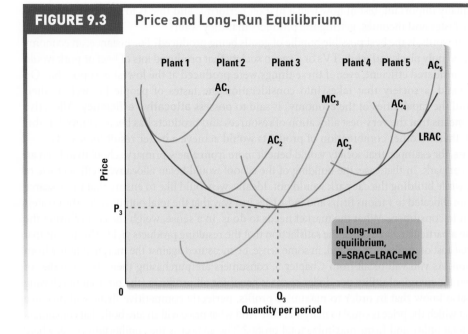

Because of economies of scale, the average firm will increase in size from plant 1 to plant 2 and to plant 3, which is the lowest-cost plant. But as this happens, the price will drop until the firm is making normal profits only at P_3.

9.2 THE BENEFITS OF PERFECT COMPETITION

We have already seen one of the major benefits of perfectly competitive markets: they encourage innovation by offering the reward of short-term economic profits. Conversely, they penalize firms that refuse to innovate by causing them to incur economic losses, which will ultimately force them out of business. Competition is the spur which brings about this result.

In addition to encouraging innovation, perfect competition forces firms to be both productively and allocatively efficient.

LO2 Explain the benefits of perfectly competitive markets.

Productive and Allocative Efficiency

Concentrating on the average costs in **Figure 9.3** for a moment, we can see that in the long run, the firm will produce at the point where price equals short-run average cost and long-run average cost.

This conclusion illustrates the concept of **productive efficiency**. This means that a product is being produced at the lowest possible average cost, that is, in the most efficient plant size and at the most efficient output level for that particular plant size. Furthermore, customers are the main beneficiaries of this because they are paying a price just equal to this lowest possible average cost. This means that the firms are making normal profits only.

productive efficiency: production of an output at the lowest possible average cost.

Productive efficiency is where P = minimum AC.

Productive efficiency is one way in which economists try to evaluate all forms of markets. They ask: does this particular system result in goods and services being produced at their lowest costs, and does the price of the product reflect that cost? You can see from our analysis so far that in the long run a perfectly competitive market easily passes this test.

But producing products at their lowest costs is not much use if nobody wants to buy those products or if customers are buying them only because no alternatives are available. There is a second, equally important, test of how well a market performs, and that is to ask: are consumers, given their tastes and incomes, getting the products that they want?

In other words, is the best possible bundle of goods being produced? For instance, an economy that produced only black and white TVs or a vegan society that produced lots of beef or pork would hardly be considered efficient, even if these things were produced at the lowest cost possible. On the other hand, a society that takes into consideration the tastes of people (as well as their incomes and the capabilities of the economy) is said to possess **allocative efficiency**. Allocative efficiency means that the very best allocation of resources and products has been achieved. If this is the case, then no other combination of products would achieve a better result for society.

Suppose, for example, that society would benefit more from a new primary school than from an additional car park. In that case, the building of the school would be an allocatively efficient use of resources, while building the car park would not. Ideally, we would like to ensure that these scarce resources are allocated to various firms and industries in a way that the total output yields the greatest satisfaction to consumers. What the market needs to do is, in a sense, weigh the cost of using the resources in a particular way against the satisfaction that the resulting products yield. This means that the marginal cost of production should, in some sense, be measured against the marginal utility from consumption. As you will recall from Chapter 5, consumers are purchasing their "best bundle" of goods when the marginal utility per dollar spent is equal for all products (the optimal purchasing rule). We also know that in order to maximize profits, perfectly competitive firms will produce an output at which the price is equal to marginal cost. And what price will ensure both that consumers maximize total utility and firms maximize total profits? The answer is the equilibrium price, where quantity demanded and quantity supplied are equal. Allocative efficiency implies, then, not only the maximization of consumers' utility but also the maximization of producers' profits. And it also means:

Allocative efficiency occurs where P = MC.

In short, allocative efficiency balances the tastes and incomes of consumers against the availability of the economy's resources.

What perfectly competitive markets do is adjust production and consumption among different products until no further gain could accrue to either producers or consumers from any other combination of goods. This is the essence of productive and allocative efficiency and is a major characteristic of perfectly competitive markets. **Figure 9.4** illustrates this outcome.

Figure 9.4A shows that in a perfectly competitive environment the typical firm produces an output where both short-run and long-run costs are at a minimum and price equals marginal costs. The summation of each firm's marginal cost curve gives us the market supply curve in **Figure 9.4B**. When we add the market demand curve, we get the equilibrium price of $3 and an equilibrium quantity of 3000 as determined by the interaction of supply and demand.

The dark shaded triangle in **Figure 9.4B** above the price line but below the demand curve represents consumer surplus, as we discussed in Chapter 5. It is the difference between what consumers are willing to pay and actual price of the product. In a very similar sense, the light shaded triangle represents **producer surplus**, since producers received a price for each unit supplied, up until the very last one, which exceeds the amount that they would be willing to accept. Therefore, another way of thinking of productive and allocative efficiency is to realize that it means that consumer and producer surplus has been maximized. The addition of consumer and producer surplus gives us what economists call **economic surplus**.

In summary, we can say that in the long run perfectly competitive markets produce an output of goods:

- from the most efficient plant size for their industry (lowest LRAC)
- at the most efficient output level for that particular plant size (lowest SRAC)

The significance of this is that both productive and allocative efficiencies have been achieved and economic surplus has been maximized.

allocative efficiency: the allocation of scarce productive resources toward the production of goods and services that society values most.

producer surplus: the difference between the amount that producers would be willing to accept for each unit of output and the price they receive when the output is sold.

economic surplus: the summation of consumer surplus and producer surplus.

| FIGURE 9.4 | Producer and Consumer Surplus in Long-Run Equilibrium |

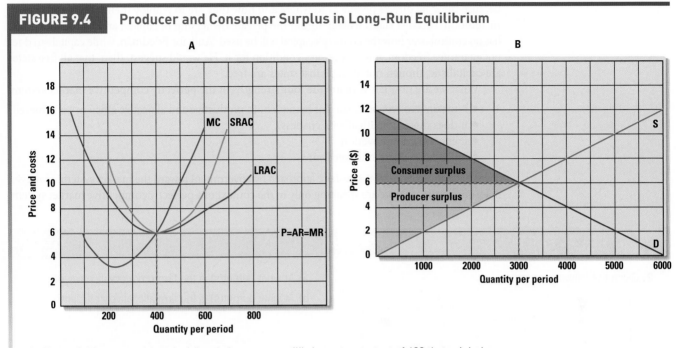

In Figure 9.4A, we see the typical firm in long-run equilibrium at an output of 400 that minimizes both short-run and long-run average costs and P = MC = $6. In Figure 9.4B, we see the market outcome after summing up the marginal cost curves of each firm to get the market supply curve and adding the market demand curve. The market equilibrium price is $6, and quantity is 3000.

Other Benefits of Competitive Markets

Productive efficiency and allocative efficiency are the two main standards by which economists try to evaluate markets, but they are not the only benefits that result from competition. As we have previously mentioned, another advantage that the market system (whether competitive or not) has over a planned economy is that markets are a collection of the interaction of millions of producer and consumer decisions happening all at once. There is no one coordinating them and no government organization framing them. That is, the system is automatic and is free of expensive administrative costs. In this sense, the system is costless.

We also need to add the intuitive argument that perfect competition encourages innovation. It is not hard to imagine active, energetic business people who continuously try to break out of the market constraints of normal profits by introducing innovative, cost-cutting techniques (shifting both the MC and the AC curves down). In a competitive market, such an advantage will not last long, however, since competitors will eventually imitate the innovation—sometimes rather quickly.

A final benefit of the market system is one that is definitely open to debate. Many people would suggest that any idea of freedom is meaningless unless people are guaranteed economic freedom. A quote from Adam Smith will help give meaning to the term *economic freedom*.

> Every man, as long as he does not violate the laws of justice, is left perfectly free to pursue his own interest in his own way, and to bring both his own industry and his own capital into competition with those of any other man, or order of men.[2]

This theme has been taken up in modern days by, among many others, Milton Friedman, the Nobel Prize–winning economist. Friedman argues that freedom is impossible in a socialist state

[2] Ibid., p. 651.

because the state directs people as to where and how they are to employ their labour and capital. In addition, socialist states usually forbid the private ownership of capital, and so the individual has no control over how the country's capital will be used. And, for Friedman, while capitalism does not guarantee freedom, it is a necessary condition for it. He would suggest, then, that all free states are capitalistic, though not all capitalist states are free.

What we are now left with are the four strengths of the perfectly competitive market system:

- it maximizes economic surplus because both productive and allocative efficiency is achieved.
- it does this automatically (is costless).
- it encourages innovation.
- it promotes economic freedom.

This is the case for a laissize-faire approach by government toward the market system. However, note, once again, that we are speaking only in the context of a perfectly competitive market system.

✓ SELF-TEST

2. Given the following graph:

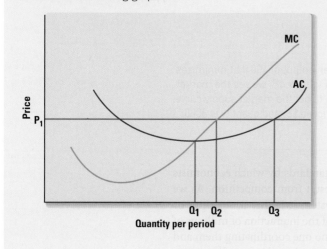

Quantity per period

a) At what output(s) is the firm productively efficient?

b) At what output(s) is the firm allocatively efficient?

9.3 MARKET FAILURES

L03 Understand the five reasons why perfect competition might fail to achieve desirable results.

market failures: the defects in competitive markets that prevent them from achieving an efficient or equitable allocation of resources.

Despite the advantages of the market system, it has been criticized over the years on many grounds. The remainder of the chapter will examine some of these criticisms, called **market failures**. We will look at five types of market failures.

First, it is said that the market is no guarantor of fairness, and *income and wealth inequalities* often seem endemic to competitive markets. Second, *competitive markets are often unstable* and periodically seem to move, without warning, from an expansionary boom to a recessionary slump. Third, competitive markets seem to contain the seeds of their own destruction because they easily admit *forces that work to destroy competition*. Fourth, competitive markets do not ensure the production of a number of important goods and services known as public goods. Finally, competitive markets often encourage the overproduction of some products and the underproduction of other products because the market has difficulty in integrating what are known as *externalities*.

We will look at each of these criticisms in turn and try to understand why many observers think that governments have an important role in correcting some of these deficiencies.

Income and Wealth Inequalities

When evaluating a particular economic system, the question of fairness is particularly pertinent. Critics of competitive markets point out that allocative efficiency, while desirable in some ways, does not guarantee fairness. Allocative efficiency means that resources are allocated in the most efficient manner, *given the tastes and income distribution of the people of that society*.

However, the competitive market system expresses no concern about what that income distribution actually is. In other words, if the income distribution were to change in ways that most consider undesirable, the competitive market system would automatically adjust the allocation of resources so as to make the new allocation also efficient. Even a society that has a vast number of poor people and a very few very rich people could have an economy that was allocatively efficient. In short, competition is blind to the fate of its participants.

For most people, an important aspect of fairness is that the rewards are commensurate with the amount of effort expended. In many respects, competitive markets do reward greater effort with greater incomes. However, the competitive market system does not always guarantee that this will be so. In particular, many people earn great rewards without putting forth any effort because they are owners of resources. Resource ownership is not evenly distributed in competitive societies and is handed down from generation to generation. The result is that the incomes that flow from this wealth are sometimes the result of parentage rather than effort. In short, competitive markets may perpetuate existing inequalities.

Most populations include people with no marketable resources and who, without government intervention, would be left destitute by the competitive market. This is the case when people do not have even their own labour to sell, perhaps because they are mentally ill or physically infirm, are too young or too old, or must look after family members full time. The perfectly competitive market would normally fail to provide such people with any income at all. The result may be a distinctly skewed distribution of incomes and wealth, causing a big disparity between the earnings of the very rich and the very poor.

In fact, this has been happening in Canada to a lesser degree over the years. Twenty years ago the top 20 percent of income earners received 43 percent of total after-tax income; the figure has now risen to 47 percent.

One graphic way of showing the wide disparity between the rich and poor in Canada is using the metaphor of the *parade of the giants*, first described by the Dutch economist Jan Penn. Suppose everybody in Canada were to march past you in a two-hour parade with the marchers organized in terms of income, the poorest going first and the richest last. Now, suppose the heights of the people are proportional to their income, those with twice the average income being twice the height of the average. What would the parade look like? Well, it is easy to imagine a parade where the people get steadily taller. But that would miss out some of the important details. In fact, the parade of giants would be more like a parade of dwarfs.

At first, you would have great difficulty peering down at the people as they would be just a few inches in height—old people, youngsters, and welfare recipients. After 15 minutes, the height of the dwarfs is still less than 10 inches. Next come the lower-skilled members of the labour force—manual and retail workers—all of them below waist height. In fact, it would take over 50 minutes for them all to pass, there are so many of them. Halfway through the two-hour parade, you would expect to be looking people in the eye—people of average height should be in the middle. But that is not so. In fact, it is only in the last 40 minutes or so that you encounter people of your own height. After that, heights begin to surge with the arrival of doctors, lawyers, and senior civil servants, 20 feet tall and more.

The real excitement, though, only begins in the last few minutes as the bankers, stockbrokers, and successful corporate executives arrive, peering down from 50, 100, 500 feet above you. Only in the last seconds do you get a fleeting glimpse of the pop stars, movie stars, and the super-rich—at least you can see parts of them: their heads are way up in the sky, a mile above you. The last person in the parade is Jim Balsillie of Research in Motion who earned a whopping $54 million in 2007, putting him almost in orbit at nearly two miles above the parade.

ADDED DIMENSION   The Rich and the Poor

The are a number of ways to measure income inequality. One is the GINI index. This index measures the difference between how a country's income is distributed compared with a base that assumes perfectly equal distribution and would, therefore, have a zero coefficient. Using this method, the country with the most even income distribution is Denmark with a coefficient of 24.7. Others with relatively equal distributions include Japan (24.9), Sweden (25) and Germany (28.3). Countries with less equal distributions (higher coefficients) are the United States (40.8), China (46.9), and Brazil (57). Namibia (74.3) has the most unequal distribution.

Country	Gini Coefficient	Country	Gini Coefficient
Denmark	24.7	Italy	36.0
Japan	24.9	India	36.8
Sweden	25.0	Russia	39.9
Czech Republic	25.4	USA	40.8
Germany	28.3	Iran	43.0
Canada	32.6	China	46.9
France	32.7	Argentina	51.3
Ireland	34.3	Brazil	57.0
Spain	34.7	Bolivia	60.1
Australia	35.2	Namibia	74.3

Source: International Bank for Reconstruction and Development/The World Bank: *World Development Indicators*, 2007.

Another way of looking at income distribution within a country is to measure the percentage of income received by the highest 10% in income earners. Here are some examples.

Country	% of total income	Country	% of total income
Denmark	21%	USA	30%
Sweden	22%	China	31%
Japan	22%	India	31%
Germany	23%	Russia	34%
Norway	25%	Kenya	38%
Canada	25%	Mexico	41%
Australia	25%	Chile	43%
France	25%	Brazil	43%
Italy	27%	Rwanda	44%
UK	29%	S. Africa	58%

Richest 10% by Country: World Development Indicators, World Bank 2011

Denmark and Sweden's income distribution are the most equal in the world and as you can see, Canada's income distribution is more equal than that in most countries of the world.

In summary:

The fair distribution of income is an issue that the market simply does not address.

Instability of Competitive Markets

Since the dawn of the industrial age, observers have noticed that competitive economies do not grow at a steady pace despite a general upward trend in production and incomes. Instead, they seem to be prone to business cycles of booms and slumps. A period of rapid economic growth and full employment eventually comes to an end, followed by a period of low or even negative growth and high unemployment. In other words, recessions seem endemic to the market system. Such fluctuations are unpredictable and not fully understood. They can, and often do, cause great distress for some, and for this reason governments generally need to intervene in the economy to minimize these fluctuations. Such intervention has often been criticized, but the truth remains that the competitive market by itself fails to prevent such harmful booms and recessions. Since the attempts of government policy to manage the economy make up a large part of the subject of *macro*economics, we will not pursue this idea any further here.

The Forces of Uncompetition

As we saw in Chapter 8, the market system encompasses the idea that producers and consumers are free to buy and sell whatever they wish, whenever and wherever they choose. Laissez-faire implies freedom from government constraint. But the troubling thought for many observers is this: does this freedom mean that firms can choose NOT to compete with each other? Adam Smith was always wary of business people:

> "People of the same trade seldom meet together, even for merriment and diversion, but the conversation ends in a conspiracy against the public, or in some contrivance to raise prices."[3]

However, having raised the possibility that firms might collude, he quickly dismissed the idea. He believed that should a number of firms collude or one big firm try to dominate an industry, it would lead to profitable opportunities for those firms that refused to collude. They could simply undercut the prices of the big firms.

But Smith ignored the fact that big firms have an advantage over smaller firms. They can achieve economies of scale and can, therefore, operate at lower costs; thus, they can undercut the prices of small firms and drive them out of business. Once this is done, the competitive market ceases to exist.

In the automobile, oil refining, and hydroelectric industries, for instance, the benefits from economies of scale can be enormous. The twentieth century saw a tremendous increase in the number of very big firms, and many industries today are dominated by a few giant companies. All of this forces us to conclude that the *ideal* of a perfectly competitive market may not be possible, given the dynamics of the *actual* market, and therefore may not produce the benefits that we have looked at. An important consequence when the forces of imperfect competition take hold in the economy is that the size of the economic surplus—made up of consumer and producer surplus—will decline as prices of goods rise and quantities produced fall. We will have more to say about this in Chapter 10.

 ADDED DIMENSION   The Theory of Second Best

In the 1950s, Canadian economist, Richard Lipsey raised a serious challenge to idea that competition in the marketplace actually yields the impressive benefits that the model implies. The restricted assumptions that underlie the perfectly competitive market model—the absence of market power for large firms to influence prices, no uncertainty about the future and perfect information—are obvious. Nonetheless, some of the many proponents of laissize-faire capitalism argue that even though perfect competition is always an abstraction and never a reality, the closer we can move markets towards the state of perfect competition, the better off we will all be. They are saying that any increase in the level of competition within a particular market is an improvement and the social benefits of such a movement are always positive.

Lipsey successfully discredited this view and we can borrow an analogy from Joseph Heath to illustrate how. Imagine that you really want to go to Hawaii for a winter holiday but you have a fixed budget that you must adhere to. You check with your travel agent about prices only to discover that you simply cannot afford to go to Hawaii. You then begin to think about an alternative destination and discover that your budget will allow you to go to

Las Vegas for a few days. Las Vegas is only one half as desirable as Hawaii but you simply cannot afford Hawaii, and so you settle for the second best alternative.

Then, out of the blue, your agent calls back to say that she has found a package that will fly you 90 percent of the way to Hawaii for a price within your budget. In the abstract, 90 percent of your first choice is preferable to the second best alternative, which is only one half as desirable. But—and this is the big but—90 percent of the way to Hawaii is nonsense. You would spend the holiday in the ocean somewhere!

The point of this analogy is that while the proponents of free market capitalism admit that perfect competition is not possible, they continue to argue that any move toward getting the economy closer to fulfilling the conditions of perfect competition is an improvement. Lipsey says, not necessarily so. An example here would be the opening up of the North American market to free trade in automobiles in the 1970s. This was a move toward a more competitive economy. Whether it made the two North American societies better places in which to live is an open debate.

---

[3] Ibid., p. 129.

Provision of Public Goods

Many goods and services consumed in Canada are provided by government. Some of these products could just as easily be provided by the private market. In many other countries, they are. So, why do governments, in general, feel that they should be responsible for providing *any* goods and services, especially when doing so requires the imposition of taxes? In a sense, the provision of public goods is a retreat from the idea of personal freedom because it means, for instance, that you and I do not have complete freedom to choose what we want to buy or not buy.

Nonetheless, there are a number of compelling reasons that throughout history, governments have felt it desirable to provide certain products. The most obvious case is the one in which private firms would simply not provide them because they would not be able to make a profit doing so. To understand why, we need to look in more detail at what exactly economists mean by a public good (some economists prefer the term collective goods).

Strictly defined, **public goods** have two features that distinguish them from **private goods**. First, all public goods are **nonrival goods**. For example, my watching a popular TV show every week does not in any way prevent you from enjoying the same show: the quality of the broadcast signal remains the same no matter how many people are watching it at the same time. With a private good, the situation is very different. If, for example, you help yourself to a can of beer (a private good) from my fridge during a commercial, there is one less can of beer available to me. Other examples of public goods that are nonrival are knowledge and fresh air. If I acquire more knowledge of a subject or breathe more deeply, it does not diminish the amount of those valuable resources available to others. As far as a government-provided service is concerned, military defence is also an example of a nonrival good, since the fact that I am defended does not reduce the amount by which you are defended.

The second feature of all public goods is that they are **non-excludable**. A classic example of a good which is non-excludable is a lighthouse. Imagine a small fishing village where the fishers are often coming to grief because of the hidden presence of a reef just offshore. Someone, quite rightly, decides that the construction of a lighthouse would provide sufficient warning. A lighthouse company constructs the needed lighthouse and charges a fee to all the fishers who are going to use its services. But you can easily see that in this situation, there will be no need for individual fishers to pay such a fee because it will be very difficult for the lighthouse company to exclude nonsubscribers from looking at the lighthouse. That being so, the lighthouse company will soon go out of business, and the only way that a future lighthouse could be built is by government financing it out of tax revenues (or through voluntary contributions).

public goods: goods or services whose benefits are not affected by the number of users and from which no one can be excluded.

private goods: goods or services whose benefits can be denied to nonbuyers and whose consumption by one person reduces the amount available for others.

nonrival goods: one person's consumption does not reduce the amount available for others.

non-excludable: a feature of certain goods that means that it is impossible (or extremely costly) to prevent nonbuyers from enjoying the benefits.

Another example of a non-excludable good is policing. If the amount of crime in a town is reduced because of efficient policing, all citizens of the town will benefit. To sell policing as a private good would be very difficult because it would be impossible to prevent those people who were not prepared to pay for the services from receiving a benefit. (This is often referred to as the "free rider" problem.)

Many products are both nonrival and non-excludable, including lighthouses, military defence, and policing, as well as snow-removal from highways, swamp-clearance, and the provision of laws and the court system. As a result, these are truly public goods and must be provided by governments, since the market system would be unable to provide them. But lest you should think that all products that are nonrival are also non-excludable, think, for instance, of cable television or an art gallery. In both these cases, it is certainly possible to prevent nonsubscribers from enjoying these services (thus they are excludable), but in each case, the addition of one more user does not really affect the provision of services to others (thus they are nonrival). It is also possible for something to be rival but non-excludable: for example, fisheries on the high seas are definitely rival (over-fishing will certainly deplete the fish stock), but it is almost impossible to exclude fishing vessels from the high seas. In short:

A lighthouse is a public good.

Perry Mastrovito/Creatas/PictureQuest

A public good is one that is both nonrival and non-excludable.

Quasi-Public Goods

It is true to say that public goods must be provided by government, but that does not mean that all goods actually provided by government are public goods—some, in fact, are private goods! For example, education is not a public good. Indeed, most countries have a private-school sector, since it is easy to exclude nonsubscribers. The same is true of private health services (treatment by doctors and hospitals), postal delivery, and the provision of social infrastructure, such as highways and harbours. All of these services could be produced by the private sector but are often provided by government. Such goods do not meet the strict definition of a public good. Thus, if they are provided by government, they are known as **quasi-public goods** (they "look like" public goods). There are three main reasons why governments decide to provide these quasi-public goods.

> **quasi-public goods:** private goods that are provided by government because they involve extensive benefits for the general public.

First, in some cases, the costs (to the firm and to consumers) of collecting revenues in a private market might be prohibitive. This is the case with urban roadways, for example. Although a toll charge could be imposed on major highways, it would be expensive to install toll booths (or some other collection device) on all urban and suburban streets or on little-used country roads. To prevent this possibility, the provision and maintenance of roads is usually financed through taxation. Or consider the case of Canada's health care system. If one accepts the validity of universal health care coverage then Canada's single-payer system has proven itself to be very efficient. This statement is supported by the fact that the administration costs of health care expenditures in the United States is 7.5 percent compared with only 2.5 percent in Canada.

A second reason for the provision of quasi-public goods by government is a situation in which competition is inefficient because it would involve wasteful duplication. This is particularly true when large economies of scale are involved. Rather than allow a number of competing electricity distribution and public transportation systems, for instance, a government might take sole responsibility for providing such services.

In 1998, HMCS Ojibwa, one of Canada's three Oberon-class submarines, ceased sea-going operations and was eventually decommissioned. Canada acquired four modern Upholder-class submarines from Britain to replace the Oberons.

The final, and probably the most important, reason governments provide health and education services is that these quasi-public goods are important not only to the people who currently use the services but to society as a whole. These services involve what are known as external costs and benefits, a subject to which we now turn.

Externalities

The fifth failure of the competitive market is its inability to take into account the costs and benefits not just to producers and consumers of products but to the rest of society as well. The true social costs of any product include the private costs of production as well as the **external costs**. Similarly, the social benefits include both the private benefits enjoyed by the users of the product as well as the **external benefits** enjoyed by others. The production of most products involve a certain amount of these **externalities**, but with some products the externalities are so great that by ignoring them, the market totally distorts the prices and quantities produced. Let us look at some examples of externalities and see why they arise.

> **external costs:** costs that are incurred by people other than the producers or consumers of a product.
>
> **external benefits:** benefits that are enjoyed by people other than the producers or consumers of a product.

Examples of Externalities

When you pay for a product, it is usually assumed that you are paying for the full costs of producing that product. Often, however, this is not the case. Suppose that fishers cast their nets and earn their livelihoods downstream from a pulp mill. What is to prevent the mill from maximizing its profits by discharging its effluent by the cheapest method possible—by simply dumping it into a nearby river? This has enormous implications for the fishers (not to mention the fish).

> **externalities:** benefits or costs of a product experienced by people who neither produce nor consume that product.

Photodisc/Getty Images

Air pollution from a pulp and paper mill is just one of many examples of external costs.

There are any number of examples of external costs besides the obvious ones of water and air pollution. Noise pollution is experienced by anyone living near a major airport or near the lines of an urban railroad. Aesthetic pollution is suffered by anyone whose scenic views from home or office are suddenly destroyed by a new monster house or skyscraper. It is now acknowledged that these external costs to society are as important as the private costs of production.

And it is not just with *production* that external costs occur. The *consumption* of products can also impose external costs on others. For example, we are all aware these days of the harmful effects of cigarette smoking, not just to smokers but also to those forced to breathe second-hand smoke. Similarly, the consumption of alcohol combined with driving can also impose great harm on others. The competitive market, however, does not include these additional costs in the overall costs of production. The result of this is that the prices of many products are *lower* than they would otherwise be and the quantity demanded is higher, and thus, too much of certain products are being produced. In a sense, then, producers and consumers of these polluting products are enjoying a benefit partly at the cost of other members of society.

It is true that the production and consumption of certain products cause external costs, but there are many cases where the production and consumption of other products may well lead to external benefits. For instance, if I spend money on having my front yard landscaped, I enjoy the benefits of greater aesthetic enjoyment and an increase in the value of my property. And my neighbours would also enjoy an increase in property values—they also receive an external benefit. However, this is usually a "free" benefit, unless I go from door to door asking for contribution. Not a good idea—at least not in my neighbourhood!

Another example of an external benefit would be the symbiotic relationship between an orange orchard and a neighbouring honey farm. The production of oranges produces a clear external benefit for the honey farm, since the bees have a ready source of nectar. But the orange orchard also derives an external benefit from the convenient proximity of the honey farm; by pollinating the orange blossoms, the bees help in the production of oranges. However, it is more usual that the consumption of goods gives rise to external benefits. For instance, it is clear that if you were given a flu vaccine you would derive a benefit, but it also helps others because their chance of contracting the illness from you is reduced. We all derive enormous external benefits when our fellow citizens are healthy and well educated.

We can now summarize the five types of market failures:

- The market creates gross inequalities of income and wealth.
- A market economy may be quite unstable.
- Competition, the market's internal regulator, may disappear.
- The market provides no public goods.
- The market ignores externalities.

SELF-TEST

3. Which of the following goods are nonrival, and which are non-excludable?

a) art galleries

b) high-seas fisheries

c) national defence

d) a seat in a movie theatre

e) highways

Are any of these *both* nonrival and non-excludable?

ADDED DIMENSION   Canada and the Kyoto Accord

The Kyoto Accord is the first binding agreement among nations to control greenhouse gases (GHG). The six gases—carbon dioxide, methane, nitrous oxide, sulphur hexafluoride, hydrofluorocarbons, and perfluorocarbons—that are created mainly by human activity comprise only 1 percent of gases in the atmosphere, yet are the main culprits in causing global warming. The Accord was ratified in February 2005 by 141 countries, including every major industrial nation, except for the United States (the world's biggest emitter of GHG), Australia (since signed on to the accord), and Monaco. Its objective was to reduce GHG emissions by roughly 5 percent (the exact figure varied from country to country) below 1990 levels between 2008 and 2012. The Accord does not specify how countries are to meet their targets; this is left up to the countries themselves. Canada ratified the agreement in December 2002, agreeing to reduce its emissions to 6 percent below its 1990 levels.

Developing nations were exempt from emission reduction targets until the next phase of Kyoto on the grounds that it is the industrialized nations that have released massive amounts of GHGs over the last 100 years. In addition, the industrialized nations have already developed technologies to reduce GHG emissions that are not widely available to developing nations. The result of their exclusion means that China and India, two of the world's fastest growing polluters, were exempted from these

reductions. They do not have to start making emission cuts until after 2012.

And just how well are countries doing? Well, the results are something of a mixed bag. In readiness for UN climate change talks in Bali in November 2007, the organizing committee published the latest data on GHG emission changes from 1990 to 2002. Some countries have made impressive progress: Latvia's reduction was 59 percent, the Russian Federation 29 percent, Germany 18 percent, and the U.K. 15 percent.

Others have actually increased their emissions appreciably: Turkey by 74 percent, Spain by 53 percent, Australia by 26 percent, and the United States by 16 percent. And Canada? Its GHG emissions in 1990 were 596 million tonnes; with a target reduction of 5 percent, it was aiming to reduce the figure to 563 million tonnes. By 2005, its emissions totalled 747 million tonnes, meaning that, with three years to go, it was already 33 percent above its target. By the end of the first commitment period of the Kyoto Protocol in 2012, a new international framework needs to have been negotiated and ratified that can deliver the stringent emission reductions that are clearly needed according to mainstream scientific thinking.

Exactly who are the worst offenders in terms of GHG? The following tables show the total emissions as of 2005:

Top Ten Polluters		Top Ten Polluters per Capita	
Country	Tonnes of Emissions (in thousands)	Country	Tonnes of Emissions Per Person
USA	7241	Australia	26.3
China	4057	USA	25.1
Russian Federation	2132	Canada	24.1
Japan	1360	Estonia	20.9
India	1214	Ireland	17.5
Germany	1001	Russian Federation	14.8
Canada	747	Czech Republic	14.6
UK	657	Belgium	14.4
Italy	580	Finland	13.8
France	558	France	13.8
		China	3.2
		India	1.2

Source: United Nations Framework Convention on Climate Change, UNFCCC /SB1/2007/30.

9.4 DEALING WITH EXTERNAL COSTS

L04 Understand how governments try to deal with external costs, such as pollution.

It is clear that, as social animals, each of us affects other people—for good or for ill. But trying to address each and every externality would be impossible as well as a little foolish. However, action often needs to be taken in cases where the externality is of particular importance. The difficult task for policymakers is to estimate the value of the externality and then attempt to integrate this into the production process—what economists term *integrating external costs*. As far as external costs are concerned, the major methods are:

- legislative controls
- taxation
- cap and trade

And among a number of methods, two ways of integrating external benefits are:

- provision of quasi-public goods
- subsidies

Let us look at each of these methods in turn.

Legislative Controls to Limit Pollution

Legislative control is one method of curtailing the production of pollutants. For instance, government could decree quotas on the levels of production or on the level of pollutants; or it could set up pollution emission standards, and fine or prosecute offending producers who exceed the limits; or it might decree that certain types of anti-pollution devices be installed at the polluters' expense.

Each of these methods has been tried, with varying degrees of success. However, the offences are sometimes difficult to detect, prove, or successfully prosecute. There are many examples of attempts to enforce pollution control regulations that end up in long courtroom battles that give law firms more business but do not help the environment much at all. Furthermore, a serious drawback to legislative controls is the fact that there is no incentive for producers to go beyond the minimum standard and reduce the level of their pollution further.

In Canada, the protection of health and the environment is covered by the 1999 *Canadian Environmental Protection Act* (CEPA) which comprises a set of regulations, including laws concerning ocean dumping, waste reduction, the reduction of acid rain, the production of fuels, the protection of the ozone layer, and the control of toxic chemicals. These laws and other provincial and municipal regulations protect individuals and the environment from banned substances, including PCBs, asbestos, mercury, and DDT; restrict such things as the use of wood stoves and leaded gasoline, and outdoor burning of garden waste; and require emission controls on cars.

Besides regulations, however, there are other economic methods a government can use to reduce pollution.

Taxation to Limit Pollution

A second method of integrating the costs of pollution into the overall cost of production (and price) is by *imposing taxes on the polluter*. This could be done by way of an excise tax, or general "pollution tax," that varies with the amount of production. Suppose that the marginal costs of production in a particular industry are as shown in **Figure 9.5**. If you recall, this is the same as the firm's supply curve. However, we have relabelled it here as the **marginal private cost**, or MPC, curve to reflect the fact that these are the internal costs incurred by the private producer of the product.

But these are not the only costs associated with producing this product; this industry imposes serious costs on the rest of society in the form of air and water pollution. We call these additional societal costs *external costs*. Suppose that we were able to measure these extra costs and estimated that they were equal to a per-unit amount of external cost, as shown in **Figure 9.5**.

marginal private cost: the extra internal (or private) cost to the producer of increasing production by one additional unit.

FIGURE 9.5	Marginal Private Costs and Marginal Social Costs

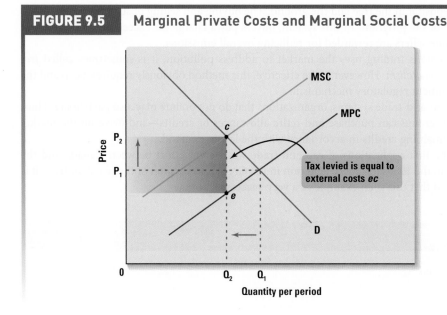

The MPC curve shows the marginal private costs of production. Given the demand for the product D, the market price is P_1 and quantity is Q_1. Adding the external costs equal to ce gives us the curve labelled marginal social costs (MSC). If government imposes a pollution tax of ec, then the new supply curve would be synonymous with the MSC curve, and the new price would be P_2 and the new quantity Q_2.

If we add both the marginal private costs *and* the external costs, *ec*, then the total costs to society are represented by the higher curve labelled *MSC*, or **marginal social costs**. These are the true costs of production—the direct production costs and the costs of the associated pollution. If the firms do not have to worry about these external costs, the resulting price, P_1, is too low and the production level, Q_1, is too high from society's point of view. One way to force producers to recognize these costs would be to impose an excise tax equal to the external costs, *ec*.

The effect of the tax will be to increase the price from P_1 to P_2 and reduce production from Q_1 to Q_2. Just how much the price increases or the output decreases will depend on the elasticities of demand and supply. This, in turn, will determine how much of the tax is paid by consumers of this product in the form of higher prices and how much is absorbed by producers in the form of lower profits. However the tax is split, those people most directly involved with the product are being forced to pay the true cost. In addition, government will be deriving a tax revenue equal to the rectangular shaded area, which it could use to clean up some of the effects of pollution or help those suffering as a result of pollution.

marginal social costs: the additional costs to both the producer (internal costs) and society (external costs) of producing additional units of a product.

Cap and Trade

There is a third way society might choose to deal with the problem of pollution and green house gases. It is called the "cap and trade system" and is designed to provide economic incentives for achieving reductions in pollution. The overall goal of the cap and trade approach is to minimize the cost of meeting a predetermined emissions target called the *cap*. It is usually envisioned that this cap would start off near the current level of admissions and then be lowered from one year to the next. Thus, over time, total emissions would be reduced.

A governmental body sets the *cap* on the total amount of a pollutant, say carbon emissions, that can be released into the atmosphere. Individual companies would then be allocated their share of this total such that the sum of allowances does not exceed the cap. Companies that want to increase their actual emissions, perhaps to increase production, must buy additional carbon credits from one of two sources. The first source is other firms that have reduced their emissions below their allocated amount through the installation of less-polluting equipment. The second source is companies that produce carbon credits directly by, for example, creating plantations of purpose-grown trees or grasses. These vast plantations, in effect, pull carbon out of the atmosphere and deposit it in the tree and the ground. The buying and selling of such carbon credits is the *trade* part of the program. In this system, buyers pay a charge for exceeding their pollution allowance, while sellers are rewarded for reducing overall emissions.

Since emissions trading uses the market to address pollution, it is sometimes called *free market environmentalism*. However, to be effective, this method obviously requires a cap and the cap is a government regulatory mechanism.

In some cap-and-trade systems, organizations that do not pollute may also participate. Thus, environmental groups can purchase and retire allowances or credits—and drive up the market price of the remaining credits in accordance with the law of demand.

One of the first applications of cap and trade was a joint effort between Canada and the United States in the 1980s to reduce acid rain in the Great Lakes region of the two countries. It is widely accepted that this is an example of a very successful policy.

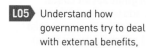

SELF-TEST

4. What are three ways to integrate external costs?

L05 Understand how governments try to deal with external benefits, such as education.

9.5 INTEGRATING EXTERNAL BENEFITS

Government has a number of methods to encourage the production of goods and services that provide a lot of external benefits. Two of the more popular are for government to provide the product directly, or for government to subsidize private production, thereby encouraging private firms to produce more.

The Provision of Quasi-Public Goods

It would be wrong to suggest that the prime reason most governments provide public education and public medical care is that they recognize the extent of external benefits. The truth is that in many cases, people over the centuries have demanded and even fought for access to the basic "right" to free public education and medical care. Such services have usually been regarded as necessities, more so than, say, food, housing, or clothing. The interesting result of this political process is that, to a certain extent, how well a person is dressed, fed, or accommodated is usually regarded as a matter of private concern, whereas the health and education of people are regarded as being of public concern.

Many governments responded to these demands after World War II and dramatically increased the provision of government services and products. As the public sector increased appreciably, it often extended access from what was considered basic coverage. Public education began to include postsecondary education; health service coverage was extended to dental, chiropractic, and psychiatric medicine; transportation began to include not only the building and maintenance of highways and harbours but also the provision of airports; communication started to include not just postal services but also telephone, radio, and television services.

In addition to this, in many countries, a number of other industries, including the hydroelectric and mining industries, were nationalized; in other countries, governments started competing with private industry in the provision of gasoline, concert theatres, and racetracks. This massive proliferation in public services led to a public outcry in the 1980s, and the movement back toward "privatization" began. The balance these days between the provision of public and private goods varies considerably from country to country, and is in a state of flux as countries search for the ideal mixture.

Providing Subsidies

The direct provision of goods and services is not the only way that government can encourage more production of certain products; it can also offer subsidies to private firms. A subsidy is merely a reverse tax, in which government pays the producer a certain amount for each unit produced.

As an example, suppose that government is convinced that the provision of day-care services involves not only benefits for the children and parents who use them but also external benefits to the rest of society. Our conventional demand curve has been relabelled as the **marginal private benefits**, or MPB, curve. A demand curve represents how much of a product people are willing and able to purchase at different prices. But it also reflects the value that people place on a product. **Figure 9.6** shows, for instance, that 50 000 parents would be willing to place their children in day care at a monthly fee of $500. It also suggests that 50 000 parents feel that a place in the day care is worth at least $500 to them; that is, they would each receive a private benefit equivalent to at least $500. Let us say that in addition, it has been determined that there are external benefits to day-care places that equal an amount *eb* for each child. The total benefits, both private and external, are shown as the higher curve labelled MSB, or **marginal social benefits**.

MPC, the supply curve, represents the marginal private costs. If both external and private benefits are considered, giving us the marginal social benefits curve, we have the equilibrium price of $550 and quantity of 60 000 day-care places. On the other hand, if only private benefits are taken into consideration, the result is a lower equilibrium price and lower number of places—50 000 and $500, respectively. Thus, ignoring social benefits results in both a quantity and a price that are lower than the socially desirable levels.

One way to encourage the provision of more day-care spaces would be to subsidize them. But should the subsidy be given to parents or to the day-care centres? Does it make any difference who receives it? Suppose government wants to increase the number of day-care spaces from 50 000 to 60 000 per our last example and decides to give a subsidy to day-care operators that will induce them to build extensions to their premises and employ additional staff. Let us say the amount of the subsidy comes to $100 per child per month. The introduction of such a subsidy would be represented graphically by a rightward shift in the supply (or MPC) curve, to the MPC + subsidy (curve), as shown in **Figure 9.7**. This would have the desired effect of increasing the number of spaces to 60 000.

marginal private benefits: the extra benefits that the buyer derives from consuming additional quantities of a product.

marginal social benefits: the extra benefits to both the consumer (internal benefits) and to society (external benefits) of additional quantities of a product.

FIGURE 9.6   **Marginal Private Benefits and Marginal Social Benefits**

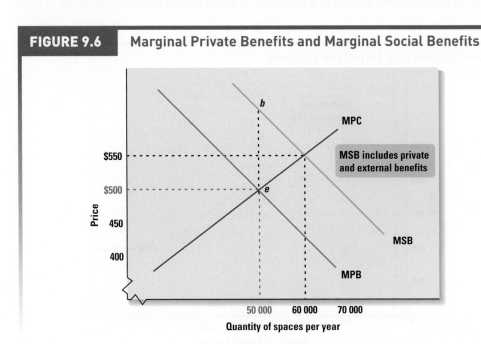

The demand curve for a product, MPB, shows the benefits users derive from it. The amount of benefits that nonusers enjoy is shown as the amount *eb*. The total of the private and external benefits gives us the marginal social benefits (MSB). Given the supply curve MPC, the equilibrium quantity and price, if external benefits are included, is 60 000 places and $550, respectively.

FIGURE 9.7   Subsidizing Day-Care Operators

One way in which government could increase the number of day-care places from 50 000 to 60 000 would be to grant a subsidy to day-care operators. In this graph, the subsidy amounts to $100 per month for each day-care place. The result of the subsidy will be to increase the number of places and also to reduce the day-care fee from $500 to $450 per month.

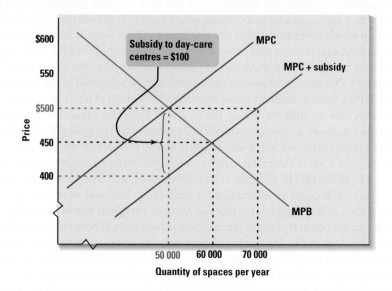

But note that it would also lead to a *decrease* in the monthly day-care charge to $450. So, who gains in this case? Well, society gains by having an additional 10 000 spaces, but who gains financially from the subsidy? It is true that the day-care centres are receiving $100 from government, but because of the increased supply, the price has dropped by $50 to $450. In other words, they end up with a net gain of $50. The same is true for parents; they, too, gain $50, since fees are now that much lower.

What would happen if the same subsidy were given to the parents instead? Since it is parents who are receiving it, the effect graphically will be to increase the demand (the MPB) curve by the amount of the subsidy, from MPB to MPB + subsidy as shown in **Figure 9.8**. The result would again be an increase in the amount of spaces from 50 000 to 60 000, but the higher demand from

FIGURE 9.8   Subsidizing Parents that Use Day-Care Centres

A subsidy of $100 per child to parents shifts the demand for day-care places (MPB) to the right, resulting in the MPB + subsidy curve. This results in the sociably desirable price and quantity of $550 and 60 000 places, respectively.

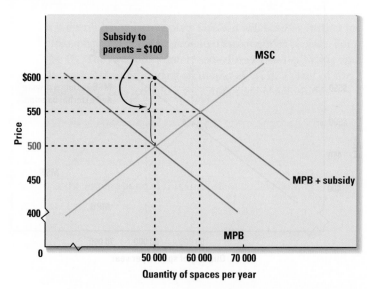

parents would result in the price increasing from $500 to $550. As with the case of the subsidy to day-care operators, parents will gain $50, since they are receiving a subsidy of $100 directly from government but have to pay an extra $50 in fees. Similarly, the day-care centres gain $50, the amount of the increased fees. (In reality, the way in which the $100 would be "shared" between parents and day-care centres depends on the elasticities of demand and supply.)

In summary, then, it does not really matter too much who receives the subsidy, since both parents and day-care centres will gain, as will society because it will have more available day-care spaces. However, if we are concerned that the price of products should more accurately reflect the real value (including externalities) of products, then the subsidy should be given to parents because that would produce a higher price.

 SELF-TEST

5. If a subsidy is given to parents of day-care children in the form of a cash payment, is there a danger that the money might not be used to contribute toward the day-care fee and might, instead, be used for other purposes? Does it matter?

6. In Figure 9.7, after the subsidy has been given to day-care operators, how many spaces would be offered at $500 per month? Why does the monthly fee drop to $450 after the subsidy?

Review

CHAPTER SUMMARY

In this chapter, you first examined the arguments that suggest competitive markets are both efficient and desirable. Then you looked at the various ways in which competitive markets can fail to achieve desirable results. Finally, you learned a number of the methods used to correct the effects of some of these failures.

9.1a Competitive markets adjust to *technological change* very well; firms that do not keep up with desirable changes will often simply fail to remain in business.

9.1b As firms grow in size, both average cost and price will drop in the long run.

9.2 Other direct *benefits* of a competitive market are that it:
- maximizes economic surplus because both productive and allocative efficiency is achieved
- does this automatically (is costless)
- encourages innovation
- promotes economic freedom

9.3 A competitive market can *fail* because:
- it may create gross income and wealth inequalities
- it can be quite unstable

- it cannot prevent the rise of monopolies
- it is unable to provide certain desirable goods, called *public goods*, that are nonrival and non-excludable
- it ignores external costs and benefits

9.4 The classic example of an *external cost* is pollution, the effects of which can be addressed by:
- legislative controls on pollution levels
- imposing a per-unit pollution tax on production
- using a cap-and-trade system to control pollution emissions

9.5a Government can integrate external benefits by providing public (or quasi-public) goods.

9.5b The day-care example illustrates how subsidies could be used to incorporate external benefits that the perfectly competitive market would otherwise ignore. This can be done in two ways:
- a subsidy to day-care operators, which would raise the quantity traded and *lower* the price
- a subsidy to parents, which would raise the quantity traded and *raise* the price

NEW GLOSSARY TERMS

allocative efficiency   274
economic surplus   274
external benefits   281
external costs   281
externalities   281
laissez-faire   270

marginal private benefits   287
marginal private costs   284
marginal social benefits   287
marginal social costs   285
market failures   276
non-excludable   280

nonrival goods   280
private goods   280
producer surplus   274
productive efficiency   273
public goods   280
quasi-public goods   281

STUDY TIPS

1. It is important to realize that the production of most products involves both private costs and external costs. The private costs are included in the price of the product and are paid for by the purchaser. The external costs are paid for (though not in money terms) by others who have no part in the production and consumption of the product. Also, most products involve both private and external benefits. The private benefits are the reward of consuming the product, and external benefits are the indirect benefits that nonbuyers often receive. It is

almost impossible to prevent external costs and benefits from occurring, but the chapter analyzes a number of ways in which such externalities can be accounted for and integrated into the market.

2. Another possible point of confusion for students is in regard to the two features of a public good. A true public good must be a nonrival good, *and* it must be non-excludable.

3. You should realize that since external costs and benefits are not usually bought and sold in the marketplace, their value is merely an estimate. It is very difficult to put an *exact* valuation on the cost of noise pollution or on the societal benefits of having an educated populace.

That does not mean that they are unimportant, but do not be misled into thinking that a precise figure can be attached to them.

4. Taxes and subsidies are often used by governments to adjust prices and outputs of privately produced goods. Remember that if the seller is responsible for paying the tax, graphically, the supply curve will shift left, as it did in Chapter 4 in the sales tax case. On the other hand, if the buyer is responsible for paying, the demand curve will shift left. If the subsidy is given to the seller to encourage more production, it will shift the supply curve right; if the subsidy is given to the buyer to encourage greater consumption, it will shift the demand curve right.

Answered Questions

These questions can also be found online on Connect.

Indicate whether the following statements are true or false:

1. **(LO 1) T or F**   A market is productively efficient if the price of a product equals the minimum average cost.

2. **(LO 1) T or F**   When a competitive market is in long-run equilibrium, the firms will be making economic profits but not normal profits.

3. **(LO 3) T or F**   The provision of private goods is an example of a market failure.

4. **(LO 1) T or F**   Long-run equilibrium in competitive markets implies that P = MC = AC.

5. **(LO 3) T or F**   By non-excludability, economists mean the inability of some firms to prevent certain people from buying a product.

6. **(LO 5) T or F**   An externality is a benefit or cost experienced by people who neither produce nor consume that product.

7. **(LO 4) T or F**   A subsidy granted to a polluting firm would be one way of integrating external costs.

8. **(LO 5) T or F**   Marginal social benefits are the total of both marginal private benefits and marginal external benefits.

9. **(LO 4) T or F**   By introducing a pollution permit fee for a lake, government allows the polluters to decide for themselves the acceptable level of pollution.

10. **(LO 5) T or F**   If external benefits are not integrated into the market, insufficient quantities of a product will be produced.

Basic (Questions 11–25)

11. **(LO 1)** What does the doctrine of laissez-faire mean?
    a) That government works best with limited market interference
    b) That the market works best with limited government interference
    c) That all externalities need to be corrected by government action
    d) That social costs are as important as private costs

McGraw Hill **connect™**

12. **(LO 3)** Which of the following is an example of a public good?
    a) A prescription drug
    b) Postsecondary education
    c) A lighthouse
    d) An orange orchard alongside a honey farm

13. **(LO 3)** What is a quasi-public good?
    a) A private good provided by government
    b) A public good sold privately to individuals
    c) A private good provided by the market
    d) A public good provided by government

14. **(LO 2)** What is producer surplus?
    a) It is the difference between the price that consumers are willing to pay and the actual market price.
    b) It is the difference between the higher market price and the price that producers are willing to accept.
    c) It is the difference between the price that producers are willing to accept and the lower market price.
    d) It is the total profits made by all forms in a particular industry.

15. **(LO 3)** Why does the market fail to produce public goods?
    a) Because normally there is no demand for such goods
    b) Because it is impossible for the producer to exclude nonbuyers from enjoying the benefit
    c) Because such products usually entail large external costs
    d) Because their production normally leads to increased income inequality

16. **(LO 3)** All of the following, except one, are features of a public good. Which is the exception?
    a) Public goods are products whose benefits are not affected by the number of users.
    b) Public goods could be produced by the market.
    c) Public goods are provided by government.
    d) Public goods could not be produced by private firms at a profit.

17. **(LO 3)** All of the following, except one, are examples of market failures. Which is the exception?
    a) Competitive markets do not result in an equitable distribution of incomes and wealth.
    b) Competitive markets do not ensure that the economy will be stable.
    c) Competitive markets do not ensure that competition will continue.
    d) Competitive markets do not ensure that individuals get the type of jobs they would like.
    e) Competitive markets do not take externalities into consideration.

18. **(LO 1)** When does allocative efficiency occur?
    a) When the price of the product is equal to its short-run average cost
    b) When the price of the product is equal to its long-run average cost
    c) When the price of the product is equal to its marginal cost
    d) When the price of the product is below its marginal cost

19. **(LO 3)** Which of the following statements is correct regarding the term *marginal social cost*?
    a) It includes only the private costs of production.
    b) It includes only the external costs of production.
    c) It includes both the private and the external costs of production.
    d) It is the difference between external costs and private costs of production.

20. **(LO 1)** What does *productive efficiency* mean?
    a) A product is being produced at the lowest possible short-run average cost but not necessarily at the lowest long-run average costs.
    b) A product is being produced at the lowest possible long-run average cost but not necessarily at the lowest short-run average costs.
    c) A product is being produced at the lowest possible short- and long-run average costs.
    d) A product is being produced at the lowest possible marginal costs.

21. **(LO 1)** What does *allocative efficiency* mean?
    a) That a product is produced where its price is equal to its marginal costs
    b) That a product is produced where its price is below its marginal costs
    c) That a product is produced where its price is equal to its average costs
    d) That a product is produced where its price is below its average costs

22. **(LO 3)** What does the term *forces of uncompetition* refer to?
    a) The tendency in the market for some firms to grow larger and drive other firms out of business, thereby eroding perfect competition
    b) The inability of firms to provide all the products that people want
    c) The inevitable wealth and income inequalities resulting from the market
    d) The tendency of governments to take over certain firms

23. **(LO 3)** All the following, except one, are benefits of the perfectly competitive market system. Which is the exception?
    a) It is productively efficient.
    b) It ensures that income is fairly distributed.
    c) It is allocatively efficient.
    d) It is a costless system.

Use **Table 9.1**, which shows the toll charges on a particular highway, to answer questions 24 and 25.

TABLE 9.1

Toll Charge	Vehicles per Hour
$0	5000
1	4000
2	3000
3	2500
4	2200
5	2000
6	1800
7	1600

24. **(LO 4)** If using the road was presently free, what toll charge would be necessary to reduce traffic by 40 percent?
    a) $1
    b) $2
    c) $3
    d) $4

25. **(LO 4)** If the toll charge was presently $1, what *increase* in the toll charge would be necessary to reduce traffic by 2000 vehicles per hour?
    a) $1
    b) $2
    c) $3
    d) $4

Intermediate (Questions 26–32)

26. **(LO 4)** If the price of a product is less than its marginal social costs, then:
    a) Society would prefer more of this product being produced
    b) Society would prefer less of this product being produced
    c) External costs must be zero
    d) Short-run average costs must be at minimum

27. **(LO 1)** What does the long-run equilibrium of a perfectly competitive market suggest?
    a) That the price is equal to the lowest SRAC but not necessarily the lowest LRAC
    b) That the price is equal to the lowest LRAC but not necessarily the lowest SRAC
    c) That the price is equal to both the lowest SRAC and the lowest LRAC
    d) That price cannot equal marginal cost

28. **(LO 3)** All of the following, except one, are benefits of perfectly competitive markets. Which is the exception?
    a) Competitive markets promote personal economic freedom.
    b) Competitive markets eliminate externalities.
    c) Ignoring externalities, competitive markets are productively efficient.
    d) Competitive markets are costless to implement.
    e) Ignoring externalities, competitive markets are allocatively efficient.

29. **(LO 3)** Which form of pollution control would one expect environmental groups to favour the most?
    a) Legislative controls, because of the built-in incentive firms have to reduce pollution below the required minimum.
    b) A pollution tax, because the producer pays all of the tax and the consumer none.
    c) The pollution tax, because the consumer pays all of the tax and the producer none.
    d) The marketing of pollution permits, because the environmental group has the option of directly reducing pollution by buying permits and not using them.

Figure 9.9 shows the demand and supply of a product in a competitive market. Refer to this figure to answer questions 30 to 32.

30. **(LO 4)** Suppose this graph represents a polluting industry and that government wishes to decrease its output by 10 units. Which of the following will produce this result?
    a) Imposing an excise tax of $2
    b) Imposing an excise tax of $1
    c) Granting a subsidy of $2 to producers
    d) Granting a subsidy of $1 to producers
    e) Granting a subsidy of $2 to consumers

FIGURE 9.9

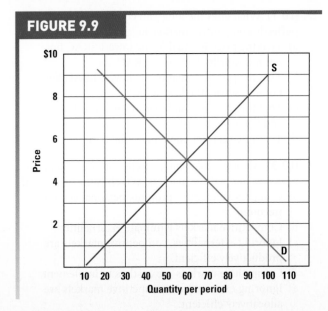

FIGURE 9.10

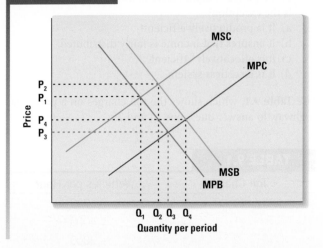

31. **(LO 5)** Suppose that this graph represents an industry with big external benefits and that government wishes to increase its output by ten units and lower its price. Which of the following will produce this result?
    a) Imposing an excise tax of $2
    b) Imposing an excise tax of $1
    c) Granting a subsidy of $2 to producers
    d) Granting a subsidy of $1 to producers
    e) Granting a subsidy of $2 to consumers

32. **(LO 5)** Suppose that this graph represents an industry with big external benefits and that government wishes to increase its output by ten units and raise its price. Which of the following will produce this result?
    a) Imposing an excise tax of $2
    b) Imposing an excise tax of $1
    c) Granting a subsidy of $2 to producers
    d) Granting a subsidy of $1 to producers
    e) Granting a subsidy of $2 to consumers

Advanced (Questions 33–35)

Refer to **Figure 9.10** to answer questions 33 to 35.

33. **(LO 4, 5)** Which of the following statements is correct regarding an unregulated competitive market?
    a) Its price of P_1 would be lower than a price that included all externalities.
    b) Its price of P_1 would be higher than a price that included all externalities.
    c) Its price of P_2 would be higher than a price that included all externalities.
    d) Its price of P_3 would be lower than a price that included all externalities.
    e) Its price of P_4 would be lower than a price that included all externalities.

34. **(LO 4, 5)** Which of the following statements is true if external costs are recognized but external benefits are not?
    a) The price would be P_1.
    b) The price would be P_2.
    c) The price would be P_3.
    d) The price would be P_4.

35. **(LO 4, 5)** Compared with the ideal quantity, which of the following statements is correct regarding an unregulated competitive market?
    a) It would be overproducing at quantity Q_1.
    b) It would be underproducing at quantity Q_2.
    c) It would be overproducing at quantity Q_2.
    d) It would be overproducing at quantity Q_3.
    e) It would be underproducing at quantity Q_4.

Parallel Problems

ANSWERED PROBLEMS

36A. **(LO 4, 5) Key Problem** The graph in **Figure 9.11** shows the marginal private benefits and the marginal private cost per year of a program at the flight-training school in London. Suppose that research indicates that the marginal external benefits from having well-trained pilots is $6000 per student.
  a) Draw in the new marginal social benefits curve in **Figure 9.11**, and label it MSB.
  b) Given the new MSB curve, what is the ideal number of students in this program? _____
  c) Now suppose that further research indicates that there are marginal social costs equal to $3000 per student due to more traffic and congestion at the college. Draw in the MSC curve in **Figure 9.11**.
  d) Now what is the optimum number of students in this program when both marginal social benefits and costs are considered? _____ .

Basic (Problems 37A–43A)

37A. **(LO 3)** In Canada today, which of the following products is a private good, a public good, or a quasi-public good?
  a) Military defence _____ .

b) Domestic airline flights. _____ .
c) The post office. _____ .
d) Cable TV. _____.

38A. **(LO 5)** **Figure 9.12** shows the market for polio vaccinations in Narnia. The market is presently in equilibrium. If the marginal external benefit is estimated at an additional $12 per vaccination, draw in the MSB curve. What are the optimal price and quantity from society's point of view?
  Price: $ _____ ; quantity: _____ .

39A. **(LO 4)** The Government of Malaca has decided to sell pollution permits that will allow people to discharge pollutants into its largest freshwater lake. Each permit is a right to discharge one tonne of pollutants. Malaca has determined that the lake will tolerate a maximum of 40 tonnes of pollutants per year and has decided to sell the permits using a Dutch auction. This means that the auction starts at a very high price, which is successively reduced until the price reaches a level that will result in all 40 tonnes of pollution permits being sold at the same price. The results of the bidding are shown in **Table 9.2**.

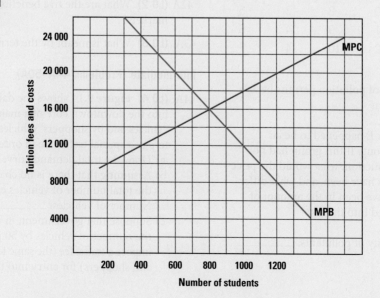

FIGURE 9.11

FIGURE 9.12

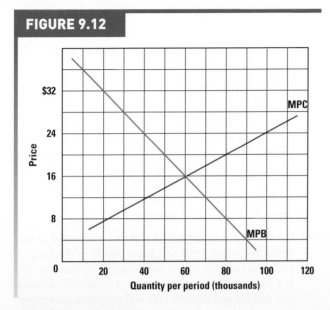

TABLE 9.2

Price per Pollution Permit	Bidder A	Bidder B	Bidder C	Bidder D	Bidder E
$6000	2				
5500	4	6			
5000	6	6	1	1	1
4500	8	7	2	2	2
4000	10	7	4	3	3
3500	12	9	6	3	4
3000	14	10	8	3	5
2500	16	11	9	4	6
2000	18	12	10	4	7

a) What will the price of pollution permits be as a result of this auction?
Price: $ _____ .

b) Suppose that Bidder E happened to be an environmentalist group. If this group had not participated in the auction, what would the price of pollution permits have been, and what difference would there have been in the amount of pollutants discharged into the lake?
Price: $ _____
Difference in quantity of pollutants: _____

40A. **(LO 1)** In order for an industry to achieve productive as well as allocative efficiency, three conditions must be fulfilled: a) the firms must be producing at economic capacity; b) the firms must be producing out of plants of minimum efficient scale; and c) the firms must be making only normal profits. In **Figure 9.13** draw the appropriate price and costs curves that indicate equilibrium at P = $10 and Quantity = 400.

FIGURE 9.13

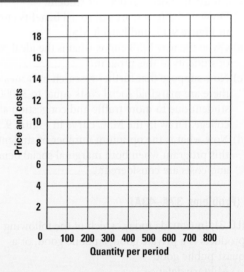

41A. **(LO 1)** What is meant by the term *productive efficiency*? If an economy is productively efficient, what conditions must be true?

42A **(LO 2)** What are the five benefits of competitive markets?

43A. **(LO 3)** What is meant by the term *market failure*?

Intermediate (Problems 44A–50A)

44A. **(LO 4)** **Figure 9.14** shows the daily demand for entry into the downtown core of a major city by commuter vehicles and by shoppers' vehicles if they were required to pay a special traffic fee in order to enter.
a) Draw the total demand curve.
b) Assuming that there is no charge for entry, what is the total number of vehicles entering downtown? Number of vehicles: _____ .
c) Suppose that government, in an effort to reduce the number of vehicles by 50 percent, decides to impose a traffic fee (the same fee for both commuters and shoppers) for entry into the downtown area.

FIGURE 9.14

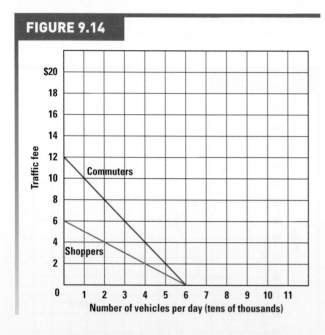

What will be the amount of the fee, and how many of each group will enter downtown?
Fee: $ _____
Number of commuter vehicles: _____
Number of shoppers' vehicles: _____ .

d) Assume that government, alternatively, decides to have a two-fee system but still wishes to reduce the traffic by 50 percent of the no-fee entry level. If it decides to charge shoppers $3, how much will it have to charge commuters? Commuter fee: $ _____ .

45A. **(LO 3, 4, 5)** Figure 9.15 shows the demand and supply of a certain product.

FIGURE 9.15

$50
45
40
35
30
25
20
15
10
5
0   10 20 30 40 50 60 70 80 90 100 110 120 130 140
Quantity per period

MSC   MPC
MPB   MSB
Price

a) In an unregulated market, what would be the equilibrium price and quantity?
Price: $ _____ ; quantity: _____ .
b) If this product were taxed by an amount equal to the external costs, what would be the equilibrium price and quantity?
Price: $ _____ ; quantity: _____ .
c) Alternatively, if buyers of this product were subsidized by an amount equal to the external benefits, what would be the equilibrium price and quantity?
Price: $ _____ ; quantity: _____ .
d) Finally, if this product were both taxed and subsidized by an amount equal to the external costs and benefits, what would be the equilibrium price and quantity?
Price: $ _____ ; quantity: _____ .

46A. **(LO 4)** Table 9.3 shows the demand for pollution permits to emit hydrocarbons in a particular industrial park. Each permit allows the owner to release one tonne of pollutants into the atmosphere.

TABLE 9.3

Price per Pollution Permit	Quantity of Permits
$4500	100
4000	200
3500	300
3000	400
2500	500
2000	600
1500	700

a) If no fee for a pollution permit were charged, how many tonnes of pollutants would be discharged into the atmosphere, assuming a straight-line demand curve? _____ tonnes.
b) Suppose government were to set a fee of $3000 per pollution permit. How many tonnes of pollutants would now be dumped? What is the total revenue received by government? _____ tonnes; government revenue: $ _____ .
c) Suppose that a new technology allows for a significant reduction in hydrocarbons at a relatively low cost so that the demand for pollution permits in the industrial park drops by 200 tonnes. Assuming that government holds the permit fee at $3000, how many tonnes of pollutants would now be dumped?

What would be the total revenue received by government? _____ tonnes; government revenue: $ _____ .

d) After the change in demand in c), what would happen if instead of maintaining the fee of $3000, government wants to maintain the same level of pollutants as in b)? What fee would it have to charge, and what would be its new revenue?
Fee: $ _____ ;
government revenue: $ _____ .

47A. **(LO 4, 5)** Figure 9.16 illustrates the market for Solarium, a product that has both extensive social benefits and extensive social costs.

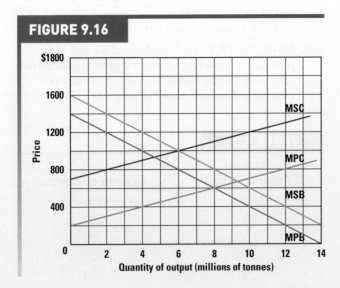

FIGURE 9.16

a) In an unregulated market, what would be the equilibrium price and quantity?
Price: $ _____ ; quantity: _____ .

b) At the unregulated equilibrium, what is the value of external benefits per tonne? What is the value of external costs per tonne?
Value of external benefits: $ _____ per tonne;
value of external costs: $ _____ per tonne.

c) At the unregulated equilibrium, what is the value of total external benefits? What is the value of total external costs?
Value of external benefits: $ _____ ;
value of external costs: $ _____ .

d) What are the most desirable price and quantity from society's point of view?
Price: $ _____ ; quantity: _____ .

48A. **(LO 4)** Figure 9.17 illustrates the private costs and benefits of producing Trisenian, a new miracle drug.

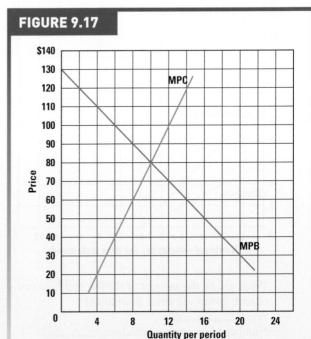

FIGURE 9.17

a) Draw the MSB and MSC curves on the graph, assuming that the external benefits are estimated at $50 per unit and the external cost at $20 per unit.

b) What are the most desirable price and quantity from society's point of view?
Price: $ _____ ; quantity: _____ .

c) If government wanted to increase the quantity to the amount in b) above, what subsidy would it need to give to producers?
Value of subsidy: $ _____ ; per unit.

d) If, instead, government wanted to increase the quantity to the amount in b) above, what subsidy would it need to give to consumers?
Value of subsidy: $ _____ ; per unit.

49A. **(LO 1)** Explain how competition forces firms to be innovative.

50A. **(LO 4)** Explain three ways in which external costs can be addressed.

Advanced (Problems 51A–54A)

51A. **(LO 5)** Table 9.4 shows the market for private long-term-care beds in two countries, Gothum and Camdon, which have identical demands but different supplies.

    a) What are the present equilibrium fee and number of available beds in each country?

        Gothum's fee: —————— Quantity: ——————

        Camdon's fee: —————— Quantity: ——————

    b) If demand were to decrease by 400 in each country, what would be the new equilibrium fee and quantity in each country? What explains the different effects in the two countries?

        Gothum's fee: —————— Q ——

        quantity: —————— —— .

        Camdon's fee: —————— Q ——

        quantity: —————— .

        Reason for the difference: —————— .

    c) From the initial situation in a), suppose the governments in each country wished to increase the quantity of beds available in long-term-care facilities by 300. They have decided to give subsidies to long-term-care residents to encourage this increase. How much subsidy must be given in each country? Explain the difference in the two countries.

        Gothum's subsidy: —————— —————— .

        Camdon's subsidy: —————— —————— .

        Reason for the difference: —————— .

TABLE 9.4

Monthly Fee	Quantity Demanded Gothum and Camdon	Quantity Supplied Gothum	Quantity Supplied Camdon
$ 700	2800	2200	1600
800	2700	2300	1900
900	2600	2400	2200
1000	2500	2500	2500
1100	2400	2600	2800
1200	2300	2700	3100
1300	2200	2800	3400

52A. **(LO 3)** In what ways are competitive markets part of the problem of income and wealth inequalities, and in what ways are they part of the solution?

53A. **(LO 1)** Explain why competitive markets ensure that in the long run, prices and outputs are both productively and allocatively efficient.

54A. **(LO 4)** What effect does a pollution tax have on the price and quantity produced? Who pays for the pollution tax?

CHAPTER 10

MONOPOLY

At the end of this chapter, you should be able to...

LO1 define a monopoly and explain how they come into existence and why they must reduce their prices to sell more.

LO2 understand how the profit-maximizing output and price are determined for a monopolist.

LO3 explain five grounds on which monopolies can be criticized.

LO4 explain the significant difference between monopoly and perfect competition.

LO5 explain three grounds on which monopolies can be defended.

LO6 discuss ways that governments can change the behaviour of monopolies.

This chapter looks at what is meant by a monopoly and what conditions lead to its creation. We focus on how a monopolist firm goes about determining the price and output that will ensure the greatest profit. We next compare a monopoly market with a perfectly competitive market to find out which of these two quite different market structures is better and why. In doing this, we also mention some of the social costs and benefits that may result from monopolies. Finally, the chapter looks at various ways in which governments have tried to deal with monopolies, either through taxation, price setting, or outright government purchase of the monopoly.

A Question of Relevance...

You might well live in an area where there is only one supplier of electricity or natural gas. Have you ever wondered why this is so? What is good about monopolies like these? Is there anything bad about them? Is Microsoft a monopolist? Should Petro-Canada have been privatized? Should government allow large firms to merge? Should government have any say in such questions at all? And how do such questions affect you, a typical consumer? The answers to some of these questions might surprise you.

From the competitive world of the last two chapters, we now turn to its extreme opposite: **monopoly**. A firm is a monopolist if it is the sole producer of a product for which there are no close substitutes. The firm not only dominates the industry, the firm *is* the industry. There is no competition for the monopolist, which leaves it in a very powerful position. The study of monopoly, then, is a study in market power. People have always been suspicious of monopolies because of the distinct possibility that the monopolist might use its power to exploit its customers, suppliers, and employees. Self-interest is unlikely to lead to exploitation in the case of competitive markets because competition itself provides a check and balance on the behaviour of competitors. However, this constraint is largely absent in monopoly markets, and therefore, the possibility of abuse of market power is greater.

L01 Define a monopoly...

monopoly: a market in which a single firm (the monopolist) is the sole producer.

In a market economy, private ownership allows owners of resources a degree of freedom and gives them licence to exercise very wide discretion in the use of those resources without public input. After all, as members of the public, we do not get to vote for the presidents and executives of firms. However, most people do not feel disenfranchised because of this, since they can at least vote with their money. We cast votes for the products we like when we buy them. If we do not like a certain product, the "democracy of the marketplace" means that the product will not be successful. In addition, we do not feel uncomfortable with this lack of accountability because in the case of the competitive market, the firm represents such a small portion of the industry or the whole economy that any damage it might do is limited.

However, none of this is true with monopolies, which replace the democracy of the competitive market with the despotism of the sole producer. As a result, most countries, including Canada, curtail the power of monopolies in various ways, which we will look at later in the chapter. In addition to this, one of the major criticisms made by economists is that monopoly power wastes an economy's resources. It does this, as we shall see, because monopolies restrict their outputs, so they produce less than the optimum amount.

Identifying what is, or what is not, a monopoly is not always straightforward. Certainly, the monopolist is the sole producer of a product in the market. But what is the market? What is a product? And if we look for close substitutes, what exactly is a substitute, and how close is close? For instance, we need to consume liquids to stay alive, and there are certainly no substitutes for drinkable liquids. Drinkable liquids, however, is a product group, not a product. Pop is a subgroup of drinkable liquids, and there are many different types of pops. Colas are a further subgroup of pops, and there are fewer types of colas than there are pops in general. Pepsi is only one type of cola but it could be suggested that this product is unique, and therefore, Pepsi is a monopoly producer. You can see then that Pepsi could be considered either a monopolist or a very competitive producer, depending upon how the product is defined.

As for the definition of the market, if a particular small town has only one gas station and the next town is 50 kilometres away, to all intents and purposes, that gas station is a monopolist. But in the whole of the province or the country, that gas station is only one of thousands of gas stations. The wider the market, in the sense of accessibility for consumers, the less likely it is that a single firm will be able to dominate. With easier and cheaper transport and communications these days, we are able to buy from firms around the world, which means that a Canadian monopolist has to compete with foreign firms. Its power in the domestic market is therefore considerably reduced.

Nonetheless, given the above cautions, most people would agree that Rogers Cable television and the only gas station in a remote town are examples of monopolies.

Woman pumping gasoline into a minivan.

10.1 HOW MONOPOLIES COME INTO EXISTENCE

L01 ... explain how monopolies come into existence and why they must reduce their prices to sell more.

barriers to entry: obstacles that make it difficult for new participants to enter a market.

How do monopolies come into existence in the first place, and how are they able to keep out competing firms? The answer lies in the concept of **barriers to entry**, whereby the monopoly is protected from new competitors in the market. The variety of barriers can be categorized under three headings: technical barriers, legal barriers, and economic barriers.

Technical barriers are those that make it difficult for other firms to duplicate a monopolist's production methods because the monopolist is the sole owner of a resource or technique. For instance, the International Nickel Company (Inco) once controlled most of the world's supply of nickel, and the De Beers Company of Kimberly, South Africa, owns or controls the majority of the world's diamond mines. Sole ownership of a resource confers a monopoly status on the producer. Similarly, a firm is a monopolist if it is the sole owner of the technical knowledge necessary to produce the product. IBM, for instance, had a monopoly on computer expertise for many years, until other companies caught up.

Legal barriers prevent other firms from competing in a particular industry by force of law. In certain instances, this is designed to grant a monopoly to the production of a good or service, as is the case with many crown corporations in Canada, such as Canada Post, or provincial government liquor boards. These are known as public franchises. Other types of legal restriction are designed to give private firms protection from competition and may take the form of a government licence (to fish commercially for salmon, for example) or of a patent or copyright, in which the originator of the idea is given a monopoly for a number of years. For example, the NCR company had the first patent on cash registers, and Xerox held the patent on photocopying using a dry-ink method (xerography).

Economic barriers are present whenever there are extensive startup costs for new firms. It is difficult to compete internationally with the major automobile firms unless you are ready to invest billions of dollars. It should be noted that this investment needs to encompass not only the fixed costs of the factory buildings and assembly line but also the cost of a distribution network and marketing plan, as well as sufficient funds to hire the highly paid design engineers and executives who are able to put all this together. The bigger this initial investment, the more difficult it is for new entrants to join the industry. Automobile firms tend to be large because of extensive economies of scale, which allow big firms to produce at much lower unit costs than can small firms. The existence of the huge corporations and international conglomerates that we see these days is often the result of the drive for higher profits through growth. Sometimes, the growth

⏵ ADDED DIMENSION   Patents and Exclusive Rights

The rationale for patent legislation is that it provides the original inventor with a period during which the invention is protected from competition so that the inventor will be able to make monopoly profits through direct sales or by charging others a royalty, if they wish to use the invention. In Canada, registered patents are granted 20 years' protection. In this way, it is hoped that research and development will be encouraged.

A number of problems associated with patents, however, deserve at least brief mention. For instance, if the registered description of the invention is too narrow, it will allow others to introduce and try to patent something that is merely a slight modification of the original. For this reason, many firms seeking patent protection try to define the patent as broadly as possible

("a motorized conveyance with four wheels," for instance) so as to keep out all competition. However, patent offices tend to dismiss patents that are too widely defined, such as "computers," or those in the form of broad ideas or theories, such as "the law of relativity," for example. Additionally, if patent protection was granted only for a short time, it would tend to inhibit research, but one that extends the period too much is likely to inhibit competition.

Finally, it should be noted that in order to register a patent, the inventor must give complete disclosure of the product and the process. But since this might reveal far too much to the competition, a number of inventions (such as the specific formula for Coca-Cola) have never been registered but remain, instead, trade secrets.

has been "organic," but more often than not, it has been the result of mergers and acquisitions. In summary, barriers to market entry by new firms can take the form of:

- technical barriers, such as sole ownership of a resource
- legal barriers, such as public franchise, licences, patents, and copyrights
- economic barriers caused by economies of scale

 SELF-TEST

1. Entry into the following industries is very difficult. What type of barrier to entry is involved?

a) Computer operating systems

b) Commercial aircraft manufacturing

c) West coast wild salmon fishing

Total, Average, and Marginal Revenues

The sole producer of a product is in a very powerful position. That does not mean, however, that it has unlimited power over the market. To a certain extent, the consumer is still sovereign and makes the ultimate decision whether or not to buy that product and if, as a result, the monopolist will be successful. Nonetheless, the monopolist, unlike the competitive producer, is a *price maker* rather than a *price taker*, which means that it is able to set the price at whatever level it chooses rather than having to accept the market-determined price. Even so, consumers will decide how much they will buy at that price. Alternatively, the monopolist could determine the size of production and leave it to the market to determine the maximum price at which that output can be sold. Therefore:

> The monopolist can determine either the price or the quantity sold; it cannot determine both the price *and* quantity sold.

All this can be expressed another way: since the monopolist and the industry are one and the same, it faces the market demand for the product, and that demand is represented by a downward-sloping demand curve. From the consumers' point of view, this means that if the price drops, they will buy more. From the monopolist's perspective, it means that in order to sell more—assuming that the same price is charged to all customers—the monopolist must lower the price. A monopolist cannot sell all it wants at any given price; it is forced to decrease the price in order to sell more.

This has important implications for the monopolist's revenues. As a result, it has a downward-sloping demand curve, whereas a perfectly competitive firm has a perfectly elastic, horizontal, demand curve. We should note at this point that throughout our analysis, we are assuming that the monopolist is selling all of its units at a single price; in other words, it is not practising price discrimination. Later in the chapter, we will look at the implications of the monopolist charging different prices to different customers.

Suppose that through mergers and acquisitions, a monopoly brewer emerged in Canada calling itself Boundary Bay Brewers. The first two columns of **Table 10.1** show the quantities (in millions of cases per day) that would be sold at various prices of beer; that is, they represent the demand for Boundary Bay Beer.

The terms *total*, *average*, and *marginal revenues* were introduced in Chapter 8. Note that as with the competitive firm, the average revenue (TR/Q) is the same thing as the price. Note also that the total revenue increases with quantity sold but only up to a point. Here, that point is a quantity of 10. If Boundary Bay Brewers wishes to increase the number of cases sold to 11, it must drop the price to $10; it will have no effect, however, on the total revenue. The company's total revenue will remain at $110. Should the monopolist wish to increase output and sales to 12, the price will have to come down to $9, with the result that total revenue will start to fall. Unlike a competitive firm, then, the monopolist is faced with a maximum sales revenue.

TABLE 10.1	Total, Average, and Marginal Revenues of the Monopolist			
Quantity (millions)	Price (per case)	Total Revenue	Average Revenue (AR)	Marginal Revenue (MR)
1	$20	$ 20	$20	$20
2	19	38	19	18
3	18	54	18	16
4	17	68	17	14
5	16	80	16	12
6	15	90	15	10
7	14	98	14	8
8	13	104	13	6
9	12	108	12	4
10	11	110	11	2
11	10	110	10	0
12	9	108	9	−2

Table 10.1 also shows that for the monopolist, the marginal revenue (ΔTR/ΔQ) is not equal to the average revenue. The extra (marginal) sales revenue that the monopolist receives for selling one more unit is not equal to the price. This is because when the monopolist sells one more unit, it *gains revenue* equal to the price at which it sells that unit, but it *loses revenue* because it is forced to drop the price not only on the additional unit sold but on *every* unit it sells.

Suppose, for instance, that the brewery is presently selling 5 million cases of beer per week at a price of $16 per case, for a total revenue of $80 million. If it reduces the price to $15, it will be able to sell one million more units and will, therefore, gain revenue equal to 1 million × $15 = $15 million. However, it will lose revenue because it is dropping the price by $1 on the previous 5 million it was selling; that is, it will lose revenue equal to $1 million × $5 = $5 million. It gains $15 million but loses $5 million so that its net gain is only $10 million, which is its extra revenue for the additional one million cases sold. Because the demand curve is downward sloping, the extra amount of revenue the monopolist gains from an additional sale will always be less than the price. In summary:

> In order to increase its sales, a monopolist is forced to reduce its price not just on the last units sold, but on the whole of its output.

These points are illustrated in **Figure 10.1**.

In **Figure 10.2**, we bring together graphs of the total revenue and of the average and marginal revenues to show the relationships between them.

Up to an output of 10, the total revenue curve is upward sloping, but the slope gets smaller and smaller with increasing output. The slope, which is the same thing as the marginal revenue, measures the rate at which total revenue changes. In other words, as **Figure 10.2B** shows, the marginal revenue decreases as the output increases. Note that the total revenue curve rises to a maximum at an output of 11 (and 10) and thereafter declines. Note also that the average revenue curve is the same thing as the demand curve. The marginal revenue curve is consistently below the average revenue curve and is twice as steep; every time the average revenue (price) drops by $1, the marginal revenue drops by $2.

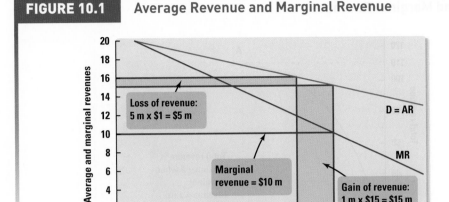

FIGURE 10.1 Average Revenue and Marginal Revenue

By cutting the price by $1, the producer is losing $1 times his present output of 5 (million) = $5 (million). However, he gains from the fact that he increases output sales by 1 million at the lower price of $15 = $15 million. The marginal revenue is the net gain of $10 (million) which is lower than the price of $15.

This is true for all straight-line demand curves: however steep the demand (AR) curve, the corresponding marginal revenue curve will be twice as steep. (It also means that wherever the demand curve intersects the horizontal axis, the marginal revenue curve will cross it at half that value.) As long as the marginal revenue is positive, even though it is falling, then total revenue must be increasing. When it becomes negative, after an output of 11, the total revenue must be falling. Thus:

> Total revenue is at a maximum when the marginal revenue is neither positive nor negative, that is, when it is zero.

If you examine **Figure 10.2**, you will see that the MR curve intersects the horizontal axis (that is, MR = 0) exactly at the output (of 11), where the TR is at its highest point (TR is at a maximum).

This monopolist will never produce an output greater than 11 units because a higher output will presumably increase the total costs but lower total revenue: at outputs greater than 11, marginal revenue is negative. Graphically, in **Figure 10.2**, this means that the monopolist will produce an output of less than 11 or, in other words, on the upper portion of the demand curve. Since the top portion of any demand curve is elastic, it means that:

> A monopolist will produce only where the demand is elastic.

In order to analyze the behaviour of monopolists a bit more thoroughly, we need to know exactly at what output a monopolist will produce. To do this, we need to know not only the revenue but also the costs and, therefore, the profitability of the monopolist.

 SELF-TEST

2. Suppose that a monopolist was charging a price of $50 for its product and was selling 15 units. It has now lowered its price to $48 and is selling 16 units. What is the marginal revenue? What is the price elasticity of demand over this price range?

FIGURE 10.2   **Total, Average, and Marginal Revenues**

Up to a point, the total revenue of the monopolist increases as more units are sold. However, the rate of increase (the slope of the TR curve) declines throughout. The total revenue reaches a maximum at an output of 11. After that, the total revenue starts to decline.

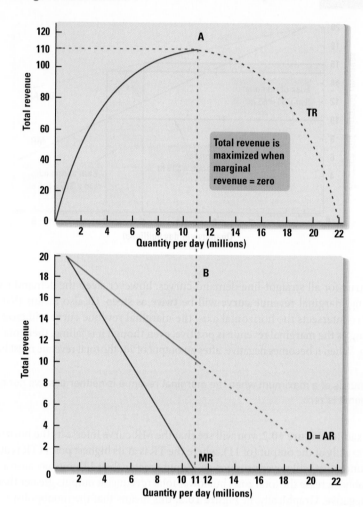

The average revenue curve is identical to the demand curve, which means that additional units can only be sold if the price is lowered. In this graph, the price must drop by $1 in order to increase sales by one unit; that is, the slope of the demand curve has a value of 1. The slope of the MR curve, however, is 2, since it drops by $2 for each additional unit sold. This means that the MR curve drops twice as steeply as the AR curve.

10.2 PROFIT-MAXIMIZING OUTPUT FOR THE MONOPOLIST

L02 Understand how the profit-maximizing output and price are determined for a monopolist.

In the short run, the cost structure for the monopolist is no different from that of the competitive producer. In the short run, the monopolist similarly enjoys the advantages of the division of labour as it produces more and later faces diminishing returns as it is constrained by the size of its operations. In **Table 10.2**, we have added the total costs of Boundary Bay Breweries (which has a TFC of $30) to the total revenue data from **Table 10.1** to calculate the total profits at the various output levels.

Given the data in **Table 10.2**, the profit-maximizing output for Boundary Bay Brewers is either an output of 5 or 6. (There are technical reasons, which we will explain in a moment, why the "correct" answer is an output of 6.) The price at this output level would be $15 per case, which will give the monopolist a total profit of $14 million. These points are shown on the graph in **Figure 10.3**.

Break-even outputs are at 3 and 8. The maximum profit point is at an output level of 6, where the vertical distance between the two total curves is at its greatest. Additionally, the maximum profit point is shown explicitly on the total profit curve, where it occurs at the highest point.

TABLE 10.2	Calculating Total Profits of the Monopolist			
Quantity (millions of cases per day)	Price (= AR)	Total Revenue (TR)	Total Cost (TC)	Total Profit (Tπ)
1	$20	$ 20	$ 40	$−20
2	19	38	48	−10
3	18	54	54	0
4	17	68	58	10
5	16	80	66	14
6	15	90	76	14
7	14	98	89	9
8	13	104	104	0
9	12	108	121	−13
10	11	110	140	−30
11	10	110	161	−51
12	9	108	184	−76

FIGURE 10.3	Total Costs, Revenues, and Profits for the Monopolist

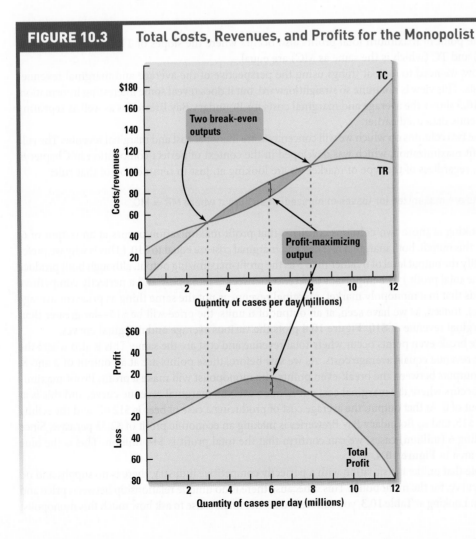

Break-even occurs where the TR and TC curves intersect, that is, at outputs of 3 and 8. Between those two outputs, TR is greater than TC, and therefore, any output will be profitable. Maximum profits occur at an output of 6. At this output, the vertical distance between the two curves is greatest. The total profit curve shows explicitly the amount of economic profit at each output and confirms these points.

TABLE 10.3	Calculating Total Profits of the Monopolist Using the Marginal Approach						
Quantity	Price (= AR)	Total Revenue (TR)	Total Cost (TC)	Average Cost (AC)	Marginal Cost (MC)	Marginal Revenue (MR)	Total Profit (Tπ)
1	$20	$20	$40	$40.00	—	20	$−20
2	19	38	48	24.00	8	18	−10
3	18	54	54	18.00	6	16	0
4	17	68	58	14.50	4	14	10
5	16	80	66	13.20	8	12	14
6	**15**	**90**	**76**	**12.67**	**10**	**10**	**14**
7	14	98	89	12.71	13	8	9
8	13	104	104	13.00	15	6	0
9	12	108	121	13.44	17	4	−13
10	11	110	140	14.00	19	2	−30
11	10	110	161	14.63	21	0	−51
12	9	108	184	15.33	23	−2	−76

The point of maximum total profits also occurs where the slopes of TR (which is the same as MR) and TC (which is the same as MC) are equal.

Now, we need to look at things using the perspective of the average and marginal revenues and costs. This view is not quite so straightforward, but it does reveal some interesting information. **Table 10.3** shows the average and marginal costs for Boundary Bay Breweries as well as repeating the revenue data used earlier.

The two columns on which we will concentrate are marginal cost and marginal revenue. The rule for profit maximization, which was developed in the context of perfect competition in Chapter 8, applies, regardless of the type of market we are looking at. Just to remind you of that rule:

Profits are maximized (or losses minimized) at an output where MR = MC.

Looking at those two columns confirms that profit maximization occurs at an output of 6, since at this output, both marginal revenue and marginal cost are equal to $10. (This is why we prefer to identify the output level of 6 rather than 5 as the profit-maximizing output, although both produce the same total profit.) The important difference between a monopoly and a perfectly competitive market is that in a monopoly market, marginal revenue is not the same thing as price (or average revenue). Indeed, as we have seen, at an output of 6 units, the price will be $15—far greater than the marginal revenue of $10. **Figure 10.4** plots the various average and marginal curves.

The break-even points occur where total revenue and cost are the same. This is also where the average revenue equals average costs. As we saw before, these points are at an output of 3 and 8. At any outputs between the break-even points, the monopolist will make a profit. Profit maximization occurs where the marginal cost curve intersects the marginal revenue curve, and this is at an output of 6. At that output, the average cost of producing a case of beer is $12.67, and the selling price is $15, and so Boundary Bay Breweries is making an economic profit of $2.33 per case. Since it is selling 6 (million) cases, we can confirm that the total profit is $14 million. This is the blue shaded area in **Figure 10.4**.

Note that unlike the situation with a perfectly competitive industry, there is no supply, and no supply curve, for the monopolist. This is because there is no unique relationship between price and quantity. Looking at **Table 10.3**, you can see it does not make sense to ask how much this monopolist

FIGURE 10.4   Average and Marginal Costs and Revenues for the Monopolist

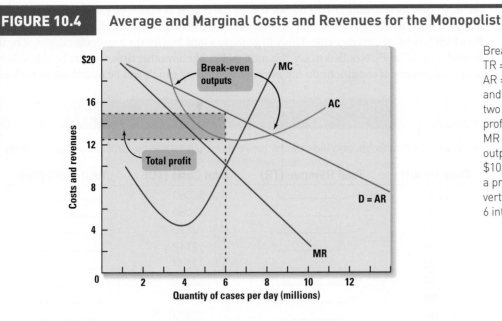

Break-even occurs where TR = TC. This must also be where AR = AC, that is, at outputs of 3 and 8. Every output between those two points is profitable. Maximum profit occurs where the MC and MR curves intersect. This is at an output of 6, where MC = MR = $10. This output would be sold at a price of $15, that is, where the vertical line from the output of 6 intersects the demand curve.

would produce at, say, a price of $18, since, given its cost structure, an output level of 3 at a price of $18 is a combination that the monopolist would never choose. For each demand faced by the monopolist, there is only a single appropriate price and a single appropriate quantity.

We should mention that being a monopolist does not guarantee profitability. If you return to **Table 10.3** and assume that average costs were increased by $5 at every output level, you can see that no output would be profitable. Therefore, it is simply not true, as many people believe, that almost by definition, monopolists are always profitable. Though many are profitable, monopolists can and do make losses from time to time. This is illustrated in **Figure 10.5**.

Suppose that, in **Figure 10.5**, the once-profitable monopolist now faces a reduced demand for its product. The demand is so low that the demand curve is below the average cost curve at every output. Assuming that it is still able to cover its variable costs, the monopolist will still produce in

FIGURE 10.5   Minimizing Losses for the Monopolist

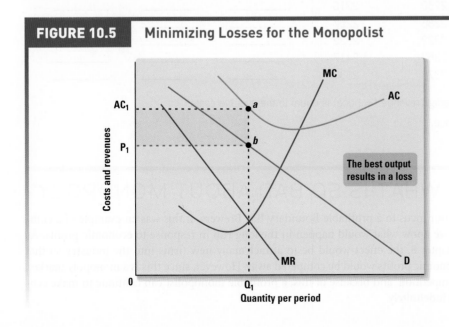

For this monopolist, its present AC curve is higher than the demand curve at all output levels. Its best option will be to minimize its losses by producing at the point where its marginal revenue equals its marginal cost; that is, where these two curves intersect at a quantity of Q_1. It would charge a price of P_1 and would incur an economic loss denoted by the shaded area, AC_1abP_1.

the short run. Its loss-minimizing output will be the output at which its marginal cost equals its marginal revenue. This occurs at output of Q_1. The maximum price it can charge for this output is P_1, which is below the average cost. This will generate a total loss for the monopolist depicted by the shaded area, $AC_1 ab P_1$. Needless to say, this monopolist, like any other firm, will not be able to incur losses indefinitely. If conditions do not improve in the long run, it will be forced out of business.

 SELF-TEST

3. Complete the following table for Onan, the monopolist, and indicate the break-even outputs and the profit maximizing output:

Quantity	Price (= AR)	Total Revenue (TR)	Total Costs (TC)	Total Profit (Tπ)
20	$100	_____	$2060	_____
21	98	_____	2080	_____
22	96	_____	2112	_____
23	94	_____	2142	_____
24	92	_____	2177	_____
25	90	_____	2216	_____
26	88	_____	2257	_____
27	86	_____	2322	_____
28	84	_____	2417	_____
29	82	_____	2530	_____

4. Using the data below, complete the table, and:

Quantity	Price	Total Revenue (TR)	Total Costs (TC)	Average Costs (AC)	Marginal Costs (MC)	Marginal Revenue (MR)
20	$100	$2000	$2067	_____	_____	_____
21	98	2058	2087	_____	_____	_____
22	96	2112	2112	_____	_____	_____
23	94	2162	2142	_____	_____	_____
24	92	2208	2177	_____	_____	_____
25	90	2250	2216	_____	_____	_____
26	88	2288	2257	_____	_____	_____
27	86	2322	2322	_____	_____	_____
28	84	2352	2417	_____	_____	_____
29	82	2378	2530	_____	_____	_____

a) show that at break-even outputs, the average revenue (= price) is equal to the average costs.

b) find the profit-maximizing output and price.

10.3 WHAT IS SO BAD ABOUT MONOPOLY?

L03 Explain five grounds on which monopolies can be criticized.

Let us return our focus to a profitable Boundary Bay Brewers. If this was an example of a competitive firm, we know what would happen in the long run in response to economic profits. As we saw in Chapter 8, the effect would be to attract many new firms into the industry so that eventually economic profits would be competed away. However, since this is a monopoly market, there is no competition, and because of this, a profitable monopolist can continue to make economic profits indefinitely.

Furthermore, the monopolist is reasonably secure because it is protected by various barriers to entry. Of course, like any firm, monopolists might incur losses, which could not be sustained indefinitely and would eventually force the monopolist out of business. However, the existence of monopoly profits do not lead to any change, except to make the monopoly owners richer. This implies that the monopolist is both productively and allocatively inefficient.

Remember from Chapter 9 that *productive efficiency* means that the producer is producing the product at the lowest possible average cost. This is not true for the monopolist. A glance back at **Figure 10.3** shows that Boundary Bay Brewers, like all monopolists, will produce an output below economic capacity and, therefore, have average costs that are higher than minimum average cost. But not only that: the price being charged is above even these high costs. This means that consumers pay a higher price than would be the case in a competitive industry because the average cost is higher than it need be and because the monopolist is making economic profits. In addition to consumers, society as a whole loses out because the existence of monopolies may lead to a more unequal distribution of income and wealth. With competitive industries, the [lower] profits are spread among many producing firms, whereas with a monopoly the [higher] profits may be concentrated in the hands of only a few owners.

In addition, **Figure 10.3** shows that at the profit-maximizing output (where MC = MR), the price is above the marginal cost. This means that the monopoly is also *allocatively inefficient* and that consumers' desire for this product at the margin, as measured by the price, is higher than its cost. In other words, consumers would be willing to pay for more additional units of a product than the monopolist would be happy to accept. However, the monopolist restricts the quantity available in order to increase its profit. In contrast, *if* this market was competitive then a greater quantity would be produced. Besides these criticisms, there is one other aspect of monopolies that is a cause for concern, and that is their ability to practise price discrimination. Although less damaging, perhaps, than some of the other charges laid against monopolies, it, nevertheless, tilts the balance of power away from consumers and into the hands of the monopolist. Let us look at the reasons for this.

Price Discrimination

As we saw in Chapter 5, price discrimination is how producers attempt to capture at least some of the existing consumer surplus. They are able to do this by selling a product at different prices. But to be able to do this, the producer needs to have a degree of market power: it has to have control over the price of the product. Certainly, firms in all forms of imperfectly competitive markets have some control over the price, and so we can see product discrimination being practised in these markets. But it is a significant feature of many monopoly markets as well. Thus, we often witness it in the fields of transportation (buses, railroads, and airlines) and communications (telephones and so on).

There are two major forms of price discrimination: discrimination among units purchased and discrimination among buying groups. Discrimination among units purchased arises because of the law of diminishing marginal utility, which suggests that buyers do not value all units of a product equally; the first unit purchased has greater value than the second unit, the second unit more than the third, and so on. For example, one consumer might value a first giant pizza at $16, but a second pizza may be worth, say, only half of that, or $8. The only way that this consumer could be induced to buy two pizzas would be if the price was $8 each. This means that the pizza shop would receive a total revenue of $16. But this is true only if there is a single price for pizzas. But what if, instead, the pizza shop charged a different price for each pizza? How could it do this? Simple. It would sell a single pizza for $16 but would offer a second bonus pizza for the low price of $6. That certainly sounds like a deal, especially since the customer values a second pizza at $8. As a result, the pizza shop is able to increase its total revenue to $22.

Discrimination among units purchased occurs whenever you see a two-for-one sale ("get a second meal for free" or "a 50-percent discount when a first meal of equal value is purchased") or when you get a card punched and receive, say, a free coffee for every six purchased. There are many other examples like this where the consumer is able to buy additional units for a lower price. However, we must be careful here, since just because a consumer can obtain a lower price by buying in large volumes does not necessarily mean the seller is practising price discrimination. That is because price discrimination exists only where a product is being sold at different prices for reasons not associated with costs. Sellers generally would prefer to sell by the case load, since it is cheaper for them in terms of storage and transaction costs and it pays them to pass on some of these savings to the customer.

Discrimination among buyer groups occurs because different groups of consumers have different demands for products and, therefore, value products differently. Some people are desperate to see first-run movies and, accordingly, are willing to pay more for the pleasure. Others are willing to wait till the movie has been out for a few months, when they can see it at reduced prices. Similarly, many new products, including movie DVDs, cell phones, and plasma TVs are initially sold at high prices because the manufacturers realize that many people are prepared to pay premium prices in order to be the first kid on the block to own the latest toy. Generally, it is often only a matter of months before the price drops to the point where the average customer is willing to buy. Finally, as we noted in Chapter 5, in addition to the fact that the price discriminator has control over the price and that different groups of consumers have different elasticities of demand, there is a third condition for price discrimination: there must be no possibility of resale.

We also saw in Chapter 5 that there are a number of ways groups differ: age, gender, when they want to buy or use a service, and so on. Being able to charge different prices to different groups will undoubtedly increase the sales revenue of the seller. This is illustrated in **Figure 10.6**, which shows the demand for haircuts at the "Hair Today, Gone Tomorrow" barber shop.

Graph A shows the daily demand by adults, graph B the demand by seniors, and graph C the total demand. The demand by adults is more inelastic than is the case for seniors, since the latter are perhaps not so self-conscious about their appearance. If Hair Today could only charge a single price, then its sales revenue would be maximized at a price of $15, which would attract 50 adults and 30 seniors. Its total revenue would be equal to $1200 (a total of 80 customers at $15 each), as illustrated in graph C.

However, if Hair Today were to charge different prices to the two groups, then it could increase its total revenue from both groups and, therefore, overall. Because the demand by adults is fairly inelastic, it will increase its total revenue by *raising* the price to, say, $18. Its customer base would only

FIGURE 10.6   The Demand for Haircuts by Two Different Groups

Figure A shows the demand for haircuts by adults and is inelastic. Figure B is the demand by seniors and is elastic. The total demand by both groups is shown in Figure C. If only one price could be charged, Figure C shows that the price that maximizes revenue is $15, which would produce revenue of $1200 ($15 × 80). If price discrimination is practised, the barber's shop should increase the adults' price to $18 in Figure A giving a revenue of $810 ($18 × 45) and lower the price for seniors at $12 in Figure B (for a revenue of $480). Its total revenue from the two groups would then be $1290.

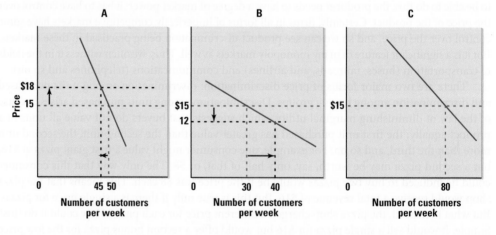

drop to 45 customers, resulting in a higher total revenue of $810 (45 at $18 compared with previous $750) as can be seen in graph A. Conversely, since the demand from seniors is fairly elastic, Hair Today will gain increased revenue by *decreasing* the price for them. Graph B shows that a reduction of the price to $12 increases the number of customers to 40, resulting in a new total revenue of $480 (40 at $12) compared with the previous $450 (30 at $15). Consequently, the overall total revenue increases to $1290 compared with the $1200 of total revenue earned with a single price.

As we saw in this example, charging different prices to the two groups increases the total revenue of the seller. However, if the seller could divide up the client base even further into three, four, or five groups it would gain even more revenue. At the ultimate, if it could charge every single customer a separate price—the maximum that each one is prepared to pay—it could really boost its business. But **perfect price discrimination** is a sellers' dream rather than a reality.

That being said, many companies these days do try to subdivide their clientele into as many different groups as their ingenuity allows. The result, as many of us are aware, is that on a flight from Vancouver to Toronto it is not uncommon to find as many as twenty different fares charged to passengers, with prices ranging from as little as $350 to as high as $3000. The amount that individual customers pay depends on their age, when they booked, who they booked with, when they fly, how long they are staying at their destinations, whether they are staying over a weekend, and so on.

Similarly, cell phone companies offer a bewildering variety of options designed to tailor a specific "package" for each of its customers. Now, of course, some of these options do mean a higher cost to the cell phone firms, but most do not. As a result, you get to choose the type of phone you would like, its ring tones, the term of the lease (one year, three years, five years), and whether or not it includes free weekends or evenings, voice-mail, text messaging, Internet access, and many, many other options.

The result of price discrimination is higher revenues and profits for the firm and a loss of consumer surplus for the consumer. However, balanced against that is the fact the output is greater than it would be for the single-price monopolist. In addition, the consumer may have a greater variety of options to choose from, although it may cost a great deal of time to find out the costs of those options.

In summary, monopolies are criticized for:

- being able to make economic profits indefinitely
- being both productively and allocatively inefficient
- producing less and charging a higher price than would occur in a competitive industry
- creating a more unequal distribution of income and wealth within society
- using their power to practise price discrimination

perfect price discrimination: a situation where customers are charged the highest price they are willing to pay for each unit of a product bought.

✓ SELF-TEST

5. The following table shows the demand for haircuts at Quick Cuts Inc.:

Price	Quantity
$20	1
19	2
18	3
17	4
16	5
15	6

a) If this was a single-price barber, what would be the total revenue for doing six haircuts?

b) If this barber were able to practise perfect price discrimination by charging each customer the maximum they would pay, what would be the total revenue for doing six haircuts?

10.4   MONOPOLY AND PERFECT COMPETITION CONTRASTED

L05 Explain the significant difference between monopoly and perfect competition.

We can show the comparison between a monopoly and a perfectly competitive industry graphically. Suppose that **Figure 10.7** illustrates a perfectly competitive mushroom industry that consists of 100 small mushroom growers all producing an identical type of mushroom. The supply curve represents the total supply of mushrooms from these growers, and the demand curve is the total market demand from millions of mushroom eaters.

The competitive price of mushrooms is $6 per kilo, and the total production is 60 000 kilos per month.

Suppose, now, that a monopolist were to buy out all the mushroom growers in the area. Having consolidated all the farms into one big combine, the monopolist sets out to maximize profits. How does it do this? By finding the output at which marginal cost is equal to marginal revenue. This will be the profit-maximizing point. Graphically, the supply curve of the perfectly competitive industry, you may remember, is synonymous with its marginal cost curve. Deriving the marginal revenue curve is reasonably straightforward because the demand curve is the same thing as the average revenue curve. Given the straight-line demand curve in **Figure 10.7**, the marginal revenue can be drawn as a curve falling twice as steeply. In other words, since the demand (average revenue) curve cuts the horizontal axis at an output of 160, then the marginal revenue curve will cut it at half that value, that is, at an output of 80.

The intersection of the marginal cost and revenue curves occurs at an output of 40 000 kilos. To find the maximum price at which this quantity could be sold, we graphically extend the output curve up to the demand curve, which establishes that this quantity could be sold at a maximum price of $8 per kilo.

In simple terms, the monopolist can make maximum profits by restricting the output, thereby pushing up the price of the product. In summary:

- Monopolies charge higher prices than perfectly competitive firms.
- Monopolies produce lower outputs than perfectly competitive firms, and these outputs are below economic capacity.
- Monopolies, unlike perfectly competitive firms, may make economic profits in the short run and in the long run.

FIGURE 10.7   Monopoly and Perfect Competition Contrasted

The competitive market's equilibrium occurs where the quantities demanded and supplied are equal. This occurs at a price of $6 and an output of 60 000 kilos. If, on the other hand, this were a monopoly industry, the monopolist would produce at the point where MR equals MC. The profit-maximizing output for the monopolist, then, is at an output of 40 000 kilos, which could be sold at a price of $8 per kilo.

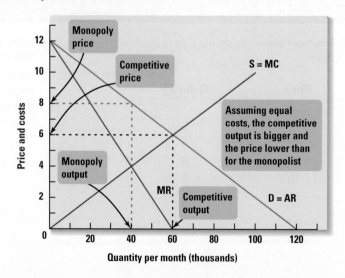

We could express the shortcomings of monopoly in different terms: monopolies are both productively inefficient and allocatively inefficient. We saw earlier that a monopolist will produce an output at which the price is well above the average cost of production: it is productively inefficient. It also produces an output where the price is above the marginal cost: it is allocatively inefficient. Let us elaborate a little on this last point. As we saw in Chapter 9, perfectly competitive markets are supremely efficient in the sense that the equilibrium output maximizes the amount of economic surplus. In contrast, the amount of economic surplus in the case of monopoly is considerably less as **Figure 10.8** shows.

You will recall from Chapter 9 that the economic surplus is the total of the consumer and producer surplus. In the case of the perfectly competitive market depicted in **Figure 10.8A**, the consumer surplus amounts to $180 000 (60 000 × $6/2) and the producer surplus is also $180 000, for a total economic surplus of $360 000. However, the monopolist shown in **Figure 10.8B** will produce at a lower output of 40 000 and sell this quantity at a price of $8. The consumer surplus

---

FIGURE 10.8   Economic Surplus, Perfect Competition versus Monopoly

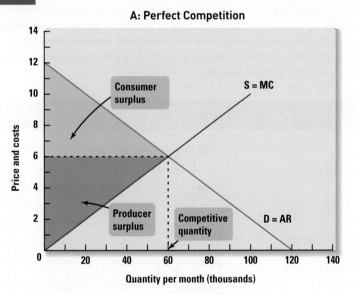

A: Perfect Competition

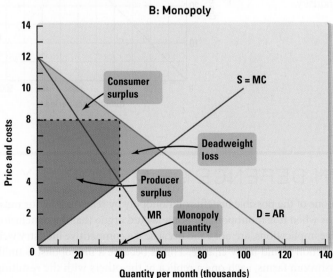

B: Monopoly

In Figure A, the competitive price is $6 and the quantity is 60 000. The consumer surplus (the green triangle) is equal to $180 000. The producer surplus (the blue triangle) is also $180 000. The economic surplus is therefore the total of $360 000. In Figure B, the monopoly price is $8, and the quantity is 40 000. The consumer surplus (the green triangle) is equal to $80 000, and the producer surplus (the blue area) is equal to $240 000. The economic surplus is, therefore, $320 000, leaving a deadweight loss (the small triangle) of $40 000.

in this case is only $80 000 (40 000 × $4/2) and the producer surplus has increased to $240 000 for a total economic surplus of $320 000. This means that consumers have lost $100 000 in consumer surplus and the monopolist has gained $60 000 in producer surplus. The result is that the economic surplus (the total of both) is $40 000 less in the case of the monopolist than it would be in the case of perfect competition. This loss in economic surplus is referred to as the **deadweight loss** and is equal to the size of the small triangle in **Figure 10.8B**. The deadweight loss is the total surplus lost, compared with an efficient market, due to market imperfections. Those imperfections result in either the over- or under-production of a product and may be the result of such things as taxes, price controls, or imperfect markets (of which monopoly is a prime example).

We can begin to see why governments have often interceded in the market by regulating monopolies and have at times outlawed private monopolies or broken up existing ones. But while this may be true on some occasions, it is fair to say that the history of anti-monopoly legislation and its enforcement in North America over the past century shows a singular lack of consistency. In certain periods, even the slightest suggestion that some firms were seeking to merge, or were thought to be behaving in an uncompetitive way, was greeted with a chorus of protests and vigorous action by legislators. In other periods, trusts, monopolies, and mergers have been treated with benign indifference by governments. What is the reason for this ambivalence, even allowing for the fact that other political considerations may be at work? One major explanation is that many people—and that includes economists—are not convinced that monopolies are necessarily all bad. They point out that monopolies possess a number of advantages over competitive markets. Let us take a look at some of these benefits.

deadweight loss: the total surplus lost relative to an efficient market due to market imperfections, taxes, or other factors.

✓ SELF-TEST

6. Given the graph on the right:

   a) If this graph depicts a competitive market, what is the equilibrium price and quantity?

   b) If this graph depicts a monopolist, what is the equilibrium price and quantity?

7. In **Figure 10.7**, what would be the total revenue earned by the perfectly competitive industry? What would be the total revenue earned by the monopolist industry? In light of your answer, explain why the monopolist is not charging the same price as the competitive industry.

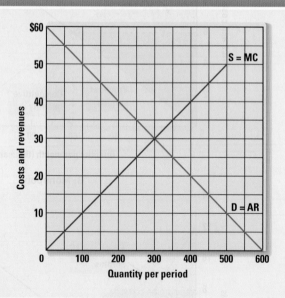

10.5 IN DEFENCE OF MONOPOLY

L05 Explain three grounds on which monopolies can be defended.

We can focus on one of the possible benefits of monopoly by returning to our mushroom industry and what happens when it is monopolized. Some would argue that the conclusions made earlier, with their negative implications, are not valid because if a competitive industry were monopolized, the costs of production would likely change. This is because a monopolist is unlikely to preserve 100 separate mushroom farms, each one a replica of the others with the resulting duplication of

FIGURE 10.9	Natural Monopoly

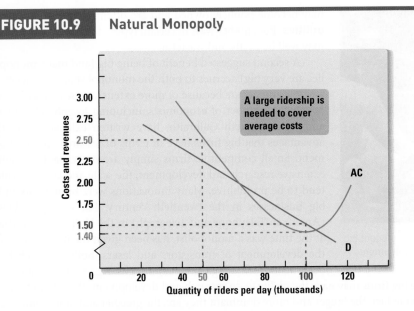

The graph shows that extensive economies of scale result in minimum AC at 100 000 riders. If the rail fare is set at $1.50, then the quantity demanded will be 100 000, and a single transit company could make a profit, since at this level of ridership the average cost is $1.40. If the market were shared between two rail companies serving, say, 50 000 riders each, then the average cost would be $2.50, which is well above the fare of $1.50.

many functions. More likely, the monopolist would rationalize the industry in an attempt to achieve *economies of scale*. It certainly would not require a hundred managers, a hundred accountants, a hundred crating machines, and so on.

If it is true that costs are lower under a monopoly, then graphically, this would mean that the whole average cost curve will be lower, resulting in a correspondingly lower price and a larger output than is shown in **Figure 10.7**. In fact, if costs were significantly lower, the profit-maximizing price could be lower and the output larger than under perfect competition. In fact, economies of scale in some industries are so extensive that in order for a firm to reduce costs sufficiently to make a profit, it may have to produce an output that is very big relative to the size of the market. Under these conditions, the market may only be able to support a single monopoly firm. It is cases like this—where *competing firms simply would not be profitable*—that give rise to what are called **natural monopolies**. This situation is illustrated in **Figure 10.9**.

Suppose the graph illustrates the demand and costs for an urban rail system in a particular city. Because of the very high costs of the railbed and all the rolling stock, the system needs to operate with at least 100 000 users a day to reduce the average cost enough for the system to be profitable. With 100 000 users, it can charge a price of $1.50 per ride, and since this is above the average cost of $1.40, the system will be profitable. (For the sake of simplicity, the MC curve has been omitted.)

natural monopoly: single producer in a market (usually with large economies of scale) that is able to produce at a lower cost than competing firms could.

However, given the size of this particular market, it would be impossible for it to support two competing firms. If each firm had a ridership of 50 000, the average costs for each firm would be $2.50 per ride, well above the $1.50 price that would attract 100 000 users. Because two firms could not make a profit in this market, we have a natural monopoly. Natural monopolies occur whenever startup costs in an industry are so high that the market can support only one profitable firm. A small city in Canada simply could not support more than one competing urban rail system, whereas Tokyo possesses a number of competing rail companies, some privately and one publicly owned. In most small urban markets (and in a number of large ones), such industries as water, electricity, and natural gas supply, urban bus and rail transportation, and telecommunications tend to be natural monopolies. Since they are also extremely important to a community, they

Toronto's GO Transit is an example of a natural monopoly.

Joseph Schumpeter and John Kenneth Galbraith both thought big firms have advantages in terms of research and development.

public utilities: goods or services regarded as essential and, therefore, usually provided by government.

may become publicly owned and are often referred to as **public utilities**. Put another way: in certain types of markets, competition may well be costly and wasteful.

A second suggested benefit of being big (and many monopolies are very big) accrues to both the monopolist and to society as a whole and occurs because of more extensive *research and development*. A number of economists, including Joseph Schumpeter and John Kenneth Galbraith, have written extensively on the advantages that big firms have in terms of research and development. Small competitive firms simply are not capable of doing extensive research and development, the scale and costs of which tend to be prohibitive. Many innovations were brought about by big businesses in the twentieth century. For example, AT&T (American Telephone and Telegraph) in the United States, which at the time was a monopolist, has been given the major credit for the development of transistors and lasers, both of which have been major technological breakthroughs. Against this, critics suggest that while big firms may have the *ability* to do research and development, they do not always have the *desire*; in fact, the bigger and more dominant they are, the greedier and more complacent they may become. As a result, instead of using their energies and resources to improve technology, they use them to create bigger barriers to entry in an effort to keep out competition.

Even worse than this, there are many examples of new ideas that have, in fact, been suppressed by big business because it was not in their own interests to introduce them. For instance, it was a long time before fluorescent tubing came on the market, despite the fact that the technology had been known for years. After all, why introduce a product that can last for years when incandescent bulbs burn out every few months?

A third and final advantage that large corporations, such as monopolies, may have over smaller firms is that they can *offer better salaries and conditions to their employees* and as a result attract a higher quality of staff. In addition, perhaps because their size makes them conspicuous or because they have the finances, big corporations often have better labour practices and are more consumer-aware than are their smaller cousins.

Many observers, recognizing these benefits of monopoly, suggest that government should take a laissez-faire attitude toward monopolies. There are, they suggest, other ways of curbing any possible excesses of the monopolist. Monopolists are not all-powerful because they will always be at the mercy of consumers, who may simply choose not to buy the product. The fear of the possible public scrutiny of their operations and the surrounding bad publicity that will accompany it often serve as a sufficient brake on abuses. In addition, while the monopoly, by definition, does not have to worry about any present competition, it does have to worry about possible future competition. In other words, the barriers to entry are seldom totally insurmountable, and the attraction of high profits may be a sufficient incentive to newcomers to try to overcome these barriers. In summary, the existence of monopolies can be defended on the following grounds:

- They capture large economies of scale in production.
- They engage in extensive research and development into new techniques of production and new products.
- They attract high-quality staff by offering relatively high wages and good working conditions.

SELF-TEST

8. In **Figure 10.9**, suppose there are two competing rail companies, each capturing 50 percent of the market. What would be the total profit or loss of each firm if they both charged a fare of $1.50?

ADDED DIMENSION John Kenneth Galbraith: A Canadian Iconoclast

John Kenneth Galbraith (1908–2006) was an economist who earned a reputation as a critic of orthodox economic theory. Born in rural Ontario, Galbraith was educated at the University of Toronto and the University of California, Berkeley. During his varied career, he played many different roles, including adviser to the U.S. government during World War II, member of the board of directors of *Fortune* magazine, and U.S. ambassador to India in the Kennedy administration. He was, for decades, a respected teacher at Harvard University, and he was a recognized expert on Far Eastern art. His prolific writings include *The Affluent Society*

and *The New Industrial State*, in which he criticizes American big business for creating consumer demand through advertising rather than simply satisfying existing demand.

Galbraith saw today's multinational corporations as being controlled by a small elite, which he termed the *technostructure*, rather than by shareholders or directors. Some of his colleagues have attacked his work for being fuzzy-minded social criticism, but his elegant writings enjoy the rare status of being widely read by both economists and the general public.

10.6 CONTROLLING THE MONOPOLIST

In the past, governments have seldom been persuaded that public scrutiny or the threat of competition are, in themselves, sufficient to address the possible damage that can be caused by monopoly. They, therefore, feel impelled to take more direct action. We will consider three possible courses of direct action: taxation, price setting, and nationalization.

L06 Discuss ways that governments can change the behaviour of monopolies.

Government's aim in regulating monopoly is usually to bring about a more competitive result: ideally, to force the monopolist to reduce its price and profits and increase its output. As we shall see, a number of measures have been attempted with varying degrees of success. Let us look at the first of these: taxation of the monopolist.

Taxing the Monopolist

Two major types of tax could be levied on the monopolist: a profits tax and a monopoly sales tax. We will examine both of them. Suppose that **Figure 10.10**, depicts a monopolist. Government decides to allow it to remain in business and to control its own affairs, but in return, it will have

FIGURE 10.10   **Profits Tax Levied on a Monopolist**

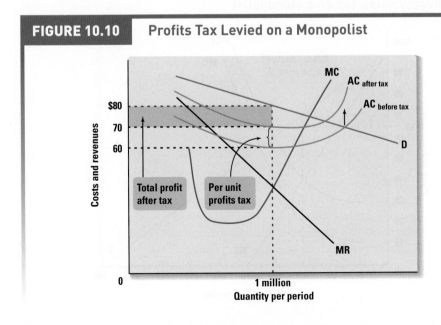

Before the imposition of the profits tax, the monopolist was maximizing its profits at the point where MC = MR, producing an output of one million units at a selling price of $80 per unit. The effect of a fixed tax of $10 million will be to increase the average costs of the monopolist, which increases from $60 to $70 at the one million level of output. As a result, the monopolist will continue to produce one million units at a price of $80. However, its profits will decline by the $10 million tax.

to pay an annual lump-sum profits tax of $10 million. What effect will this have on the monopolist? In particular, will the monopolist end up paying this tax, or will it simply pass this tax on to its customers? Let us look at the results graphically.

Suppose that before the imposition of the tax, the monopolist was producing a profit-maximizing output of one million units, which were being sold at $80 per unit. What effect will the lump-sum tax have on output and price? The important point to bear in mind is that the monopolist must pay this $10 million tax regardless of the level of profits or output. In other words, the tax represents a fixed cost to the monopolist and will increase the average costs of production *while leaving the marginal cost unaffected*. In **Figure 10.10**, the average cost curve will reflect this new tax by shifting up $10 at the present one million output from $AC_{before\ tax}$ to $AC_{after\ tax}$. However, since the variable costs are unaffected by this tax, the marginal cost curve does not change. As a result, the profit-maximizing output remains unaffected. Given the new costs, the best output level is still one million and the best price is still $80 per unit. The only thing that has been affected is the profitability of the monopolist.

Since the output and price levels are unaffected by a lump-sum profit tax, such a policy has its limitations, though it does at least return some of the excess profits to society by way of increased tax revenue to government. The provincial government in British Columbia imposed this type of tax on the mining industry in the 1970s. The industry's response was to reduce their presence in the province considerably and a new government quickly reversed the policy.

Instead of a profits tax, a government might decide to introduce a *monopoly sales tax* on the monopolist's output. In this case, what effect, if any, will this tax have on the monopolist, and again will the tax be passed on to the consumer? Since a monopoly sales tax, unlike the lump-sum profits tax, is a tax on each unit sold, it will affect the marginal cost, as shown in **Figure 10.11**.

The average cost curve has been omitted in the graph because we do not need it to bring out the main points. Prior to the tax, the output level is 140, the marginal cost and revenue equal $30, and the price is $65. Suppose that government now imposes a monopoly sales tax of $20 per unit. The result will be that the marginal cost curve will shift upward by $20 at every level of output, from MC_1 to MC_2. As a result, the new profit-maximizing output is reduced to 120, and the new price will be $70. Part of the new tax of $20 does get passed on to the customer, since the price has increased by $5. The other $15 is absorbed by the monopolist.

FIGURE 10.11   The Effect of a Monopoly Sales Tax on a Monopolist

Prior to the tax, the monopolist was producing where the MC and MR curves intersect—at an output of 140, this gives a selling price of $65. Imposing a $20 per unit sales tax means that MC increases by $20 at every output level. This is shown by an upward shift in the MC curve from MC_1 to MC_2. The new profit-maximizing equilibrium now occurs at the point where the MC_2 curve intersects the MR curve, that is, at an output of 120. The resulting price at which this output can be sold is $70.

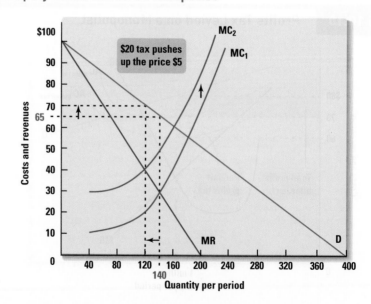

The extent to which the monopolist is able to shift the tax onto the consumer depends, in good part, on the price elasticity of demand. In most cases, the cost is shared between the producer and consumer, and as a result, the total profit of the monopolist will be reduced. However, this type of tax fails abysmally to reduce prices and increase output—in fact, just the opposite effect. The province of Alberta raised the royalty rate on the Athabasca Oil Sands project near Fort McMurray in 2007. Since this royalty is calculated by multiplying output times price times the royalty rate, its effect is the same as a sales tax.

Government Price Setting

In Canada, large monopolies are often regulated by commissions, such as the Canadian Radio and Television Commission (CRTC), Ontario Hydro Commission, and the Canadian Transport Commission. Such commissions are made up of representatives from government, industry, and the public and have the power to approve, or not, any price change the monopoly might propose.

We also see the use of the more direct method of *price setting* to counter the effects of monopoly power. For example, airports are often seen as monopolies and, as such, they are subject to price regulation on the landing fees that airline companies must pay to land their planes. Also, there is evidence that price regulation by the federal government on new pharmaceutical drugs (where the manufacturer enjoys a monopoly position via a patent) results in a lower price than would result from an unregulated market.

Governments, in theory, have the power to force the monopolist to sell at any price as long as this does not impose losses on the monopolist (and thus force the firm out of business). However, some prices are better than others. From society's point of view, the most allocatively efficient solution would be to force the monopolist to charge a price that is equal to the marginal cost of production. This is known as the **socially optimum price** and is illustrated in **Figure 10.12**.

Suppose that without government regulation, the monopolist would produce the quantity Q_{UM} (unregulated monopolist) at a price P_{UM}. Assume now that government decides to regulate the monopolist and forces it to charge a price equal to its marginal cost. If you think of the demand curve as being the price curve, then it is easy to find the socially optimum price because it is located at the point where the MC curve cuts the demand curve. (You might recall from an earlier discussion that if this were a perfectly competitive industry, then marginal cost is the same as supply so that the socially optimum position is equivalent to the equilibrium between demand and supply.)

socially optimum price: the price that produces the best allocation of products (and, therefore, resources) from society's point of view: P = MC.

FIGURE 10.12   The Socially Optimum and Fair-Return Prices

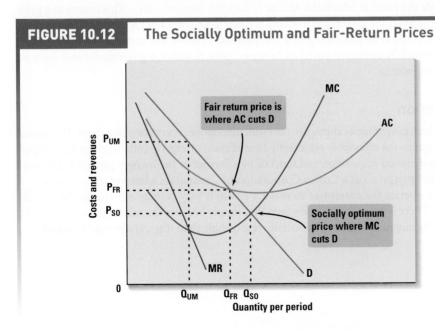

With no intervention by government, the monopolist would maximize profits, where MC = MR. This occurs at the output marked Q_{UM} and at a price of P_{UM}. The socially optimum price is where price is equal to MC at an output of Q_{SO} and a price of P_{SO}. However, this price is below AC, so the monopolist would be forced to incur a loss. Instead, government might impose a fair-return price at which price is equal to AC. This occurs at the point AC intersects the demand curve and produces the output Q_{FR} and a price of P_{FR}.

ADDED DIMENSION Government and Monopolies: An Uneasy Relationship

Since monopolies produce both benefits and costs, governments have often differed in their approach to them. Unlike the United States, Canada has tended to look at monopolists not so much as problems in themselves but as part of a wider problem of restrictive practices, in which firms often combine to restrain competition. As such, the first anti-combines legislation was passed in Canada in 1889 and sought to not only prevent the formation of monopolies or near-monopolies but also forbade collusion among firms to raise prices or restrict supplies to their customers or to do anything which would "unduly lessen competition."

Over the years, this legislation has been revised and updated, the last revision coming in the form of the 1986 Competition Act. This act forbids actions that would lessen competition but does not outlaw mergers or monopolies, per se; it forbids only the "abuse of dominant position." In fact, it explicitly recognizes that some mergers may be warranted as being in the public interest if, for example, this would allow Canadian firms to compete better in world markets.

The socially optimum price, therefore, is P_{SO}, and at this price, the quantity purchased will be Q_{SO}. This regulated price will have the desired effect of reducing the price (and profits) of the monopolist and inducing an increase in output.

Wherever possible, the socially optimum price is the best. In certain circumstances, however, the imposition of such a price might result in the monopolist operating at a loss. This is particularly true where, as in **Figure 10.12**, the costs of production are high relative to the demand at the relevant price. A price of P_{SO} in the above example is below the average costs of production, regardless of the output produced. In circumstances like this, it would not be possible for government to force the monopolist to incur losses. In other words, government will need to ensure that the monopolist is able to earn at least a reasonable profit.

And what is a reasonable profit? Presumably, it is an amount sufficient to keep the company in business and to prevent the owners from looking for other avenues for their financial investment. This is what economists mean by normal profits, and if you remember, normal profits are regarded as a cost of production and are, therefore, included in the average cost shown in **Figure 10.12**. A **fair-return price**, in other words, is a price that allows the monopolist to earn a normal profit and no more. This means that the price should be set equal to average costs. To find it in **Figure 10.12**, we need to locate the point at which the AC curve cuts the demand curve. This occurs at a price of P_{FR}, and at this price, the quantity purchased is equal to an output of Q_{FR}. You can see that the fair-return price tends to be something of a compromise between the unregulated monopolist's position and the socially optimum position. In many cases, however, a government may have no choice but to compromise.

fair-return price: a price that guarantees that the firm will earn normal profits only, that is, where P = AC.

Nationalization

A final way in which governments attempt to deal with monopolies is to nationalize them. This means that the state acquires the monopoly reluctantly (sometimes) or eagerly (often), either by compulsory and uncompensated acquisition (seldom) or by a buyout of the owners (usually). The state then operates the enterprise (as a Crown Corporation in Canada) on whatever terms it sees fit. It may or may not operate the enterprise to make a profit; it may or may not charge the socially optimum price. There is no guarantee, however, that simply because the monopoly is operated by the state, it will be any more efficient or socially responsible than if it were privately owned.

ADDED DIMENSION   Nationalization or Regulation?

Attempting to ensure that certain monopoly and oligopoly industries act in the public interest, some countries have gone to the extreme measure of taking over the industries completely (with or without compensation). Supposedly, government can then appoint its own managers, who will presumably have full knowledge about the costs of production and can ensure that "fair" prices and a "proper" level of production are maintained. In the United Kingdom, after World War II, a number of industries, such as coal mining, steel, and railways, were nationalized by the then-ruling Labour government and run by government-appointed boards. In contrast, in the United States, these and other industries were left in private hands but regulated by government-appointed bodies.

As might be expected, Canada has a more flexible approach to this question. Some firms and whole industries have been nationalized, some are still privately owned but regulated, and some others remain privately owned and unregulated. The nationalized firms (called *Crown Corporations* in Canada) include federally controlled corporations, such as the CBC and Canada Post, but former Crown Corporations, such as Canadian National (CN), Air Canada, and Petro-Canada, have now been privatized. In addition, many provinces have Crown Corporations producing electricity, while at the municipal level, urban transit, the water system, and garbage collection are usually public enterprises.

SELF-TEST

9. The accompanying figure shows the costs and revenue for a monopolist. On the graph, indicate the following:

a) the price (P_{UM}) and quantity (Q_{UM}) if the monopolist is unregulated

b) the price (P_{SO}) and quantity (Q_{SO}) if the monopolist is required to charge the socially optimum price

c) the price (P_{FR}) and quantity (Q_{FR}) if the monopolist is required to charge the fair-return price

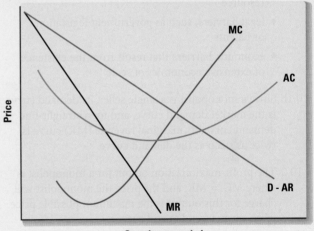

Review

CHAPTER SUMMARY

In this chapter, you learned that defining what is and what is not a monopoly, and whether monopolies are a good or a bad thing for society in general, are not perfectly clear cut. In addition, you learned how the concept of the profit-maximizing output and price are extended from the equality of P and MC under perfect competition to the equality of MR and MC under monopoly.

10.1a The existence of monopolies is a result of barriers to entry, which come in three types:

- technical barriers, such as sole ownership of a resource
- legal barriers, such as government legislation or patents
- economic barriers that result from the existence of extensive economies of scale

10.1b Since a monopolist is a single seller, its demand curve is the market demand curve, and for a straight-line demand curve, its marginal revenue (MR) curve is twice as steep as the demand curve.

10.2 The profit-maximization output for a monopolist is where MC = MR, and the price the monopolist will charge for this output is the maximum possible price, given the market demand curve.

10.3 Monopolies can be criticized for:

- being able to make economic profits even in the long run
- being both productively and allocatively inefficient
- producing a lower output and charging a higher price than would be done in a competitive industry
- creating a more unequal distribution of income
- using their power to practise price discrimination

10.4 Compared with perfect competition, all things being equal, the monopolist charges a higher price and produces a smaller output. In addition, monopoly entails a deadweight loss which means that the economic surplus is less than with perfect competition.

10.5 On the other hand, monopolies can be defended on the grounds that:

- they capture large economies of scale and are, therefore, efficient
- they engage in extensive research and development into new technology and new products
- they offer relatively good wages and working conditions for their employees

10.6 Governments can attempt to change the behaviour of monopolies in three ways:

- taxing the monopolist
- requiring that they sell at a specific price, either a socially optimum price (where P = MC) or a fair return price (where P = AC)
- converting a privately owned monopoly into a crown corporation

NEW GLOSSARY TERMS

barriers to entry   302
deadweight loss   316
fair-return price   322

monopoly   301
natural monopoly   317
perfect price discrimination   313

public utilities   317
socially optimum price   321

STUDY TIPS

1. Students initially have problems understanding why marginal revenue is less than price. The best way to understand the difference is to make up a few tables for yourself, with quantities increasing by one unit and price decreasing by any constant amount. Work out total and marginal revenues, and think out what is happening. Now, put it into words. If you are able to do this, then you understand the concept.

2. **Figure 10.4** is probably the single most complicated graph that you have encountered so far. It is very important that you are able to draw it for yourself and understand what it says. It is probably a good idea to first draw a smooth, saucer-shaped average cost curve with a clearly identifiable lowest point. Now, draw the marginal cost curve intersecting this lowest point. Next, put on the demand curve so that it intersects the average cost curve to the right of the lowest point. Finally, draw in the marginal revenue curve. Strictly, this is supposed to be twice as steep as the demand

curve and should cut the horizontal axis at the halfway point between the origin and the demand curve's intersection with the horizontal axis. But do not worry if it is not exact and you find you have to cheat a little. Once you have located the intersection between the marginal cost and revenue curves, draw a vertical line down to the quantity axis to get the profit-maximizing output. Then, continue this vertical line upward until you hit the demand curve. Go across to the price axis to get the profit-maximizing price.

3. The other graph in this chapter that is difficult to draw is **Figure 10.12**, which shows the effect of government price-setting. Since you want to set up a situation in which the socially optimum price involves a loss for the monopolist, proceed as you would for the normal monopoly diagram. However, when you draw in the demand curve, make sure that it intersects the average cost curve to the *left* of the latter's lowest point.

Answered Questions

These questions can also be found online on Connect.

Indicate whether the following statements are true or false:

1. **(LO 1) T or F** A monopolist is free to charge any price it wishes for its product.

2. **(LO 1) T or F** A patent is an example of a barrier to entry.

3. **(LO 1) T or F** At any given output the marginal revenue of the monopolist may be equal to, greater than, or less than its average revenue.

4. **(LO 5) T or F** A natural monopoly exists when a single producer is able to produce at a lower cost than competing firms could.

5. **(LO 2) T or F** At the profit-maximizing output of the monopolist, the price will be equal to the marginal cost.

6. **(LO 2) T or F** A monopolist will only be able to make a profit if, at some output level, the average revenue exceeds the average cost.

7. **(LO 6) T or F** A lump-sum profit tax imposed on a monopolist will cause the monopolist to increase the price and reduce output in order to maximize its profits.

8. **(LO 6) T or F** A fair-return price is a price set equal to a firm's lowest average cost.

9. **(LO 6) T or F** A socially optimum price is a price set equal to a firm's marginal cost.

10. **(LO 2) T or F** A monopolist will break even if it is producing an output at which the average revenue is equal to the average cost.

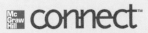

Basic (Questions 11–23)

11. **(LO 1, 2)** All of the following statements, except one, are true about a monopolist. Which is the exception?
    a) Its demand curve is downward sloping.
    b) Average revenue and price are the same.
    c) Marginal revenue and price are the same.
    d) Marginal revenue and marginal cost are equal at the profit maximizing output.

12. **(LO 1)** Sole ownership of a particular resource is an example of:
    a) A natural monopoly
    b) A technical barrier to entry
    c) An economic barrier to entry
    d) A public utility

13. **(LO 2)** Which of the following is true of a private monopoly?
    a) It cannot make economic losses in the short run.
    b) It cannot make economic losses in the long run.
    c) It always makes economic profits.
    d) It never makes economic profits.

14. **(LO 5)** All of the following, except one, are true statements about a natural monopoly. Which is the exception?
    a) It is able to produce at a lower cost than competing firms could.
    b) It has economies of scale and a declining LRAC over the relevant range of demand.
    c) The demand for its product is perfectly elastic.
    d) They are often found in public utility industries.

15. **(LO 1)** All of the following statements, except one, are true about a monopolist. Which is the exception?
    a) The monopolist can determine the price, but the market will determine the quantity purchased.
    b) The monopolist can determine the quantity offered for purchase but the market will determine the price.
    c) The monopolist can determine both the quantity offered for purchase and the price.
    d) The monopolist faces a downward-sloping market demand curve.

16. **(LO 1)** Which of the following statements is true regarding the marginal revenue curve of the monopolist?
    a) It is twice as steep as the average revenue curve.
    b) It could also be called a price curve.
    c) It is a horizontal line.
    d) It is the same as its average revenue curve.

17. **(LO 1)** All of the following, except one, are examples of barriers to entry. Which is the exception?
    a) Economies of scale
    b) Minimum-wage legislation
    c) Copyrights
    d) Government licences

Figure 10.13 depicts the cost and revenue curves for a monopolist. Use it to answer questions 18 to 20.

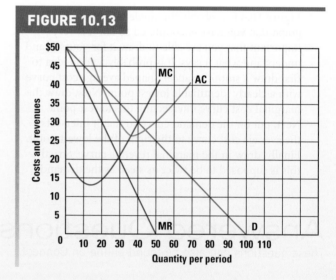

FIGURE 10.13

18. **(LO 2)** What are the profit-maximizing level of output and price, respectively?
    a) 30 and $20
    b) 30 and $35
    c) 35 and $27.50
    d) 40 and $30
    e) 42 and $28

19. **(LO 2)** At the profit-maximizing level of output, what is the amount of total costs?
    a) $20
    b) $600
    c) $900
    d) $1200
    e) Cannot be determined from this information

20. **(LO 2)** What is the level of profits at the profit-maximizing output?
    a) 0
    b) $20
    c) $150
    d) $450
    e) $600

21. **(LO 1)** All of the following, except one, are true at the output where a monopolist's marginal revenue is equal to zero. Which is the exception?
    a) It is the output that maximizes total revenue.
    b) It is the output that maximizes average revenue.
    c) It is the output that is associated with the midpoint of the AR curve.
    d) It is the output where average revenue must be greater than marginal revenue.

22. **(LO 1)** Suppose a monopolist was charging a price of $120 for its product and was selling 80 units. If it lowers its price to $119 and, as a result, sells 81 units, what is the marginal revenue for the product?
    a) 0
    b) $1
    c) $39
    d) $9639

23. **(LO 2)** All of the following, except one, are true at the output(s) where a monopolist breaks even. Which is the exception?
    a) TC = TR
    b) Profits are maximized
    c) AR = AC
    d) Economic profits are zero

Intermediate (Questions 24–33)

24. **(LO 2)** Under what circumstances will a profit-maximizing monopolist be forced to shut down?
    a) If the average revenue exceeds the average costs of production
    b) If the average revenue exceeds the average variable costs of production
    c) If the average variable costs of production exceeds the average revenue
    d) If marginal revenue exceeds average revenue

25. **(LO 6)** How will a monopoly sales tax affect a monopolist's output?
    a) It will lead to an increase in the price and a reduction in output.
    b) It will lead to an increase in price but will have no effect on output.
    c) It will lead to a reduction in output but will have no effect on price.
    d) It will have no impact on price or output.

Table 10.4 outlines the cost and revenue data for a monopolist. Use it to answer questions 26 and 27.

TABLE 10.4

Quantity Demanded	Price	Total Cost
0	/	$ 40
1	$45	58
2	40	73
3	35	87
4	30	100
5	25	118
6	20	143

26. **(LO 2)** What are the profit-maximizing level of output and price, respectively?
    a) 3 and $35
    b) 4 and $30
    c) 5 and $25
    d) 5 and $30
    e) 6 and $20

27. **(LO 2)** What is the level of profits at the profit-maximizing output?
    a) 0
    b) $7
    c) $15
    d) $20
    e) $120

Refer to **Figure 10.14** to answer questions 28 and 29.

FIGURE 10.14

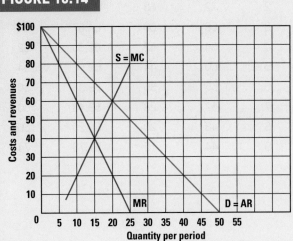

28. **(LO 4)** Suppose this graph depicts a perfectly competitive industry. What will be the equilibrium price and output, respectively?
    a) $40 and 15
    b) $40 and 30
    c) $60 and 20
    d) $60 and 25
    e) $70 and 15

29. **(LO 4)** Suppose this graph depicts a monopoly industry. What will be the profit-maximizing price and output, respectively?
    a) $40 and 15
    b) $40 and 30
    c) $60 and 20
    d) $60 and 25
    e) $70 and 15

30. **(LO 6)** Which of the following is a correct statement about the socially optimum price?
    a) It is a price equal to average cost.
    b) It is a price equal to marginal cost.
    c) It is a price equal to the lowest average cost.
    d) It is a price equal to marginal revenue.

Refer to **Table 10.5**, which contains data for a monopolist, to answer questions 31 and 32.

TABLE 10.5

Output	Price ($)	Marginal Revenue ($)	Average Cost ($)	Marginal Cost ($)
0	80	/	/	/
1	76	76	92	54
2	72	68	72	52
3	68	60	64.67	50
4	64	52	61.50	52
5	60	44	60	54
6	56	36	59.33	56
7	52	28	59.43	60
8	48	20	60.25	66
9	44	12	61.78	74

31. **(LO 6)** What would be the output and price if this firm was an unregulated, profit-maximizing firm?
    a) 4 and $52
    b) 4 and $64
    c) 5 and $60
    d) 6 and $56
    e) 9 and $44

32. **(LO 6)** What would be the output and price if this firm was regulated and required to charge a fair-return price?
    a) 4 and $52
    b) 4 and $64
    c) 5 and $60
    d) 6 and $56
    e) 9 and $44

33. **(LO 6)** What would be the output and price if this firm was regulated and required to charge a socially optimum price?
    a) 4 and $52
    b) 4 and $64
    c) 5 and $60
    d) 6 and $56
    e) 9 and $44

Advanced (Questions 34–35)

34. **(LO 2)** All, except one, of the following statements regarding the profit-maximizing output of the monopolist are correct. Which one is false?
    a) At that output, marginal cost will be equal to price.
    b) At that output, marginal profit is zero.
    c) At that output, the difference between total revenue and total cost will be at a maximum.
    d) At that output, marginal cost will equal marginal revenue.
    e) At that output, average revenue will exceed marginal revenue.

35. **(LO 4)** Suppose that a perfectly competitive industry is monopolized. If the costs of production remain unchanged, which of the following statements is correct?
    a) Both the price and the output of the perfectly competitive industry will be higher than those of the monopoly industry.
    b) Both the price and the output of the perfectly competitive industry will be lower than those of the monopoly industry.
    c) The perfectly competitive price will be higher, and the output will be lower.
    d) The perfectly competitive price will be lower, and the output will be higher.
    e) Output and price will remain unchanged.

Parallel Problems

ANSWERED PROBLEMS

36A. **(LO 2, 4, 6) Key Problem Table 10.6** depicts the metal keg industry which is perfectly competitive. (All units, apart from the price are in thousands per week).
  a) Complete the table, and, in **Figure 10.15**, draw in the demand and supply curves for the industry. (Recall that the supply curve for a perfectly competitive industry is the same as its MC curve.)
  b) What are the equilibrium values of price, quantity traded, and total profit (or loss) in the industry? Label the competitive equilibrium as e_1 on the graph.
    Price: $ _____ ; quantity: _____ ;
    profit/loss: $ _____ .
  c) Suppose instead that the table depicts a monopolist. What will be the profit-maximizing price, quantity, and profits? (*Hint:* Draw in the AC and MR curves on your graph in **Figure 10.15**.)
    Price: $ _____ ; quantity: _____ ;
    profit/loss: $ _____ .
  d) Now, suppose that the government is not satisfied with the monopolist's situation and decides to impose a monopoly tax of $3000. What will be the price, quantity, and profits?
    Price: $ _____ ; quantity: _____ ;
    profit/loss: $ _____ .

  e) What if, instead of the tax, the government decides to impose a socially optimum price. What will be the price, quantity, and profits?
    Price: $ _____ ; quantity: _____ ;
    profit/loss: $ _____ .
  f) Finally, suppose that instead of the socially optimum price, the government imposes a fair-return price. What will be the price, quantity, and profits?
    Price: $ _____ ; quantity: _____ ;
    profit/loss: $ _____ .

FIGURE 10.15

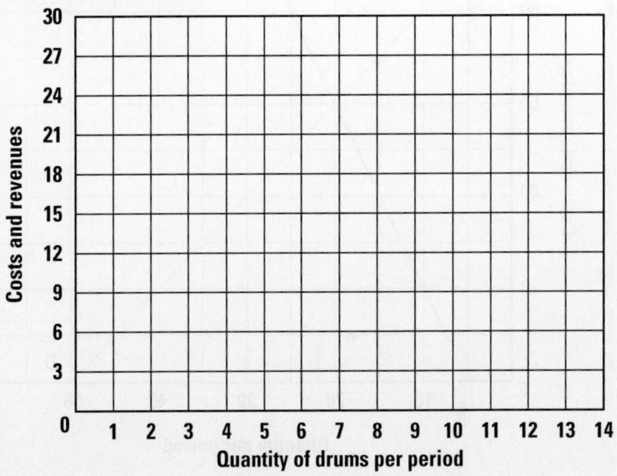

Price ($)	Quantity Demanded	TR ($)	MR ($)	MC ($)	TC ($)	Tπ ($)	AC ($)
30	0	_____	/	/	28	_____	/
28	1	_____	_____	_____	48	_____	_____
26	2	_____	_____	_____	59	_____	_____
24	3	_____	_____	_____	67	_____	_____
22	4	_____	_____	_____	83	_____	_____
20	5	_____	_____	_____	100	_____	_____
18	6	_____	_____	_____	118	_____	_____
16	7	_____	_____	_____	138	_____	_____
14	8	_____	_____	_____	163	_____	_____
12	9	_____	_____	_____	193	_____	_____

TABLE 10.6

Basic (Problems 37A–43A)

37A. (LO 2) Figure 10.16 shows the demand and marginal cost curves for the monopolist Mr. Peanut.
  a) Draw in the marginal revenue curve.
  b) What are the values of the profit-maximizing output and price?
     Output: _____ ; price: _____ .
  c) What are the values of output, price, and total revenue, when the firm's total revenue is maximized?
     Output: _____ ; price: _____ .

FIGURE 10.16

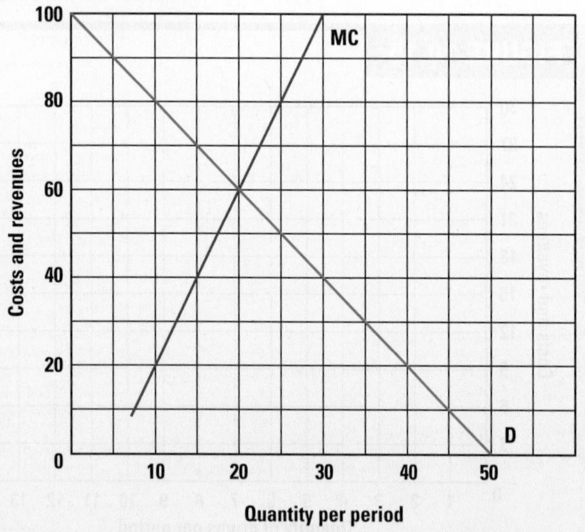

38A. (LO 2) Figure 10.17 refers to the monopolist Ms. Get It Right.
  a) At what output(s) does the firm break even?
     _____ and _____ .
  b) At what output does the firm maximize its profits?
     _____ .
  c) That is the amount of this profit? _____ .
  d) Draw the total profit curve in Figure 10.17B.

39A. (LO 2)
  a) Complete Table 10.7, which shows the costs and revenues of Solo the monopolist. (You may assume that the demand curve is a straight line.)
  b) What are the values of the profit-maximizing output, price, and total profit or loss?
     Output: _____ Price: $ _____
     Total Profit/Loss: $ _____
  c) At what output will total revenue be maximized, and what will be the value of total revenue?
     Output (units): _____
     Total revenue: $ _____
  d) What is the value of MR when profits are maximized and when total revenue is maximized?
     MR is _____ when profits are maximized.
     MR is _____ when total revenue is maximized.

40A. (LO 2) Figure 10.18 shows the demand for the product of Primo the monopolist.
  a) From this information, complete Table 10.8, and add the MR curve to Figure 10.18.
  b) At what output level is total revenue maximized? What is the marginal revenue at this output?
     Output (units): _____
     Marginal revenue: $ _____

TABLE 10.7

Quantity per Period	Price	TR	MR	MC	TC
0	/	/	/	/	$ 65
1	$32	___	___	$ 8	73
2	___	___	___	7	80
3	28	___	___	6	86
4	___	___	___	5	91
5	___	120	___	6	97
6	___	___	___	7	104
7	20	___	___	8	112
8	___	___	___	9	121
9	___	___	___	10	131
10	___	___	___	12	143

FIGURE 10.17

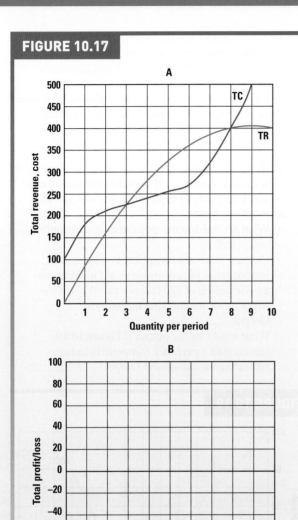

FIGURE 10.18

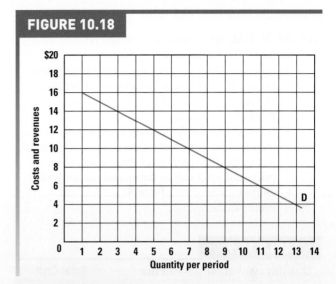

TABLE 10.8

Quantity Demanded	Price = AR ($)	TR ($)	MR ($)
1	___	___	___
2	___	___	___
3	___	___	___
4	___	___	___
5	___	___	___
6	___	___	___
7	___	___	___
8	___	___	___
9	___	___	___
10	___	___	___
11	___	___	___

c) What is the maximum output the monopolist would produce? Output of: _____ .

d) What is the elasticity of demand for outputs greater than the quantity in c)?
Answer: _____ .

e) What general rule can you derive from these observations?
Answer: _____
_____ .

41A. **(LO 2)** The monopolist Mr. Pop It Right is considering whether it is worthwhile producing an additional 20 units per day of his large bags of popcorn. Doing so would

cost him an additional $42 in total. He is currently selling 48 bags per day at $4 each. In order to sell the additional 20 bags every day, however, he would have to lower his price to $3.50. What do you recommend?
Answer: _____
_____

42A. **(LO 3)** Explain the difference between discrimination among units and discrimination among buying groups.

43A. **(LO 1)** What is meant by *barriers to entry*? What are the three types of barriers? Give an example of each.

Intermediate (Problems 44A–50A)

44A. (LO 2) Table 10.9 shows the cost and revenue data for Molly the monopolist.

a) What are Molly's profit-maximizing output and price, and what will be the amount of her profit?

Output: _____ Price: $ _____

Profit: $ _____

b) Suppose that the demand for Molly's product increased by three units at every price level. What will be her new profit-maximizing output and price, and what will be the amount of her profit?

Output: _____ Price: $ _____

Profit: $ _____

TABLE 10.9

Quantity per Period	Price	Total Cost
0	$30	$ 4
1	28	32
2	26	54
3	24	72
4	22	86
5	20	98
6	18	112
7	16	134
8	14	160
9	12	192

45A. (LO 2, 4) Table 10.10 shows the costs and demand for the Clove Oil industry.

TABLE 10.10

Quantity	Price	Total Cost
0	$20	$ 9
1	19	23
2	18	33
3	17	48
4	16	64
5	15	82
6	14	102
7	13	124
8	12	148

a) If this industry was perfectly competitive, what would be the output, price, and total industry profit?

Output: _____ ; price: $ _____ ;

profit: $ _____ .

b) If this industry was a monopoly industry, what would be the output, price, and total industry profit?

Output: _____ ; price: $ _____ ;

profit: $ _____ .

46A. (LO 2, 4) Sol-Motors is the only auto manufacturer in West Lidia, a country that prohibits the importation of cars. Figure 10.19 depicts the demand and the costs for Sol-Motors.

a) What are Sol-Motors' price-maximizing output and price?

Output: _____ ; price: $ _____ .

b) Suppose that the government of Lidia imposes a price ceiling of $20 000 per car. What is the firm's profit-maximizing output now?

Output: _____ .

c) What would be the output if Figure 10.19 represented a perfectly competitive industry rather than a monopoly? Output: _____ .

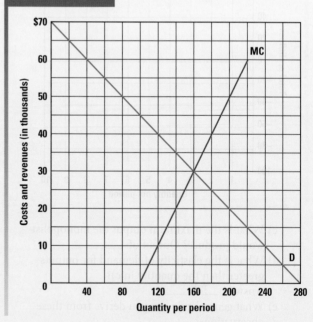

FIGURE 10.19

47A. (LO 2, 6) Figure 10.20 shows the cost and revenue information for Shitotsu the monopolist.

What are the levels of price, output, total (sales) revenue, and total profits if the monopolist were to produce at the positions a) through d) indicated in Table 10.11?

FIGURE 10.20

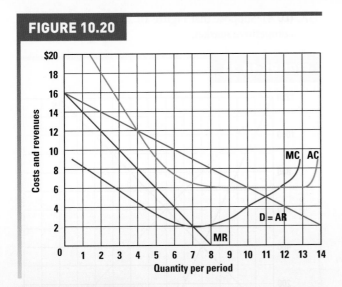

TABLE 10.11

	Price ($)	Output	Total Revenue ($)	Total Profits ($)
a) Total revenue maximization	___	___	___	___
b) Profit maximization	___	___	___	___
c) Socially optimum price	___	___	___	___
d) Fair-return price	___	___	___	___

48A. **(LO 3)** Ivan runs a small independent movie theatre in Scarborough, which presently attracts 1200 customers per week at a ticket price of $8. His customer base comprises 1000 adult customers and 200 seniors. He would like to increase his total revenue by practising price discrimination. He knows that the demand by adults is fairly inelastic and that a change in the admission price of $1 would change the quantity by 80 customers. He also recognizes that the demand by seniors is fairly elastic and a $1 change in the price would result in a change of 50 customers.
   a) What is Ivan's present total revenue? _____ .
   b) Should he increase or decrease the price for adults? _____ . Should he increase or decrease the price for seniors? _____ .
   c) What price will maximize the total revenue from adult customers? _____ .
   d) What price will maximize the total revenue from seniors? _____ .

e) What will be the total revenue from both groups? _____ .

49A. **(LO 1)** Explain why the average revenue of the monopolist is not the same thing as the marginal revenue.

50A. **(LO 6)** Why would a lump-sum tax have no impact on either the price or the output of a monopolist?

Advanced (Problems 51A–55A)

51A. **(LO 2)** Tom, the only steel drum manufacturer in Narnia, can sell a single drum for $30. However, for every extra drum he wants to sell, he is forced to reduce the price (for all his customers) by $2. The total fixed costs in his workshop are $15, and the variable cost of the first drum produced is $25. For each extra drum thereafter, the cost drops by $5 up to, and including the fifth drum. After that, the cost of each extra drum increases by $5.
   a) Draw the AR, MR, AC, and MC curves in **Figure 10.21**.
   b) What is Tom's profit-maximizing output, price, and total profit or loss?
      Output: _____ ; price: $ _____ ;
      profit/loss: $ _____ .

FIGURE 10.21

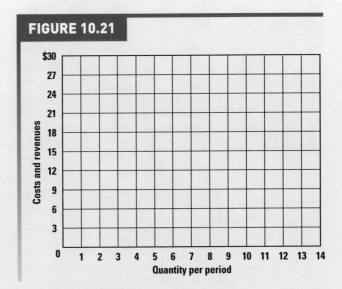

52A. **(LO 2, 3)** **Figure 10.22** shows the demand curve facing Jill the monopolist who cannot sell partial units.
   a) Using **Figure 10.22**, fill in columns 2, 3, and 4 in **Table 10.12**.
   b) Draw in the MR1 curve in **Figure 10.22**.
   c) What is the level of output when Jill's total revenue is maximized? What is her total revenue?
      Output: _____ . TR: _____ .

FIGURE 10.22

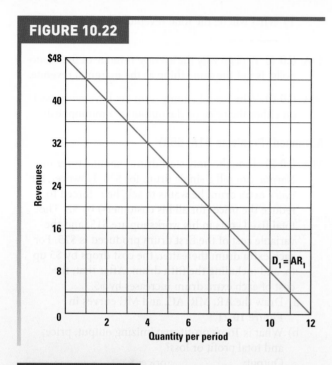

TABLE 10.12

(1) Quantity	(2) AR$_1$	(3) MR$_1$	(4) TR$_1$	(5) AR$_2$	(6) MR$_2$	(7) TR$_2$
1	___	___	___	___	___	___
2	___	___	___	___	___	___
3	___	___	___	___	___	___
4	___	___	___	___	___	___
5	___	___	___	___	___	___
6	___	___	___	___	___	___
7	___	___	___	___	___	___
8	___	___	___	___	___	___
9	___	___	___	___	___	___
10	___	___	___	___	___	___
11	___	___	___	___	___	___
12	___	___	___	___	___	___

d) Suppose that Jill could practise perfect price discrimination by selling each unit at a different price (the first at $44, the second at $40, the third at $36, etc.). Fill in columns 5, 6, and 7 in **Table 10.12**.

e) Now, what is Jill's maximum total revenue?
Answer: _____.

53A. **(LO 4)** Suppose that **Figure 10.23** depicts a perfectly competitive market.

FIGURE 10.23

a) What are the equilibrium price and quantity? At what equilibrium, what are the values of the producer surplus, the consumer surplus, and the economic surplus?
Price: _____ Q; quantity: _____
producer surplus _____
consumer surplus: _____
economic surplus: _____

Suppose instead that **Figure 10.23** depicts a monopoly.

b) What would be the monopolist's price, quantity, producer surplus, consumer surplus, economic surplus and deadweight loss?
Price: _____; quantity: _____;
producer surplus _____
consumer surplus: _____;
economic surplus: _____;
Deadweight loss: _____.

54A. **(LO 1)** A monopolist would never produce in the price range at which the demand was inelastic. Why not?

55A. **(LO 2)** In terms of both totals and averages/marginals, identify the profit-maximizing output for the monopolist.

CHAPTER 11

IMPERFECT COMPETITION

LEARNING OBJECTIVES

At the end of this chapter, you should be able to...

LO1 understand the importance and effects of product differentiation, including advertising.

LO2 understand the differences between the two types of imperfect competition.

LO3 explain why monopolistically competitive firms tend to have excess capacity and are unlikely to earn long-run economic profits.

LO4 understand the main characteristics of oligopoly markets.

LO5 understand why large firms are often tempted to collude and form cartels.

LO6 understand price leadership and why oligopolistic firms are reluctant to change prices very often.

WHAT'S AHEAD...

This chapter looks at the behaviour of firms operating in two types of imperfectly competitive markets, referred to as oligopoly and monopolistic competition. We begin by looking at the common features of both and see how firms try to distinguish their products through advertising and other types of product differentiation. We then look at equilibrium in both markets and evaluate how the results compare with perfect competition. In the case of the monopolistically competitive firm, we show why the distinction between the short run and the long run is important. In the case of the oligopolistic firm, we emphasize the importance of interdependence among firms. This means there is no single theory of oligopoly, and the behaviour of the oligopolistic firms depends upon whether they collude or not.

A Question of Relevance...

Baseball caps, video cameras, haircuts, beer, books, TV programs, cell phones, cigars, calculators, and airline flights. What do all these products have in common, apart from the fact that they are of interest to most students and their professors? They are all produced by firms that are neither perfect competitors nor monopolies. Instead, all the firms associated with these products operate in a market structure that economists call *imperfect competition.*

ADDED DIMENSION   Joan Robinson: Filling the Void

Joan Robinson (1903–1983) was a long-time professor of economics at Cambridge University and a student of Alfred Marshall's. Although she was neither a member nor a founder of any particular school of thought, she made some significant contributions to economic theory, including a critique of Marxist economics from the position of a friendly detractor. Her most important contribution, however, was *Economics of Imperfect Competition* (1933). This book filled a huge void in economics: the analysis of market structures that lie between the extremes of monopoly and perfect competition.

Her work was published at the same time as that of the American economist Edward Chamberlin, who wrote on the same theme. The two provided similar, though not identical, analyses. Chamberlin praised imperfect competition for adding increased consumer choice. Robinson criticized it for leading to the waste caused by under-utilized resources. She concluded that firms in imperfect competition are likely to reduce output in order to maintain price, and this results in a great deal of idle capacity and under-utilized resources. Consequently, she believed that government should intervene to discourage this form of market structure.

So far, we have examined two market structures: monopoly and perfect competition. There are only a few examples of a pure monopoly, and as we have seen, the model of perfect competition is more of an abstraction (albeit a very useful abstraction) than a description of our present world. Lying between these two extremes is the market for a multitude of familiar products that millions of people buy. The term **imperfect competition** is used by economists to refer to these more familiar market situations, and it describes much of modern capitalism reasonably well. As we shall see, there are, in fact, two different forms of imperfect competition: *monopolistic competition* and *oligopoly*. We will discuss the differences between the two shortly. Many of the ideas in this chapter were developed independently in the 1930s by Edward Chamberlin of Harvard University and Joan Robinson of Cambridge University.

imperfect competition:
a market structure in which producers are identifiable and have some control over price.

11.1 PRODUCT DIFFERENTIATION

L01 Understand the importance and effects of product differentiation, including advertising.

product differentiation:
the attempt by a firm to distinguish its product from that of its competitors.

Imperfect competition is competition between firms based on something other than price. One example of this is **product differentiation**. Product differentiation is the attempt by a seller to offer a product that is *seen* by the consumer as different, and presumably better, than the others on the market. There are several ways this may be done. A recognizable logo is a popular form of product differentiation. Nearly everyone recognizes the Nike "swoosh" that is seen on television ads, T-shirts, baseball hats, and billboards. To many consumers, the widely recognized symbol adds to the desirability of owning a pair of Nike shoes. This increases the demand for Nike products and enables the company to charge a higher price than its rivals do. Perhaps the world's most recognizable symbol is McDonald's golden arches. The success of this company speaks volumes about the rewards of effective product differentiation.

Besides using a logo, firms try to create a special image for their products through distinctive brand names. There are several highly successful examples that one could think of: a Hoover is a vacuum cleaner; Kleenex is really facial tissue; a Band-Aid is an adhesive dressing; Saran Wrap is quite ordinary plastic sheeting; and Scotch tape is just one of many types of adhesive tape. In each of these cases, the generic product has come to be commonly identified with a brand name. Besides the use of recognizable symbols or brand names, firms sometimes try to differentiate their products through distinctive packaging of different sizes, colours, shapes, or textures. Infants, for instance, can recognize their own favourite brands of cereal or candy long before they are able to read.

Product differentiation may take a different form. Think of a business, such as a retail outlet, in which location and service are often significant differentiators. This explains, for example, why some dry-cleaning shops do brisk business, while others do not, or why a supermarket chain retains a strong presence in older neighbourhoods where it has attractive, long-established locations and a reputation for service.

Another type of product differentiation occurs when firms introduce a new and supposedly improved version of their product. A prime example of this occurs annually in the auto industry, where new models are introduced every year and each new version is reported to be an improvement that will better meet customer needs. This same phenomenon has spread to other industries, resulting in, for example, the annual new models of television sets or, almost unbelievably, of mattresses.

Finally, let us look in some detail at the way firms attempt to differentiate their products through advertising. There may, in fact, be no difference between two brands of motor oil, but if people think there is a difference, then product differentiation has occurred. Successfully convincing consumers that one motor oil is better than another often involves extensive advertising effort.

Advertising by rival firms can be thought of as a very expensive and very important form of nonprice competition. In many people's minds, the word *advertising* conjures images of expensive television commercials, which only very large firms can afford. However, adver-

Roadside signs are one way in which sellers try to differentiate their products.

tising comes in other forms as well—from flyers delivered directly to households to sign boards in a mall. These are ways that smaller firms attempt to differentiate themselves from their rivals. Larger firms, on the other hand, can afford national television exposure.

There is debate within the discipline of economics over the benefits of advertising to society as a whole. We will look at both sides of the argument and examine the views of both the supporters of advertising and its critics.

Supporters point out that advertising provides the consumer with vital information about the availability, quality, and location of products, which helps greatly to cut down on the consumers' search time in acquiring information. For instance, it would be very time consuming if, because of the lack of advertising, you could obtain information about buying a car only by driving from dealer to dealer.

A second argument in favour of advertising is that it increases the degree of competition in the market because new firms are better able to enter an industry when they can announce their entry through advertising. For example, you can imagine the near impossibility for a firm, such as Hyundai, to break into the North American car market without the benefits of national advertising. An extension of this argument is that the development and introduction of new products is also greatly enhanced by the presence of advertising. The point is sometimes made that advertising creates an atmosphere that encourages new-product development so that technological change is encouraged.

The third argument of supporters is that advertising can actually lower the price of many products that are extensively advertised. There are two reasons for this. The first is that increased competition, mentioned above, would be expected to heighten consumer knowledge about prices and thereby force down prices and decrease profit margins for the representative firm. In addition, it has been argued that advertising enables a firm to expand its size and thereby enjoy economies of scale in production. This lowers average costs and thus, ultimately, leads to a lower price for the final product.

Lastly, another benefit credited to advertising is the increased availability of the magazines and television shows financed by sponsors' ads. Whether this improves our overall standard of living is a value judgment best left to the reader.

In summary, supporters of advertising believe it is beneficial because:

- it provides the consumer with vital information
- it enhances competition between firms
- it lowers the prices of products
- it finances magazines and television shows

ADDED DIMENSION   Too Many Breakfast Cereals?

A trip to the local supermarket reveals some interesting insights into product differentiation and competition. A bewildering choice of products is on display: 20 types of laundry detergents, a dozen brands of coffee, 50 tempting bags of cookies and at least 30 different breakfast cereals. This is competition in action. Or is it? Although we have spent time in this text looking at the markets for various products and figuring out what determines the price and output of each, it is firms—not products—that compete.

A closer look at the cereal aisle reveals that while there may well be 30 competing brands on display, the majority are produced by only four competing firms: General Mills, Quaker, Post, and Kellogg's. Combined, they account for 80 percent of sales. General Mills manufactures Cheerios, Cinnamon Toast Crunch, and Wheaties among many others; Quaker is responsible for Life and Quaker Oats; Post sells Raisin Bran, Cap'N Crunch, and Shreddies; and Kellogg's produces their famous Cornflakes, as well as Vector, Fruit Loops, Rice Krispies, Special K, and so on.

In all, these four companies produce well over a hundred brands. But why would a company sell more than one brand—in essence competing against itself? The companies themselves would suggest that are simply catering to consumer demands and increasing the choices available. However, the real answer lies in simple arithmetic. Suppose, for instance, that you are trying to enter the breakfast cereal industry, and suppose further that each of the four major companies produced only one brand each. With luck and good sales promotion you are hoping to take market share away from the others with your new brand of appealing, nutritious cereal. Assume that you are successful and you are now one of the big five, and as a result, the older companies have seen their market share drop from 25 percent to 20 percent each and you have captured 20 percent.

Now, back to the real world. What if you entered the market with your new product and faced competition from 50 other brands? Probably, the best you can expect to capture is a proportional share of the market—just 2 percent. Multi-branding, in other words, is just one way for firms to establish and maintain market share. As such, it acts as a big barrier for new entrants into the market.

In rather dramatic contrast, critics of advertising argue that it is wasteful because even if all advertising were eliminated tomorrow, total consumption expenditures in the economy would not decline. Expenditure patterns may well change—as fewer products that were highly advertised are bought—but more of other products would be purchased, so total consumer spending would be little affected. This argument goes on to state that the billions of dollars spent on trying to persuade consumers to buy a certain brand of product could then be spent in much more socially desirable ways. This argument discounts the informational value of advertising by pointing out that most advertising (TV in particular) is aimed at persuasion, and its effectiveness is cancelled out by a rival firm's large expenditures with the same goal in mind. For instance, millions of dollars are spent by both Procter & Gamble and its rival Johnson & Johnson as they go head-to-head in the shampoo wars on television. We might ask, after all is said and done, if the consumer is any better off as a result.

Critics of advertising also challenge the idea that advertising increases competition by arguing that it is just as likely that huge advertising budgets used to promote brand loyalty can create a barrier to entry that could encourage the emergence of monopoly tendencies.

Finally, critics hold that expenditures on advertising must raise the price of products. Someone pays for the billions of dollars spent every year on advertising, and that someone must be either the producer of the product or the consumer of it. If the producer ended up paying, it would seem logical for it to not advertise. But, the argument goes, it is the consumer who pays, and it is very unlikely that anyone's hair is cleaner or more beautiful because of advertising—but the shampoo is probably more expensive than it would otherwise be.

In summary, critics offer these arguments against advertising:

- It is mostly non-informative and wasteful.
- It encourages concentration within industries.
- It raises prices to the detriment of consumers.

As you can see, points on both sides of this argument seem quite valid, and empirical studies have not succeeded in ending this argument. Let us bring this discussion on product differentiation to a close by summarizing the ways that firms attempt to do this:

- developing a recognized brand name, product logo, or packaging
- securing a superior location or developing a reputation for exceptional service
- engaging in product redevelopment and improvement
- developing an effective advertising strategy

 SELF-TEST

1. Assume that two firms dominate the running-shoes industry. One of these firms hires a high-profile sports figure to endorse its product by appearing in its advertising.

   a) What would you expect the other firm to do in response, and why?

   b) After the second firm has reacted in the way you said it would, what do you think each firm's relative share of the market would be?

   c) Given your answer in b), what might these two firms be tempted to do?

11.2 THE DIFFERENCE BETWEEN THE TWO TYPES OF IMPERFECT COMPETITION

We can distinguish between two types of market structures that come under the general heading of imperfect competition. **Monopolistic competition** is a market containing many relatively small firms, whereas **oligopoly** is a market with a few large firms. One way of emphasizing this distinction is to compare industry concentration ratios. These **concentration ratios** measure the percentage of an industry's total sales that the largest few (for example, four) firms control. Suppose, for instance, that the combined sales revenue of the four biggest firms in the asphalt industry is $320 million and the total sales revenue of the whole industry is $400 million. The concentration ratio in that industry, therefore, would be $320/$400 × 100 = 80 percent.

High concentration ratios would occur in industries dominated by a few large firms which, together, produce a big percentage of total output. This often occurs when large output levels are required to capture economies of scale. The automobile, aluminum, oil refining, beer, soft drink, and airline industries are all oligopolies. On the other hand, industries in which economies of scale are not significant tend to have low concentration ratios. These industries, such as real estate agencies, brake and muffler shops, travel agencies, hair salons, and dry-cleaning shops, contain many small firms and are therefore monopolistically competitive.

Table 11.1 provides some data on selected Canadian industries that are highly concentrated and whose markets are, therefore, oligopolistic. An industry with a concentration ratio above 40 percent is regarded as highly concentrated and therefore oligopolistic. The figures indicate the percentage of total industry output produced by the largest four firms in the industry.

It should be noted that some oligopoly industries, breweries for example, may contain not only a few dominant firms but also a number of small firms. Deciding whether a particular industry is an example of monopolistic competition or an oligopoly is a matter of degree and a question of fact. In other words, when looking at any industry, we need to ask, "Would the total supply of this industry be seriously affected or not by the exit of its largest firm?" If yes, then it is clearly an oligopoly industry. If no, then it is monopolistically competitive.

L02 Understand the differences between the two types of imperfect competition.

monopolistic competition: a market in which there are many firms that sell a differentiated product and have some control over the price of the products they sell.

oligopoly: a market dominated by a few large firms.

concentration ratio: a measurement of the percentage of an industry's total sales that is controlled by the largest few firms.

TABLE 11.1	Highly Concentrated Canadian Industries	
	Concentration Ratio (Top Four Producing Firms) % of Total Industry Sales	
Industry	**1990**	**2005**
Motor Vehicles	87.2%	100.0%
Petroleum	75.6	99.9
Tobacco	98.8	99.8
Cement	72.0	99.7
Fertilizers	56.7	99.4
Tires	86.2	99.3
Breweries	90.6	99.2
Sugar and Confectionary	47.8	98.7
Household Appliances	61.6	98.5
Coffee and Tea	76.5	97.8
Sporting and Athletic Goods	22.7	92.8
Wineries	48.5	92.2

Source: Statistics Canada, *Concentration Ratios in the Manufacturing Industries*, Cat. 31C0024.

 SELF-TEST

2. The Canadian grummit industry consists of ten companies whose annual sales are as shown.

   a) Calculate the (four-)firm concentration ratio for this industry.

   b) In what type of market does the grummit industry operate?

Company	Sales (in $millions)
A	22
B	6
C	17
D	12
E	8
F	15
Next four companies (total)	12

11.3 MONOPOLISTIC COMPETITION

L03 Explain why monopolistically competitive firms tend to have excess capacity and are unlikely to earn long-run economic profits.

Monopolistic competition is the third type of market structure we study. Some examples of monopolistically competitive markets were mentioned above. Others include almost all retailing, from ladies' clothes stores to gasoline retailing; almost all of the services that are provided directly to the retail consumer, including travel agents, hairdressing, shoe repair, and tax accounting; almost all services aimed at the home owner, such as roofers, plumbers, carpet layers, and painters; most of the growing cottage-industry sector, from software designers to authors and proofreaders; and some manufacturing markets, such as the textile, footwear, and furniture industries.

A monopolistically competitive industry has four characteristics. The first is that the industry is made up of *many relatively small firms* that act independently of each other. Across any metropolitan area are dozens of shops, agencies, and small businesses, each of which tries to distinguish itself from its competition. Similarly, across the whole economy are dozens of T-shirt or chair manufacturers acting in the same way.

Second, there is *freedom of entry* into the industry for new firms. This is analogous to the perfect-competition model. Free entry does not mean that entry requires no money. What it does mean is that there are no significant barriers to entry, as discussed in the previous chapter.

Third, firms within a monopolistically competitive industry have *some control over the price* of the products they sell. This is unlike the firms in a perfectly competitive industry. Despite such control, there often is very little price competition among firms. Instead, competition centres on attempts by individual firms to differentiate the products they sell.

The fourth characteristic of a monopolistically competitive industry is the fact that each firm sells a differentiated product. Many would suggest that product differentiation is the major defining characteristic of monopolistic competition. This is because a new entrant into the market has a degree of control, not only over the price it charges, but also over the product itself. In contrast, a new corn farmer, for instance, has little choice but to sell its corn at the same price as every other corn farmer. But further than that, the farmer has almost no chance of making his product unique. Corn is corn. However, if you are thinking of opening a new restaurant you not only have control over the prices of the menu items but you can also decide what type of food you want to serve and what clientele you want to appeal to.

In summary, the characteristics of a monopolistically competitive industry are:

- many small firms
- freedom of entry
- some control over price
- differentiated products

The Short-Run and Long-Run Equilibrium for the Monopolistically Competitive Firm

The costs of production of firms in a monopolistically competitive industry tend to be very similar—the cost of running one hair salon is not much different from the cost of another. On the other hand, the presence of nonprice competition and product differentiation does result in the possibility that the demand faced by one firm can be quite different from that facing another. This is why our analysis of this type of market structure focuses on the role of the demand faced by the individual firm. Usually, the individual firm faces a highly elastic demand curve, although it is not perfectly elastic as in the case of the perfectly competitive model.

To launch the analysis of the monopolistically competitive model, let us imagine a trendy restaurant that is currently doing well. Could this firm be making economic profits? **Figure 11.1** will provide us with an answer.

In this figure, we have an elastic demand curve (D_1) that the restaurant faces, along with its associated marginal revenue curve (MR_1). The demand curve for a representative firm is more elastic than the market demand curve for the whole industry because it is so easy for customers to stop coming to this establishment and go to a competitor instead. In fact, the firm's elasticity of demand will depend on the amount of competition as well as the degree of product differentiation it has achieved.

If there is very little competition for a firm or if its product is very different from the competition's product, then the demand will be inelastic. At the opposite extreme, if there was extensive competition and the product was indistinguishable from that of the competition, then the demand would be perfectly elastic, and we would be describing perfect competition. Since there is a degree of product differentiation with monopolistic competition but a great deal of competition and the ability to control price, then its demand is likely to be fairly elastic.

On the graph is the average cost curve (AC) and its associated marginal cost curve (MC). These two curves are the same as those developed in Chapter 6. In fact, you will notice that the graph is identical to that for a monopolist and for every firm that is not perfectly competitive. Much of what we said about the monopolist will apply here, too.

Next, recall the two basic questions that any firm must answer: what is the right output level at which to operate, and what is the right price to charge? The answer to the first question is: the output level that maximizes total profits, which in **Figure 11.1** is quantity Q_1. This is the point

FIGURE 11.1   The Monopolistically Competitive Firm in Short-Run Equilibrium

D_1 is an elastic demand curve with its associated marginal revenue curve MR_1. AC and MC are the normal U-shaped cost curves. The area P_1aQ_10 represents total revenue. Similarly, C_1bQ_10 represents total costs. If we subtract costs from revenue, we get economic profits, represented by area P_1abC_1.

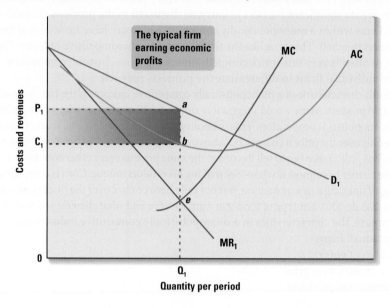

The typical firm earning economic profits

Costs and revenues

Quantity per period

where the marginal cost equals marginal revenue (point e). The right price is the highest price that the firm can charge and still sell the optimum quantity—in this case, price P_1.

To find out the amount of total profit the restaurant is making, remember that total revenue equals price times quantity. This is represented on the graph by the area P_1aQ_10. Similarly, total cost equals average cost times quantity, and this is represented by the area C_1bQ_10. Total revenue less total cost is total profit, and this is represented by the area P_1abC_1. Remember that these are economic profits, since normal profits by definition are incorporated in the costs.

We now come to the crucial point in understanding how monopolistically competitive industries function. What will be the response of outsiders not yet in the industry to the fact that this restaurant is making economic profits? The answer is that some of these outsiders will want a share of these profits and will enter the industry as new firms. And what will be the effect of this entry?

First, the restaurant will notice that business just is not as good as it used to be. At its current price, it will find that it now has fewer customers. In graphical terms, the demand curve that the restaurant faces (the same one we saw in **Figure 11.1**) shifts to the left and also becomes more elastic. This is because the restaurant in question must now share the market with new competitors. **Figure 11.2** illustrates the eventual result of this entry.

As always, the firm's best output level is at the point where marginal cost equals marginal revenue (point e), which occurs at quantity Q_2. The best price is the highest that can be charged and still sell quantity Q_2. This is price P_2. The crucial thing to note about the graph is that the new demand curve (D_2) faced by the restaurant has shifted to the left (because of the entry of new firms) and has become more elastic so that it is now tangent to the average costs curve at point a. Given this point of tangency between the AC curve and the demand curve (which is also the average revenue curve), the area P_2aQ_20 represents both the restaurant's total revenue and its total cost. Therefore, economic profits are zero. Another way of stating this is that the firm is making only normal profits.

How can we be sure that economic profits will end up at zero in the long run? Well, as long as even some economic profits continue to be made by the representative firm, then more entry will occur, and graphically this additional entry will mean that the demand curve faced by the representative firm will continue to shift back until all economic profit has disappeared. This will occur when the demand curve is eventually tangent to the average total costs curve. In short, the existence of economic profit triggers a reaction that continues until that profit disappears.

FIGURE 11.2	The Long-Run Equilibrium for the Firm

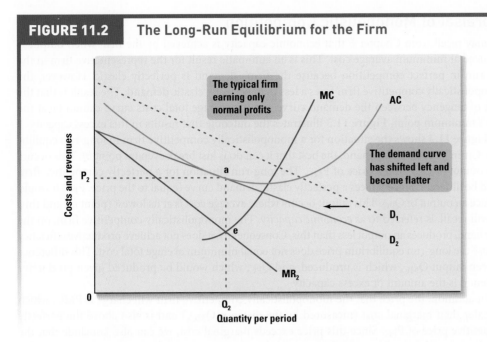

The equilibrium price and quantity are P_2 and Q_2. Further, since the demand curve is tangent to the average cost curve at point *a*, the area P_2aQ_20 represents both total revenue and total cost. This is the case of zero economic profit.

We are now ready for the main conclusion from our analysis of the monopolistically competitive industry model:

> In the long run, the representative firm in a monopolistically competitive market makes only normal profits.

In other words, in the long run there are no economic profits to be made in, say, the dry-cleaning, shoe repair, hardware retailing, or textile manufacturing businesses. Think of it this way: if there were economic profits to be made in doing something as simple as running a dry-cleaning shop, wouldn't some of you start doing that? And if enough of you did open your own shops, what would happen to those economic profits? They would disappear.

Now, this last point should not be interpreted to mean that there are *no* monopolistically competitive firms that make economic profits in the long run. We are probably all aware of some travel agent or gas station or convenience store that seems, even in the long run, to be so busy it must be making an economic profit. Such exceptional firms do exist, and usually, the reason for their success can be summed up in two words: product differentiation. This could be the result of an excellent location, exceptional service, or some other similar reason. However, for every one of these success stories, there are three or four other stories of firms that entered the same industry, hung on until the owner's money was gone, and then went out of business. If we subtract these firms' losses from the profits of the successful firms, we would more closely approximate zero economic profits in the long run in the *whole industry*.

 SELF-TEST

3. Since there are hundreds of small family-owned restaurants in any large Canadian urban area, why are these markets considered to be monopolistically competitive and not perfectly competitive?

4. Assume that a representative firm in monopolistic competition is experiencing economic losses. What series of events will occur to return this firm to its long-run equilibrium?

Appraisal of Monopolistic Competition

You may recall from Chapter 6 that economic capacity is achieved by the firm when output is produced at minimum average cost. This is an automatic result for the representative firm in the long run in perfect competition because the firm's demand is perfectly elastic. However, the monopolistically competitive firm faces a less than perfectly elastic demand. The result is that the point of tangency between the demand curve and the average total costs curve cannot be at the latter's minimum point. **Figure 11.3** illustrates the outcome that results in this excess capacity.

Figure 11.3 shows the situation for a monopolistically competitive firm in long-run equilibrium. Given its costs and demand, the best that it can do is just break even (at point *b*). This occurs at an output of Q_{MC} and a price of P_{MC}. The long-run situation for a perfectly competitive firm would be different. Since it faces a perfectly elastic demand curve (equal to the price, P_{PC}) it would produce an output of Q_{PC}. This output occurs where average cost is at its lowest (point *a*), and this, you will recall, is referred to as *economic capacity*. The monopolistically competitive firm, on the other hand, produces an output less than this. Consequently, it does not achieve productive efficiency because the long-run equilibrium price does not equal minimum average total cost. This difference between output Q_{MC}, which is produced, and Q_{PC}, which would be produced given productive efficiency, is the amount of excess capacity.

In addition, the price that the monopolistically competitive firm will charge is PMC, which is greater than marginal cost (measured by the distance Q_{MCc}) and is also above the perfectly competitive price of P_{PC}. Since this price exceeds marginal cost, we can also conclude that the firm does not achieve *allocative efficiency* as defined in Chapter 9.

At the root of this excess capacity is product differentiation. Each firm's attempt to differentiate itself, or its product, from all the others in the market results in the overall market being fragmented. Excess capacity is the result.

The result of this fragmentation is that the representative firm in each industry finds its profit-maximizing output to be one at which average total costs are not at the minimum. This means that the total output of a monopolistically competitive market could be produced at a lower cost. Examples of excess capacity are seen in the large number of hairdressing salons, gas stations, and travel agencies that dominate the urban landscape, all working at less than capacity.

FIGURE 11.3   Excess Capacity

The long-run equilibrium for a perfectly competitive firm with a perfectly elastic demand curve, D_1, is at point *a*. This is the point of minimum average total cost. The long run equilibrium for a monopolistically competitive firm with a downward-sloping demand curve, D_2, is not at the point of minimum average cost, as can be seen by point *b*. The difference in the two outputs $Q_{PC} - Q_{MC}$ is referred to as *excess capacity*.

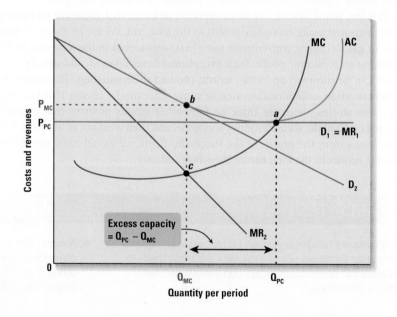

Does this mean that public policy should somehow restrain firms from fragmenting the market by attempting to differentiate themselves? Almost certainly not. Not only is it difficult to prevent, there are benefits from differentiation. The most important is the fact that consumers have a wide choice of variations of the same general product, which makes it more likely that diverse consumer tastes will be fully satisfied. There are many gasoline stations, convenience stores, and shoe styles available to choose from in our economy. Most people see this as a strength of the market system rather than a weakness. However, this wide choice does come with a cost to the consumer, which is that production could be technically more efficient if the representative firm could raise its output to the level at which average costs are at a minimum.

✓ SELF-TEST

5. Consider the accompanying graph for a monopolistically competitive firm.

   a) What output will this firm produce?

   b) How much excess capacity exists at this output level?

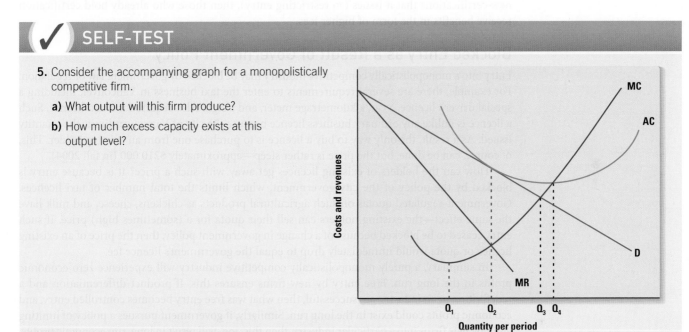

Explaining the Franchise Phenomenon

It should be clear from the discussion so far that there are no economic profits in a monopolistically competitive industry in the long run because it is easy for new firms to enter the industry. We can turn this observation around and deduce that if entry could somehow be blocked, the chances for most firms to experience economic profits would be greatly increased. How would it be possible to block entry, to make a monopolistically competitive industry less competitive?

If a product could be successfully differentiated so that it is somehow regarded as "unique" and cannot be duplicated by rival firms, then it is possible to restrict production of that product to member firms that alone are given permission to produce it. This is the explanation for the enormous growth in the franchise phenomenon, where, for an initial fee and payment of royalties, individuals are given exclusive rights to sell a product. We find such groupings in the fast-food industry, real estate agencies, auto repair specialists, and convenience stores, among others.

The many potential advantages to franchising include bulk purchasing, national advertising, and in particular, brand identification. In addition, it allows individuals to own their own businesses without having to accumulate the large sums of money it would take to get started on a national level. If such brand identification becomes strong enough that going out for a hamburger is redefined as going out to McDonald's, then the meaning of the term "industry" is changed. This means that entry can be controlled, since each franchise holder has a contractual commitment from the franchiser that entry into his or her territory is blocked.

Now, there is no guarantee that a rival grouping will not enter the same territory, but entry by a new firm selling the same differentiated product is controlled. Proof that even this limited blocking of entry is valuable is found in the fact that the purchase price of an established franchise firm is often quite high.

Professional associations also try to redefine the industry in which their members practise. They do this by trying to create the perception in the public's mind that members of the association are better qualified to do a certain kind of work than are nonmembers. If hiring an accountant is redefined, through advertising, to mean hiring a certified general accountant (CGA), then the demand for CGAs will increase. If the professional association is also able to limit the number of new certifications that it issues (so restricting entry), then those who already hold certification receive benefits in the form of higher fees.

Blocked Entry as a Result of Government Policy

Entry into a monopolistically competitive industry may be blocked by government law or regulation. For example, there are several requirements to enter the taxi business in Vancouver, including a special driver's licence, a car, a kilometrage meter, and a sign. Also required is a taxi licence. Such a licence is unlike any ordinary business licence because the city of Vancouver limits the quantity issued. As a result, the only way to buy a licence is to purchase one from an existing holder. This, of course, can be done, but the price is rather steep—approximately $210 000 (in fall 2004).

How can the holders of existing licences get away with such a price? It is because entry is blocked by the policy of the city government, which limits the total number of taxi licences. Government-regulated quotas on such agricultural products as chickens, cheese, and milk have the same effect—the existing holders can sell their quota for a (sometimes high) price. If such entry ceased to be blocked because of a change in government policy, then the price of an existing licence or quota would immediately drop to equal the government's licence fee.

In summary, a purely monopolistically competitive industry will experience zero economic profits in the long run. Free entry by new firms ensures this. If product differentiation and a redefinition of an industry are successful, then what was free entry becomes controlled entry, and economic profits could exist in the long run. Similarly, if government pursues a policy of limiting entry by new firms into a particular industry, then this, too, will result in long-run economic profits.

11.4   OLIGOPOLY

L04 Understand the main characteristics of oligopoly markets.

Let us now turn to the last of our four market models—oligopoly. As mentioned earlier, an oligopoly is characterized first of all by the fact that the industry is made up of a *few large firms that dominate the market*, which means that the concentration ratio is high.

Oligopolies can be found both in industries that produce differentiated products and in industries that produce a standardized product. Examples of oligopolistic industries in which the products are differentiated include tobacco, breweries, automobiles, major appliances, electronic goods, and batteries. Examples of industries in which the few firms produce a standardized product include steel, aluminum, lumber, and pulp. Individual oligopolistic firms are generally large enough to be commonly known by most people. They include all the "Generals"—General Motors, General Foods, General Tire, General Electric, General Paint—plus a host of other household names from Phillips to Nikon to Air Canada.

New firms do occasionally enter an oligopoly industry. Yet, and this is our second characteristic, *entry is difficult*—much more so, for example, than in a monopolistically competitive industry. Let us examine why this is so. Note that the firms mentioned above concentrate on the production of physical products, such as cars, tires, TV sets, or boxes of cereal. This is no coincidence because the production of almost any physical product involves economies of scale, and such economies result in falling average cost as output is increased. Thus, at the early stages of a new industry, those firms that are able to increase the size of operation will gain a tremendous advantage over rivals that lag behind. This leads to the dominance of an industry by the few firms that grew fastest in the beginning. Thus, once the industry has grown beyond its early stages, barriers to entry become more significant.

As discussed earlier in the chapter, such oligopoly firms as those in monopolistic competition engage in a great deal of *nonprice competition*. This is especially so when product differentiation is present. This can be considered the third characteristic.

The fourth characteristic is the ability of the firm to have significant control over the price that it charges for its product. However, this control is limited by consumer demand because it is consumers who determine how much to buy and, therefore, how successful the firm will be. But in determining the price, the oligopolist's control is limited by what is called **mutual interdependence**, which is the fifth characteristic of this market structure. Mutual interdependence exists when one firm, before it makes a decision, must consider the reactions of rival firms. It is this phenomenon of mutual interdependence that, more than any other characteristic, distinguishes oligopoly from the other types of market structures.

For example, let us imagine a typical oligopolistic industry in which a large percentage of the total output is produced by only two firms (the soft-drink industry in North America is a typical example). Each firm is large and powerful and would, presumably, be able to set the price of its own product. Yet, any pricing decision that either firm might decide on could generate a response from the rival firm. Thus, the power of firm A is very much constrained by the anticipated reaction of firm B. Such interdependence plays a crucial role in any oligopoly environment. Because of this mutual interdependence and because of the uncertainty of how competitors will react to pricing and output changes, there is no single oligopoly theory of price and output. As a result, a number of theories have been developed to explain oligopoly markets.

In summary, an oligopoly industry has five characteristics:

- It is dominated by a few large firms.
- Entry by new firms is difficult.
- Nonprice competition between firms is widely practised.
- Each firm has significant control over its price.
- Mutual interdependence exists between firms.

mutual interdependence: the condition in which a firm's actions depend, in part, on the reactions of rival firms.

 SELF-TEST

6. Since both oligopoly and monopolistically competitive firms practise price differentiation and have control over their own prices, in what ways are they different?

11.5 THE TEMPTATION TO COLLUDE

To a large extent, the world of oligopoly is a struggle between cooperating and competing. It pays for oligopoly firms to cooperate because that is how they can make the most *joint* profits. But even when they cooperate, there is still the incentive to compete and outdo the rival, which could result in even greater *individual* profits for one of the firms. Cooperation among rivals is called **collusion**, which is an agreement or understanding among firms for the purposes of setting prices and/or dividing up the market. As we shall see later in this chapter, collusion often means that the colluding firms tend to act as though they are a single monopolist with the results we saw in the last chapter: productive and allocative inefficiency. Societies are poorly served by such arrangements and so collusion between firms is illegal in most countries and usually carries stiff fines or other penalties. However, collusion between countries is a different matter, as we shall see, and is impossible to prosecute.

L05 Understand why large firms are often tempted to collude and form cartels.

collusion: an agreement among suppliers to set the price of a product or the quantities each will produce.

FIGURE 11.4   The Demand for Drinking Water in an Ancient Persian Village

The maximum price for water is 10 shekels, and the maximum quantity is 100 jugs. Given this demand curve, the marginal revenue drops twice as steeply and crosses the quantity axis at 50 (half of 100). This is the revenue (and profit) maximizing output; that is, total revenue is maximized where MR = 0. The maximum price for this quantity is 5 shekels (half the maximum price of 10 shekels). The total revenue equals 250 shekels (50 × 5 shekels).

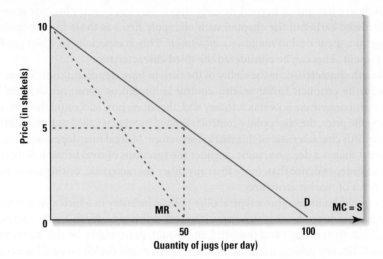

To help you understand this "compete versus cooperate" dilemma, let us look at a simple example. Imagine an isolated village in a remote, mountainous region of ancient Persia, which possesses an abundant supply of drinking water from the local well to which the villagers have free access. The marginal cost of the water is zero, and since it is identical to the supply curve, it plots as a horizontal straight line in **Figure 11.4**, which also shows the demand. The (perfectly competitive) market price, therefore, is equal to zero (where demand equals supply), and the quantity consumed each day is 100 jugs.

Now, suppose that the village sheik, whose name is Aman, is granted ownership of the well in return for exceptional services rendered to the empire's sultan. As the new monopoly owner, he is trying to decide how much to charge the villagers for the water. Since the cost of the water is zero, Aman needs only to look at revenues and decide which price will give him the maximum revenue. **Table 11.2** shows that the best price to charge is 5 shekels per jug, since total revenue at that price is at a maximum of 250 shekels.

TABLE 11.2   Total Revenue for Aman

Price (in shekels)	Quantity per Day	Total Revenue
10	0	0
9	10	90
8	20	160
7	30	210
6	40	240
5	50	250
4	60	240
3	70	210
2	80	160
1	90	90
0	100	0

(We could also confirm that this is the revenue-maximizing point by adding a marginal revenue curve to our graph. This shows that it crosses the horizontal axis at an output of 50, which would imply a price of 5 shekels.)

Suppose that a few weeks later, a village shepherd, Omar, while digging some large stones out of the ground to give his sheep better access to a nearby mountain trail, discovers a bountiful spring of fresh water. Knowing that Aman is charging 5 shekels a jug, he decides that he would like a piece of the action; he offers his water for sale to the villagers at 4 shekels per jug. The result is that all the villagers desert the village well and start buying their water from Omar. Understandably, Aman is furious and decides to drop the price of his water to 2 shekels. Omar retaliates and drops his price even lower to 1½ shekels. A price war has broken out, and it is clear that the price will continue to drop. But how low can it go? Well, since the cost of the water is zero, we already know that the competitive price will eventually fall to zero. But Aman and Omar also realize this and so decide to hold a summit meeting. At a shady spot between the well and the newly found spring. a truce is declared in the price war. They come to an agreement to divide the market equally between them. Aman explains that the revenue- and profit-maximizing price is 5 shekels and the maximum output should be 50 jugs. So, they decide to limit the output to 25 jugs per day each, which will earn each of them a profit of 125 shekels.

All goes fine for a few weeks until Aman gets a bit greedy. Although 125 shekels are better than zero, which would have been the outcome if the price war had continued, it is, nevertheless, only half of what he used to earn. He starts to wonder what would happen if he were to renege on his promise to Omar and increase his output by 10 jugs, to 35 jugs. He realizes that the total output would rise to 60 jugs (25 by Omar and 35 by himself), which would cause the price to drop to 4 shekels. But that would still give him greater revenue, since 35 jugs at 4 shekels amounts to 140 shekels, 15 more than his present earnings. (It would be tough luck for Omar, whose revenue, as a result, would drop to 100 shekels—25 jugs at 4 shekels each). What about increasing his output even further to, say, 45 jugs? The total would then be 70 jugs, forcing the price down even further to 3 shekels. His revenue would, therefore, be 135 shekels. No, not so good; an increase to 35 jugs would be ideal.

But, of course, Omar is thinking exactly the same thing and has also concluded that an increase in output to 35 jugs would be in his best interests.

So, as rational profit-maximizers, what should they do? We can present their choices by making use of **game theory**. Game theory was first developed by economists John Neumann and Oskar Morgenstern in the 1940s to analyze strategic behaviour. This idea can be applied not just to oligopoly theory but also to any situation where people seek to work out the best possible action, taking into consideration the possible reactions of rivals. The various strategies and outcomes (or payoffs) are usually presented in the form of a matrix. The payoff matrix for Aman and Omar is shown in **Figure 11.5**.

game theory: a method of analyzing firm behaviour that highlights mutual interdependence among firms.

FIGURE 11.5 **The Payoff Matrix for Aman and Omar**

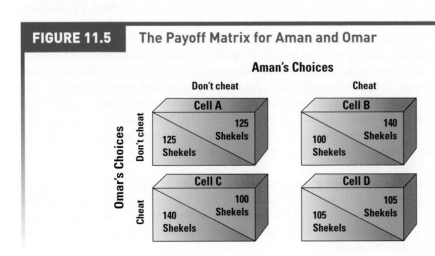

Cell A shows the outcome if Aman and Omar stick to their agreement. This is the best outcome for them jointly. Cell B shows the result if Aman cheats but Omar does not (better for Aman but worse for Omar). Cell C shows what happens if, instead, Omar cheats but Aman does not (better for Omar, but worse for Aman). Cell D shows the likely outcome when they both cheat, which produces the worst joint outcome for them.

ADDED DIMENSION   John Nash, the Beautiful Mind

In the early 1950s, a young graduate student at Princeton University, John Nash, wrote a series of articles and mathematical proofs that laid the groundwork for the game theory revolution that swept through economics in the 1980s and 1990s. Nash became a tenured faculty member at the Massachusetts Institute of Technology at the unbelievably young age of 29 in 1958. In that same year, he was struck by paranoid schizophrenia and, as a result, lost his faculty position. He wandered around Europe and North America—in and out of mental institutions—for the next few decades. The effects of his illness began to recede in the early 1980s when he returned to Princeton, though he was seen or spoken with only rarely and thus came to be known as the "Phantom of Fine Hall." In 1994, Nash received the Nobel Prize in Economics for his work of 40 years earlier. Hollywood's version of his story is told in the movie *A Beautiful Mind*.

There are four possible payoffs, labelled cells A through D. Cell A shows the results if neither of them cheats and they stick to their original agreement to produce an output of 25 jugs. Cell B shows what will happen if Aman cheats but Omar sticks to the agreement. Cell C shows, on the contrary, what will happen if Omar cheats but Aman sticks to the agreement. Finally, Cell D shows what would happen if they both cheat.

If both Aman and Omar stick to the agreement, the payoff, as shown in cell A, is 125 shekels to each of them. If, on the other hand, Aman cheats and increases his output to 35, but Omar sticks to the agreement, cell B shows the outcome would be a profit of 140 shekels to Aman but a profit of only 100 shekels to Omar. Cell C shows the results if the positions were reversed and Omar cheats but Aman sticks to the agreement. Now, Omar would end up with 140 shekels, with Aman's dropping to 100. Finally, cell D shows what would happen if they both cheat. In this case, if they both decide to increase output by 10 jugs, the total output would increase to 70 jugs causing the price to drop to 3 shekels, with the result that each would receive 105 shekels. Looking at each of the four payoffs, it is clear that the best option for them would be to stick to the agreement, since the monopoly position definitely guarantees the greatest joint profits. But is that likely to happen?

Look at things from Aman's point of view. He is thinking: "If I were to stick to our agreement, the best that could happen is that I will end up with a profit of 125 shekels (if Omar also sticks to the agreement)—cell A—and the worst thing is a profit of only 100 shekels (if Omar cheats)—cell C. On the other hand, what will happen if I cheat? The best would be a profit of 140 shekels (if Omar does not cheat)—cell B—and the worst is 105 shekels (if he does)—cell D. Given that his best is better by cheating and his worst is also better by cheating, it is clear that he should cheat. But this is equally true for Omar. So, what will happen? They will both cheat despite the fact that this is, by far, the worst result for them jointly. This result is what is referred to as a **Nash equilibrium**, named after the Nobel Prize winner in Economics John Nash.

Nash equilibrium: a situation where each rival chooses the best actions given the (anticipated) actions of the other(s).

This story highlights some important aspects of oligopoly markets. First, competition may well lead to a price war, causing prices to drop to the point where oligopolists may not be able to make profits or may even make losses. Second, cooperation, in contrast, can offer far greater rewards for oligopoly firms—it can offer them the prospect of making monopoly profits. The temptation to collude, therefore, is very high despite the fact that collusion is illegal and is banned in most countries. Third, these collusive agreements seldom last long, since the temptation for one (or all) of the parties to cheat is too attractive. Since collusion implies cheating on consumers, it is perhaps only a further small step to cheating on your business partners. Or, as the saying goes, there is no honour among thieves.

The existence of interdependence and the possibility of collusion among firms results in oligopoly theory that is complex and a little messy. For this reason, there is not a single oligopoly model but rather several possible variants, each of which has a different focus. We will investigate a couple of examples of collusive oligopoly and then look at two examples of how oligopoly firms behave, assuming that they do not collude.

Collusive Oligopoly

If rivals decide that they are going to collude instead of competing, the collusion can take many different forms.

Firms might divide up the market on the basis of geography (you stay south of the river, and we will stay north). Alternatively, the whole market could be divided up according to existing client lists, or simply by general agreement on an output quota for each firm. The most obvious form of collusion, of course, is for the colluding firms to agree on a fixed price. When both price fixing and quotas are used, the firms are acting as if they were a single monopolist. This means that they need to determine the profit-maximizing output for the group as a whole and then divide up this output in some agreed-on fashion. Whether the collusion is out in the open or secret, the term **cartel** is used to describe a formal agreement of cooperation among firms.

cartel: an association of sellers acting in unison.

The classic example of an open cartel is that of the Organization of Petroleum Exporting Countries (OPEC), which came into existence in 1961. Within a few years, it controlled more than 85 percent of the world's oil exports.

OPEC did not draw much worldwide attention until 1973, when the member countries agreed to restrict their (combined) output, thereby decreasing the market supply of oil. To accomplish this they set a total output target and then assigned each member a quota based on that (restricted) quantity. This had a dramatic effect on world markets, and some straightforward elasticity analysis will help us understand why.

Prior to this point in OPEC's history, the demand faced by any of the twelve member countries was undoubtedly elastic. But world demand for oil is inelastic, and once member countries agreed to act in concert, the organization created a near-monopoly on oil exports. Thus OPEC, as an organization, faced a highly *inelastic demand*. **Figure 11.6** shows the effect of OPEC's policy of restricting the output of oil.

The decision to restrict oil output is represented by a shift to the left in the supply curve from S_1 to S_2. Remember that our definition of supply is the amount that producers are able and *willing* to put on the market at various different prices. What we are saying here is that the OPEC producers were, at each and every price, only willing to put on the market less than before. The inelastic demand curve in **Figure 11.6** means that a relatively modest 20 percent restriction in quantity (from 30 million barrels a

In the future, a gas price of $131.4 per litre may seem ridiculously low.

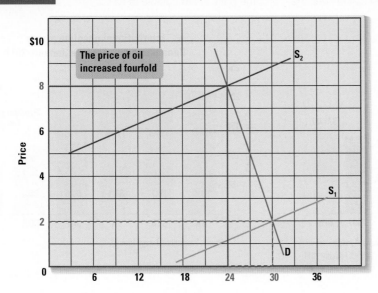

| **FIGURE 11.6** | **The Effect of OPEC's Policy on the World Market for Oil** |

The price of oil increased fourfold

By forming a cartel, the 12 members of OPEC were able to reduce the world's supply of oil, which resulted in the supply curve shifting to the left from S_1 to S_2. Since the world demand for oil is inelastic, this resulted in a dramatic increase in the price of oil from $2 to $8.

day to 24 million) causes a dramatic 400 percent increase in price (from $2 a barrel to $8). Note what happened to OPEC's revenues. They rose from $60 million a day (30 million × $2)—the red-dashed rectangle—to $192 million a day (24 million × $8)—the blue-lined rectangle.

Each of the 12 member nations was selling less oil than before, but combined they were receiving over three times the previous revenue. This was the beginning of a very significant shift in wealth among the world's economies, and it all came about because former rivals acted cooperatively and behaved like one big monopoly. How long could this last? Seemingly, as long as each of the 12 stuck to their assigned quotas and *trusted* that others were doing the same.

However, like most things, OPEC's stranglehold on the world oil-export market changed. On the supply side of things, the high price of oil (it peaked at about $35 a barrel in the early 1980s) brought new productive capacity to the market by countries not in OPEC but keen to enter the market at these high prices. In addition, the world's demand for oil was reduced as a result of conservation efforts that prompted some new technology and through the development of some alternative sources of energy.

All of this caused the world price of oil to start to drop. Then, when the worldwide recession of 1981–1983 hit, the price of oil began to plummet even further, and the OPEC countries found that cutting their quotas again and again did not stop the trend toward much lower prices. Oil revenues to the OPEC-12 fell dramatically, which was quite a shock given that these countries had come to assume they would enjoy fantastic revenues forever and were spending accordingly. In the face of falling revenues and growing excess capacity, various members of OPEC began to cheat. They sold their quota at the official (agreed-upon) price and then also tried to sell additional quantities under the table at a reduced price. The net effect of this was a further increase in the world's supply of oil and an even greater downward pressure on the price.

Each member country had to choose between cooperating (sticking to the agreement) or competing (breaking the agreement). We can, again, analyze this fundamental dilemma using game theory. In **Figure 11.7**, we set up a simple payoff matrix in which we assume there are only two countries, Rani and Raqi.

ADDED DIMENSION   The Escalating Price of Oil

The following graphs help to put oil prices into some context. The first graph shows how oil prices have escalated over the past 35 years.

The next graph shows comparative gas prices and how much of the price is attributable to excise taxes.

Source: 1970–78, *Petroleum Energy Weekly*; 1979 forward, *Weekly Petroleum Status Report* / International gasoline prices, Canadian cents per litre, OECD/IEA February 2011.

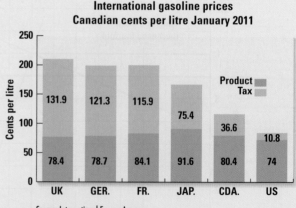

Source: International Energy Agency.

FIGURE 11.7	Rani and Raqi's Payoff Matrix

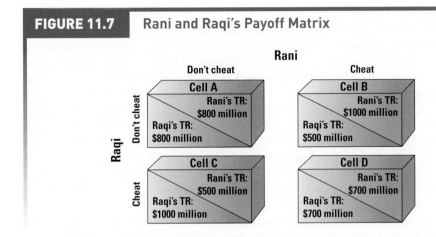

The figures in each cell show the (hypothetical) total revenues resulting from the four possible outcomes. (Once again, these figures are simply made up; it is the way in which they change that matters.) Joint revenue between the countries is maximized at $1600 million ($800 million each), as seen in cell A, and can be achieved if both countries cooperate and stick to the agreement.

Cell B shows us what will happen if Rani cheats on the agreement but Raqi does not. In this case, Rani's revenue will increase to $1000 million, while Raqi's will drop to $500 million. Their situation would be reversed, however, if it was Raqi that cheated and Rani did not, as seen in cell C. Then, Raqi's revenue would increase to $1000 million while Rani's would drop to $500 million. If they both cheated, they will each see their revenues drop to $700 million, as shown in cell D.

Suppose that the two countries had this full information and knew exactly the consequences of cheating. It is clear that the best outcome for them jointly would be to stick to the agreement and earn a total combined income of $1600 million. The worst outcome would be if they *both* cheated. Then, they would end up with a combined income of only $1400 million.

So, what do they do? You have probably guessed the answer: they will cheat! Think of things from Rani's point of view. Since its fortune depends on what Raqi does, it asks, "What is the best thing that can happen to my country if Raqi does, indeed, stick to the agreement? If we stick to the agreement we will earn $800 million, but if we cheat we will earn $1000. No question, we should cheat. But what if Raqi cheats? Then, the worst outcome is that we do not cheat and earn $500 million. The best option is if we do cheat. Then, we will earn $700 million." So, irrespective of what Raqi does, Rani's best option would be to cheat. Raqi will, of course, have figured things out the same way. As a result, they will both end up cheating.

Cartels are difficult to hold together; the temptation to cheat is just too great. As a result, by 1985, OPEC officially abandoned its system of quotas, and the power of the most significant cartel of the century was weakened. In summary, we can say that:

Cartels work to the advantage of members only if there is no cheating among the participants.

In the last few years, the economies of several developing nations have been growing at extraordinary, nearly double-digit rates. This growth has put both China and India in the spotlight since these two have the potential to become among the world's largest economies. Such growth has also increased the demand for commodities in general, and oil in particular, dramatically pushing up its price to over $130 a barrel (in April 2008). The effect that OPEC has on prices is less conspicuous than in the past, but it is still significant. Although non-OPEC producers now account for about 60 percent of the world's oil production, they are all producing flat-out and cannot raise output. The OPEC members—the other 40 percent of output—could increase their output but have not, thus keeping oil prices at record levels.

Our next example of collusion comes from the world of advertising. Suppose that in Canada, two big breweries, Eastern and Western, presently advertise extensively and are splitting the market equally. However, they realize that the effect of much of this advertising is self-cancelling and that if neither firm were to advertise, they would still split the market equally with the added difference that their costs would be considerably lower and their profits higher. Given this, suppose that they come to an agreement to reduce their advertising budgets to the bare minimum.

The outcome is illustrated in **Figure 11.8**. Cell A shows that each firm receives $500 million in profits per year. There is, however, an enormous potential reward involved if either firm decides to cheat on the agreement, as can be seen by examining the results in cells B and C. If either firm chooses a large budget strategy and its rival chooses a small budget strategy, then its profits will increase significantly, while its rival's profits decrease. For example, if Western goes with a large budget and Eastern goes with a small budget, then Western's profits will rise to $800 million while Eastern's profits will fall to $150 million (cell B).

The reason for this is not hard to understand. If Western greatly increases the advertising expenditure on its product, while Eastern does not, then Western will gain market share at its rival's expense. The demand for Western's product will increase, while Eastern's demand will decrease, with the result that profits will rise in the one case and fall in the other. Cell C illustrates the situation in which Western chooses a small advertising budget, while Eastern goes with a large one. From this, we can see that each firm, being aware of the possible disaster that could result from choosing a small budget strategy, reasons that it has no choice but to cheat on the agreement and go with a large budget strategy. The result of this reasoning is represented in cell D, in which each firm ends up with only $300 million profit. This helps explain the large expenditures on advertising in today's market economy.

Now, you may well ask: wouldn't it be advantageous for the two firms to stick with the agreement and not use the large-budget strategy? On the surface the answer to this question would seem to be yes, but for this solution (represented by cell A) to persist, both firms must trust each other and, as we saw in earlier examples this is unlikely to happen.

There are numerous real-life examples of collusion between competitors on record. In the mid-eighties, it was widely accepted that Major League Baseball (MLB) owners were restricting players' salaries to increase their profits. This led to a long strike by the players and, eventually, to a new contract that included a free-agency clause for players. Another example involves the conviction of several food manufactures in the United States for conspiring to fix the prices of food services to the U.S. Army and to U.S. colleges and universities. In late 2007, three Canadian companies—Hershey Canada Inc., Mars Canada Inc., and Nestle Canada Inc. were charged in court with conspiracy to fix the price of—you guessed it—chocolate bars, through clandestine meetings between executives in various coffee shops, restaurants, and at industry conventions over the previous five years.

FIGURE 11.8   Rival Firms' Advertising Strategies

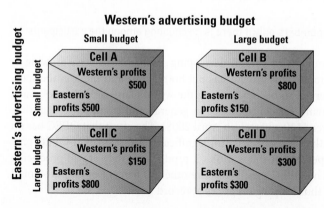

SELF-TEST

7. Suppose that Spartan Inc. and Trojan Ltd., the only two firms in the industry, have entered into a collusive agreement to share the industry's total profits of $50 million equally. However, if either of them cheats, it will increase its profits by $10 million at a cost of $10 million to the other firm. If they both cheat, they will each reduce their profits by $5 million.

a) Construct a matrix showing the various options.

b) Which option will they likely chose?

11.6   NONCOLLUSIVE OLIGOPOLY

Both the OPEC example and the advertising example suggest that although cooperation through collusion produces the greatest joint rewards, individual rivals still end up competing because the incentive to cheat is strong. Will this always be the result? Not necessarily. Certainly, it will not be the result if rivals learn from bitter experience. This is particularly true when competition takes the form of price cutting. Often, such activity has led to an outright price war. Such price rivalry leads to "death by a thousand cuts," causing great losses and bankruptcies. There are a couple of ways in which firms can avoid this. The first is through the practice of price leadership.

L06 Understand price leadership and why oligopolistic firms are reluctant to change prices very often.

Price Leadership

In price leadership, rival firms engage in what amounts to price fixing without overt collusion. Instead, industrial history and a process of trial and error lead the firms in an industry to concede the role of price leader to a single firm—usually the largest or most efficient firm. The leader monitors its cost and revenue patterns with the long view in mind—ignoring the day-to-day fluctuations in demand and costs. When conditions change sufficiently that a price increase seems urgent, the leader will balance the advantages of a large increase with the risks of creating a tempting opening for a new entrant into the industry. Having decided on a price increase that is profitable but not too high to risk new entry, the leader announces this price increase in some very public way, and the rival firms in the industry quickly follow suit by also increasing their prices by a similar amount. As far as prices go, this has the same effect as overt collusion would, but it is accomplished without doing anything technically illegal. This also allows firms in an industry to adjust prices without triggering a price war. At various times in the past, Canada Cement Ltd., Canadian General Electric, American Airlines, and Tesco supermarkets (in the United Kingdom) have been price leaders in their industries.

The Kinked Demand Curve

In certain circumstances, the choice of action by an oligopoly firm is not clear cut. In some cases, rival firms may want to compete, and at other times they might wish to cooperate. This is the case with the model known as the *kinked demand curve*, which was developed in the 1930s by economist Paul Sweezy to explain price rigidities often observed in oligopoly markets. The basic proposition of this model is that any one interdependent firm, say, Wonder Inc., will reason that if it increases the price of its product, rival firms will see this as a golden opportunity to gain market share at the expense of Wonder by simply *not* increasing their prices.

The demand curve that Wonder faces for all prices above the prevailing price is quite elastic, and we know that increasing the price of a product that has an elastic demand is not advantageous to the firm because its total revenue would fall. At the same time, Wonder Inc. reasons that if it were to lower its price, its rivals may well interpret this as a very aggressive move on Wonder's part to attempt to steal customers from them. They would have no option, Wonder reasons, but

FIGURE 11.9	The Kinked Demand Curve

Wonder Inc. thinks that any price decrease that it might initiate will be matched by its rivals, which will result in inelastic demand below the prevailing price. Further, it thinks that if it raises the price of its product, its rivals will not raise their prices, which will result in elastic demand above the prevailing price. Thus, Wonder Inc. views its demand curve as kinked at the prevailing price of P_1.

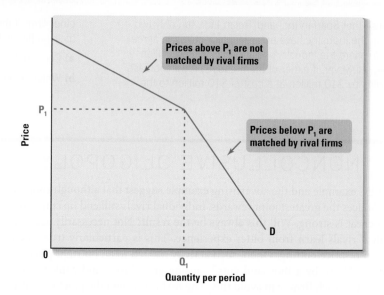

to compete by matching the lower price, and the overall distribution of market share between firms would not change. This means that Wonder's lower price would attract very few new customers; in effect, the demand curve that Wonder faces for all prices below the prevailing price is inelastic. Of course, lowering the price of a product with inelastic demand is not advantageous because this, too, would decrease total revenue.

In other words, the behaviour of its competitors is not symmetrical. They will match any price decrease but will ignore any price increase. This leads to the conclusion that the demand curve faced by Wonder Inc., given its view of the way that rivals would react to any price change it might initiate, is kinked at the prevailing price. This is illustrated in **Figure 11.9**.

Given this, then, it is a case of "damned if you do, and damned if you don't." The best action that Wonder Inc. could take is no action at all. This is an explanation of the often-observed phenomenon of oligopoly rivals charging very similar prices for competing products. Furthermore, these prices do not change often. What is of additional interest about the kinked demand curve is that the marginal revenue curve associated with this peculiar demand curve has a discontinuity in it, as shown in **Figure 11.10**.

The marginal revenue curve associated with the kinked demand curve D_1D_2 is *abcd*. It turns out that this discontinuity in the marginal revenue curve could be of some significance. The intersection of MC_1 with the marginal revenue curve, *abcd*, at *c* confirms that the prevailing price of P_1 is the profit-maximizing price. Next, observe what happens if Wonder Inc.'s marginal cost rises to MC_2. Wonder's profit-maximizing price and quantity remain P_1 and Q_1.

Now, in normal circumstances, an increase in a firm's cost of production will be (at least partially) passed on to the customer in the form of a higher price. But this does not happen here because the firm is afraid of the loss of business from increases in its price and will be forced, reluctantly, to absorb the higher costs. This means that it is common to observe very stable prices in oligopoly industries despite changes in demand and cost conditions. For example, prices of some cars or fridges can remain unchanged for months, if not years, at a time. However, there is another simple reason big firms are often reluctant to pass on cost increases to their customers, and that is that changing prices in itself can be very expensive. These *menu costs*, as they are called, include the costs of reprinting brochures and price lists, as well as updating prices in cash registers and computers. Such changes can be prohibitively expensive and, therefore, may only be done infrequently and reluctantly.

| **FIGURE 11.10** | **The Kinked Demand Curve and Marginal Revenue Curve** |

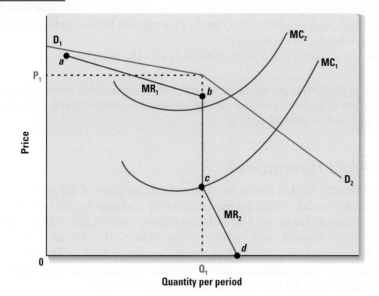

The discontinuity in the marginal revenue curve is the result of the kink in the demand curve. MC_1 is the original marginal cost curve. Quantity Q_1 is the profit-maximizing output that results in price P_1. An increase in marginal cost from MC_1 to MC_2 results in no change in equilibrium price or quantity.

One rather serious qualification about the kinked demand theory needs to be added before we leave it. If you go back and quickly re-read this section, you will notice that nowhere in the analysis did we explain how the prevailing price of was P_1 originally established! Thus, although it is a rather neat and logical explanation for price rigidity, it cannot explain how that price came about in the first place.

An Appraisal of Oligopoly

From an overall economic point of view, how do oligopolies measure up—are they an efficient form of market structure? The typical oligopoly firm possesses a degree of market power, which means that its demand curve is downward sloping. Thus, it will not operate on the minimum point of its average cost curve. This means that it will not achieve economic capacity. Moreover, an oligopoly firm will charge a price that exceeds average cost. These two points lead us to our first conclusion: an oligopoly firm does not achieve productive efficiency. Second, an oligopoly firm will charge a price higher than its marginal costs. Thus, it will also not achieve allocative efficiency. When we compare these realities with those of firms in perfect competition, we see that oligopolies do not stack up very well at all.

Some people have even gone so far as to argue that monopolies are preferable to oligopolies. At least it is politically feasible to regulate monopolies, whereas oligopoly industries, which often produce very similar outcomes to those in monopoly industries, go unregulated.

On the other hand, it has been argued that oligopolies operate in an environment that is highly conducive to the vital research and technological change that our economy needs to remain competitive by world standards. John Kenneth Galbraith was a leading proponent of this view and pointed out that modern research is very expensive. For this reason, large oligopoly firms are the most likely ones to be able to finance research. In addition, the barriers to entry that they enjoy give them some assurance that they will be able to recover the cost of research before the new technology or new product is imitated by others.

If this view is correct, it will mean that an oligopoly industry, over the long haul, will foster technological change and improvement. This would reduce its average cost, with the result that prices would fall and output levels would rise. On the other hand, many suggest that oligopoly industries, because they are protected by barriers to entry, may well become greedy and complacent and lose their competitive edge. In addition, they often spend their time and energy in nonprice competition, such as advertising (thereby creating even higher barriers to entry) rather than in initiating research and development.

Once again, you can see a sharp point of debate within the discipline:

> Some believe that oligopolies are too powerful and produce inefficiently; others take the view that oligopolies are at the cutting edge of new technological development and, in the long run, push the average costs of production down.

Are Firms Profit Maximizers?

John Kenneth Galbraith's work is also at the centre of another point of debate within the discipline. All four market models—from perfect competition to oligopoly—contain an underlying assumption that we need to examine. This is the assumption that the firm behaves in a way that maximizes its profits. If demand, costs, or taxes change, then the firm will adjust its output level and (if it can) its price level so as to continue making maximum total profits. This assumption underlies the concept of firm equilibrium and is at the heart of microeconomics. This can be seen by the following quote from the University of Chicago's George Stigler:

> [Profit maximization is] the strongest, the most universal, and the most persistent of the forces governing entrepreneurial behaviour.[1]

Galbraith challenged this fundamental assumption in his work *The New Industrial State* (1967), in which he pointed out that a characteristic feature of the large multinational corporation of today is that management and ownership have become divorced. Ownership of publicly traded companies is typically very diverse and is often unknown to the hired managers who make corporate decisions, whom Galbraith calls the technostructure. Galbraith goes on to say,

> So long as earnings are above a certain minimum, it would be agreed that management has little to fear from the stockholders. Yet [the discipline of economics assumes that] it is for these stockholders, remote, powerless and unknown, that management seeks to maximize profits.[2]

Most would find, argued Galbraith, that the proposition that individual managers seek to maximize their own return—to make as much income for themselves as possible—is reasonable and sound. For managers to maximize the profits of the corporation, they would have to show great restraint in what they pay themselves. In effect, they would have to forgo personal reward in order to enhance it for others. Galbraith says,

> Accordingly, if the traditional commitment to profit maximization is to be upheld, they [the managers] must be willing to do for others, specifically the stockholders, what they are forbidden to do for themselves.[3]

---

[1] George J. Stigler, *The Theory of Price*, rev. ed., (New York: MacMillan, 1952), p. 149.

[2] John Kenneth Galbraith, *The New Industrial State*, (Boston: Houghton Mifflin Co., 1967), p. 115.

[3] Ibid., p. 117.

ADDED DIMENSION   The World's Largest Economic Entities

The following is a list of the world's 80 largest economic entities. Countries are ranked by 2009 GDP and corporations by 2009 revenue, both in billions of American dollars.

Rank	Entity	Value ($ billion U.S.)	Rank	Entity	Value ($ billion U.S.)
1	United States	14 266	41	ConocoPhillips	231
2	Japan	5 049	42	Colombia	229
3	China	4 758	43	United Arab Emirates	229
4	Germany	3 235	44	**ING Group Netherlands**	**227**
5	France	2 635	45	Ireland	227
6	United Kingdom	2 198	46	Portugal	220
7	Italy	2 090	47	Israel	216
8	Brazil	1 482	48	Hong Kong SAR	209
9	Spain	1 438	49	**Sinopec China**	**208**
10	Canada	1 319	50	Malaysia	207
11	Russia	1 255	51	**Toyota Motor Japan**	**204**
12	India	1 243	52	**Japan Post Holdings Japan**	**199**
13	Australia	920	53	Czech Republic	190
14	Mexico	866	54	Egypt	188
15	Korea	800	55	**General Electric U.S.**	**183**
16	Netherlands	790	56	**China National Petroleum China**	**181**
17	Turkey	594	57	**Volkswagen Germany**	**167**
18	Indonesia	515	58	Pakistan	167
19	Switzerland	484	59	Nigeria	165
20	Belgium	461	60	**State Grid China**	**164**
21	**Royal Dutch Shell Netherlands/U.K.**	**458**	61	Singapore	163
22	**Exxon Mobil U.S.**	**443**	62	**Dexia Group Belgium**	**161**
23	Poland	423	63	Romania	161
24	**Wal-Mart Stores U.S.**	**406**	64	**ENI Italy**	**159**
25	Sweden	398	65	Philippines	159
26	Saudi Arabia	380	66	Chile	150
27	Austria	374	67	**General Motors U.S.**	**149**
28	Norway	369	68	**Ford Motor U.S.**	**146**
29	**BP U.K.**	**367**	69	**Allianz Germany**	**142**
30	Taiwan Province of China	357	70	**HSBC Holdings U.K.**	**142**
31	Venezuela	353	71	**Gazprom Russia**	**141**
32	Greece	338	72	**Daimler Germany**	**140**
33	Iran, Islamic Republic of	332	73	**BNP Paribas France**	**136**
34	Denmark	308	74	Algeria	135
35	Argentina	301	75	**Carrefour France**	**129**
36	South Africa	277	76	Peru	127
37	Thailand	266	77	**E.ON Germany**	**127**
38	**Chevron U.S.**	**263**	78	**PDVSA Venezuela**	**126**
39	Finland	242	79	**ArcelorMittal Luxembourg**	**125**
40	**Total France**	**235**	80	Hungary	124

Source: Fortune 500 and International Monetary Fund

If the behaviour of today's modern corporations is not driven by profit maximization, how might one understand their behaviour? Galbraith believed the *multiple* goals of today's corporations included earning sufficient profits to keep the shareholders happy, obtaining autonomy of decision making, developing state-of-the-art technology, achieving high rates of growth, and even such social goals as the design and manufacture of a superior space vehicle, which would greatly enhance the company's image and give the corporation's management a great sense of pride. There need not be a particular hierarchy in such a list of possible goals because one corporation's ranking of goals may not be the same as another corporation's. The point is that modern management is often motivated to pursue a number of goals rather than solely attempting to maximize profit.

Again, we neither feel any particular ability nor see any particular need to try to resolve this issue. We do, however, find it important and interesting that something as fundamental as the assumption of profit maximization has not gone without challenge. This is evidence that the discipline of economics is alive and that its ideas continue to be debated and developed.

✓ SELF-TEST

8. Given the following graph:

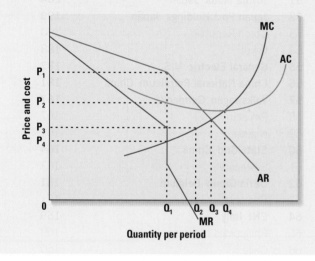

a) What output should this firm produce in order to maximize its profits?

b) What price should this firm charge?

9. a) Explain how one might argue that the existence of oligopolies means higher prices for consumers.

b) Explain how one might argue that the existence of oligopolies means lower prices for consumers.

STUDY GUIDE

Review

CHAPTER SUMMARY

In this chapter, you examined the two remaining types of market structure that come under the general heading of imperfect competition. First you examined monopolistic competition, which is representative of the hundreds of retail shops seen in any major city, and discovered that the model used to analyze it is straightforward. Then, you looked at oligopoly, which is representative of any of the scores of large, often multinational, firms with which most of us are familiar. You also learned that firm interdependence means oligopoly theory is not straightforward.

11.1a Product differentiation is a characteristic of the monopolistic–competitive market structure and most of the oligopoly market structure (though some oligopoly industries are made up of firms that sell identical products).

11.1b There is debate within economics about the benefits of advertising. Supporters believe advertising is beneficial because it:

- provides the consumer with vital information
- enhances competition among firms
- lowers prices of products
- finances magazines and television shows

Critics of advertising argue that it:

- is mostly noninformational and wasteful
- encourages concentration within industries
- raises prices to the detriment of consumers

11.2 A concentration ratio measures the percent of an industry's sales controlled by the top four firms. A high concentration ratio is a characteristic of oligopoly markets.

11.3a Monopolistic competition is a market in which:

- there are many small firms
- there is freedom of entry by new firms
- firms have some control over price
- firms sell differentiated products

11.3b In the long run, the typical firm in monopolistic competition:

- makes no economic profit
- charges a price above minimum average cost and is, therefore, not productively efficient
- charges a price above minimum marginal cost and is, therefore, not allocatively efficient

11.4 Oligopoly is a market in which:

- there is domination by a few large firms
- entry by new firms is difficult because of barriers to entry
- nonprice competition among firms is widely practised
- each firm has significant control over price
- mutual interdependence exists among firms

11.5a Oligopoly firms sometimes collude in order to avoid the risk of a price war. However, such illegal agreements are seldom long-lasting because of the temptation to cheat on the agreement.

11.5b Game theory is a method of analyzing firm behaviour that highlights the mutual interdependence between firms. Its first application in the chapter was to analyze two possible advertising strategies between two firms.

11.5c Cartels involve overt collusion between firms and can be analyzed effectively using game theory.

- The OPEC example explained why the member countries found it to their collective advantage to agree to quotas and why those countries later found it to their individual advantage to cheat on the agreement.

- The advertising example shows why rival oligopolists often have big advertising budgets, even though much of it is self-cancelling and, therefore, ineffective.

11.6a Price leadership involves tacit collusion between firms. Kinked demand curve theory is effective in explaining the often observed phenomenon of stable prices within oligopoly industries.

11.6b Oligopolies are productively and allocatively inefficient though some argue that they foster technological change.

11.6c Galbraith and others believe that profit maximization is not the sole or even the most important goal for many corporations. They propose other motives behind firm behaviour.

NEW GLOSSARY TERMS

cartel   351
collusion   347
concentration ratio   339
game theory   349

imperfect competition   336
monopolistic competition   339
mutual interdependence   347

Nash equilibrium   350
oligopoly   339
product differentiation   336

STUDY TIPS

1. Students often relate well to this chapter because it is able to explain some observations they make about the real world. If that describes your reaction, this has probably been an enjoyable chapter. Do not think that you must be missing something because "it seems so obvious."

2. Two important concepts were used in this chapter to evaluate market performance:
   Productive efficiency occurs when the firm is producing at an output that results in minimum AC and is charging a price equal to AC.
   Allocative efficiency occurs when the firm is charging a price equal to MC.

3. **Figure 11.2** is the key to understanding firm equilibrium under conditions of monopolistic competition. In stark contrast, oligopoly theory comes in three variants.

4. When you are asked to draw a graph illustrating the long-run equilibrium of a monopolistically competitive firm, you need to ensure that the demand curve is just tangent to the AC curve and that this point of tangency is at the same output level where MR = MC. Therefore, leave the drawing of the marginal revenue curve until last.

Answered Questions

These questions can also be found online on Connect.

Indicate whether the following statements are true or false:

1. **(LO 2) T or F**   Imperfect competition is characterized by firms competing on price.

2. **(LO 2) T or F**   One characteristic of monopolistic competition is the existence of many firms operating in the same industry.

3. **(LO 3) T or F**   Monopolistically competitive firms typically make economic profits in the long run.

4. **(LO 3) T or F**   The franchise system attempts to limit the entry of new firms into an existing industry.

5. **(LO 4) T or F**   Mutual interdependence is a significant characteristic of a monopolistically competitive industry.

6. **(LO 6) T or F**   Both the kinked demand curve and the price leadership variants of oligopoly theory assume that firms collude with each other.

7. **(LO 3, 6) T or F**   Productive efficiency occurs when firms charge a price that is equal to minimum AC.

8. **(LO 3, 6) T or F**   Allocative efficiency is absent if price exceeds marginal cost.

9. **(LO 6) T or F**   Galbraith argues that oligopoly firms can be efficient because of the research they engage in and the technological change they foster.

10. **(LO 6) T or F**   The assumption that firms attempt to maximize sales revenue underlies much of the analysis in microeconomics.

Basic (Questions 11–24)

11. **(LO 1)** What does *product differentiation* mean?
    a) It is the attempt by the firm to offer a product similar to that of its rivals.
    b) It is the attempt by the firm to offer a product seen to be different from that of its rivals.
    c) It is the practice of many firms to sell more than one product.
    d) It is the practice of many firms to sell the same product in more than one market.

12. **(LO 2)** In which of the following market structures is entry easiest?
    a) Monopolistic competition
    b) Oligopoly
    c) Monopoly
    d) Duopoly

13. **(LO 3)** What price does a monopolistically competitive firm charge?
    a) A price equal to marginal cost
    b) A price greater than marginal cost
    c) A price equal to marginal revenue
    d) A price less than average cost

14. **(LO 3)** What is the level of economic profits earned by a firm operating in the short-run under conditions of monopolistic competition?
    a) It is positive.
    b) It is likely to be positive but could be negative.
    c) It is zero.
    d) It is negative.

15. **(LO 3)** Graphically, what will be the effect of entry by new firms into a monopolistically competitive industry?
    a) It will shift each firm's demand curve to the right.
    b) It will shift each existing firm's demand curve to the left.
    c) It will shift the market's supply curve to the left.
    d) It will shift the market's demand curve to the right.

16. **(LO 3)** What will be the long-run result of new firms entering a monopolistically competitive industry?
    a) The price charged by the representative firm will be equal to marginal cost.
    b) The representative firm will certainly incur losses.
    c) While the representative firm will not make economic profits, it will be able to make normal profits.
    d) The representative firm will be able to maintain economic profits.

17. **(LO 3, 6)** What is meant by the term *allocative efficiency*?
    a) A firm is producing an output that equals minimum AC.
    b) A firm is producing an output and charging a price that equals minimum AC.
    c) A firm is charging a price equal to MC.
    d) A firm has achieved its MES.

18. **(LO 2)** All of the following, except one, are oligopoly industries. Which is the exception?
    a) The manufacture of automobiles
    b) The manufacture of cigarettes
    c) The provision of accounting services
    d) Breweries

19. **(LO 5)** All of the following statements, except one, are correct concerning the cartel variant of oligopoly theory. Which is the exception?
    a) An effective cartel restricts the supply of the product being sold.
    b) The individual members of the cartel must agree to and respect quotas on their output.
    c) The primary threat to the success of a cartel is government regulation.
    d) The output and the price of the cartel is often similar to that of a monopoly.

20. **(LO 5)** All of the following statements, except one, are correct about game theory analysis. Which is the exception?
    a) It has led some economists to conclude that the likelihood of cheating is a more effective barrier to collusion than government legislation.
    b) It emphasizes the importance of mutual interdependence.

c) It is an attempt to explain firm behaviour.
d) It shows that it is rational for each firm to trust the other.
e) It is able to predict a likely outcome of two firms engaged in considering a specific action.

21. **(LO 6)** Most economic theory is based on the assumption that firms have one goal. Which of the following is that goal?
a) Profit maximization
b) Continued growth of the corporation's sales and size of operations
c) The achievement of management autonomy in decision making
d) Development of state-of-the art technology
e) Enhancement of the company's image and the management's pride

22. **(LO 1)** Product differentiation includes all, except one, of the following. Which is the exception?
a) Developing a recognized brand name or product logo
b) Securing a superior location or developing a reputation for exceptional service
c) Engaging in product development or improvement
d) Developing an effective advertising strategy
e) Charging a price lower than the competitor's

Answer questions 23 and 24 using the data in **Table 11.3**.

TABLE 11.3

Quantity	MC	AC	MR
640	120	175	150
700	128	165	145
760	140	160	140
820	154	156	135
880	170	158	130
940	188	162	125

23. **(LO 3)** What output will this firm produce?
a) 700
b) 760
c) 820
d) 880

24. **(LO 3)** If the firm produces its profit-maximizing output, how much excess capacity will it have?
a) 60
b) 120
c) 300
d) More information is needed to answer the question

Intermediate (Questions 25–32)

25. **(LO 3)** Which of the following describes excess capacity?
a) The difference between what is being produced and the level of production that maximizes profits
b) The difference between what is being produced and economic capacity
c) The difference between what is being produced and the level of production that minimizes short-run marginal cost
d) The difference between the level of production that minimizes short-run average cost and that which achieves economic capacity

26. **(LO 5)** Which of the following statements is correct when comparing a monopoly market and an oligopoly market?
a) The price and quantity would be the same in both markets.
b) Both price and quantity would be lower in the monopoly market than in the oligopoly market.
c) The price would be lower and the quantity would be higher in the monopoly market than in the oligopoly market.
d) The price would be higher and the quantity would be lower in the monopoly market than in the oligopoly market.

27. **(LO 6)** All, except one, of the following statements about the kinked demand curve theory of oligopoly are correct. Which is the exception?
a) It explains why the prices charged by rival firms are often similar.
b) It explains why rival firms that charge similar prices may not be in collusion.
c) It explains why the prices charged by rival firms sometimes go for months, or even years, without changing.
d) It explains, particularly well, how the prevailing price in the industry first got established.

28. **(LO 6)** If we assume that price leadership prevails in a particular industry, what might prevent the leader from announcing a dramatic increase in the price of the product sold?
a) The fear that the AC of the other firms within the industry would decrease
b) The fear that new firms would be tempted to enter the industry
c) The fear that one of the other firms would break ranks and increase their price even more
d) The fear that such action would provide proof that the firms are engaged in overt collusion

29. **(LO 4, 5)** All of the following, except one, could explain a price war between firms. Which is the exception?
    a) A breakdown in the collusive agreement between firms
    b) The intense competition that one finds in a perfectly competitive industry
    c) An aggressive young firm challenging the established price leadership of a rival firm
    d) The action taken by established firms to ward off the possible entry of a new firm

30. **(LO 1)** All, except one, of the following statements are valid arguments in favour of advertising. Which one is the exception?
    a) Advertising provides consumers with information.
    b) Advertising reduces the search time needed by consumers to acquire products.
    c) Advertising increases the barriers to entry into an industry and thereby enhances competition.
    d) Advertising can lower the prices of products by reducing the firms' average cost through increased output levels.
    e) Advertising increases the availability of radio and television program choices for the consumer.

Answer questions 31 and 32 using **Figure 11.11** below.

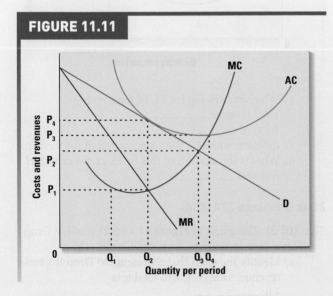

FIGURE 11.11

31. **(LO 3)** What output level will the firm produce?
    a) Q_1
    b) Q_2
    c) Q_3
    d) Q_4
    e) More information is needed to answer this question

32. **(LO 3)** What price will the firm charge?
    a) P_1
    b) P_2
    c) P_3
    d) P_4

Advanced (Questions 33–35)

33. **(LO 6)** Which of the following statements is correct about oligopoly firms?
    a) They typically achieve economic capacity.
    b) They may or may not charge a price higher than marginal cost.
    c) They maximize profits by equating marginal revenue and marginal cost.
    d) They operate in an intensely competitive atmosphere in which the market dictates price.
    e) They produce an output that puts them graphically on the rising portion of the AC curve.

34. **(LO 4)** All of the following statements, except one, are valid statements regarding barriers to entry and the existence of large profits in an oligopoly industry. Which statement is not valid?
    a) Barriers to entry enable firms to spend large sums on research that can then be recovered in future sales.
    b) Barriers to entry lead to lower profits.
    c) The large profits enable firms to finance the development of new technology.
    d) The barriers to entry help maintain large-sized firms within the industry, which enhances the ability of these firms to capture economies of scale.
    e) The barriers to entry increase the prospect of downward shifts in the short-run average cost curves.

35. **(LO 3, 5)** All of the following statements, except one, are correct about a firm operating under conditions of either monopolistic competition or oligopoly. Which is the exception?
    a) Graphically, it faces a downward-sloping demand curve.
    b) It charges a price above marginal cost in both the short run and the long run.
    c) It charges a price equal to average cost in both the short run and the long run.
    d) It fails to achieve economic efficiency.
    e) It fails to achieve productive efficiency.

Parallel Problems

ANSWERED PROBLEMS

36A. **(LO 3) Key Problem** The graph in **Figure 11.12** is for Chic and Sharpe Ltd., a firm in the women's garment industry, which is monopolistically competitive.
   a) Label the four curves in **Figure 11.12**.
   b) What areas in **Figure 11.12** represent:
      Total cost: _____
      Total revenue: _____
      Economic profit: _____

   The graph in **Figure 11.13** represents the market supply and demand for the women's garment industry.

FIGURE 11.12

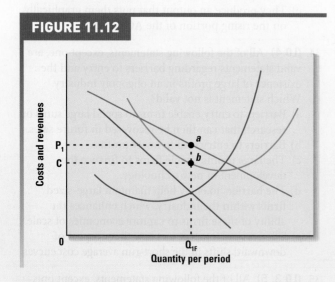

Quantity per period

FIGURE 11.13

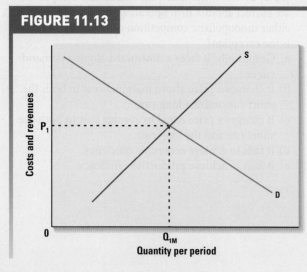

Quantity per period

c) On **Figure 11.13**, sketch in the effect of entry by new firms into this industry, and label the new price and quantity traded as P_2 and Q_{2M}.
d) Using the average/marginal cost curves in **Figure 11.14** (which are the same as in **Figure 11.12**), sketch in the firm's new demand and marginal revenue curves that would be consistent with zero economic profits. Label the equilibrium price and quantity traded as P_2 and Q_{2F}.

FIGURE 11.14

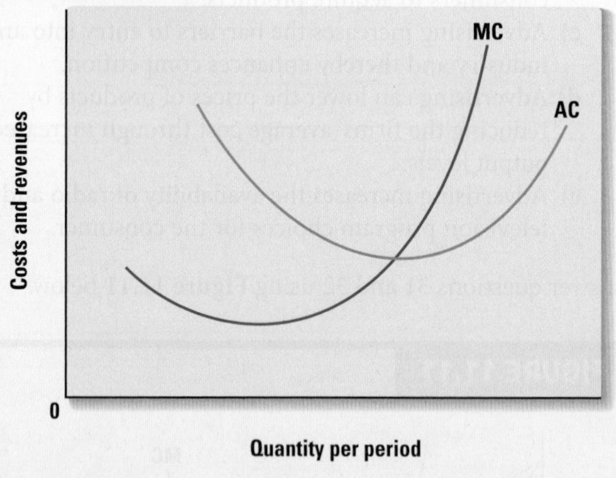

Quantity per period

e) What areas in **Figure 11.14** represent:
   Total revenue: _____
   Total costs: _____
f) Indicate, with Q_C, the capacity output for the firm.
g) What is the amount of this firm's excess capacity?
   Answer: _____ .

Basic (Problems 37A–43A)

37A. **(LO 3)** The graph in **Figure 11.15** is that of Do Drop In, a shop in the dry-cleaning industry.
   a) Identify the areas that represent Do Drop In's total revenue, total cost, and total loss.
      TR: _____
      TC: _____
      Total loss: _____
   b) If this firm made a rational decision to continue to produce, despite the loss, average variable cost must be below what level at output Q?
      AVC must be less than _____

FIGURE 11.15

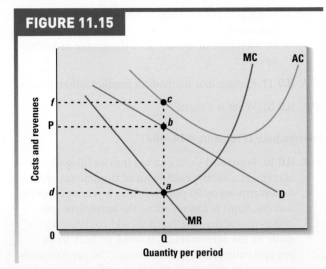

FIGURE 11.16

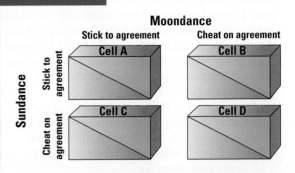

38A. (LO 5) Assume that the only two firms in the industry, Sundance Inc. and Moondance Ltd., have entered a collusive agreement to reduce their advertising budgets to a minimum. The result is that they expect to make profits of $120 million each. However, if either of them cheats, the cheater will increase its profits by $30 million at a cost of $30 million to the other firm. If they both cheat, they will each reduce their profits by $15 million.

a) Complete the matrix in **Figure 11.16** showing the options facing the two firms.

b) Explain which option they will likely choose, and why.

39A. (LO 3) **Table 11.4** contains some revenue and cost data for the Rising Moon T-shirt Company (quantities for packets of a dozen shirts), which is in long-term equilibrium.

a) Complete **Table 11.4**.

b) What is the profit-maximizing price and output for Rising Moon?
   Price: _____; output: _____

c) At the profit-maximizing output, what are MC and MR?
   MC: _____; MR: _____

d) At the profit-maximizing output, what are AC and AR?
   AC: _____; AR: _____

e) Given your answers above, what type of market must Rising Moon be operating in?
   _____

TABLE 11.4

Quantity	Price	TR	MR	TC	MC	AC
0	/	$ /	/	$122	/	/
1	___	64	___	154	___	___
2	___	124	___	184	___	___
3	___	180	___	216	___	___
4	___	232	___	250	___	___
5	___	280	___	286	___	___
6	___	324	___	324	___	___
7	___	364	___	364	___	___
8	___	400	___	406	___	___
9	___	432	___	450	___	___
10	___	460	___	498	___	___

40A. **(LO 3)** Aruna owns a small firm, Pottery Plus, that produces terra cotta pots for sale in the Edmonton area. Pottery Plus has two rival firms, and the current price that each firm charges for a dozen pots is $12. Aruna is convinced that she dare not raise her price because her rivals will not raise their prices, and she dare not decrease prices because her rivals will simply match her lower price.

a) On the graph in **Figure 11.17**, sketch in the demand and marginal revenue curves (which start at price $16) that fit Aruna's perception of the market. Aruna is currently producing 8 dozen pots per period.

b) Next, sketch in two marginal cost curves, MC_1 and MC_2, that are at different levels but still indicate that Aruna is maximizing profits at the current $12 price.

FIGURE 11.17

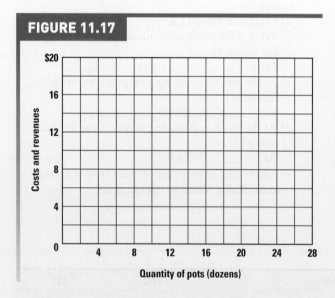

41A. **(LO 2)** The Costa Rican gimble industry consists of 14 firms whose annual sales are as shown in **Table 11.5**.

TABLE 11.5

Firm	Sales (in millions)
A	18
B	5
C	6
D	8
E	10
F	12
Next eight firms (total)	21

a) What is the (four-)firm concentration ratio for this industry?

b) In what type of market does the gimble industry operate?

42A. **(LO 1)** Explain four methods of product differentiation.

43A. **(LO 5)** What is a cartel?

Intermediate (Problems 44A–48A)

44A. **(LO 5)** Popsi and Cuke entered into an (illegal) agreement whereby each reduced the amount spent on advertising by 50 percent. After a year of apparent success, Popsi is uneasy about the agreement and begins to wonder whether it should continue to abide by the agreement or, instead, go back to its pre-agreement level of advertising. The payoff matrix, expressed in million of dollars of profits per year, for Popsi and Cuke's choices is shown in **Figure 11.18**. What do you think Popsi should do, and why?

FIGURE 11.18

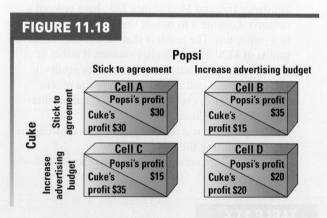

45A. **(LO 5)** The graph in **Figure 11.19** shows the demand for Cosmic shampoo.

Suppose there are no fixed costs and marginal cost is a constant $60.

a) What are the perfectly competitive price and output?
Price: _____ ;
output: _____ .

b) What are the cartel (monopoly) price and output?
Price: _____ ;
output: _____ .

c) If there are only four firms in the cartel, what are the price and output of each firm, assuming equal shares?
Price: _____ ;
output of each firm: _____ .

FIGURE 11.19

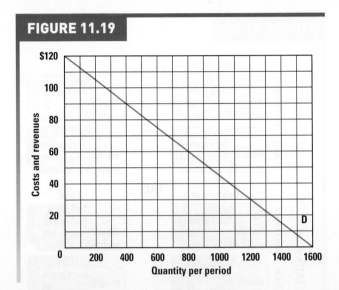

46A. **(LO 5)** **Figure 11.20** shows the demand for nectar in Gardenia.

FIGURE 11.20

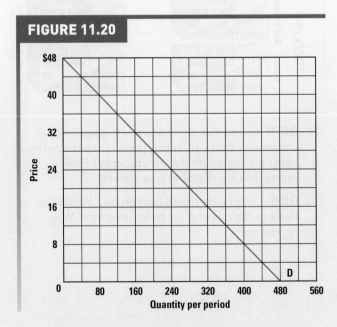

Suppose that there are only two firms, Ace and Pace, producing nectar, and they decide to act as a (monopoly) cartel and share the market equally.
a) What price and output will maximize their joint total *revenue*, and what amount is that?
Price: _____
Output: _____
Total revenue: _____

FIGURE 11.21

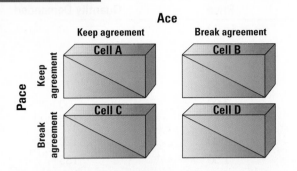

b) In the payoff matrix in **Figure 11.21**, show in cell A the amount of total revenue each will receive if they stick to the agreement.
c) Suppose that Ace believes that Pace will honour the agreement by maintaining his present output. However, Ace decides to cheat and increase his output by one-third. What will be Ace's and Pace's total revenues? Show Ace's and Pace's results in cell B.
d) Now, assume that the positions are reversed and that Pace decides to cheat while assuming that Ace will stick to the agreement. Show Ace's and Pace's resulting revenues in cell C.
e) Finally, in cell D show the total revenue of Ace and Pace that would result if they *both* cheat.

47A. **(LO 3)** In the short run, is it possible for the typical monopolistically competitive firm to make an economic profit?

48A. **(LO 4)** What is meant by *mutual interdependence*?

Advanced (Problems 49A–52A)

49A. **(LO 5)** **Table 11.6** is the demand faced by The Tienshan Company, a monopolist, which enjoys zero variable cost in its production.
a) What is the price Tienshan will charge, and what quantity of output will it produce?
Price: _____ ;
output: _____ .

Suppose that Endless Journey Inc., which also has zero variable cost, enters this industry and assumes that Tienshan will continue to produce its current output.
b) What output will Endless Journey choose to produce, and what will be the new market price, given both firms' output?
Endless Journey's output: _____ ;
new price: _____ .

TABLE 11.6

Price	Quantity Demanded
$5.00	30
4.50	45
4.00	60
3.50	75
3.00	90
2.50	105
2.00	120
1.50	135
1.00	150
.50	165
0	180

FIGURE 11.22

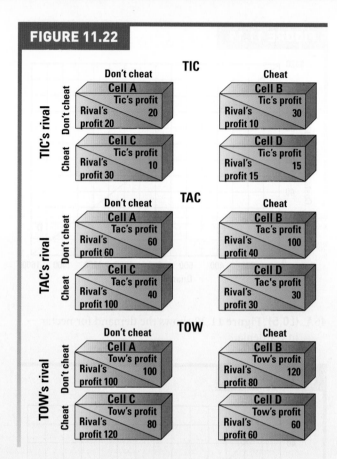

50A. **(LO 5)** You are the consultant to three firms, Tic, Tac, and Tow, each of which belongs to a different cartel. Each firm is trying to decide whether it is better to honour its present agreement or to cheat. The numbers in the payoff matrix in **Figure 11.22** show the total profits the three companies can make and the profits of each of their rival firms. What would you recommend to each of the three firms after analyzing the four possible outcomes faced by each?

Tic: _____

_____ .

Tac: _____

_____ .

Tow: _____

_____ .

51A. **(LO 3)** In long-run equilibrium, a monopolistically competitive firm's AC equals price. Given this, why hasn't it achieved productive efficiency? How is excess capacity related to your answer?

52A. **(LO 6)** "High risks means high profits." Would this likely be the motto of the technostructure? Why, or why not?

CHAPTER 12

THE FACTORS OF PRODUCTION

At the end of this chapter, you should be able to...

LO1 understand that the demand for labour depends on the productivity of labour.

LO2 understand other important factors operating in the labour market.

LO3 explain why factors that are highly inelastic in supply require special analysis.

LO4 recognize the relevance of the right rate of exploitation in the natural resource market.

LO5 understand that the demand for capital goods depends on the productivity of capital goods.

LO6 explain the two views on the ultimate source of profits.

WHAT'S AHEAD...

In this chapter, we shift our focus from the structure of the market for goods and services to that of the market for the factors of production. The key concept here is the productivity of those factors, whether labour, land, or capital. You will learn that both productivity and the prices of the output produced lie behind the demand for any factor. We also examine the supply of each of the factors, putting particular emphasis on the supply of labour, and we explain the reasons behind different wage rates.

A Question of Relevance...

You, like most students today, probably spend a lot of time wondering about what kind of job you will end up with and spend even more energy worrying about whether the job will be satisfying and well paid. There are a number of other questions students sometimes ask as well. Is it a good idea to chase the elusive dollar, or should you sacrifice some income to gain a satisfying career? You might also wonder if it makes sense to take risks while you are young and leave caution for middle age. Or perhaps you wonder why professional athletes get paid so much while day-care workers get paid so little. This chapter will give you some insights into these questions and others like them.

The first 11 chapters of this book wove their way through the topics of supply and demand, costs, and market structure. There was a common theme to all of this discussion. The focus was on the **product market**, for example, the demand for orange juice and gasoline, the supply of automobiles by oligopolistic firms, and the supply of or demand for shoes from a monopolistically competitive firm.

We now shift the focus to the **factor market** and look at the supply of and demand for the factors of production—labour, natural resources (land), capital, and enterprise—as well as some of the more interesting issues that arise from this discussion. One comment about the demand for factors can be made now. Factor demand is a derived demand; that is, since people want automobiles, there is a demand for auto workers.

product market: the market for consumer goods and services.

factor market: the market for the factors of production.

12.1 THE LABOUR MARKET

The Demand for Labour

L01 Understand that the demand for labour depends on the productivity of labour.

To ask what determines the demand for labour is equivalent to asking: what factors does an employer consider when deciding whether or not to hire one more employee or pay for more hours of labour? The discussion in Chapter 6 on marginal productivity is key to formulating an answer. What the employer has to keep in mind in making such a decision is the benefit derived from one more hour of labour compared with the cost of employing that person. If the benefit outweighs the cost, then the additional hour will be bought. If, however, the cost outweighs the benefit, no new work will be created.

So, what does the firm gain from one more hour (or day or week) of labour? The answer is that it gains from what that labour can produce, that is, its marginal product. In money terms, it gains revenue as a result of selling that marginal product. In other words, it benefits as a result of receiving **marginal revenue product**, which is equal to the marginal product times the price at which the marginal product is sold. That is:

marginal revenue product: the increase in a firm's total revenue that results from the use of one more unit of input.

$$\text{Marginal revenue product (MRP)} = \text{marginal product (MP)} \times \text{price (P)} \qquad \textbf{[12.1]}$$

Now, since the marginal product is equal to $\Delta Q / \Delta L$, where Q is the quantity of output and L is the quantity of labour, we could rewrite the last equation as:

$$\text{Marginal revenue product (MRP)} = \frac{\Delta Q}{\Delta L}$$

Given that $\Delta Q \times P$ is the same thing as the change in total revenue, an alternative way of defining the marginal revenue product is:

$$\text{Marginal revenue product (MRP)} = \frac{\Delta \text{ total revenue } (\Delta TR)}{\Delta \text{ labour}} \qquad \textbf{[12.2]}$$

And what is the cost of employing this labour? It is simply the (hourly, daily, weekly) wage rate. We can envision the employer balancing the cost, for instance, of one more hour of hired employment, with the marginal revenue product of the person supplying that extra hour. **Table 12.1** will help clarify this.

The concepts contained in the first three columns of **Table 12.1** were introduced in Chapter 6 and need no comment. The fourth column indicates that the per-unit price of the product is $1.50 and, further, that this price does not change as more and more output is produced and sold. (We are assuming that the producer is selling its output in a perfectly competitive market.) The figures in the Total Revenue column are obtained by multiplying the total product by the $1.50 price per unit. The marginal revenue product of labour figures can be obtained by either using equation 12.1 or 12.2.

TABLE 12.1	Marginal Revenue Product of Labour Data				
Hours of Labour	Total Product	Marginal Product of Labour	Unit Price of Product	Total Revenue	Marginal Revenue Product of Labour
0	0	/	$1.50	0	/
1	10	10	1.50	$ 15.00	$15.00
2	25	15	1.50	37.50	22.50
3	45	20	1.50	67.50	30.00
4	75	30	1.50	112.50	45.00
5	100	25	1.50	150.00	37.50
6	120	20	1.50	180.00	30.00
7	135	15	1.50	202.50	22.50
8	145	10	1.50	217.50	15.00
9	150	5	1.50	225.00	7.50
10	150	0	1.50	225.00	0

For instance, using equation 12.1, when eight hours of labour are employed, the MRP is equal to:

$$MRP = MP(10) \times P(\$1.50) = \$15$$

Or, using equation 12.2 gives us:

$$MRP = \frac{\Delta TR(\$217.50 - \$202.50)}{\Delta labour\ (l)} = \$15$$

Having identified the marginal revenue product of labour, we now want to know, in our hypothetical example, how many hours of labour would an employer hire if the wage rate is, for example, $15 per hour? The answer can be read directly from **Table 12.1**. Eight hours of labour would be hired. That is because each of the 8 hours hired add more to total revenue—each has a marginal revenue product that either equals or exceeds the $15 wage rate. The ninth hour of labour would not be hired because its marginal revenue product ($7.50) is less than the hourly wage of $15.

We are now in a position to make a significant generalization. An employer, operating under conditions of a perfectly competitive labour market, will hire up to the point at which the marginal revenue product of labour equals the wage rate. Profit maximization occurs when for the last unit of labour employed:

$$MRP_L = W \qquad\qquad\qquad [12.3]$$

In fact, we can generalize by saying that *any* factor (capital, labour, or land) will be bought up to the point where its MRP just equals its price. If the marginal revenue product of capital, for example, is $600 per unit and its price is $550, it will be bought. If, however, its marginal revenue product is only $500, it will not be bought. Generally, as long as the marginal benefit (MRP) of employing or purchasing an additional unit of a factor exceeds its marginal cost (price), the firm should employ it. This idea is analogous to the optimal purchasing rule we saw in Chapter 5, where we concluded that consumers would maximize utility by equating the marginal utility per dollar spent on each product with its price. Here, the firm, not the consumer, is maximizing profits rather than utility.

Now, let us return to the data in **Table 12.1** and ask how many hours of labour would be hired if the wage rate decreased to $7.50? We can see that the MRPL of the ninth hour of labour is also $7.50 and, applying the rule above, 9 hours of labour would be hired.

Let us now turn to **Figure 12.1**, where we graph the marginal revenue product data from **Table 12.1**. The MRP curve has the same shape as the familiar MP curve, since it is derived by multiplying MP by the constant price. If the wage rate was, say, $15, the firm would hire 8 hours of labour. A ninth hour of labour would be hired only if the wage rate dropped to $7.50. In general, the demand by firms for any factor depends on that factor's marginal revenue product, which is illustrated by the downward-sloping portion of its MRP curve. In short:

> The downward-sloping portion of the MRP curve is the firm's demand curve for that factor.

The above illustration of the firm's demand for labour assumed that the firm was selling its output in a perfectly competitive product market. Would our analysis change if the firm operated in, say, an oligopolistic product market? The basic answer is no, since the only change would be that the marginal revenue product of labour would decline faster. This is because using more of any factor always increases output, and this increase in output would mean that the firm would be forced to decrease price in order to sell the increased quantities. That is to say, the marginal revenue for competitive firms is constant and equal to price, whereas for imperfectly competitive firms it declines with output, driving marginal revenue product down faster.

The Supply of Labour

labour force: the total number of people over the age of 15 who are willing and able to work.

labour force supply: the total hours that those in the labour force are willing to work.

An economy's **labour force** is, simply, the number of people over the age of 15 who are willing and able to work at paid employment. The total amount of hours that these people are willing to work is the **labour force supply**.

We know that the labour force supply tends to expand as the wage rate increases. There are two explanations for this upward-sloping supply of labour. First, as the wage rate increases, the rate at which the population is willing to participate in the labour force increases because the higher wage rate makes employment more attractive. For example, younger people enter the labour force sooner, older workers tend not to retire as quickly, and others who were previously not participating in the labour force are more likely to enter it. Second, extra hours supplied might come as a result of present employees working longer hours.

FIGURE 12.1	The Firm's Marginal Revenue Product of Labour

The downward-sloping portion of the firm's MRP_L curve represents its demand curve for labour. For instance, when the wage rate is $15, eight hours of labour will be hired. At a wage rate of $7.50, nine hours of labour would be hired.

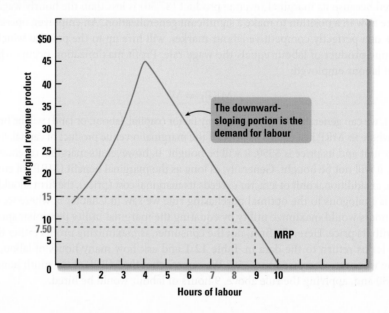

But how would those already in the labour force respond to a higher wage rate? Wouldn't everyone be willing to work more hours through taking on overtime work or a second job? Some would, and some would not. The reason for this is that such decisions involve more than just the maximization of income. For instance, either of your authors could work weekends at McDonald's and increase his income. Why don't we? The answer involves what economists call the *income effect* and the *substitution effect*. It is certainly true that a higher wage will make working additional time more attractive. However, working more hours also means less leisure. As one's income rises, there is a point reached where leisure becomes more valuable, and at this point, a further increase in the wage rate means that the same level of income can be obtained with less work and more of the valuable leisure time can be enjoyed.

The net effect of these two opposing alternatives is that economists know that the supply curve for labour is upward sloping but relatively inelastic so that a 10-percent rise in the wage rate (for example) will result in something less than a 10-percent increase in the quantity of labour supplied. This is illustrated in **Figure 12.2**.

Theoretically, if we were to imagine a very high wage rate so that a majority of people valued more leisure over more income, then the number of hours people would be willing and able to work would, in fact, decline. Graphically, the labour force supply curve would start to bend back to the left as it continued to rise. However, we will ignore this possibility.

As **Figure 12.2** shows, an increase in the wage from W_1 to W_2 results in an increase in the quantity of hours that the population is willing to work, as indicated in the movement up on the labour force supply curve, S, from point *a* to point *b*.

Figure 12.2 illustrates the supply of labour curve for the *market*. We know from our earlier discussion that a single firm's demand for labour curve is determined by that firm's marginal revenue product. Just as we did in Chapter 2, we could horizontally sum each firm's demand for labour to obtain a market demand for labour curve. When we put the *market* demand for labour curve together with market supply of labour curve, as we do in **Figure 12.3**, we get the equilibrium wage, W_1, for labour.

FIGURE 12.2	The Labour Force Supply Curve

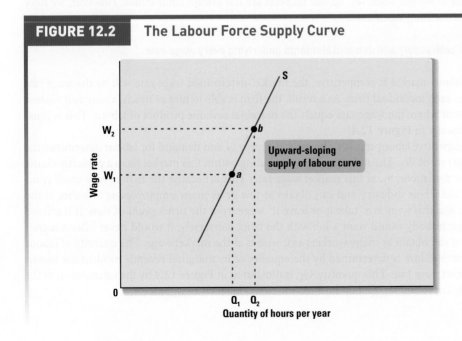

An increase in the wage rate from W_1 to W_2 results in the quantity of labour supplied rising from Q_1 to Q_2: that is, from point *a* to *b*. This indicates that the supply-of-labour curve is upward sloping with a relatively steep slope.

FIGURE 12.3   **The Market Equilibrium Wage Rate**

Given the upward-sloping supply-of-labour curve and the downward-sloping demand-for-labour curve, the equilibrium wage rate is W_1 and the equilibrium quantity is Q_1.

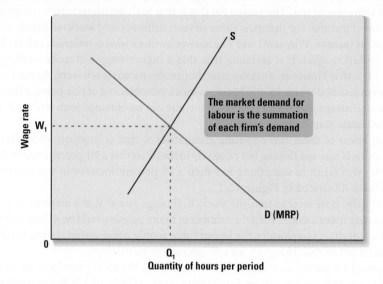

The market demand for labour is the summation of each firm's demand

Market Equilibrium

Given the market demand for labour, D, and the market supply of labour, S, we obtain the equilibrium wage rate, W_1, and the equilibrium quantity of hours, Q_1, that are bought and sold.

The answer to the very important question of what determines the wage rate for labour is the rather conventional answer: the supply of and demand for labour. We do not mean to imply that this general answer has universal application. There are, after all, many wage rates for labour, not just one, and as we will soon see, labour markets are not always competitive. However, we have uncovered something significant:

> There are both supply and demand elements underlying every wage rate.

If the labour market is competitive, the market-determined wage rate will be the wage rate applicable to each individual firm. As a result, the firm is able to hire as much labour as it wishes, up to the point where the wage rate equals the marginal revenue product of labour. This is illustrated graphically in **Figure 12.4**.

In a competitive labour market, the market supply of and demand for labour determines the market wage rate of W_1. The individual firm operating within this market faces a perfectly elastic supply curve for labour, S_1, at this market wage rate. This is because the firm is very small compared with the whole industry and can obtain as few or as many employees as it wishes at the going wage, and this wage is a "take it or leave it" wage from the firm's point of view. If it offered a lower wage, nobody would want a job with the firm; conversely, it would never offer a higher wage, since it can obtain as many workers as it wishes at the market wage. The quantity of labour that this firm will hire is determined by the equality of its marginal revenue product for labour and the market wage rate. This quantity, Q_1, is illustrated in **Figure 12.4** by the intersection of the firm's supply curve and the demand for labour curve, labelled $D_{(MRP)}$.

| FIGURE 12.4 | The Firm's Equilibrium Quantity of Labour in a Competitive Labour Market |

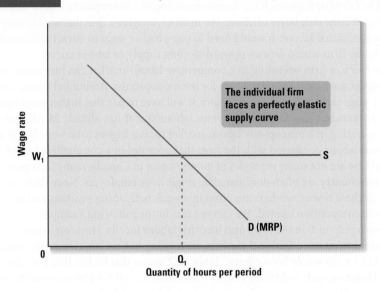

The individual firm faces a perfectly elastic supply curve

Given this market-determined wage rate, W_1, the individual firm faces a perfectly elastic supply of labour curve, S. The quantity of labour this firm would hire is determined by the intersection of the firm's MRP curve with the perfectly elastic supply curve, resulting in quantity Q_1 being hired.

 SELF-TEST

1. a) Given the data in the following table, and assuming that the output of Sparky the Plug Maker can be sold for $3 per unit, fill in the blanks below:

Hours of Labour	Total Product	Marginal Product	Marginal Revenue Product
0	0	/	/
1	3	___	___
2	7	___	___
3	13	___	___
4	18	___	___
5	22	___	___
6	25	___	___
7	27	___	___
8	28	___	___

b) If the firm can hire all the labour it wants for $9 per hour, how many hours per week will it hire, and what output will it produce?

2. The economy's supply and demand for labour are as follows:

Wage Rate	Supply of Labour (billions of hours)	Demand of Labour (billions of hours)
$12	12	16
14	13	15
16	14	14
18	15	13
20	16	12

Data for Ruby's Rhubarb are as follows:

Hours of Labour Hired	MRP_L
180	$18
220	16
260	14
300	12
340	10

a) How many hours of labour will Ruby's hire?

b) If the supply of labour increased by two billion at every wage rate, what effect would this have on the quantity of hours that Ruby's hires?

The Case of Monopsony

Next, we need to ask what happens if the firm is operating in a **monopsony** labour market, that is, a market in which it is the only buyer of labour. For instance, imagine a firm that was the only employer of some highly specialized labour. It would need to pay a higher wage to attract additional workers. In other words, the firm would face an upward-sloping supply of labour curve.

As we have seen, a firm operating in a competitive labour market can hire *additional* labour at the going market wage rate. This is not true for the monopsonist. Additional labour can be hired only if a higher wage rate is offered. Furthermore, it will have to pay that higher wage rate not only to additional workers but also to all the previous labour that it has already hired. The net result is that a firm operating in a monopsony labour market faces a higher total wage bill as a result of hiring additional labour compared with the firm that operates in a competitive labour market.

Although there are not many examples of monopsonies in Canada, many "company towns" in rural areas of the country are often dominated by single large employers. Since there are few other opportunities in these towns, workers are often in a weak bargaining position and are often paid less than if more competition existed. We can see this in the following example.

Sonny runs a pulp mill in the town and hires his labour locally. However, since he is the only employer, in order to attract additional workers, he is going to have to increase the wage not only for new hires but for the whole labour force. **Table 12.2** shows that he can hire a single worker for $15 per hour. However, each additional worker means that he will have to increase the wage by $1 for all the workers. His total wage cost is simply the total cost of hiring each quantity of workers. It is the last column which is significant. The **marginal wage cost** (MPC) shows how much extra it will cost Sonny to hire each additional worker. For instance, to hire a total of 5 workers will cost Sonny $95 at $19 per hour for each worker. However, if he wants to hire a sixth worker he is going to have to increase the wage to $20, not just for the sixth worker but for all workers.

The hourly wage and marginal wage cost, along with Sonny's demand for labour are illustrated in **Figure 12.5**.

If this were a competitive labour market, then the equilibrium wage would be $22 and 8 workers would be hired. However, in order to maximize his profits, the monopsonist would hire workers up to the point at which the extra cost (MWC) is equal to the extra revenue (MRP). This occurs when 6 workers are hired at which the MWC and MRP are both $25. However, in order to hire this quantity of workers, the monopsonist would only have to pay an hourly wage of $20. The conclusion is:

The monopsonist hires fewer workers and pays a lower wage than would a competitive firm.

TABLE 12.2	Total and Marginal Wage Costs for a Monopsonist		
# of Workers	Hourly wage	Total Wage Cost (TWC)	Marginal Wage Cost (MWC)
1	$15	$ 15	$15
2	16	32	17
3	17	51	19
4	18	72	21
5	19	95	23
6	20	120	25

FIGURE 12.5	The Firm's Equilibrium in a Monopsony Market

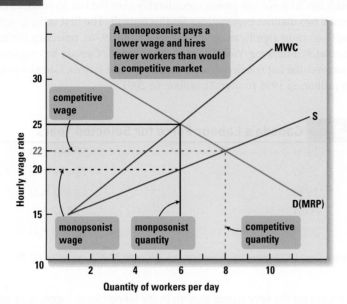

The monopsonist would hire workers to the point where the MWC equals the MRP. This occurs at the employment of 6 workers where each worker would be paid $20. If this were a competitive labour market, the equilibrium wage would be $22, and 8 workers would be hired.

 SELF-TEST

3. Syn Inc. is a monopsonist and has the following demand and supply of labour:

(1) Number of Workers	(2) Hourly Wage	(3) Total Wage Cost	(4) Marginal Wage Cost	(5) Marginal Revenue Product (= Demand)
1	16	_____	_____	28
2	17	_____	_____	27
3	18	_____	_____	26
4	19	_____	_____	25
5	20	_____	_____	24
6	21	_____	_____	23
7	22	_____	_____	22
8	23	_____	_____	21

a) Complete columns (3) and (4).

b) How many workers will Syn Inc. employ, and what will be the wage rate?

The Long-Run Supply of Labour

The size of Canada's labour force has grown considerably over the last 35 years, as can be seen in **Table 12.3**. There are two distinct explanations for this growth. The first is the growth in population. This influence was most significant in the late 1960s and 1970s, reflecting the high birth rate in the years immediately following World War II. In addition, Canada has experienced a great deal of immigration over the last few decades. As a result of these factors, Canada's population grew from just over 16 million in 1956 to over 31 million in 2001.

TABLE 12.3	Canada's Labour Force for Selected Years
1976	10 491 300
1986	13 272 100
1996	14 853 500
2004	17 182 300
2009	18 368 700

Source: Adapted from the Statistics Canada CANSIM database http://cansim2.statcan.ca, table number 282-0002, retrieved March 11, 2011.

The second reason for the very strong growth in the labour force supply is an increase in the rate at which the population participates in the labour force. Since 1950, the percentage of the female population in the labour force supply has steadily grown, from under 30 percent to approximately 66 percent by 2001, while the male participation rate has declined, in the same period, only slightly from nearly 80 percent to about 73 percent.

In explaining the cause of the growth in the labour force, we raise the question of exactly how to define the labour force supply. Since we earlier defined the supply as total hours worked rather than as the number of individuals working, the average number of hours worked per week also is relevant. It is interesting to note that although the average hours worked per week has steadily declined during the century, it has, in fact, been increasing in the last few years.

The overall increase in an economy's supply of labour will not fall evenly across every industry in the economy. Some industries will experience a larger increase in the supply of labour than others. For example, young people today seem to put a great deal of importance on maximizing their chances for getting a good entry-level job. Thus, more high school graduates are choosing to extend their formal education in colleges, universities, and technical institutes. And the areas they are choosing to focus on tend to be the more "practical" subjects, such as accounting, dental assisting, or computer studies. At the same time, most people want a chance to be creative in their work and to enjoy good working conditions. Thus, the supply of labour for any industry that seems to offer a good prospect for getting started, as well as being interesting, will be high. Examples of these industries include the software, medical services, and petroleum industries. Meanwhile, the supply of labour is decreasing for the more traditional industries that are not growing much, such as mining, forestry, and fishing.

The Long-Run Demand for Labour

We have established the importance of the marginal revenue product of labour in determining the demand for labour. Our discussion so far has assumed that technology and the size of the economy's capital stock remain unchanged. Yet, of course, technology improves and the capital stock grows over time. The effect of this can be seen in the growth of labour productivity, which has the effect of increasing each firm's marginal product and thus graphically shifting its MRP_L curve out to the right.

In addition to an increase in productivity, the demand for any factor is a derived demand. This means that an increase in the demand for an industry's product will cause an increase in its price in the short run and an increase in the number of firms in that industry in the long run. Both will result in an increase in the demand for labour.

Therefore, an increase in the demand for labour in any industry could occur because of increases in labour productivity in that industry or simply because demand for the product is growing.

We can put these trends together in **Figure 12.6**, where we see a shift to the right in the demand for labour curve (D_1 to D_2) because of increases in overall labour productivity or in the demand for the industry's product. In this figure, we also show an increase in the supply of labour: people might be attracted to the industry because they know it is growing and offers the possibility of interesting jobs with attractive working conditions. As shown in the figure, if the demand for labour increases more than the supply does, then the equilibrium quantity of labour will rise (from Q_1 to Q_2) and so will the wage rate (from W_1 to W_2). This, for example, could illustrate what is happening in the computer software industry. Recent graduates, trained in management information systems, are being offered entry-level jobs at several thousand dollars more per year than students whose major was in the more conventional subjects.

Does training in computer science mean better job prospects?

Productivity and the Real Wage

To extend the discussion of the importance of productivity, let us ask this question: what was fictional castaway Robinson Crusoe's real wage? By **real wage**, we mean the purchasing power of any given wage. In contrast, the **nominal wage** is the dollar-and-cents figure received from work. That is to say:

$$\text{Real wage} = \frac{\text{nominal wage}}{\text{price level}} \qquad [12.4]$$

Returning to the question above, Robbie's real wage is whatever he is able to produce for himself. If he produces nothing, his real wage would be nothing. If he produced more this month than he produced the previous month, his real wage has risen.

real wage: the purchasing power of the nominal wage; that is, nominal wage divided by the price level

nominal wage: the wage rate expressed as a dollar-and-cents figure

---

| FIGURE 12.6 | The Long-Run Trend in Labour Force Supply and Demand |

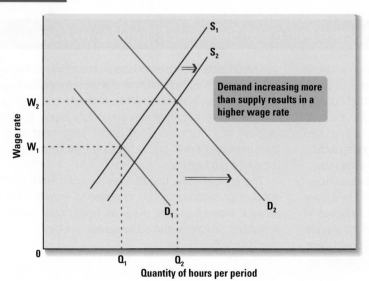

Increases in labour productivity and the growth in overall output for this industry cause the demand for labour curve to shift to the right, as illustrated by D_1 to D_2. The supply of labour curve also shifts to the right, as illustrated by S_1 to S_2. Since the demand for labour increased more than the supply, both the equilibrium quantity of labour and the wage rate rise.

| **FIGURE 12.7** | **Trend in Business-Sector Real Hourly Compensation and Productivity, Canada, 1990–2010** |

Productivity, and real hourly compensation have both risen steadily in the last 20 years, but productivity has increasingly lagged behind increases in compensation.

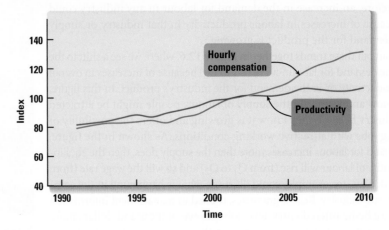

What is true for Robinson Crusoe, who lived alone on an uninhabited island, is also true for a whole economy. Given the labour force supply, the real wage for Canadians depends on how much is produced by Canadians, and, generally speaking, the more Canada produces, the higher will be Canadians' real wage. This inevitable relationship between productivity and the real wage is illustrated in **Figure 12.7**.

What is really being said here is that:

An economy's real output and real income are the same thing.

Thus, an economy's real income (real wage rate) per worker can only increase at about the same rate as its output per worker. In summary:

- Both supply and demand are determinants of wage rates.
- There are distinct long-run trends of growth in both the labour supply and demand.
- The average real wage for labour for the whole economy has increased over time, and this increase is closely related to increases in labour productivity.

 ADDED DIMENSION   Why the Prices of Services Continue to Rise

Many people have observed that the prices of tickets to a concert or the theatre have become almost prohibitive. There is an explanation for this. Live performances require direct contact between those who consume the service and those who provide it. In contrast, the consumer (buyer) of, say, a DVD player has no idea who worked on it or how much labour time went into its production; that is, there is no contact between producer and consumer.

Next, consider the fact that technological change saves labour time in producing the DVD player and often results in a lower price—one that is not achieved at the cost of a reduction in product quality. On the other hand, few such innovations are possible in providing live theatre or musical performances, and therefore, it is difficult to increase the productivity of a live performer.

The possible increases in labour productivity in manufacturing that come from technological change increase the wage rates paid throughout that sector. When wages for common labour in manufacturing rise, musicians and actors expect to receive an increase, too. Such increased labour costs must be paid for from increased ticket prices because they cannot come from increased productivity.

This general point, that the service sector faces rising (real) costs of production, can be extended to include most public services workers as well, such as health care professionals, firefighters, teachers, and social service workers.

Having established these quite general, but important, points, we now need to understand why wage rates for specific groups of individuals differ. In other words, we need to examine the wage rate differentials between pipefitters and nurses, and between medical doctors and helicopter pilots.

12.2 THE EFFECTS OF TRADE UNIONS AND PROFESSIONAL ASSOCIATIONS

Many individuals who earn a living by selling their labour belong, in association with their fellow workers, to a trade union, such as the Canadian Auto Workers' union, or to a professional association, such as the Nova Scotia Medical Association. From an economist's point of view, the broad objectives of such groups are to (a) increase the work available to their members, (b) increase the compensation received by their members, and (c) improve the working conditions of their members. If such unions and associations have any influence on how labour markets perform, their existence forces our analysis to go beyond the context of perfectly competitive markets.

As far as increased work and increased compensation are concerned, organizations use three basic approaches to achieve these objectives. **Figure 12.8** looks at the first approach—the attempt to increase the demand for the type of work their members perform.

Figure 12.8 could refer to any type of work, such as that of a medical practitioner, gas line plumber, or tailor. Let us choose the latter for our illustration. D_1 and S are the demand for and supply of labour in a non-unionized environment. This yields a wage of \$12 and an equilibrium quantity of 10 000 hours per week.

Now, suppose that the clothing workers become unionized and that their union is able to increase the demand for this type of work. The result is that the demand curve shifts out to D_2. This results in the wage rate increasing to \$14 and the equilibrium quantity increasing to 13 000 hours. This is obviously to the advantage of the organization and its members.

But how might the organization achieve this increase in demand for its members? One way is for the union to spend its own funds to advertise the employer's product. An ad campaign to encourage people to buy only clothes with a "union made" label would increase the demand for union-made clothing and thus increase the demand for the union members that make it.

LO2 Understand other important factors operating in the labour market.

FIGURE 12.8   The Effects on Wage Compensation of an Increase in Demand for Tailors

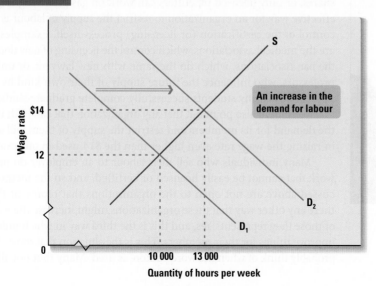

The non-unionized demand and supply for clothing makers is D_1 and S. Equilibrium occurs at an equilibrium wage of \$12 and quantity of 10 000. Effective unionization could result in the demand for labour shifting to the right, as illustrated by D_2. This would increase the wage rate to \$14 and the quantity to 13 000.

| **FIGURE 12.9** | **The Effects of Supply Restriction on Wage Compensation** |

Restricting the supply of labour shifts the supply curve from S_1 to S_2. As a result, the wage rate rises to $14, but equilibrium quantity declines to 6000.

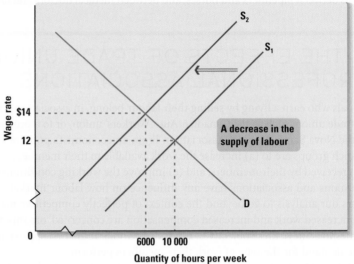

Another example would be a "Hire a CGA" campaign paid for by the organization aiming to increase the demand for its members.

Some organizations may not be able to use the above method to increase the demand for their members. A second approach to improving pay or employment is to restrict the supply of those who are qualified to do the work. **Figure 12.9** illustrates this situation.

The effect of restricting the supply of labour as shown by the shift from S_1 to S_2 is to cause the wage rate to rise from the non-unionized $12 per hour to $14 per hour. However, in this case the equilibrium quantity declines from the original 10 000 hours per week to only 6000. This approach is not as desirable to the organization and its members as was the one of increasing the demand, which raised both the equilibrium wage rate and quantity hired.

How might an organization restrict the supply of labour? One way is for the organization to successfully lobby for laws that restrict those who can perform a certain task; for example, only those who are certified as brokers can legally sell shares, or only licensed pipefitters can work on gas plumbing. The most effective way for an organization to restrict the supply of labour is to gain control of the certification (or licensing) process itself. Examples of this are the medical associations, which control the licensing of new doctors, or the bar associations, which do the same with new lawyers, or university professors, who influence the future supply of their own kind by having a say in how many students successfully complete graduate studies.

We should also point out that any organization that can both increase the demand for its members *and* restrict the supply of them will succeed in raising the wage rate even higher than the $14 used in our example.

Many individuals who sell their labour to an employer do unskilled work that cannot be easily licensed or certified, and so the methods discussed above are not open to the organizations that represent them. Is there any other way that these organizations might increase the wage rate of those they represent? Yes, and this is the third way in which unions can improve things for their members. This is the situation that most students probably think of when the word "union" is used. Many (but not all) trade

Members of the Fish Food and Allied Workers union march to the Confederation Building in St. John's, Newfoundland, in 2005 to protest production quotas for the crab fishery.

| FIGURE 12.10 | A Negotiated Wage Rate above Equilibrium |

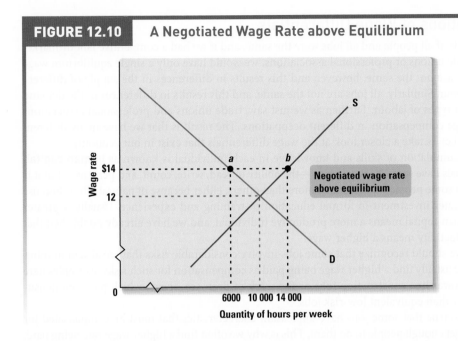

A union may succeed in obtaining a $14 wage rate in contract negotiations, but the consequence of an imposed wage settlement above equilibrium is that the quantity of hours supplied exceeds the quantity demanded by the horizontal distance *ab*, which, in this case, is 8000 hours per week.

unions are well enough organized to have sufficient bargaining power in negotiating contracts of employment to *simply impose* a wage rate that is above what would otherwise be market equilibrium. **Figure 12.10** illustrates this case.

As in the previous figure, **Figure 12.10** illustrates a market equilibrium wage rate of $12 per hour and a quantity of 10 000. If, through bargaining power, the union negotiates a contractual wage rate of $14 per hour, we would have the situation as shown here. This is analogous in many ways to price control by a government, which we examined in Chapter 3. Here, the price control is being done (with agreement from employers) by trade unions. Note that as the result of the higher negotiated wage of $14, the quantity of labour demanded has declined to 6000 hours per week at point *a*, while the quantity supplied has increased to 14 000 at point *b*. The result is that 8000 more hours per week are supplied than are demanded—the distance *ab* in **Figure 12.10**. This distance represents unemployed labour, much of it, unemployed union workers. This is essentially the phenomenon that occurs when an outsider looks enviously at a job that someone else has and wishes that he, too, had one of those jobs.

How successful are such attempts to raise the wage rate above what would be market equilibrium? Studies that attempt to measure the effect of trade unions on wage rates seem to agree that union organizations do increase the wage rate. For example, recent studies in the United States indicate a union/non-union wage differential of up to 33 percent. Similar studies in Canada indicate an hourly union/non-union wage differential of about $3. This would result in a 30 percent differential for the hourly wage rate of $10 and 12 percent for the hourly wage rate of $25.

In summary, unions can attempt to raise the wages of their members by:

- increasing the demand for their members by advertising the employer's product or their members' skills
- restricting the supply of labour for certain types of jobs by convincing government to establish legal qualifications for the work and then affecting the number of people who would obtain such qualifications
- negotiating a fixed wage rate above equilibrium

Explanations of Wage Differentials

Conceptually, if all people and all jobs were the same, and if we had a competitive labour market with no trade unions or professional associations, we would have only a single equilibrium wage rate. People are not the same, however, and this results in differences in the supply of different kinds of labour. Similarly, all jobs are not the same, and this results in differences in the demand for different types of labour. Further, as we just saw, trade unions and professional associations do alter wage compensation in different occupations. The result is that we have many different wage rates. Let us take a closer look at the wage differentials that exist in our economy.

human capital: the accumulation of all skills and knowledge acquired by individuals.

The accumulation of skills and knowledge in each individual is known as **human capital**. All individuals have some human capital—the ability to read, write, count, and perceive—but it is obvious that some people possess much more than others, either because of natural gift or because of much greater investment in formal education or training and experience. Usually, a greater level of human capital means a more productive individual, and we have already established that higher productivity means a higher wage.

Next, we should recognize that some jobs involve considerable risks that are absent in other jobs, and we usually find a higher wage being paid as compensation for such risks. Examples here would be power-line construction jobs or the work of deep-sea divers, which pay commensurately higher than equivalent low-risk jobs.

It is also true that some jobs have unpleasant characteristics that must be compensated for in order to get enough people to do them. This is why we often find a higher wage rate being paid, for example, for the night shift or for dirty, exposed work, such as that on an oil exploration rig, especially if that rig is 200 kilometres northeast of Aklavik.

Some jobs have very attractive non-pecuniary benefits that result in the wage rate being lower than it would otherwise be. These benefits range from lots of time off (for example, for school teachers), to flexible working hours (for example, for a self-employed writer), to the opportunity to be creative (for example, for a landscape architect).

We also need to mention that discrimination in the labour market results in some jobs being difficult to obtain by members of certain groups, such as women or visible minorities. This restricts the supply of labour into these kind of jobs, which raises the wage rate paid in them. In addition, the supply of labour into jobs traditionally held predominantly by women (day-care workers) or visible minorities (janitorial work) and requiring relatively low skills is greater than it might otherwise be, with the result that wage rates are lower.

This is not an exhaustive list of the reasons for wage differentials. There is, for example, an aspect of luck in all this. Some people seem to have just "lucked into" a job that they really love, and as a result, they do the job very well and get better compensation for doing so than others who

ADDED DIMENSION   Education and Earning Power

It has long been established by economic research that individuals with more formal education enjoy, on average, higher earning capacity throughout their lives. The following data from the 2006 census illustrate this point. The dollar figures are average incomes for the population over 15 years of age in Canada.

Level of Formal Education	Median Annual Income
Certificate or diploma below degree level	30 116
Bachelor's degree	52 907
Above Bachelor's degree level	69 230

SOURCE: Adapted from Statistics Canada's Summary Tables, Average earnings of the population 15 years and over by highest level of schooling, by provinces and territory (2006 Census); http://www40.statcan.gc.ca/l01/cst01/labor50a-eng.htm, retrieved October 9, 2009.

TABLE 12.4	Hourly Wages by Profession
Wage Category	**Average Canadian Hourly Wage**
Sales and services	$15.21
Labour	15.19
Clerical	18.51
Technical, occupations in health	21.47
Professional, business	29.76
Management, senior	46.72

Source: Adapted from the Statistics Canada CANSIM database http://cansim2.statcan.ca, table number 282-0069, retrieved March 11, 2011.

do the same work—imagine the really happy gardener or hairdresser. But the point is that people are different and jobs are different, so wage rates differ despite the impersonal forces of supply and demand that underlie every wage rate. In summary, wage differentials can exist because:

- the level of human capital varies among individuals
- some jobs involve more risks than others
- some jobs have unpleasant characteristics
- some jobs have attractive non-pecuniary benefits
- there is discrimination in labour markets

Table 12.4 indicates the average wage in May 2010 in Canada as a whole for six broad categories of labour.

 SELF-TEST

4. a) Draw supply and demand for labour curves for an entire economy, and label them S_1 and D_1.

b) Indicate the equilibrium wage as W_1 and the equilibrium quantity as Q_1.

c) Increase the demand for labour by drawing in D_2, and restrict the supply of labour by drawing in S_2.

d) Will the new wage rate, W_2, be higher or lower than W_1?

e) Will the new quantity, Q_2, be higher or lower than Q_1?

f) Give two reasons for the increase in the demand for labour and for the decrease in the supply of labour referred to in c).

12.3 THE CONCEPT OF ECONOMIC RENT

The original concept of economic rent is rooted in the work of the nineteenth-century classical economist David Ricardo. Ricardo focused on land and assumed that this factor had a single use: agriculture. Since the quantity of land is fixed, he went on to argue that it was perfectly inelastic in supply. Therefore, Ricardo saw the price of land as being purely demand driven. If land is in high demand, its price will be high, as was the case in Ricardo's England. However, if the demand for land is low, as it was in nineteenth-century North America, its price is very low (in many cases it was free). Whatever the price of land might be, this is the price that the owners of land earn. Ricardo called this **economic rent**.

If we do suppose that the supply of land is perfectly inelastic, as shown in **Figure 12.11**, and demand is relatively high, as with D_1, then the rent will be R_1. A decrease in demand, as illustrated by D_2, will result in the rent decreasing to R_2. Even if the price of land is zero, its supply is

L03 Explain why factors that are highly inelastic in supply require special analysis.

economic rent: the return to any factor of production above what is required to keep the factor in its present use.

FIGURE 12.11   The Concept of Economic Rent as Applied to Land

If we assume that land has only one use, then its supply is perfectly inelastic, as illustrated by S. Given this, the price of land, or the rent that it receives, is purely demand driven. If demand is high, as in D_1, then rent is R_1. Low demand, as illustrated by D_2, results in the lower rent of R_2.

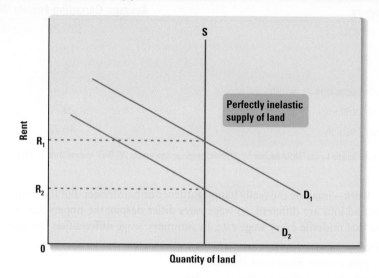

the same. Because land has this unique aspect, Ricardo considered the return to land, the economic rent, a surplus and not a cost. What this means is that the rent rate of, say, wheat land on the prairies will increase as a *result* of a higher price of wheat rather than being the *cause* of the higher wheat price.

We know today, however, that land has other uses besides agriculture. The larger the number of alternative uses that land might have, the less inelastic the supply of land for any one use. Because the supply curve of any factor is less than perfectly inelastic, we need to distinguish between rent and **transfer earnings** when discussing the return to the factor. Transfer earnings are defined as the necessary payment that a factor of production must earn in order to remain in its present use. Let us take the concept of transfer earnings and apply it to the example of another factor of production that has a very inelastic supply.

transfer earnings: a necessary payment that a factor of production must earn in order for it to remain in its present use.

Economic Rent and Professional Athletes

We are all aware of the fact that there are some well-paid professional athletes who love the game so much that they would continue to play even if they received less than they are currently earning. The wage rate that would be necessary to ensure that they continued to play is their transfer earnings. The difference between the transfer-earnings wage and the actual wage received is the economic rent. **Figure 12.12** will help us understand this concept better.

To fully understand the concept of economic rent, we need to view the supply curve, S, in **Figure 12.12** as showing the minimum price at which a given quantity is willingly supplied. Let us consider the case of a young athlete who is currently working hard but struggling in the minor leagues, but in whom the hope of making it into the big time is still alive. If the wage rate is W_1, our young athlete will play for a total of four years because he loves to play. Yet, he knows that most of his contemporaries will not make the big time and that the promise of riches will go unfulfilled. Therefore, he is not willing to play more than four years because the current wage is not sufficient for him to postpone getting on with his life any longer.

To persuade him to agree to play for a fifth year and a sixth year, a higher wage rate, W_2, for example, would have to be offered. Similarly, he will willingly play for eight years only if the wage offered is again increased, this time to W_3. The red-shaded area under the supply curve, therefore, is the transfer earnings necessary to induce our would-be pro to play for the full eight years.

FIGURE 12.12   Economic Rent and Transfer Earnings

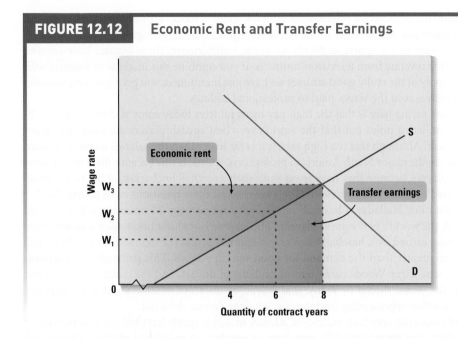

At wage rate W_1, our athlete will play for only 4 years. At wage rate W_2, he will play for 6 years. The red-shaded area is the pay that is necessary to induce him to commit to the full 8 years. Given the wage rate W_3, the entire rectangle is what he actually receives. Therefore, the blue-shaded area is his economic rent.

On the other hand, if our athlete is paid wage rate W_3 for each of the eight years, his total pay is the entire rectangle. Thus, the blue-shaded area represents his total pay less his transfer earnings, that is, his economic rent. This economic rent is a real bonus for him; it is the pay he receives over and above what he would have been willing to accept in order to continue doing what he is already doing.

Next, look at **Figure 12.13** in which the first supply curve, S_1, is elastic and S_2 is inelastic. It should be clear to you that the more inelastic the supply curve, the greater is the economic rent that the particular wage rate, either W_1 or W_2, will generate. Now, ask yourself—what is likely to be the elasticity of supply of an exceptionally good athlete who is a star in the major leagues of any professional sport? The answer is, of course, that it is *very* inelastic. This means that the majority of his earnings is an economic rent; the transfer earnings (what he could earn in the next-best alternative occupation) is small.

FIGURE 12.13   Economic Rents for Two Different Supply Elasticities

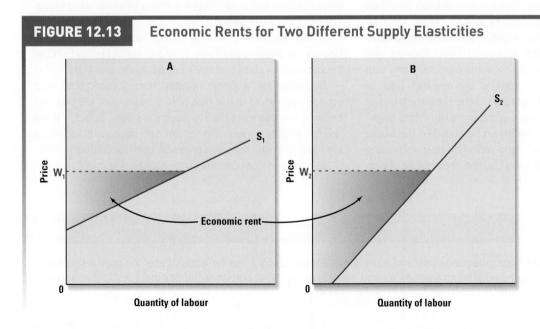

The economic rent which occurs at the same wage rate ($W_1 = W_2$) is greater in the case of the more inelastic supply curve S_2 than with the more elastic S_1.

In addition, the demand for professional athletes, some of whom are very good and some not so good, has increased dramatically in the last several years due to the expansion of the number of teams in all four major sports in North America. Furthermore, these leagues have enjoyed rapidly escalating revenue from television contracts. If you combine this increase in demand with the inelastic supply of the really good athletes we have just mentioned, you get a good explanation for the great increases in the wages paid to professional athletes.

What we are saying here is that the high pay many athletes today enjoy is *demand driven*. To clinch this point, let us point out that the world's very best squash players are paid only about $150 000 per year. Although this is a high salary, it is far lower than the salaries received by even average players in the major North American professional sports. Is this because there are so many of the squash players, because they have fewer skills than a football linebacker, or because they do not work as hard as a baseball outfielder? The answer to all these questions is, of course, "no."

So why does Roy Halladay, a baseball pitcher, get paid perhaps 20 times more than Shahid Zaman, one of the world's best squash players? The answer is that the ticket sales and television contract revenue earned by a baseball team are so enormous that the demand for good baseball players is much greater than the demand for good squash players. This demand side phenomenon explains why Tiger Woods earns tens of millions of dollars, and the concept of economic rent explains the sense, shared by many, that maybe he does not deserve all of it. In addition, Halladay has a union representing his interests, whereas Zaman does not.

As we all know, the very high salaries of athletes in major sports have led team owners to try to impose salary caps (maximums) in one form or another on individual players. The players' unions have, of course, resisted these attempts. What this dispute boils down to is a question of who (the team owner or the athlete) is entitled to what percentage of the economic rent that exists.

 ADDED DIMENSION   David Ricardo and Hockey Prices

The price of a season ticket for any of Canada's NHL teams is out of reach for many Canadian fans, sometimes as high as $6800. Even single tickets for the average family are likely to cost over $200. The reason usually given for these high prices is that to attract the best players, clubs have no choice but to offer high salaries. Even a journeyman hockey player these days can earn well over $1 million per season, with the stars earning well over $5 million. The high prices then are the result of high wages. But is that really the case?

Two centuries ago, British economist David Ricardo also pondered the cause of high prices; in his case he, along with his fellow countrymen, was alarmed at the very high price of corn (wheat) that was the direct result of the French attempt to blockade his country and starve it into submission. Prices began to escalate. The producers, the British farmers, laid the blame at the door of the landowners: farm rents had been increasing every year. As a result, the farmers claimed, they had no choice

but to increase prices. Workers complained about the high cost of food and demanded higher wages. Factory owners who were being forced to pay higher wages, in turn, blamed the farmers.

Into the fray came Ricardo, the leading economist of his age. He pointed out that since the supply of land is fixed (perfectly inelastic) then the price of corn is totally demand determined. The (economic) rent earned by the landowners is a true surplus and in no way related to costs. Put simply, rents are high because farmers can afford to pay them. They could afford to pay because the demand for corn, and therefore the price, was high.

Translated into a modern context then, Ricardo (and most economists) would argue that NHL ticket prices are high not because the salaries of hockey players are high. In fact, it is the reverse: hockey players' salaries are high because ticket prices are high. And why are ticket prices so high? Because the (insatiable) demand from Canadians for hockey is so high!

 SELF-TEST

5. Draw a normal downward-sloping demand curve and a perfectly inelastic supply curve for labour. Label the axes *wages* and *quantity of labour*. Indicate the equilibrium wage as W_1 and quantity as Q_1. What portion of the pay that goes to this labour is economic rent?

12.4   THE NATURAL RESOURCE MARKET

Natural resources are both renewable (trees and wild fish) and nonrenewable (minerals). The use of one more unit of a nonrenewable resource reduces, forever, the supply with which nature has endowed this planet. For this reason, nonrenewable resources are a topic of particular interest to both economists and the public in general. As an example, oil is nonrenewable. Does this mean that the supply of the world's oil is perfectly inelastic? In some grand sense, in the very long run, yes. However, we are certain that not all the available oil in the world has been discovered, and so we really do not know the total quantity of that perfectly inelastic supply.

LO4 Recognize the relevance of the right rate of exploitation in the natural resource market.

Furthermore, much of the oil that has been discovered is not for sale at current prices. Therefore, the present supply curve of oil is much more like S_2 in **Figure 12.14** and represents not so much the total quantity that exists but the amount currently available for sale.

Given that in the very long run, there is only a finite amount of oil available, we need to ask if the price system leads to an overly rapid exploitation of oil. Or is it possible that the future will prove our current rate of use to be too conservative?

This is a highly politicized question, but economists do have something to say about it. Let us try to follow an argument that can get rather complex. The current value of oil to consumers is the amount they are willing to pay in order to obtain one more barrel. Let us assume this figure is $20. Further, let us assume this is also the current market price for oil. An additional barrel extracted and sold now will yield $20 in revenue to the oil producer, which can be held and earn interest that we will assume is 5 percent so that the producer would have a value of $21 per year from now. Alternatively, he could leave the barrel of oil in the ground in order to extract and sell it one year from now. Which is better, to extract and sell it now and invest the proceeds or extract and sell it one year from now? The answer depends on what the price of the barrel of oil turns out to be in one year. If one year from now its price is $21.50, the producer should have left it in the ground. If, however, the price turns out to be $20.50, the producer will realize that it should have been extracted and sold a year ago. Understanding this little conundrum leads us to a very useful conclusion:

> The optimal rate of extraction of oil depends on the rate at which the price of oil is changing and on the interest rate.

FIGURE 12.14   The World's Supply of Oil

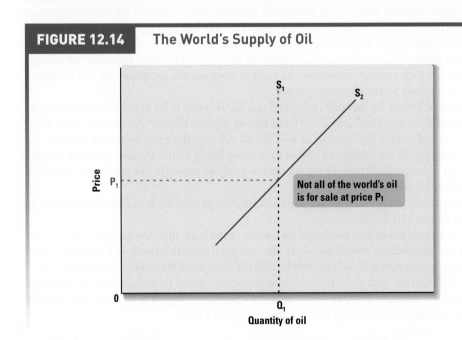

Given the facts that not all of the oil in the world has been discovered and that not all the discovered oil is for sale at the present price, say, P_1, the supply curve for oil is upward sloping, as illustrated by S_2. Only in the very long run can we think of the supply curve of oil as being perfectly inelastic, as some unknown quantity.

To nail this down, again assume that the present price of oil is $20, the rate of interest is 5 percent, and both remain unchanged so that extracting a barrel of oil today and selling it for $20 would give us approximately (an invested sum of) $25.50 in five years. If, five years from now, the price of a barrel of oil is also exactly $25.50, then our rate of extraction is exactly correct. On the other hand, if the price of oil turns out to be only $24, then we have been extracting oil far too fast. Similarly, if the price of oil turns out to be $27, then we have been conserving oil too much. Interesting, isn't it?

Let us hasten to say that we are not proposing this idea as the complete solution to the complex question of how quickly we should use up nonrenewable resources. We do, however, wish to emphasize the point that economists do have some ideas in this area.

Common Property Resources

common property resource: a resource not owned by an individual or a firm.

There is also an interesting question concerning (some) renewable resources that are called **common property resources**. This term means that no one individual or firm (or individual state, for that matter) owns the resource. Wild fish in the ocean are the classic example of a common property resource.

As we saw in the case of nonrenewable resources, such as oil, the question here is: what is the correct rate of exploitation of a common property resource? If this question is not addressed and answered by some regulatory body, we can be certain that the resource will be over-extracted and possibly disappear. Consider cod stocks in the Grand Banks, off the coast of Newfoundland. From a social point of view, these stocks should be harvested at a rate that does not exceed their natural rate of reproduction. This will ensure that there are fish to harvest next year and 10 years from now and 100 years from now.

However, from an individual fisher's point of view, the more fish harvested now, the greater the fisher's income. But isn't a sound conservation policy to that individual's long-term benefit? Yes, but only if all other fishers do not fish intensively until the stocks are all gone—something they are strongly tempted to do. You can see the need for the social regulation of a common property resource. Given the state of the East Coast cod fisheries today, one can conclude that such regulation was not done well.

The idea of overexploiting common property resources was brought home to many in an article by the biologist Garrett Hardin called "The Tragedy of the Commons," which first appeared in the journal Science in 1968. Hardin looked at the common pasture land that existed in many European countries in the Middle Ages (and in the United States into the twentieth century). In Medieval Europe, peasants were free to graze their animals, often sheep, on the common pasture without fee or payment. It was their traditional right. This was fine as long as such things as wars, poaching, and disease kept the numbers of both humans and sheep in check, but it became a problem when numbers started to rise. Now came the real risk of too many sheep for not enough pasture. However, each peasant was rational enough to work out the marginal cost and benefit of adding one more sheep to the common pasture.

The marginal benefit for any one individual was the revenue to be derived from selling one more sheep while the marginal cost came from having slightly thinner sheep, since each additional grazer would reduce the amount of feed for all. Clearly, the extra benefit of grazing one more sheep outweighed the additional cost of each sheep being a little thinner. For each peasant there would be a marginal surplus. However, for the group of peasants this is patently invalid. It is that old fallacy of composition again.

The over-production of common property resources in general leads to a deadweight loss, as illustrated in **Figure 12.15**.

If there is no restriction and no charge for the use of the land, then the marginal private cost is zero and the equilibrium would be where the marginal private benefit and cost are equal. However, there is definitely a social cost involved in the overuse of the land (a quantity of ten). If we include this external cost, then the true cost to society would be reflected in the marginal social cost, and the optimum quantity would be six. Without some type of restriction, the economy would suffer a deadweight loss—the triangle area in **Figure 12.15**.

FIGURE 12.15   Common Property Resources and the Deadweight Loss

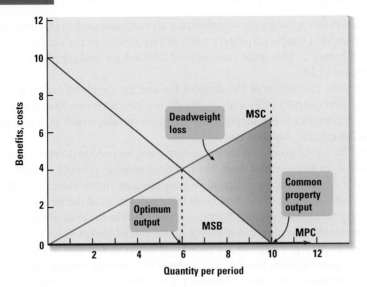

If external costs are ignored, then given the marginal private costs and demand, a quantity of 10 units of the resource would be used. If external costs are taken into consideration, then the true costs are reflected in the marginal social cost curve and the optimal quantity would be 6 units. Without regulation, there would be overproduction, and the economy would suffer a deadweight loss, as shown.

The tragedy of the commons is caused by the fact that the most people do not take into consideration the impact of their actions on others—they ignore external costs. The problem could, of course, be easily overcome if the government were to regulate the commons and limit the number of sheep, or put a tax or fee on each sheep grazed. Alternatively, they could privatize the grazing land and allow each family to enclose its own parcel of land. This is exactly what happened in Europe during the enclosure movement. But this is impossible in the case of the high seas or the atmosphere, which are quickly becoming depleted or polluted. The tragedy of the commons remains a serious challenge to society and policy makers.

Let us now leave the natural resource market and turn to the capital goods market.

✓ SELF-TEST

6. Assume that one year ago, the rate of interest was 5 percent and we decided to extract a barrel of oil for $50 and sell it. If the present price of oil is $54, what can be said about last year's decision?

7. The accompanying diagram shows the demand and marginal social costs for a common property resource.

   Assuming that there was no charge made for the use of this resource:

   a) What quantity would be used?

   b) Shade in the area that represents the deadweight loss.

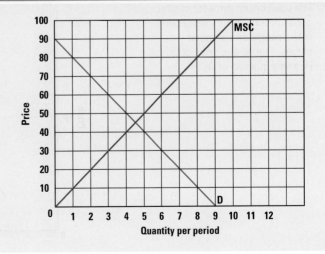

12.5   THE CAPITAL GOODS MARKET

In a sense, the market for capital goods—whether they are machines used in a factory, or a computer system for an office, or a simple carpenter's tool—is very similar to the market for any *product*, as discussed in Chapter 2. This quite conventional demand for and supply of capital goods is illustrated in **Figure 12.16**.

In the figure, the interaction of the demand for and the supply of capital goods yields an equilibrium price and quantity of P_1 and Q_1. We do not have anything to add about the supply of capital goods in reference to the supply of any particular product, such as orange juice—as the price increases, the quantity supplied rises.

The demand for capital goods is more interesting. First, we need to point out that the demand for capital goods is, in fact, derived from the marginal revenue product of capital, just as the demand for labour depended on its marginal revenue product. In this case, the MRP of capital is the additional benefit accruing to the firm from the employment of the next unit of capital and is equal to the marginal physical product it produces multiplied by the price of the product. Second, we need to recognize that the purchase of capital goods almost always needs to be financed with borrowed money. Even large firms are not able to lay out several hundred thousand dollars in cash for a new computer system. Instead, they arrange for a loan to finance the purchase, which is then paid back over time. They must, of course, pay interest on this loan, and it is because of this that the demand for capital goods is (inversely) related to the cost of financing capital purchases, which is the interest rate. In other words, the higher the interest rate, the lower the amount of borrowed funds and, therefore, the amount of spending on capital goods. The factors that determine the rate of interest are a matter for discussion in a macroeconomics course.

The demand side of the capital goods market is also interesting because an improvement in technology can certainly affect the demand for such goods. Significant improvements in technology can render existing capital goods obsolete and require that they be replaced by newer versions. This increases the demand and is illustrated graphically by a rightward shift in the demand curve for the new capital goods.

Just as technological change increases the marginal revenue product of labour, it also increases the marginal revenue product of new capital goods that incorporate the new technology, and this

---

FIGURE 12.16   **The Market for Capital Goods**

The equilibrium price for capital goods occurs at the intersection of the supply and demand curves: that is, at a price of P_1 and a quantity of Q_1.

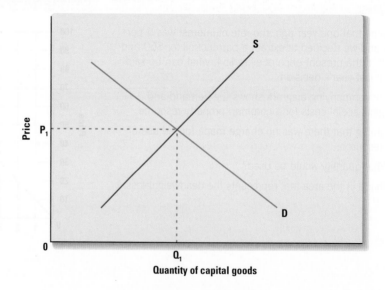

Quantity of capital goods

can result in (the newer) capital goods being more productive *relative* to labour. Firms will be very tempted to substitute the now more productive capital for labour, which has become relatively less productive and therefore relatively more expensive. In other words, when deciding on amounts of substitutable factors, such as capital and labour, a firm would take into account both productivity and the price of the factors. Thus, if:

$$\frac{MP_K}{P_K} > \frac{MP_L}{P_L}$$

it would be profitable to substitute capital for labour. In a sense, what the firm does is compare the value received for each dollar spent on labour with each dollar spent on capital. If a dollar spent on capital yields a greater return than a dollar spent on labour, then the firm will invest in more capital. This ratio of the marginal product of capital per dollar spent on capital compared with the marginal product of labour per dollar spent on labour is analogous to the equation we saw in Chapter 5, when exploring a consumer's attempt to maximize total utility. By equating the marginal product per dollar of the two factors, we know that the firm is maximizing total profits.

Such substitution of capital for labour is something that we witness almost every day. One of your authors, as a teenager, used to work after school unloading cases of beer from railway cars—one case at a time. Today, one person, using a forklift, does the work that half a dozen kids used to do. As another example, think of the labour saved at a supermarket because of the use of the conveyor belt and the bar-code reader. A third example is the use of computerized test banks in economics courses, which have replaced student graders.

When capital is substituted for labour, it raises questions about whether or not such automation destroys jobs and is, therefore, something that society needs to be concerned about. Many misconceptions about this issue can be easily cleared up. There is no question that automation does, indeed, eliminate certain types of jobs—the days of young people unloading beer from railway cars are gone. Economists call this the **factor substitution effect** of technological change. But if technological change causing the substitution of capital for labour was the whole story, we would have to wonder how it is that anyone is still working, given the fact that our economy has experienced over 200 years of dramatic changes in technology.

factor substitution effect:
one factor replaces another factor as a result of technological change.

In fact, the substitution effect is not the whole story. Capital substitution increases labour's productivity (the labour that was not replaced by capital) and thus lowers the cost of production. This, in turn, lowers the price of the final products, which increases both the quantity demanded for those products and thus total output. This increase in total output increases the demand for labour, so the **output effect** of technological change *creates* jobs. Given the fact that there are more people working in our society today than ever before, the output effect of technological change must have been stronger than the substitution effect over the last two centuries or so.

factor output effect:
rising total output leads to an increased demand for labour.

 ADDED DIMENSION   The Luddites and the Fear of Machines

Although the twentieth century saw a quantum leap in the number of machines used by society, it generally did not result in mass unemployment. In the short run, however, the replacement of labour by machines can result in loss of specific jobs. In the early days of the Industrial Revolution, these short-term effects devastated the lives of many workers. The rapid introduction of machines led to, in Karl Marx's phrase, "an industrial army of unemployed workers."

Small wonder, then, that working people at the time, still more used to country ways than city ways, feared and hated the introduction of machines. A group of them, inspired by a mythical figure called Ned Ludd, swore to fight the invasion of the machines. In the textile manufacturing areas in the north of England, Luddites went on a rampage, burning and wrecking factories. These riots peaked in 1811 and 1812 but were eventually brought to an end by the authorities. A mass trial in 1816 led to the hanging of some of the group's leaders and the deportation of others, resulting in an abrupt end to the reign of "King Ludd."

8. Given its current output, Rally Rackets Ltd. is experiencing a marginal product of capital of 60 and a marginal product of labour of 10. If the price of capital is $100 per unit and the price of labour is $25 per unit, how should this firm substitute factors?

12.6   THE ENTREPRENEURIAL MARKET

LO6 Explain the two views on the ultimate source of profits.

The fourth of our four factors of production is enterprise, or entrepreneurial talent. No economist explored the role of entrepreneurial talent in the market economy more than Joseph Schumpeter, who taught at Harvard University in the first half of the twentieth century. Schumpeter saw the entrepreneur as an innovating doer who bridged the gap between a mere idea and a productive application. Eccentric minds invented, and common businesspeople managed, but it was the risk-taking entrepreneur who had the vision and the chutzpah to take truly new and revolutionary *action*. The entrepreneur, in Schumpeter's eyes, is the engine of economic growth and development in a capitalist economy.

From the time of Adam Smith, economists have argued that competition within a capitalist economy would tend to result in (economic) profits being competed down to zero—a process we explored in the context of both the perfectly competitive and the monopolistically competitive market models. What then explained the continued existence of economic profits nearly two centuries after capitalism took root in the Western European and North American economies?

Surely, Schumpeter argued, the innovations of the entrepreneur were the source of economic profits in capitalism. New innovation created unique situations in which profits could be made. In time, a swarm of imitators would become established, and such profits would be driven to zero. However, in a dynamic and growing economy, another wave of innovation would have already occurred, and new profit opportunities would be continuously created.

While entrepreneurs create profits, they are often not the long-term beneficiaries of them. As John Kenneth Galbraith pointed out in *The New Industrial State*, the risk-taking entrepreneur sometimes loses control of his or her growing business to the impersonal forces of what Galbraith calls the *technostructure*, which is at the heart of the modern transnational corporation. When this happens, more conservative and more bureaucratic managers take over from the risk-taking entrepreneur.

Before we leave this topic, we should point out that there is an alternative explanation for profits: the existence of oligopoly and monopoly influences that inhibit the natural tendency for profits to be competed away. However, this explanation, while valid, just does not have the same zing to it as Schumpeter's.

Review

CHAPTER SUMMARY

In this chapter, you studied the factor markets for labour, land, capital, and entrepreneurial activity. You learned that it is the productivity (marginal product) of each factor that underlies the rate of return that it earns and the rate that it is employed.

12.1a The *demand for labour* is a derived demand that is determined by the marginal product of labour, which when converted to money terms, becomes

$$MRP_L = \frac{\Delta \text{ total revenue}}{\Delta \text{ labour inputs}} \text{ or } = MP_L \times P$$

12.1b The downward-sloping portion of the MRPL curve is the demand for labour curve, while the *supply of labour curve* is upward-sloping, since increases in the wage rate increase the quantity supplied of labour. The *equilibrium wage rate* is determined by the point of intersection of these two curves.

12.1c In a competitive factor market, the individual firm is able to hire all the labour it wishes at the market determined wage rate and will, in fact, *hire labour* up to the point that:

$$MRP_L = W$$

12.1d A firm operating in a *monopsony* labour market will find that if it wants to hire more labour, it will have to offer a higher wage rate to new employees, which increases the average wage rate that it must pay. Compared with competitive labour markets, monopsonies hire fewer workers and pay lower wages.

12.1e Canada's *long-run supply of labour* has been growing steadily as a result of increased population and an increase in labour force participation rates.

12.1f Increases in *labour productivity*, which depends on technological change and increases in the nation's capital stock, are closely related to:

- the long-run demand for labour
- the real wages of Canadians that is measured by:

$$\text{Real wage} = \frac{\text{nominal wage}}{\text{price level}}$$

12.2a *Trade unions and professional associations* attempt to benefit their members by increasing the demand for their work, raising their nominal wage rates, and improving their working conditions. This is done by:

- shifting the demand curve for the members' labour to the right
- shifting the supply of labour curve to the left
- imposing a negotiated wage rate above the market equilibrium rate

12.2b Wage rate *differentials* exist because:

- of variations in the level of human capital between individuals
- some jobs involve more risks than others
- some jobs have unpleasant characteristics
- some jobs have attractive nonpecuniary benefits
- there is discrimination in labour markets

12.3 The concept of *economic rent* was originally conceived as the return to land (which, it was assumed, could only be used for agriculture) and was perfectly inelastic in supply. The modern view of rent is that it is the return to a factor that is over and above that factor's transfer earnings.

Practise and learn online with Connect, where you can find the Answered Questions and the Unanswered Problems for all chapters of this textbook's Study Guide section.

12.4a Two of the interesting questions in the *natural-resource market* are:

- What is the best rate of exploitation of a non-renewable resource such as oil?
- How can we best regulate common property resources, such as wild fish?

12.4b The Tragedy of the Commons refers to the fact that common property resources tend to be over-exploited, which results in a dead-weight loss.

12.5 The demand for *capital goods*, like the demand for all factors, depends on the productivity of capital that is determined by technological change and that lowers the price of capital goods and leads to the substitution of capital for labour so as to maintain the equality:

$$\frac{MP_K}{P_K} = \frac{MP_L}{P_L}$$

12.6 The two views of *economic profits* are that they are the result of:

- entrepreneurial activities *à la* Schumpeter
- imperfect competition in the product market

NEW GLOSSARY TERMS AND KEY EQUATIONS

common property resource   392
economic rent   387
factor market   372
factor output effect   395
factor substitution effect   395

human capital   386
labour force   374
labour force supply   374
marginal revenue product   372
marginal wage cost   378

monopsony   378
nominal wage   381
product market   372
real wage   381
transfer earnings   388

Equations:

[12.1]   Marginal revenue product (MRP) = marginal product (MP) × price (P)   **page 372**

[12.2]   Marginal revenue product (MRP) = $\frac{\Delta \text{ total revenue } (\Delta TR)}{\Delta \text{ labour}}$ **page 372**

[12.3]   Profit maximization: $MRP_L = W$ **page 373**

[12.4]   Real wage = $\frac{\text{nominal wage}}{\text{price level}}$ **page 381**

STUDY TIPS

1. In this chapter, we shifted our focus from the product market to the factor market. Most of the chapter assumes a perfectly competitive factor market. This means that a firm can buy all it wants of a particular factor, say, labour, at the going wage rate; that is, the firm's hiring practices will not drive the wage rate up. Another way to put this is to say that the price of a factor remains constant because the actions of individual sellers and buyers do not affect the price. This is analogous to the perfectly competitive product market we studied in Chapter 8, in which the price of the product remains constant, regardless of the action of individual buyers and sellers.

2. You may recall that in Chapter 6, we stressed the importance of the relationship between the costs of production and productivity of inputs. Productivity

also plays a key role in this chapter, in that it determines in the long run the real return received by the factor; for example, the real wage of labour is determined by labour's productivity.

3. The calculation of the MRP of any factor can be done in one of two ways. The first is to multiply the MP of the factor by the price of the product sold. The second is to simply determine the change in total revenue resulting from the use of one unit of the factor in question.

4. Students tend to confuse the effect of a change in the price of a competitive firm's product with the effect of a change in the price of a factor that the firm hires. The former shifts the factor demand curve, while the latter results in a movement along the demand curve for the factor.

5. Even though it may seem like a small point, make sure you understand the distinction between real wage and nominal wage. This will be essential when you take on the study of macroeconomics.

6. You should not assume that the concept of economic "rent" applies only to land. Under the right conditions, any factor can receive economic rent.

Answered Questions
These questions can also be found online on Connect.

Indicate whether the following statements are true or false:

1. **(LO 1) T or F** Although supply and demand analysis can be used to analyze the product market, it cannot be used to analyze the factor market.

2. **(LO 1) T or F** Marginal revenue product is the increase in a firm's total revenue that results from the use of one more unit of input.

3. **(LO 1) T or F** An employer operating under conditions of a perfectly competitive labour market will hire labour up to the point where the marginal product of labour equals the wage rate.

4. **(LO 1) T or F** If the product market is imperfectly competitive rather than perfectly competitive, the marginal revenue product curve declines faster.

5. **(LO 1) T or F** The fact that neither of the authors works weekends at McDonald's demonstrates that they both value an extra hour of leisure over the added hourly income that they could earn.

6. **(LO 1) T or F** The size of Canada's labour force has more than doubled over the last 35 years.

7. **(LO 1) T or F** The typical range for the annual increase in labour productivity in Canada over the last 30 years has been between 3 and 5 percent.

8. **(LO 1) T or F** The real wage is defined as the nominal wage divided by labour productivity.

9. **(LO 2) T or F** Often, trade unions and professional associations have the same effect on the labour market.

10. **(LO 4) T or F** Some form of regulation is needed to ensure that a common property resource is not over-extracted.

Basic (Questions 11–22)

11. **(LO 3)** Which of the following is assumed in Ricardo's concept of economic rent?
    a) A perfectly inelastic supply curve
    b) A perfectly inelastic demand curve
    c) A perfectly elastic supply curve
    d) A perfectly elastic demand curve

12. **(LO 6)** Which of the following statements best describes Schumpeter's view of profits?
    a) Profits come in a steady stream in a capitalist economy as long as full employment is achieved.
    b) Economic profits are zero in a capitalist economy in the long run.
    c) The source of profits, whatever level they may be, is the result of entrepreneurial activity.
    d) Profits occur only when the economy is in equilibrium.

13. **(LO 1)** What is the most likely effect of an increase in the demand for a particular type of labour?
    a) The wage rate for that type of labour will rise, and the quantity hired will decrease.
    b) The wage rate for that type of labour will rise, and the quantity hired will also increase.
    c) The wage rate for that type of labour will rise, but the quantity hired will remain unchanged.
    d) The wage rate for that type of labour will fall, and the quantity hired will increase.

14. **(LO 1)** The average wage rate in Canada has increased over the last 30 years. Which of the following is the most likely explanation?
    a) The demand for labour has decreased.
    b) The supply of labour has decreased.
    c) The demand for labour has increased more than the supply of labour has decreased.
    d) The demand for labour has increased more than the supply of labour has increased.

15. **(LO 2)** All of the following statements, except one, are valid explanations for wage rate differentials. Which is the exception?
    a) All individuals possess the same amount of human capital.
    b) Different jobs involve different degrees of risk.
    c) Some jobs have unpleasant characteristics that are absent in other jobs.
    d) Some jobs have very attractive non-pecuniary benefits.

16. **(LO 1)** Suppose that the MRPL for a competitive firm is currently $50 and the hourly cost of labour is $40. Which of the following is the correct action for the firm?
    a) Since the firm must be profitable, it need not do anything.
    b) The firm should hire more labour.
    c) The firm should substitute labour for capital.
    d) The firm should raise the wage rate of its labour.

17. **(LO 1)** At what point will a competitive firm stop hiring additional labour?
    a) When its total product is maximized
    b) When the marginal product of labour is maximized
    c) When the marginal revenue product of labour is maximized
    d) When the marginal revenue product of labour is just equal to the wage rate

18. **(LO 1)** Which of the following best illustrates the factor market?
    a) The market for gasoline supplied by an oligopolistic firm
    b) The market for shoes supplied by a monopolistic firm
    c) The market for wheat supplied by a perfectly competitive firm
    d) The market for labour, natural resources, capital, and enterprise

Use **Table 12.5**, which provides data for the firm Skipper the Shoemaker, to answer questions 19 and 20.

19. **(LO 1)** What is the marginal revenue product of the fourth hour of labour?
    a) 18 units of output
    b) 90 units of output
    c) $36
    d) $180

TABLE 12.5

Hours of Labour	Total Product	Total Revenue	Marginal Revenue Product
0	0	/	/
1	20	$ 40	$40
2	48	96	56
3	72	144	48
4	90	180	36
5	104	208	28
6	112	224	16

20. **(LO 1)** If labour can be hired for $28 per hour, how many hours should the firm hire?
    a) 3
    b) 4
    c) 5
    d) 6

21. **(LO 4)** What is a common property resource?
    a) Any natural resource, such as iron ore
    b) Any resource openly bought and sold in the market place
    c) Any resource supplied by government
    d) Any resource not owned by an individual or a firm

22. **(LO 2)** All of the following, except one, is part of human capital. Which is the exception?
    a) Natural abilities
    b) Higher wage rates
    c) Formal education
    d) On-the-job experience

Intermediate (Questions 23–31)

23. **(LO 5)** The argument that technological change creates jobs assumes that:
    a) The factor substitution effect outweighs the factor output effect
    b) The factor output effect outweighs the factor substitution effect
    c) The real wage rate increases more quickly than the nominal wage rate
    d) The level of human capital in the economy is increasing

24. **(LO 4)** The world's supply of oil is:
    a) Perfectly inelastic at all prices
    b) Elastic at prices up to a certain level after which becomes perfectly inelastic
    c) Perfectly elastic
    d) Inelastic at prices up to a certain level after which becomes perfectly elastic

25. **(LO 1)** What is the most likely consequence if a monopsonist hires more labour?
    a) A decrease in the wage rate
    b) An increase in the wage rate
    c) A wage rate that neither increases nor decreases
    d) A rise in the marginal product of labour

26. **(LO 2)** Which of the following would be most advantageous to a trade union or professional association?
    a) The supply of labour is restricted.
    b) The demand for labour is decreased.
    c) The supply of labour increases by more than the demand increases.
    d) The demand for labour increases by more than the supply increases.

27. **(LO 3)** All of the following statements, except one, are correct concerning the labour market for high-profile professional athletes. Which is the exception?
    a) The supply is inelastic.
    b) The wage rate is demand driven.
    c) There is an element of economic rent in their pay.
    d) There are no transfer earnings involved in their pay.

28. **(LO 4)** What do most economists think is the socially optimum extraction rate of a natural resource, such as oil?
    a) One that equals the MRP of the resource
    b) A rate that ensures that the price of oil increases at the same rate as the interest rate
    c) One that is less than the rate of discovery of new sources
    d) One that is less than 2 percent of known reserves so as to guarantee at least 50 years' supply at all times

29. **(LO 5)** If the MP_K/P_K is greater than the MP_L/P_L, which of the following is correct?
    a) The firm should substitute labour for capital.
    b) The firm should substitute capital for labour.
    c) The firm should raise the wage rate of its labour.
    d) The firm should decrease its output.

30. **(LO 1)** Graphically, which of the following would cause a shift to the right in the demand curve for a factor?
    a) A decrease in the price of that factor
    b) An increase in the price of a substitute factor
    c) A decrease in the price of the product produced by the factor
    d) An increase in the marginal product of a substitute factor

31. **(LO 1)** If most people's desire for leisure increases, which one of the following statements is correct?
    a) The wage rate would fall, and the quantity of products produced would rise.
    b) Both the wage rate and the quantity of products produced would fall.
    c) The wage rate would fall, and the demand for labour would increase.
    d) The wage rate would rise, and the quantity of products produced would fall.
    e) Both the wage rate and the quantity of products produced would rise.

Advanced (Questions 32–35)

32. **(LO 3)** All of the following statements, except one, concerning the concept of economic rent are correct. Which is the exception?
    a) The more inelastic the supply of a factor, the more economic rent that factor earns.
    b) A factor that has a perfectly inelastic supply will earn no transfer earnings.
    c) It is possible for a factor to receive both economic rent and transfer earnings.
    d) If we assume that land has only one use, such as agriculture, then all of its return is economic rent.
    e) The higher the transfer earnings of a factor, the higher its economic rent will be.

33. **(LO 1)** When is the marginal revenue product of a factor at a maximum?
    a) When its marginal product is at a maximum
    b) When the firm's total product is at a maximum
    c) When its marginal product is at a minimum
    d) When both its marginal product and the firm's total product are at a maximum
    e) When average product is at its maximum

34. **(LO 1)** If a firm is operating in a monopsony market, which of the following statements is correct?
    a) The firm can hire additional labour at the same wage rate it is currently paying.
    b) The firm would hire more labour in the monopsony situation than in the competitive situation.
    c) The firm faces an upward-sloping supply of labour curve.
    d) The MPR_L declines faster in the case of the monopsony situation than in the competitive one.
    e) The firm's demand for labour curve is downward sloping in the situation of the monopsony market and horizontal in the case of the competitive one.

35. **(LO 2)** All of the following statements, except one, are correct when a trade union successfully imposes a wage rate above equilibrium. Which is the exception?
    a) There will be more workers willing to work than are hired.
    b) The firm's total wage bill will definitely be higher.
    c) The average firm is not operating in a competitive factor market.
    d) The quantity of workers hired will be less after the imposition of the higher wage than it was before.
    e) Neither the demand for nor the supply of labour has changed.

Parallel Problems

ANSWERED PROBLEMS

36A. **(LO 1)** **Key Problem** Heavenly Bubbles is a small soap company whose main product is hand soap, which sells in a competitive market for $2 per bar. The bars are produced at autonomous workstations that feature a specially designed machine. The output per hour of each workstation varies with the amount of labour used, as the data in **Table 12.6** indicate. Labour costs $16 per hour.
   a) Fill in the Marginal Product, Total Revenue 1, and Marginal Revenue Product 1 columns in **Table 12.6**.
   b) How many hours of labour should the firm assign to each workstation?
      Hours of labour: _____ .

   c) Assuming the firm has six workstations, construct the firm's demand for labour curve (and label it D_1) on the graph in **Figure 12.17**. Indicate, with the letter a, the total amount of labour that the firm will hire at a wage rate of $16.
   d) Assume that there is an increase in employment taxes (the employers share of EI and CPP), which raises the cost of labour to $24 per hour. Now, how many workers per hour should the firm assign to each workstation, and how many should it hire in total?
      Number of workers: _____ ;
      number of workers in total: _____ .
   e) On the graph in **Figure 12.17** indicate, with the letter b, the effect of this increase in the cost of labour.

TABLE 12.6

Quantity of Labour	Output per Hour	Marginal Product	Total Revenue 1	Marginal Revenue Product 1	Total Revenue 2	Marginal Revenue Product 2
0	0	/	/	/	/	/
1	24	___	___	___	___	___
2	44	___	___	___	___	___
3	60	___	___	___	___	___
4	72	___	___	___	___	___
5	80	___	___	___	___	___
6	84	___	___	___	___	___

FIGURE 12.17

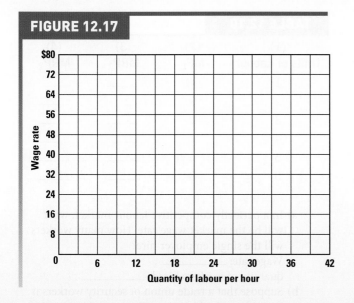

f) Suppose the price of each bar of soap rises to $3. Fill in the Total Revenue 2 column and Marginal Revenue Product 2 column in **Table 12.6**, and indicate the effect of this change on the graph in **Figure 12.17** by drawing in the new demand curve and labelling it D₂.

g) Assuming that the cost of labour remains at the $24 per hour level, how much labour per hour will the firm now hire? Label it *c* on the graph. Number of workers: _____

h) Suppose that, instead, there is a 25-percent increase in labour productivity (that is, the MP of labour increases by 25 percent) over that shown in **Table 12.6**. If the price of soap is $2, fill in **Table 12.7**.

i) On the graph in **Figure 12.17**, draw in the demand for labour curve that reflects the increase in productivity, and label it D₃.

j) Compare the changes in d), f), and h).

_____

_____

_____

Basic (Problems 37A–43A)

37A. (LO 1) Complete **Table 12.8**, which gives the data for Gimlets Inc.

TABLE 12.7

Quantity of Labour	Output per Hour	Marginal Product	Total Revenue	Marginal Revenue Product
0	____	/	/	/
1	____	____	____	____
2	____	____	____	____
3	____	____	____	____
4	____	____	____	____
5	____	____	____	____
6	____	____	____	____

TABLE 12.8

Quantity of Labour	1	2	3	4	5	6
Total product	10	28	45	60	70	78
Marginal product	____	____	____	____	____	____
Price	$6	$6	$6	$6	$6	$6
Total revenue	____	____	____	____	____	____
Marginal revenue product	____	____	____	____	____	____

38A. **(LO 1)** Table 12.9 gives the data for Gumbles Ltd.

TABLE 12.9

Quantity of Labour	1	2	3	4	5	6	7
Marginal revenue product (hourly)	$10	$15	$14	$12	$10	$8	$5

How many workers should Gumbles hire at the following wage rates?
a) $15 per hour: _____
b) $12 per hour: _____
c) $9 per hour: _____
d) $6 per hour: _____

39A. **(LO 1)** Suppose that in the country of Gardenia the nominal wage rate is $18 per hour and the price level is 1.2.
a) What is the value of the real wage rate?
_____.
b) If the nominal wage rate increases by 10 percent, what will be the new value of the real wage rate?
_____.
c) If, instead, the price level were to increase by 10 percent, what will be the new value of real wages?
_____.

40A. **(LO 1)** Table 12.10 shows the data for a small company, Willie the Pickle Maker. The marginal product figures are for cases of pickles per day.
a) Fill in column 3 in the table, assuming that the firm sells its products in a competitive market for $24 a case (situation A). Then, fill in column 4, assuming that the price of a case of pickles increases to $27 (situation B).
b) If labour costs $216 per day, how much labour will Willie the Pickle Maker hire in each of the two situations? Situation A: _____ workers Situation B: _____ workers
c) What has happened to the demand curve for labour when comparing these two situations?
Answer: _____.

41A. **(LO 1, 2)** The graph in Figure 12.18A shows the market demand and supply of security personnel. The graph in Figure 12.18B is the MRP of labour (demand for labour) by a single firm that employs security personnel.

TABLE 12.10

(1) Units of Labour	(2) MP_L	(3) MRP_1	(4) MRP_2
1	10	_____	_____
2	9	_____	_____
3	8	_____	_____
4	7	_____	_____
5	5	_____	_____
6	3	_____	_____

a) In a perfectly competitive labour market, what will be the market wage rate. How many workers will the single employer hire?
Wage rate: _____ ; quantity of workers hired: _____.
b) Suppose that a trade union of security workers is formed and is able to negotiate a wage rate of $16 per hour for its members. What will be the resulting surplus of workers? How many employees will the firm now hire?
Surplus: _____ workers; quantity of workers hired: _____.

42A. **(LO 1)** What is MRP? How can it be calculated?

43A. **(LO 1)** Distinguish between the *real wage* and the *nominal wage*.

Intermediate (Problems 44A–49A)

44A. **(LO 1)** Table 12.11 shows the daily production of simple lawn chairs by Sit Right Inc. The firm is able to hire as many workers as it wishes for $12 per hour and sells the chairs to department stores for $4 each. How many workers and hours will the firm employ?
Answer: _____ workers.
How many workers and hours will the firm employ?
Answer: _____ workers.

45A. **(LO 1)** The demand for film animators is illustrated in Figure 12.19.
a) Draw in a supply curve from the origin showing that the quantity increases by 100 for each $10 increase in the wage rate.
b) What are the total earnings per period of the animators as a group?
Answer: _____.

FIGURE 12.18

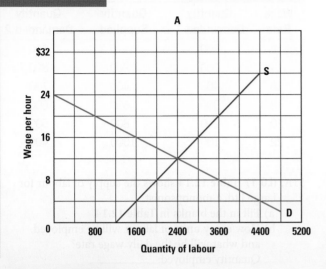

A

B

TABLE 12.11

Number of Hours Worked	Total Production
1	5
2	12
3	18
4	23
5	26
6	28
7	29
8	29

c) How much of the earnings in b) are transfer earnings, and how much is economic rent?
Transfer earnings: _____ ;
economic rent: _____ .

d) If the supply of animators increased, would the total earnings for the group increase or decrease?
Answer: _____ .

46A. **(LO 5)** Table 12.12 lists some productivity data for the firm Omir in the country of Hanu.

a) Assume that both the price of capital and labour is $1 per unit. If the present MP of capital is the column MP$_K$1, what is the right capital–labour ratio for Omir to use?
Ratio: _____ .

FIGURE 12.19

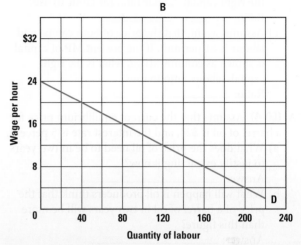

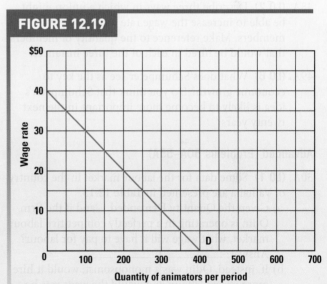

TABLE 12.12

Units	MP$_K$1	MP$_L$	MP$_K$2
1	23	11	50
2	21	10	45
3	18	8	38
4	14	6	30
5	10	3	11
6	5	0	10

b) Assume that the price of capital remains at $1 but the price of labour increases to $2. Now what is the right capital–labour ratio for Omir to use?
Ratio: _____ .

c) Assume, again, that the price of both capital and labour is $1 per unit. If the present MP of capital is shown as column MP_K2, what is the right capital–labour ratio to use?
Ratio: _____ .

47A. **(LO 4)** Assume that the current equilibrium price for a barrel of oil is $24, and the interest rate is 5 percent.
a) What does the price of oil need to be in two years to justify extracting it now?
Answer: _____ .
b) What will happen if oil producers think that the price of a barrel of oil in two years will be more than this figure?
Answer: _____ .

48A. **(LO 2)** Describe three ways in which a union might be able to increase the wage rate received by its members. Make reference to the quantity of members that would be hired in each of the three instances.

49A. **(LO 6)** What does Schumpeter see as the key to economic growth? Do you think that Schumpeter's idea is likely to become more important in the next twenty years?

Advanced (Problems 50A–55A)

50A. **(LO 1)** Some data for the labour market in the country of Valhalla are presented in **Table 12.13**.
a) Given the Quantity Demanded 1, and if the firm Odin is operating in a perfectly competitive labour market, what wage will it have to pay for labour?
Answer: _____ .
b) If, instead, Odin was a monopsonist, would it hire more or less labour, and would the wage rate be higher or lower?
Quantity hired: _____
Wage rate: _____ .
Now, assume that the quantity of labour demanded increased as illustrated by the last column in **Table 12.13**.
c) Given the same conditions as in a), what is your answer to that question now?
Answer: _____ .

TABLE 12.13

Wage Rate	Quantity Demanded 1	Quantity Supplied	Quantity Demanded 2
$12	600	0	900
14	500	200	800
16	400	400	700
18	300	600	600
20	200	800	500
22	100	1000	400

51A. **(LO 1)** **Table 12.14** shows the supply of labour for Large Ltd. a monopsonist.
a) Fill in the blanks in **Table 12.14**.
b) How many units of labour will be employed, and what will be the daily wage rate?
Quantity employed: _____
Wage rate: _____

TABLE 12.14

Quantity of Daily Labour	Wage Rate	MRP	Total Wage Cost	Marginal Wage Cost
1	$ 60	$160	_____	_____
2	70	170	_____	_____
3	80	160	_____	_____
4	90	150	_____	_____
5	100	140	_____	_____
6	110	120	_____	_____
7	120	90	_____	_____
8	130	50	_____	_____

52A. **(LO 3)** The two supply curves in **Figure 12.20** represent the supply of workers in two different occupations.
a) At an annual wage of $60 000 per year, what are the amounts of economic rent and transfer earnings for S_1?
Economic rent: $ _____
Transfer earnings: $ _____
b) At an annual wage of $60 000 per year, what are the amounts of economic rent and transfer earnings for S_2?
Economic rent: $ _____
Transfer earnings: $ _____
c) Which of the two curves is more inelastic?
_____

FIGURE 12.20

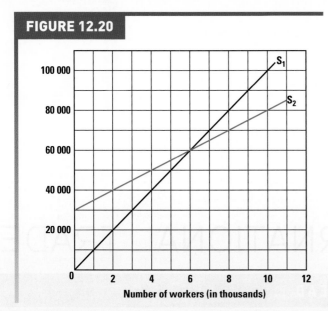

Number of workers (in thousands)

Columns 1 and 2 in **Table 12.15** show the supply of labour.

TABLE 12.15

(1) Number of Workers	(2) Daily Wage	(3) Total Wage Cost	(4) Marginal Wage Cost
1	$150	_____	_____
2	155	_____	_____
3	160	_____	_____
4	165	_____	_____
5	170	_____	_____
6	175	_____	_____
7	180	_____	_____
8	185	_____	_____

53A. **(LO 1)** **Figure 12.21** shows the demand for pulp workers in a small town in Northern Ontario.

FIGURE 12.21

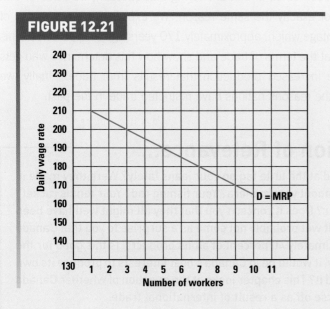

Number of workers

a) Draw in the supply curve in **Figure 12.21**.
b) If the labour market were perfectly competitive, what are the equilibrium values of daily wage and number of workers?
   Daily wage: $ _____
   Number of workers: _____
c) Suppose that there was a single monopsonist pulp mill in the town. Fill in columns 3 and 4 in **Table 12.15**.
d) Draw in the marginal wage cost in **Figure 12.21**.
e) What are the equilibrium values of daily wage and number of workers?
   Daily wage: $ _____
   Number of workers: _____

54A. **(LO 1)** Use the theory of marginal productivity and the concept of real wage to discuss whether you think Robinson Crusoe's standard of living increased or decreased when Friday came onto the scene.

55A. **(LO 2)** Discuss the following statement: "The Canadian Medical Association is perhaps the most powerful union in the country."

CHAPTER 13

INTERNATIONAL TRADE

At the end of this chapter, you should be able to...

LO1 explain why nations trade with each other.

LO2 explain why nations import certain goods, even though they can be made more cheaply at home.

LO3 explain how the gains from trade are divided between trading partners.

LO4 describe why some groups win and others lose as a result of freer trade, and explore trade restrictions.

LO5 identify some arguments against free trade.

We start this look at the international market of trade and finance by asking why people trade with each other, and in answering that question, we discover that all nations trade for exactly the same reason. We explain Ricardo's theory of comparative advantage which, approximately 170 years ago, helped sort all this out. We then look at the terms of trade and show how this determines who gets what share of the increased production that results from trade. Finally, we examine some of the reasons nations have restricted trade in the past.

A Question of Relevance...

Have you looked at the little tag on your jeans lately? Were they made in Canada? What about your camera? Your fishing rod? Your tennis racket? Your MP3 player? Does it concern you that they all might well have been made abroad? It will probably not come as a surprise to you that Canada imports approximately 40 percent of all its products. Is this good for the country? Surely, it would be in Canada's best interests to produce its own goods. Or would it? This chapter looks at the question of whether Canada is better or worse off as a result of international trade.

People have traded in one form or another since the dawn of time, and most of the great powers in history have also been famous traders: the Phoenicians and the Greeks; medieval Venice and Elizabethan England; the early American colonies and modern Japan. It seems obvious that great benefits are obtained from trading, but there has always been the underlying suspicion that someone also loses as a result. For many, a great trading nation is one that consistently, and through shrewd practice, always manages to come out on top during trade negotiations. This "beggar thy neighbour" attitude was no great concern for writers immediately preceding Adam Smith, who thought it was part of the natural state of affairs that there are always winners and losers in trade. It was the job of policy makers, they felt, to ensure that their own country was always on the winning side.

It took the mind of Adam Smith to see that whenever two people enter into a voluntary agreement to trade, both parties must gain as a result. If you trade a textbook in exchange for your friend's new Guns 'n' Butter CD, you obviously want that CD more than the textbook, and your friend must want the textbook more than the CD. Trade is to the advantage of both of you, otherwise it would not take place. When we look at international trade between nations, we are simply looking at this single transaction multiplied a billion-fold. It is not really nations that trade, but individual people and firms buying from foreign individuals and firms. In many ways, the reason you trade with a friend is the same reason you buy products from a Toronto brewery, Winnipeg car dealer, or Tokyo fishing rod manufacturer: you hope to gain something as a result, and what you give up in return (usually money) is of less value to you than the thing you obtain in return.

All of which raises the question of why you personally (or a whole nation for that matter) would want to buy something rather than make it at home. In other words, why are people not self-sufficient? Why do they not produce everything that they personally consume? Well, Adam Smith had an answer for this (as for many things):

> It is the maxim of every prudent master of a family, never to make at home what it will cost him more to make than to buy.[1]

There, in essence, is the main argument for trade: why make something yourself if you can buy it cheaper elsewhere? If it takes Akio three hours to make a certain product, but he can buy it elsewhere from the income he gets from one hour's work in his regular job, then why would he bother? It would pay him to do his own job for three hours; he could afford to buy three units of the product. An additional consideration is the fact that Akio cannot make most of the things he wants—or could make them only after extensive training and with the help of very expensive equipment.

Winners from free trade

- Consumers of imported goods
- Producers of exported goods

Losers from free trade

- Consumers of exported goods
- Producers of imported goods

---

[1] Adam Smith, *Wealth of Nations* (Edwin Cannan edition, 1877), p. 354.

13.1 SPECIALIZATION AND TRADE

LO1 Explain why nations trade with each other.

Specialization is the cornerstone of trade. As we have seen in earlier chapters, big advantages can be gained from specialization. From an individual point of view, each of us is better suited to one thing than to another. Rather than trying to grow all our own food, make our own clothes, brew our own beer, and so on, it makes more sense to specialize in our chosen occupation and, with the proceeds, obtain things that other people can make better and more cheaply. Similarly, firms will be far more productive if they specialize in the production process, that is, make use of the division of labour. As we shall see in this chapter, there are also great benefits to be enjoyed by countries that specialize rather than trying to be self-sufficient.

Specialization and trade go hand in hand, so it follows that more specialization means more trading. Modern nations, firms, and individuals have become increasingly specialized, and with this has come a huge increase in the volume of trade, domestically and internationally. But is there a limit to specialization? From a technical point of view, Smith thought not. But he did believe that specialization would be limited by the size of the market: the smaller the market, the smaller is the output and, therefore, the less the opportunity or need for extensive specialization. The larger the market, the greater is the opportunity for specialization which would then lower the cost of producing goods. The prime driving force behind the expansion of markets is that it enables firms to produce in higher volumes at a lower cost. All things being equal (including demand), it is the cost of production, and therefore the price of the product, that induces trade. If you can produce a product more cheaply than I can, then it makes no sense for me to try to produce it myself. And why are you able to produce certain products more cheaply than I can? The answer presumably is that you possess certain advantages over me. Let us look at these advantages.

▶ ADDED DIMENSION   Canada, the Great Trader

Canada is certainly one of the world's great trading nations, at least in relative terms. In 2010, for example, Canada exported $475 billion worth of goods and services and imported $507 billion. Each of these figures represents approximately 30 percent of Canada's GDP. Only a few developed countries, such as Austria and the Netherlands, trade a larger fraction. The United States and Japan, in comparison, trade only about 12 percent of their

GDPs (though, of course, in actual dollars, this represents a lot more). The United States is Canada's predominant trading partner, purchasing more than all other countries combined (buying approximately 70 percent of our exports). In fact, Canada sells over twice as much to the United States as it does to all other countries combined and buys approximately 62 percent of all of its imports from the United States.

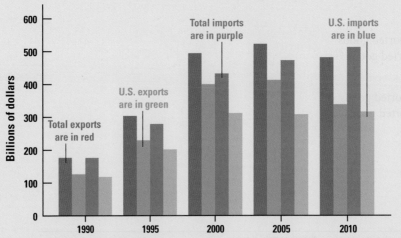

Source: Adapted from the Statistics Canada CANSIM database http://cansim2.statcan.ca, table number 376-0003, retrieved May 9, 2011.

Factor Endowment

One person has an advantage in production over others if he or she is endowed with certain natural or acquired skills or has more or better equipment or other resources. Just as there are many reasons why some people are better gardeners or truck drivers or hockey players than others, so it is with countries. A country will have a great advantage in producing and trading pineapples, for instance, if it possesses the right type of soil and climate. But the same country may well be at a disadvantage in growing coniferous trees. Another country has an advantage in producing electronic equipment if it has the right capital, the technical expertise, and a well-educated labour force. It may not, however, be able to compete with other countries in raising sheep. Just as with people, countries are well endowed in certain areas and impoverished in others. Japan has a well-educated and motivated workforce, possesses great technical expertise, and is highly capitalized, yet it is very poorly provided with arable land and possesses very few mineral resources.

It is often suggested that countries trade primarily to buy resources that they do not naturally possess. Although there is some truth in this, it often obscures the main motivation. Canada, for instance, is not endowed with a warm and sunny climate throughout the year and is unable to produce bananas commercially. However, using geodesic domes with artificial light and heating, it could grow its own bananas, but the cost would be enormous. The reason it does not grow bananas is not because it cannot but because it is cheaper to buy them from countries that grow them more easily. Most countries can overcome a resource deficiency by using different methods or other resources, but it does not make sense if this production method results in more expensive products than those obtainable from abroad.

Theory of Absolute Advantage

A country will gravitate to producing in those areas where, because of its own factor endowments, it possesses a cost advantage over other producing countries: Canada produces wheat, lumber, and minerals; Chile produces copper and other metal ores; Australia exports mineral fuels; Japan produces cars and electronic equipment; and so on. **Figure 13.1** shows the distribution of exports for these particular countries. This is what Adam Smith proposed when he put forward his *theory of absolute advantage*. Nations, like firms and individuals, should specialize in producing goods and services for which they have an advantage, and they should trade with other countries for goods and services for which they do not enjoy an advantage.

Let us work through a simple example of this theory. We will concentrate on just two countries and suppose that they produce just two products. We will assume that the average cost of producing each product remains constant. In addition, to begin with, we will further assume that each country is self-sufficient and that no trade is taking place. **Table 13.1** shows the productivity per worker (average product) of producing wheat and beans in Canada and Mexico.

We can see at a glance that Canada is more productive than Mexico at producing wheat, whereas Mexico is more productive than Canada at producing beans. Let us examine the possibility of gains if both countries were to specialize—Canada in wheat and Mexico in beans.

TABLE 13.1	Output per Worker by Country and Industry		
	NUMBER OF BUSHELS PER DAY		
	Wheat		**Beans**
Canada	3	or	2
Mexico	1	or	4

Assume that initially the two countries do not trade with each other and that the working population in each country is 16 million, divided equally between the two industries. **Table 13.2** shows what the two countries produce.

FIGURE 13.1 — Merchandise Exports 2009

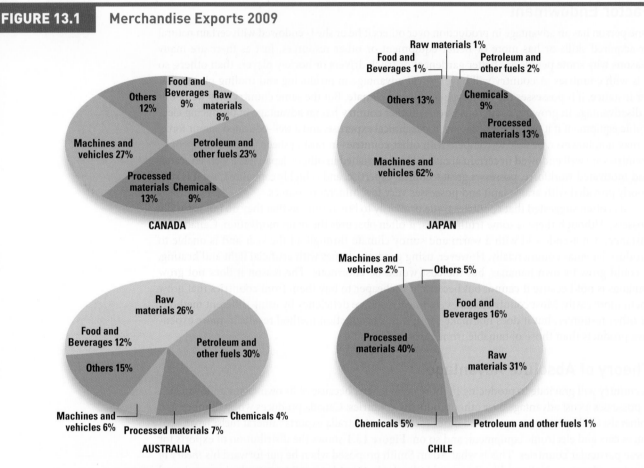

Source: *Commodity Trade Statistics Database*, United Nations, 2010. The United Nations is the author of the original material.

TABLE 13.2 — Total Outputs before Trade

	TOTAL NUMBER OF BUSHELS PER DAY (in millions)	
	Wheat	Beans
Canada	24	16
Mexico	8	32
Total	32	48

In this case, half the working population of Canada—8 million workers—is producing wheat. Since each person is capable of producing 3 bushels of wheat, the total production of wheat is 8 million times 3, or 24 million bushels. The other figures are similarly derived.

Now, suppose that the two countries decide to enter into a free trade agreement, with each country totally specializing in what it does best: Canada producing wheat and Mexico producing beans. With the whole of the working population of 16 million in Canada producing wheat and all 16 million people producing beans in Mexico, the totals can be seen in **Table 13.3**.

With specialization, the two countries combined could produce an additional 16 million bushels of wheat (48 minus the previous 32) and an additional 16 million bushels of beans (64 minus the

TABLE 13.3	Total Outputs after Trade	
	TOTAL NUMBER OF BUSHELS PER DAY (in millions)	
	Wheat	**Beans**
Canada	48	0
Mexico	0	64
Total	48	64

previous 48). These are referred to as the *gains from trade*. Strictly speaking, the increased total production is really the result of increased specialization. But if a country is going to specialize, it will need to trade in order to obtain those products that it is not producing. Specialization, then, implies trade, and it would be impossible to have one without the other.

 SELF-TEST

1. The following table shows the productivity per worker in the beer and wine industries of Freedonia and Libraland:

Output in Hundreds of Litres

	Beer		**Wine**
Freedonia	4	or	1
Libraland	3	or	4

a) Which country should specialize in which product?

b) Suppose that initially the working population of each country is 20 million, with 10 million working in each industry. What is the total output of the two countries?

c) Now, suppose that each country decides to specialize in the product in which it has an advantage. What will be the total output of each product, and what are the gains from trade?

13.2 THEORY OF COMPARATIVE ADVANTAGE

The eminent economist David Ricardo, following in the footsteps of Adam Smith, agreed in principle with Smith, adding a subtle but important refinement to Smith's theory of trade. To see the effect of his modification, let us change our example to that of theoretical trade between the United States and the Philippines, keeping the same two products, wheat and beans. The output per worker in each country is shown in **Table 13.4**.

 L02 Explain why nations import certain goods, even though they can be made more cheaply at home.

TABLE 13.4	Output per Worker by Country and Industry	
	NUMBER OF BUSHELS PER DAY	
	Wheat	**Beans**
United States	4	4
Philippines	1	3

You can see from the table that U.S. wheat production is four times that of the Philippines; similarly, the United States is one and one-third times as productive as the Philippines in producing beans. If we were to follow Smith's dictum, then presumably the United States should produce both products itself. After all, how can it possibly be of any advantage to trade with the Philippines, since it could produce both products more cheaply? The heart of Ricardo's idea is

comparative advantage:
the advantage that comes from producing something at a lower opportunity cost than others are able to do.

that it is not *absolute advantage* but **comparative advantage** that provides the mutual gains from trade. Let us see exactly what this means, through an example.

Suppose you happened to be absolutely the best lawyer in town. Not only that, but you are also its greatest secretary. Given this, why would you bother to hire a secretary to do your clerical work, since you are faster and, by all measurements, more efficient than anyone you could possibly hire? The answer is that you would still hire a secretary because you could not afford not to. That is because you are very productive. Your high productivity is both a blessing and a curse. It is a blessing because you earn a great deal as a lawyer; it is a curse because you sacrifice a great deal in not being a secretary. In other words, your opportunity cost of being a lawyer is the lost salary of not being a secretary. Your opportunity cost of being a secretary is your lost earnings as a lawyer. But because you can earn *comparatively* more as a lawyer than as a secretary, you would be advised to concentrate on that career and hire someone (admittedly less productive than yourself) to act as your secretary.

Ricardo's idea of comparative advantage directs attention away from making comparisons between countries and, instead, focuses on the comparison between products. In **Table 13.4**, for instance, we might ask: how much does it cost for the United States to produce wheat? One way to answer this would be to express it in dollars and cents. However, knowing that the value of money varies over time and that it is often misleading to translate one currency into another, Ricardo was at pains to express costs in more fundamental terms. One way of doing this is to express costs in terms of the number of hours it takes to produce something. For instance, if in our example the average worker in the United States can produce 4 bushels of beans in an average 8-hour day, then the cost of one bushel of beans would be 8/4, or 2 hours. In contrast, the cost of one bushel of beans in the Philippines would be 8/3, or about 2.66 hours. So, beans are more expensive to produce in the Philippines. However, it is more illuminating to measure costs is in terms of *opportunity costs*. This is the method chosen by Ricardo.

You will remember that the opportunity cost of producing one thing can be measured in terms of another thing that has to be sacrificed in order to get it. As far as the United States and the Philippines are concerned, the cost of producing more wheat is the sacrifice of beans, and the cost of increased bean production is the loss of wheat. Let us work out these costs for each country. The cost of employing a worker in the wheat industry is what that worker could have produced in the bean industry, assuming that the country is fully employed. In other words, for every 4 bushels of wheat that an American worker produces, the country sacrifices 4 bushels of beans. In per-unit terms, in the United States 4 bushels of wheat costs 4 bushels of beans, so 1 bushel of wheat costs 1 bushel of beans, and 1 bushel of beans costs 1 bushel of wheat.

In the Philippines the cost of 1 bushel of wheat is 3 bushels of beans, and the cost of 1 bushel of beans equals 1/3 bushel of wheat. Let us summarize these figures in **Table 13.5**.

TABLE 13.5	Opportunity Costs of Production	
	COST OF PRODUCING ONE UNIT	
	Wheat	**Beans**
United States	1 beans	1 wheat
Philippines	3 beans	1/3 wheat

Now you can understand the significance of comparative costs. If you measure the costs in absolute terms, using hours as we did in our example above, then beans are cheaper to produce in the United States. But in comparative terms, they are very *expensive*. Why is that? Because to produce beans, the United States has to make a big sacrifice in the product in which it is even more productive: wheat. Similarly, although beans, in absolute terms, are very expensive in the Philippines, they are cheap in comparative terms; to produce them the Philippines sacrifices little in wheat production because productivity in the wheat industry is low.

In this example then, the United States should specialize in producing wheat, since the opportunity cost is only one unit of beans compared with three units of beans in the Philippines. Conversely, the Philippines can produce beans comparatively cheaply, at the cost of 1/3 unit wheat, while in the United States, the cost is one unit of wheat. Although the United States has an absolute advantage in both products, it has a comparative advantage only in wheat production, and the Philippines has a comparative advantage in bean production.

Let us extract some further insights by showing the production possibilities of the two countries on the assumption that the size of the labour force in both the United States and the Philippines is 100 million, and that unit costs are constant.

We are assuming constant unit costs to keep the analysis simple. If you remember from Chapter 1, in reality, the law of increasing costs applies, which means that the slope of the production possibilities curve is concave. Assuming constant costs means that the production possibilities curves in this chapter plot as straight lines.

The respective production possibilities for the United States and the Philippines are shown in **Table 13.6**. The 400 bushels of wheat, under option A in the United States, is the maximum output of wheat if all of the 100 (million) workers were producing 4 bushels of wheat each. Similarly, if the 100 million American workers produced only beans and no wheat, then they would also produce 400 bushels of beans as seen under option F. The figures for B, C, D, and E are derived by calculating the output if 80, 60, 40, and 20 million workers are employed in wheat production, while 20, 40, 60, and 80 million workers are, correspondingly, employed in bean production. The figures for the Philippines are similarly obtained.

TABLE 13.6	**Production Possibilities**					
UNITED STATES: OUTPUT (millions of bushels per day)						
	A	**B**	**C**	**D**	**E**	**F**
Wheat	400	320	240	160	80	0
Beans	0	80	160	240	320	400
PHILIPPINES: OUTPUT (millions of bushels per day)						
	A	**B**	**C**	**D**	**E**	**F**
Wheat	100	80	60	40	20	0
Beans	0	60	120	180	240	300

Suppose that initially the countries do not trade with each other, with the United States producing combination C and the Philippines producing combination B. Before specialization and trade, therefore, their joint totals are as shown in **Table 13.7**.

TABLE 13.7	**Output of Both Countries before Specialization and Trade**	
TOTAL OUTPUT (millions of bushels per day)		
	Wheat	**Beans**
United States	240	160
Philippines	80	60
Total	320	220

If the two countries now specialize, the United States producing wheat and the Philippines producing beans, their output levels would be as shown in **Table 13.8**.

TABLE 13.8	Output of Both Countries after Specialization and Trade	
	TOTAL OUTPUT (millions of bushels per day)	
	Wheat	**Beans**
United States	400	0
Philippines	0	300
Total	400	300

You can see by comparing the before and after specialization positions of the two countries that production of both products is now higher. **Table 13.9** outlines the gains from trade.

TABLE 13.9	Gains from Specialization and Trade
TOTAL OUTPUT (millions of bushels per day)	
Wheat	**Beans**
+80	+80

Thus, we can conclude that:

> As long as there are differences in comparative costs between countries, regardless of the differences in absolute costs, there is a basis for mutually beneficial trade.

What this example shows is that it is possible for both countries to gain from trade, but several questions remain. Will they? How will the increased production be shared? Will it be shared equally, or will one country receive more than the other? Discussion of the terms of trade will help answer these questions.

 SELF-TEST

2. Suppose that the labour force in Freedonia is 10 million: 6 million people are producing apples, and the rest are producing pears. Libraland's labour force is 16 million, divided equally between the production of apples and the production of pears. The labour productivity in the two countries is given in the following table:

Output per Worker (bushels per day)

	Apples		Pears
Freedonia	5	or	2
Libraland	1	or	3

Make a production possibilities table for Fredonia (A to F) and for Libraland (A to E).

a) Which is Fredonia's present combination (A–F)?

b) Which is Libraland's present combination (A–E)?

3. a) Given the data in Self-Test 2, what is the total output of the two countries for both products?

b) If each country were to specialize in the product in which it has a comparative advantage, what will be the total output of the two countries for both products?

c) What will be the gains from trade?

ADDED DIMENSION   WTO: Forum for International Cooperation or Engine of Destruction?

The World Trade Organization (WTO), created in 1995 and with 153 member nations, is the only international organization that deals with the rules of trade among nations. It catapulted into people's consciousness during the violent street protests in Seattle in November 1999. Thousands of protestors voiced their displeasure with the trend toward globalization—which they saw as being fostered by the WTO—by disrupting the organization's meetings. While the intensity of the debate about the "good" or "evil" of globalization and the WTO has subsided recently, the issue is still an important one. Let us list some of the pros and cons of the issue.

Pros:
1. Most of those who work within the organization are seasoned bureaucrats or academics from well-known universities around the globe. The importance of growing world trade can be seen in the fact that every post-World War II example of a nation breaking out of the vicious cycle of poverty and underdevelopment has been a nation that dramatically increased its exports.
2. It is easier for concerned nations with strong labour, safety, and environmental standards to put pressure for change on nations whose standards are weak, if they are already participants in the WTO.
3. Increased trade, fostered by the WTO, has shown some dramatic benefits. An example comes from a World Bank study (using 2000–2001 data) concluding that the number of people in the world living on less than $1 a day decreased in the last twenty years by over 600 million. At no time in human history have such a large number of people been lifted out of abject poverty in so short a period.

Cons:
1. The WTO is an undemocratic organization whose members are not elected. It poses one of the biggest threats to the sovereignty of independent nations and ignores the social and cultural differences among nations.
2. Globalization reduces the effectiveness of labour, safety, and environmental standards across the globe as each nation becomes trapped in a race to the bottom while competing to attract more foreign investment from the large transnational corporations.
3. Globalization increases the income gap between the rich and poor nations of the world. It also increases the disparity of incomes within a country, since a few big business people gain at the expense of ordinary citizens.
4. The WTO's dispute resolution panels are loaded with members who represent a corporate bias, which works against the interests of ordinary people.

We hasten to add that some very famous economists—Alan Blinder and Paul Krugman, for example—are raising serious concerns about the process of freer trade and globalization as they might affect Canada. They argue that communications technology, which allows services to be delivered electronically from afar, will put many North American middle-class jobs in jeopardy in the next two decades. The late Paul Samuelson, a giant among economists, said that "most economists oversimplify the complexities about globalization" and that we need to slow this trend to help poor nations build domestic industries and give rich nations more time to retain displaced workers.

13.3   TERMS OF TRADE

The expression **terms of trade** refers to the price at which a country sells its exports compared with the price at which it buys its imports. Statistics Canada regularly measures Canada's terms of trade using the following formula:

$$\text{Terms of trade} = \frac{\text{Average price of exports}}{\text{Average price of imports}} \times 100 \qquad \textbf{[13.1]}$$

If the worldwide demand for Canadian softwood lumber were to increase, for example, it would increase the average price of Canadian exports, with the result that the terms of trade would be said to have moved in Canada's favour. The result would be the same if Canadian prices remain the same but the price of imports drops. In either case, the sale of our exports would enable us to purchase more imports. On the other hand, the terms of trade would shift against Canada if Canadian export prices dropped and/or the price of imported goods rose (see **Figure 13.2**).

 L03 Explain how the gains from trade are divided between trading partners.

terms of trade: the average price of a country's exports compared with the price of its imports.

FIGURE 13.2   Terms of Trade

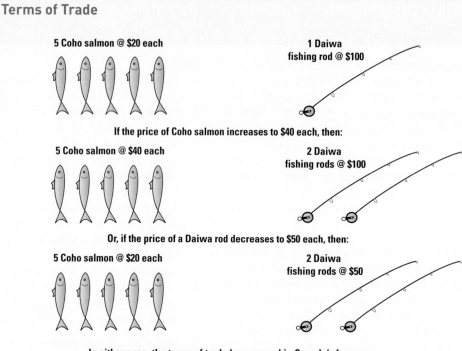

5 Coho salmon @ $20 each   1 Daiwa
fishing rod @ $100

If the price of Coho salmon increases to $40 each, then:

5 Coho salmon @ $40 each   2 Daiwa
fishing rods @ $100

Or, if the price of a Daiwa rod decreases to $50 each, then:

5 Coho salmon @ $20 each   2 Daiwa
fishing rods @ $50

**In either case, the terms of trade have moved in Canada's favour;
that is, Canada now gets more imports for the same amount of exports.**

Changes in the terms of trade can have a significant effect on Canada's economic performance. This ratio of our exports to import prices directly affects our nominal trade balance, and indirectly affects the level of real GDP in Canada. A higher ratio reflects a situation in which most Canadians are better off, since our exports would be high—which means more jobs—and the price of imports that Canadians buy would be lower. Canada's terms of trade peaked at a ratio of approximately 112 in 1973 when world commodity prices were very high, then declined to 70 in 1998. By 2003, the ratio had risen to 106 and has continued to rise as Canada's oil exports from the Alberta oil sands continue to grow and the price of oil remains high.

In our previous United States/Philippines example, we found that the country which gains the most from trade depends upon the terms of trade. But let us look at what would be acceptable prices from the two countries' points of view. Remember that the United States is the wheat producer and exporter. A glance back at **Table 13.5** shows that *in the United States, one bushel of wheat costs one bushel of beans*. Given this, what price would it be willing to sell its wheat for? Presumably for as high a price as it can get, but certainly not for less than one bushel of beans. What about the Philippines? How much would it be willing to pay for wheat? Remember, **Table 13.5** tells us that *in the Philippines, one bushel of wheat costs three bushels of beans*. Therefore, we can conclude that the Philippines would certainly not pay any higher than this price and would be happy to pay less. As long as the price is above the American minimum and below the Philippines' maximum, both countries would be willing to trade. In other words, trade is possible if the price of one unit of wheat is anywhere between one and three units of beans.

We could have just as easily expressed things in terms of beans, and a glance back at **Table 13.5** shows that feasible terms of trade would be anywhere between one-third and one bushel of wheat for one bushel of beans. In other words, the feasible terms of trade will be between the costs of each product in the two countries. The final terms of trade will depend on the strength of demand in the two countries for these products.

Let us choose one particular rate among the many possible terms of trade and work out the consequences. Suppose, for instance, that the terms end up at *1 bushel of wheat = 2 bushels of beans (or 1 bushel of beans = 1/2 bushel of wheat)*. Let us now assume, since we need some point to start from, that the Philippines is quite happy consuming the 60 million bushels of beans that it was producing before it decided to specialize, as was shown in **Table 13.6**. However, because of specialization, it is now producing only beans and will, therefore, have 300 − 60 = 240 million bushels of beans available for export, which it sells to the United States at a rate of one bushel of beans for half a bushel of wheat. It will receive back 120 million bushels of wheat and will finish up with 60 million bushels of beans and 120 million bushels of wheat. Because of trade, it will have gained an additional 40 million bushels of wheat compared with its self-sufficient totals shown in the "Before Trade" column in **Table 13.10**.

The United States will also gain. It was the sole producer of wheat, and of the total of 400 million bushels produced, it has sold 120 million bushels to the Philippines in exchange for 240 million bushels of beans. It will end up with 280 million bushels of wheat and 240 million bushels of beans, which is 40 million bushels of wheat and 80 million bushels of beans more than when it was producing both products as shown by comparing the "Before Trade" and "After Trade" columns for the United States. In reviewing **Table 13.10**, recall that we are assuming that the Philippines consumes the same 60 million bushels of beans before and after trade.

Terms of Trade and Gains from Trade, Graphically

Let us now look at each country's trading picture separately. Using a graphical approach, **Figure 13.3** shows the production possibilities curve for the United States. Before it decided to trade, this was also its consumption possibilities curve, since it could obviously not consume more than it produced. The slope of the curve is 1, which is the cost of 1 bushel of beans (that is, it equals 1 bushel of wheat). The curve to the right is its trading possibilities curve, which shows how much the

TABLE 13.10

		PHILIPPINES	
		Before Trade	**After Trade**
	Beans produced	60	300
	Beans exported	0	−240
Beans consumed		**60**	**60**
	Wheat produced	80	0
	Wheat imported	0	+120
Wheat consumed		**80**	**120**
		Gain = 40 Wheat	
		UNITED STATES	
		Before Trade	**After Trade**
	Beans produced	160	0
	Beans imported	0	+240
Beans consumed		**160**	**240**
	Wheat produced	240	400
	Wheat exported	0	−120
Wheat consumed		**240**	**280**
		Gain = 80 Beans and 40 Wheat	

United States could obtain through a combination of specializing its production and trading. Note that the slope of the trading possibilities curve is equal to 0.5. This is the terms of trade established between the two countries: 1 bushel of wheat for 2 bushels of beans.

You can see from this graph that the United States, at one extreme, could produce the maximum quantity of 400 million bushels of wheat and keep all of it. However, before trade, the maximum amount of beans available was 400 million bushels. Now, if it wished, the United States could produce 400 million bushels of wheat, trade *all* of it, and receive in exchange 800 million bushels of beans. (We presume it is able to buy these beans from other countries as well as from the Philippines, given that the latter can only produce 300 million bushels of beans.) More likely, of course, it will opt to have a combination of both products, such as 280 million bushels of wheat and 240 million bushels of beans, as in our numerical example above.

 ADDED DIMENSION   Public Opinion about NAFTA

In 1993, Canada, the United States, and Mexico formalized the North American Free Trade Agreement (NAFTA) despite considerable political opposition in both Canada and the United States. This agreement was an expansion of the earlier Canada–U.S. Free Trade Agreement of 1988. Unlike the European Union, NAFTA does not create a set of supranational governmental bodies, nor does it create a body of law that supersedes national law.

Since NAFTA, trade has increased dramatically among the three nations. For instance, from 1993–2004, total trade between Canada and the United States increased by 129.3 percent. Public opinion in Mexico, Canada, and the United States tends to be positive toward NAFTA. A July 2004 survey conducted in Mexico showed that 64 percent of the Mexican public favoured NAFTA. A Canadian poll conducted in June 2003 found that 70 percent of Canadians supported NAFTA. Another survey reported in January 2004 that 47 percent of Americans thought NAFTA has been good for the United States, while 39 percent thought it had been bad for the country.

Despite their support for NAFTA, polls in Canada and Mexico have tended to show that citizens see their own country as the loser in NAFTA, and see the United States as the winner. The U.S. public has viewed Mexico as the winner and has been narrowly divided about whether the United States is a winner or loser in NAFTA.

FIGURE 13.3   **U.S. Production and Trading Possibilities Curves**

The slope of the production possibilities curve shows that the cost of producing beans in the United States is equal to 1 bushel of wheat = 1 bushel of beans. The slope of the trading possibilities curve shows the terms of trade and equals 1 bushel of wheat = 2 bushels of beans. The previous maximum obtainable quantity of beans was 400 million bushels, when the United States was self-sufficient. Its new maximum, as a result of trading, is now 800 million bushels.

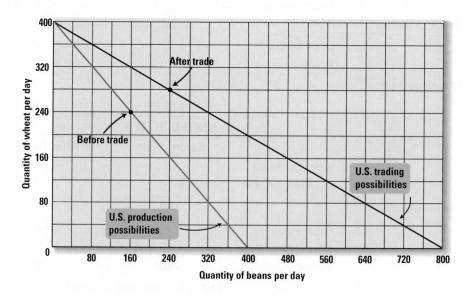

FIGURE 13.4   **Philippines' Production and Trading Possibilities Curves**

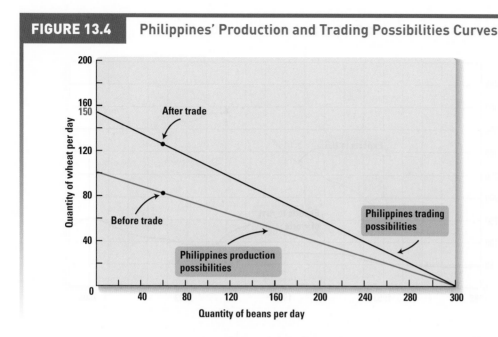

The Philippines specializes in the production of beans, and its trading possibilities curve lies to the right of the production possibilities curve. In other words, regardless of whether it trades or not, the cost of beans remains the same; the cost of wheat, however, is now lower as a result of trade, since it can now obtain wheat at a cost of 2 bushels of beans per 1 bushel of wheat, whereas producing its own wheat costs 3 bushels of beans per 1 bushel of wheat.

Figure 13.4 shows the situation from the point of view of the Philippines. The inside curve is its production (and therefore its consumption) possibilities curve, representing the maximum of both products that can be produced when the country is self-sufficient. The slope of the curve represents the cost of 1 bushel of beans and is equal to 1/3 bushel of wheat. The outer curve is the trading possibilities curve if the terms of trade are 1 bushel of beans = 1/2 bushel of wheat. You can see that trading allows the Philippines to enjoy increased consumption as well. After specialization, the maximum amount of beans remains unchanged at 300 million bushels. However, the maximum amount of wheat has increased from 100 (if produced in the Philippines) to 150 (by trading all of its 100 million bushels of beans for this quantity of wheat).

The Benefits of Free Trade

Ricardo's theory of comparative advantage, which we have been looking at, is very important because it clearly highlights the major benefits of trade. Free and unrestricted trade gives nations and individuals the opportunity to sell in world markets, and this will enable them to specialize in products where they enjoy a cost advantage over others. The effect will be lower costs of production generally, which translates into *lower prices* for consumers. This, in turn, will reduce the cost of living and enable them to enjoy a higher standard of living. In addition, free trade will increase the levels of output worldwide and will mean *higher levels of incomes*, which, in turn, will lead to improved standards of living.

This boils down to the fact that specialization increases productivity, so people as a group are better off as the result of lower production costs and higher incomes. But not only that, countries that do not specialize and trade will generally have to make do with domestically produced products of lower quality and of limited choice; with global markets, the variety and quality of products are much greater.

A final benefit of free trade is that all companies are exposed to international competition. This means that they cannot sit complacently behind protective barriers but are forced to compete for business with firms around the world. This also tends to discourage the formation of monopolies, since it is much more difficult to be a monopolist in the world market than it is to be a monopolist in the home market. In summary, free trade has the following advantages:

FIGURE 13.5   Canadian Exports to the United States and the Rest of the World

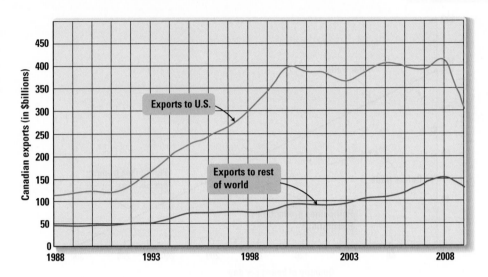

- Lower prices as the result of lower costs of production
- Higher incomes
- A greater variety and quality of products
- Increased competition

The 1988 Free Trade Agreement with the United States caused a dramatic increase in the volume of trade that Canada has done with that country, as **Figure 13.5** demonstrates.

Some Important Qualifications

We need to point out that when comparing the wage rates of two countries engaged in international trade, the country with lower nominal wages will not necessarily have an advantage over a country that has higher nominal wages. The productivity of the workers in the two countries must also be considered. If the higher wage country also has a labour force that has higher labour productivity, then they may not be at a disadvantage.

These are, indeed, powerful arguments in favour of free trade, but before we leave the topic, let us look at some of the qualifications that must be introduced. First, free trade is never free because there will always be transport, insurance, and other freight charges, which must be added to the cost of production and which will usually reduce the trading advantage of foreign sellers. (However, in a country as large as Canada, it is often cheaper to transport products to the American states bordering the country than it is to transport them from one end of the country to the other.)

In addition, selling in a foreign country is always going to be more difficult (and often more expensive) than selling in the domestic market because of the differences in language, culture, taxation, regulations, and so on. Besides cost differences, the analysis we have presented so far has assumed constant costs. This leads to the result in our examples that countries should specialize in, perhaps, a single product and produce that product to a maximum. However, as we learned in Chapter 1, if any country tries to concentrate on a single product, its production is subject to the law of increasing costs. This means that one country only enjoys a cost advantage over others *up to a point*. As it tries to push production levels higher, its cost will start to increase so that it no longer enjoys a competitive advantage. This is the reason why few countries specialize entirely and why many countries both produce *and* import the same product. The presence of increasing costs will also lessen the advantages that one country enjoys over another in trade.

ADDED DIMENSION Other Organizations of Major Importance for Trade

IMF: The International Monetary Fund (IMF) was created at the Bretton Woods Conference in 1944 in response to the experience of the interwar period (1918–1939) when world trade collapsed. Headquartered in Geneva, Switzerland, the IMF has 184 member countries and is dedicated to the promotion of international monetary cooperation, exchange stability, economic growth, and international trade. It makes loans to national governments—at the request of governments themselves—and provides a very sophisticated level of technical assistance.

OECD: The Organization for Economic Cooperation and Development (OECD) is a Paris-based organization with 30 developed-nation members and working relationships with some 70 less developed countries. The mission of the OECD is to promote policies that achieve sustainable economic growth and development of the world economy, help countries realize sound economic expansion and development, and help world trade grow on a multilateral, nondiscriminatory basis.

EU: The European Union (EU) currently has 27 members and grew out of the six-member former European Economic Community, which was established in 1957. The EU has its capital in Brussels and is the largest economic/social experiment ever attempted among nations. It continues to be a work in progress. Over time, the EU has established a common market for goods, services, capital, and labour. Given the size of its population (495 million people) and huge contribution to the world's GDP, its decisions on competition, labour and safety standards, and environmental policies have profound effects on the behaviour of other nations.

G8: This group of 8 nations consists of Canada, the United Kingdom, France, Germany, Italy, Japan, the United States, and, recently, Russia. It represents (along with China and Spain) the 10 largest economies in the world. The heads of state of these eight countries hold summits (in various locations around the globe) in which the world's pressing economic, political, and social issues are discussed.

G20: This is an expanded version of the **G8**. In this case, the ministers of finance and heads of the central banks of the 20 member nations meet to promote financial stability in the world's markets.

UNCTAD: The United Nations Conference on Trade and Development (UNCTAD) was established in 1964 and is located in Geneva. UNCTAD aims to help developing countries integrate into the world economy. UNCTAD provides a forum for intergovernmental discussions while also supporting research, data collection, and policy analysis helpful to the developing countries, along with the provision of some technical assistance.

NAFTA Secretariat: The North American Free Trade Agreement (NAFTA) Secretariat was established with the signing of the 1994 agreement that formed the world's largest free trade area made up of Canada, the United States, and Mexico. The mandate of the Secretariat is to provide administrative support to panels and committees established by the agreement to provide dispute resolutions. The Secretariat has three locations: Ottawa, Mexico City, and Washington, D.C.

Even allowing for these cautions, it is still true that there are a number of benefits to be obtained from trade. This leads us to ask: why does free trade tend to be the exception rather than the rule throughout history? Why does the question of free trade still divide countries and lead to such acrimonious debate? To understand part of the reason, let us look at an example illustrating that not everyone within a country will benefit from free trade.

 SELF-TEST

4. The following table shows the average productivity in Freedonia and Libraland:

Output per Worker (bushels per day)

	Apples		Pears
Freedonia	6	or	3
Libraland	3	or	2

Assuming the two countries wish to trade, would terms of trade of 1 bushel of pears = 2.5 bushels of apples be feasible? What about 1 bushel of pears = 1 bushel of apples? 1 bushel of pears = 1.75 bushels of apples?

5. From the data contained in **Figure 13.3** or **Table 13.6**, how many beans can the United States obtain if it is self-sufficient and producing 240 million bushels of wheat? If, instead, it specializes in wheat production and can trade at terms of 1 bushel of wheat = 2 bushels of beans, how many bushels of beans could it have to accompany its 240 million bushels of wheat? What if the terms were 1 bushel of wheat = 3 bushels of beans?

13.4   THE EFFECT OF FREE TRADE

Let us set up a scenario in which initially we have two self-sufficient countries, France and Germany, each producing wine. The demand and supply conditions in the two countries are different, of course, with both the demand and supply being greater in France than in Germany, as is shown in **Table 13.11**.

TABLE 13.11   The Market for Wine in France and Germany (millions of litres per month)

FRANCE			GERMANY		
Price ($ per litre)	Quantity Demanded	Quantity Supplied	Price ($ per litre)	Quantity Demanded	Quantity Supplied
3	19	7	3	17	2
4	17	11	4	15	3
5	**15**	**15**	5	13	4
6	13	19	6	11	5
7	11	23	7	9	6
8	9	27	**8**	**7**	**7**

The equilibrium price in France is $5 per litre and the equilibrium quantity is 15. In Germany, the equilibrium price and quantity are $8 and 7, respectively. These are shown graphically in **Figure 13.6**.

Now, suppose that the two countries decide to engage in free trade. To keep things simple, let us assume there are no transport costs. If free trade is now introduced, what will be the price of wine in the two countries? Since we have assumed there are no transport costs, the price in the two countries should be the same. To find this price, all we need to do is look at the combined market of France and Germany. In other words, we simply need to add the demands and supplies of the two countries, as shown in **Table 13.12**.

The total market demand is obtained by adding together the French demand and the German demand at each price. For instance, at $3 per litre, the quantity demanded in France is 19 and in Germany 17, giving a total for the two countries of 36. Similarly, the quantity supplied at $3 is 7 in France and 2 in Germany, giving a total market supply of 9. This is done for all prices. The new market price (let us call it the world price), then, will be $6 per litre, and at that price, a total of 24 million litres will be produced and sold.

FIGURE 13.6   Demand and Supply of Wine in France and Germany

In France, the demand and supply of wine are both higher than in Germany. The consequence is a greater quantity of wine traded in France: 15 million litres, compared with 7 million in Germany. The price of wine, however, is lower in France than in Germany.

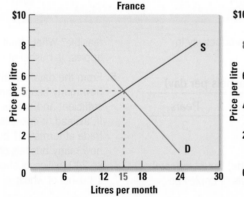

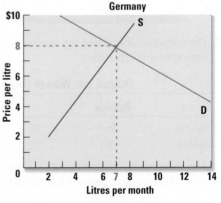

TABLE 13.12	**Deriving the Total Market Demand and Supply of Wine for France and Germany (in millions of litres per month)**					
	FRANCE		GERMANY		TOTAL MARKET	
Price ($ per litre)	Demand	Supply	Demand	Supply	Demand	Supply
3	19	7	17	2	36	9
4	17	11	15	3	32	14
5	15	15	13	4	28	19
6	13	19	11	5	**24**	**24**
7	11	23	9	6	20	29
8	9	27	7	7	16	34

Now, let us look at the effect in each market. French winemakers are delighted at the situation because the world price for wine is higher and their volume of business is higher. French winemakers are now producing 19 million litres, up from the 15 million litres produced before trade, and the price they receive is $6, up from $5. Note also that in France, the quantity produced (19) exceeds the demand from French consumers (13). What happens to the surplus of 6 million litres? It is being exported to Germany. And what is the situation in that country? Well, certainly German consumers are delighted because the new world price of $6 is lower than the previous domestic price of $8. But we can imagine that the German winemakers are far from happy. The new lower world price has caused a number of producers to cut back production, and presumably some producers are forced out of business and some employees have lost their jobs. Therefore, while the populations of both France and Germany as a whole benefit, not everyone within those populations gains. At the world price of $6, German producers are only producing 5 million litres, below the German demand of 11 million litres. How is this shortage going to be made up? The answer is: from the import of French wine. This simply means that the French export of 6 million litres equals the German import of 6 million litres. These points are illustrated graphically in **Figure 13.7**.

Bottled wine aging in storage.

FIGURE 13.7	**Demand and Supply of Wine in France and Germany with Free Trade**

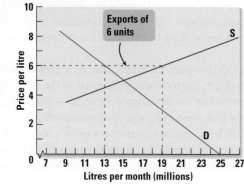 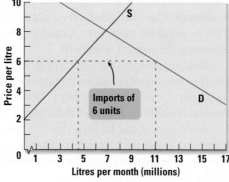

The new world price of wine is above the previous French price but below the previous German price. The result is a surplus of wine in France of 6 million litres but a shortage in Germany of 6 million litres.

So, who loses and who gains as a result of markets being opened up? The answer in our example is that both German wine consumers and French wine producers gain, and French wine consumers and German wine producers lose. Free trade has cost French consumers $1 a litre, and it has cost German winemakers $2 per litre. Previously, German winemakers were selling 7 million litres at $8 per litre, for a total revenue of $56 million. Now, they are selling only 5 million litres for $6 per litre, for a total revenue of $30 million. In total, then, these producers, of whom there may be fewer than 100, have collectively lost $26 million in revenue. It is easy to see why these producers may not be in favour of free trade! In fact, it would pay them to lobby their own parliament and to launch publicity campaigns in an attempt to keep out "cheap" French wines. If they are successful and efforts do not cost more than $26 million, they will be ahead of the game.

It is easy to see why powerful lobby and special interest groups have been very vocal throughout history in trying to persuade government and the public that it is in the country's interests to ban or curtail foreign imports. This is an activity that economists call *rent seeking*. Such **protectionism** can take many forms, which we will now examine.

protectionism: the economic policy of protecting domestic producers by restricting the importation of foreign products.

quota: a limit imposed on the production or sale of a product.

The Imposition of Import Quotas

The most obvious way to restrict imports is to ban them entirely or partially, and this is exactly what is meant by a **quota**. An import quota can take a variety of forms, ranging from a total restriction to a maximum limit being placed on each individual foreign exporter, or perhaps the requirement that each foreign exporter reduce its exports by a percentage of the previous year's sales. The essence of an import quota is to reduce or restrict the importation of certain products. And what will the effect of such restriction be? Suppose, in our wine example, that German winemakers were successful in their efforts to keep out French wines, and the German government imposed a total ban on French wines. At the current price of $6 per litre, there will be an immediate shortage in Germany. The result of the shortage is to push up the price of wine. It will continue to rise, encouraging increased German production until the price returns to the pre–free-trade price of $8. In France, the immediate effect of the German quota will be to cause a surplus of French wine, which will depress the price of French wine until it, too, is back at the pre-trade price of $5 per litre.

Let us move on from our European example and look at trade from the Canadian perspective. Unlike our example where the market price was determined by the total demand and supply in just two countries, in reality, the prices of wine and of most products traded internationally are determined by the world's demand and supply. That is to say, for any one small country, such as Canada, the world price is a given; the country's action will have little impact on the world price. This situation is illustrated in **Figure 13.8**.

Figure 13.8 shows the domestic demand (D_d) and supply (S_d) of wine in Canada. P_d would be the domestic price and Q_d the domestic production if Canada was totally closed to foreign trade. Suppose that the world price is Pw and that Canada now freely allows imports into the country. This means that if the world price of P_w prevails within Canada, the amount produced by domestic Canadian producers is *a*, and the amount demanded is *c*. Since Canadian consumers want to purchase more than Canadian producers are willing to produce, the difference of *ac* represents the amount of imports.

Now, suppose that the Canadian government yields to pressure from Canadian wine producers and imposes a quota of *ab* on imported wine. In effect, the total supply is equal to the domestic supply plus the amount of the quota. This is represented by the new supply curve, $S_d +$ *quota*. Since the total available has now been reduced, the price will increase to P_q, and the quantity will fall to Q_q.

From this, it can be seen that the losers will be Canadian consumers (who are paying a higher price and are having less quantity and variety of wines) and foreign winemakers whose exports are being restricted. The winners will be Canadian winemakers, who are producing more wine and receiving a higher price.

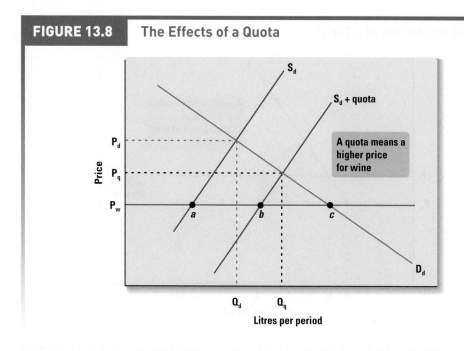

FIGURE 13.8   **The Effects of a Quota**

A quota means a higher price for wine

Initially, the Canadian domestic demand and supply are D_d and S_d, and the world price is P_w. The quantity demanded in Canada at the world price P_w equals c, of which Canadian producers would produce a and foreign producers would export ac to Canada. A quota of ab would raise the price to P_q. As a result, domestic production will increase, and imports would drop to the amount of the quota.

The Imposition of Tariffs

A second way of restricting imports is by the use of a **tariff**, which is a tax on imports. It is implemented more often than import quotas because governments can derive considerable revenue from tariffs. The effects of a tariff are much the same as those of a quota because in both cases the price of the product will increase. With a quota, however, the domestic producers get the whole benefit of the higher price, whereas with a tariff the benefit is shared between the domestic producers and government. An additional benefit of a tariff over a quota is that a quota tends to treat foreign producers indiscriminately because each and every producer is treated in the same way; with a tariff, only the more efficient producers will continue to export, since only they will be able to continue to make a profit. A tariff discriminates against the less efficient producers, and therefore, from an efficiency point of view, it is superior to a quota.

In **Figure 13.9**, suppose, again, that we are describing the Canadian wine market. At the world price of P_w, Canadian producers are supplying a, and Canadian consumers are buying b. The difference, ab, is the amount of imported wine. Suppose that the Canadian government imposes a tariff of t per unit. The price in Canada will rise to P_t. Note that at the higher price, Canadian producers (who do not pay the tariff) will receive the whole price P_t, and will increase production to Q_f. Canadian consumers will reduce consumption to Q_g. In addition, imports will fall to a level represented by the distance $Q_f - Q_g$. The result is very similar to what we saw in the analysis of quotas. Again, it is Canadian consumers and foreign producers who lose out and Canadian producers who gain.

The other winner in this scenario is the Canadian government, which will receive tax revenue equal to the shaded rectangle in **Figure 13.9**.

tariff: a tax (or duty) levied on imports.

Other Trade Restrictions

Besides the two most popular protectionist measures of tariffs and quotas, a number of other available methods deserve mention. **Currency-exchange controls** are similar to quotas, but instead of restricting the importation of goods, currency exchange controls limit the availability of foreign currencies (that is, foreign exchange). The effect is the same because foreigners wish to be paid in their own currencies, and importers who are unable to get their hands on the appropriate currency will not be able to buy the foreign goods.

currency-exchange controls: government restrictions limiting the amount of foreign currencies that can be obtained.

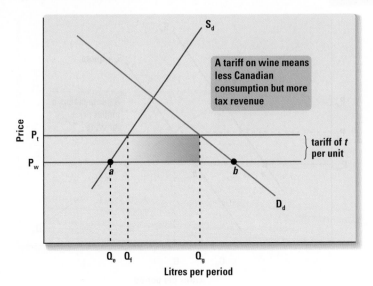

FIGURE 13.9   The Effects of the Imposition of a Tariff

The imposition of a tariff, t, will increase the price of wine in Canada to P_t from P_w. As a result, Canadian production will increase from Q_e to Q_f and imports will drop to $Q_g - Q_f$. The tax revenue to government is equal to t times the quantity of imports, $Q_g - Q_f$, the shaded area.

A tariff on wine means less Canadian consumption but more tax revenue

tariff of t per unit

The controls might be across-the-board restrictions or restrictions on particular currencies or on particular products or industries. The effect in all cases will be to increase the domestic price of the products affected, which will be to the benefit of the domestic producer at the expense of the domestic consumer. Another more subtle but often equally effective way to cut imports is by way of *bureaucratic regulations*, though not all regulations have that intent. A government might make trade so difficult or time-consuming for the importer that the amount of trade is significantly reduced. For instance, the customs department of a particular country might tie the importer up with red tape by requiring that all imports must be accompanied by ten different forms (all in triplicate) obtainable from ten different government departments. Or perhaps the product must meet certain very unrealistic standards of safety or packaging, or hygiene standards that are not required for domestically produced items.

A more recent type of trade restriction is known as **voluntary export restrictions (VERs)**. Rather than imposing tariffs and import quotas, the importing country requests that the exporting country itself voluntarily restrict the amount being exported. In this way, the exporting country is given the power to administer the quotas, which will also prevent the importing country from receiving tariff revenue on the imports. Since the restrictions are voluntary, the exporting country does not have to comply. However, since the importing country has other weapons at its disposal, these restrictions are usually adhered to.

In summary, there are five types of trade protection:

voluntary export restriction (VER): an agreement by an exporting country to restrict the amount of its exports to another country.

- Import quotas
- Tariffs
- Currency-exchange controls
- Bureaucratic regulations
- Voluntary export restrictions

 SELF-TEST

6. In **Table 13.12**, if the demand for wine in Germany increased by nine (million litres) at every price, how much wine would now be produced in Germany, and how much would be imported from France?

ADDED DIMENSION The Softwood Lumber Dispute

In 2006, Canada and the United States finally reached an agreement to end the dispute over Canadian exports of softwood lumber to the United States. The seven-year agreement removed a U.S. tariff on softwood lumber that Canada claimed was illegal under the terms of NAFTA. However, it also included an export tax imposed on Canadian shipments of wood to the United States if the market price dropped below a certain level. This tax ranges from 5 percent to 15 percent, depending on how low the market price dropped below a certain base level. This long simmering dispute centred on the stumpage fees that Canadian provincial governments impose on lumber companies for the right to harvest trees on crown land. The Americans felt that these fees were too low, which resulted in a de facto subsidy to Canadian lumber companies.

13.5 PROTECTIONISM

In this chapter, we have tried to avoid making an outright declaration in favour of free trade, though the flavour of the chapter would suggest that there are many benefits to be derived from trade, and probably the majority of economists feel that the freer the trade, the better. But even a notable free-trader, such as the astute Adam Smith, recognized that there may be occasions when a degree of protectionism in the way of tariffs and quotas might be called for. He suggested, for instance, that a country's strategic industries should be offered protection so that, for instance, the country does not become dependent on foreign manufacturers for the production of military hardware and related technology. The problem with this *strategic industry argument*, however, is that most industries would claim that they are of "strategic importance" to a nation and, therefore, deserve similar protection from foreign competition.

L05 Identify some arguments against free trade.

In addition, Smith suggests that, in order to have a level playing field for both domestic and foreign producers, if the produce of domestic industry is being taxed then foreign imports should be taxed by a similar amount. He also felt that if a foreign country is placing tariffs and import quotas on your country's exports, then you should do likewise to its exports—not, it should be noted, for retaliation but to help the foreign country to recognize the folly of its actions and to persuade it to restore free trade.

Finally, Smith was prescient enough to realize that if a country has had a long history of protectionism, the sudden arrival of free trade is likely to cause dramatic shifts of labour and capital away from industries that can no longer compete to those industries that are growing. This dislocation may cause a great deal of suffering in the short term, so Smith felt that a wise government would introduce free trade gradually, to mitigate any suffering. This caveat is of particular importance in terms of the North American Free Trade Agreement discussions. Although many felt that there would be great long-term benefits for all the participating countries, it is equally certain that in the short term a great deal of suffering would be experienced by those industries, firms, and individuals who, through no fault of their own, found themselves unable to compete. This is why tariffs were reduced in stages over a 10-year period.

It should also be mentioned that some economists believe certain "infant" industries should be given a helping hand by government until they are sufficiently mature to take on foreign competition. This *infant industry argument* is strongest when government feels that undue reliance on the exportation of a few staple products would leave the country in a vulnerable position if a future change in demand or technology were to occur. In order to diversify the economy and develop other industries, many feel that these "infants" should be sheltered from competition. The trouble is, these infant industries often never grow up! In addition, even if there are persuasive arguments in favour of protecting or assisting certain industries, it may be better for government to give this aid in the form of direct subsidies rather than by interfering with normal trading patterns through the imposition of tariffs and quotas.

A third argument against free trade is the *cultural identity argument*. This one is difficult to dismiss solely on economic grounds. Many commentators feel that free trade brings with it mass production and standardization, which may harm the importing country's sense of individuality and cultural identity. As a result, some are totally against free trade, while others feel that it should not extend into such areas as communications, health, and education. They firmly believe that a country's radio and television stations, its newspapers and magazines, and its educational institutions and hospitals should not be owned or controlled from abroad.

A fourth argument is the belief that the environmental and labour standards of developed nations may be eroded as they try to compete with countries whose standards may be considerably lower and who may have a cost advantage as a result. This could trigger a "race to the bottom" as standards are lowered in all countries.

In summary, there are four arguments against free trade:

- The strategic industry argument
- The infant industry argument
- The cultural identity argument
- The lower environmental and labour standards argument

SELF-TEST

7. Which industry in Canada do you feel deserves protection in each of the following categories:

a) Strategically important

b) Infant industry

c) Culturally important

d) Environmentally important

ADDED DIMENSION   Does Free Trade Cost Jobs?

During the recession that began in 2008, a number of countries introduced rescue packages designed to boost their own industries. Many thought that such aid should only be given to those firms and industries able to guarantee that money would flow directly into boosting domestic production and jobs. There was a concern that a great deal of the extra spending might instead benefit foreign producers. In the United States, for example, President Barack Obama was enjoined to ensure that any stimulus spending by the government would be to "Buy American." There is nothing new in this. Whenever a country is suffering economically, there are always those who advocate restrictions on foreign imports on the basis that it costs jobs and that by buying from abroad, jobs are, in effect, exported to other countries.

There is some truth in this. Certainly in the case of Canada, employment in the textile industry has declined as jobs have shifted to India and other countries. But before we jump to the conclusion that Canada needs protection from low-wage countries that are able to "unfairly" compete with us, let us stop to consider who have been the top trading nations in the world over the last half century. The list would surely include the United States, Japan, Germany, the United Kingdom, and—Canada. And which countries have the highest wage rates in the world? Again, the United States, Japan, Germany, the United Kingdom, and—

Canada. The reason for this is straightforward. It may be true that labour costs determine which country can produce certain products more cheaply, but labour costs are not determined solely by wage rates. For example, suppose that a Canadian steelworker earns $30 an hour while the going wage in Mexico is just $5 an hour. A big advantage to Mexico, it would seem. However, let us further suppose that the Canadian worker is able to produce 15 units of steel an hour compared with only 2 units by the Mexican. The cost of a unit of steel in Canada is, therefore, equal to $30/15 or $2 per unit, whereas in Mexico a unit of steel costs $5/2 or $2.50. In summary, Canada will be more competitive than Mexico in steel production because although it has higher wage rates, it has even higher productivity rates.

But let us return to the original idea: does buying abroad cost us jobs in Canada? In a sense, the answer is yes, since we are importing products made by foreign labour and, therefore, exporting jobs. But whenever we export products, we are importing jobs into Canada. So, what jobs should we export, and what should we import? Presumably we should specialize in products and jobs where we have some expertise: automobile production, high-tech electronics, financial services, and telecommunications. And we should buy products and jobs that other countries can produce more cheaply: T-shirts, textiles, and soy beans.

Review

CHAPTER SUMMARY

In this chapter, you learned that the benefits of free trade are rooted in specialization and that a nation's comparative advantage determines what products it should export. The way that the gains from trade are divided between trading partners is determined by the terms of trade between them. You also learned that when a nation embraces free trade, there are both winners, usually consumers, and losers, usually inefficient producers of certain products.

13.1a If trade is voluntary, then both parties to the trade must benefit.

13.1b Differences in factor endowments between nations and the theory of absolute advantage explain why, for example, Canada exports lumber and imports bananas.

13.2a The theory of comparative advantage explains why one nation is willing to trade with another nation, even though it may be more efficient in producing both (all) the products involved.

13.2b The trade in any two products between any two nations will result in gains from trade unless the opportunity costs of production happen to be exactly the same in each country.

13.3a The way in which the gains from trade are divided between the trading partners is determined by the terms of trade, calculated as the average price of exports divided by the average price of imports times 100.

13.3b The major benefits of free trade are:
- lower prices
- higher incomes
- a greater variety and quality of products
- increased competition

13.4a While the population of a country as a whole gains from free trade, not everyone within that population wins.

13.4b The two most common forms of *trade restrictions* are tariffs and quotas, both of which:
- increase the domestic price of a product that is imported
- reduce the quantities traded of that product

The other two types of restrictions are:
- exchange controls
- voluntary exports restrictions

13.5 Four arguments against free trade are:
- the strategic industry argument
- the infant industry argument
- the cultural identity argument
- the lower environmental and labour standards argument

NEW GLOSSARY TERMS AND KEY EQUATION

comparative advantage 414
currency-exchange controls 427
protectionism 426

quota 426
tariff 427
terms of trade 417

voluntary export restriction (VER) 428

Practise and learn online with Connect, where you can find the Answered Questions and the Unanswered Problems for all chapters of this textbook's Study Guide section.

Equations:

[13.1] $\text{Terms of trade} = \dfrac{\text{Average price of exports}}{\text{Average price of imports}} \times 100$ page 417

STUDY TIPS

1. The argument for free trade is based on Ricardo's theory of comparative advantage. It is important that you fully understand the basic idea of opportunity costs that lies behind this theory. A good way to test yourself is to make up your own figures for a two-country, two-product world, draw the corresponding production possibilities curves, and work out which country has an advantage in which product and why.

2. Some students have difficulty understanding that if we are dealing with only two products, and if a country has a comparative advantage at producing one product, it must by definition have a comparative *disadvantage* in the other product.

3. To get an understanding of the terms of trade, again make up some numbers for yourself, and plot them on a production possibilities diagram. For instance, start off with a country that could produce 30 units of wool or 20 computers and has an advantage in wool production. If it could trade at 1 wool = 1/2 computer, what combinations could it have? Try 1 unit of wool = 1 computer, 1 unit of wool = 2, 3, 5 computers and so on.

Draw each resulting trading possibilities curve. Note that both the trading and production possibilities curves reflect opportunity costs. The former case shows what must be given up in trading; the latter case shows what must be given up in production.

4. To understand the idea behind world markets, note, as in **Figure 13.7**, that what one country is exporting, another country must be importing. This means that if one country produces a trade surplus, then the other country must be experiencing a trade deficit. In the exporting country, the world price must be higher than the domestic price. In the importing country, the world price must be lower than the domestic price.

5. You will get a good grip on the effects of tariffs and quotas by drawing a simple demand-and-supply curve and noting, first, the effect of a price set above market equilibrium (which is what a tariff produces) and, second, a quantity below market equilibrium (which is what an import quota produces). This approach suggests that the effect of both tariffs and import quotas is to produce higher prices and lower quantities.

Answered Questions

These questions can also be found online on Connect.

Indicate whether the following statements are true or false:

1. **(LO 2) T or F** A country has a comparative advantage over another only if it is able to produce all products more cheaply.

2. **(LO 2) T or F** David Ricardo first introduced the theory of comparative advantage.

3. **(LO 1) T or F** If a country wishes to specialize its production, it will also want to engage in trade.

4. **(LO 2) T or F** If a country is able to produce all products more cheaply than any other country, then there is no advantage in trade.

5. **(LO 3) T or F** The terms of trade relate to the laws and conditions that govern trade.

6. **(LO 3) T or F** If the prices of a country's exports decrease and the prices of imports increase, then the terms of trade will move in its favour.

7. **(LO 3) T or F** If a country's trading possibilities curve lies to the right of its production possibilities curve, there are no gains from trade.

8. **(LO 5) T or F** Protectionism is the economic policy of protecting domestic producers by putting restrictions on exports.

9. **(LO 4) T or F**   A tariff is a tax on exports; a quota is a tax on imports.

10. **(LO 5) T or F**   Domestic producers gain and domestic consumers lose as a result of the imposition of tariffs or quotas.

Basic (Questions 11–26)

11. **(LO 1)** What is the meaning of the term *gains from trade*?
    a) The surplus of exports over imports
    b) The increase in output resulting from international trade
    c) The fact that everyone gains from international trade
    d) The increase in revenue that government receives from tariffs

12. **(LO 4)** What is a tariff?
    a) It is a tax imposed on an import.
    b) It is a tax imposed on an export.
    c) It is a tax imposed on production.
    d) It is a tax imposed on consumption.

13. **(LO 1)** What are the two largest categories of goods that Canada exports?
    a) Energy and forestry products
    b) Agricultural and forestry products
    c) Forestry products and industrial materials
    d) Automotive products and machinery/equipment products

14. **(LO 3)** What is the definition of *terms of trade*?
    a) It is the average price of a country's imports divided by the average price of its exports.
    b) It is the average price of a country's exports divided by the average price of its imports.
    c) They are the rules and regulations governing international trade.
    d) The value of a country's currency compared with that of its biggest trading partner.

15. **(LO 2)** What does it mean if the opportunity costs differ between two countries?
    a) Then comparative costs must be the same.
    b) There can be no gains from trade.
    c) It is possible for both countries to gain from specialization and trade.
    d) Then absolute costs must be the same.

16. **(LO 3)** On what basis are the gains from trade divided between countries?
    a) According to the terms of trade
    b) According to international trade agreements

c) According to the quantity of resources possessed by each
d) According to each country's comparative advantage

17. **(LO 2)** Under what circumstances will there be no opportunity for mutually advantageous trade between two countries?
    a) When the terms of trade are the same
    b) When comparative costs are the same
    c) When comparative costs are different
    d) When tariffs exist

18. **(LO 3)** Suppose that originally the average price of Happy Island's exports was 180 and the average price of its imports was 120. Now, the price of its exports drops to 160, and the price of its imports drops to 100. What effect will this have on Happy Island's terms of trade?
    a) There will be no change in the terms of trade.
    b) The terms of trade have moved in Happy Island's favour.
    c) The terms of trade have moved against Happy Island.
    d) The terms of trade have both increased and decreased.

19. **(LO 5)** All the following, except one, are forms of protectionism. Which is the exception?
    a) Import subsidies
    b) Tariffs
    c) Exchange controls
    d) Quotas

20. **(LO 2)** Suppose that the cost of producing one unit of wine in Happy Island is two units of rice; in Joy Island, one unit of wine costs four units of rice. What does this mean for the two countries?
    a) Happy Island should specialize in rice and export it to Joy Island.
    b) Happy Island should specialize in wine and export it to Joy Island.
    c) Happy Island should specialize in rice but export wine to Joy Island.
    d) Happy Island should specialize in wine but export rice to Joy Island.

21. **(LO 3)** Suppose that the cost of producing one unit of wine in Happy Island is two units of rice; in Joy Island one unit of wine costs four units of rice. What might be possible terms of trade between the two countries?
    a) 1 rice = 3/8 wine
    b) 1 rice = 3 wine
    c) 1 rice = 6 wine
    d) 1 wine = 1 rice

22. **(LO 5)** What is the difference between a tariff and a quota?
    a) A tariff causes an increase in the price, whereas a quota does not affect the price.
    b) Both a tariff and a quota will affect the price, but a tariff has no effect on the quantity, whereas a quota will lead to a reduction.
    c) Both a tariff and a quota will affect the price, but a tariff has no effect on the quantity, whereas a quota will lead to an increase.
    d) A quota affects all foreign producers equally, whereas a tariff does not.
    e) A tariff affects all foreign producers equally, whereas a quota does not.

Refer to **Figure 13.10** to answer questions 23–26.

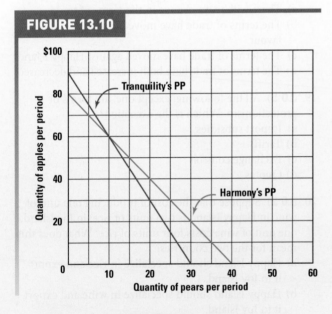

FIGURE 13.10

23. **(LO 2)** What is the opportunity cost of producing 1 apple in Harmony and in Tranquillity?
    a) 2 pears in Harmony and 3 pears in Tranquillity
    b) 1/2 pear in Harmony and 1/3 pear in Tranquillity
    c) 2 pears in Harmony and 1/3 pear in Tranquillity
    d) 1/2 pear in Harmony and 3 pears in Tranquillity
    e) 3 pears in Harmony and 2 pears in Tranquillity

24. **(LO 2)** What do the comparative opportunity costs in the two countries suggest?
    a) That there are no advantages to be gained from trade
    b) That Harmony should specialize in apples but export pears
    c) That Tranquillity should specialize in apples but export pears

d) That Harmony should specialize in pears but export apples
e) That Harmony should specialize in pears and Tranquillity should specialize in apples

25. **(LO 3)** Suppose that both Harmony and Tranquillity are producing 20 pears. What will be the total gains from trade for the two countries?
    a) 20 apples and 0 pears
    b) 30 apples and 10 pears
    c) 20 apples and 10 pears
    d) 20 apples and 30 pears
    e) 0 apple and 20 pears

26. **(LO 3)** What could be possible terms of trade between the two countries?
    a) 1 apple = 0.25 pear
    b) 1 apple = 2.5 pears
    c) 1 apple = 3 pears
    d) 1 pear = 0.5 apple
    e) 1 pear = 2.5 apples

Intermediate (Questions 27–31)

Refer to **Table 13.13** to answer problems 27–31.

TABLE 13.13

	AVERAGE PRODUCT PER WORKER			
Country	Broomsticks			Swords
Rings	1	or		4
Potter	6	or		3

27. **(LO 2)** What is the cost of producing one sword in Rings?
    a) 4 broomsticks
    b) 0.25 broomstick
    c) 0.67 broomstick
    d) 1.5 broomsticks

28. **(LO 2)** What is the cost of producing one broomstick in Potter?
    a) 2 swords
    b) 0.5 sword
    c) 0.33 sword
    d) 3 swords

29. **(LO 2)** Supposing that there are 200 workers in Rings, how many broomsticks could be produced if 200 swords were produced?
    a) 40 broomsticks
    b) 50 broomsticks
    c) 150 broomsticks
    d) 160 broomsticks

30. **(LO 2)** Supposing that there are 200 workers in Potter, how many swords could be produced if 540 broomsticks were produced?
    a) 0 swords
    b) 110 swords
    c) 120 swords
    d) 330 swords

31. **(LO 2)** Supposing that there are 200 workers each in Rings and Potter. If, originally, half the workers were employed in each industry, what would be the gains from trade if the countries completely specialized in the products in which they have a comparative advantage?
    a) + 200 broomsticks, − 100 swords
    b) + 200 broomsticks, + 100 swords
    c) + 500 broomsticks, + 100 swords
    d) + 700 broomsticks, + 700 swords

Advanced (Questions 32–35)

Refer to **Figure 13.11**, which shows the market for cloth in Smith Island, to answer questions 32, 33, and 34.

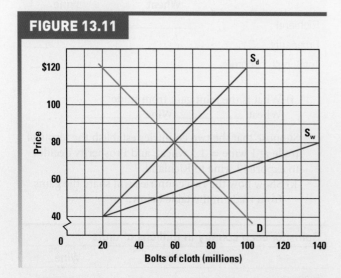

FIGURE 13.11

32. **(LO 1)** At the world price, how much is Smith Island trading?
    a) It is importing 30 units.
    b) It is importing 40 units.
    c) It is exporting 30 units.
    d) It is exporting 40 units.

33. **(LO 5)** If Smith Island introduced an import quota of 20, what would be the new price of cloth in Smith Island?
    a) $55
    b) $60
    c) $70
    d) $90

34. **(LO 5)** If Smith Island introduced an import quote of $20, how much would be imported?
    a) 0 units
    b) 10 units
    c) 20 units
    d) 40 units

Table 13.14 shows the output of kumquats per month. Refer to this table to answer question 35.

TABLE 13.14

| Price ($ per kilo) | SMITHLAND | | |
	Demand	Domestic Supply	Imports
3	100	40	30
4	90	50	40
5	80	60	50
6	70	70	60

35. **(LO 1)** What is the world (free trade) price of kumquats, and what quantity of this product is being consumed domestically?
    a) $4 and 50 kilos
    b) $4 and 90 kilos
    c) $5 and 80 kilos
    d) $6 and 70 kilos
    e) $6 and 130 kilos

Parallel Problems

ANSWERED PROBLEMS

36A. **(LO 2, 3) Key Problem** Suppose that Richland and Prosperity have the output figures shown in **Table 13.15**.

TABLE 13.15

AVERAGE PRODUCT PER WORKER			
Country	Wheat		Wine
Richland	4 bushels	or	2 barrels
Prosperity	2 bushels	or	6 barrels

Assume that cost and productivity remain constant.
a) What is the opportunity cost of producing one bushel of wheat in Richland? _____ .
b) What is the opportunity cost of producing one barrel of wine in Richland? _____ .
c) What is the opportunity cost of producing one bushel of wheat in Prosperity? _____ .
d) What is the opportunity cost of producing one barrel of wine in Prosperity? _____ .
e) In what product does Richland have a comparative advantage? _____ .
f) In what product does Prosperity have a comparative advantage? _____ .
Suppose that the labour force in each country is 10 million.
g) Fill in the missing production possibilities data for both countries in **Table 13.16**.

TABLE 13.16

RICHLAND'S PRODUCTION POSSIBILITIES (millions of units)					
	A	B	C	D	E
Wheat	40	30	20	10	0
Wine	___	___	___	___	___

PROSPERITY'S PRODUCTION POSSIBILITIES (millions of units)					
	A	B	C	D	E
Wheat	___	___	___	___	___
Wine	0	15	30	45	60

Suppose that both countries are presently producing combination C.
h) Fill in the blanks in the following table:

Total output in millions of units:		
	Wheat	Wine
Richland	_____	_____
Prosperity	_____	_____
Total: both countries	_____	_____

Now, suppose that each country specializes in the product in which it has a comparative advantage.
i) Show the results below:

Total output in millions of units:		
	Wheat	Wine
Richland	_____	_____
Prosperity	_____	_____
Total: both countries	_____	_____

j) What is the joint gain from trade?
   Wheat: _____ Wine: _____

Suppose that the two countries establish the terms of trade at 1 wine = 1.5 wheat, and Prosperity decides to export 12 wine to Richland.
k) Show how the two countries will share the gains from trade in the table below:

Gains for each country in millions of units		
	Wheat	Wine
Richland	_____	_____
Prosperity	_____	_____
Total: both countries	_____	_____

Basic (Problems 37A–43A)

37A. **(LO 3)** If the terms of trade for the country of Onara equals 0.9 and the average price of its imports is 1.4, what is the average price of its exports? _____ .

38A. **(LO 2)** In Onara, the average worker can produce either five bags of pummies or three kilos of clings, whereas in Traf the average worker can produce either four bags of pummies or six kilos of clings. Which country can produce pummies more cheaply and which can produce clings more cheaply? Show the cost in each country.

Pummies: _____ Cost: _____

Clings: _____ Cost: _____

39A. **(LO 2, 3)** The following shows the maximum output levels for Here and There:

	Cloth		Computers
Here	100	or	50
There	60	or	120

a) What is the cost of 1 unit of cloth and a computer in Here?
1 unit of cloth: _____
1 computer: _____

b) What is the cost of 1 unit of cloth and a computer in There?
1 unit of cloth: _____
1 computer: _____

c) In what product does each country have a comparative advantage?
Here: _____
There: _____

d) What is the range of feasible terms of trade between the two countries?
1 unit of cloth: _____
1 computer: _____

40A. **(LO 2)** The following table shows the productivity for the countries of Yin and Yang:

	Machines		Bread
Yin	2	or	10
Yang	3	or	2

a) If the working populations of Yin and Yang are both 40 million, divided equally between the two industries in each country, how many machines and bread are currently being produced in Yin and Yang?

	Machines	Bread
Yin	_____	_____
Yang	_____	_____
Total	_____	_____

b) If the two countries decide to specialize, in which product does each country have a comparative advantage?
Yin: _____ Yang: _____

c) If the two countries were to totally specialize, show the totals in the table below.

	Machines	Bread
Yin	_____	_____
Yang	_____	_____
Total	_____	_____

d) What are the gains from trade?

	Machines	Bread
	_____	_____

41A. **(LO 2, 3)** Table 13.17 shows the production possibilities curves for Concordia and Harmonia.

TABLE 13.17

CONCORDIA'S PRODUCTION POSSIBILITIES

Product	A	B	C	D	E
Pork	4	3	2	1	0
Beans	0	5	10	15	20

HARMONIA'S PRODUCTION POSSIBILITIES

Product	A	B	C	D	E
Pork	8	6	4	2	0
Beans	0	6	12	18	24

a) What are the costs of the two products in each country?
Concordia: 1 unit of pork costs _____
1 unit of beans costs _____
Harmonia: 1 unit of pork costs _____
1 unit of beans costs _____

b) What products should each country specialize in and export?
Concordia: _____
Harmonia: _____

c) If, prior to specialization and trade, Concordia produced combination C and Harmonia produced combination B, what would be the total gains from trade?
Pork: _____
Beans: _____

d) What would be the range of feasible terms of trade between the two countries?

_____ .

42A. **(LO 3)** What is meant by *terms of trade*?

43A. **(LO 1)** What is meant by *factor endowment*?

Intermediate (Problems 44A–50A)

44A. **(LO 2)** The graph in **Figure 13.12** shows the domestic supply of and demand for mangos in India.

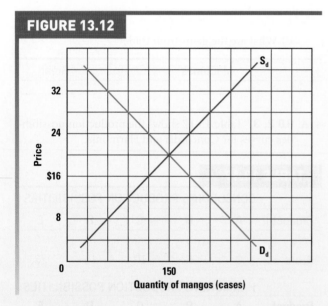

FIGURE 13.12

The world price is $16 a case, and India is open to free trade.
a) Will India export or import mangos?
b) What quantity will domestic producers supply?

_____ .

c) What quantity will India export or import?

_____ .

d) If the world price is $28, will India export or import mangos?
How much? _____
(Exports/import): _____
Quantity: _____

45A. **(LO 1, 5)** Table 13.18 shows the market for wool in Canada, which is closed to trade.
a) What is the present equilibrium price and domestic production?
Price: _____
Domestic production: _____
b) Suppose that Canada now opens to free trade and the world price of wool is $2000 per tonne.

TABLE 13.18

Price per Tonne ($)	Quantity Demanded Domestically	Quantity Supplied Domestically
1700	145	45
1800	140	60
1900	135	75
2000	130	90
2100	125	105
2200	120	120
2300	115	135
2400	110	150

How much wool will Canada produce domestically, and how much will it import?
Domestic production: _____
Imports: _____
c) Assume that the Canadian government, under pressure from the Canadian wool industry, decides to impose an import quota of 20 tonnes. What will be the new price, and how much will the Canadian industry produce? Price: _____
Domestic production: _____
d) Now, suppose that the Canadian government decides to replace the import quota with a tariff. If it wishes to maintain domestic production at the same level as with a quota, what should be the amount of the tariff, and how much revenue will government receive? Tariff: $ _____
Tariff revenue: $ _____

46A. **(LO 4)** Table 13.19 shows the production possibilities for Canada and Japan. Prior to specialization and trade, Canada is producing combination D, and Japan is producing combination B.

TABLE 13.19

CANADA'S PRODUCTION POSSIBILITIES					
Product	A	B	C	D	E
DVD players	30	22.5	15	7.5	0
Wheat	0	10	20	30	40

JAPAN'S PRODUCTION POSSIBILITIES					
Product	A	B	C	D	E
DVD players	40	30	20	10	0
Wheat	0	5	10	15	20

a) On the graph (Figure 13.13), draw the production possibilities curve for each country, and indicate their present output positions.

b) Suppose that the two countries specialize and trade on the basis of 1 DVD player = 1 wheat. Draw the corresponding trading possibilities curves.

FIGURE 13.13

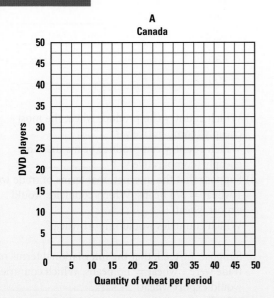

A
Canada

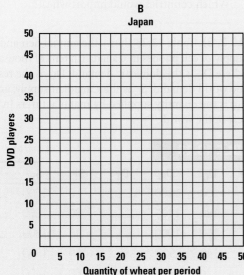

B
Japan

47A. **(LO 2)** The following incomplete table (**Table 13.20**) shows the productivity levels of producing beer and sardines in Canada and Mexico.

TABLE 13.20

	PRODUCTION PER WORKER (average product)	
	Beer	**Sardines**
Canada	6	4
Mexico	3	_____

In order for there to be no advantage gained from trade, what would the Mexican productivity per worker in the sardine industry need to be?

48A. **(LO 5)** Suppose the Canadian demand for and the Japanese supply of cars to Canada is shown in **Table 13.21** (quantities in thousands).

a) The present equilibrium price is $ _____ and quantity is _____ (thousand).

b) Suppose that the Canadian government imposes a $2000 per car tariff on imported Japanese cars. Show the new supply in the last column above.

c) The new equilibrium price is $ _____ and quantity is _____ (thousand).

d) The total revenue received by government will be $ _____ .

e) Assume, instead, that government imposes an import quota of 100 000 cars. The new equilibrium price is $ _____ and quantity is _____ (thousand).

f) Does government now receive any revenue? _____ .

49A. **(LO 1)** How are trade and specialization related?

50A. **(LO 3)** List three arguments against free trade.

Advanced (Problems 51A–55A)

51A. **(LO 2, 3, 4)** Latalia has a labour force of 12 million, half works in the wool industry, and half is employed in rice farming. The labour productivity in the wool industry is 40 kilos per worker per year, and in rice farming, it is 100 kilos per worker per year. Latalia has discovered that the international terms of trade are two kilos of rice per one kilo of wool. It is happy with its current consumption of rice but would like to obtain more wool.

a) Assuming constant per-unit costs, on the graph in **Figure 13.14**, draw the production and trading possibilities curves for Latalia.

b) If Latalia were to specialize and trade, what product should it produce? _____ .

c) What would be Latalia's gain from trade? _____ .

d) On the graph, indicate the consumption levels before and after trade.

TABLE 13.21

Price ($)	Quantity Demanded	Quantity Supplied (before tariff)	Quantity Supplied (after tariff)
$12 000	180	60	_____
13 000	160	80	_____
14 000	140	100	_____
15 000	120	120	_____
16 000	100	140	_____
17 000	80	160	_____
18 000	60	180	_____
19 000	40	200	_____

FIGURE 13.14

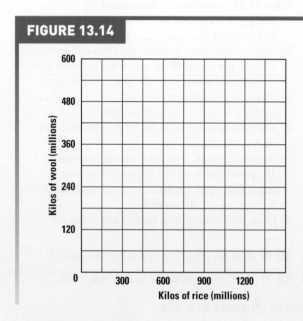

52A. **(LO 2, 3)** Suppose three countries have the productivity data shown in **Table 13.22**.

TABLE 13.22

	PRODUCTIVITY PER WORKER	
	Wheat	Beans
Alpha	1	2
Beta	4	2
Gamma	2	2

a) What is the cost of wheat in each country?
In Alpha, 1 unit of wheat costs _____ .
In Beta, 1 unit of wheat costs _____ .
In Gamma, 1 unit of wheat costs _____ .

b) Which country can produce wheat the most cheaply (comparatively)?
c) Which country can produce beans the most cheaply (comparatively) ? _____ .
d) Suppose that the international terms of trade were 1 wheat = 3/4 beans. Which countries would export wheat? _____ .
Which countries would import wheat?

_____ .

e) Suppose, instead, that the international terms of trade were 1 wheat = 1½ beans. Which countries would export wheat? _____ _____ .
Which countries would import wheat?

_____ .

53A. **(LO 2, 3)** Table 13.23 shows the annual demand and supply of cell phones in Canada (in tens of thousands), where D_C is the domestic demand, D_W is the rest of the world demand, S_C is the Canadian supply, and S_W is the quantity supplied by manufacturers in the rest of the world.

TABLE 13.23

Price	D_C	D_W	D_T	S_C	S_W	S_T
$ 25	200	1200	_____	20	1200	_____
50	180	1100	_____	30	1250	_____
75	160	1000	_____	40	1300	_____
100	140	900	_____	50	1350	_____
125	120	800	_____	60	1400	_____
150	100	700	_____	70	1450	_____
175	80	600	_____	80	1500	_____
200	60	500	_____	90	1550	_____
225	40	400	_____	100	1600	_____

a) Complete the total demand (D_T) and total supply (S_T) columns.

b) What are the world price and quantity?
Price: _____ Quantity: _____

c) If Canada was closed to international trade, what would be the price and quantity in Canada?
Price: _____ Quantity: _____

d) If Canada were open to international trade, how much would Canada import from the rest of the world? Quantity imported: _____

e) If the Canadian government were to impose a quota and limit the amount of imported cell phones to 90 (tens of thousands), what would be the new price and quantity in Canada?
Price: _____ Quantity: _____

54A. **(LO 2, 5)** If comparative cost is the basis for trade, why are the developing countries (which have very low wage rates) not the world's greatest trading nations?

55A. **(LO 1, 2)** Explain the theory of comparative advantage. How does it differ from the theory of absolute advantage?

GLOSSARY

A

allocative efficiency: the production of the combination of products that best satisfies consumers' demands; the allocation of scarce productive resources toward the production of goods and services that society values most.

average fixed cost: total fixed cost divided by the quantity of output.

average product: total product (or total output) divided by the quantity of inputs used to produce that total.

average profit: the profit per unit produced; that is, the total profit divided by the output.

average revenue: the amount of revenue received per unit sold.

average total cost: total cost divided by quantity of output.

average variable cost: total variable cost divided by total output.

B

barriers to entry: obstacles that make it difficult for new participants to enter a market.

break-even output: the level of output at which the sales revenue of the firm just covers fixed and variable costs, including normal profit.

break-even price: the price at which the firm makes only normal profits, that is, makes zero economic profits.

C

capital: human-made goods that are used to produce other products.

cartel: an association of sellers acting in unison.

ceteris paribus: other things being equal, or other things remaining the same.

change in demand: a change in the quantities demanded at every price, caused by a change in the determinants of demand.

change in supply: a change in the quantities supplied at every price, caused by a change in the determinants of supply.

change in the quantity demanded: the change in quantity that results from a price change. It is illustrated by a movement along a demand curve.

change in the quantity supplied: the change in the amounts that will be produced as a result of a price change. This is shown as a movement along a supply curve.

collusion: an agreement among suppliers to set the price of a product or the quantities each will produce.

common property resource: a resource not owned by an individual or a firm.

comparative advantage: the advantage that comes from producing something at a lower opportunity cost than others are able to do.

complementary products: products that tend to be purchased jointly and for which demand is, therefore, related.

concentration ratio: a measurement of the percentage of an industry's total sales that is controlled by the largest few firms.

constant-cost industry: an industry in which the prices of resources and products remain unchanged as the industry expands.

constant returns to scale: a firm's output increases by the same percentage as the increase in its inputs.

consumer goods and services: products that are used by consumers to satisfy their wants and needs.

consumer surplus: the difference between what a customer is willing to pay and the actual price of the product.

cross-elasticity of demand: how the quantity demanded of product A responds to a change in the price of product B.

currency-exchange controls: government restrictions imposed limiting the amount of foreign currencies that can be obtained.

D

deadweight loss: the total surplus lost relative to an efficient market due to market imperfections, taxes, or other factors.

decreasing-cost industry: an industry in which the prices of resources and products both fall as the industry expands.

decreasing returns to scale: the situation in which a firm's output increases by a smaller percentage than its inputs.

demand: the quantities that consumers are willing and able to buy per period of time at various prices.

demand schedule: a table showing the various quantities demanded per period of time at different prices.

depreciation: the annual cost of any asset that is expected to be in use for more than one year.

diseconomies of scale: bureaucratic inefficiencies in management that result in decreasing returns to scale.

division of labour: the dividing of the production process into a series of specialized tasks, each done by a different worker.

dumping: the sale of a product abroad for a lower price than is being charged in the domestic market or for a price below the cost of production.

E

economic capacity: that output at which average total cost is at a minimum.

economic profit: revenue over and above all costs, including normal profits.

economic rent: the return to any factor of production above what is required to keep the factor in its present use.

economic surplus: the summation of consumer surplus and producer surplus.

economies of scale: cost advantages achieved as a result of large-scale operations.

elastic demand: quantity demanded that is quite responsive to a change in price (coefficiency of elasticity is greater than 1).

elasticity coefficient: a number that measures the responsiveness of quantity demanded to a change in price.

elasticity of supply: the responsiveness of quantity supplied to a change in price.

enterprise: the human resource that innovates and takes risks.

equilibrium price: the price at which the quantity demanded equals the quantity supplied such that there is neither a surplus nor a shortage.

equilibrium quantity: the quantity that prevails at the equilibrium price.

excess capacity: the situation in which a firm's output is below economic capacity.

excise tax: a sales tax imposed on a particular product.

explicit cost: a cost that is actually paid out in money.

external benefits: benefits that are enjoyed by people other than the producers or consumers of a product.

external costs: costs that are incurred by people other than the producers or consumers of a product.

externalities: benefits or costs of a product experienced by people who neither produce nor consume that product.

F

factor market: the market for the factors of production.

factor output effect: rising total output leads to an increased demand for labour.

factor substitution effect: one factor replaces another factor as a result of technological change.

factors of production: the productive resources that are available to an economy, categorized as labour, capital, land, and enterprise; also **resources**.

fair-return price: a price that guarantees that the firm will earn normal profits only; that is, where P = AC.

G

game theory: a method of analyzing firm behaviour that highlights mutual interdependence among firms.

H

human capital: the accumulation of all skills and knowledge acquired by individuals.

I

imperfect competition: a market structure in which producers are identifiable and have some control over price.

implicit cost: a cost that does not require an actual expenditure of money.

income effect: the effect that a price change has on real income and therefore on the quantity demanded of a product.

income elasticity: the responsiveness of quantity demanded to a change in income.

increasing-cost industry: an industry in which the prices of resources and products both rise as the industry expands.

increasing returns to scale: a firm's output increases by a greater percentage than the increase in its inputs.

indifference curve: shows the combinations of goods that would give the same satisfaction (or total utility) to an individual (or household).

inelastic demand: quantity demanded that is not very responsive to a change in price (coefficiency of elasticity is less than 1).

inferior products: products for which demands will decrease as a result of an increase in income and increase as a result of a decrease in income.

inputs: *See* **resources**.

interest: the payment made and the income received for the use of capital.

L

labour: human physical and mental effort that can be used to produce goods and services.

labour force: the total number of people over the age of 15 who are willing and able to work.

labour force supply: the total hours that those in the labour force are willing to work.

laissez-faire: the economic doctrine asserting that an economy works best with the minimum amount of government intervention.

land: any natural resource that can be used to produce goods and services.

law of diminishing marginal rate of substitution: the more of one good a person has, the less of another good he will be willing to give up to gain an additional unit of the first good.

law of diminishing marginal utility: the amount of additional utility decreases as successive units of a product are consumed.

law of diminishing returns: as more of a variable input is added to a fixed input in the production process, the resulting increase in output will, at some point, begin to diminish.

law of increasing costs: as an economy's production level of any particular item increases, its per unit cost of production rises.

long run: the period during which all inputs are variable.

long-run average cost curve: a graphical representation of the per-unit costs of production in the long run.

M

macroeconomics: the study of how the major components of an economy interact; it includes the topics of unemployment, inflation, interest rate policy, and the spending and taxation policies of government.

margin: the extra or additional unit (also "marginal").

marginal cost: the increase in total variable costs as a result of producing one more unit of output.

marginal private benefits: the extra benefits that the buyer derives from consuming additional quantities of a product.

marginal private costs: the extra internal (or private) costs to the producer of increasing production by one additional unit.

marginal product: the increase in total product as a result of adding one more unit of input.

marginal profit: the additional economic profit from the production and sale of an extra unit of output.

marginal rate of substitution: the amount of one good a consumer is willing to give up to get one more unit of another good and still maintain the same level of satisfaction.

marginal revenue: the extra revenue derived from the sale of one more unit.

marginal revenue product: the increase in a firm's total revenue that results from the use of one more unit of input.

marginal social benefits: the additional benefits to both the consumer (internal benefits) and to society (external benefits) of additional quantities of a product.

marginal social costs: the additional costs to both the producer (internal costs) and to society (external costs) of producing additional quantities of a product.

marginal utility: the amount of additional utility derived from the consumption of an extra unit of a product.

marginal wage cost: the extra cost of hiring an additional worker.

market: a mechanism that brings buyers and sellers together and assists them in negotiating the exchange of products.

market demand: the total demand for a product by all consumers.

market failures: the defects in competitive markets that prevent them from achieving an efficient or equitable allocation of resources.

market supply: the total supply of a product offered by all producers.

microeconomics: the study of the outcomes of decisions by people and firms; it focuses on the supply and demand of goods, the costs of production, and market structures.

minimum efficient scale: the smallest-size plant capable of achieving the lowest long-run average cost of production.

minimum wage: the lowest rate of pay per hour for workers, as set by government.

monopolistic competition: a market in which there are many firms that sell a differentiated product and have some control over the price of the products they sell.

monopoly: a market in which a single firm (the monopolist) is the sole producer.

monopsony: a market structure in which there is only one buyer.

mutual interdependence: the condition in which a firm's actions depend, in part, on the reactions of rival firms.

N

Nash equilibrium: a situation where each rival chooses the best actions given the (anticipated) actions of the other(s).

natural monopoly: a single producer in a market (usually with large economies of scale) in which it is able to produce at a lower cost than competing firms could.

nominal wage: the wage rate expressed as a dollar-and-cents figure.

non-excludable: a feature of certain goods that means that it is impossible (or extremely costly) to prevent nonbuyers from enjoying the benefits.

nonrival goods: one person's consumption does not reduce the amount available for others.

normal products: products for which demand will increase as a result of an increase in income and decrease as a result of a decrease in income.

normal profit: the minimum profit that must be earned to keep the entrepreneur in that type of business.

normative statement: a statement of opinion or belief that cannot be verified.

oligopoly: a market dominated by a few large firms.

opportunity cost: the value of the next-best alternative that is given up as a result of making a particular choice.

optimal purchasing rule: in order to maximize utility, consumers should allocate their budgets so that marginal utility per dollar spent on all products is equal.

P

perfect competition: a market in which all buyers and sellers are price takers.

perfect price discrimination: a situation where customers are charged the highest price they are willing to pay for each unit of a product bought.

positive statement: a statement of fact that can be verified.

price ceiling: a government regulation stipulating the maximum price that can be charged for a product.

price controls: government regulations to set either a maximum or minimum price for a product.

price discrimination: the selling of an identical product at a different price to different customers for reasons other than differences in the cost of production.

price elasticity of demand: a measure of the percentage change of quantity demanded relative to a change in price.

price floor: a government regulation stipulating the minimum price that can be charged for a product.

private goods: goods or services whose benefits can be denied to nonbuyers and whose consumption by one person reduces the amount available for others.

producer surplus: the difference between the amount that producers would be willing to accept for each unit of output and the price they receive when the output is sold.

producers' preference: an allocation system in which sellers are allowed to determine the method of allocation on the basis of their own preferences.

product differentiation: the attempt by a firm to distinguish its product from that of its competitors.

product market: the market for consumer goods and services.

production possibilities curve: a graphical representation of the various combinations of maximum output that can be produced from the available resources and technology.

productive efficiency: production of an output at the lowest possible average cost.

profit: the income received from the activity of enterprise.

protectionism: the economic policy of protecting domestic producers by restricting the importation of foreign products.

public goods: goods or services whose benefits are not affected by the number of users and from which no one can be excluded.

public utilities: goods or services regarded as essential and, therefore, usually provided by government.

quasi-public goods: private goods that are often provided by government because they involve extensive benefits for the general public.

quota: a limit imposed on the production or sale of a product.

R

rationing: allocating products that are in short supply using ration coupons issued by government, guaranteeing a certain quantity of something per family.

real income: income measured in terms of the amount of goods and services that it will buy. Real income will increase if either actual income increases or prices fall.

real wage: the purchasing power of the nominal wage; that is, nominal wage divided by the price level.

rent: the payment made and the income received for the use of land.

rent control: a government regulation making it illegal to rent accommodation above a stipulated level.

resources: physical or virtual entities that can be used to produce goods and services.

short run: any period of time in which at least one input in the production process is fixed (cannot be increased or decreased).

shortage: at the prevailing price, the quantity supplied is smaller than the quantity demanded.

shutdown price: the price that is just sufficient to cover a firm's variable costs.

socially optimum price: the price that produces the best allocation of products (and, therefore, resources) from society's point of view, that is, P = MC.

substitute products: any products for which demand varies directly in relation to a change in the price of a similar product.

substitution effect: the substitution of one product for another as a result of a change in their relative prices.

sunk costs: costs that are unrecoverable.

supply: the quantities that producers are willing and able to sell per period of time at various prices.

supply schedule: a table showing the various quantities supplied per period of time at different prices.

surplus: at the prevailing price, the quantity demanded is smaller than the quantity supplied.

T

tariff: a tax (or duty) levied on imports.

technological improvement: changes in production techniques that reduce the costs of production.

technology: a method of production; the way in which resources are combined to produce goods and services.

terms of trade: the average price of a country's exports compared with the price of its imports.

total cost: the sum of both total variable cost and total fixed cost.

total fixed costs: costs that do not vary with the level of output.

total product: the total output of any productive process.

total revenue: the total receipts of a firm from its sales; formally, it is price multiplied by the quantity of the product sold.

total variable cost: the total of all costs that vary with the level of output.

transfer earnings: a necessary payment that a factor of production must earn in order for it to remain in its present use.

U

unitary elasticity: the point where the percentage change in quantity is exactly equal to the percentage change in price, that is, where the elasticity coefficient is equal to 1.

utility: the satisfaction or pleasure derived from the consumption of a product.

V

voluntary export restriction (VER): an agreement by an exporting country to restrict the amount of its exports to another country.

W

wages: the payment made and the income received for the use of labour.

INDEX

TOP TEN LISTS

World's Most Visited Countries

Rank	Country	Annual Number of Arrivals (in millions per year)
1	France	74.2
2	United States	54.9
3	Spain	52.2
4	China	50.9
5	Italy	43.2
6	United Kingdom	28.0
7	Turkey	25.5
8	Germany	24.2
9	Malaysia	23.6
10	Mexico	21.5

Source: UN World Tourist Organization June 2010

World's Best-Selling Global Brands

Rank	Brand	Brand Value ($ billions)
1	Coca-Cola (U.S.)	70.5
2	IBM (U.S.)	64.7
3	Microsoft (U.S.)	60.9
4	Google (U.S.)	43.6
5	General Electric (U.S.)	42.8
6	McDonalds (U.S.)	33.6
7	Intel (U.S.)	32.0
8	Nokia (Finland)	29.5
9	Disney (U.S.)	28.7
10	HP (U.S.)	26.9

Source: Interbrand's Annual Rankings, 2010

World's Cleanest Countries

Rank	Country	Environmental Performance Index (EPI)
1	Iceland	93.5
2	Switzerland	89.1
3	Costa Rica	86.4
4	Sweden	86.0
5	Norway	81.1
6	Mauritius	80.6
7	France	78.2
8	Austria	78.1
9	Cuba	78.1
10	Columbia	76.8

Source: Columbia/Yale EPI Index